TRONDHJEMITES, DACITES, AND RELATED ROCKS

Series

Developments in Petrology

Developments in Petrology 6

TRONDHJEMITES, DACITES, AND RELATED ROCKS

Edited by

F. BARKER

U.S. Geological Survey, Denver, Colorado, U.S.A.

ELSEVIER SCIENTIFIC PUBLISHING COMPANY
AMSTERDAM – OXFORD – NEW YORK   1979

ELSEVIER SCIENTIFIC PUBLISHING COMPANY
335 Jan van Galenstraat
P.O. Box 211, 1000 AE Amsterdam, The Netherlands

Distributors for the United States and Canada:

ELSEVIER/NORTH-HOLLAND INC.
52, Vanderbilt Avenue
New York, N.Y. 10017

Library of Congress Cataloging in Publication Data
Main entry under title:

Trondhjemites, dacites, and related rocks.

    (Developments in petrology ; 6)
    Includes index.
    1. Trondhjemite. 2. Dacite. I. Barker, Fred,
1928-   II. Series.
QE462.T74T76   552'.1   78-24338
ISBN 0-444-41765-6

ISBN 0-444-41765-6 (Vol. 6)
ISBN 0-444-41562-9 (Series)

Printed in The Netherlands

PREFACE

Siliceous igneous rocks of low potassium content, although mapped in the field and described by geologists for many years, were largely neglected by geochemists and petrologists until the late 1960's. These rocks have been termed trondhjemite, tonalite, soda granite, leucogranodiorite, soda rhyolite, high-silica dacite, and other names. Rocks of this general composition and cogenetic, less siliceous and more mafic rocks are now known to be a major component of Archean gneiss terranes, to occur in the volcanic and plutonic parts of Late Archean greenstone-granite terranes, to form widely scattered extrusive and intrusive bodies in plate-tectonic environments of convergent oceanic-continental and oceanic-oceanic types, and to be a prominent if volumetrically minor component of many ophiolites.

The purpose of this book is to give the reader a view, by a diverse and active group of geologists and geochemists, of the geology, geochemistry, and petrology of the several kinds of trondhjemites and dacites, and of the genetically related rocks. Many chapters focus on major and minor elements, isotope geochemistry, or petrology. Others stress the pertinent field relations as well. Individual chapters range from preliminary reports to review articles.

The name trondhjemite comes from the old spelling, "Trondhjem," of Trondheim, Norway. V. M. Goldschmidt originated the term in 1916 in his famous paper on the intrusives of the Trondheim-Oppdal region, in which he defined trondhjemite as holocrystalline, leucocratic rock that consists largely of sodic plagioclase and quartz and contains only minor biotite and potassic feldspar. For at least 40 years thereafter, few geologists outside of Fennoscandia used the term. Even the status of trondhjemite as a magmatic type was in doubt. N. L. Bowen, in his classic The Evolution of the Igneous Rocks, doubted that magmas of this composition existed; and he attributed the formation of such rocks rich in CIPW-normative albite to Na-metasomatism of common potassic granitic rocks. Bowen's point of view, however, was gradually overcome by detailed field, petrographic, and chemical studies. Reports by Hietanen in 1943 on the Proterozoic hornblende gabbro-trondhjemite suite of southwestern Finland and by Hietanen, Compton, Taubeneck, L. H. Larsen and Poldervaart; Davis; Lipman; and others in the period 1951-1965 on Mesozoic intrusives of northern California and Oregon are notable in demonstrating the existence of trondhjemitic magmas. Use of trondhjemite as a rock name by these and other workers and recent sanction of the term by the IUGS Subcommission on the Systematics of Igneous Rocks indicate that Goldschmidt's term "trondhjemite" now is well established.

I am pleased to acknowledge the help and advice given me in preparation of this volume by many members of the U.S. Geological Survey--especially Robert G. Coleman of the Branch of Field Geochemistry and Petrology, Charles L. Pillmore of the Denver Technical Reports Unit, and Flora K. Walker of the Branch of Chemical Resources.

The text was prepared and printed out by a word processor in Denver. The editor apologizes for the undetected, scattered typographical and other errors which, inevitably, seem to be found in material produced by this apparatus.

Fred Barker
June 1978
Denver, Colorado

CONTRIBUTORS

J. G. Arth, 929 National Center, U.S. Geological Survey, Reston, VA 22092, U.S.A.

F. Barker, U.S. Geological Survey, Box 25046, Denver, CO 80225, U.S.A.

D. Bridgwater, The Geological Survey of Greenland, Øster Volgade 10, DK-1350 Copenhagen K, Denmark.

W. B. Bryan, Woods Hole Oceanographic Intitution, Woods Hole, MA 02534, U.S.A.

R. G. Coleman, U.S. Geological Survey, Menlo Park, CA 94025, U.S.A.

K. D. Collerson, Department of Geology, Memorial University of Newfoundland, St. John's, Newfoundland, Canada A1C 5S7.

M. M. Donato, U.S. Geological Survey, Menlo Park, CA 94205, U.S.A.

S. A. Drury, Department of Earth Sciences, The Open University, Milton Keynes, U. K.

C. Dupuy, Laboratorie de Geochimie du Centre Geologique et Geophysique, U.S.T.L., Place E. Bataillon, 34060 Montepellier, Cedex France.

I. F. Ermanovics Geological Survey of Canada, 588 Booth Street, Ottawa, Canada K1A OE4.

A. Ewart, Department of Geology and Mineralogy, The University of Queensland, St.Lucia, Queensland, Australia 4067.

J. B. Gill, Division of Natural Sciences, University of California, Santa Cruz, CA 95064, U.S.A.

W. N. Houston, Geological Survey of Canada, 588 Booth Street, Ottawa, Canada K1A OE4.

D. R. Hunter, Department of Geology, University of Natal, Pietermaritzburg 3200, South Africa.

R. J. Knight, U.S. Geological Survey, Box 25046, Denver, CO 80225, U.S.A.

A. Leyreloup, Laboratoire de Petrologie et laboratoire associee du C. N. R. S. n° 266, U. S. T. L., Place E. Bataillon, 34060 Montepellier, France.

P. W. Lipman, U.S. Geological Survey Box 25046, Denver, CO 80225, U.S.A.

F. J. Longstaffe, Department of Geology, University of Alberta, Edmonton, Canada T6G 2E3.

J. Malpas, Department of Geology, Memorial University of Newfoundland, St. John's, Newfoundland, Canada A1C 5S7.

V. R. McGregor, The Geological Survey of Greenland, Atangmik, 3912 Sukkertoppen, Greenland, Denmark.

W. D. McRitchie, Geological Services Branch, 993 Century Street, Winnipeg, Canada R3H OW4.

H. T. Millard, Jr., U.S. Geological Survey, Box 25046, Denver, CO 80225, U.S.A.

C. Nicollet, Laboratoire associee du C. N. R. S. n° 266, U. S. T. L., Place E. Bataillon, 34060 Montpellier, Cedex France.

J. G. Payne, c/o Racey, MacCallum & Bluteau Ltd., 8205 Montreal-Toronto Blvd., Montreal, Canada.

Z. E. Peterman, U.S. Geological Survey, Box 25046, Denver, CO 80225, U.S.A.

D. W. Phelps, Department of Geology, Arizona State University, Tempe, AZ 85281, U.S.A.

A. L. Stork, Division of Natural Sciences, University of California, Santa Cruz, CA 95064, U.S.A.

D. F. Strong, Department of Geology, Memorial University of Newfoundland, St. John's, Newfoundland, Canada A1C 5S7.

J. Tarney, Department of Geological Sciences, The University of Birmingham, Birmingham B15 2TT, U. K.

J. F. Tomblin, Seismic Research Unit, University of The West Indies, St. Augustine, Trinidad, W. I.

B. L. Weaver, Department of Geological Sciences, The University of Birmingham, Birmingham B15 2TT, U. K.

CONTENTS

CHAPTER 8. GEOCHEMISTRY OF ARCHEAN TRONDHJEMITIC AND TONALITIC GNEISSES FROM
         SCOTLAND AND EAST GREENLAND
         J. Tarney, B. Weaver and S. A. Drury

CHAPTER 9. THE ROLE OF TONALITIC AND TRONDHJEMITIC ROCKS IN THE CRUSTAL
         DEVELOPMENT OF SWAZILAND AND THE EASTERN TRANSVAAL, SOUTH AFRICA
         D. R. Hunter

CHAPTER 10. PETROCHEMISTRY AND TECTONIC SETTING OF PLUTONIC ROCKS OF THE
         SUPERIOR PROVINCE IN MANITOBA
         I. F. Ermanovics, W. D. McRitchie and W. N. Houston

CHAPTER 14. PETROGENESIS OF HIGH PRESSURE TRONDHJEMITIC LAYERS IN ECLOGITES
AND AMPHIBOLES FROM SOUTHERN MASSIF CENTRAL, FRANCE
C. Nicollet, A. Leyreloup and C. Dupuy

CHAPTER 15. TWO CONTRASTING TRONDHJEMITE ASSOCIATIONS FROM TRANSPORTED
OPHIOLITES IN WESTERN NEWFOUNDLAND: INITIAL REPORT
J. Malpas

CHAPTER 16. ORIGIN OF THE TWILLINGATE TRONDHJEMITE, NORTH-CENTRAL
NEWFOUNDLAND: PARTIAL MELTING IN THE ROOTS OF AN ISLAND ARC
J. G. Payne and D. F. Strong

Chapter 1

TRONDHJEMITE: DEFINITION, ENVIRONMENT AND HYPOTHESES OF ORIGIN

F. Barker

ABSTRACT

Goldschmidt's definition (1916) of the rock name "trondhjemite," unfortunately, was not quantitative. Furthermore, the trondhjemite intrusives of the type area, south of Trondheim, Norway, have had much of their original mineralogy obliterated by metamorphism to greenschist facies. The author suggests that the IUGS definition of trondhjemite as leucotonalite be followed, except that andesine-bearing leucotonalite be termed calcic trondhjemite, and that albite-bearing leucotonalite, as well as the oligoclase variety, be termed trondhjemite.

Major-element characteristics of trondhjemite, which of course are dependent on the petrographic limits as defined and on the chemistry of the constituent mineral phases, include:

1. $SiO_2 >$ ca. 68 percent, usually <75 percent;

2. Al_2O_3 typically >15 percent @ 70 percent SiO_2 and <14 percent @ 75 percent SiO_2;

3. (FeO* + MgO) <3.4 percent, and FeO*:MgO commonly is 2-3;

4. CaO ranges from 4.4-4.5 percent in calcic trondhjemite to typical values of 1.5-3.0 percent;

5. Na_2O typically is 4.0-5.5 percent; and

6. K_2O <ca. 2.5 percent, and typically <2 percent.

The separation of trondhjemites into low-Al_2O_3 and high-Al_2O_3 types should be made at 15 percent Al_2O_3 at 70 percent SiO_2.

Most suites of trondhjemite and genetically related tonalite plot as calc-alkalic, but should be considered as a specific type of low K/Na ratio and of low (FeO* + MgO) abundance.

Generation of trondhjemite-tonalitic liquids is briefly reviewed in terms of fractionation of wet basaltic and dry low-K tholeiitic or andesitic liquid and of partial melting of quartz eclogite, amphibolite and gabbro.

Trondhjemite-tonalite suites occur largely in: (1) Archean gray gneiss terranes; (2) peripheries of Archean greenstone belts; (3a) Proterozoic and Paleozoic continental margins; and (3b) Mesozoic and Cenozoic continental margins. Trondhjemites of slightly different character are found in: (4) subvolcanic regions of island arcs; and (5) ophiolites.

The spatial relations between trondhjemite-tonalite suites and subduction zones in environments (3b) and probably (3a) are very close. The actual methods of generation of magmas of this type at or near subduction zones, however, in spite of much work and speculation are not well known.

TRONDHJEMITE: DEFINITION

Goldschmidt originally defined the term trondhjemite (1916), giving the type area as the "Trondhjem-Gebiet." He stated that the rock is leucocratic, that the plagioclase is in the range oligoclase-andesine, that biotite is the typical dark phase, and that amphibole or, rarely, diopsidic pyroxene may occur in place of biotite. Unfortunately, the type plutons in the region south of Trondheim have been metamorphosed to greenschist facies (Goldschmidt, 1916; Barker and Millard, this volume), the feldspars of liquidus crystallization mostly are altered to felted aggregates of albite, epidote, and muscovite, and only a trace of potassic feldspar is present. These rocks are not suitable for giving us a strict petrographic definition of the term trondhjemite. Goldschmidt's inclusion of andesine as a possible constituent also presents a difficulty: a tonalitic rock containing the percentage of CaO (usually more than 4) and the relatively high ratio of $CaO:Na_2O$ necessary to form plagioclase more calcic than An_{30} usually contains so much (FeO* + MgO), where FeO* = FeO + 0.9 Fe_2O_3, that the rock contains more than 10 percent dark minerals. Thus the rock is not leucocratic and cannot be termed trondhjemite. But andesine-bearing leucotonalites are found, and Davis (1963) gave the mode and major-element analysis of one from the Trinity Alps, California, and suggested it be called calcic trondhjemite.

The recent IUGS classification of igneous rocks (Streckeisen, 1976) defines trondhjemite as leucotonalite whose plagioclase is oligoclase or andesine. This definition also specifies that quartz content be 20 percent or more of the leucocratic minerals, that alkali feldspar constitute 10 percent or less of the total feldspar, and color index be 10 or less. For the most part this is an excellent definition. The writer suggests, however, that Davis' term calcic trondhjemite be used for andesine-bearing trondhjemite, and that albite-bearing (Ab_{90}-Ab_{100}) leucotonalites as well as oligoclase-bearing varieties be termed trondhjemite. These albite-bearing rocks are better referred to as "trondhjemite" than as "alkali-feldspar granite."

An approximate definition of trondhjemite also can be given in terms of major elements. The most important of these in distinguishing trondhjemite from tonalite and granodiorite are (FeO* + MgO), which is involved in determining proportions of mafic minerals and hence color index, and K_2O, a determining constituent of potassic feldspar and biotite. Analyses of biotite and hornblende from the hornblende gabbro-trondhjemite suite of southwest Finland (Arth et al., in press) show that the (FeO* + MgO) content of biotite is 28-30 percent, and that of hornblende is 27-28 percent. Thus, keeping in mind that biotite and hornblende are denser than quartz and feldspars, about 3.3 weight percent (FeO* + MgO) is contained in 10 volume percent biotite and about 3.4 percent in hornblende. Magnetite and ilmenite, of course, contain much higher percentages of FeO* than do the two mafic silicates and these two oxide minerals are much denser. Most trondhjemites, however, contain only a trace of magnetite or ilmenite and only 0.1-0.3 percent or less of the FeO* of the rock is contained in these phases. Epidote may contain a few tenths to as much as 1 percent of FeO* in altered trondhjemite. The limit of (FeO* + MgO) in trondhjemite may be taken at about 3.4 percent. K_2O comprises 10-12 percent of potassic feldspar, 9-10 percent of biotite, 0.5-0.6 percent of hornblende and approximately 0.15-0.4 percent of plagioclase, as estimated from analyses of these phases as found in calc-alkaline intrusives (Deer et al., 1963) and from analyses of biotite and hornblende (Arth et al., in press). Thus, a trondhjemite containing the maximum 10 percent each of biotite and potassic feldspar, as well as 50-60 percent of plagioclase, would contain 2.3-2.55 percent of K_2O. The maximum percentage of K_2O in trondhjemite may be taken as about 2.5 percent.

The major-element contents of trondhjemites, either as limits or as typical concentrations(Fig. 1), are:

1. SiO_2 >ca. 68 percent, usually <75 percent;

2. Al_2O_3 typically >15 percent @ 70 percent SiO_2 and <14 percent @ 75 percent SiO_2;

3. (FeO* + MgO) <3.4 percent, and FeO*:MgO commonly is 2-3;

4. CaO ranges from 4.4-4.5 percent in calcic trondhjemite to typical values of 1.5-3.0 percent;

5. Na_2O typically is 4.0-5.5 percent; and

6. K_2O <ca. 2.5 percent, and typically <2 percent.

The writer stresses that trondhjemites and tonalites, like many other plutonic rocks, often do not show a one-to-one correspondence of major-element contents to volumetric percentages of minerals (modal analyses determined by

4

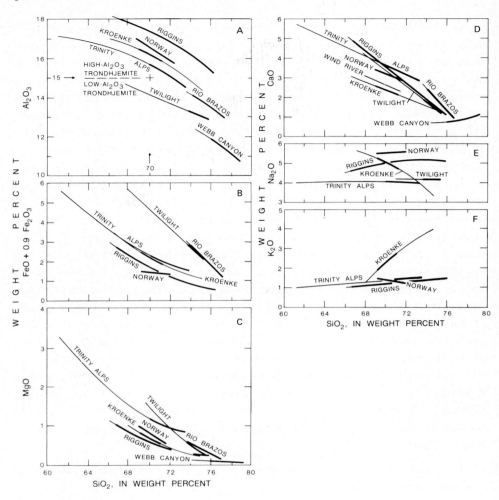

Figure 1.--Harker diagrams for the Kroenke Granodiorite, trondhjemite of Rio Brazos and Twilight Gneiss of Colorado and New Mexico (Barker et al., 1976; Barker and Millard, this volume); and gneisses of the Wilson Creek area, Wind River Mountains, Wyoming, trondhjemite and pegmatite of Riggins area, Idaho, quartz diorite-trondhjemite intrusives of the Trinity Alps, California, and Webb Canyon Gneiss, Teton Range, Wyoming (Barker et al., this volume). Note that not all suites are represented in some of the diagrams because the data points did not fall near or on smooth curves. Heavier line segments indicate rock type is trondhjemite.

one or two thin sections), considering the compositions and densities of those mineral phases. These discrepancies presumably are due to modal inhomogeneities of the rocks that are not discernable to the eye. Thus, some rocks are more accurately classified as trondhjemite or not by means of major elements rather than by modal analysis.

Classification of common siliceous igneous rocks by proportions of normative Ab, Or, and An was proposed by O'Connor (1965). His diagram is given in Figure 2A. O'Connor's plot separates trondhjemites from tonalite, granodiorite, and granite rather well, even though this type of classification does not consider mafic constituents or color index. However, some trondhjemites fall in the tonalite field of this diagram. Also, because the ratio Ab/An generally increases from tonalitic to granitic compositions, the author suggests a modification in which the boundary separating trondhjemite from tonalite and from granodiorite extends from $Ab_{30}Or_{70}$-An_{100}. These modifications are shown in Figure 2B.

Cawthorn et al. (1976) have discussed the corundum-normative character of calc-alkaline magmas, especially in relation to hornblende fractionation. Most trondhjemites and many of the associated tonalites are corundum-normative, irrespective of whether they are of the low- or high-Al_2O_3 type; e.g., the low-Al_2O_3 trondhjemite of Rio Brazos, New Mexico (Barker et al., 1976), shows as much as 5 percent normative corundum; the Twilight Gneiss of Colorado, also the low-Al_2O_3 type, shows as much as 3.6 percent. High-Al_2O_3 types, such as the Kroenke Granodiorite of Colorado and the trondhjemite of Riggins, Idaho (Barker and Millard, this volume), typically show from a fraction of a percent to about 2 percent of normative corundum. As Cawthorn et al. point out, calc-alkaline rock suites typically change from diopside-normative to corundum-normative at SiO_2 contents in the middle to high 60's. A prominent exception to this, however, is found in the gabbro-diorite-tonalite-trondhjemite suite of SW Finland (Arth et al., in press); this suite becomes corundum-normative at 57 percent SiO_2.

MAJOR-ELEMENT CHARACTER

Major-element compositions of some tonalite-trondhjemite suites are shown in the Harker diagrams of Figure 1. The superposed dashed lines in that figure show approximately which compositional region of each suite is trondhjemite. Plots of some of the constituents of the eight suites of Figure 1 do not give smooth curves and are not shown. K_2O is prominent in this regard, and curves for only four of the suites are given (Fig. 1F).

The earlier division of trondhjemites into low Al_2O_3 and high-Al_2O_3 types (Barker et al., 1976) needs to be qualified as shown in Figure 1A, the depend-

6

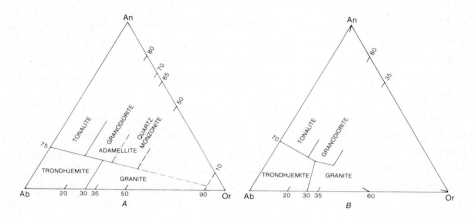

Figure 2.--Normative plots of Ab-Or-An showing fields of some siliceous plutonic rocks. A, after O'Connor, 1965; B, suggested modification.

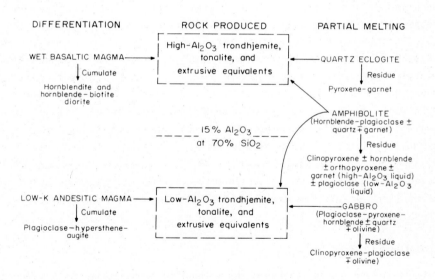

Figure 3.--Schematic diagram showing generation of high-Al_2O_3 and low-Al_2O_3 trondhjemitic-tonalitic liquids by differentiation and partial melting, modified from Barker and Arth (1976).

ence of Al_2O_3 contents on SiO_2 is rather pronounced, and so the author suggests that the two suites be separated into low-Al_2O_3 and high-Al_2O_3 types at 15 percent Al_2O_3 and 70 percent SiO_2. There is a continuum of Al_2O_3 compositions of trondhjemites, and so the separation as suggested is done for convenience. Implications of Al_2O_3 contents are discussed in the following section.

Most trondhjemite-tonalite suites, including those having dioritic or gabbroic end members, plot as calc-alkaline in terms of (Na_2O +K_2O)-SiO_2 and (Na_2O + K_2O)-FeO*-MgO (Barker and Arth, 1976). By this definition, and also by use of CaO versus (Na_2O + K_2O) on a Harker plot, the gabbro-trondhjemite suite of southwestern Finland, at least, is calc-alkaline (Barker and Arth, 1976). However, plots such as K-Na-Ca, or normative ones including Ab and Or in which Na_2O and K_2O, or derivative parameters, are separated, show that trondhjemites should be considered as a low-Na/K-ratio type of calc-alkaline rock (Barker and Arth, 1976). They also should be described as a low-(FeO* + MgO) type. Thus, the calc-alkaline quartz diorite-tonalite-granodiorite-granite suites that form the bulk of the Mesozoic circum-Pacific batholiths are rather different from trondhjemite-tonalite suites. And, even though trondhjemite-tonalite suites in some cases are found only 5-50 km oceanward of the great batholiths, there apparently is not a compositional continuum between the two.

OCCURRENCE

The trondhjemitic-tonalitic suite (not including many of the composition-ally similar dacitic suites, which are considered by other contributors to this volume) is found mostly in four geologic environments, two of which are similar:

1) Archean gray gneiss terranes, as a major rock type, often in association with basaltic rocks, and, in some cases with komatiitic rocks, to give a compositionally bimodal or trimodal suite; these rocks mostly are intru-sive but some are volcanic--many original features of emplacement have been obliterated by shearing and metamorphism in most of these terranes; usually metamorphosed to amphibolite or granulite facies, and commonly retrograded to greenschist facies; relatively potassic intrusives are specially associated in some of these terranes; see Barker and Arth, Barker and Millard, Collerson and Bridgewater, Hunter, McGregor, and Tarney in this volume,

2) Peripheries of Archean greenstone belts, as emplaced during or just after buckling of those belts; usually accompanied by plutos of granodiorite and granite; see Ermanovics et al., Hunter, and Longstaffe in this volume.

3a) Along margins of Proterozoic and Paleozoic continental margins, that apparently are related to subduction or to subsidiary back-arc spreading; the

Proterozoic occurrences, at least, typically are accompanied by much greater volumes of the suite quartz diorite-tonalite-granodiorite-granite; see Arth, Barker and Millard; Malpas; and Payne and Strong in this volume; and

3b) Along margins of Mesozoic and Cenozoic continental margins, that almost certainly are related to subduction; of relatively small volume; partly as composite intrusives oceanward of large calc-alkaline batholiths; see Arth, Barker et. al., in this volume.

Trondhjemites also are found either separately or as members of rock suites that differ from the common trondhjemite-tonalite suite in:

4) Subvolcanic regions of island arcs, either as parts of arc-tholeiitic or calc-alkaline suites; derived from the same magma system as the much better known dacitic rocks considered in this volume by Barker and Millard, Gill, Malpas, Payne and Strong, Phelps, and Tomblin in this volume; and

5) Ophiolites, as a member of the plagiogranite suite of Coleman and Peterman (1975) and as considered by Coleman and Donato in this volume, which includes diorite, quartz diorite, tonalite and albite-quartz rocks as well as trondhjemite proper.

Other environments may contain minor trondhjemitic rocks; one example is high-rank metamorphic terranes in which metabasalt has been partially melted or dissolved and precipitated to give trondhjemitic pegmatites or aplites (see Nicollet et al., this volume).

HYPOTHESES OF ORIGIN

Most workers follow Hanson and his coworkers (Hanson and Goldich, 1972; Arth and Hanson, 1972, 1975) in believing that trondhjemitic-tonalitic liquids form from basaltic sources. Other sources, such as graywacke, dacitic volcanic rocks, plutonic rocks of low K/Na ratio, and others, cannot be excluded a priori as possible parents for such liquids, but in many cases their involvement is ruled out by geochemical or petrological considerations. The generation of trondhjemitic-tonalitic liquids was briefly summarized by Barker and Arth (1976). Their schematic diagram showing four general modes of origin from basaltic rock or liquid--differentiation by crustal-liquid fractionation and partial melting under both relatively dry and relatively wet conditions--is reproduced here (Fig. 3). The reader will find more discussion on origins in this volume and in Arth et al. (in press).

Processes of fractionation and of partial melting involve such a variety of cumulate or residual minerals that liquids of all Al_2O_3 compositions may be produced by either process; that is, there is a continuum between high-Al_2O_3 and low-Al_2O_3 trondhjemitic liquids.

COMMENTS ON ARCHEAN GRAY GNEISS COMPLEXES

Trondhjemite is a major rock type or is abundant only in the Archean gray gneiss complexes. These gneiss complexes comprise much of the Earth's oldest known rocks, which are 2.8 to 3.8 b.y. old. The common association of trondhjemite and tonalite gneiss and metabasalt--and the general absence of andesitic rocks--led Barker and Arth (1976) to "suggest a variation of Green and Ringwood's second model (1968), involving partial melting of amphibolite under wet conditions. The first event in this two-stage model consists of mantle upwelling, generation of basaltic liquid by partial melting of mantle material, volcanism (probably in rift zones), and accumulation of thick piles of basalt. The lower parts of these accumulating piles were metamorphosed to hornblende-plagioclase $\pm$ quartz amphibolite, the necessary water coming from interstitial sources. Along relatively steep Archean geotherms (see discussion of Green, 1975), partial melting commenced at less than 10-kb total pressure and second-stage siliceous magmas were produced. At 15 to 30 percent fractional melting in the range 850° to $1000^{\circ}C$ and at $^a H_2 O > 0.6$, the liquids were trondhjemitic to tonalitic (Holloway and Burnham, 1972; Helz, 1973, 1976), and the residue was largely hornblende, varietal clinopyroxene, and minor magnetite and olivine. At relatively low total pressure, $^a H_2 O$, and percentage of partial melting, the residue contained plagioclase and the liquid was of the low-$Al_2 O_3$ type (Fig. 3). Typically, however, we infer that plagioclase was not a residual phase and that the liquids were of high-$Al_2 O_3$ type (Fig. 3). As the lower part of the basaltic pile reached higher pressures and temperatures, it was progressively dehydrated largely by the upward removal of the trondhjemitic-tonalitic liquids, so that conditions were reached where the hornblende-bearing residue became unstable and reacted to pyroxene, olivine, and other minerals. This dehydrated residue was below its solidus and did not undergo further fractional melting. The critical factor in this model, obviously, is that the siliceous liquid must have been removed from the residue before the fraction of melting reached about 40 percent or more and before the liquid phase became andesitic. Basaltic volcanism of the first stage continued as the trondhjemitic-tonalitic liquids rose through the basaltic pile, and so bimodal volcanism occurred in the upper parts of the pile. The ratio of basalt to dacitic rocks thus depended on two loosely related processes and so varied widely..."

These two authors further suggested that "Models of genesis of trondhjemitic-tonalitic liquids involving quartz eclogite probably are not pertinent for Archean rocks. Early Archean terranes apparently contain no eclogite, at least in present exposures. Amphibolite is ubiquitous. Many workers have suggested that heat flow was significantly higher in Archean time than at present (see, for example, Daly, 1933; Brooks and Hart, 1972, 1974). The crust and lithosphere in the early Archean also may have been thinner than at present (Daly, 1933; Green, 1975). D. H. Green also has suggested that Archean geotherms may have been so steep that they did not pass through an eclogite region, and so eclogite was absent. Even if Archean geotherms were not so steep as to obviate a stability field for eclogite, they presumably would have been sufficiently steep that the 15 to 30 percent of partial melting required to generate trondhjemitic-tonalitic liquids would have occurred well before the parental amphibolite reached the depths (50 to 60 km) where garnet would form (Wyllie, 1971; Lambert and Wyllie, 1972). Thus we propose that common amphibolite, rather than quartz eclogite or garnet amphibolite, was the predominant parental material of the bimodal Archean trondhjemitic and tonalitic liquids.

Differentiation suites of the Finnish type (Arth et al., in press), important as they may be in terranes of late Archean and younger age, are not reported to occur in the earlier parts of Archean gray gneiss complexes. Identification of the mode of generation of individual bodies of trondhjemite or tonalite, occurring in the field without closely associated diorite and gabbro, is difficult. The systematics of REE patterns with SiO_2 may be the key to distinguishing rocks formed by fractionation of basaltic liquid from those formed by partial melting."

Cawthorn and coworkers (Cawthorn and Brown, 1976; Cawthorn et al., 1976) have independently discussed the role of hornblende in the fractionation of calc-alkaline magmas.

The chapters of Collerson and Bridgewater, McGregor, and Tarney et al. in this volume consider the origin of Archean gneiss terranes in much detail.

RELATION TO SUBDUCTION

Many Phanerozoic and some Proterozoic trondhjemite bodies can reasonably be related to subduction, excepting those in ophiolites and in several minor environments. However, the actual processes of generation of trondhjemitic liquids at or above subducted oceanic crust and lithosphere remain an outstanding problem. In many publications and discussions various workers have suggested several processes by which trondhjemitic-tonalitic liquids may be formed: (1) partial melting of the basaltic part of subducted oceanic crust; (2) partial melting of scattered masses or inclusions of eclogite in the subducted lithosphere; (3) water vapor produced by dehydration reactions in the subducted slab streaming upward into the overlying partial wedge of mantle or even into the lower crust and there causing of rock of basaltic composition; (4) basaltic liquid, generated by partial melting of peridotite, fractionating by separation of hornblende and other liquidus phases; or (5) by other means. Certainly all of these processes are plausible. Much work, though, remains to be done to enable us to determine which process occurs for a given occurrence, details of that process, and which geologic, petrologic, and chemical parameters are diagnostic or indicative of process.

ACKNOWLEDGMENTS

The writer is indebted to J. G. Arth and D. C. Ross for reviewing this chapter.

REFERENCES

Arth, J. G. and Hanson, G. N., 1972. Quartz diorites derived by partial melting of eclogite or amphibolite at mantle depths. Contrib. Miner. Pet., 37: 161-174.

Arth, J. G. and Hanson, G. N., 1975. Geochemistry and origin of the Early Precambrian crust of northeastern Minnesota. Geochim. Cosmochim. Acta, 39: 325-362.

Arth, J. G., Barker, F., Peterman, Z. E. and Friedman, I., Geochemistry of the gabbro-diorite-tonalite-trondhjemite suite of southwest Finland and its implications for the origin of tonalitic and trondhjemitic magmas. J. Pet., (in press)

Barker, F., Arth, J. G., Peterman, Z. E. and Friedman, I., 1976. The 1.7- to 1.8-b.y. old trondhjemites of southwestern Colorado and northern New Mexico: Geochemistry and depths of genesis. Geol. Soc. Am. Bull., 87: 189-198.

Barker, F. and Arth, J. G., 1976. Generation of trondhjemitic-tonalitic liquids and Archean bimodal trondhjemite-basalt suites. Geology, 4: 596-600.

Barker, F. and Arth, J. G., 1974, On the significance of komatiite. Geology, 2: 107-110.

Cawthorn, R. G., Strong, D. F. and Brown, P. A., 1976. Origin of corundum-normative intrusive and extrusive magmas. Nature, 259: 102-104.

Cawthorn, R. G. and Brown, P. A., 1976. A model for the formation and crystallization of corundum-normative calc-alkaline magmas through amphibole fractionation. J. Geol., 84: 467-476.

Coleman, R. G. and Peterman, Z. E., 1975. Oceanic plagiogranite. J. Geophys. Res., 80: 1099-1108.

Daly, R. A., 1933. Igneous rocks and the deths of the Earth: New York and London, McGraw-Hill Book Co., Inc., 598 pp.

Davis, G. A., 1963. Structure and mode of emplacement of Caribou Mountain pluton, Klamath Mountains, California. Geol. Soc. Am. Bull., 74: 331-348.

Deer, W. A., Howie, R. A. and Zussman, J., 1963. Rock-forming minerals, Vol. 4, Framework silicates. Longmans, Green and Co., London: 435 pp.

Goldschmidt, V. M., 1916. Geologisch-petrographische studien im hochgebirge des südlichen Norwegens, IV. Übersicht der eruptivgesteine im Kaledonischen Gebirge zwischen Stavanger und Trondhjem. Vid. Skr. I.Mat.-Nat. Klasse, 2: 75-112.

Green, D. H., 1975. Genesis of Archean peridotitic magmas and constraints on Archean geothermal gradientsand tectonics. Geology, 3: 15-18.

Green, T. H. and Ringwood, A. E., 1968. Genesis of the calc-alkaline igneous rock suite. Contr. Miner. Pet., 18: 105-162.

Hanson, G.N. and Goldich, S. S., 1972. Early Precambrian rocks in the Saganaga Lake-Northern Light Lake area, Minnesota-Ontario--Pt. 2, Petrogenesis. In: B. R. Doe and D. K. Smith (Eds.), Studies in mineralogy and Precambrian geology. Geol. Soc. Am. Mem. 135: 179-192.

Helz, R. T., 1973. Phase relations of basalts in their melting range at P_{H_2O} = 5 kb as a function of oxygen fugacity. Pt. I. Mafic phases. J. Pet., 14: 249-302.

Helz, R. T., 1976. Phase relations of basalts in their melting ranges at P_{H_2O} = 5 kb. Pt. II. Melt compositions. J. Pet., 17: 139-193.

Hietanen, Anna, 1943. Uber das Grundgebirge des Kalantigebietes im sudwestlichen Finnland: Finlande Comm. Geol. Bull., 130, 105 pp.

Holloway, J. R. and Burnham, C. W., 1972. Melting relations of basalt with equilibrium water pressure less than total pressure. J. Pet., 13: 1-29.

Lambert, I. B. and Wyllie, P.J., 1972. Melting of gabbro (quartz eclogite) with excess water to 35 kilobars, with geological applications: J. Geol., 80: 693-708.

O'Connor, J. T., 1965. A classification for quartz-rich igneous rocks based on feldspar ratios. U.S. Geol. Surv. Prof. Pap., 525-B: 79-84.

Streckeisen, A., 1976. To each plutoic rock its proper name. Earth Sci. Rev., 12: 1-33.

Wyllie, P. J., 1971. Experimental limits for melting in the Earth's crust and upper mantle, in Heacock, J. G., ed., The structure and physical properties of the Earth's crust. Am. Geophys. Union Geophys. Mon. 14: 279-301.

Chapter 2

A REVIEW OF THE MINERALOGY AND CHEMISTRY OF TERTIARY-RECENT DACITIC, LATITIC, RHYOLITIC, AND RELATED SALIC VOLCANIC ROCKS

A. Ewart

ABSTRACT

This paper attempts to review those salic eruptives in which SiO_2 >60%, but specifically excluding peralkaline and silica-undersaturated types. The approach is based on a compilation of major and trace elements, plus phenocryst occurrence and phenocryst modal data; some 2,890 sets of rock data are included. The data are tabulated into five chemical groupings (60-63, 63-66, 66-69, 69-72, >73% SiO_2); further breakdown of data is based on geographic and/or tectonic subregions, and further chemical subdivision into low-K, calc-alkaline, and high-K series from each subregion. In this paper, the general terms siliceous andesite, dacite, and rhyolite are applied to volcanic rocks with SiO_2% of 60-63, 63-69, and >69%, respectively, except lavas specified as trachytes, for which a separate set of data are compiled.

The majority of salic volcanic magmas have been erupted within orogenic zones; i.e., the circum-Pacific regions, Indonesia, the Mediterranean arcs, and to a lesser extent, the Caribbean and Scotia arcs. An additional group of silicic magmas, dominated by rhyolites, are those of the bimodal mafic-silicic magma associations; examples are drawn from Yellowstone, Mono, Medicine Lake, and Salton Sea in the western U.S.A.: Iceland; western Scotland; and southern Queensland (Australia). Further comparative data are provided from the Hawaiian, Galapagos, and Canary Islands, and the unusual high soda-low potash lavas of Deception and Fedarb Islands.

Cluster analyses of averaged data for the various subregions suggest close correlations between the orogenic silicic magmas of the western U.S.A. (excluding Cascades), western South America, and Mediterranean regions. Further clustering is found between the eruptives of the Cascades-Aleutians, Middle Americas, and Indonesian subregions. The clustering tends to separate these orogenic magmas from the oceanic rhyolites and dacites, and the rhyolites of the bimodal associations. The trachytes exhibit no clear correlations with any of these groupings.

14

Mineralogically, the calc-alkaline orogenic salic volcanics are characterized by phenocryst assemblages comprising plagioclase, quartz, augite, hypersthene, hornblende, cummingtonite, Fe-Ti oxides, biotite, and rarely sanidine. The low-K eruptives lack biotite and sanidine, while the high-K eruptives contain much more abundant sanidine, quartz and biotite, and commonly also sphene and allanite. Detailed phenocryst assemblages are tabulated in the text. Fe-Ti oxide temperatures range from 640-780°C in high-K rhyolites of western U.S.A. (excluding those of the bimodal associations); 725-900°C in calc-alkaline rhyolites from the S.W. Pacific; and 830-1120°C for orogenic dacites from various circum-Pacific regions. These data also suggest that the orogenic silicic magmas from the western U.S.A. have equilibrated on a slightly higher f_{O_2} buffer (between NNO and HM buffers) than the orogenic magmas from other regions. It is also shown that the averaged compositions of the magmas from western U.S.A., western South America, and Mediterranean regions, and indeed the high-K eruptives from other regions, trend towards and terminate close to the lower pressure "ternary minima" in the quartz-feldspar system, and the 2-feldspar cotectic surface in the feldspar system. This is not found for the calc-alkaline and low-K series.

Rhyolites of bimodal associations often exhibit distinctive phenocryst assemblages and compositions, most notably the progressive development of strongly Fe-enriched pyroxenes, olivines, and where present, amphiboles and biotites. Fe-Ti oxide data indicate relatively high equilibration temperatures (800-985°C), and equilibration between the QFM and NNO f_{O_2} buffers (i.e., lower than most orogenic salic magmas). These rhyolites also frequently exhibit very fractionated trace element abundance patterns.

INTRODUCTION
Classification

Streckeisen (1967, p. 181-185) has summarized the diverse opinions concerning the nomenclature of salic volcanic rocks, and has proposed a very logical classification, based on the parameters Q (silica minerals), A (alkali feldspars including albite), and P (plagioclase An_{05-100} and scapolite). Unfortunately, this classification necessitates the recalculation of the chemistry of the volcanic rocks into the necessary normative mineralogy; this, of course, results from the typical volcanic two-stage (or more) crystallization history (phenocryst and groundmass) which represent distinct P-T equilibration assemblages. Rittman (1973) has proposed a rather complex system of recalculation of the chemistry into the necessary mineral molecules, but at least to this writer, the calculation procedure still seems often ambiguous and sometimes arbitrary. Nevertheless, it offers an important approach to the classification of the volcanic rocks being considered in this review.

The occurrence of Tertiary-Recent salic lavas and pyroclastics is predominantly in the island arcs and orogenic (mobile) continental marginal zones, both being regions in which subduction is interpreted to play a key role in magma genesis. Within these regions, well defined geographic and stratigraphic variations of chemistry are often recognized within volcanic sequences (e.g., Jakes and White, 1969), even within a given compositional type (e.g., dacite). Variation of K_2O is the most significant within the major elements, and three distinct series of volcanic eruptives are commonly distinguished within the subduction tectonic environment; i.e., low-K series, calc-alkali series, and high-K series. Moreover, these three series are not necessarily distinguished by routine petrography. Thus, many current workers, particularly those studying the S.W. Pacific region, prefer a simpler chemical classification scheme, based on a simple plot of SiO_2 versus K_2O (wt. %, e.g., Mackenzie and Chappell, 1972; Peccerillo and Taylor, 1976). This approach has been adopted in this review for certain aspects of the data reduction and presentation, and the scheme of Peccerillo and Taylor (1976) is followed with minor modification for nomenclature. Thus, throughout this paper, volcanic rocks for which SiO_2 >69% are referred to as rhyolites; 63-69% SiO_2 as dacites; 60-63% SiO_2 as silicic andesites. When necessary, the terms low-K, calc-alkaline, and high-K are added as prefixes.

Aims and Methods of Approach of Review

The primary aim is to present comparative data of the chemistry and mineralogy of "dacitoid" and associated magmas from diverse geographic regions. In order to cover a reasonably comprehensive range of salic volcanic rocks, the following procedures for data selection and treatment have been adopted:

(a) With the exception of peralkaline (a recent review of peralkaline volcanic rocks is to be found in Bulletin Volcanologique, Volume 38, 1974) and silica undersaturated types, all data for volcanic lavas and pyroclastics for which SiO_2 >60% (anhydrous basis) are included in the compilations.

(b) No data are included for pre-Tertiary rocks, partly because of increasing problems of secondary alteration, and partly because of increasing ambiguity as to the tectonic environment of these older volcanic series.

(c) In data selection, emphasis has been placed on obtaining both chemical (major and trace elements), mineralogical (phenocryst), and petrographic data for individual samples. Altogether, some 2,890 sets of data are utilized, based on data available to October 1977. The complete list of data sources is provided in the references. Although the literature search cannot be described as exhaustive, it is intended to provide a reasonably comprehensive coverage of salic volcanic occurrences from diverse geographic and tectonic regions. Data have only been excluded if there is clear evidence (mineralogical or chemical) of modification due to weathering, hydrothermal alteration, or leaching. By far the majority of chemical analyses utilized in the compilations included specific determinations for FeO and Fe_2O_3. Where only a total Fe value was published, the FeO and Fe_2O_3 were calculated according to the method of Le Maitre (1976).

(d) The data have been primarily subdivided on the basis of two criteria: (i) SiO_2 content, and (ii) geographic and/or tectonic region. Chemically, the following five groupings are prepared, based on $SiO_2\%$ (calculated on anhydrous basis): 60-63%; 63-66%; 66-69%; 69-73%; >73%. This procedure partly overcomes ambiguities caused by arbitrary classification divisions. In practice, the 60-63% SiO_2 group corresponds approximately to silicic andesites, the 63-66% and 66-69% divisions to most definitions of dacites and quartz latites, and the >69% divisions to most definitions of rhyodacites and rhyolites.

The geographic and/or tectonic regional groupings are as follows:

Number
(Reference to
Figs. 1-3,21-22;
Tables 1-3; and
appendices 1-3)

Regional Grouping

Number	Regional Grouping
1.	Western (Andean) South America
2.	Middle Americas (Mexico, Guatemala, El Salvador, Honduras, Nicaragua, Costa Rica).
3.	Western U.S.A.--eastern belt (zone), defined on basis of the inferred eastern subduction zone of Lipman, Prostka, and Christiansen (1972, see their Fig. 9, p. 235). The Yellowstone and Snake River plain rhyolites are excluded (see later).
4.	Western U.S.A.--western belt (zone), but excluding the Quaternary Cascades. Boundary defined as in 3 above. The Mono and Salton Sea rhyolites (California) are excluded (see later).
5.	Quaternary High Cascades of northwestern U.S.A. and Canada (including the Medicine Lake and Newberry volcanic centres), Alaska, and Aleutians.

6.	Japan (including the southern islands), Taiwan, Kuriles, Kamchatka, and Saipan.
7.	Indonesia (Sunda arc).
8.	S.W. Pacific, including Papua, New Guinea, Soloman Islands, New Hebrides, Fiji, Tonga-Kermadec Islands and New Zealand.
9.	Tonga-Kermadec Islands (considered as a separate subdivision).
10.	Mediterranean region, comprising the Eolian and and Aegean island arcs (e.g., Barberi et al., 1974).
11.	Caribbean (Lesser Antilles) island arc.
12.	South Sandwich Islands (Scotia arc).
13.	Deception Island (within South Shetland islands)
14.	Western Scotland and Northern Ireland (Slieve Gullion complex).
15.	Iceland
16.	Galapagos Islands
17.	Canary Islands.

The complete averaged data (chemical and mineralogical) divided according to the criteria set out above, are presented in Tables 1-A and 1-B.

(e) For further consideration and discussion of the compilations, the data for the orogenic volcanic sequences have been further divided into "low-K," "calc-alkaline," and "high-K" groupings, based on slightly modified chemical subdivisions proposed by Peccerillo and Taylor (1976), a plot of which is shown in Figure 1. Selected averaged data, subdivided into three chemical series, are presented in Appendices 1, 2, and 3.

(f) Trace and minor element data are also included in the compilations of Tables 1 and Appendices 1, 2, and 3. The average concentrations are based as all available data (for which adequate accompanying major element data are given), irrespective of the analytical technique used. This has the obvious disadvantage that data of variable quality are mixed (e.g., optical spectrographic and isotope dilution data). In the interests of obtaining as wide a coverage as possible, however, this "blanket" approach was preferred.

(g) Petrographic data on phenocryst phases, presented in Tables 1-3 and Appendices 1-3 are based on both modal abundances (only limited data available), and also in terms of the % frequency occurrence of each mineral phase present within a given grouping. This is based on the stated occurrence of a given mineral phase in published petrographic descriptions. It must be noted, however, that many accounts which may present excellent chemical data, are

Table 1 - A - Compilation of total major and trace element data for salic volcanic eruptives, grouped according to geographic and/or tectonic region. The data are averaged into five SiO₂ intervals. Major element analyses are recalculated to 100% on an anhydrous basis.

	Region No ‡	1				2				
	Region ‡	Western (Andean) South America				Middle Americas				
SiO₂ interval	60-63	63-66	66-69	69-73	>73	60-63	63-66	66-69	69-73	>73
SiO₂	61.83	64.49	67.36	70.45	75.51	61.62	64.71	67.47	71.02	75.95
TiO₂	0.86	0.74	0.62	0.46	0.20	0.82	0.69	0.53	0.41	0.19
Al₂O₃	16.91	16.25	15.76	15.43	13.21	16.83	16.67	16.40	15.54	13.05
Fe₂O₃	3.25	2.50	2.69	1.76	1.06	2.60ˣ	2.27ˣ	1.90ˣ	1.74	1.16
FeO	2.35	2.25	1.45	0.98	0.21	2.94ˣ	2.38ˣ	1.83ˣ	1.05	0.66
MnO	0.09	0.08	0.07	0.05	0.06	0.11	0.11	0.11	0.09	0.04
MgO	2.83	2.23	1.35	0.84	0.35	3.11	2.07	1.41	0.63	0.28
CaO	5.18	4.39	3.46	2.27	1.18	5.57	4.51	3.28	2.26	0.78
Na₂O	3.71	3.71	3.51	3.72	3.68	4.18	4.22	4.32	3.56	3.41
K₂O	2.72	3.12	3.49	3.90	4.48	2.02	2.22	2.65	3.59	4.42
P₂O₅	0.26	0.22	0.23	0.14	0.05	0.21	0.16	0.11	0.09	0.06
n	31	37	27	17	28	47	42	27	15	20
Trace elements⁺ (p.p.m.)										
Rb	101(18)⁺	124(15)	169(13)	173(9)	132(7)	53(18)	52(20)	56(7)	124(1)	160(7)
Ba	798(8)	718(4)	510(2)	570(1)	649(9)	588(11)	546(10)	560(3)	565(1)	318(6)
Sr	582(18)	430(15)	288(14)	214(10)	126(16)	465(18)	480(20)	462(7)	97(1)	48(7)
Zr	178(13)	140(12)	99(12)	79(6)	307(10)	72(18)	172(1)	172(1)	n.d.	n.d.
Zn	95(4)#	97(7)#	122(10)	90(5)	56(1)	n.d.	60(19)	52(6)	25(1)	37(7)
La	n.d.	n.d.	n.d.	n.d.	n.d.	n.d.	n.d.	n.d.	n.d.	n.d.
Ce	47(3)	45(8)	47(2)	n.d.	n.d.	n.d.	137(1)	143(1)	n.d.	n.d.
Yb	2.1(3)#	1.4(8)	1.4(2)	n.d.	n.d.	n.d.	n.d.	n.d.	n.d.	n.d.
Y	7(8)	6(4)	n.d.	n.d.	15(9)	n.d.	n.d.	n.d.	n.d.	n.d.
Cu	33(13)	29(11)	31(11)	16(6)	4(1)	19(20)	12(20)	11(6)	1.7(1)	2.8(7)
Ni	49(14)	16(20)	12(14)	13(5)	5(10)	43(19)	28(21)	19(7)	7.2(1)	8.6(7)
Co	20(13)	12(11)	9(12)	8(6)	n.d.	n.d.	n.d.	n.d.	n.d.	n.d.
Cr	58(8)	26(4)	22(1)	n.d.	n.d.	92(20)	63(21)	41(7)	5.2(1)	18(7)
V	128(8)	107(4)	104(2)	40(1)	32(9)	n.d.	n.d.	n.d.	n.d.	n.d.
Nb	n.d.	n.d.	n.d.	n.d.	n.d.	n.d.	n.d.	n.d.	n.d.	n.d.
Li	n.d.	n.d.	48(1)	n.d.	30(4)	9(18)	10(19)	10(6)	n.d.	n.d.
Pb	n.d.	n.d.	n.d.	n.d.	57(9)	n.d.	n.d.	n.d.	n.d.	n.d.
Hf	n.d.	n.d.	n.d.	n.d.	n.d.	n.d.	n.d.	n.d.	n.d.	21(2)

	Region No[‡]	3					4				
	Region[‡]	Western U.S.A. – Eastern Belt					Western U.S.A. – Western Belt				
	SiO₂ interval	60-63	63-66	66-69	69-73	>73	60-63	63-66	66-69	60-73	>73
SiO₂		61.77	64.51	67.56	71.11	75.78	61.58	64.53	67.69	71.60	75.94
TiO₂		0.89	0.74	0.55	0.40	0.18	0.83	0.72	0.54	0.35	0.14
Al₂O₃		16.63	16.52	16.20	15.06	13.08	16.90	16.65	16.21	15.02	13.16
Fe₂O₃		3.72	3.31	2.63	1.75	1.01	3.11	2.74	2.32	1.46	0.75
FeO		1.98	1.33	0.82	0.65	0.39	2.64	1.74	1.18	0.89	0.50
MnO		0.09	0.10	0.08	0.07	0.06	0.10	0.08	0.07	0.05	0.05
MgO		2.32	1.49	0.92	0.64	0.23	2.72	1.81	1.11	0.50	0.21
CaO		4.76	3.66	2.72	1.83	0.68	5.66	3.94	3.17	1.96	0.83
Na₂O		4.02	4.15	4.27	3.82	3.68	3.70	3.92	3.79	3.73	3.59
K₂O		3.44	3.92	4.07	4.58	4.86	2.50	3.62	3.75	4.34	4.79
P₂O₅		0.37	0.27	0.19	0.11	0.04	0.26	0.24	0.17	0.09	0.04
n		62	59	74	84	59	47	63	29	55	145
Trace elements[+] (p.p.m.)											
Rb		102(6)	125(5)	93(3)	163(6)	231(2)	127(3)	199(8)	n.d.	140(6)	192(25)
Ba		1680(13)	1420(23)	1700(34)	1330(19)	409(13)	1700(16)	1700(25)	1614(14)	1324(17)	363(44)
Sr		1000(18)	768(24)	547(35)	339(22)	118(15)	1070(16)	1098(27)	893(14)	455(17)	79(44)
Zr		330(14)	253(23)	243(34)	248(19)	172(13)	225(16)	216(25)	245(14)	176(17)	129(44)
Zn		95(1)	n.d.	68(1)	n.d.	n.d.	58(2)	79(4)	n.d.	43(5)	36(9)
La		110(10)	96(19)	88(18)	77(14)	75(8)	89(14)	79(14)	125(6)	95(15)	53(32)
Ce		215(8)	292(11)	271(8)	174(6)	100(11)	146(14)	143(9)	208(6)	184(11)	93(13)
Yb		2.3(10)	2.6(20)	2.8(24)	2.5(14)	3.0(12)	2.2(9)	2.1(15)	2.1(11)	3.8(9)	4.5(23)
Y		25(12)	30(23)	31(33)	29(19)	29(12)	23(16)	22(25)	18(14)	29(17)	33(43)
Cu		25(14)	25(23)	15(34)	13(18)	5(13)	34(15)	18(24)	10(14)	12(17)	6(41)
Ni		36(11)	29(2)	5(24)	5(18)	-1(12)	32(16)	24(25)	10(13)	8(12)	2(36)
Co		13(12)	10(21)	6(23)	3(15)	2(13)	20(14)	27(24)	21(13)	8(9)	4(36)
Cr		61(14)	31(22)	6(32)	4(17)	2(12)	94(16)	47(25)	22(14)	15(15)	2(35)
V		89(14)	73(20)	56(27)	26(13)	14(13)	110(16)	74(25)	49(14)	27(15)	5(35)
Nb		18(10)	16(16)	19(14)	18(10)	36(11)	18(13)	17(12)	24(6)	17(13)	19(41)
Li		n.d.	n.d.	n.d.	n.d.	n.d.	26(2)	21(11)	19(7)	12(1)	42(13)
Pb		24(11)	33(20)	34(30)	30(18)	30(12)	29(15)	24(25)	19(14)	28(16)	40(42)
Hf		n.d.	n.d.	n.d.	n.d.	n.d.	n.d.	n.d.	n.d.	n.d.	n.d.

‡   See Introduction.

‡   Numbers in brackets refer to number of data used to calculate average for each trace element.

+   Number of data used to calculate average for each element.

n   Number of data used to calculate average for each element.

n.d.   Insufficient data.

x   Fe₂O₃/FeO values adjusted according to method of Le Maitre (1976) for much of data used in compilation of these analyses.

Ignoring one anomalously high Zn value in each group.

Table 1-A-continued (2)

Region No.	5					6				
Region	High Cascades		Alaska	Aleutians		Japan	Taiwan	Kuriles	Kamchatka	Saipan
SiO$_2$ interval	60-63	63-66	66-69	69-73	>73	60-63	63-66	66-69	69-73	>73
SiO$_2$	61.60	64.42	67.60	71.34	74.18	61.58	64.34	67.46	70.88	75.37
TiO$_2$	0.79	0.63	0.58	0.34	0.23	0.71	0.68	0.60	0.48	0.26
Al$_2$O$_3$	17.25	16.78	16.08	14.85	13.93	16.86	16.27	15.70	14.96	13.33
Fe$_2$O$_3$	2.18	1.94	1.74	1.17	0.57	2.74	2.57	2.03	1.51	0.98
FeO	3.52	2.73	2.06	1.57	1.41	3.83	3.25	2.61	1.67	1.12
MnO	0.11	0.10	0.09	0.06	0.04	0.13	0.14	0.12	0.09	0.06
MgO	2.60	2.27	1.37	0.61	0.31	2.87	2.16	1.42	0.83	0.45
CaO	5.88	5.07	3.39	1.99	1.37	6.20	5.17	4.22	3.02	1.83
Na$_2$O	4.22	4.19	4.47	4.78	4.17	3.39	3.61	3.98	3.98	3.86
K$_2$O	1.60	1.68	2.45	3.18	3.73	1.52	1.64	1.69	2.44	2.62
P$_2$O$_5$	0.25	0.18	0.16	0.10	0.06	0.19	0.18	0.17	0.13	0.12
n	74	57	27	53	35	200	144	97	96	78
Trace elements (p.p.m.)										
Rb	39(25)	59(11)	69(4)	125(18)	136(14)	25(15)	58(3)	64(4)	107(2)	76(10)
Ba	716(25)	738(15)	493(9)	873(14)	840(14)	738(13)	685(6)	383(9)	566(7)	464(6)
Sr	624(39)	954(21)	698(11)	361(15)	154(11)	274(23)	291(8)	197(19)	201(9)	106(15)
Zr	160(19)	173(14)	188(9)	185(12)	207(11)	120(2)	n.d.	n.d.	n.d.	125(1)
Zn	85(8)	63(2)	n.d.	122(3)	68(8)	80(14)	66(5)	86(9)	88(1)	82(1)
La	20(9)	15(3)	21(1)	25(6)	25(7)	15(10)	12(7)	8(6)	15(3)	7.2(4)
Ce	60(11)	46(3)	100(1)	45(2)	43(5)	37(10)	32(7)	24(6)	38(3)	21(4)
Yb	1.8(14)	1.5(9)	1.9(7)	2.5(4)	2.8(6)	2.7(10)	3.7(6)	4.0(6)	2.9(3)	3.7(4)
Y	61(15)	32(13)	34(9)	35(11)	41(9)	19(10)	18(5)	12(15)	10(9)	12(5)
Cu	32(24)	28(12)	17(9)	18(5)	14(8)	38(21)	14(7)	6(12)	1(7)	3(6)
Ni	27(19)	34(13)	24(8)	4(7)	2(9)	42(17)	29(5)	20(9)	22(1)	19(2)
Co	16(23)	15(12)	13(8)	4(8)	5(12)	23(26)	15(8)	15(11)	10(3)	6(3)
Cr	39(24)	44(14)	32(8)	5(10)	3(10)	54(24)	16(8)	9(12)	5(3)	14(3)
V	117(18)	92(14)	83(8)	27(8)	13(7)	130(10)	70(5)	26(15)	19(6)	14(5)
Nb	4.6(6)	6.5(6)	5(2)	n.d.	5(2)	4.4(2)	n.d.	n.d.	n.d.	0.5(1)
Li	35(2)	57(3)	n.d.	65(4)	93(3)	8(16)	11(5)	13(9)	6.5(1)	8(1)
Pb	5.5(11)	7.5(5)	8.3(2)	15(8)	18(6)	9(7)	16(3)	7(8)	7(6)	9(5)
Hf	n.d.	n.d.	n.d.	6.3(2)	4.2(3)	3.3(9)	4.4(4)	3.1(3)	4.5(2)	3.2(2)

Region No.	7					8				
Region	Indonesia					S.W. Pacific				
SiO_2 interval	60-63	63-66	66-69	69-73	>73	60-63	63-66	66-69	69-73	>73
SiO_2	60.43	63.87	66.64	70.91	75.49	61.24	64.50	67.27	71.28	75.15
TiO_2	0.68	0.73	0.68	0.35	0.24	0.69	0.67	0.57	0.42	0.25
Al_2O_3	17.67	16.17	15.76	15.10	13.81	16.47	15.57	15.45	14.49	13.28
Fe_2O_3	2.93*	2.83*	2.42*	1.68	0.80	2.59	2.13	1.94	1.43	0.88
FeO	3.50*	3.10*	2.20*	1.30	0.67	3.75	3.73	2.76	1.75	1.01
MnO	0.13	0.10	0.10	0.05	0.03	0.12	0.13	0.11	0.08	0.06
MgO	2.66	2.05	1.27	0.77	0.16	3.23	2.31	1.40	0.65	0.31
CaO	6.05	4.85	3.33	2.58	1.21	6.22	5.24	4.26	2.44	1.52
Na_2O	3.54	3.73	4.28	3.53	3.97	3.55	3.73	4.06	4.57	4.23
K_2O	2.19	2.43	3.16	3.67	3.56	1.92	1.78	1.99	2.81	3.27
P_2O_5	0.23	0.16	0.17	0.07	0.05	0.23	0.20	0.18	0.09	0.05
n	21	10	9	8	5	145	89	54	44	100
Trace elements* (p.p.m.)										
Rb	71(18)	86(8)	105(9)	154(4)	n.d.	48(90)	36(43)	43(25)	100(22)	108(42)
Ba	414(8)	420(1)	460(2)	n.d.	n.d.	506(89)	515(48)	462(24)	762(24)	782(54)
Sr	349(18)	277(8)	259(9)	155(4)	n.d.	473(98)	478(48)	456(25)	152(22)	103(42)
Zr	162(17)	183(5)	271(6)	n.d.	n.d.	140(46)	114(46)	167(20)	351(22)	176(42)
Zn	n.d.	n.d.	66(1)	49(4)	n.d.	77(24)	86(28)	79(17)	62(20)	32(16)
La	17(2)	n.d.	31(1)	n.d.	n.d.	20(44)	15(36)	17(19)	48(22)	28(38)
Ce	34(2)	n.d.	59(1)	n.d.	n.d.	38(44)	28(37)	35(18)	76(20)	55(20)
Yb	2.3(2)	n.d.	2.4(1)	n.d.	n.d.	2.0(13)	2.2(7)	2.4(4)	7.7(5)	3.4(9)
Y	30(17)	35(5)	47(1)	35(4)	n.d.	25(68)	28(44)	27(25)	51(22)	25(41)
Cu	23(8)	37(1)	25(2)	n.d.	n.d.	47(86)	26(44)	17(23)	7(22)	7(41)
Ni	9(8)	1(1)	1(2)	n.d.	n.d.	26(83)	21(42)	10(22)	3(20)	3(18)
Co	12(8)	10(1)	7(2)	n.d.	n.d.	19(32)	13(26)	9(13)	7(3)	4(4)
Cr	26(8)	3(1)	3(2)	n.d.	n.d.	68(88)	38(44)	11(23)	13(22)	4(41)
V	104(8)	74(1)	44(2)	n.d.	n.d.	138(90)	88(44)	61(23)	13(22)	10(41)
Nb	9.4(2)	n.d.	6(1)	n.d.	n.d.	6(24)	7(15)	9(6)	35(17)	17(17)
Li	n.d.	n.d.	n.d.	n.d.	n.d.	16(2)	n.d.	10(1)	29(2)	35(23)
Pb	12(2)	n.d.	17(1)	25(3)	n.d.	10(59)	12(25)	14(18)	14(19)	16(21)
Hf	3.4(2)	n.d.	4.7(1)	n.d.	n.d.	3.1(10)	2.4(5)	4.2(4)	8.9(5)	4.7(10)

* Fe_2O_3/FeO values adjusted according to method of Le Maitre (1976) for much of data used in compilation of these analyses.

Table 1-A-continued (3)

Region No.	9			10					11			
Region	Tonga – Kermadec Islands			Mediterranean					Caribbean [++]			
SiO$_2$ interval	60–63	63–66	66–69	60–63	63–66	66–69	69–73	>73	60–62	62–64	64–66	>66
SiO$_2$	61.37	65.07	66.79	61.84	64.33	67.60	70.56	75.61	60.99	62.94	64.97	67.86
TiO$_2$	0.71	0.59	0.62	0.70	0.68	0.51	0.41	0.17	0.60	0.52	0.43	0.38
Al$_2$O$_3$	14.94	14.31	13.75	17.14	16.45	15.72	15.05	13.33	17.27	16.97	16.71	15.55
Fe$_2$O$_3$	3.20	1.76	1.32	2.84	2.55	2.21	1.67	0.94	1.74	1.48	1.40	1.25
FeO	6.37	5.93	6.28	2.17	2.45	1.65	1.09	0.44	4.82	4.19	3.89	3.47
MnO	0.20	0.17	0.14	0.10	0.10	0.08	0.07	0.05	0.16	0.14	0.14	0.13
MgO	2.46	2.07	1.54	2.42	1.83	1.24	0.85	0.34	2.29	1.90	1.33	1.02
CaO	7.11	6.02	5.43	5.70	4.49	3.74	2.73	1.02	7.06	6.41	5.79	5.30
Na$_2$O	2.92	2.96	3.17	3.46	3.77	3.85	3.76	3.18	3.30	3.41	3.43	3.24
K$_2$O	0.60	0.96	0.79	3.36	3.11	3.25	3.69	4.80	1.08	1.38	1.35	1.50
P$_2$O$_5$	0.13	0.16	0.17	0.26	0.23	0.16	0.12	0.11	0.12	0.11	0.11	0.08
n	5	17	7	82	85	39	44	27	93	95	90	26
Trace elements (p.p.m.)												
Rb	8(5)	14(15)	11(3)	69(24)	95(15)	126(12)	138(8)	356(7)	37(93)	49(95)	46(90)	52(26)
Ba	180(5)	272(16)	243(3)	1032(14)	776(7)	959(3)	484(2)	26(3)	298	352	281	242
Sr	231(5)	257(16)	218(3)	486(24)	353(16)	299(12)	204(8)	13(7)	394	416	328	283
Zr	45(5)	51(15)	63(3)	191(8)	177(6)	129(1)	205(1)	51(3)	116	117	111	106
Zn	102(5)	102(14)	124(3)	69(8)	67(9)	57(4)	51(2)	40(7)	66	60	54	48
La	4.0(5)	4.0(15)	3.9(3)	22(14)	23.3(5)	19(1)	56(1)	16(3)	n.d.	n.d.	n.d.	n.d.
Ce	9.5(5)	10.1(15)	11.9(3)	53(4)	51.9(5)	71(1)	132(1)	59(3)	n.d.	n.d.	n.d.	n.d.
Yb	1.3(1)	2.3(2)	3.9(1)	2.4(3)	1.5(12)	n.d.	n.d.	n.d.	n.d.	n.d.	n.d.	n.d.
Y	24(5)	26(15)	27(3)	23(9)	28(6)	29(1)	41(1)	97(3)	26	23	23	22
Cu	76(5)	31(15)	16(3)	25(17)	21(12)	19(4)	43(2)	13(7)	46	45	40	40
Ni	3(5)	6(15)	3(3)	14(11)	12(12)	9(4)	6(3)	4(7)	33	40	32	30
Co	23(5)	15(14)	12(3)	13(11)	12(9)	8(6)	5(3)	3(7)	n.d.	n.d.	n.d.	n.d.
Cr	7(5)	19(15)	3(3)	10(4)	16(6)	6(3)	17(2)	35(3)	96	130	110	107
V	209(5)	102(15)	64(3)	105(8)	85(6)	47(3)	35(1)	n.d.	109	93	71	35
Nb	1.5(1)	3.1(2)	1(1)	24(3)	21(5)	n.d.	n.d.	n.d.	5	6	4	4
Li	n.d.	n.d.	n.d.	14(7)	17(6)	26(3)	18(1)	26(4)	n.d.	n.d.	n.d.	n.d.
Pb	2.7(4)	3.4(6)	4(2)	6.2(4)	7.0(3)	n.d.	n.d.	n.d.	n.d.	n.d.	n.d.	n.d.
Hf	0.72(1)	1.2(1)	2.2(1)	5.5(3)	3.4(2)	n.d.	n.d.	n.d.	n.d.	n.d.	n.d.	n.d.

Region No.	13						14	
Region	Deception Island			Fedarb Island	Western Scotland		Northern Ireland	
SiO_2 interval	60-63	66-69	69-73	66-69	63-66	66-69	69-73	>73
SiO_2	61.79	67.83	70.98	68.28	63.35	67.59	70.89	75.71
TiO_2	1.30	0.70	0.49	0.82	0.97	0.96	0.77	0.27
Al_2O_3	16.25	15.12	14.28	15.16	14.74	13.46	13.14	11.96
Fe_2O_3	1.21	1.57	1.31	1.63	1.56	2.06	2.38	1.17
FeO	5.60	3.18	2.36	2.19	5.91	4.34	2.80	1.31
MnO	0.17	0.15	0.10	0.15	0.20	0.24	0.14	0.12
MgO	1.67	0.54	0.87	1.16	2.02	1.02	0.67	0.20
CaO	4.03	2.09	3.58	3.02	4.17	3.21	1.88	0.97
Na_2O	6.37	6.77	5.17	5.90	3.68	3.93	3.56	3.79
K_2O	1.28	1.89	0.80	1.46	3.11	3.00	3.55	4.43
P_2O_5	0.34	0.16	0.06	0.23	0.29	0.19	0.14	0.07
n	4	6	1	2	3	7	10	18

Trace elements (p.p.m.)

Rb	19(3)	29(1)	n.d.	19(2)	84(1)	n.d.	89(6)	147(11)
Ba	295(2)	340(1)	n.d.	347(2)	1559(1)	n.d.	986(6)	384(10)
Sr	210(3)	135(1)	n.d.	436(2)	216(1)	n.d.	115(6)	102(11)
Zr	353(3)	535(1)	n.d.	87(2)	414(1)	n.d.	325(6)	319(10)
Zn	n.d.	n.d.	n.d.	24(2)	101(1)	n.d.	210(1)	56(8)
La	n.d.	n.d.	n.d.	56(2)	n.d.	n.d.	63(6)	113(9)
Ce	n.d.	n.d.	n.d.	2,8(1)	n.d.	n.d.	82(3)	85(1)
Yb	49(3)	57(1)	n.d.	31(2)	n.d.	n.d.	n.d.	n.d.
Y	n.d.	n.d.	n.d.	24(2)	25(1)	n.d.	45(4)	33(9)
Cu	19(1)	n.d.	n.d.	<5(2)	1(1)	n.d.	15(3)	5.3(9)
Ni	29(2)	5(1)	n.d.	n.d.	n.d.	n.d.	4(3)	2.4(9)
Co	25(1)	n.d.	n.d.	26(2)	n.d.	n.d.	2(3)	1.9(9)
Cr	55(1)	tr(1)	n.d.	30(2)	n.d.	n.d.	4(3)	3.5(9)
V	n.d.	n.d.	n.d.	n.d.	n.d.	n.d.	14(3)	11(9)
Nb	37(2)	48(1)	n.d.	n.d.	n.d.	n.d.	16(3)	17(9)
Li	n.d.	n.d.	n.d.	16(2)	n.d.	n.d.	15(3)	23(9)
Pb	n.d.	n.d.	n.d.	n.d.	n.d.	n.d.	15(1)	19(8)
Hf	n.d.	n.d.	n.d.	n.d.	n.d.	n.d.	n.d.	n.d.

++ Data taken directly from Brown et al (1977).

Table 1 - A - Continued (4)

Region No. Region	15 Iceland*					16 Galápagos Islands		
SiO$_2$ interval	60-63	63-66	66-69	69-73	>73	60-63	66-69	69-73
SiO$_2$	61.47	64.26	67.99	72.19	75.06	60.67	66.86	70.62
TiO$_2$	1.03	0.95	0.58	0.33	0.23	1.87	0.68	0.70
Al$_2$O$_3$	15.85	14.62	14.73	13.86	12.77	14.75	14.70	13.25
Fe$_2$O$_3$	2.59	3.45	2.34	1.03	1.16	3.51	5.61	1.94
FeO	5.98	3.67	2.65	2.65	1.43	4.74	1.61	2.67
MnO	0.24	0.15	0.12	0.10	0.07	0.16	0.11	0.10
MgO	1.64	1.36	0.99	0.14	0.16	2.16	0.33	0.63
CaO	4.88	4.11	3.54	1.60	1.38	4.99	1.08	1.16
Na$_2$O	4.13	4.77	4.44	4.89	4.52	4.42	5.97	5.62
K$_2$O	1.79	2.45	2.46	3.13	3.15	2.22	2.94	3.25
P$_2$O$_5$	0.39	0.20	0.16	0.06	0.05	0.50	0.11	0.05
n	7	5	10	4	29	2	1	1
Trace element (p.p.m.)								
Rb	n.d.	n.d.	81(2)	n.d.	113(12)	n.d.	n.d.	n.d.
Ba	n.d.	n.d.	1300(1)	n.d.	1046(12)	300(1)	460(1)	520(1)
Sr	n.d.	n.d.	200(2)	n.d.	114(12)	245(1)	157(1)	170(1)
Zr	n.d.	n.d.	493(2)	n.d.	386(12)	551(1)	1016(1)	1170(1)
Zn	n.d.	n.d.	185(1)	105(1)	122(12)	n.d.	n.d.	n.d.
La	n.d.	n.d.	150(1)	n.d.	167(12)	39(1)	98(1)	61.5(1)
Ce	n.d.	n.d.	n.d.	n.d.	n.d.	n.d.	n.d.	n.d.
Yb	n.d.	n.d.	n.d.	n.d.	n.d.	n.d.	n.d.	n.d.
Y	n.d.	n.d.	41(2)	n.d.	44(12)	41(1)	66(1)	100(1)
Cu	n.d.	n.d.	0.5(1)	9(1)	10(12)	33(1)	9(1)	14(1)
Ni	n.d.	n.d.	0.5(1)	0.9(1)	0.7(12)	10(1)	9(1)	13(1)
Co	n.d.	n.d.	1.1(1)	2.1(1)	1.3(12)	20.8(1)	3.5(1)	4.2(1)
Cr	n.d.	n.d.	n.d.	n.d.	5(12)	10(1)	n.d.	15(1)
V	n.d.	n.d.	20(1)	n.d.	15(12)	98(1)	5(1)	19(1)
Nb	n.d.	n.d.	25(1)	n.d.	27(12)	34(1)	73(1)	n.d.
Li	n.d.	n.d.	20(1)	n.d.	13(12)	n.d.	n.d.	n.d.
Pb	n.d.	n.d.	10(1)	10(1)	9(12)	n.d.	n.d.	n.d.
Hf	n.d.	n.d.	n.d.	n.d.	n.d.	12.4(1)	23.7(1)	22.9(1)

| Region No. | | | 17 | | | | |
| Region | Hawaii | Zephyr Shoal Lau Basin | Tenegua Volcano Canary Islands | | Potassic | Trachytes | | |
SiO₂ interval	66-69	63-66	69-73	>73	60-63	63-66	66-69	69-73
SiO_2	67.77	64.72	71.76	74.81	62.00	64.88	67.77	70.14
TiO_2	0.57	0.54	0.33	0.25	0.75	0.75	0.60	0.37
Al_2O_3	15.70	14.90	16.04	14.52	17.85	16.25	15.37	15.10
Fe_2O_3	1.37	3.16	0.32	0.43	2.68	2.74	1.96	1.73
FeO	1.37	2.61	0.70	0.35	2.42	1.15	1.51	1.08
MnO	0.06	0.09	0.02	0.02	0.19	0.09	0.10	0.07
MgO	1.53	3.50	0.46	0.92	0.88	1.02	0.58	0.17
CaO	2.79	5.28	0.29	1.05	2.59	2.56	1.53	0.76
Na_2O	4.51	4.13	5.71	5.58	5.54	4.78	4.90	5.18
K_2O	3.69	1.01	4.29	2.04	4.82	5.51	5.53	5.36
P_2O_5	0.32	0.05	0.06	0.03	0.28	0.26	0.14	0.05
n	3	2	2	1	17	24	21	5
Trace element (p.p.m.)								
Rb	n.d.	7.8(1)	115(1)	35(1)	114(4)	116(11)	140(11)	134(2)
Ba	n.d.	100(1)	748(1)	1162(1)	1073(5)	1726(12)	1040(13)	1103(2)
Sr	n.d.	170(1)	58(1)	324(1)	323(5)	1087(13)	591(15)	101(2)
Zr	n.d.	72(1)	696(1)	688(1)	1020(4)	611(12)	682(10)	742(2)
Zn	n.d.	n.d.	31(1)	26(1)	121(4)	72(10)	121(9)	201(2)
La	n.d.	4.1(1)	129(1)	113(1)	71(3)	82(11)	85(10)	64(2)
Ce	n.d.	9.0(1)	n.d.	n.d.	118(4)	128(11)	141(10)	122(2)
Yb	n.d.	0.85(1)	n.d.	n.d.	3.4(2)	2.9(5)	3.0(5)	n.d.
Y	n.d.	8(1)	134(1)	130(1)	58(4)	24(11)	36(8)	67(2)
Cu	n.d.	n.d.	16(1)	18(1)	27(2)	105(10)	58(11)	1(2)
Ni	n.d.	n.d.	33(1)	14(1)	2(2)	22(11)	12(9)	2(2)
Co	n.d.	n.d.	n.d.	n.d.	n.d.	n.d.	4(3)	n.d.
Cr	n.d.	n.d.	32(1)	n.d.	0.5(4)	43(11)	17(8)	3(2)
V	n.d.	n.d.	n.d.	n.d.	13(4)	97(11)	60(8)	1(2)
Nb	n.d.	4.2(1)	n.d.	n.d.	105(4)	16(11)	30(7)	48(2)
Li	n.d.	n.d.	n.d.	n.d.	15(1)	n.d.	52(2)	n.d.
Pb	n.d.	3(1)	n.d.	n.d.	16(4)	22(10)	23(7)	16(2)
Hf	n.d.	1.7(1)	n.d.	n.d.	15.7(1)	11.7(3)	13(1)	n.d.

* Granophyres specifically excluded in compilation.

Table 1 - B - Compilation of total mineralogical (phenocryst) data for salic
volcanic eruptives, grouped according to geographic and/or tectonic region.
The data are arranged into five SiO2 intervals, all divisions corresponding
to those presented in Table 1 - A.

Region No[+]	1					2				
Region	Western (Andean) South America					Middle Americas				
SiO$_2$ interval	60-63	63-66	66-69	69-73	>73	60-63	63-66	66-69	69-73	>73
Phenocryst modes (volume %):										
Sa*	0.31	0	0	8.1	n.d.	0	0	0	0	4.1
Pl	23.2	21.3	14.5	5.9	n.d.	25.5	23.3	14.3	18.6	4.6
Qtz	0.06	0	0	7.7	n.d	0	0	0.01	0	10.1
Ol	0.03	0.04	0	0	n.d.	0.29	0	1.0	0.13	0
Cpx	1.1	1.1	0.7	0.13	n.d.	2.3	1.1	1.0	0.20	0
Opx	2.2	2.9	1.8	0.17	n.d.	4.7	2.3	0.74	0.67	0
Hb	6.9	2.9	0.27	0.17	n.d.	0.38	0.75	0.90	2.1	0
Bi	0.34	1.4	0.03	1.8	n.d.	0 .	0	0.23	0	0.34
Sphene	0.04	0	0	0	n.d.	0	0	0	0	0
Fe-Ti oxides	1.8	1.1	0.97	0.57	n.d.	1.0	1.3	0.49	0.03	0
Σ	36.0	30.7	18.3	24.5	-	34.2	28.8	17.7	21.7	19.1
n**	9	12	3	3		8	4	7	3	7
% Frequency occurrence of phenocryst phases										
Sa	7	3	13	54	96	0	0	4	8	92
Pl	93	100	100	100	96	86	93	96	100	67
Qtz	31	24	50	46	92	0	3	15	25	58
Ol	14	8.8	0	0	0	39	0	4	0	0
Cpx	79	65	54	46	4	97	80	85	67	8
Opx	79	85	67	38	0	100	87	77	75	0
Hb	69	68	75	31	50	33	67	65	50	0
Bi	45	62	75	77	100	0	7	8	50	67
Sphene	7	0	8	23	0	0	0	0	0	0
Fe-Ti oxides	59	74	100	100	69	75	93	81	83	0
n**	29	34	24	13	26	36	30	26	12	12

Region No[+]		Western U.S.A. 3 - Eastern Belt					Western U.S.A. 4 - Western Belt				
SiO$_2$ interval		60-63	63-66	66-69	69-73	>73	60-63	63-66	66-69	69-73	>73
Phenocryst modes (volume %):											
Sa*		0.9	1.8	3.5	4.2	8.4	1.3	1.3	1.5	2.9	3.3
Pl		16.6	14.9	18.2	10.9	3.8	20.9	21.8	19.0	12.0	2.4
Qtz		0.10	0.31	0.89	2.6	3.7	0.21	0.25	4.4	3.1	2.7
Ol		0.08	0.01	<0.01	0	0	0.16	0.05	0	0	<0.01
Cpx		2.5	0.89	0.46	0.15	0.02	2.2	1.1	0.44	0.17	0.03
Opx		1.6	0.65	0.09	0.15	0	1.8	0.47	0.67	0.08	0.01
Hb		2.6	1.5	1.3	0.24	0.07	3.3	2.5	0.40	0.66	0.04
Bi		1.7	2.3	2.8	2.0	0.83	2.0	3.9	2.9	2.2	0.32
Sphene		0	<0.01	0.05	0.01	0.01	0	0.02	<0.01	0.03	0.01
Fe-Te oxides		1.4	0.86	1.3	0.61	0.32	0.9	0.48	0.68	0.38	0.10
Σ		27.5	23.2	28.6	20.9	17.2	32.8	31.9	30.0	21.5	8.9
n**		40	47	54	53	30	20	22	21	23	69
% Frequency occurrence of phenocryst phases											
Sa		16	49	73	70	93	4	12	54	54	81
Pl		89	93	100	96	75	100	100	96	98	80
Qtz		10	24	46	52	76	11	33	71	88	75
Ol		7	2	1	0	10	4	5	0	0	6
Cpx		84	63	43	34	10	89	75	79	32	13
Opx		50	17	5	11	0	76	43	46	20	11
Hb		55	63	65	49	19	52	69	82	68	33
Bi		44	73	93	94	90	48	77	96	81	70
Sphene		0	3	18	24	5	0	7	14	34	19
Fe-Ti oxides		73	73	92	82	61	93	93	93	81	69
n**		62	59	74	83	59	46	61	28	41	118

+   See introduction
n.d. Insufficient data
n**   Number of data used in compilation of each set of data.
*   Abbreviations: Sa = Sanidine; Pl = plagioclase; Qtz = Quartz; Ol = olivine; Cpx = clinopyroxene; Opx = orthopyroxene; Hb = hornblende;
         Bi = biotite; Fe-Ti oxides = iron-titanium oxide phases.

Table 1 - B - continued (2)

Region No.	5					6				
Region	High Cascades - Alaska - Aleutians					Japan - Taiwan - Kuriles - Kamchatka - Saipan				
SiO_2 interval	60-63	63-66	66-69	69-73	>73	60-63	63-66	66-69	69-73	>73

Phenocryst modes (volume %):

	60-63	63-66	66-69	69-73	>73	60-63	63-66	66-69	69-73	>73
Sa	0	0	0	0	0	0	0	0	0	0
Pl	20.7	19.1	7.6	9.2	0.91	12.1	10.1	14.6	11.8	11.1
Qtz	0	0.05	0	0.19	0.05	0	1.2	4.0	1.1	4.0
Ol	<0.01	0.02	0.02	<0.01	0	0.03	0.10	0	0	0
Cpx	2.4	1.6	0.72	0.40	0.03	1.3	0.29	0.32	0.38	0.05
Opx	2.7	2.7	0.38	0.64	0.11	2.1	1.3	1.4	1.2	0.40
Hb	1.9	0.7	1.2	0.81	<0.01	0.8	2.1	2.0	0.20	0.25
Bi	0	0.05	0	0.13	0.07	0.02	0.04	0.01	0	0
Sphene	0	0	0	0	0	0	0	0	0	0
Fe-Ti oxides	0.83	0.66	0.35	0.35	0.12	0.43	0.5	0.77	0.55	0.21
Σ	28.5	24.9	10.3	11.7	1.3	16.8	15.6	23.1	15.2	16.0
n	12	10	6	22	12	20	22	15	30	12

% Frequency occurrence of phenocryst phases

	60-63	63-66	66-69	69-73	>73	60-63	63-66	66-69	69-73	>73
Sa	0	0	0	0	0	0	0	0	0	4
Pl	100	100	100	88	94	99	95	98	97	97
Qtz	11	18	27	10	13	10	18	20	28	54
Ol	13	6	12	2	0	14	12	2	7	1
Cpx	86	68	77	84	45	80	68	81	71	53
Opx	94	76	77	88	87	92	84	87	88	58
Hb	29	44	65	59	23	39	43	37	45	26
Bi	2	4	8	14	3	13	12	11	12	21
Sphene	0	0	4	0	0	0	0	0	0	0
Fe-Ti oxides	87	90	89	89	87	86	87	87	85	68
n	63	50	26	49	31	196	139	94	92	72

| Region No. | 7 | | | | | 8 | | | | |
| Region | Indonesia | | | | | S.W. Pacific | | | | |
SiO$_2$ interval	60-63	63-66	66-69	69-73	>73	60-63	63-66	66-69	69-73	>73
Phenocryst modes (volume %):										
Sa	0	2.0	1.3	2.6	n.d.	0.01	0	0	0.01	0.05
Pl	22.1	19.0	14.8	18.1	n.d.	17.8	12.4	10.9	9.0	7.3
Qtz	0	0	0	8.7	n.d.	0.01	0.32	0.30	1.2	1.8
Ol	0.29	0.20	0.25	0	n.d.	0.08	0.04	0	0	<0.01
Cpx	3.5	3.4	1.6	0.03	n.d.	3.0	2.0	1.3	0.41	0.05
Opx	3.8	2.4	2.0	0.03	n.d.	2.3	1.1	1.2	0.62	0.35
Hb	1.1	0.40	0.73	1.2	n.d.	1.7	1.1	1.3	0.52	0.17
Bi	0.06	0	0	3.0	n.d.	0.33	0.41	0.01	0.04	0.17
Sphene	0	0	0	0	n.d.	0	0	0	0	0
Fe-Ti oxides	1.0	1.0	0.90	0.30	n.d.	0.81	0.76	0.60	0.41	0.28
Σ	31.9	28.4	21.6	34.0	-	26.0	18.1	15.6	12.2	10.2
n	17	5	4	4	-	104	62	35	32	77
% Frequency occurrence of phenocryst phases										
Sa	0	57	25	63	100	0.7	0	0	7	2
Pl	100	100	100	100	100	98	100	100	95	98
Qtz	0	29	0	100	50	4	11	19	24	48
Ol	28	14	25	0	0	20	9	4	2	3
Cpx	94	71	100	38	0	79	90	87	61	19
Opx	94	86	75	63	100	69	85	76	73	80
Hb	33	57	25	100	100	37	30	36	34	51
Bi	11	29	0	100	100	16	11	17	20	27
Sphene	0	0	0	0	0	0	0	0	0	0
Fe-Ti oxides	100	100	100	100	100	78	92	87	90	85
n	18	7	4	8	2	138	88	53	41	93

Table 1 - B - Continued (3)

Phenocryst modes (volume %):

Region No.	9			10					11		
Region	Tonga-Kermadec Islands			Mediterranean					Caribbean		
SiO$_2$ interval	60-63	63-66	66-69	60-63	63-66	66-69	69-73	>73	60-63	63-66	66-69
Sa	0	0	0	2.7	2.2	0	0	15.2	0	n.d.	n.d.
Pl	4.0	6.1	5.2	23.3	22.3	25.1	19.1	8.5	25.0	n.d.	n.d.
Qtz	0	0	0	<0.01	<0.01	0.09	0.18	14.4	0.88	n.d.	n.d.
Ol	0	<0.01	0	0.02	1.3	2.4	0.22	0	0.08	n.d.	n.d.
Cpx	0.58	1.6	0.63	3.2	2.2	0.43	0.92	0	0.71	n.d.	n.d.
Opx	0.28	0.72	0.47	1.5	2.9	2.3	2.6	0	3.6	n.d.	n.d.
Hb	0	0	0	3.1	4.2	0.29	0.38	3.6	1.5	n.d.	n.d.
Bi	0	0	0	3.6	0	0	0	0	0.06	n.d.	n.d.
Sphene	0	0	0	0	0	0	0	0	0	n.d.	n.d.
Fe-Ti oxides	0.28	0.35	0.27	0.69	0.41	2.03	0.76	0	1.1	n.d.	n.d.
Σ	5.1	8.8	6.6	38.1	35.5	32.6	24.2	41.7	32.9	-	-
n	5	15	3	21	15	9	5	12	12	-	-

% Frequency occurrence of phenocryst phases

	60-63	63-66	66-69	60-63	63-66	66-69	69-73	>73	60-63	63-66	66-69
Sa	0	0	0	27	26	13	32	92	0	0	0
Pl	100	100	100	100	100	97	100	100	100	100	100
Qtz	0	0	0	17	19	36	52	100	30	40	67
Ol	0	12	0	7	7	0	5	0	0	0	0
Cpx	100	94	100	84	66	59	30	0	91	80	50
Opx	100	100	100	48	66	49	36	0	100	90	83
Hb	0	0	0	65	49	67	73	8	85	90	67
Bi	0	0	0	65	52	62	68	96	6	0	50
Sphene	0	0	0	0	8	13	14	0	0	0	0
Fe-Ti oxides	100	100	100	61	68	79	73	12	97	100	100
n	5	17	7	82	85	39	44	26	33	10	6

| Region No. | 13 | | | Fedarb Island | 14 | | | |
| Region | Deception Islands | | | | Western Scotland-Northern Ireland | | | |
SiO$_2$ interval	60-63	66-69	69-73	66-69	63-66	66-69	69-63	>73
Phenocryst modes (volume %):								
Sa	n.d.	0	n.d.	0	n.d.	0	0	4.0
Pl	n.d.	4.2	n.d.	6.7	n.d.	14.3	14.2	2.1
Qtz	n.d.	0	n.d.	0	n.d.	0	2.3	3.9
Ol	n.d.	0	n.d.	0	n.d.	0	0.05	0.14
Cpx	n.d.	0.7	n.d.	0.6	n.d.	4.7	3.4	0.28
Opx	n.d.	0.5	n.d.	0.2	n.d.	0.1	0.03	0
Hb	n.d.	0	n.d.	0	n.d.	0	0	0.01
Bi	n.d.	0	n.d.	0	n.d.	0	0	0
Sphene	n.d.	0	n.d.	0	n.d.	0	0	0
Fe-Ti oxides	n.d.	0.5	n.d.	0.4	n.d.	1.3	1.2	0.05
Σ	-	5.9	-	7.9	-	20.4	21.2	10.5
n	-	1	-	2	-	1	4	13
% Frequency occurrence of phenocryst phases								
Sa	0	0	0	0	0	0	40	33
Pl	100	100	100	100	67	100	60	78
Qtz	0	0	0	0	0	0	40	67
Ol	75	83	100	0	67	0	30	61
Cpx	50	100	0	100	67	100	70	67
Opx	75	100	100	100	0	33	20	11
Hb	0	0	0	0	0	0	0	6
Bi	0	0	0	0	0	0	0	0
Sphene	0	0	0	0	0	0	0	0
Fe-Ti oxides	50	100	100	100	67	83	50	28
n	4	6	1	2	3	6	10	18

Table 1 - B - Continued (4)

Phenocryst modes (volume%):

	Iceland 60-63	Iceland 63-66	Iceland 66-69	Iceland 69-73	Iceland >73	Galápagos Islands 60-63	Galápagos Islands 66-69	Hawaii 66-69	Zephyr Shoal Lau Basin	Potassic Trachytes 60-63	Potassic Trachytes 63-66	Potassic Trachytes 66-69	Potassic Trachytes 69-73
Sa	n.d.	0	0	0	1.1	n.d.	n.d.	0	0	8.5	6.7	24.2	7.7
Pl	n.d.	4.9	4.1	8.1	1.8	n.d.	n.d.	12.0	30	2.1	9.4	0.68	2.0
Qtz	n.d.	0	0	0.7	0.7	n.d.	n.d.	0	0	0	0	0.16	0
Ol	n.d.	0.80	0.60	1.6	0.03	n.d.	n.d.	0	0	0.15	0.10	0.65	0.10
Cpx	n.d.	0	0.28	0	0.13	n.d.	n.d.	0.75	10	0.63	0.66	0.01	0.23
Opx	n.d.	0	0.03	0	0.01	n.d.	n.d.	6.7	5	0	0	0.70	0
Hb	n.d.	0	0	0	0	n.d.	n.d.	2.3	0	0.23	0	0.06	0
Bi	n.d.	0	0	0	0	n.d.	n.d.	0	0	0.20	0.53	0.38	0
Sphene	n.d.	0	0	0	0	n.d.	n.d.	0	0	0.02	0.09	0.26	0
Fe-Ti oxides	n.d.	0	0.10	0.6	0.09	n.d.	n.d.	1.1	2	0.23	0.49	0	0.10
Σ	-	5.7	5.1	11.0	3.9	-	-	22.9	47	12.1	18.0	27.1	10.1
n	-	3	4	1	20	-	-	2	2	6	7	8	3

% Frequency occurrence of phenocryst phases

	Iceland 60-63	Iceland 63-66	Iceland 66-69	Iceland 69-73	Iceland >73	Galápagos Islands 60-63	Galápagos Islands 66-69	Hawaii 66-69	Zephyr Shoal Lau Basin	Potassic Trachytes 60-63	Potassic Trachytes 63-66	Potassic Trachytes 66-69	Potassic Trachytes 69-73
Sa	0	0	0	0	7	0	0	0	0	64	57	81	100
Pl	100	60	100	100	79	100	100	100	100	57	52	19	50
Qtz	0	0	10	0	4	0	0	0	0	0	0	0	0
Ol	67	20	40	75	36	0	0	0	0	64	30	33	50
Cpx	83	80	90	100	57	100	100	100	100	71	87	76	100
Opx	17	20	30	0	4	0	0	100	100	7	9	5	0
Hb	0	0	20	0	0	0	0	0	0	21	9	24	25
Bi	0	0	10	0	0	0	0	0	0	14	35	19	25
Sphene	0	0	0	0	0	0	0	0	0	14	9	10	0
Fe-Ti oxides	17	0	60	50	46	100	100	100	100	57	52	62	100
n	6	5	10	4	28	2	1	2	2	14	23	21	4

TABLE 2.--Frequency distribution of low-K (L-K), calc-alkaline (C-A), and
high-K (H-K) compositional types from different geographic/
tectonic regions considered within this compilation

Regional Group and	Compo- sitional type	% Frequency occurrence and total number of samples within each subdivision		
		60-63% SiO_2	63-69% SiO_2	>69% SiO_2
Western South America (1)	C-A H-K	19% 81% 31	14% 86% 64	2% 90% 45
Middle Americas (2)	C-A H-K	77% 23% 47	74% 26% 69	17% 83% 35
Western U.S.A.-- eastern zone (3)	C-A	5% 95% 62	5% 95% 133	1% 99% 143
Western U.S.A.-- western zone (exclud- ing Cascades) (4)	L-K C-A H-K	0% 45% 47 55%	1% 23% 92 76%	0% 5% 200 95%
Cascades-Alaska- Aleutians (5)	L-K C-A H-K	3% 86% 74 11%	2% 83% 84 14%	0% 42% 88 58%
Japan - Taiwan - Kuriles - Kamchatka - Saipan (6)	L-K C-A H-K	22% 60% 200 18%	34% 55% 241 12%	19% 59% 174 22%
Indonesia (7)	C-A H-K	62% 38% 21	37% 63% 19	23% 77% 13
S.W. Pacific (8)	L-K C-A H-K	12% 60% 145 28%	34% 51% 143 15%	10% 44% 144 46%
Mediterranean arcs	L-K C-A H-K	1% 24% 82 74%	0% 39% 124 61%	0% 25% 72 75%
Caribbean (11)	L-K C-A	36% 64% 33	18% 82% 17	-
W. Scotland and N. Ireland	C-A H-K	- -	40% 60% 10	18% 82% 28
Iceland	C-A H-K	14% 86% 7	67% 33% 15	52% 48% 33

* See Introduction

Table 3 - A - Compilation of major and trace element chemistry of selected orogenic dacites (defined on basis of 63-69%SiO₂). The averaged composition of the potassic trachyte data is also presented for comparison. Major element analyses presented recalculated to 100% on an anhydrous basis. Data from tables 1 and appendix 1.

Region No. ++ / Region ‡	1 Western South America	2 Middle Americas	3 Western U.S.A.- Eastern Belt	4 Western U.S.A.- Western Belt	5 High Cascades- Alaska- Aleutians	6 Japan Taiwan- Kuriles- Kamchatka- Saipan	8 S.W. Pacific	10 Mediterranean	9 Tonga- Kermadec Islands	12 South Sandwich‡ Islands	6 Low-K dacites; Japan- Kurile- Saipan region	Average Potassic trachyte
SiO_2	65.70	65.79	66.21	65.53	65.44	65.60	65.55	65.36	65.57	65.4	65.79	65.45
TiO_2	0.69	0.63	0.63	0.66	0.61	0.65	0.63	0.63	0.60	0.8	0.69	0.67
Al_2O_3	16.04	16.56	16.34	16.51	16.56	16.04	15.52	16.22	14.15	13.8	15.63	16.29
Fe_2O_3	2.58	2.13	2.93	2.61	1.88	2.35	2.06	2.44	1.63	1.3	2.53	2.40
FeO	1.91	2.16	1.05	1.56	2.51	2.99	3.36	2.20	6.03	7.1	3.39	1.58
MnO	0.08	0.11	0.09	0.08	0.10	0.13	0.12	0.09	0.16	0.2	0.15	0.12
MgO	1.86	1.81	1.17	1.59	1.98	1.86	1.97	1.64	1.92	1.4	1.79	0.78
CaO	4.00	4.03	3.14	3.70	4.53	4.79	4.87	4.25	5.85	4.7	5.19	2.11
Na_2O	3.63	4.26	4.11	3.88	4.28	3.76	3.85	3.80	3.02	4.0	3.81	5.04
K_2O	3.28	2.39	4.11	3.66	1.93	1.66	1.86	3.15	0.91	1.1	0.86	5.33
P_2O_5	0.22	0.14	0.23	0.22	0.17	0.18	0.19	0.21	0.16	0.2	0.17	0.23
n	64	69	133	92	84	241	143	124	24	2	81	67
Trace elements⁺ (p.p.m.)												
Rb	145(28)	53(27)	113(8)	199(8)	62(15)	61(7)	39(68)	109(27)	13(18)	n.d.	3.2(1)	126(28)
Ba	649(6)	549(13)	1587(57)	1671(39)	646(24)	504(15)	497(72)	831(10)	267(19)	n.d.	343(8)	1306(32)
Sr	361(29)	475(27)	247(57)	266(39)	866(32)	225(27)	470(73)	330(28)	251(19)	n.d.	174(15)	709(35)
Zr	120(24)	172(2)	68(1)	79(4)	179(23)	n.d.	130(66)	170(7)	53(18)	n.d.	n.d.	705(28)
Zn	112(17)	58(25)	92(37)	93(20)	63(2)	79(14)	83(45)	64(13)	106(17)	n.d.	94(10)	108(25)
La	n.d.	n.d.	n.d.	n.d.	21(4)	10(13)	15(55)	23(6)	4.0(18)	n.d.	8.4(9)	81(26)
Ce	46(10)	140(2)	283(19)	169(14)	60(4)	28(13)	30(55)	55(6)	10.4(18)	n.d.	23(9)	131(27)
Yb	1.4(10)	n.d.	2.7(44)	2.1(26)	1.7(16)	3.8(12)	2.3(11)	1.5(2)	2.8(3)	n.d.	3.9(8)	3.0(12)
Y	6(4)	n.d.	31(56)	21(39)	33(22)	14(20)	28(69)	28(7)	26(18)	n.d.	14(14)	37(25)
Cu	30(11)	12(26)	19(57)	15(38)	23(21)	9(19)	23(67)	21(16)	29(18)	n.d.	9(11)	70(25)
Ni	14(34)	26(28)	16(44)	19(38)	30(21)	23(14)	17(64)	11(18)	6(18)	n.d.	23(10)	15(24)
Co	10(23)	n.d.	8(44)	27(37)	14(20)	15(19)	12(39)	10(15)	14(17)	n.d.	16(13)	4(3)
Cr	25(5)	n.d.	16(54)	38(39)	40(22)	12(20)	29(67)	13(9)	16(18)	n.d.	10(13)	25(25)
V	106(6)	58(28)	63(47)	65(39)	89(22)	37(20)	79(67)	72(9)	96(18)	n.d.	28(14)	64(25)
Nb	n.d.	n.d.	17(30)	19(18)	6(8)	n.d.	10(1)	21(5)	2.4(3)	n.d.	n.d.	38(24)
Li	48(1)	n.d.	n.d.	20(18)	57(3)	12(14)	13(43)	20(9)	3.6(8)	n.d.	8(10)	40(3)
Pb	n.d.	10(25)	34.(50)	22(39)	8(7)	9(11)	3.2(9)	7(3)	1.7(2)	n.d.	6(5)	21(23)
Hf	n.d.	n.d.	n.d.	n.d.	n.d.	3.8(7)	n.d.	3.4(2)	n.d.	n.d.	3.3(3)	13(5)

++   see Introduction

n   Number of data used in each major element compilation

‡‡   After Baker (1968a)

+   Numbers in brackets refer to number of data used to calculate average for each trace element

n.d.   Insufficient data

Table 3 - B - Compilation of mineralogical (phenocryst) data of selected orogenic dacites (63-69%SiO$_2$). Data corresponds to those in Table 3 - A.

Region No.	1	2	3	4	5	6	8	10	9	12	6	
Region	Western South America	Middle Americas	Western U.S.A.- Eastern Belt	Western U.S.A.- Western Belt	High Cascades Alaska-Aleutians	Japan-Taiwan-Kamchatka-Saipan-Kuriles	S.W. Pacific	Mediterr-anean	Tonga Kermadec Islands	South Sandwich Islands	Low-K dacite; Japan-Kurile-Saipan region	Average potassic trachyte
Phenocryst modes (volume%)*:												
Sa	0	0	2.7	1.4	0	0	0	1.4	0	n.d.	0	13.1
Pl	19.9	17.6	16.7	20.4	14.8	11.9	11.9	23.4	5.9	n.d.	8.2	3.7
Qtz	0	0	0.62	2.3	0.03	2.3	0.31	0.04		n.d.	2.0	0
Ol	0.03	<0.1	<0.01	0.03	0.02	0.06	0.03	0	<0.01	n.d.	0.14	0.13
Cpx	0.98	1.1	0.66	0.76	1.3	1.3	1.7	1.7	1.4	n.d.	0.58	0.60
Opx	2.7	1.3	0.35	0.57	1.8	2.0	1.2	1.5	0.71	n.d.	0.92	<0.01
Hb	2.4	0.85	1.4	1.5	0.88	0.30	1.2	2.7	0	n.d.	0.05	0.29
Bi	1.1	0.15	2.6	3.4	0.03	0.03	0.27	2.7	0	n.d.	0	0.22
Sphene	0	0	0.03	0.01	0			0	0	n.d.		0.16
Fe-Ti oxides	1.1	0.77	1.1	0.58	0.54	0.63	0.70	1.0	0.34	n.d.	0.35	0.30
Σ	28.2	21.8	26.2	31.0	19.4	18.5	17.3	34.4	8.4	-	12.2	18.5
n	15	11	101	43	16	37	97	24	18		13	24
% Frequency occurrence of phenocryst phases												
Sa	7	2	62	25	0	0	0	22	0	0	0	69
Pl	100	95	97	99	100	96	100	99	100	(100)	91	42
Qtz	34	8	36	45	21	19	14	24	0	0	18	0
Ol	5	2	2	3	8	8	7	5	8		6	40
Cpx	60	82	52	76	71	73	89	64	96	(100)	87	81
Opx	78	82	11	44	76	85	82	60	100	(100)	86	6
Hb	57	64	64	73	51	41	32	55	0	0	18	18
Bi	67	7	84	83	5	11	14	55	0	0	0	24
Sphene	3	0	11	9	1	0	0	10	0		0	10
Fe-Ti oxides	84	87	83	93	89	87	90	72	100	(100)	86	60
n	58	56	133	89	76	233	141	124	24	2	78	62

* Abbreviations as in Table 1 - B.

n.d. Insufficient data

surprisingly ambiguous with regard to the petrography and mineralogy of the analyzed samples. This is particularly the case for the Fe-Ti oxides, and the averaged data for these oxides are likely to be less reliable than for the other mineral phases. Other aspects of the treatment of the data follows that in Ewart (1976).

Rhyolites of Essentially Bimodal Basalt-Rhyolite Associations

Christiansen and Lipman (1972) have emphasized the occurrence in the Western U.S.A. of predominantly mafic-salic volcanic associations, in which these bimodal associations occur. The bimodal volcanism occurs contemporaneously with crustal extension and normal faulting. The salic volcanic representatives of this association are commonly high silica, low Ca and Mg, and alkali-rich rhyolites.

Reference to the literature suggests that such associations are present in many volcanic provinces, although intermediate compositions are sporadically developed (often as metaluminous quartz trachytes), and the salic members of the associations (usually rhyolites) vary in their relative abundance. Where sufficient data are available, these have been incorporated into the compilations for comparative purposes. The following rhyolitic associations were specifically included from this category into the compilations:

(1) Yellowstone rhyolite plateau and eastern Snake River Plain, Wyoming and Idaho, U.S.A. (Boyd, 1961; Hamilton, 1959, 1963, 1965).

(2) Medicine Lake volcanic centre, California. (Anderson, 1933, 1941; Condie and Hayslip, 1975).

(3) Mono Craters and Glass Mountain, Long Valley volcanic centre. The latest phase is evidently bimodal, although not the earlier salic volcanic phases; the rhyolites exhibit, however, a fractionated chemistry (e.g., Bailey et al., 1976; Carmichael, 1967; Loney, 1968; Noble et al., 1972).

(4) Salton Sea geothermal field, California (Robinson, Elders, and Muffler, 1976).

(5) Iceland.

(6) Western Scotland and N. Ireland.

(7) Southern Queensland, Australia, in which several distinct volcanic centres occur, characterized by largely bimodal associations (Ewart et al., 1976, 1977). Several distinct series of rhyolites are recognized, two of which are considered here; the Binna Burra rhyolites and the hedenbergite-fayalite-bearing rhyolites.

(8) St. Andrew Strait volcanoes Papua New Guinea (Johnson et al., 1974, in press).

Although peralkaline rocks are specifically excluded in this review, data for one strictly peralkaline volcanic unit is included, namely the Devine Canyon welded tuff, southeastern Oregon (Greene, 1973), which is of interest as it evidently represents a transition between peralkaline and metaluminous rhyolites when both mineralogical and chemical criteria are considered.

CHEMISTRY

The Dacite-Rhyolite Associations of Island Arcs and Orogenic Continental Margins

In Figure 1, a simple SiO_2 versus K_2O plot is presented of the composite averaged data from each geographic region being considered and these can be compared to the "low-K,"calc-alkali," and "high-K" division of Peccerillo and

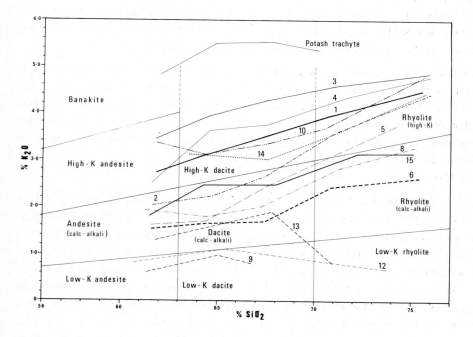

Figure 1.--A plot of K_2O versus SiO_2 (wt.%) for the total averaged data (Table 1) for each of the salic volcanic series from the various geographic and/or tectonic subregions considered within this review. The trends for each region are based on the averaged compositions from each of the five SiO_2 compositional groupings (60-63, 63-66,66-69, 69-73, >73%). The rock boundaries and nomenclature are slightly modified from Peccerillo and Taylor (1976). The numbers refer to the specific subregions represented by each trend line, as listed in the Introduction.

Taylor (1976). This plot clearly shows that: (a) The salic volcanic suites of the western U.S.A. (excluding Cascades), the Andean province of western South America, and the Mediterranean arcs are characterized by high-K magma suites; (b) the island arc systems of the western and southwestern Pacific regions are dominantly calc-alkaline in their chemical affinities; (c) the Cascades-Aleutian province, and the Middle Americas are somewhat transitional in their overall chemical characteristics, with only the siliceous compositions lying within the high-K fields.

A summary of the actual frequency occurrence of the high-K, calc-alkali, and low-K compositional types is given in Table 2 for the various geographic regions, and the figures simply confirm the general picture emerging from composite plots of Figure 1. Worthy of additional note, however, is the further increase in the frequency occurrence of high-K eruptives in the eastern zone of the western U.S.A., compared to the western zone. The low-K series of eruptives reach their most prominent development within the Tonga-Kermadec Islands, South Sandwich Islands, the .Caribbean arc, parts of New Britain, and within the Huzi volcanic zone of Japan and its continuation into the Izu Islands, and Marianas Islands. These are typically regions of sub-continental and relatively young crust, and/or intra-oceanic island arcs.

Within Tables 3 and 4 are presented complete chemical (and mineralogical) compilations of the weighted average values of dacitic (63-69% SiO_2) and rhyolitic (>69% SiO_2) eruptives from selected orogenic regions, the data being in part derived from Table 1 and Appendix 1. Further aspects of the regional variations in chemistry shown by these salic volcanic compositions will be deferred to later discussion in this paper.

Trace Elements

Ba.--The general behaviour, as is well known, is closely correlated with K during magmatic crystallization. Thus, the relatively high Ba abundances in the silicic andesite and dacite eruptives of the western U.S.A. and the Mediterranean arcs correlates with their high-K characteristics. Nevertheless, the western U.S.A. abundances are apparently considerably higher than those of the Mediterranean, although all these three groupings exhibit marked Ba depletions within the rhyolites, at differentiation indices (D.I.) $\geq$80. Similarly, the high-K dacites are Ba-enriched compared to the calc-alkaline dacites from any given region (Appendices 2 and 3), with the low-K suites showing lowest overall Ba abundances (Appendix 1). With the exceptions noted above, the remaining salic volcanic suites evidently show no overall systematic pattern of Ba with D.I.

Rb and Sr.--Sr is also characteristically high in the western U.S.A.

volcanics, although exhibiting a general depletion with increasing D.I. In fact, the progressive decrease of Sr with increasing D.I. is a feature shown by all the averaged trends. As with Ba, both Rb and Sr are most enriched in the high-K dacites and rhyolites relative to the calc-alkaline, and especially the low-K siliceous volcanics, from each region. A Rb versus K/Rb/plot (Fig. 4) illustrates the general abundance relations within these three series; the low-K volcanics are characterized by very low Rb and high K/Rb rations, whereas the high-K volcanics are characterized by higher Rb and lower K/Rb ratios. The calc-alkali dacite-rhyolitic volcanoes are essentially intermediate in terms of Rb abundances, but exhibit completely overlapping K/Rb ratios to the high-K types.

<u>Nb, Zr, Pb, La, Ce</u>.--These elements again are closely correlated with K, and are enriched, within a given region or province, in the high-K silicic magmas, relative to the low-K types. The calc-alkali dacites and rhyolites are typically intermediate in their abundance levels. It is also noteworthy that the western U.S.A. suites (excluding the Cascades) are characterized by rather higher abundances of Nb, La, and Ce than found in the high-K suites of the other island arc and continental margin orogenic provinces.

<u>Cr, Ni, V</u>.--These elements each show a systematic depletion with increasing D.I., although several of the suites apparently undergo a small, late-stage increase in Cr in the most silica-rich rhyolitic compositions. Also worthy of note are the relative abundance levels of these elements within the various suites, at the lower D.I. values; i.e., silicic andesite-dacite compositions. For example, the V abundances in the dacitic lavas from Tonga-Kermadec Islands (low-K suite) are relatively high (correlating with the Fe-enriched compositions of these lavas), but these lavas are very depleted in Cr and Ni; this has been explained in terms of low pressure pyroxene-plagioclase fractionation (Ewart, Bryan, and Gill, 1973). In contrast, the averaged Cr levels of the dacitic and related magmas of the Middle Americas and Western U.S.A. suites are rather high. A recent compilation of data from the Caribbean arc (Brown et al., 1977) indicates relatively high Cr and Ni in the dacitic lavas of some of the islands within this province, notably those in which the lavas are more K-enriched.

<u>The Biotite Rhyolites of Western U.S.A.</u>.--During the course of the compilation of data from both the western and eastern volcanic zones of the Western U.S.A., it became apparent that there existed a fairly distinctive group of rhyolites, typically characterized by the ferromagnesian assemblage biotite + clinopyroxene (+ sanidine, plagioclase, and quartz). These rhyolites, which evidently represent late phases from many volcanic centres of predominantly intermediate composition, exhibit many of the chemical

40

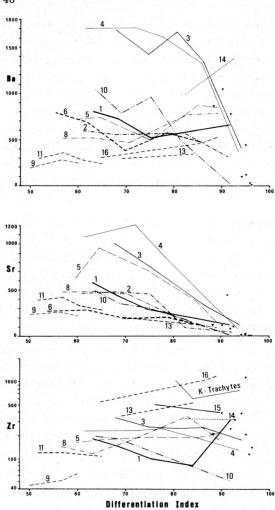

Figure 2.--The averaged trends (based on total data, Table 1) of Ba, Sr, and Zr
abundances (ppm) versus Differentiation Index, for the various salic
volcanic series. Individual trends are compiled from each of the five
averaged SiO_2 compositional groupings. Numbers refer to the specific
subregions réprsented by each trend line, as listed in the Introduction.
Inverted triangles are rhyolites of bimodal associations.

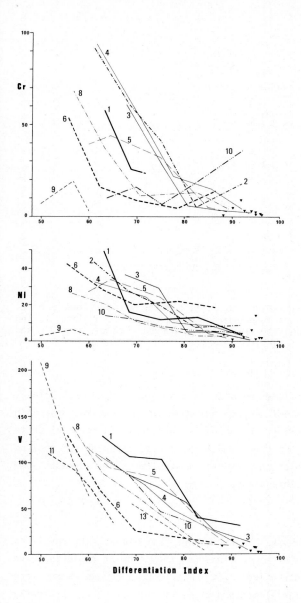

Figure 3.—The averaged trends (based on total data, Table 1) of Cr, Ni, and V
abundances (ppm) versus Differentiation Index, for the various salic
volcanic series. Compilation and symbols as in Figure 2.

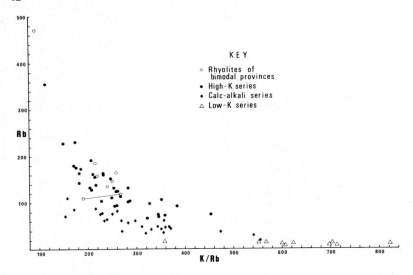

Figure 4.--Rb versus K/Rb, based on averaged data, for the various low-K, calc-alkali, and high-K data groups presented in Appendices 1, 2, and 3, and Table 5.   Dotted line joins the averaged Icelandic "calc- alkali" and "high-K" rhyolites.

characteristics of rhyolites of the bimodal associations (described below). They are high silica (>75%), tend to be depleted in Ca and Mg, and with $K_2O > Na_2$; averaged data are presented in Tables 4-A and 4-B.   In terms of trace elements, they are also similar to the bimodal rhyolites, although not showing the same degree of Ba and Sr depletion. Their chemistry certainly suggests some degree of late stage crystal fractionation.

Rhyolites of Bimodal Associations

These are typically high silica, low Ca and Mg, and high-alkali rhyolites (Tables 5-A and 5-B).   In terms of trace elements, they show Sr depletion, and rapidly decreasing Ba with increasing D.I. (Fig. 2).   Zr abundances are variable, while the ferromagnesian elements such as Cr, Ni, and V are typically very strongly depleted; Nb, Pb, La, Ce and related elements exhibit varying degrees of enrichment, which may be correlated with increasing D.I.   The overall geochemical characterisics of these rhyolites indicate a control by crystal fractionation, at least at the later stages of development of these magmas.

Iceland.--Although included broadly within the bimodal associations, this is of special interest in view of the oceanic setting. Sigurdsson (1971a) has pointed out the existence of two rhyolitic magma types--an alkali enriched group (roughly equivalent to the high-K division used in this review) which is associated with volcanic centres rich in alkali or transitional basalts, and a "calc-alkali" series associated with volcanic centres with tholeiitic affinities. Walker (1966) has noted the chemical similarity of these latter rhyolites to the calc-alkaline rhyolites of island arc regions (e.g., the Taupo rhyolites of New Zealand). Comparative data, based on available published data, are presented in Tables 1 and 5. In terms of their trace elements, the rhyolites are characterized by relatively high Ba and Zr abundances, and apparently also by surprisingly high La abundances.

Dacitic and Rhyolitic Lavas from Other Oceanic Islands

Comparative data are presented in Table 1, from the Galapagos Islands (McBirney and Williams, 1969), Hawaii (Bauer et al., 1973; Macdonald and Katsura, 1964), Canary Islands (Arana and Ibarrola, 1973), and the Zephyr Shoal in the Lau Basin (Hawkins, 1976; Gill, 1976). Each suite of silicic lavas from these various locations shows its own characteristics. For example, the Canary Islands rhyolites are noteworthy for high Na/K ratios, high Ba, Sr, La and Zr abundances, but relatively depleted Rb. The Galapagos "dacitic" lavas have definite similarities to the icelandites from Iceland, as clearly recognized by McBirney and Williams (1969); these Galapagos lavas are also characterized by relatively enriched Ba, Zr, La, Nb, Y, and Hf abundances, and depleted Ni and Cr abundances. The Hawaiian rhyodacites, which are evidently very uncommon, are notably K-rich; no trace element data are available. The Zephyr Shoal dacite is quite distinct from the previously described oceanic dacites and rhyolites. It is a low-K dacite, with very low Rb, Ba, Sr, REE, Nb, and Hf abundances, and high K/Rb (1054). This dacite, in fact, shows similar chemical and mineralogical characteristics to the Tonga-Kermadec dacites (occurring on the Tonga-Kermadec ridge adjacent to the Lau Basin), although it is less Fe enriched.

Soda-Rich-Potash-Poor Magmas

The magmas erupted from Deception Island (within the South Shetland Group) are all unusual in containing abnormally high Na_2O, but also low K_2O (Baker et al., 1969, 1975; Hawkes, 1961; Gonzalez-Ferran and Katsui, 1970). Similar compositions are found in the dacites of Fedarb Island, St. Andrew Strait, Papua New Guinea (Johnson et al., 1974, 1978).

Both areas in which these magmas occur are probably regions in which subduction has ceased in the relatively recent geologic past. These lavas are relatively low in Rb (with K/Rb ratios 540-640), Ni, Cr, and V, and possibly enriched in Zr. In other respects, these lavas are not readily distinguished from other orogenic dacites.

Table 4 - A - Compilation of major and trace element chemistry of selected orogenic rhyolites (defined on basis >69%SiO$_2$). Major element analyses presented recalculated to 100% on an anhydrous basis.

Region and Type [++]	Low-K rhyolite:- S.W. Pacific region	Low-K rhyolite:- Japan-Kurile-Saipan region	South Sandwich Islands-pumice*	Metis shoal Pumice (Tonga)-Residual Glass**	Western U.S.A.-Western Belt. All data	Western U.S.A.-Eastern Belt. All data	Western U.S.A. Western Belt. Biotite [++] rhyolites	Western U.S.A. Eastern Belt. Biotite [++] rhyolites	Western South America	Cascades-Alaska-Aleutions; excluding Medicine Lake rhyolites	Taupo Volcanic Zone, New Zealand	[x]
SiO$_2$	72.31	72.33	73.74	73.69	74.75	73.04	76.41	75.92	73.60	74.56	74.92	
TiO$_2$	0.46	0.46	0.30	0.52	0.20	0.31	0.13	0.16	0.30	0.21	0.25	
Al$_2$O$_3$	13.70	14.09	13.74	12.30	13.67	14.24	13.10	13.13	14.05	13.92	13.47	
Fe$_2$O$_3$	1.42	1.80	0.70	1.31	0.95	1.44	0.65	0.98	1.32	0.62	1.01	
FeO	2.40	1.75	2.15	2.71	0.61	0.54	0.34	0.36	0.50	1.21	0.89	
MnO	0.09	0.10	0.08	0.06	0.05	0.07	0.05	0.06	0.06	0.05	0.06	
MgO	0.86	0.78	0.50	1.07	0.29	0.47	0.18	0.21	0.54	0.29	0.32	
CaO	3.65	3.35	3.28	3.61	1.14	1.36	0.76	0.62	1.59	1.31	1.57	
Na$_2$O	3.93	4.07	4.70	3.17	3.63	3.76	3.54	3.73	3.70	4.28	4.18	
K$_2$O	1.06	1.12	0.68	1.47	4.67	4.70	4.80	4.80	4.26	3.48	3.27	
P$_2$O$_5$	0.11	0.18	0.12	0.07	0.05	0.08	0.03	0.03	0.08	0.06	0.05	
n	15	33	1	1	200	143	54	46	45	22	83	

Trace elements[+] (p.p.m.)

	Low-K rhyolite:- S.W. Pacific region	Low-K rhyolite:- Japan-Kurile-Saipan region	South Sandwich Islands-pumice*	Metis shoal Pumice (Tonga)-Residual Glass**	Western U.S.A.-Western Belt. All data	Western U.S.A.-Eastern Belt. All data	Western U.S.A. Western Belt. Biotite [++] rhyolites	Western U.S.A. Eastern Belt. Biotite [++] rhyolites	Western South America	Cascades-Alaska-Aleutions; excluding Medicine Lake rhyolites	Taupo Volcanic Zone, New Zealand	[x]
Rb	12(7)[+]	n.d.	n.d.	21(1)	182(31)	180(8)	n.d.	256(1)	155(16)	129(10)	111(25)	-
Ba	283(7)	420(5)	n.d.	610(1)	631(61)	957(32)	531(15)	356(11)	641(10)	687(7)	849(39)	783[x]
Sr	173(7)	201(6)	n.d.	130(1)	184(61)	249(32)	118(15)	107(11)	160(26)	210(4)	113(25)	132[x]
Zr	88(7)	n.d.	n.d.	68(1)	142(61)	217(32)	101(15)	172(11)	222(16)	215(4)	159(25)	219[x]
Zn	63(4)	85(2)	n.d.	46(1)	39(14)	n.d.	n.d.	n.d.	84(6)	82(6)	n.d.	28[x]
La	4.3(4)	6.7(2)	n.d.	n.d.	66(47)	76(22)	48(12)	72(6)	n.d.	18(3)	26(24)	56[x]
Ce	11(4)	22(2)	n.d.	n.d.	135(24)	163(7)	175(2)	100(1)	n.d.	32(3)	43(4)	56[x]
Yb	n.d.	4.9(2)	n.d.	n.d.	4.3(32)	2.7(26)	2.6(15)	3.0(10)	n.d.	3(4)	3.6(4)	4.3[x]
Y	33(6)	11(6)	n.d.	25(1)	32(60)	29(31)	22(15)	28(10)	n.d.	55(4)	24(25)	38[x]
Cu	26(6)	2(6)	n.d.	120(1)	8(58)	10(31)	10(15)	4(11)	15(15)	13(4)	6(25)	-
Ni	2(6)	29(2)	n.d.	4(1)	4(48)	3(30)	2(7)	1(10)	12(6)	1(4)	<2	-
Co	5(6)	11(3)	n.d.	10(1)	5(45)	3(28)	2(7)	2(11)	6(16)	4(5)	<2	-
Cr	2(6)	16(3)	n.d.	7(1)	6(50)	3(29)	2(15)	2(11)	n.d.	3(7)	1(25)	-
V	36(6)	8(5)	n.d.	130(1)	12(50)	20(26)	7(15)	14(11)	33(10)	16(4)	9(25)	-
Nb	n.d.	n.d.	n.d.	n.d.	19(54)	27(21)	22(15)	41(9)	n.d.	n.d.	5.6(4)	8.3[x]
Li	n.d.	7(2)	n.d.	n.d.	40(14)	n.d.	n.d.	n.d.	30(4)	n.d.	35(25)	-
Pb	3(4)	10(2)	n.d.	4.2(1)	37(58)	30(30)	47(15)	29(10)	57(9)	10(1)	18(4)	17[x]
Hf	3.4(2)	3.7(1)	n.d.	n.d.	n.d.	n.d.	n.d.	n.d.	n.d.	4.2(3)	4.5(4)	5.9[x]

[++] See Introduction

n   Number of data used in each major element compilation.

[+]   Numbers in brackets refer to number of data used to calculate average for each trace element

[++] See text for further explanation of thee biotite rhyolites

n.d. Insufficient data

*   From Gass et al (1963)

**   After Ewart et al (1973)

[x]   Based on spark source mass spectrographic analyses of 19 tephra glasses by Howorth and Rankin (1975)

Table 4 – B – Compilation of mineralogical (phenocryst) data of selected orogenic rhyolites (>69%SiO$_2$). Data corresponds to those in Table 4 – A.

Phenocryst modes (volume %)*:

Region and Type	Low-K rhyolites: S.W. Pacific region	Low-K rhyolite: Japan-Kurile-Saipan region	South Sandwich Islands-pumice**	Metis Shoal Pumice (Tonga): Residual glass***	Western U.S.A.:- Western Belt. All data	Western U.S.A.:- Eastern Belt. All data	Western U.S.A.:- Western Belt. Biotite rhyolites++	Western U.S.A.:- Eastern Belt. Biotite rhyolites++	Western South America	High Cascades-Alaska-Aleutians (excluding Medicine Lake)	Taupo Volcanic Zone; New Zealand
Sa	0	0	0	0	3.2	5.7	2.6	7.8	8.1	0	0.06
Pl	11.5	8.1	~17	(10.5)	4.8	8.3	2.1	3.7	5.9	1.5	8.7
Qtz	0.33	1.5	0	0	2.8	3.0	2.1	4.0	7.7	0.20	2.1
Ol	0.88	0.28	0	(<0.1)	<0.01	0	0	0	0	0	<0.01
Cpx	0.66	0.58	~2.5	(11.6)	0.07	0.10	0.01	0.01	0.13	0	0.03
Opx	0.04	0.03	0	(5.5)	0.03	0.10	0	0	0.17	0.07	0.49
Hb	0	0	0	0	0.20	0.18	0	0	0.17	0.03	0.33
Bi	0	0	0	0	0.79	1.60	0.28	0.64	1.8	0.27	0.19
Sphene	0	0	0	0	0.02	0.01	<0.01	0.01	0	0	0
Fe-Ti oxides	0.56	0.25	~0.5	(0.2)	0.17	0.51	0.13	0.24	0.57	0.17	0.30
Total	14.0	10.7	~20	(27.8)	12.1	19.5	7.2	16.4	24.5	2.2	12.2
n	9	4	1	1	92	83	28	21	3	3	74

% Frequency occurrence of phenocryst phases

	Low-K rhyolites: S.W. Pacific region	Low-K rhyolite: Japan-Kurile-Saipan region	South Sandwich Islands-pumice**	Metis Shoal Pumice (Tonga): Residual glass***	Western U.S.A.:- Western Belt. All data	Western U.S.A.:- Eastern Belt. All data	Western U.S.A.:- Western Belt. Biotite rhyolites++	Western U.S.A.:- Eastern Belt. Biotite rhyolites++	Western South America	High Cascades-Alaska-Aleutians (excluding Medicine Lake)	Taupo Volcanic Zone; New Zealand
Sa	0	0	0	0	74	80	88	91	82	0	5
Pl	100	93	100	(100)	84	87	79	74	97	95	97
Qtz	14	41	0	0	79	62	83	78	77	20	62
Ol	14	14	0	(100)	5	0	0	0	0	0	1
Cpx	93	76	100	(100)	18	24	4	7	18	0	9
Opx	14	83	0	(100)	13	6	6	0	13	60	94
Hb	0	38	0	0	42	37	0	0	44	80	58
Bi	0	0	0	0	72	92	85	89	92	35	30
Sphene	0	0	0	0	23	16	6	4	8	5	0
Fe-Ti oxides	86	69	100	(100)	72	73	60	52	79	80	96
n	14	29	1	1	159	142	52	46	39	20	77

* Abbreviations as in Table 1 – B.
++ See text for further explanation of these biotite rhyolites
** From Gass et al. (1963)
*** From Ewart et al. (1973)

Table 5 - A - Compilation of major and trace element chemistry of rhyolites ($>69\%SiO_2$) from predominantly bimodal mafic-silicic volcanic associations

Region and Type	Yellowstone and Snake River Plain; Western U.S.A.	Medicine Lake Centre, California	Mono Craters and Glass Mt., California	Salton Sea Centre, California	Iceland; "Calc-alkali" type	Iceland; "High-K" type	Western Scotland; Northern Ireland	Southern Queensland; Binna Burra Rhyolites	Southern Queensland; Ferrohedenbergite-Fayalite-Bearing Rhyolites	Devine Canyon; Oregon, U.S.A. **
SiO_2	76.59	73.49	76.61	73.77	74.62	74.81	74.02	76.72	76.02	76.02
TiO_2	0.16	0.27	0.06	0.23	0.24	0.24	0.45	0.07	0.17	0.20
Al_2O_3	12.36	13.93	12.77	13.40	12.95	12.85	12.38	12.57	12.30	11.47
Fe_2O_3	1.08	0.50	0.40	0.60	1.10	1.20	1.60	0.77	0.72	2.22
FeO	0.56	1.75	0.56	2.04	2.01	1.14	1.84	0.46	1.16	0.62
MnO	0.03	0.02	0.05	0.04	0.08	0.07	0.13	0.01	0.03	0.05
MgO	0.14	0.35	0.08	0.17	0.19	0.12	0.37	0.03	0.15	0.26
CaO	0.54	1.45	0.57	0.89	1.87	0.92	1.30	0.44	0.68	0.43
Na_2O	3.47	4.00	4.04	4.68	4.38	4.77	3.71	3.60	3.42	3.93
K_2O	5.04	4.15	4.82	4.15	2.52	3.81	4.12	5.31	5.32	4.75
P_2O_5	0.02	0.05	0.04	0.03	0.05	0.06	0.10	0.01	0.02	0.05
n	21	13	24	5	17	16	28	10	18	14
Trace elements[+] (p.p.m.)										
Rb	n.d.	156(4)	185(18)	142(3)	109(7)	119(5)	127(17)	471(10)	165(16)	n.d.
Ba	537(15)+	849(7)	25(19)	540(5)	1079(7)	1000(5)	1235(16)	11(10)	96(16)	112(14)
Sr	27(15)	121(7)	8(19)	37(5)	126(7)	98(5)	107(17)	11(10)	11(16)	19(14)
Zr	203(15)	202(7)	111(19)	300(5)	384(7)	388(5)	321(16)	137(10)	387(16)	1114(14)
Zn	n.d.	25(2)	38(7)	n.d.	124(7)	116(6)	73(9)	147(10)	145(16)	n.d.
La	97(15)	30(4)	39(10)	68(5)	149(7)	192(5)	93(15)	26(9)	77(15)	106(14)
Ce	167(12)	60(2)	56(7)	133(3)	n.d.	n.d.	83(4)	60(9)	168(15)	194(8)
Yb	6.5(15)	2.5(2)	3.0(3)	12(5)	n.d.	n.d.	n.d.	9(1)	5(1)	15(14)
Y	54(15)	30(5)	25(19)	110(5)	40(7)	50(5)	37(13)	95(10)	74(16)	131(14)
Cu	7(15)	15(4)	2(19)	7(5)	10(7)	9(6)	8(12)	11(10)	8(15)	11(14)
Ni	-1(15)	3(5)	2(19)	n.d.	0.8(7)	0.7(6)	3(12)	2(10)	6(14)	14(14)
Co	-1(7)	6(7)	5(19)	1.5(1)	1.3(7)	1.4(6)	2(12)	n.d.	1(6)	n.d.
Cr	2.5(15)	1(3)	2(12)	2(4)	6.4(7)	3(5)	4(12)	<1(10)	<1(14)	-1(14)
V	7(7)	9(3)	2(12)	7(1)	15(7)	14(5)	12(12)	1(9)	3(14)	7(14)
Nb	41(15)	5(2)	17(19)	23(5)	24(7)	30(5)	17(13)	58(10)	35(15)	70(14)
Li	n.d.	93(3)	46(9)	n.d.	11(5)	14(5)	21(12)	n.d.	n.d.	n.d.
Pb	20(15)	20(5)	36(19)	13(2)	9(7)	10(6)	19(9)	44(10)	22(16)	36(14)
Hf	n.d.	n.d.	n.d.	n.d.	n.d.	n.d.	n.d.	5.1(1)	9.5(1)	n.d.

‡   See Introduction.   n = Number of data used in each major element compilation

+   Numbers in brackets refer to number of data used to calculate average for each trace element

n.d.   Insufficient data

**   Chemically, this is strictly just peralkaline, but not mineralogically.

Table 5 – B – Compilation of mineralogical (phenocryst) data of rhyolites from predominantly bimodal mafic–silicic volcanic associations. Data corresponds to those in table 5 – A.

Phenocryst modes (volume %)*:

Region and Type	Yellowstone and Snake River Plain; Western U.S.A.	Medicine Lake Centre, California	Mono Craters and Glass Mt., California	Salton Sea Centre, California	Iceland; "Calc-alkali" type	Iceland; "High-K" type	Western Scotland; Northern Ireland	Southern Queensland; Binna Burra Rhyolites	Southern Queensland; Ferrohedenbergite-Fayalite-Bearing Rhyolites	Devine Canyon; Oregon, U.S.A.
Sa	3.2	0	0.31	n.d.	0	2.1	3.1	1.2	11.9	-11
Pl	1.0	0.70	0.07	n.d.	1.6	2.6	4.9	0.19	0	0
Qtz	1.4	0	0.27	n.d.	0	1.3	3.5	0.66	3.5	-2
Ol	0.06	0	0.01	n.d.	0.04	0.08	0.12	0	0.23	0
Cpx	0.08	0.04	0	n.d.	0.09	0.29	1.0	0	0.67	-0.1
Opx	0	0.12	0.03	n.d.	0.02	0	<0.01	0	0	0
Hb	0	0	0.02	n.d.	0	0	<0.01	0	0	0
Bi	0	0	0	n.d.	0	0	0	0.05	0	0
Sphene	0	0	0	n.d.	0	0	0	0	0	0
Fe-Ti oxides	0.08	0.10	0.04	n.d.	0.06	0.15	0.32	0.08	0.10	-0.1
Σ	5.8	0.96	0.75	-2	1.8	6.5	12.9	2.2	16.4	-13.2
n	8	9	19	-	10	11	17	8	15	7

% Frequency occurrence of phenocryst phases:

Sa	95	0	46	100	0	13	36	100	100	100
Pl	48	91	46	100	81	81	71	90	0	0
Qtz	86	0	46	100	0	6	57	100	100	100
Ol	38	0	8	100	44	38	50	0	89	100
Cpx	48	18	0	100	62	62	68	0	100	100
Opx	0	100	21	0	6	0	14	0	0	0
Hb	0	0	8	100	0	0	4	0	0	0
Bi	5	0	21	0	0	0	0	50	0	0
Sphene	0	0	0	0	0	0	0	0	0	0
Fe-Ti oxides	52	100	50	100	37	56	36	80	100	100
n	21	11	24	5	16	16	28	10	18	14

*   Abbreviations as in Table 1 – B.
n.d. Insufficient data

Trachytes

Data on quartz-bearing, metaluminous, potash-rich trachytes (these were based on the published descriptions of the rocks as trachytes), both of continental and oceanic occurrences, were accumulated during the compilation of the dacitic-rhyolitic data. Their main chemical feature is the high total alkalis, distinctly higher than the average values for high-K dacites and andesites (Fig. 1). Nevertheless, it does appear from the literature that some gradation occurs between trachytic and high-K (latitic) compositions. Other chemical characteristics of the trachytic magmas include relatively high Al_2O_3, low MgO and CaO, and depleted Ni, Cr, and V abundances, while Ba, Sr, Zr, REE, Y, and Nb abundances are typically enriched relative to equivalent dacitic compositions. These chemical characteristics of trachytes are presumably the result of crystal fractionation processes.

PHENOCRYST MINERALOGY
Total Phenocryst Contents

A compilation of total phenocryst contents (volume %) of orogenic dacites and rhyolites, plus additional rhyolitic groups, is illustrated in histogram form in Figure 5. It is clear that very wide variations occur within the various silica composiional groupings, in the degree of crystallinity, which ranges from zero to more than 50%. Nevertheless, a subtle change in the overall pattern of crystallinity does occur with increasing SiO_2 contents. Thus, in the 60-63% SiO_2 grouping (corresponding to siliceous andesites), there is evidence of the persistence of the bimodal distribution of phenocryst contents which was previously found in the less silicic andesites and basalts of orogenic regions (Ewart, 1976a), with the main bulk of eruptives having crystal contents in the 30-40% range. With increasing SiO_2, there is a tendency for the distributions of crystallinity to move towards lower values,this becoming particularly marked in the most SiO_2-rich rhyolite group (>73%). Reference to the averaged modal data of the various geographic and silica groupings (Table 1-B) show little significant difference of crystallinity of a given compositional group between the different geographic regions.

In the two top histograms of Figure 5 are compared the phenocryst contents of the rhyolites of the bimodal associations, with the "calc-alkaline" rhyolites of the Taupo region, New Zealand (Table 4), the latter rhyolites interpreted as derived by upper crustal partial fusion (e.g., Ewart and Stipp, 1968; Ewart et al., 1975). The bimodal rhyolites are clearly characterized by extremely low crystal contents, consistent with their relatively high

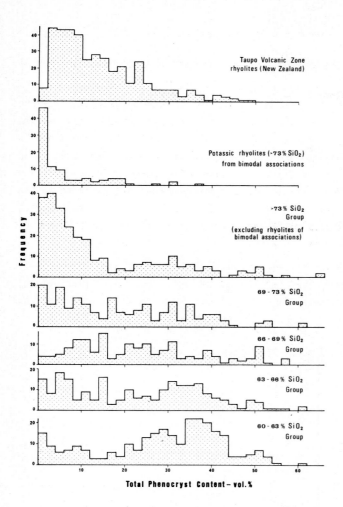

Figure 5.--Histogram showing the distributions of total phenocryst contents of salic volcanic rocks. The lower five histograms illustrate these distributions in the five SiO_2 compositional groupings of orogenic eruptives. The two top histograms illustrate the distributions in rhyolites of bimodal associations, and the predominantly calc-alkali rhyolites of the Taupo Volcanic Zone, New Zealand (after Ewart, 1966).

equilibration temperatures (see later). The New Zealand rhyolites show a wider range of crystallinity, dominantly between about 2-15%; moreover, it has been previously shown that they exhibit no overall differences of crystallinity (or mineralogy) between lavas and pyroclastics (Ewart, 1966). Futhermore, this trend towards higher crystal contents is consistent with relatively lower equilibration temperatures of these New Zealand rhyolites (see later).

Phenocryst Occurrences and Phenocryst Assemblages

The dacite and rhyolite associations of island arcs and orogenic continental margins

Low-K dacites and rhyolites (Tables 1, 3, and 4; Appendix 1; Fig. 6).--The magmas of this series are dominated by plagioclase, hypersthene, augite, and Fe-Ti oxides (typically titanomagnetite in the dacites). Hornblende and quartz occur sporadically, but in significantly lower frequency percentages than found in the calc-alkaline and high-K suites. Olivine also occurs infrequently, and where the composition is Mg-rich, it is presumably xenocrystic, as found in the 1967-68 Metis Shoal eruption. Tonga (Melson et al, 1970). An important aspect of the phenocryst assemblages in these low-K magmas is the persistence of pyroxenes throughout the compositional range from dacite to siliceous rhyolite.

Some typical phenocryst assemblages commonly reported (excluding Fe-Ti oxides) are: (abbreviations used for the assemblages are: pl = plagioclase; aug = augite; hyp = hypersthene; hb = hornblende; qtz = quartz; bi = biotite;

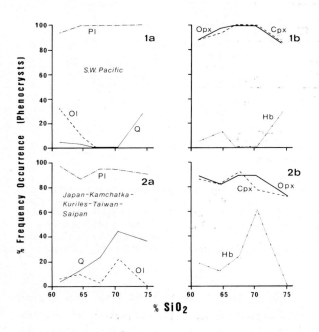

Figure 6.--Percent frequency occurrence of major phenocryst phases in the low-K lavas of the S.W. Pacific and the Japan subregions, plotted as a function of averaged whole rock compositions (expressed as SiO_2%). Data based on the five averaged SiO_2 compositional groupings presented in Appendix 1. Abbreviations (Figs. 6-8): Pl = plagioclase; Q = quartz; Ol = olivine; Opx = orthopyroxene; Cpx = clinopyroxene; Hb = hornblende; Bi = biotite; Sph = sphene; Sa = sanidine.

sph = sphene; ol = olivine; sa = sanidine; cumm = cummingtonite; af = alkali feldspar):

   pl + aug + hyp (the most common assemblage)

   pl $\pm$ qtz + aug + hyp + hb

   pl + qtz + aug + hyp

   pl + ferroaugite + ferropigeonite + ferrohypersthene (rare)

   pl + fayalite + ferrohypersthene + ferropigeonite + ferro-augite (rare)

Calc-alkaline dacites and rhyolites (Tables 1, 3, and 4; Appendix 2; Fig. 7).--The phenocryst assemblages become more varied with quartz and hornblende more frequent in occurrence, and the appearance of biotite in 10-20% of the rocks. The frequency of pyroxene occurrence shows a relative decrease in the most silica-rich rhyolites. All assemblages are dominated by plagioclase. Commonly reported assemblages (excluding Fe-Ti oxides) include:

   pl $\pm$ qtz + aug + hyp

   pl $\pm$ qtz + aug + hyp + hb

   pl $\pm$ qtz $\pm$ aug + hyp + hb + bi

   pl $\pm$ qtz + hb

   pl $\pm$ qtz + hb + bi

   pl + hb + bi

   pl + qtz + bi

   pl + ferrohortonalite + ferrohypersthene (rare)

   pl + qtz + fayalite + ferroaugite (rare)

   pl + qtz + ferrohortonalite + eulite + ferroaugite (rare)

   pl + qtz + sa + bi + hb $\pm$ hyp.

In addition, of particular interest is the occurrence of phenocrystic cummingtonite, occurring in the following assemblages:

   pl $\pm$ qtz + cumm + hb $\pm$ hyp

   pl + qtz + bi + cumm + hb $\pm$ hyp

   pl + aug + hyp + cumm + hb

High-K dacites and rhyolites (Tables 1, 3, and 4; Appendix 3; Fig. 8).-- There is further increase in the diversity of phenocryst assemblages, with sanidine and biotite as common phenocrysts. Sphene is a notable accessory, most frequently occurring in magmas in the 67-72% SiO_2 range. Allanite is also reported as an accessory in a significant number of rhyolites from the western U.S.A.

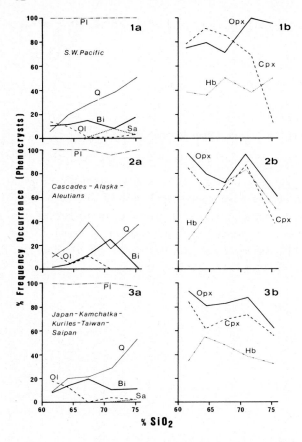

Figure 7.--Percent frequency occurrence of major phenocryst phases in the calc-alkali series of salic volcanic rocks from S.W. Pacific, the High Cascades-Alaska-Aleutians, and the Japan subregions, plotted as a function of averaged whole rock compositions. Data from Appendix 2. Abbreviations as in Figure 6.

Figure 8 compares the relative frequency occurrences of the dominant phenocrysts from the two volcanic zones of the western U.S.A., western South America, and the Mediterranean arcs. Compared to the low-K and calc-alkaline suites, these high-K series are notable for the strong increase in sanidine with increasing SiO_2, increased abundances of quartz and biotite, and the strong decrease in the frequency of occurrences of the pyroxenes with increasing SiO_2. Plagioclase is again the dominant phenocryst, except in some of the high silica biotite rhyolites.

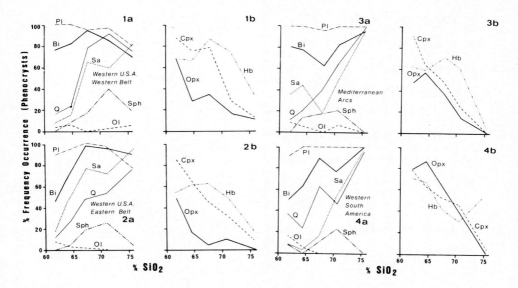

Figure 8.--Percent frequency occurrence of major phenocryst phases in the high-K series of the western U.S.A. (eastern and western belts), the Mediterranean arcs, and western South America, plotted as a function of averaged whole rock compositions. Data from Appendix 3. Abbreviations as in Figure 6.

Commonly reported phenocryst assemblages are as follows, with those of dacitic and rhylitic eruptions shown separately:

<u>Dacites</u> (63-69% SiO_2)

pl + sa $\pm$ qtz + bi

pl + sa $\pm$ qtz $\pm$ aug + bi

pl + sa $\pm$ qtz $\pm$ aug + hb + bi $\pm$ sph

pl + bi $\pm$ aug $\pm$ sph

pl $\pm$ qtz + hb + bi $\pm$ aug $\pm$ sph

pl + hyp + aug

pl + hyp + aug + hb

pl + hb $\pm$ bi

pl + hb $^{\pm}$ aug

pl + qtz + hyp + aug + hb + bi

pl + aug + hyp + bi

<u>Rhyolites</u> (>69% SiO_2)

sa $^{\pm}$ pl + qtz + hb + bi $^{\pm}$ aug $^{\pm}$ sph $^{\pm}$ allanite

sa $^{\pm}$ pl + qtz + bi $^{\pm}$ aug $^{\pm}$ sph $^{\pm}$ allanite

pl $^{\pm}$ qtz + hyp + hb $^{\pm}$ aug

pl $^{\pm}$ qtz + hb + bi $^{\pm}$ aug $^{\pm}$ sph $^{\pm}$ allanite

sa $^{\pm}$ pl $^{\pm}$ qtz + hb $^{\pm}$ aug $^{\pm}$ sph

sa + pl + qtz + aug

pl + aug + hyp

pl + hyp + aug + bi

pl $^{\pm}$ qtz + hb $^{\pm}$ hyp $^{\pm}$ aug

pl $^{\pm}$ qtz + hb + bi

pl + qtz + hyp + hb + bi

sa + pl + qtz + bi + cordierite (Roccastrada, Tuscan igneous province, Italy).

Rhyolites of the Bimodal Associations

These are rather variable in mineralogy, but some of the phenocryst assemblages are evidently quite characteristic of this association. The following are some reported assemblages (excluding Fe-Ti oxides):

Sa $^{\pm}$ pl + qtz + ferroaugite-ferrohedenbergite + fayalite + chevkinite (examples from Yellowstone and Island Park, western U.S.A.; southern Queensland; western Scotland and N. Ireland).

pl $^{\pm}$ qtz + ferroaugite-ferrohedenbergite + Fe-rich olivine (examples from Iceland and western Scotland).

pl + qtz + ferropigeonite $^{\pm}$ hyp(-ferrohypersthene) $^{\pm}$ aug (-ferroaugite) (examples from western Scotland; southern Queensland).

sa + pl + qtz + bi $^{\pm}$ allanite (Mono Craters, U.S.A.; southern Queensland).

sa + pl + qtz + hyp(-ferrohypersthene) (Mono Craters, southeastern Queensland).

sa + pl + qtz + Fe-rich ol + hb $^{\pm}$ ferroaugite (-ferrohedenbergite) (Mono Craters; southern Queensland; Salton Sea).

pl + aug + hyp + hb (Medicine Lake).

Iceland and W. Scotland.--The rhyolites are considered above, but in both these regions, various "dacitoid" compositions also occur sporadically, including the icelandites and 'inninmoreites.' These lavas contain predominantly plagioclase + pyroxene phenocryst assemblages as follows:

pl + pigeonite + aug (-ferroaugite)

pl + aug (-ferroaugite)

pl + aug + hyp

pl + Fe-rich ol + ferroaugite + ferrohypersthene

pl + qtz + aug + hyp + hb + bi

pl + aug + hb

The two latter assemblages are recorded by Hald, Noe-Nygaard and Pedersen (1971) in icelandic dacites, although such assemblages are evidently uncommon in the lavas of Iceland.

The "Dacitic" Lavas of Hawaii and the Galapagos Islands

The Hawaiian rhyodacites are reported to contain the assemblage pl + bronzite + hb + bi. The Galapagos icelandites and dacites contain the assemblages pl + pigeonite and pl + hedenbergite + hb (hastingsite), respectively.

The Soda-Rich-Potash-Poor Lavas of Deception and Fedarb Islands

These are characterized by assemblages pl + hyp + Fe-rich ol, and pl + aug + hyp.

Plagioclase is reported to be oligoclase-andesine, zoned to anorthoclase, and the olivine Fa_{47-84}.

Trachytes

Probably the main features of the phenocryst mineralogy are the relative decrease of plagioclase in relation to alkali feldspar, the latter becoming completely dominant in the more siliceous trachytes, and the absence of phenocrystic quartz. The ferromagnesian assemblages are variable. The following assemblages are reported:

pl + af + aug + hyp (trachyandesites)

pl + af + hb + bi

pl + af + aug (-ferroaugite) + hb + sph

pl + af + aug (-ferroaugite) + hb + bi + sph

pl + af + aug + bi $\pm$ sph

pl + af + aug

af $\pm$ pl + Fe-rich olivine + ferroaugite (-ferrohedenbergite) $\pm$ allanite

aug + bi

Phenocryst Compositions

Feldspars

Dacitic and rhyolitic associations of island arcs and orogenic continental margins.--Plagioclase is the dominant phenocrystic feldspar, and characeristically exhibits strongly developed normal oscillatory zoning, frequently resulting in ranges of composition of 20-30% or even more. The overall compositions reported in orogenic dacitic and rhyolitic volcanics range from oligoclase to anorthite.

Some specific comparative data are presented in Figure 9, based on detailed microprobe studies of dacites and rhyolites from various active S.W. Pacific volcanic provinces, representing low-K and calc-alkali suites. The plagioclase compositions of the low-K dacites of Tonga are predominantly bytownite, with narrow rims of calcic andesine-labradorite. In comparison, the calc-alkaline dacites of New Zealand and New Britain are characterized by plagioclase dominantly of calcic andesine-labradorite composition, while the rhyolitic plagioclases of the Taupo Volcanic Zone (mostly calc-alkaline), New Zealand, are predominantly andesine (zoned in some rocks to oligoclase); the compositions of these rhyolitic plagioclases are, however, correlated with the type of coexisting ferromagnesian assemblage (Fig. 9, e-g), which are again temperature dependent (Ewart et al., 1975). These general compositional ranges are generally consistent with the quoted compositions from comparable volcanic rocks from other orogenic regions. Thus, low-K dacites characteristically contain plagioclase of labradorite-bytownite composition, while low-K rhyolites contain andesine-labradorite. Plagioclases from calc-alkaline dacites are generally quoted to be in the range calcic andesine to bytownite, and in calc-alkaline rhyolites between oligoclase and calcic labradorite.

There is a dearth of published comparative microprobe data for plagioclases in high-K dacites and rhyolites. Compositions most commonly reported for the dacites span the range andesine to sodic labradorite, with rims zoned to oligoclase. Rhyolites of the high-K type typically contain oligoclase, some extending to sodic andesine. Bulk compositions (based on mineral separates) of coexisting plagioclase-sanidine pairs from high-K lavas of the western U.S.A. are illustrated in Figure 10g.

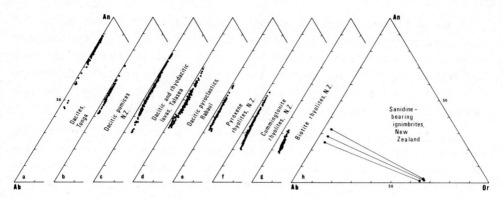

Figure 9.--Microprobe analyses (a-g) of phenocryst plagioclases from selected
low-K and calc-alkali dacites and rhyolites from Tonga, New Britain, and
the Taupo Volcanic Zone of New Zealand, all active volcanic regions within
the S.W. Pacific. Data in Figure h represents bulk compositions of
coexisting plagioclase-sanidine pairs (joined by tie-lines) separated from
three rhyolitic ignimbrites. All compositions in mol. %. Data from Ewart
(1969, 1976), Ewart et al. (1975), Heming and Carmichael (1973), and Lowder
(1970).

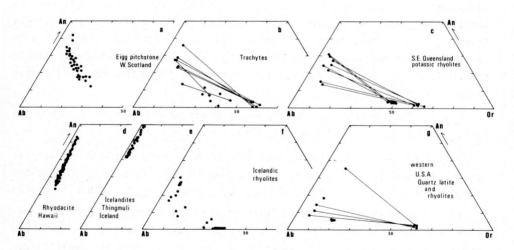

Figure 10.--Comparison of feldspar phenocryst compositions (mol. %) from
oceanic silicic lavas of Hawaii and Iceland; from a pitchstone of W.
Scotland; potassic rhyolites of the bimodal associations of southeastern
Queensland (Australia); from potash trachytes; and from a high-K dacite
(quartz latite) and high-K rhyolites of the western U.S.A. Figures a, d,
and e represent microprobe analyses of individual crystals, while the other
plots represent averaged microprobe data from a single rock, or mineral
separate analyses. Tie-lines join coexisting compositions. Data after
Bauer et al. (1973), Carmichael (1960b, 1963a, 1965, 1967b), Ewart et al.
(1976, 1977), Ridley (1971), Robinson et al. (1976), and Sigurdsson (1970a,
b).

Sanidine becomes a major phenocryst phase only in the high-K dacites and rhyolites, and compositions are reported to range from Or_{40-65}. Sanidine does occur rarely in calc-alkaline rhyolites, such as shown in Figure 9h for three New Zealand rhyolitic ignimbrites; these, however, are crystal-rich and the residual liquid has therefore fractionated sufficiently to intersect the two-feldspar cotectic surface (Ewart, 1969; see later discussion).

Rhyolites of the bimodal associations.--With the exception of the Icelandic rhyolites, rhyolites within this category are typically characterized by two feldspars, oligoclase and sanidine. The sanidine compositions are reported to lie in the range Or_{35-65}, average compositions being Or_{60-65}. Examples of coexisting feldspars within this group are illustrated in Figure 10c, based on averaged microprobe analyses of Miocene rhyolites of southeastern Queensland. In this particular suite, rhyolites from certain volcanic centres contain a slightly more calcic plagioclase (sodic andesine) which occurs as strongly resorbed cores enclosed within the sanidine phenocrysts, themselves more sodic than average ($\sim Or_{50}$). Robinson et al. (1976) report anorthoclase plus oligoclase xenocrysts in the Salton Sea rhyolites (Fig. 10g).

Iceland (Figs. 10e-f).-- The "calc-alkaline" rhyolites contain a single phenocryst feldspar whose compositions range from sodic andesine to anorthoclase; the more alkali-rich rhyolites also contain only a single feldspar, the compositions of which are more potassic, being low-Ca anorthoclase to sodic sanidine (Carmichael, 1963; Sigurdsson, 1971a). Within the icelandites, andesine-labradorite represents the phenocrystic feldspar phase.

Hawaii.--The rhyodacitic lavas contain a single feldspar, plagioclase of dominantly andesine composition (Fig. 10d).

Trachytes (Fig. 10b).--The phenocrystic feldspar relations within trachytes are complex and variable. Some contain two distinct feldspars, plagioclase (andesine-oligoclase) and sanidine (approximately Or_{60-65}). Other trachytes contain essentially a single zoned feldspar of calcic anorthoclase composition. Gradations exist between the two types, and some trachytes are found to contain, with detailed microprobe studies, either two discrete anorthoclase compositions, or calcic-anorthoclase plus sanidine phases. One feature of the chemistry of many of these trachytic feldspars is their extensive ternary solid solution, presumably a function of both the trachyte bulk chemistry and relatively high crystallization (see later).

Pyroxenes and Olivines

<u>Dacitic eruptives of island arcs and orogenic continental margins</u> (Figs. 11-13).--Two phenocryst pyroxenes are characteristically present in the silicic andesites and dacites (and many rhyolites) of these orogenic regions; these are a Ca-rich pyroxene (typically augite, some compositions just lying within the diopside field), and an orthopyroxene (bronzite-hypersthene). Appreciable ranges of solid solutions are found, due to zoning, within most rocks on which detailed microprobe analyses are made (Figs. 11c, 12a,e,f). The significant aspect is that the pyroxenes of these orogenic silicic magmas very rarely exhibit any tendency for strong Fe-enrichment. Kuno (1969) has described rare examples of Fe-enriched phenocryst assemblages, containing ferrohypersthene, ferropigeonite, fayalitic olivine, and ferroaugite, from low-K andesites and dacites of the Asio and Sidara districts, Japan. Kuno further compares these rocks and mineral assemblages with the Skaergaard, and implies that these re-enriched dacites and andesites are derived by crystal fractionation from a tholeiitic parental magma. Such mechanism may not be appropriate for many other silicic orogenic magmas.

Excluding these Japanese examples described above, the strongest Fe-enrichment so far observed, considering a whole suite, is probably found within the low-K and rather Fe-rich lavas of Tonga (Fig. 12h; Ewart et al., 1973), but even within the Tongan dacites, pyroxene compositions still project within the augite and hypersthene compositional fields, and no Fe-rich olivine is present. The groundmass pyroxenes of these Tongan dacites exhibit a greater degree of Fe-enrichment; perhaps more sigificant, however, is their wide variability across the subcalcic pyroxene compositional range (Fig. 12i), a mineralogical charcteristic that may be widespread in low-K island arc lavas.

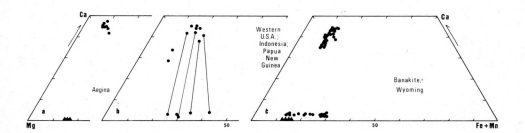

Figure 11.--Pyroxene and olivine phenocryst compositions, plotted in terms of Ca, Mg, and Fe + Mn (atomic %), from various high-K dacites and siliceous andesites. Figures a and b based on averaged microprobe analyses; figure c is based as individual microprobe analyses. Filled circles are Ca-rich pyroxenes and orthopyroxenes; filled triangles are olivines. Data after Fodor (1971); Jakes (1970), Joplin et al. (1972); Nicholls and Carmichael (1969); Pe (1973); Stormer (1972); and Witkind (1969).

Olivine compositions within orogenic dacites are essentially bimodal; they are either very Mg-rich (e.g., Fig. 11), in which case the olivines are usually described as being resorbed or enclosed by reaction rims (and are presumably xenocrystic), or the olivines are Fe-rich as described in certain Japan dacites (see above).

Rhyolitic eruptives of island arcs and orogenic continental margins.-- Relatively little microprobe data are published on the pryoxenes within modern orogenic rhyolites. Rhyolitic and rhyo-dacitic pyroxenes from Lassen (California), Talasea (New Britain), and the Taupo region of New Zealand are

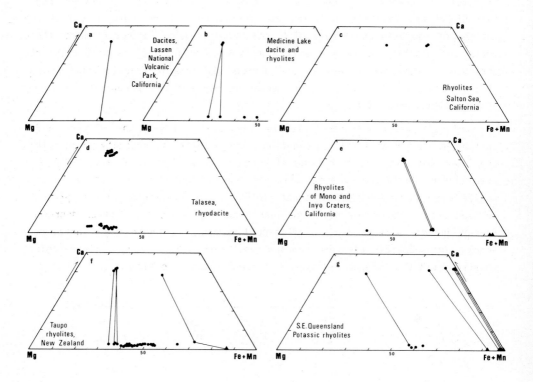

Figure 12.--Pyroxene compositions, plotted in terms of Ca, Mg, and Fe + Mn (atomic %) of selected calc-alkali and low-K silicic andesites and dacites. Data are for phenocryst phases except where otherwise stated. Coexisting compositions are joined by tie-lines. Filled circles are Ca-rich pyroxenes and orthorhombic pyroxenes (in Fig. i, filled circles represent all groundmass pyroxenes); hollow triangles represent phenocryst pigeonite. Figures a, e, f, and i are based on individual microprobe spot analyses; remaining figures are based on averaged probe data, or mineral separate analyses. Data after Aramaki and Haramura (1975); Black (1970); Ewart (1971, 1976); Kuno (1938a, 1969); Lowder(1970); Nicholls (1971); Oba (1966); Smith and Carmichael (1968); Tiba (1976); Ui (1971); and Ujike (1972).

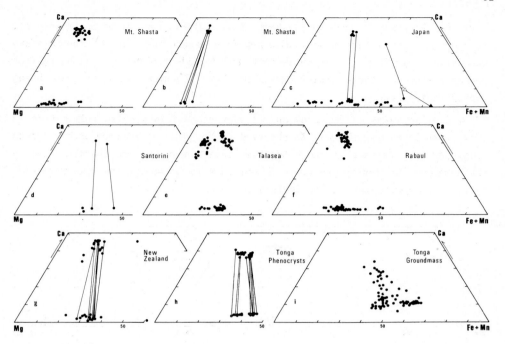

Figure 13.--Pyroxene and olivine phenocryst compositions, plotted in terms of
Ca, Mg, and Fe + Mn (atomic %) from rhyolitic eruptives of the western
U.S.A., New Britain, the Taupo Volcanic Zone of New Zealand, and
southeastern Queensland (Australia). The rhyolites from Medicine Lake,
Salton Sea, Mono Craters, and Queensland represent orogenic rhyolites.
Figure d is based on individual microprobe analyses; other figures are
based on rock averaged microprobe data. Filled circles are Ca-rich
pyroxenes and orthorhombic pyroxenes; filled triangles are olivines. Tie-
lines join coexisting compositions. Data after Carmichael (1967a); Ewart
(1971); Ewart et al. (1975, 1976, 1977); Lowder (1970); and Robinson et al.
(1976).

illustrated in Figures 13a, d, and f, from which it is clear that these
rhyolites most commonly contain relatively Mg-rich pyroxenes, typically augite
and hypersthene. In only one New Zealand rhyolite (of several hundred
examined) has an Fe-enriched assemblage been found (Fig. 13f). The controls on
the compositions of the pyroxenes is dependent on several factors; for example,
orthopyroxene compositions are interdependent on f_{O_2}, temperature, a_{SiO_2} of
the liquid and P_{total} (Ewart et al., 1975).

Rhyolites of the bimodal associations.--Published data on rhyolites of this
association are presented in Figures 13b, c, e, and f, and 14c, d, and e. Of
particular significance are the range of compositions exhibited by the
pyroxenes; these range, for example, from hypersthene + augite in the Medicine
Lake rhyolites, through assemblages containing ferrohypersthene and/or

fayalite, as found in the Inyo Craters, Mono Craters, and Salton Sea rhyolites, to virtually pure ferrohedenbergite-fayalite assemblages in the southeastern Queensland rhyolites. It is noteworthy that fayalitic olivine replaces Fe-rich orthopyroxene in these assemblages, the most Fe-rich orthopyroxenes being approximately fs_{70}.

A similar range of pyroxene and olivine compositions, also culminating in very Fe-enriched compositions, as observed in the western sequence is considered (Fig. 14d,e). Certain of these Scottish lavas, however, are characterized by the presence of ferropigeonite, in addition to orthopyroxene and a Ca-rich pyroxene (Emeleus, Dunham, and Thompson, 1971).

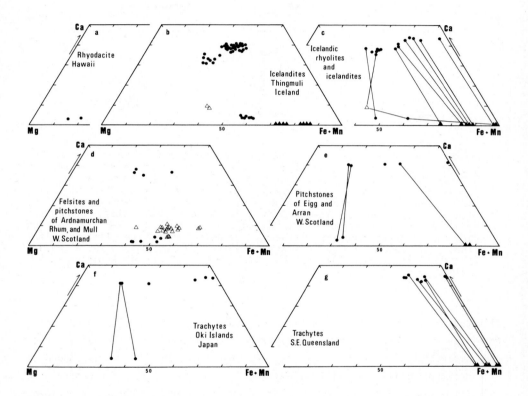

Figure 14.--Pyroxene and olivine phenocryst compositions, plotted in terms of Ca, Mg, and Fe + Mn (atomic %), from selected salic lavas from Hawaii, the bimodal associations of Iceland and W. Scotland, and potassic trachytes from Japan and southeastern Queensland (Australia). Figures b and d based on individual microprobe analyses; other figures based on averaged microprobe data or mineral separate analyses. Tie-lines join coexisting compositions. Filled circles are Ca-rich pyroxenes and orthopyroxenes; open triangles are phenocryst pigeonite; filled triangles are olivines. Data after Bauer et al. (1973); Carmichael (1960a, 1963b, 1964, 1967a and b); Emeleus et al. (1971); Ewart et al. (1976, 1977); Ridley (1971); Sigurdsson (1971b); Uchimizu (1966); and Virgo and Ross (1973).

Iceland (Fig. 14b and c).--The icelandites and rhyolites for which analytical data are available again show progressive Fe-enrichment from coexisting augite + hypersthene, through coexisting ferroaugite + ferrohortonalite, to ferrohedenbergite + fayalite pairs. In addition, certain of the icelandites contain pigeonite. Although these pyroxene assemblages appear to be most common in the Icelandic lavas, it is again noted that biotite and hornblende have been recorded, although no analytical data are available (Hald et al., 1971).

Hawaii (Fig. 14a).--Mineralogically, the described Hawaiian rhyodacites are very different from the oceanic dacites and rhyolites of Iceland. The Hawaiian rhyodacites contain a bronzite as the only pyroxene phenocryst phase.

Quartz trachytes.--The pyroxene-olivine assemblages from two trachyte suites (Fig. 14f-g, Oki Island (Japan) and southeastern Queensland), indicate a similar pattern of compositional behaviour as in the bimodal suites considered previously; that is, progressive Fe-enrichment from augite + hypersthene in "trachyandesites" to the pure ferrohedenbergite-faalite assemblages found in the more siliceous trachytes of southeastern Queensland.

Amphiboles

Calciferous amphiboles.--These are by far the most common amphibole type occurring in orogenic dacitic and rhyolitic volcanic rocks; inspection of available analyses suggests that almost all can be classified as belonging to the common hornblende series. Nevertheless, considerable variation exists in the solid solution relations of the major cations. This is illustrated in Figure 15 in terms of Si, Ca + alkalis, Al, and Mg + Fe + Mn; the data are subdivided according to the SiO_2% of the parent (host) rock in which the hornblendes occur, plus a fourth group comprising hornblendes in the rhyolites from bimodal associations. It is seen from Figure 15 that, with the exception of the bimodal rhyolites, there is a general tendency for a systematic change of hornblende composition to occur with increasing SiO_2 of the host rock. Thus, in the Si versus Ca+Na+K plot, the compositions tend towards the pargasite $NaCa_2(MgFe)_4AlSi_7AlO_{22}(OH)_2$ end member in the amphiboles from the least silicic dacites and siliceous andesites, and trend towards hornblende $NaCa_2(MgFe)_4AlSi_7AlO_{22}(OH)_2$ in the rhyolitic hornblendes; i.e., by decreasing Ca+Na+K and increasing Si. In the Al versus Mg+Fe+Mn plot the trend is from the pargasitic towards the edenitic end members; i.e., decreasing Al and increasing Mg+Fe+Mn with increasing SiO_2 of the host rock. Few of the amphiboles, however, can be regarded as edenitic in their overall chemistry.

The amphiboles from the bimodal rhyolites fall in the same general field as

64

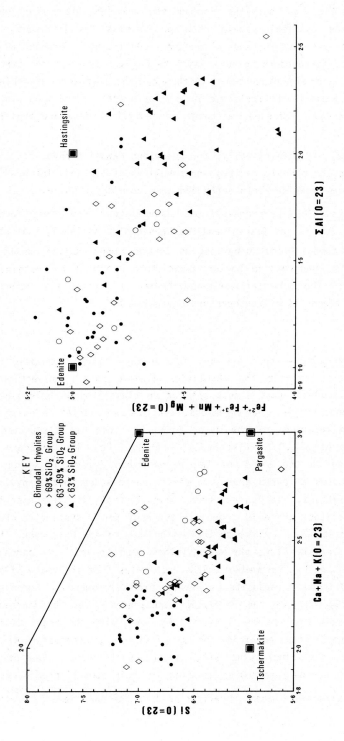

Figure 15.--Compilation of published calcic amphibole (phenocryst) analyses from silicic andesites, dacites, and rhyolites, plotted in terms of number of cations per structural formula unit (0 = 23). Data subdivided according to the compositions of the whole (host) rock for the orogenic eruptives; the rhyolites of bimodal associations are indicated by a separate symbol.

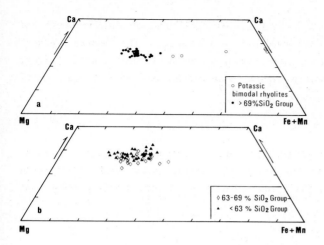

Figure 16.--Compilation of published calcic amphibole (phenocryst) analyses from silicic andesites, dacites, and rhyolites, plotted in terms of Ca, Mg, and Fe + Mn (atomic %). Data subdivided according to the compositions of the whole (host) rocks for orogenic eruptives, while the rhyolites of bimodal associations are indicated by a separate symbol.

the amphiboles from the dacites and rhyolites described above, but show a rather wider range of solid solution than found in the equivalent orogenic rhyolites.

The hornblendes are replotted in Figure 16 in terms of their Mg:Fe ratios. The hornblendes from the orogenic acid andesites, dacites and rhyolites exhibit completely overlapping Mg:Fe ratios, and all these amphiboles contain more Mg than Fe on a molecular basis. In contrast, the hornblendes of the bimodal rhyolites exhibit the tendency for progressive Fe-enrichment, consistent with the pyroxene data. In certain of the rhyolites of southern Queensland, the amphiboles become completely Mg-deficient; these amphiboles lie between the ferroedenite and hastingsite end member compositions.

Cummingtonites.--Primary phenocrystic cummingtonite, coexisting with (or sometimes included within) hornblende, has been described from dacitic and rhyolitic lavas and pumices from Japan (Kuno, 1938b), the Cascades of the western U.S.A. (Wilcox, 1965; Klein, 1968), West Indies (Robson and Tomblin, 1966, p. 42; Bryan, 1972), and New Zealand (Ewart et al., 1971, 1975). Figure 17 illustrates the compositions of the analyzed cummingtonites, and the coexisting hornblendes.

Detailed minralogical studies of the New Zealand cummingtonite-bearing rhyolites (Ewart et al., 1975) suggest that the upper stability limit of cummingtonite is close to $760^{\circ}C$ (Fe-Ti oxide equilibration temperatures) and that phenocryst equilibration occurred under P_{H_2O} P_{total}. The important aspect is that cummingtonite coexisting with orthopyroxene constitutes a water buffer, and will allow, given appropriate mineral assemblages, estimates to be made of f_{H_2O} for phenocryst equilibration.

Biotite

A compilation of published analyses are presented in Figure 18, which emphasizes the Mg-Fe ratios to the biotites. Again, no systematic difference is apparent in biotites from the volcanic rocks of differing SiO_2 contents, at

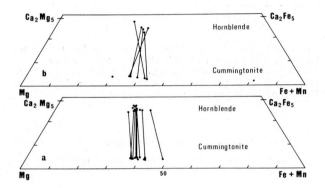

Figure 17.--Compositions of phenocrystic cummingtonite and of calcic hornblendes coexisting with cummingtonite, plotted in terms of Ca, Mg, and Fe + Mn (atomic %). Tie-lines join coexisting compositions. Figure a plots data from ryholites of the Taupo Volcanic Zone, New Zealand, while Figure b presents data from dacites and rhyolites of the Cascades of western U.S.A., and the Caribbean (no coexisting hornblende analysis). Data after Bryan (1972); Ewart et al. (1971, 1975); and Klein (1968).

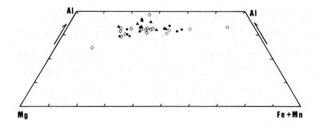

Figure 18.--Compilation of published analyses of biotite phenocrysts from silicic andesites, dacites, and rhyolites, plotted in terms of Al, Mg, and Fe + Mn (atomic %). Data subdivided according to compositions of whole (host) rocks in which the biotites occur; symbols as in Figure 15.

least in the 60-76% SiO_2 range, except for those biotites occurring in the rhyolites of the bimodal provinces. These again exhibit a tendency for a greater degree of Fe-enrichment, in conformity with the pyroxene-olivine-amphibole data previously presented.

Temperature-f_{O_2} Relationships

Figures 19 and 20 summarize published data for T-f_{O_2} relations in rhyolitic and dacitic eruptives, based on equilibrations between coexisting Fe-Ti oxides (after Buddington and Lindsley, 1964). It should be noted that the values of T and f_{O_2} quoted in the literature are not always based on exactly identical procedures for recalculating the titanomagnetite and ilmenite analyses (mostly microprobe analyses) but the published values are incorporated in Figures 19 and 20 without modification. The data in each diagram are compared with three buffer curves, hematite-magnetite (HM), nickel-nickel oxide (NNO), and quartz-fayalite-magnetite (QFM). Figure 19 illustrates data from the western U.S.A. and Alaska, whereas Figure 20 is based on data from other regions of the world, predominantly the S.W. Pacific. In each diagram, the individual data points are

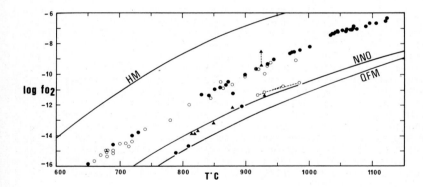

Figure 19.--Compilations of T °C-f_{O_2} data based on equilibration of co-existing Fe-Ti oxides, for silicic andesites, and dacitic and rhyolitic lavas and pyroclastics from the western U.S.A. and Alaska. The curves labelled HM, NNO, and QFM refer to the hematite-magnetite, nickel-nickel oxide, and quartz-fayalite-magnetite buffer curves (1 atmos.), after Eugster and Wones (1962) and Wones and Gilbert (1969). Symbols indicate type of coexisting ferromagnesian phenocryst assemblage; solid circles are hornblende-bearing (± pyroxene; no biotite); hollow circles are biotite-bearing; solid circles are pyroxene-bearing (no hornblende or biotite). The group of data plotting close to, and between the NNO and QFM curves represent the data for the Recent rhyolites from the bimodal associations of Mono and Inyo Craters, and Medicine Lake, California. Dotted lines join alternative estimates of f_{O_2} and T where compositional inhomogeneity occurs in the Fe-Ti oxides. Data after Carmichael (1967a); Lerbekmo et al. (1975); Lipman (1971); and Stormer (1972).

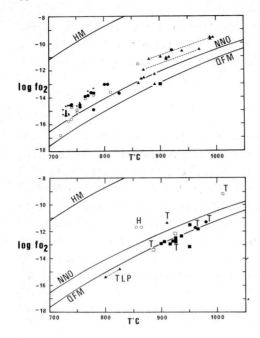

Figure 20.--Compilation of f_{O_2}-T°C data, based on equilibration of coexisting
Fe-Ti oxides, for: <u>Top</u> diagram: rhyolites and dacites from the Taupo
Volcanic Zone of New Zealand, New Britain (Talasea and Rabaul), Santorini,
and Japan. <u>Bottom</u> diagram: rhyolites of the St. Andrew Strait islands
(Papua New Guinea, "<u>TLP</u>" Series); rhyodacites from Hawaii (H); trachytes
(T); rhyolites and icelandites from Iceland; rhyolites from Arran, western
Scotland; and rhyolites from southeastern Queensland (Australia). Dotted
lines join alternative estimates of f_{O_2} and T where compositional
inhomogeneity occurs in the Fe-Ti oxides. Symbols indicate type of
coexisting phenocryst ferromagnesian assemblage: Small filled circles are
cummingtonite-bearing (no biotite); large filled circles are hornblende-
bearing (no cummingtonite or biotite); hollow circles are biotite-bearing;
filled triangles are pyroxene-bearing (no amphiboles or biotite); hollow
squares indicate no coexisting ferromagnesian phase. Data after Bauer et
al. (1973); Carmichael (1964, 1967a and b); Ewart et al. (1971, 1975, 1976,
1977); Heming and Carmichael (1973); Johnson et al (1978); Lowder (1970);
Nicholls (1971); and Ui (1971).

subdivided broadly according to the presence or absence of key ferromagnesian
phases as phenocrysts, namely pyroxene, hornblende, and biotite.

Reference to all data plotted in Figures 19 and 20 suggests that the
volcanic magmas equilibrated on three broadly differing buffer curves or
systems:

(a) The high-K and calc-alkaline lavas and pyroclastics of the western
U.S.A. "orogenic" series, including the modern Cascades, but excluding the
rhyolites of the bimodal associations. These magmas define a buffer curve

between the NNO and HM buffers, and are noteworthy for the common occurrence of sphene.

(b) The predominantly calc-alkaline silicic lavas and pyroclastics of the S.W. Pacific island arcs, Japan and Santorini. These magmas define a buffer curve above the NNO buffer, but clearly below that defined by the western U.S.A. orogenic silicic magmas. Sphene is absent from these volcanic series.

(c) The rhyolitic lavas of the predominantly bimodal associations of Iceland; Arran (Scotland); southern Queensland; St. Andrew Strait (Papua, New Guinea); Mono and InyoCraters and Medicine Lake, California. These magmas lie essentially on or between the NNO and QFM buffer curves.

The equilibration temperatures of the various dacitic and rhyolitic eruptives are sumarized in Table 6, in which the phenocryst assemblages are also listed. From these compilations, three points emerge.

First the lower range of equilibration temperatures found for the high-K western U.S.A. rhyolites (640-780°C) are lower than found for the predominantly calc-alkaline rhyolites of the S.W. Pacific (720-900°C), and as shown in the next section, this is consistent with the chemistry of these different rhyolitic series when considered in terms of the experimental quartz-feldspar systems; moreover, the relatively low temperatures suggest that the magmas were water saturated.

Secondly, the equilibration temperatures of the rhyolites of the bimodal associations are, in general, significantly higher than found in the orogenic calc-alkaline and high-K rhyolites and even dacites. This observation is consistent with their very low phenocryst contents, and with the Fe-enriched phenocryst assemblages occurring within these bimodal rhyolites, indicating equilibration under very low water fugacities.

Thirdly, the data for the western U.S.A. silicic lavas show very little evidence of a systematic correlation of the dominant ferromagnesian phenocryst phases (biotite, hornblende, pyroxenes) with equilibration temperatures or a change in f_{O_2} buffer, perhaps suggesting that these western U.S.A. silicic magmas have been externally buffered. Correlations between ferromagnesian assemblages, equilibration temperatures, and f_{O_2} are found in the S.W. Pacific rhyolites (e.g., Ewart et al., 1975).

INTERRELATIONSHIPS BETWEEN MINERALOGY AND CHEMISTRY

The averaged total, low-K, calc-alkaline, and high-K chemical data from Table 1 and Appendices 1, 2, and 3, recalculated in terms of normative mineralogy (C.I.P.W.), are compared in the ternary quartz-feldspar and feldspar

Table 6. Summary of Fe-Ti oxide equilibration temperatures, in relation to phenocryst assemblages, of dacitic and rhyolitic eruptives from various geographic and tectonic localities. Sources of data as in Figs 19 and 20.

Phenocryst Assemblage	Range of Fe-Ti oxide equilibration temperatures (°C)	General Location
1. Orogenic dacites and silicic andesites		
pl + sa + bi + aug	845–940	Western U.S.A.
pl + qtz + cumm + hb + hyp	770–780	Japan
pl + qtz + hb + bi + hyp	740–810	Japan
pl + hb	880	Western U.S.A.
pl + hyp + hb	930–1120	Alaska
pl + hyp + aug + hb	920	Talasea (New Britain)
pl + hyp + aug	870–990	Rabaul (New Britain); Japan; Santorini
hyp + aug + ol	925	Western U.S.A.
2. Orogenic rhyolitic lavas and pyroclastics		
sa + qtz + bi + sph	670–680	Western U.S.A.
sa + pl + qtz + bi	680–710	Western U.S.A.
sa + hb + sph	640–730	Western U.S.A.
sa + pl + bi + sph	715–720	Western U.S.A.
sa + pl + bi + hb + sph ± aug	700–780	Western U.S.A.
pl + qtz + cumm + hb + hyp	725–755	New Zealand
pl + qtz + bi + hb ± hyp	720–765	New Zealand; Japan
pl + qtz + hb + hyp ± aug	740–805	New Zealand
pl + hb + hyp ± aug	770–825	New Zealand
pl + qtz + hyp + aug	865–890	New Zealand
pl + hyp + aug	800–915	New Zealand; Rabaul (New Britain); Santorini

	Mineral assemblage	Temperature (°C)	Locality
	pl + qtz + ferroaugite + eulite + ferrohortonalite	900	New Zealand
	pl ± qtz + hyp + aug + hb + bi	860–980	Talasea (new Britain); Western U.S.A.
3.	**Rhyolites of bimodal Association**		
	pl + Fe-rich cpx + Fe-rich ol	900–925	Arran (W. Scotland); Medicine Lake (California); St. Andrew Strait (Papua New Guinea)
	pl + hyp + aug	800–930	
	sa + hb ± ferrohedenbergite ± fayalite	920–980	Southern Queensland
	sa + pl + qtz + bi + allanite	830–930	Southern Queensland
	sa + Fe-rich cpx + fayalite + ferrohypersthene	890–940	Southern Queensland
	sa + pl + qtz + fe-rich ol + hb	790–810	Mono Craters (California)
	hyp ± sa ± pl ± qtz	815–850	Mono Craters (California)
	sa + pl + qtz + hyp + aug + hb + bi	920–985	Inyo Craters (California)
4.	**Oceanic 'dacitic' lavas**		
	pl + aug ± hyp + ol	905–965	Iceland (icelandites)
	pl + hyp + hb + bi	855–865	Hawaii
5.	**Trachytes**		
	pl + sa + hyp + aug + hb + bi + sph	1010	Cantal, France
	sa + pl + hyp + aug	910	Eigg, Scotland
	sa + pl + ferrohedenbergite + fayalite	925	Southern Queensland

systems in Figures 21 and 22, respectively. The plotted trends are compared with the quartz-feldspar and two-feldspar boundary curves determined by James and Hamilton (1969) for 1 kb P_{H_2O}. From these plots, the following two points emerge:

(a) The total data (i.e., for the five SiO_2 groups) for each of the western

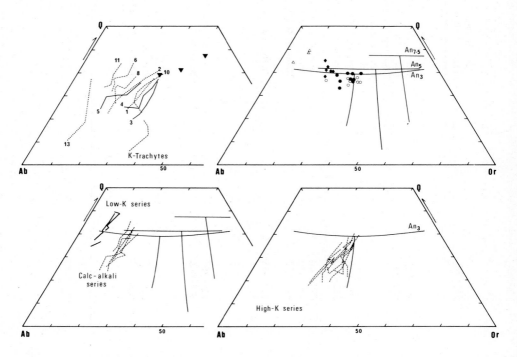

Figure 21.--Normative (C.I.P.W.) Q, Ab, and An components of averaged chemical analyses (total data) from Tables 1, 4, and 5, and the averaged analyses of the low-K, calc-alkaline, and high-K compositions from different subregions, partly from Appendices 1, 2, and 3.
Upper left: Total data compositional trends for each of the geographic and/or tectonic subregions considered in this review; numbers refer to the specific subregion represented by each trend, as listed in the Introduction.
Upper right: Averaged compositions of high SiO_2 rhyolites (>73%); these are divided into low-K types (hollow triangles); calc-alkali (solid diamonds); high-K types (solid circles); and those of bimodal associations (hollow circles).
Lower left: Averaged low-K and calc-alkali compositional trends from the various orogenic regions.
Lower right: Averaged high-K compositional trends from the various orogenic regions.
Each trend line is based on the averaged composition, for each subregion, region, for the five SiO_2 groupings (60-63, 63-66, 66-69, 69-73, >73%). K-Trachytes refer to potassic trachyte trend line. Also shown on each figure is the projection of the quartz-feldspar and the two-feldspar boundary curves (1kb P_{H_2O}) for the three An compositions as labelled (after James and Hamilton, 1969).

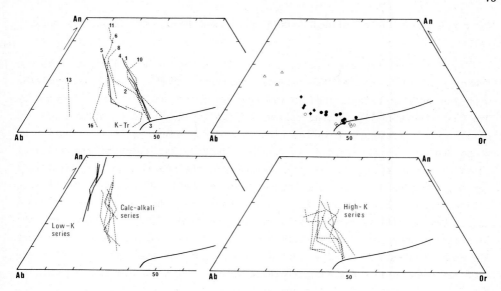

Figure 22.--Normative (C.I.P.W.) Ab, Or, and An components of averaged chemical
   analyses (total data) from Tables 1, 4, and 5, and the averaged analyses of
   the low-K, calc-alkaline, and high-K compositions from various subregions,
   partly from Appendices 1, 2, and 3. Symbols, abbreviations, and methods of
   compilation as in Figure 21.
   Lower left: Averaged low-K and calc-alkali compositional trends.
   Upper left: Total data compositional trends for each subregion. K-Tr refers
   to potassic trachyte compositional trend.
   Upper right: Averaged compositions of high-SiO$_2$ rhyolites (>73%).
   Lower left: Averaged low-K and calc-alkali compositional trends.
   Lower right: Averaged high-K compositional trends.
    Also shown on each figure is the projection of the quartz-saturated two-
   feldspar boundary curve for 1 kb H$_2$0, after James and Hamilton (1969).

U.S.A., western South America, and the Mediterranean regions, together with the
corresponding data for the high-K series from these and other geographic
regions, all exhibit well-defined directional trends towards the "ternary
minima" compositions in the quartz-feldspar systems, and the highest SiO$_2$
compositions (>73% group), in fact, terminate in close proximity to the An$_3$
piercing point (1 kb H$_2$0) in this system,(Fig. 21). Similarly, these high-SiO$_2$
rhyolite compositions also terminate in close proximity to the quartz-saturated
two-feldspar curve (Fig. 22).

    (b) The trends exhibited by the sets of data for the various calc-alkaline
and low-K series do not show this same tendency to terminate at the "ternary
minima" compositions. The high SiO$_2$ rhyolite compositions (>73% SiO$_2$) within
these two series show increasing normative quartz and anorthite, relative to
the high-K rhyolites; this relative increase in normative quartz and anorthite

is particularly well defined within the low-K rhyolites, which are notably calcic.

The fact that the analyses of the high-K series project closer to both the "ternary minima" and the two-feldspar boundary curve, is readily correlated with the previously described mineralogy, in which two feldspars plus quartz are characteristically present as phenocrysts in the high-K rhyolites, and are also commonly present within the high-K dacites. Clearly, crystallization of these high-K magmas results in the residual liquid reaching the critical boundary curves at a relatively early stage of the process. In the calc-alkali series, sanidine is much less common, and in the low-K series it is absent; reference to Figures 21 and 22 clearly shows that the compositions of these less-potassic silicic magma series lie progressively farther removed from the two-feldspar boundary curves which are thus unlikely to be intersected except at advanced stages of crystallization. Figure 21 indicates, however, that the same restriction does not apply to the crystallization of quartz. Furthermore, the increased normative quartz and anorthite components of the averaged calc-alkali and low-K rhyolitic compositions can be correlated with the shift of the quartz-feldspar boundary curve towards more quartz-rich compositions with increasing anorthite component within the Ab-Or-An-Q systems (e.g., James and Hamilton, 1969).

Some degree of correlation also exists between the lower ranges of Fe-Ti oxide equilibration temperatures and the magma compositions. Thus the western U.S.A. high-K rhyolites have equilibration temperatures determined in the range 640-780°C for the dominantly calc-alkaline rhyolites of the Taupo region, New Zealand. Winkler (1976, p. 279-299) has clearly shown that liquid compositions lying closest to the "ternary minima" compositions will, other factors remaining equivalent, exist at lower temperatures than liquids whose compositions lie further removed from the "ternary minima," although still perhaps lying on a cotectic surface. Clearly, the low-K rhyolites and dacites should have the highest equilibration temperatures, but data are not available to check this.

The averaged compositions of the rhyolites from the essentially bimodal provinces are also found to project very close to the lower pressure "ternary minima" compositions (with the notable exception of the "calc-alkali" Icelandic rhyolites), although Fe-Ti oxide equilibration temperatures are relatively high (800-985°C). This is certainly indicative of crystallization under very low f_{O_2}, and is consistent with their very low phenocryst contents, Fe-enriched phenocryst compositions, and equilibration at lower f_{O_2} than characteristic for the majority of the orogenic rhyolites and dacites.

Reference to the compositional trend of the averaged potassic trachyte data (60-63, 63-66, 66-69, 69-73% SiO_2) in Figure 21 shows clearly why phenocrystic quartz is absent, even within the most silicic trachytes. In both Figures 21 and 22, the averaged trachyte trend exhibits a marked curvature, suggesting that the compositions are being controlled along the two-feldspar boundary surface; this receives support from the proximity of the SiO_2-rich part of the trachyte trend to the quartz-saturated feldspar boundary curve in Figure 22 and the fact that these potassic trachytes typically contain either two coexisting phenocryst feldspars, or a calcic anorthoclase.

REGIONAL VARIATIONS OF DACITIC AND RHYOLITIC MAGMAS

It is obvious that rather pronounced differences exist in the chemical, and thus mineralogical characteristics of silicic volcanic magmas from different geographic and tectonic environments, and clearly, these must reflect variations in the petrogeneses of these magmas.

In order to attempt to obtain a reasonably objective view of these differences and interrelationships, the final averaged data of the five SiO_2 groupings (60-63, 63-66, 66-69, 69-73, >73%) for the different geographic and tectonic regional divisions have been subject to Q-mode cluster analyses. These have utilized weighted pair group averaging, using both distance and correlation coefficients (with correlations applied to standardized data). The input data used included all averaged major and trace element data, plus phenocryst mode and phenocryst occurrence data, as listed in Tables 1, 3, 4, and 5, a total maximum of 5 variables per input sample set. The results obtained by using distance and correlation coefficients are substantially in agreement and three dendrograms are illustrated in Figures 23-25 for the 60-63, 66-69, and >73 SiO_2% groups, based on correlation coefficients.

The following general conclusions can be drawn from the clustering calculations:

Silicic andesites and silicic dacite (Figs. 23-24): (a) The eruptives from the two western U.S.A. zones, western South America, and the Mediterranean are always most closely correlated together, but significantly, the eruptives of the High Cascades-Alaska-Aleutian subregion are clearly excluded. In all dendograms, the western and eastern zones of the western U.S.A. are very closely correlated. (b) There is a general tendency for a clustering together of the data for the High Cascades-Alaska-Aleutians subregion with those of the Middle Americas, Indonesia, and the Caribbean. (c) The silicic andesites and dacites of the S.W. Pacific and the Japan-Taiwan-Kamchatka-Saipan subregions are closely clustered as a subgroup. (d) There is a generalized grouping of

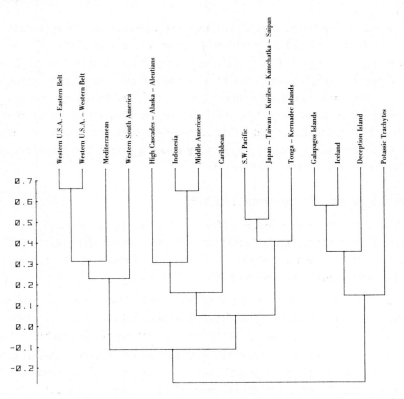

Figure 23.--Dendrogram, based on Q-mode cluster analysis using correlation
coefficients, showing interrelationships and groupings between silicic
"andesites" (60-63% SiO_2) from different orogenic and oceanic subregions.
Correlations based on total average major and trace element data, and
phenocryst occurrence and modal data, from Table 1.

the oceanic lavas from Iceland and the Galapagos Islands, with those of
Deception and Fedarb Islands (these two islands being of the high soda-low
potash type); significantly, the dacitic lavas of western Scotland also
consistently fall within this clustering. (e) The potassic trachyte data in
all dendograms, especially those based on distance coefficients, exhibit little
tendency to closely cluster with any of the other volcanic divisions,
emphasizing that the trachytes are not likely to be derived from, or closely
related to, the high-K orogenic silicic magmas.

Rhyolites (Fig. 25): The data presentation is more complex owing to the
greater variety of averaged rhyolitic types included. On the most generalized
basis, the dendrogram suggests a possible overall two-fold split into potassic
rhyolites from the bimodal associations and also the orogenic associations of
'mobile' continental margins, and secondly, the less-potassic rhyolites of

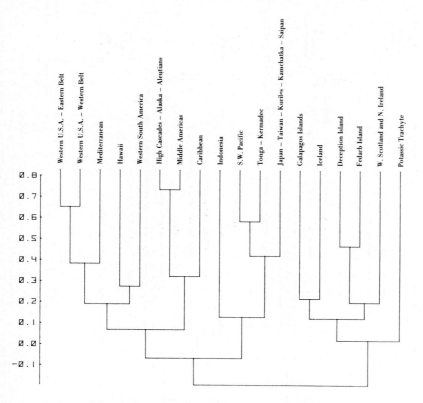

Figure 24.--Dendrogram, based on Q-mode cluster analysis using correlation coefficients, showing interrelationships and groupings between silicic dacites (66-69% SiO_2) from different orogenic and oceanic subregions. Correlations based on total averaged major and trace element data, and phenocryst occurrence and modal data, from Tables 1 and 3.

island arcs, oceanic islands, and actively spreading continental margins (Salton Sea, and western Scotland (Eocene)).

At the higher levels of correlation, the following four-fold clustering is indicated by the data: (a) The orogenic potassic rhyolites of the western U.S.A. (excluding High Cascades), western South America, Middle Americas, and the Mediterranean arcs. (b) Potassic rhyolites belonging to bimodal associations; e.g., Yellowstone and Mono, western U.S.A., and southern Queensland. Significantly, the slightly peralkaline Devine Canyon rhyolite correlates within this grouping. (c) The low-K and predominantly calc-alkaline rhyolites of the S.W. Pacific and Japan-Taiwan-Kurile-Kamchatka-Saipan subregions. (d) A grouping of less potassic rhyolites form the bimodal provinces of Iceland, western Scotland, and Salton Sea (California). These rhyolites are less potassic, have slightly lower differentiation indices, and their trace element

78

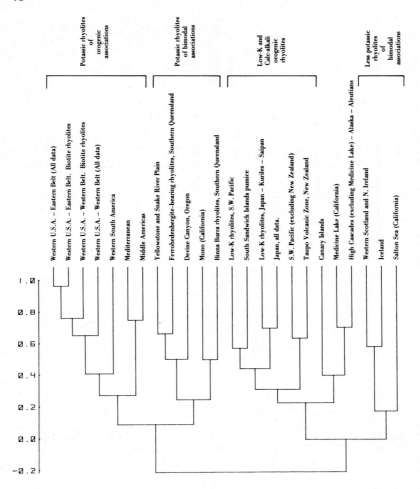

Figure 25.--Dendrogram, based on Q-mode cluster analysis using correlation
coefficients, showing interrelationships and groupings between high-SiO$_2$
rhyolites (>73% SiO$_2$) from different orogenic and oceanic subregions and
associations. Correlations based on averaged major and trace element data,
and phenocryst occurrence and modal data from Tables 1, 4, and 5.

abundance patterns suggest that they are less fractionated than the previous
group of potassic rhyolites of bimodal associations.

A full discussion of the possible petrogenetic significance of these
regional variations of chemistry is beyond the scope of this review, if for no
oher reason than it would also require a corresponding compilation of both
isotopic and more extensive trace element data (e.g., REE). Nevertheless, it
is clear that a correlation exists between various tectonic and crustal

environments, and the chemistry of the salic magmas occurring within them. If it is accepted that the magmas responsible for the voluminous outpourings of rhyolites and dacites in such regions as the western U.S.A., Japan, New Zealand, Sumatra, western South America, etc., owe their origin in a large part to derivation by crustal fusion, then the composition of these magmas, including trace element abundances, must reflect the overall chemistry of the parental crustal rocks. Crustal structure, however, may influence the ultimate chemistry of the magmas in additional respects; i.e., the thickness, density, rigidity (viscosity), and heterogeneity of the crust are likely to control the dynamics of magma rise, and the emplacement and structure of magma chambers (e.g., Ramberg, 1970), thereby influencing the importance of superimposed crystal fractionation and assimilation processes.

For example, it has been shown that the averaged compositions of the salic magmas from the western U.S.A. (excluding Cascades), western South American and Mediterranean regions, and indeed the high-K series from othe regions, trend towards and terminated close to the lower pressure "ternary minima" compositions in the quartz-feldspar system. This certainly is readily explicable in terms of crystal fractionation controlling the development of the most silicic magma composition, and the trace and minor element data for the high-SiO_2 rholitic compositions from the western U.S.A. (excluding the Cascades; Tables 1-A and 4-A) certainly lends support to this interpretation. Fractional crystallization within one specific centre, producing rhyodacite and rhyolite derivatives, has been described by Zielinski and Lipman (1976). Moreover, some Sr isotopic studies have indicated that crustal assimilation has occurred during fractional crystallization of silicic volcanic magmas within some volcanic centres of the western U.S.A. Province (e.g., Noble and Hedge, 1969; Bikerman, 1976; Stinnett, 1976; see also Scott et al., 1971). Such assimilation could clearly also modify or buffer the major element chemistry of the magmas; e.g., potassium, f_{O_2}.

In contrast to the high-K magmas discussed above, the calc-alkali salic magmas of especially the island arc regions show much less convincing chemical evidence for control of their compositions by fractional crystallization, as previously noted. In the specific example of the Taupo Volcanic Zone of New Zealand, it has been argued that the rhyolites and dacites represent increasingly advanced stages of partial fusion of volcanogenic Mesozoic graywacke-argillite sediments; i.e., melting extending into the upper crust (Ewart and Stipp, 1968; Ewart et al., 1975, 1977). The low-K salic magmas, however, which appear to occur predominantly in regions of subcontinental and relatively young crust, or within intra-oceanic island arcs, are evidently erupted on a smaller scale than many of their calc-alkali equivalents. In the example of low-K dacites of the Tongan Islands, a model of low pressure crystal fractionation from parental low-K basaltic andesites seems to fit the available data most satisfactorily (Ewart et al., 1973).

Finally, attention is drawn to the rhyolites of the bimodal associations, which have been included within this compilation. The geochemistry of certain of these rhyolites indicate that fractional crystallization has been an important process in their petrogenesis, at least in the later stages of their development; e.g., the rhyolites of the Yellowstone region (western U.S.A.) and southern Queensland. Moreover, as described, these rhyolites exhibit certain mineralogical assemblages and mineral compositions which distinguish them from the majority of orogenic rhyolites; these bimodal rhyolites are also noteworthy for higher equilibration temperatures, and equilibration at relatively lower oxygen fugacities. Such an origin could certainly be consistent with derivation from a predominantly basaltic parental material, either by conventional fractional crystallization, or even partial melting as suggested, for example, by Gibson (1969) and Johnson et al., (in press), with superimposed later fractional crystallization.

ACKNOWLEDGMENTS

The writer is particularly indebted to A. S. Bagley, University of Queensland, for his continued help in the computer processing of the data and with programming.

REFERENCES (including data sources; cited references are marked by asterisk)

*Anderson, C. A., 1933. Volcanic history of Glass Mountain, northern California. Am. J. Sci., 26: 485-506.

*Anderson, C. A., 1941. Volcanoes of the Medicine Lake Highlands, California. Univ. Calif. Publ. Bull. Dept. Geol. Sci., 25: 347-422.

Anderson, F. W. and Dunham, K. C., 1966. The geology of Northern Skye. Mem. Geol. Surv. Scotland: 1-216.

Ando, S., 1971. Minor element abundances in the Quaternary volcanic rocks in Hokkaido, Japan. Part 1: The rocks from southwestern Hokkaido. Jap. Assoc. Min., Pet., and Econ. Geol. J., 66: 213-227 (in Japanese).

Ando, S., 1972. Minor element abundances in the Quaternary volcanic rocks in Hokkaido, Japan. Part 2: The rocks from eastern and central Hokkaido. Jap. Assoc. Min. Pet., and Econ. Geol. J., 67: 151-157 (in Japanese).

Ando, S., 1975. Minor element geochemistry of the rocks from Mashu volcano, eastern Hokkaido. J. Fac. Sci. Hokkaido Univ., Ser. IV, 16: 553-566.

Aoki, Ken-ichiro, 1959. Petrology of alkali rocks of the Iki Islands and Higashi-matsuura District, Japan. Sci. Rep. Tohoku Iniv., Ser. III, 6: 261-310.

Aramaki, S., 1963. Geology of Asama Volcano. J. Fac. Sci. Univ. Tokyo, Sec. II, 14: 229-443.

*Aramaki, S. and Haramura, H., 1975. Geochemical Notes (1): Chemical and mineral compositions of Ejecta of 1973 eruption, Asama volcano. Bull. Earthquake Res. Inst., 50: 109-114.

Aramaki, S. and Ui, T., 1966. The Aira and Ata pyroclastic flows and related caldera and depressions in Southern Kyushu, Japan. Bull. Volcan. 29: 29-47.

Arana, V., Badiola, E. R. and Hernan, F., 1973. Peralkaline acid tendencies in Gran Canaria (Canary Islands). Contrib. Miner. Pet., 40: 53-62.

*Arana, V. and Ibarrola, E., 1973. Rhyolitic pumice in the basaltic pyroclasts from the 1971 eruption of Teneguia volcano, Canary Islands. Lithos, 6: 273-278.

Arculus, R. J., Delong, S. E., Kay, R. W., Brooks, C. and Sun, S. S., 1977. The alkalic rock suite of Bogoslof Island, eastern Aleutian Arc, Alaska. J. Geol., 85: 177-186.

Ayranci, B. and Weibel, M., 1973. Zum chemismus der ignimbrite des Ericyes-Vulkans (Zentral-Anatolien). Sond. Schweiz. Miner. Pet. Mitt., 53: 49-60.

Bailey, E. B., Clough, C. T., Wright, W. B., Richey, J. E. and Wilson, G. V., 1924. Tertiary and post-Tertiary geology of Mull, Loc Aline, and Oban. Mem. Geol. Surv. Scotland: 445 pp.

*Bailey, R. A., Falrymple, G. B., and Lanphere, M. A., 1976. Volcanism structure, and geochronology of Long Valley Caldera, Mono Country, California. J. Geophys. Res., 81: 725-744.

*Baker, P. E., 1968a, Comparative volcanology and petrology of the Atlantic island-arcs. Bull. Volcan., 32: 189-206.

Baker, P. E., 1966b. Petrology of Mt. Misery volcano, St. Kitts, West Indies. Lithos, 1: 124-150.

*Baker, P. E., Davies, T. G. and Roobol, M. J., 1969. Volcanic activity at Deception Island in 1967 and 1969. Nature, 244: 553-560.

Baker, P. E. and Holland, J. G., 1973. Geochemical variation in a pyroclastic succession on St. Kitts, West Indies. Bull. Volcan., 37: 472-499.

*Baker, P. E., McReath, I., Harvey, M. R., Roobol, M. J. and Davies, T. G., 1975. The geology of the south Shetland Islands: V, Volcanic evolution of Deception Island. Brit. Antarctic Surv. Sci. Rep., 78: 1-81.

Baldridge, W. Scott, McGetchin, T. R., Frey, F. A., and Jarosewich, E., 1973. Magmatic evolution of Hekla, Iceland. Contrib. Miner. Pet., 42: 245-258.

*Barbero, F., Innocrnti, F., Ferrara, G., Keller, J. and Villari, L., 1974. Evolution of Eolian arc volcanism (Southern Tyrrhenian Sea). Earth Planet. Sci. Lett: 269-276.

Barth, T. F. W., 1956. Geology and petrology of the Pribilof Islands, Alaska. U.S. Geol. Surv. Bull., 1028-F: 101-160.

Bateman, P. C., 1965. Geology and tungsten mineralization of the Bishop District, California. U.S. Geol. Surv. Prof. Pap., 470: 1-208.

Bauer, G. R., 1970. The geology of Tofua Island, Tonga. Pac. Sci., 24: 333-350.

Bauer, G. R., Fodor, R. V., Husler, J. W., and Keil, K., 1973. Contributions to the mineral chemistry of Hawaiian rocks. III. Composition and mineralogy of a new rhyodacite occurrence on Oahu, Hawaii. Contrib. Miner. Pet., 40: 183-194.

Beckinsale, R. D., 1974. Rb-Sr and K-Ar age determinations, and oxygen isotope data for the Glen Cannel Granophyre, Isle of Mull, Argyllshire, Scotland. Earth Planet. Sci. Lett., 22: 267-274.

Becraft, G. E., Pinckney, D. M. and Rosenblum, S., 1963. Geology and mineral deposits of the Jefferson City quadrangle, Jefferson and Lewis and Clark Counties, Montana. U.S. Geol. Surv. Prof. Pap., 428: 1-101.

*Bikerman, M., 1976. Initial $Sr^{87}Sr^{86}$ ratios and K-Ar dates of some volcanic rocks from Catron County, New Mexico. Abstracts with programs, Geol. Soc. Am., 8, No. 5: 569.

*Black, P. M., 1970. Observations on White Island volcano, New Zealand. Bull. Volcan., 34: 158-167.

Blake, D. H., 1968. Post Miocene volcanoes on Bougainville Island, Territory of Papua and New Guinea. Bull. Volcan., 32: 121-138.

Blake, D. H., and Ewart, A., 1974. Petrography and geochemistry of the Cape Hoskins volcanoes, New Britain, Papua New Guinea. J. Geol. Soc. Aust., 21: 319-331.

Blake, D. H., and Miezitis, Y., 1967. Geology of Bougainville and Buka Islands, New Guinea. Bur. Miner. Res., Geol. Geophys. (Aust.) Bull., 93: 1-56.

Blake, M. C., McKee, E. H., Marvin, R. F., Silberman, M. L., and Nolan, T. B., 1975. The Oligocene volcanic center at Eureka, Nevada. J. Res. U.S. Geol. Surv., 3: 605-612.

Bloomfield, K., 1975. A late-Quaternary monogenetic volcano field in central Mexico. Geol. Rundschau, 64: 476-497.

Borchardt, G. A., Harward, M. E., and Schmitt, R. A., 1971. Correlation of volcanic ash deposits by activation analysis of glass separates. Quat. Res., 1: 247-260.

Borsi, S., Ferrara, G., Innocenti, F., and Mazzuoli, R., 1972. Geochronology and petrology of Recent volcanics in the Eastern Aegean Sea (west Anatolia and Lesvos Island). Bull. Volcan., 36: 473-496.

*Boyd, F. R., 1961. Welded tuffs and flows in the Yellowstone Plateau of Yellowstone Park, Wyoming. Geol. Soc. Am. Bull., 72: 387-426.

*Brown, G. M., Holland, J. G., Sigurdsson, H., Tomblin, J. F., and Arculus, R. J., 1977. Geochemistry of the Lesser Antilles volcanic island arc. Geochim. Cosmochim. Acta, 41: 785-801.

Brown, G. M. and Schairer, J. F., 1971. Chemical and melting relations of some calc-alkaline volcanic rocks. Geol. Soc. Am. Mem., 130: 139-157.

Bryan, W. B., 1968. Low-potash dacite drift pumice from the Coral Sea. Geol. Mag., 105: 431-439.

Bryan, W. B., 1971. Coral Sea drift pumice stranded on Eua Island, Tonga, in 1969. Geol. Soc. Am. Bull., 82: 2799-2812.

*Bryan, W. B., 1972. Cummingtonite-dacite drift pumice stranded at West Palm Beach, Florida. Geol. Soc. Am. Bull., 83: 3745-3746.

Buddington, A. F. and Lindsley, D. H., 1964. Iron-titanium oxide minerals and synthetic equivalents. J. Pet., vol. 5: 310-357.

Burbank, W. S., 1932. Geology and ore deposits of the Bonanza Mining District, Colorado. U.S. Geol. Surv. Prof. Pap., 169: 1-166.

Burri, C. and Soptrajanova, G., 1967. Petrochemie der jungen Vulkanite der Inselgruppe von Milos (Griechenland) und deren Stellung im Rahmen der Kykladenprovinz. Vierteljahrsschrift Naturforschenden Ges. Zürich, 112: 1-27.

Byerly, G. R., Melson, W. G. and Vogt, P. R., 1976. Rhyodacites, andesites, ferro-basalts and ocean tholeiites from the Galapagos spreading center. Earth Planet. Sci. Lett., 30: 2155-221.

Byers, F. M., 1961. Petrology of three volcanic suites, Umnak and Bogoslof Islands, Aleutian Islands, Alaska. Geol. Soc. Am. Bull., 72: 93-128.

*Carmichael, I. S. E., 1960a. The pyroxenes and olivines from some Tertiary acid glasses. J. Pet., 1: 309-336.

*Carmichael, I. S. E., 1960b. The feldspar phenocrysts of some Tertiary acid glasses. Miner. Mag., 32: 587-608.

Carmichael, I. S. E., 1962. A note on the compositions of some natural acid glasses. Geol. Mag., 99: 253-264.

*Carmichael, I. S. E., 1963a. The crystallization of feldspar in volcanic acid liquids. Quart. J. Geol. Soc. Lond., 119: 95-131.

*Carmichael, I. S. E., 1963b. The occurrence of magnesian pyroxenes and magnetite in porphyritic acid glasses. Miner. Mag., 33: 394-403.

*Carmichael, I. S. E., 1964. The petrology of Thingmuli, a Tertiary volcano in Eastern Iceland. J. Pet., 5: 435-460.

*Carmichael, I. S. E., 1965. Trachytes and their feldspar phenocrysts. Miner. Mag., 34: 107-125.

*Carmichael, I. S. E., 1967a. The iron-titanium oxides of salic volcanic rocks and their associated ferromagnesian silicates. Contrib. Miner. Pet. 14: 36-64.

*Carmichael, I. S. E., 1967b. The mineralogy of Thingmuli, a Tertiary volcano in eastern Iceland. Am. Min., 52: 1815-1841.

Carmichael, I. S. E. and McDonald, A., 1961. The geochemistry of some natural acid glasses from the North Atlantic Tertiary volcanic province. Geochim. Cosmochim, Acta, 25: 25: 189-222.

Chen, Cheng-Hong, 1975. Petrological and chemical study of volcanic rocks from Tatum volcano group. Proc. Geol. Soc. China (Taipei, Taiwan), 18: 59-72.

Chen, Ju-Chin, 1975. Geochemistry of andesites from the Coastal Range, eastern Taiwan. Proc. Geol. Soc. China (Taipei, Taiwan), 18: 73-88.

Chiba, M., 1966. Genesis of magmas producing pumice flow and fall deposits of Towada Caldera, Japan. Bull. Volcan., 29: 545-558.

Church, S. E. and Tilton, G. R. 1973. Lead and strontium isotopic studies in the Cascade Mountains: Bearing on andesite genesis. Geol. Soc. Am. Bull., 84: 431-454.

Christiansen, R. L. and Lipman, P. W., 1966. Emplacement and thermal history of a rhyolite lava flow near Fortymile Canyon, southern Nevada. Geol. Soc. Am. Bull., 77: 671-684.

*Christiansen, R. L. and Lipman, P. W., 1972. Cenozoic volcanism and plate-tectonic evolution of the western United States. II. Late Cenozoic. Phil. Trans. Roy. Soc. Lond. A., 271: 249-284.

Clark, R. H., 1960. Petrology of the volcanic rocks of Tongariro Subdivision. New Zealand Geol. Surv. Bull., 40 (n.s.): 107-123.

Coats, R. R., 1959. Geologic reconnaissance of Semisopochnoi Island, Western Alaska, Aleutian Islands, Alaska. U.S. Geol. Surv. Bull., 1028-0: 477-519.

Coats, R. R., 1952. Magmatic differentiation in Tertiary and Quaternary volcanic rocks from Adak and Kanaga Islands, Aleutian Islands, Alaska. Geol. Soc. Am. Bull., 63: 485-514.

Coats, R. R., 1968. The Circle Creek rhyolite, a volcanic complex in northern Elko County, Nevada. Geol. Soc. Am. Mem., 116: 69-106.

Cole, J. W., 1970. Petrography of the rhyolite lavas of Tarawera volcanic complex. New Zealand J. Geol. Geophys., 13: 903-924.

Cole, J. W. (in press). Andesites of the Tongariro volcanic centre, North Island, New Zealand. J. Volcan. Geotherm. Res.

Cole, J. W. and Nairn, I. A., 1975. Catalogue of the active volcanoes of the world including solfatara fields. Part 22. New Zealand. Int. Assoc. Volc. and Chem. of Earth's Interior, 156 pp.

Colley, H. and Warden, A. J., 1974. Petrology of the New Hebrides. Geol. Soc. Am. Bull. 85: 1635-1646.

*Condie, K. S. and Hayslip, D. L., 1975. Young bimodal volcanism at Medicine Lake volcanic centre, northern California. Geochim. Cosmichim. Acta, 39: 1165-1178.

Condie, K. C. and Swenson, D. H., 1973. Compositional variation in three Cascade stratovolcanoes: Jefferson, Rainier, and Shasta. Bull. Volcan., 37: 305-230.

Cook, H. E., 1968. Ignimbrite flows, plugs, and dikes in the southern part of the Hot Creek Range, Nye County, Nevada. Geol. Soc. Am. Mem., 116: 107-152.

Coombs, H. A., 1939. Mt. Baker, a Cascade volcano. Geol. Soc. Am. Bull., 50: 1492-1510.

Corbett, M. K., 1968. Tertiary volcanism of the Specimen-Lulu-Iron Mountain area, north-central Colorado. Quart. Colorado School Mines, 63: 1-37:

Coulon, C., Baque, L. and Dupuy, 1973. Les andésites cénozoiques et les les laves associées en Sardaigne Nord-Occidentale (Province du Logudoro et du Bosano) - Caractères mineralogique et Chimiques. Contrib. Miner. Pet., 42: 125-139.

Coulon, C. and Demant, A., 1972. Un épisode du volcanisme cénozoique calco-alcalin de la Sardaigne nord-occidentale: le cycle "andésitique terminal" de la region Mara-Romana. Bull. Volcan., 36: 418-442.

Curtis, G. H., 1951. Geology of the Topaz quadrangle and eastern half of the Ebbetts Pass quadrangle. Ph. D. thesis (unpubl), Univ. California, 316 pp.

Dengo, G., 1962. Tectonic-igneous sequence in Costa Rica: In: Petrologic Studies: A volume to honour A. F. Buddington. Geol. Soc. Am.: 133-161.

Dings, M. G. and Robinson, C. S., 1957. Geology and ore deposits of the Garfield quadrangle, Colorado: U.S. Geol. Surv. Prof. Pap., 289: 1-110.

Dupuy, C., McNutt, R. H. and Coulon, C., 1974. Determination de $^{87}Sr/^{86}Sr$ dans les andésites cénoziques et les laves associées de Sardaigne Nord occidentale (Italie). Geochim. Coismochim. Acta, 38: 1287-1296.

Dunjam, A. C., 1968. The felsites, granophyre, explosion breccias and tuffi-sites of the northeastern margin of the Tertiary igneous complex of Rhum, Inverness-shire. Quart. J. Geol. Soc. Lond., 123: 327-352.

Eastwood, R. L., 1970. A geochemical-petrological study of Mid-Tertiary vol-canism in parts of Pima and Pinal Counties, Arizona. Ph. D. thesis (unpubl.), Univ. Arizona, 212 pp.

Ekren, E. B., Anderson, R. E., Rogers, C. L. and Noble, D. C., 1971. Geology of Northern Nellis Air Force Base bombing and gunnery range, Nye County, Nevada. U.S. Geol. Surv. Prof. Pap., 651: 1-91.

Ekren, E. B. and Byers, F. M., 1976. Ash-flow fissure vent in west-central Nevada. Geology, 4: 247-251.

El-Hinnawi, E. E., Pichler, H. and Zeil, W., 1969. Trace element distribution in Chilean ignimbrites. Contrib. Miner. Pet., 24: 50-62.

Elston, W. E., 1957. Geology and mineral resources of Dwyer quadrangle, Grant, Luna, and Sierra Counties, New Mexico. New Mexico Bur. Min. Miner. Res. Bull., 38: 1-86.

Emeleus, C. H., 1962. The porphyritic felsite of the Tertiary ring complex of Slieve Gullian. Co. Armagh. Proc. Roy. Irish Acad., 62, Sect. B: 55-76.

*Emeleus, C. H., Dunham, A. C. and Thompson, R. N., 1971. Iron-rich pigeonites from acid rocks in the Tertiary igneous province of Scotland. Am. Miner., 56: 940-951.

Ericksen, G. E., Wedow, H., Eaton, G. P. and Leland, G. R., 1970. Mineral resources of the Black Range primitive area, Grant, Sierra, and Catron Counties, New Mexico. U.S. Geol. Surv. Bull., 1319-E: 1-162.

Ernst, W. G., 1968. Amphiboles, crystal chemistry, phase relations and occurrence. Springer-Verlag, New York/Heidelberg/Berlin.

*Eugster, H. P. and Wones, D. R., 1962. Stability relations of the ferruginous biotite, annite. J. Pet., 3: 82-125.

Ewart, A., 1963. Petrology and petrogenesis of the Quaternary pumice ash in the Taupo area, New Zealand. J. Pet., 4: 392-431.

Ewart, A., 1965. Mineralogy and petrogenesis of the Whakamaru ignimbrite in the Maraetai area of the Taupo Volcanic Zone, New Zealand. New Zealand. J. Geol. Geophys., 8: 611-677.

*Ewart, A., 1966. Review of mineralogy and chemistry of the acidic volcanic rocks of Taupo volcanic Zone, New Zealand. Bull. Volcan., 29: 147-171.

Ewart, A., 1968. The petrography of the central North Island rhyolitic lavas. Part 2. New Zealand J. Geol. Geophys., 11: 478-545.

*Ewart, A., 1969. Petrochemistry and feldspar crystallization in the silicic volcanic rocks, central North Island, New Zeland. Lithos, 2: 371-388.

Ewart, A., 1971a. Chemical changes accompanying spherulitic crystallization in rhyolitic lavas, central volcanic region, New Zealand. Miner. Mag., 38: 424-434.

*Ewart, A., 1971b. Notes on the chemistry of ferromagnesian phenocrysts from selected volcanic rocks, central volcanic region. New Zealand J. Geol. Geophys., 14: 323-340.

*Ewart, A., 1976a. Mineralogy and chemistry of modern orogenic lavas--some statistics and implications. Earth Planet. Sci. Lett., 31: 417-432.

*Ewart, A., 1976b. A petrological study of the younger, Tongan andesites and dacites, and the olivine tholeiites of Niua Foou Island, S.W. Pacific. Contrib. Miner. Pet., 58: 1-21.

*Ewart, A., Brothers, R. N. and Mateen, A., 1977. An outline of the geology and geochemistry, and the possible petrogenetic evolution of the volcanic rocks of the Tonga-Kermadec-New Zealand island arc. J. Volcan. Geotherm. Res., 2: 205-250.

Ewart, A., Bryan, W. B. and Gill, J. B., 1973. Mineralogy and geochemistry of the younger volcanic islands of Tonga, S.W. Pacific. J. Pet., 14: 429-465.

*Ewart, A., Green, D. C., Carmichael, I. S. E. and Brown, F. H., 1971. Voluminous low temperature rhyolitic magmas in New Zealand. Contrib. Miner. Pet., 33: 128-144.

*Ewart, A., Hildreth, W. and Carmichael, I. S. E., 1975. Quaternary acid magma in New Zealand. Contrib. Miner. Pet., 51: 1-27.

*Ewart, A., Mateen, A. and Ross, J. A., 1976. Review of mineralogy and chemistry of Tertiary central volcanic complexes, S.E. Queensland-N.E. New South Wales. In: R. W. Johnson (Ed.), Volcanism in Australasia. Elsevier: 21-39.

*Ewart, A. Oversby, V. M. and Mateen, A., 1977. Petrology and isotope geo-chemistry of Tertiary lavas from the northern flank of the Tweed volcano, southeastern Queensland. J. Pet., 18: 73-113.

*Ewart, A. and Stipp, J. J., 1968. Petrogenesis of the volcanic rocks of the central North Island, New Zealand, as indicated by a study of Sr^{87}/Sr^{86} ratios and Sr, Rb, K, U, and Th abundances. Geochim. Cosmochim. Acta, 32: 699-735.

Ewart, A., Taylor, S. R. and Capp, A. C., 1968. Trace and minor element chemistry of the rhyolitic volcanic rocks, central North Island, New Zealand. Contrib. Miner. Pet., 18: 76-104.

Fenner, C. N., 1926. The Katmai magmatic province. J. Geol., 34: 673-772.

Fenner, C. N., 1936. Bore-hole investigations in Yellowstone Park. J. Geol., 44: 225-315.

Fenner, C. N., 1938. Contact relations between rhyolite and basalt on Gardiner River, Yellowstone Park. Geol. Soc. Am. Bull., 49: 1441-1484.

Fenner, C. N., 1950. The chemical kinetics of the Katmai eruption. Am. J. Sci., 248: 593-627.

Fernandez, A., Hörmann, P. K., Kussmaul, S., Meave, J., Pichler, H. and Subieta, T., 1973. First petrologic data on young volcanic rocks of SW Bolivia. Tschermaks Min. Pet. Mitt., 19: 149-172.

Fisher, R. V., 1966. Geology of a Miocene ignimbrite layer, John Day Formation, eastern Oregon. Univ. Calif. Pub. Geol. Sci., 67: 1-58.

Fiske, R. S., Hopson, C. A. and Waters, A. C., 1963. Geology of Mount Rainier National Park, Washington. U.S. Geol. Surv. Prof. Pap., 444: 1-93.

*Fodor, R. V., 1971. Fe content in pyroxenes from a calc-alkalic volcanic suite, New Mexico. U.S.A. Earth Planet. Sci. Lett., 11: 385-390.

Fodor, R. V., 1975. Petrology of basalt and andesite of the Black Range, New Mexico. Geol. Soc. Am. Bull., 86: 295-304.

Fodor, R. V., 1976. Volcanic geology of the northern Black Range, New Mexico. In: W. E. Elston and S. A. Northrop (Eds.), Cenozoic volcanism in southwestern New Mexico. New Mexico Geol. Soc. Spec. Publ., 5: 68-70.

Francis, P. W., Roobol, M. J., Walker, G. P. L., Cobbold, P. R. and Coward, M., 1974. The San Pedro and San Pablo volcanoes of northern Chile and their hot avalanche deposits. Geol. Rundschau, 63: 338-357.

Fraser, G. D. and Barnett, H. F., 1959. Geology of the Delarof and westernmost Andreanof Islands, Aleutian Islands, Alaska. U.S. Geol. Surv. Bull. 1028-I: 211-248.

Fujimaki, H., 1975. Rare earth elements in volcanic rocks from Hakone volcano and northern Izu Peninsula, Japan. J. Fac. Sci. Univ. Tokyo, Sec. II, 19: 81-93.

*Gass, I. G., Harris, P. G. and Holdgate, M. W., 1963. Pumice eruption in the area of the south Sandwich Islands. Geol. Mag., 100: 321-330.

Gates, O., Powers, H. A. and Wilcox, R. E., 1971. Geology of the Near Islands, Alaska. U.S. Geol. Surv. Bull., 1028-U: 709-822.

Gibson, D. L., 1969. Origin and development of the Star Mountain rhyolite. Bull. Volcan., 33: 438-474.

*Gibson, I. L., 1969. Origin of some Icelandic pitchstones. Lithos, 2: 343-349.

Gilbert, C. M., 1941. Late Tertiary geology southeast of Mono Lake, California. Geol. Soc. Am. Bull., 52: 781-816.

Gill, J. B., 1972. The geochemical evolution of Fiji. Ph. D. thesis (unpubl.), Australian Natl. Univ., 140 pp.

*Gill, J. B., 1976. Composition and age of Lau Basin and Ridge volcanic rocks: Implications for evolution of an interarc basin and remnant arc. Geol. Soc. Am. Bull., 87: 1384-1395.

Gilluly, J., 1956. General geology of central Cochise County, Arizona. U.S. Geol. Surv. Prof. Pap., 281: 1-169.

Gilluly, J. and Gates, O., 1965. Tectonic and igneous geology of the northern Shoshone Range, Nevada. U.S. Geol. Surv. Prof. Pap., 465: 1-152.

Gilluly, J. and Masursky, H., 1965. Geology of the Cortez quadrangle, Nevada. U.S. Geol. Surv. Bull., 1175: 1-117.

*Gonzalez-Ferran, O. and Katsui, Y., 1970. Estudio integral del volcanismo cenozoico superior de las Islas Shetland del sur, Antarctica. Instituto Antarctico Chileno, Serie Cientifica, 1: 125-174.

Gonzalez-Ferran, O. and Vergara Martinez, M., 1962. Reconocimiento geologico de la Cordillera de los Andes entre los paralelos 35° y 38° latitud Sur. Univ. de Chile, Inst. Geologia, Publ., 24: 21-121.

Gorshkov, G. S., 1970. Volcanism and the upper mantle. Investigations in the Kurile Island Arc. Translated by C. P. Thornton. Plenum Press, New York/London, 385 pp.

Gorton, M. P., 1974. The geochemistry and geochronology of the New Hebrides. Ph. D. thesis (unpubl.), Australian Natl. Univ., 295 pp.

Grange, L. I., 1937. The geology of the Rotorua-Taupo Subdivision. New Zealand Geol. Surv. Bull., 37 (n.s.): 1-138.

Greene, R. C., 1968. Petrography and petrology of volcanic rocks in the Mount Jefferson area, High Cascade Range, Oregon. U.S. Geol. Surv. Bull., 1251-G: 1-48.

*Greene, R. C., 1973. Petrology of the welded tuff of Devine Canyon, southeastern Oregon. U.S. Geol. Surv. Prof. Pap., 797: 1-26.

Guest, J. E., 1968. Banded pumice in a Chilean ignimbrite. Geol. Mag., 105: 177-184.

Guest, J. E., 1969. Upper Tertiary ignimbrites in the Andean Cordillera of part of the Antofagasta Province, northern Chile. Geol. Soc. Am. Bull., 80: 337-362.

Guest, J. E. and Sanchez, R., 1969. A large dacite lava flow in northern Chile. Bull. Volcan., 33: 778-790.

Gumowska-Wdowiak, Z., Maneki, A., Narebski, W. and Paulo, A., 1974. Mineralogical and chemical study of dacite from Quilotoa volcano in Ecuador. Mineralogia Polonica, 5: 3-20.

Gunn, B. M. and Mooser F., 1970. Geochemistry of the volcanics of central Mexico. Bull. Volcan., 34: 577-616.

Gunn, B. M., Roobol, M. J., and Smith, A. L., 1974. Petrochemistry of the Pelean-type volcanoes of Martinique. Geol. Soc. Am. Bull., 85: 1023-1030.

Hail, W. J., 1968. Geology of southwestern North Park and vicinity, Colorado. U.S. Geol. Surv. Bull., 1257: 1-119.

*Hald, N., Noe-Nygaard, A. and Pedersen, A. K., 1971. The Kroksfjördur central volcano in northwest Iceland. Acta Nat. Islandica, II, no. 10: 1-29.

Halsley, J. H., 1953. Geology of parts of the Bridgeport, California and Wellington, Nevada quadrangles. Ph. D. thesis (unpubl.), Univ. California, 502 pp.

*Hamilton, W., 1959. Yellowstone Park area, Wyoming: A possible modern lopolith. Geol. Soc. Am. Bull., 70: 225-228.

*Hamilton, W., 1963. Petrology of rhyolite and basalt, northwestern Yellowstone Plateau. U.S. Geol. Surv. Prof. Pap., 475-C: 78-81.

*Hamilton, W., 1965. Geology and petrogenesis of the Island Park caldera of rhyolite and basalt, eastern Idaho. U.S. Geol. Surv. Prof. Pap., 504-C: 1-37.

Hantke, G. and Parodi, I., 1966. Catalogue of the active volcanoes of the world including solfatara fields. Part 19. Columbia, Equador, and Peru. Int. Assoc. Volc. and Chem. of the Earth's Interior, 73 pp.

Hattori, H. and Katoda, M., 1963. Trachytic rocks near Mt. Daisen, Tottori Prefecture, western Japan. Jap. Assoc. Min., Pet., J. 50: 199-207.

Hausen, H., 1938. Zur Kenntnis der magmengesteine der Chilenischen Atacama-Wüste, Neues Jahrbuch fur Mineral. Palaeont., 73. Abt. A: 151-238.

*Hawkes, D. D., 1961. The geology of the South Shetland Islands. II. The geology and petrology of Deception Island. Falk. Isl. Dep. Surv. Sci. Rep., 27: 1-43.

Hawkes, L., 1924. On an olivine dacite in the Tertiary volcanic series of eastern Iceland: The Rauthaskritha (Hamerfjord). Quart. J. Geol. Soc. Lond., 80: 549-566.

Hawkes, L. and Harwood, H. F., 1932. On the changed composition of an anorthoclase-bearing rock-glass. Miner. Mag., 23: 163-174.

*Hawkins, J. W., 1976. Petrology and geochemistry of basaltic rocks of the Lau Basin. Earth Planet. Sci. Lett., 28: 283-297.

Hearn, B. C., Pecora, W. T. and Swadley, W. C., 1964. Geology of the Rattlesnake quadrangle, Bearpaw Mountains, Blaine County, Montana. U.S. Geol. Surv. Bull., 1181-B: 1-66.

Hedge, C. E. and Lewis, J. F., 1971. Isotopic composition of strontium in three basalt-andesite centers along the Lesser Antilles Arc. Contrib. Miner. Pet., 32: 39-47.

Heming, R. F., 1974. Geology and petrology of Rabaul caldera, Papua New Guinea. Geol. Soc. Am. Bull., 85: 1253-1264.

Heming, R. F., and Carmichael, I. S. E., 1973. High-temperature pumice flows from the Rabaul caldera, Papua, New Guinea. Contrib. Miner. Pet., 38: 1-20.

Higgins, M. F., 1973. Petrology of Newberry volcano, central Oregon. Geol. Soc. Am. Bull., 84: 455-488.

Holland, J. G., and Brown, G. M., 1972. Hebridean tholeiitic magmas: A geochemical study of the Ardnamurchan cone sheets. Contrib. Miner. Pet. 37: 139-160.

Hörmann, P. K., Pichler, H. and Zeil, W., 1973. New data on the young volcanism in the Puna of NW-Argentina. Geol. Rundschau, 62: 397-418.

*Howorth, R. and Rankin, P. C., 1975. Multi-element characterisation of glass shards from stratigraphically correlated rhyolitic tephra units. Chem. Geol., 15: 239-250.

Hughes, C. J., 1960. The Southern Mountains igneous complex, Isle of Rhum. Quart. J. Geol. Soc. Lond., 116: 111-138.

Hutton, C. O., 1944. Some igneous rocks from the New Plymouth area. Trans. Roy. Soc. New Zealand, 74: 125-153.

Innocenti, F. and Mazzuoli, R., 1972. Petrology of the Izmir-Karaburun volcanic area (west Turkey). Bull. Volcan., 36: 83-104.

Ishikawa, T., Minato, M., Kuno, H., Matsumoto, T. and Yagi, K., 1956. Welded tuffs and deposits of pumice flow and nuée ardente in Japan. Int. Geol. Cong., 20th Sess., Mexico, Sec. I, 1: 137-150.

Isshiki, N., 1963. Petrology of Hachijo-Jima volcano group, seven Izu islands, Japan. J. Fac. Sci. Univ. Tokyo, Sec. II, 15: 91-134.

Izett, G. A., 1968. Geology of the Hot Sulphur Springs quadrangle, Grand County, Colorado. U.S. Geol. Surv. Prof. Pap., 586: 1-79.

Jack, R. N. and Carmichael, I. S. E., 1969. The chemical 'fingerprinting' of acid volcanic rocks. In: Short contributions to California geology. California Div. Mines and Geology Spec. Rept., 100: 17-32.

*Jakes, P., 1970. Analytical and experimental geochemistry of volcanic rocks from island arcs. Ph. D. thesis (unpubl.), Australian Natl. Univ.

Jakes, P., 1970. Rare earth elements and the island arc tholeiite series. Earth Planet. Sci. Lett., 9: 17-28.

Jakes, P. and Smith, I. E., 1970. High potassium calc-alkaline rocks from Cape Nelson, eastern Papua. Contrib. Miner. Pet., 28: 250-271.

*Jakes, P. and White, A. J. R., 1969. Structure of the Melanesian arcs and correlation with distribution of magma types. Tectonophysics, 8: 223-236.

James, D. E., Brooks, C. and Cuyubamba, A., 1976. Andean Cenozoic volcanism: Magma genesis in the light of strontium isotopic composition and trace element geochemistry. Geol. Soc. Am. Bull., 87: 592-600.

*James, R. S. and Hamilton, D. L., 1969. Phase relations in the system $NaAlSi_3O_8-KAlSi_3O_8--CaAl_2Si_2O_8-SiO_2$ at 1 kilobar water vapour pressure. Contrib. Miner. Pet., 21: 111-141.

Jenks, W. F. and Goldich, S. S., 1956. Rhyolitic tuff flows in southern Peru. J. Geol., 64: 156-172.

Jicha, H. L., 1954. Geology and mineral deposits of Lake Valley quadrangle, Grant, Luna, and Sierra Counties, New Mexico. New Mexico Bur. Mines Bull., 37: 1-93.

Johnson, R. W., 1970. Likuruanga volcano, Lolobau Island, and associated volcanic centres, New Britain: Geology and petrology. Bur. Miner. Res., Geol. Geophys. (Aust.) Rec. No. 1970/42.

Johnson, R. W., 1971. Bamus volcano, Lake Hargy area, and Sulu Range, New Britain: Volcanic geology and petrology. Bur. Miner. Res. Geol. Geophys. (Aust.), Rec. No. 1971/55.

Johnson, R. W., 1977. Distribution and major-element chemistry of late Cainozoic volcanoes at the southern margin of the Bismarck Sea, Papua, New Guinea. Bur. Miner. Res., Geol. Geophys. (Aust.), Report 188: 1-170.

Johnson, R. W. and Blake, D. H., 1972. The Cape Hoskins area, southern Willaumez Peninsula, the Witu Islands, and associated volcanic centres, New Britain: Volcanic geology and petrology. Bur. Miner. Res., Geol. Geophys. (Aust.), Rec. No. 1972/133.

Johnson, R. W., Davies, R. A. and Palfreyman, W. D., 1971. Cape Gloucester area, New Britain: Volcanic geology, petrology, and eruptive history of Langila craters up to 1970. Bur. Miner. Res., Geol. Geophys. (Aust.), Rec. No. 1971/14.

*Johnson, R. W. and Smith, I. E., 1974. Volcanoes and rocks of St. Andrew Strait, Papua, New Guinea. J. Geol. Soc. Aust., 21: 333-351.

*Johnson, R. W., Smith, I. E. M. and Taylor, S. R., 1978. Hot-spot volcanism in St. Andrew Strait, Papua, New Guinea: Geochemistry of a Quaternary bimodal rock suite. Bur. Miner. Res., Geol. Geophys. (Aust.), 3: 55-69.

Johnson, R. W., Taylor, G. A. M. and Davies, R. A., 1972. Geology and petrology of Quaternary volcanic islands off the north coast of New Guinea. Bur. Miner. Res., Geol. Geophys. (Aust.), Rec. No. 1972/21.

Johnson, R. W., Wallance, D. A. and Ellis, D. J., 1976. Feldspathoid-bearing potassic rocks and associated types from volcanic islands off the coast of New Ireland, Papua, New Guinea: A preliminary account of geology and petrology. In: R. W. Johnson (Ed.), Volcanism in Australasia. Elsevier: 297-316.

Jones, W. R., Hernon, R. M. and Moore, S. L., 1967. General geology of Santa Rita quadrangle, Grant County, New Mexico. U.S. Geol. Surv. Prof. Pap., 555: 1-144.

Joplin, G. A., Kiss, E., Ware, N. G. and Widdowson, J. R., 1972. Some chemical data on members of the shoshonite association. Miner. Mag., 38: 936-945.

Katsui, Y., 1961. Petrochemistry of the Quaternary volcanic rocks of Hokkaido and surrounding areas. J. Fac. Sci. Hokkaido Univ., Ser. IV, 11: 1-58.

Katsui, Y., 1963. Evolution and magmatic history of some Krakatoan calderas in Hokkaido, Japan. J. Fac. Sci. Hokkaido Univ., Ser. IV, 11: 631-650.

Katsui, Y., Ando, S. and Inaba, K., 1975. Formation and magmatic evolution of Mashu volcano, east Hokkaido, Japan. J. Fac. Sci. Hokkaido Univ., Ser. IV, 16: 533-552.

Katsui, Y. and Gonzalez-Ferran, O., 1968. Geologia del area neovolcanicade los Nevados de Payuchata. Universidad de Chile, Fac. de Ciencias, Fisicas y Matematicas, Dept. Geologia, Publ. 29: 1-61.

Katsui, Y. and Katz, H. R., 1967. Lateral fissure eruptions in the southern Andes of Chile. J. Fac. Sci. Hokkaido Univ., Ser. IV, 13: 433-448.

Kawano, Y. and Aoki, Ken-ichiro, 1960. Petrology of Hachimantai and surrounding volcanoes, northeastern Japan. Sci. Rep. Tohoku Univ., Ser. III, 6: 409-429.

Kawano, Y., Yagi, K. and Aoki, Ken-ichiro, 1961. Petrography and petrochem-
    istry of the volcanic rocks of Quaternary volcanoes of northeastern Japan.
    Sci. Rep. Tohoku Univ., Ser. III, 7: 1-46.

Keller, J., 1969. Origin of rhyolites by anatectic melting of granitic
    crustal rocks. The example of rhyolitic pumice from the island of Kos
    (Aegean Sea). Bull. Volcan., 33: 942-959.

Keller, J., 1974. Petrology of some volcanic rock series of the Aeolian arc,
    southern Tyrrhenian Sea: Calc-alkaline and shoshonitic associations.
    Contrib. Miner. Pet., 46: 29-47.

Keller, J. and Villari, L., 1972. Rhyolitic ignimbrites in the region of
    Afyon (Central Anatolia). Bull. Volcan., 36: 342-358.

Kerr, P. F., Brophy, G. P., Dahl, H. M., Green, J. and Woolard, L. E., 1957.
    Marysvale, Utah, uranium area. Geol. Soc. Am. Spec. Pap., 64: 1-212.

King, B. C., 1955. The Ard Bheinn area of the central igneous complex of
    Arran. Quart. J. Geol. Soc. Lond., 110: 323-356.

*Klein, C., Jr., 1968. Coexisting amphiboles. J. Pet., 9: 281-330.

Klerkx, J., 1965. Ètude petrologique de laves des volcans Villarica, Calbuco,
    Osorno, Llaima (Chili central). Ann. Soc. Geol. de Belgique, 88: 451-
    470.

Knopf, A., 1936. Igneous geology of the Spanish Peaks region, Colorado.
    Geol. Soc. Am. Bull., 47: 1727-1784.

Koga, M., 1972. Geology and petrology of Tara-Dake volcano, northwestern
    Kyushu. Sci. Rep. Tohoku Univ., Ser. III, 11: 203-238.

Krushensky, R. D., 1976. Neogene calc-alkaline extrusive and intrusive rocks
    of the Karalar-Yesiller area, northwest Anatolia, Turkey. Bull. Volcan.,
    39: 336-360.

Kuellmer, F. J., 1954. Geologic section of the Black Range at Kingston, New
    Mexico. New Mexico Bur. Mines Bull., 33: 1-100.

*Kuno, H., 1938a. Hypersthene from Odawara-mati, Japan. Proc. Imperial
    Acad., 14: 218-220.

*Kuno, H., 1938b. On the occurrence of a primary cummingtonitic hornblende in
    some dacites from Japan. Proc. Imperial Acad., 14: 221-224.

Kuno, H., 1950. Petrology of Hakone volcano and the aejacent areas, Japan.
    Geol. Soc. Am. Bull., 61: 957-1020.

Kuno, H., 1962. Catalogue of the active volcanoes of the world including sof-
    fatara fields. Part II. Japan, Taiwn and Marianas. Int. Assoc. Volcan.
    and Chemistry of the Earth's Interior, 332 pp.

*Kuno, H., 1969. Pigeonite-bearing andesite and associated dacite from Asio, Japan. Am. J. Sci., Schairer vol., 267-A: 257-268.

Kurasawa, H., 1965. Petrology and chemistry of Quaternary volcanic rocks in the western part of Chugoku Provinces, southwest Japan. Japan Geol. Surv. Bull., 16: 217-226.

Lacroix, A., 1936. Composition mineralogique et chemique des laves des volcans des Iles de L'ocean Pacifique situees entre L'equateur et le Tropique du Capricorne, le 175° de longitude ouest et le 165° de longitude est. Academie des Sciences de L'Institute de France, Mem., 63: 1-97.

Laidley, R. A. and McKay, D. S., 1971. Geochemical examination of obsidians from Newberry caldera, Oregon. Contrib. Miner. Pet., 30: 336-342.

Larsen, E. S. and Cross, W., 1956. Geology and petrology of the San Juan region, southwestern Colorado. U.S. Geol. Surv. Prof. Pap., 258: 1-303.

Larsen, E. S., Irving, J., Gonyer, F. A. and Larsen, E. S., 1936. Petrologic results of a study of the minerals·from the Tertiary volcanic rocks of the San Juan region, Colorado. 1. Geologic setting. 2. The Silica Minerals. 3. Pyroxenes. 4. Olivine. Am. Min., 21: 679-701.

Larsen, E. S., Irving, J., Gonyer, F. A. and Larsen, E. S., 1937. Petrologic results of a study of the minerals from the Tertiary volcanic rocks of the San Juan region, Colorado. 5. The amphiboles. 6. Biotite. Am. Miner., 22: 889-905.

Larsen, E. S., Irving, J., Gonyer, F. A. and Larsen, E. S., 1938a. Petrologic results of a study of the minerals from the Tertiary volcanic rocks of the San Juan region, Colorado. 7. The plagioclase feldspars. Am. Miner., 23: 227-257.

Larsen, E. S., Irving, J., Gonyer, F. A. and Larsen, E. S., 1938b. Petrologic results of a study of the minerals from the Tertiary volcanic rocks of the San Juan region, Colorado. 8. Orthoclase. Am. Miner., 23: 417-429.

Larsson, W., 1935. Vulkanische asche vom asubruch des Chilenischen vulkans Quizapu (1932) in Argentina gesammelt. Bull. Geol. Inst. Univ. Uppsala, 26: 27-52.

Larsson, W., 1941. Petrology of interglacial volcanics from the Andes of northern Patagonia. Bull. Geol. Inst. Univ. Uppsala, 28: 191-405.

*Le Maitre, R. W., 1976. Some problems of projecting chemical data into mineralogical classifications. Contrib. Miner. Pet., 56: 181-189.

Lerbekmo, J. F. and Campbell, F. A., 1969. Distribution, composition and source of the White River Ash, Yukon Territory. Can. J. Earth Sci., 6: 109-116.

*Lerbekmo, J. F., Westgate, J. A., Smith, D. G. W. and Denton, G. H., 1975. New data on the character and history of the White River volcanic eruption, Alaska. In: R. P. Suggate and M. M. Cresswell (eds.), Quaternary Studies. Roy. Soc. New Zealand Bull., 13: 203-209.

Lewis, J. F., 1968. Tauhara volcano, Taupo Zone. Part II - Mineralogy and petrology. New Zealand J. Geol. Geophys., 11: 651-684.

Lipman, P. W., 1967. Mineral and chemical variations within an ash-flow sheet from Aso caldera, southwestern Japan. Contrib. Miner. Pet., 16: 300-327.

Lipman, P. W., 1968. Geology of the Summer Coon volcanic center, eastern San Juan Mountains, Colorado. Quart. Colorado School Mines, 63: 211-236.

*Lipman, P. W., 1971. Iron-titanium oxide phenocrysts in compositionally zoned ash-flow sheets from southern Nevada. J. Geol., 79: 438-456.

Lipman, P. W., 1975. Evolution of the Platora Caldera Complex and related volcanic rocks, southeastern San Juan Mountains, Colorado. U.S. Geol. Surv. Prof. Pap., 852: 1-128.

Lipman, P. W., Christiansen, R. L. and O'Connor, J. T., 1966. A compositionally zoned ash-flow sheet in southern Nevada. U.S. Geol. Surv. Prof. Pap., 524-F: 1-47.

*Lipman, P. W., Prostka, H. J. and Christiansen, R. L., 1972. Cenozoic volcanism and plate-tectonic evolution of the Western United States. I. Early and Middle Cenozoic. Phil. Trans. Roy. Soc. Lond. A., 271: 217-248.

*Loney, R. A., 1968. Flow structure and composition of the Southern Coulee, Mono Craters, California--A pumiceous rhyolite flow. Geol. Soc. Am. Mem., 116: 415-440.

Longwell, C. R., 1963. Reconnaissance geology between Lake Mead and Davis Dam, Arizona-Nevada. U.S. Geol. Surv. Prof. Pap., 374-E: 1-51.

Love, L. L., Kudo, A. M. and Love, D. M., 1976. Dacites of Bunsen Peak, the Birch Hills, and the Washakie Needles, northwestern Wyoming, and their relationship to the Absaroka volcanic field, Wyoming and Montana. Geol. Soc. Am. Bull., 87: 1455-1462.

Lovering, T. S., 1957. Halogen-acid alteration of ash at fumarole No. 1, Valley of Ten Thousand Smokes, Alaska. Geol. Soc. Am. Bull., 68: 1585-1604.

*Lowder, G. G., 1970. The volcanoes and caldera of Talasea, New Britain; and caldera of Talasea, New Britain: Mineralogy. Contrib. Miner. Pet., 26: 324-340.

Lowder, G. G., and Carmichael, I. S. E., 1970. The volcanoes and caldera of Talasea, New Britain: Geology and petrology. Geol. Soc. Am. Bull., 81: 17-38.

*Macdonald, G. A., and Katsura, T., 1964. Chemical composition of Hawaiian Lavas. J. Pet., 5: 83-133.

Macdonald, G. A., and Katsura, T., 1965. Eruption of Lassen Peak, Cascade Range, California, in 1915: Example of mixed magmas. Geol. Soc. Am. Bull., 76: 475-482.

Mackenzie, D. E., 1976. Nature and origin of late Cainozoic volcanoes in western Papua, New Guinea. In: R. W. Johnson (Ed.), Volcanism in Australasia. Elsevier: 221-238.

Mackenzie, D. E., and Chappell, B. W., 1972. Shoshonite and calc-alkaline lavas from the Highlands of Papua, New Guinea. Contrib. Miner. Pet., 35: 50-62.

Marakis, G. and Sideris, C., 1972. Petrology of the Edassa area volcanic rocks, western Macedonia, Greece. Bull. Volcan., 36: 462-472.

Masuda, Y., Nishimura, S., Ikeda, T. and Katsui, Y., 1975. Rare-earth and trace elements in the Quaternary volcanic rocks of Hokkaido, Japan. Chem. Geol., 15: 251-271.

Mathews, W. H., 1957. Petrology of Quaternary volcanics of the Mount Garibaldi map-area, southwestern British Columbia. Am. J. Sci., 255: 400-415.

Matsui, Y., 1963. The geochemistry of rocks from Asama volcano, Japan. New approaches in the quantitative interpretation of the chemical composition of volcanic rocks. Pap. Inst. Thermal. Spring Res. Okayama Univ.., no. 32: 1-85.

Matsumoto, H., 1960. The chemical characteristics of the lavas from Ryukyu volcanic zone, Kyusyu, Japan. Kumamoto J. Sci., Ser. B, Sec. 1, 4: 13-29.

Matsumoto, H., 1963. Petrological study on rocks from Aso volcano. Kumamoto J. Sci., Ser. B. Sec. 1, 5: 1-67.

Mazzuoli, R., 1967. Le vulcaniti di Roccastrada (Grosseto). Studio Chimico-petrografico e geologico. Atti Soc. Toscana Sci. Nat. Mem., Ser. A, 74: 315-373.

McBirney, A. R., 1968. Petrochemistry of the Cascade andesite volcanoes. In: H. M. Dole (Ed.), Andesite Conf. Guidebook. Dept. Geol. Min. Ind. State of Oregon Bull., 62: 101-107. McBirney, A. R. and Williams, H., 1965. Volcanic history of Nicaragua. Univ. Calif. Publ. Geol. Sci., 55: 1-65.

*McBirney, A. R. and Williams, H., 1969. Geology and petrology of the Galapagos Islands. Geol. Soc. Am. Mem., 118: 1-197.

McKee, E. H., 1976. Geology of the northern part of the Toquima Range, Lander, Eureka, and Nye Counties, Nevada. U.S. Geol. Surv. Prof. Pap., 931: 1-49.

McKee, E. H. and Anderson, C. A., 1971. Age and chemistry of Tertiary volcanic rocks in north-central Arizona and relation of the rocks to the Colorado Plateaus. Geol. Soc. Am. Bull., 82: 2767-2782.

*Melson, W. G., Jarosewich, E. and Lundquist, C. A., 1970. Volcanic eruption at Metis Shoal, Tonga, 1967-1968: Description and petrology. Smithsonian Contrib. Earth Sci., 4: 1-18.

Merriam, C. W. and Anderson, C. A., 1942. Reconnaissance survey of the Roberts Mountains, Nevada. Geol. Soc. Am. Bull., 53: 1675-1728.

Minami, E. and Matsui, Y., 1960. Composition of the main chemical components in the rocks from Hotoke-iwa volcanic body of Mt. Asama. Bull. Earthquake Res. Inst., 38: 291-305.

Mitchell, A. H. G. and Warden, A. J., 1971. Geological evolution of the New Hebrides island arc. J. Geol. Soc. (Lond.), 127: 501-529.

Moorbath, S. and Bell, J. D., 1965. Strontium isotope abundance studies and rubidium-strontium age determinations on Tertiary igneous rocks from the Isle of Skye, northwest Scotland. J. Pet., 6: 37-66.

Moore, R. B., Wolfe, E. W. and Ulrich, G. E., 1976. Volcanic rocks of the eastern and northern parts of the San Francisco volcanic field, Arizona. J. Res. U.S. Geol. Surv., 4: 549-560.

Moore, W. J., 1973. Igneous rocks in the Bingham Mining District, Utah. U.S. Geol. Surv. Prof. Pap., 629-B: 1-42.

Mooser, F., Meyer-Abich, H. and McBirney, A. R., 1958. Catalogue of the active volcanoes of the world including solfatara fields. Part 6. Central America. Int. Assoc. Volcan. and Chemistry of the Earth's Interior, 146 pp.

Morgan, W. R., 1966. A note on the petrology of some lava types from east New Guinea. J. Geol. Soc. Aust., 13: 538-591.

Morimoto, R., Huzita, K. and Kasama, T., 1956. Cenozoic volcanism in southwest Japan with special reference to the history of the Setouch (Inland Sea) geologic province. Int. Geol. Cong., 20th Sess., Mexico, Sec. I, 1: 161-170.

Muessig, S., 1967, Geology of the Republic quadrangle and a part of the Aeneas quadrangle, Ferry County, Washington. U.S. Geol. Surv. Bull., 1216: 1-135.

Mukae, M., 1958. Volcanostratigraphical study on the Miocene volcanism in the Shimane Prefecture, Japan. J. Sci. Hiroshima Univ., Ser. C, 2: 129-171.

Mullineaux, D. R., 1974. Pumice and other pyroclastic deposits in Mount Rainier National Park, Washington. U.S. Geol. Surv. Bull., 1326: 1-83.

Nagashima, K., 1953. Geochemistry of the Kita-Izu and Hakone volcanic rocks, Shidara volcanic rocks, and Hamada nepheline basalts. Bull. Fac. Agr., Tokyo Univ. Agr. Technol., 1(2): 1-39.

Nagasawa, H., 1973. Rare-earth distribution in alkali rocks from Oki-Dogo Island, Japan. Contrib. Min. Pet., 39: 301-308.

Negendank, J. F. W., 1972. Volcanics of the Valley of Mexico. Part I. Petrography of the volcanics. N. Jb. Miner. Abh., 116: 308-320.

Nelson, W. H., 1959. Geology of Segula, Davidof and Khvostof Islands, Alaska. U.S. Geol. Surv. Bull., 1028-K: 257-266.

*Nicholls, I. A., 1971. Petrology of Santonini volcano, Cyclades, Greece. J. Pet., 12: 67-119.

Nicholls, J. and Carmichael, I. S. E., 1969. A commentary on the Absarokite-Shoshonite-Banakite series of Wyoming, U.S.A. Schweiz. Miner. Pet. Mitt., 49: 47-64.

Noble, D. C. and Christiansen, R. L., 1974. Black Mountain volcanic center, Nye County, Nevada. Nevada Bur. Mines and Geol. Rept., 19: 27-34.

*Noble, D. C. and Hedge, C. E., 1969. $Sr^{87}Sr^{86}$ variations within individual ash-flow sheets. U.S. Geol. Surv. Prof. Pap., 650-C: 133-139.

Noble, D. C., Korringa, M. K., Church, S. E., Bowman, H. R., Silberman, M. L. and Herepoulos, C. E., 1976. Elemental and isotopic geochemistry of non-hydrated quartz latite glasses from the Eureka Valley Tuff, east-central California. Geol. Soc. Am. Bull., 87: 754-762.

*Noble, D. C., Korringa, M. K., Hedge, C. E. and Riddle, G. O., 1972. Highly differentiated subalkaline rhyolite from Glass Mountain, Mono County, California. Geol. Soc. Am. Bull., 83: 1179-1184.

Noble, D. C., Sargent, K. A., Mehnert, H. H., Ekren, E. B. and Byers, F. M., 1968. Silent Canyon volcanic center, Nye County, Nevada. In: E. B. Eckel (Ed.), Geol. Soc. Am. Mem. 110: 65-75.

Nockolds, S. R., and Allen, R., 1953. The geochemistry of some igneous rock series. Geochim. Cosmochim. Acta, 4: 105-142.

Noe-Nygaard, A., 1952. A group of Liparite occurrences in Vatnajökull, Iceland. Folia Geographica Danica, 1, No. 3: 1-59.

Noe-Nygaard, A., 1956. Some liparite dykes from Raudheller in Morsardalur, Iceland. Meddel. Dansk Geol. Foren., 13: 118-123.

Nolan, T. B., 1935. The Gold Hill mining district, Utah. U.S. Geol. Surv. Prof. Pap., 177: 1-172.

Oba, Y., 1960. On the rocks of the Niseko volcanic group, Hokkaido. J. Geol. Soc. Japan, 66: 788-799.

*Oba, Y., 1966. Geology and petrology of Usu volcano, Hokkaido, Japan. J. Fac. Sci. Hokkaido Univ., Ser. IV, 13: 185-236.

Olson, J. C., Hedlund, D. C. and Hansen, W. R., 1968. Tertiary volcanic stratigraphy in the Powderhorn-Black Canyon region, Gunnison and Montrose Counties, Colorado. U.S. Geol. Surv. Bull., 1251-C: 1-29.

Oversby, V. M. and Ewart, A., 1972. Lead isotopic compositions of Tonga-Kermadec volcanics and their petrogenetic significance. Contrib. Min. Pet., 37: 181-210.

Oyarzun, J. and Villalobos, J., 1969. Recopilacion de analisis quimicos de rocas Chilenas. Univ. de Chile, Fac. de Ciencias, Publ. No. 33: 1-47.

Paraskevopoulos, G. M., 1956. Über den Chemismus und die Provinzialen Verhältnisse der tertiären und quartären Ergussgesteine des äaischen Raumes und der benachbarten Gebieten. Tchermaks Min. Pet. Mitt., 6: 13-72.

Parker, R. L. and Calkins, J. A., 1964. Geology of the Curlew quadrangle, Ferry County, Washington. U.S. Geol. Surv. Bull., 1169: 1-95.

*Pe, G. G., 1973. Petrology and geochemistry of volcanic rocks of Aegina, Greece. Bull. Volcan., 37: 491-514.

Pe, G. G., 1975. Strontium isotope ratios in volcanic rocks from the northwestern part of the Hellenic arc. Chem. Geol., 15: 53-60.

Pe, G. G. and Gledhill, A., 1975. Strontium isotope ratios in volcanic rocks from the southeastern part of the Hellenic arc. Lithos, 8: 209-213.

Peacock, M. A., 1924. A contribution to the petrography of Iceland. Trans. Geol. Soc. Glascow, 17: 271-333.

*Peccerillo, A. and Taylor, S. R., 1976. Geochemistry of Eocene calc-alkaline volcanic rocks from the Kastamonu area, northern Turkey. Contrib. Miner. Pet., 58: 63-81.

102

Peck, D. L., Griggs, A. B., Schlicker, H. G., Wells, F. G. and Dole, H. M., 1964. Geology of the central and northern parts of the western Cascade Range in Oregon. U.S. Geol. Surv. Prof. Pap., 449: 1-56.

Peterman, Z. E., Carmichael, I. S. E. and Smith, A. L., 1970. Sr^{87}/Sr^{86} ratios of Quaternary lavas of the Cascade Range, northern California. Geol. Soc. Am. Bull., 81: 311-318.

Pichler, H., 1963. Beiträge zur Geologie der Insel Salina (Aolische Archipel, Sizilien). Geol. Rundschau, 53: 800-821.

Pichler, H. and Kussmaul, S., 1972. The calc-alkaline volcanic rocks of the Santorini group (Aegean Sea, Greece). N. J. Miner. Abh., 116: 268-307.

Pichler, H. and Weyl, R., 1975. Magmatism and crustal evolution in Costa Rica (Central America). Geol. Rundschau, 64: 457-475.

Pichler, H. and Zeil, W., 1969. Die quartäre "Andesit"-Formation in der Hoch-kordillere Nord-Chiles. Geol. Rundschau, 58: 866-903.

Powers, H. A. and Wilcox, R. E., 1964. Volcanic ash from Mount Mazama (Crater Lake) and from Glacier Peak. Science, 144: 1334-1336.

Puxeddu, M., 1971. Studio chimico-petrografico delle vulcaniti de M. Cimino (Viterbo). Atti Soc. Toscana Sci. Nat., Mem., Ser. A, 78: 329-394.

Rabone, S. D. C., 1975, Petrography and hydrothermal alteration of Tertiary andesite-rhyolite volcanics in the Waitekauri Valley, Ohinemuri, New Zealand. New Zealand J. Geol. Geophys., 18: 239-258.

*Ramberg, H., 1970. Model studies in relation to intrusion of lutonic bodies. In: G. Newall and N. Rast (Eds.), Mechanism of igneous intrusion. Geol J., Spec. Issue, 2: 261-286.

Randle, K., Goles, G. G. and Kittleman, L. R., 1971. Geochemical and petro-logical characterization of ash samples from Cascade Range volcanoes. Quart. Res., 1: 261-282.

Ransome, F. L., 1898. Some lava flows of the western slope of the Sierra Nevada, California. U.S. Geol. Surv. Bull., 89: 1-74.

Ransome, F. L., 1923. Geology of the Oatman Gold District, Arizona. U.S. Geol. Surv. Bull., 743: 1-58.

Ratte, J. C., and Steven, T. A., 1964. Magmatic differentiation in a volcanic sequence related to the Creede Caldera, Colorado. U.S. Geol. Surv. Prof. Pap., 475-D: 49-53.

Ratte, J. C., and Steven, T. A., 1967. Ash flows and related volcanic rocks associated with the Creede Caldera, San Juan Mountains, Colorado. U.S. Geol. Surv. Prof. Pap., 524-H: 1-58.

Rea, W. J., 1974. The volcanic geology and petrology of Montserrat, West Indies. J. Geol. Soc. Lond., 130: 341-366.

Reed, J. J., 1951. Hornblende andesite rocks from Solander Island. Trans. Roy. Soc., New Zealand, 79: 119-125.

Rhodes, R. C., 1976a. Volcanic geology of the Mogollon Range and adjacent areas, Catron and Grant Counties, New Mexico. In: W. E. Elston and S. A. Northrop (Eds.), Cenozoic Volcanism in Southwestern New Mexico. New Mexico Geol. Spec. Publ., 5: 42-50.

Rhodes, R. C., 1976b. Petrologic framework of the Mogollon Plateau volcanic ring complex, New Mexico--surface expression of a major batholith. In: W. E. Elston and S. A. Northrop (Eds), Cenozoic volcanism in Southwestern New Mexico. New Mexico Geol. Soc. Spec. Publ., 5: 103-112.

Rhodes, R. C. and Smith, E. I., 1976. Stratigraphy and structure of the northwestern part of the Mogollon Plateau volcanic province, Catron County, New Mexico. In: W. E. Elston and S. A. Northrop (Eds.), Cenozoic volcanism in Southwestern New Mexico. New Mexico Geol. Soc. Spec. Publ., 5: 57-62.

Richey, J. E. and Thomas, H. H., 1930. The geology of Ardnamurchan. Northwest Mull and Coll. Mem. Geol. Surv. Scotland: 393 pp.

*Ridley, I., 1971. The petrology of some volcanic rocks from the British Tertiary Province: The Islands of Rhum, Eigg, Canna, and Muck: Contrib. Min. Pet., 32: 251-266.

Rinehart, C. C. and Ross, D. C., 1964. Geology and mineral deposits of the Mount Morrison quadrangle, Sierra Nevada, California. U.S. Geol. Surv. Prof. Pap., 385: 1-106.

*Rittman, A., 1973. Stable mineral assemblages of igneous rocks. Springer-Verlag, Berlin/Heidelberg/New York, 262 pp.

Roberts, R. J. and Peterson, D. W., 1961. Suggested magmatic differences between welded "ash" tuffs and welded crystal tuffs, Arizona and Nevada. U.S. Geol. Surv. Prof. Pap., 424-D: 73-79.

Robinson, H. H., 1913. The San Franciscan volcanic field. U.S. Geol. Surv. Prof. Pap., 76: 1-213.

Robinson, P. T., 1972. Petrology of the Potassic Silver Peak volcanic center, western Nevada. Geol. Soc. Am. Bull., 83: 1693-1708.

*Robinson, P. T., Elders, W. A., and Muffler, L. J. P., 1976. Quaternary volcanism in the Salton Sea geothermal field, Imperial Valley, California. Geol. Soc. Am. Bull., 87: 347-360.

*Robson, G. R. and Tomblin, J. F., 1966. Catalogue of the active volcanoes of the world including solfatara fields. Part 20. West Indies. Int. Assoc. Volcan. and Chemistry of the Earth's Interior, 56 pp.

Rogers, N. W. and Gibson, I. L., 1977. The petrology and geochemistry of the Creag Dubh composite sill, Whiting Bay, Arran, Scotland. Geol. Mag., 114: 1-8.

Rose, W. I., 1972, Santiaguito volcanic dome, Guatemala. Geol. Soc. Am. Bull., 83: 1413-1434.

Rose, W. I., Grant, N. K., Hahn, G. A., Lange, I. M., Powell, J. L., Easter, J. and Degraff, J. M., 1977. The evolution of Santa Maria volcano, Guatemala. J. Geol., 85: 63-87.

Ross, J. A., 1977. The Tertiary Focal Peak shield volcano, southeast Queensland--A geological study of its eastern flank. Ph. D. thesis (unpubl.), Univ. of Queensland, 207 pp.

Rubel, D. N., 1971. Independence volcano: A major Eocene eruptive center, northern Absaroka Volcanic Province. Geol. Soc. Am. Bull., 82: 2473-2494.

Ruxton, B. P., 1966. A late Pleistocene to Recent rhyodacite-trachybasalt-basaltic latite volcanic association in northeast Papua. Bull. Volcan., 29: 347-374.

Sargent, K. A., 1969. Petrography and heavy minerals of three groups of rhyolitic lavas, Pahute Mesa, Neva Test Site. U.S. Geol. Surv. Prof. Pap., 650-C: 18-24:

Schmidt, R. G., 1957. Geology of Saipan, Mariana Islands. Chapt. B. Petrology of the volcanic rocks. U.S. Geol. Surv. Prof. Pap., 28-B: 127-175.

Schmidt, R. G., Pecora, W. T. and Hearn, B. C., 1964. Geology of the Cleveland quadrangle, Bearpaw Mountains, Blaine County, Montana. U.S. Geol. Surv. Bull., 1141-P: 1-26:

*Scott, R. B., Nesbitt, R. W., Dasch, E. J. and Armstrong, R. L., 1971. A strontium isotope evolution model for Cenozoic magma genesis, Eastern Great Basin, U.S.A. Bull. Volcan., 35: 1-26:

Sendo, T. Matsumoto, H. and Imamura, R., 1967. Geology and petrography of Unzen volcano. Kumamoto J. Sci., Ser. B, Sec. 1. 7: 31-89.

Sheridan, M. F., 1970. Fumarolic mounds and ridges of the Bishop Tuff, California. Geol. Soc. Am. Bull., 81: 851-868.

Sheridan, M. F., Stuckless, J. S. and Fodor, R. V., 1970. A Tertiary silicic cauldron complex at the northern margin of the Basin and Range Province, central Arizona, U.S.A. Bull. Volcan., 34: 649-662.

Shuto, K., 1974. The strontium isotopic study of the Tertiary acid volcanic rocks from the southern part of northeast Japan. Sci. Rep. Tokyo Kyoiku Daigaku, Sec. C, 12: 75-140.

Siegers, A., Pichler, H. and Zeil, W., W. 1969. Trace elements in the "Andesite" Formation of northern Chile. Geochim. Cosmochim. Acta, 33: 882-887.

*Sigurdsson, H., 1971a. Feldspar relations in Icelandic alkalic rhyolites. Miner. Mag., 38: 503-510.

*Sigurdsson, H., 1971b. Feldspar relations in a composite magma. Lithos, 4: 231-238.

Simons, F. S., 1964. Geology of Klondyke quadrangle, Graham and Pinal Counties, Arizona. U.S. Geol. Surv. Prof. Paper., 461: 1-173.

Smedes, H. W., 1966. Geology and igneous petrology of the northern Elkhorn Mountains, Jefferson and Broadwater Counties, Montana. U.S. Geol. Surv. Prof. Paper., 510: 1-116.

*Smith, A. L. and Carmichael, I. S. E., 1968. Quaternary lavas from the southern Cascades, western U.S.A. Contrib. Miner. Pet., 19: 212-238.

Smith, D. G. W. and Westgate, J. A., 1969. Electron probe technique for characterising pyroclastic deposits. Earth Planet. Sci. Lett., 5: 313-319.

Smith, E. I., 1976. Structure and petrology of the John Kerr Peak dome complex, southwestern New Mexico. In: W. E. Elston and S. A. Northrop (Eds.), Cenozoic volcanism in southwestern New Mexico. New Mexico Geol. Soc. Spec. Publ., 5: 71-78.

Smith, G. I., 1964. Geology and volcanic petrology of the Lava Mountains, San Bernardino County, California. U.S. Geol. Surv. Prof. Pap., 457: 1-97.

Smith, I. E. M., 1976a. Volcanic rocks from southeastern Papua. The evolution of volcanism at a plate boundary. Ph. D. thesis (unpubl.), Australian Natl. Univ., 290 pp.

Smith, I. E. M., 1976b. Peralkaline rhyolites from the D'Entrecasteaux Islands, Papua, New Guinea. In: R. W. Johnson (Ed.), Volcanism in Australasia. Elsevier: 275-285.

Snyder, G. L., 1959. Geology of Little Sitkin Island, Alaska. U.S. Geol. Surv. Bull., 1028-H: 169-210.

Spencer, E., 1930. A contribution to the of moonstone fromm Ceylon and other areas and of the stability-relations of the alkali feldspar. Miner. Mag., 22: 291-367.

Staatz, M. H., 1964. Geology of the Bald Knob quadrangle, Ferry and Okanogan Counties, Washington. U.S. Geol. Surv. Bull., 1161-F: 1-79.

Steiner, A., 1958. Petrogenetic implications of the 1954 Ngauruhoe lava and its xenoliths. New Zealand J. Geol. Geophys., 1: 325-363.

Steiner, A., 1963. Crystallization behavior and origin of the acidic ignimbrite and rhyolite magma in the North Island of New Zealand. Bull. Volcan., 25: 217-241.

Steven, T. A. and Ratté, J. C., 1960. Geology and ore deposits of the Summitville District, San Juan Mountains, Colorado. U.S. Geol. Surv. Prof. Pap., 343: 1-70.

Stinnett, J. W., 1976. A strontium isotopic and geochemical study of volcanic rocks from the Datil-Mogollon field, southwestern New Mexico. Abs. with Programs, Geol. Soc. Am., 8, no. 5: 636-637.

*Stormer, J. C., 1972. Mineralogy and petrology of the Raton-Clayton volcanic field, northeastern New Mexico. Geol. Soc. Am. Bull., 83: 3299-3322.

*Streckeisen, A. L., 1967. Classification and nomenclature of igneous rocks. Neues Jahrb. Miner. Abhandl, 107: 144-240.

Stuckless, J. S. and O'Neill, J. R., 1973. Petrogenesis of the Superstition-Superior volcanic area as inferred from strontium- and oxygen-isotope studies. Geol. Soc. Am. Bull., 84: 1987-1998.

Swanson, D. A., 1966. Tieton volcano, a Miocene eruptive center in the southern Cascade Mountains, Washington. Geol. Soc. Am. Bull., 77: 1293-1314.

Swanson, D. A. and Robinson, P. T., 1968. Base of the John Day Formation in and near the Horse Heaven Mining District, north-central Oregon. U.S. Geol. Surv. Prof. Pap., 600-D: 154-161.

Tabor, R. W. and Crowder, D. F., 1969. On batholiths and volcanoes--intrusion and eruption of late Cenozoic magmas in the Glacier Peak area, North Cascades, Washington. U.S. Geol. Surv. Prof. Pap., 604: 1-67.

Takeuchi, T. and Abe, H., 1967. Alteration processes of volcanic rocks under hydrothermal conditions (Hydrothermal studies on the wall-rock alteration I). Sci. Rep. Tohoku Univ., Ser. III, 10: 151-172.

Tanida, K., 1961. A study on salic effusive rocks. Sci. Rep. Tohoku Univ., Ser. III, 7: 47-100.

Tanida, S., 1975. Geological and petrological studies of the "Shirasu" in south Kyushu, Japan. Mem. Fac. Sci. Kyushu Univ., Ser. D, 23: 295-201.

Taniguchi, H. 1974. The study of the physical and chemical properties of some volcanic acid glasses. Sci. Rep. Tohoku Univ., Ser. III, 12: 189-237.

Taylor, G. A., 1958. The 1951 eruption of Mount Lamington, Papua. Bur. Miner. Res., Geol. Geophys. (Aust.), Bull. 38: 10117.

Taylor, S. R., Capp, A. C., Grahamm, A. L., and Blake, D. H., 1969. Trace element abundances in andesites II. Saipan, Bougainville and Figi. Contrib. Miner. Pet., 23: 1-26.

Taylor, S. R. and White, A. J. R., 1966. Trace element abundances in andesites. Bull. Volcan., 29: 177-194.

Thayer, T. P., 1937. Petrology of later Tertiary lavas and Quaternary rocks of the north-central Cascade Mountains in Oregon, with notes on similar rocks in western Nevada. Geol. Soc. Am. Bull., 48: 1611-1652.

Thiele, R. and Katsui, Y., 1969. Contribucion al conocimiento del volcanismo post-Miocenico de los Andes en la Provincia de Santiago, Chile. Univ. de Chile, Fac. de Ciencias, Fisicas y Matematicas, Dept. Geologia, Publ. 35: 1-23.

Thompson, B. N., Kermode, L. O. and Ewart, A. (Eds.), 1965. New Zealand Volcanology. Central Volcanic Region. New Zealand Dept. Sci. Ind. Res., Inf. series, 50: 1-211.

Thompson, G. A. and White, D. E., 1964. Regional geology of the Steamboat Springs area, Washoe County, Nevada. U.S. Geol. Surv. Prof. Pap., 458-A: 1-52.

Thompson, R. N. and Dunham, A. C., 1972. Major element variation in the Eocene lavas of the Isle of Skye, Scotland. J. Pet., 13: 219-253.

Thorarinsson, S., 1944. Tefrokronologiska studier pa Island. Geografiska Annaler, 26: 1-217.

Thorarinsson, S., 1967. The eruptions of Hekla 1947-1948. I. The eruptions of Hekla in historical times. A tephrochronological study. Soc. Scientiarum Islandica: 1-170.

Thorarinsson, S. and Sigvaldason, G. E., 1972. The Hekla eruption of 1970. Bull. Volc., 36: 269-288.

Thorpe, R. S., Potts, P. J. and Francis, P. W., 1976. Rare earth data and petrogenesis of andesite from the North Chilean Andes. Contrib. Miner. Pet., 54: 65-78.

Thorpe, R. S. and Francis, P. W., 1975. Volcan Ceboruco: A major composite volcano of the Mexican volcanic belt. Bull. Volcan., 39: 201-213.

Tiba, T., 1966. Petrology of the alkaline rocks of the Takakusayama District, Japan. Sci. Rep. Tohoku Univ., Ser. III, 9: 541-610.

*Tiba, T., 1976. Hornblende megacrysts in andesite from Hakusan volcano. Bull. Natl. Sci. Mus. Tokyo, Ser. C. (Geol.), 2: 115-119.

Tonking, W. H., 1957. Geology of Puertecito quadrangle, Socorro County, New Mexico. New Mexico Bur. Mines Bull., 41: 1-67.

Tryggvson, T., 1965. The eruption of Hekla 1947-1948. IV-Petrographic studies on the eruption products of Hekla. Soc. Scientiarum Islandica, 6: 1-13.

Tsuya, H., 1937. On the volcanism of the Huzi volcanic zone, with special reference to the geology and petrology of Idu and the southern islands. Tokyo Imp. Univ. Earthquake Res. Inst., Bull., 15: 215-357.

Tuttle, O. F. and Bowen, N. L., 1958. Origin of granite in the light of experimental studies in the system $NaAlSi_3O_8$-$KAlSi_3O8$-SiO_2-H_2O. Geol. Soc. Am. Mem., 74 1-153.

Tyrrell, G. W., 1928. The geology of Arran. Mem. Geol. Surv. Scotland: 292 pp.

Tyrrell, G. W., 1932. Report on rock specimens from Thule Island, South Sandwich Islands. Discovery Reports, 3: 191-197.

*Uchimizu, M., 1966. Geology and petrology of alkali rocks from Dogo, Oki Island. J. Fac. Sci., Univ. Tokyo, Sec. II, 16: 85-160.

Ui, T., 1971. Genesis of magma and structure of magma chamber of several pyroclastic flows in Japan. J. Fac. Sci., Univ. Tokyo, Sec. II, 18: 53-127.

Ui, T., 1972. Recent volcanism in Masaya-Granada area, Nicaragua. Bull. Volcan., 36: 174-190.

*Ujike, O., 1972. Petrology of Tertiary calc-alkaline volcanic rock suite from northeastern Shikoku and Shodo-Shima Island, Japan. Sci. Rep. Tohoku Univ., Ser. III, 11: 159-201.

Van Alstine, R. E., 1969. Geology and mineral deposits of the Poncha Springs NE quadrangle, Chaffee County, Colorado. U.S. Geol. Surv. Prof. Pap., 626: 1-52.

Van Bemmelen, R. W. and Rutten, M. G., 1955. Table mountains of Northern Iceland (and related geological notes). Leiden, E. J. Brill, 217 pp.

Verhoogen, J., 1937. Mount St. Helens: A recent Cascade volcano. Univ. Calif. Publ. Bull. Dept. Geol. Sci., 24: 263-302.

Viramonte, J. G. and Di Scala, L., 1970. Summary of the 1968 eruption of Cerro Negro, Nicaragua. Bull. Volcan., 34: 347-351.

*Virgo, D. and Ross, M., 1973. Pyroxenes from Mull andesites. Ann. Rep. Director Geophys. Lab., Carn. Inst. Wash., 72: 535-540.

Vlodavetz, V. I. and Piip, B. I., 1959. Catalogue of the active volcanoes of the world including solfatara fields. Part 8. Kamchatka and continental areas of Asia. Int. Assoc. Volc. and Chem. of the Earth's Interior, 110 pp.

Wager, L. R., Vincent, E. A., Brown, G. M. and Bell, J. D., 1965. Marcosite and related rocks of the western Red Hills Complex, Isle of Skye. Phil. Trans. Roy. Soc. Lond., 257, Ser. A: 273-307.

Wahlstrom, E. E., 1944. Structure and petrology of Specimen Mountain, Colorado. Geol. Soc. Am. Bull., 55: 77-90.

Walker, G. P. L., 1962. Tertiary welded tuffs in eastern Iceland. Quart. J. Geol. Soc. Lond., 118: 275-293.

Walker, G. P. L., 1963. The Breiddalur central volcano, eastern Iceland. Quart. J. Geol. Soc. Lond., 119: 29-63.

*Walker, G. P. L., 1966. Acid rocks in Iceland. Bull. Volcan., 29: 375-402.

Washington, H. S., 1926. Santorini eruption of 1925. Geol. Soc. Am. Bull., 37: 349-384.

Westercamp, D., 1976. Petrology of the volcanic rocks of Martinique, West Indies. Bull. Volcan., 39: 175-200.

Westermann, J. H. and Kiel, H., 1961. The geology of Saba and St. Eustatius. Natuurwetenschappelijke Studiekring voor Suriname en de Nederlandse Antillen, Utrecht, 175 pp.

Westerveld, J., 1947. On the origin of the acid volcanic rocks around Lake Toba, north Sumatra. Kon. Akad. van Wetensch., Verh., Afd. Natuurkunde, Tweede Sectie, 43: 1-51.

Westerveld, J., 1952. Quaternary volcanism of Sumatra. Geol. Soc. Am. Bull., 63: 561-594.

Weyl, R., 1954a. Beiträge zur Geologie El Salvadors. IV. Die Bimsaschen in der Umgebung san Salvadors. N. Jb. Geol. u. Palaeontol. Monatscheffe: 49-70.

Weyl, R., 1954b. Beträge zur Geologie El Salvadors. V. Die Schmelztruffe der Balsamkette. N. Jb. Geol. u. Palaeontol., Abh., 99: 1-32.

Weyl, R., 1955. Beiträge zur Geologie El Salvadors. VI. Die laven der jungen Vulkane. N. Jb. Geol. u. Palaeontol., Abh., 101: 12-38.

Weyl, R., 1961. Die Geologie Mittelamerikas. Berlin/Nikolassee, 226 pp.

Whitford, D. J., 1975. Geochemistry and petrology of volcanic rocks from the Sunda Arc, Indonesia. Ph. D. thesis (unpubl.), Australian Natl. Univ., 449 pp.

Wilcox, R. E., 1954. Petrology of Paricutin volcano, Mexico. U.S. Geol. Surv. Bull., 965-C: 281-353.

*Wilcox, R. E., 1965. Volcanic-ash chronology. In: H. E. Wright, Frey, D. G. (Eds.). The Quaternary of the United States. Princeton Univ. Press: 807-816.

Williams, H., 1929. Geology of the Marysville Buttes, California. Univ. Calif. Publ. Bull. Dept. Geol. Sci., 18: 103-220:

Williams, H., 1932a. The history and characters of volcanic domes. Univ. Calif. Publ. Bull. Dept. Geol. Sci., 21: 51-146.

Williams, H., 1932b. Geology of the Lassen Volcanic National Park, California. Univ. Calif. Publ. Bull. Dept. Geol. Sci., 21: 195-385.

Williams, H., 1934. Mount Shasta, California. Zeit. Für Volkanologie, 15: 225-253.

Williams, H., 1935. Newberry volcano of central Oregon. Geol. Soc. Am. Bull., 46: 253-304.

Williams, H., 1942. The geology of Crater Lake National Park, Oregon. Carnegie Inst. Washington Publ., 540: 1-161.

Williams, H., 1950. Volcanoes of the Paricutin region, Mexico. U.S. Geol. Surv. Bull., 965-B: 165-275.

Williams, H., 1952. Volcanic history of the Mesata Central Occidental Costa Rica. Univ. Calif. Publ. Geol. Sci., 29: 145-180.

Williams, H. and Curtis, G. H., 1977. The Sutter Buttes of California. Univ. Calif. Publ. Geol. Sci., 116: 1-56.

Williams, H., and McBirney, A. R., 1969. Volcanic history of Honduras. Univ. Calif. Publ. Geol. Sci. 85: 1-101.

Williams, H., McBirney, A. R. and Dengo, G., 1963. Geologic reconnaissance of southeastern Guatemala. Univ. Calif. Publ. Geol. Sci., 50: 1056.

Williams, H. and Meyer-Abich. H., 1955. Volcanism in the southern part of El Salvador. Univ. Calif. Publ. Geol. Sci., 32: 1-64:

*Winkler, H. G. F., 1976. Petrogenesis of metamorphic rocks. Springer-Verlag, New York/Heidelberg/Berlin, 334 pp.

Wise, W. S., 1969. Geology and petrology of the Mt. Hood area: A study of High Cascade volcanism. Geol. Soc. Am. Bull., 70: 969-1006.

*Witkind, I. J., 1969. Clinopyroxenes from acidic, intermediate, and basic rocks, Little Belt Mountains, Montana. Am. Miner., 54: 1118-1138.

*Wones, D. R. and Gilbert, M. C., 1969. The fayalite-magnetite-quartz assemblage between 600° and 800°C. Am. J. Sci., Schairer Vol., 267-A: 480-488.

Wrucke, C. T. and Silberman, M. L., 1975. Cauldron subsidence of Oligocene age at Mount Lewis, northern Shoshone Range, Nevada. U.S. Geol. Surv. Prof. Pap., 876: 1-20.

Yagi, K., 1953. Recent activity of Usu volcano, Japan, with special reference to the formation of Syowa Sinzan. Am. Geophys. Union Trans., 34: 449-456.

Yajima, T., Higuchi, H. and Hagasawa, H., 1972. Variation of rare earth concentrations in pigeonitic and hypersthenic rock series from Izu-Hakone region, Japan. Contrib. Miner. Pet., 35: 235-244.

Yamasaki, M., Nakanishi, N. and Kaseno, Y., 1964. Nuée ardente deposit of Hakusan volcano. Sci. Rep. Kanazawa Univ., 9: 189-201.

Yamasaki, M., Nakanishi, N. and Mijata, K., 1966. History of Tateyama volcano. Sci. Rep. Kanazawa Univ., 73-92.

Zeil, W. and Pichler, H., 1967. Die Känozoische Ryolite-Formation im mittleren Abschnitt der Anden. Geol. Rundschau, 57: 48-81.

*Zielinski, R. A. and Lipman, P. W., 1976. Trace element variations at Summer Coon volcano, San Juan Mountains, Colorado, and the origin of continental-interior andesites. Geol. Soc. Am. Bull., 87: 1477-1485.

Appendix 1 - A - Compilation of major and trace element chemistry of Low-K salic volcanic rocks from the S.W. Pacific, and the Japan - kuriles - Saipan regions. Major element analyses recalculated to 100% on anhydrous basis.

Region	Japan - Kuriles - Saipan					S.W. Pacific				
SiO_2 interval	60-63	63-66	66-69	69-73	>73	60-63	63-66	66-69	69-73	>73
SiO_2	61.19	64.33	67.45	70.35	75.01	61.24	64.82	66.97	70.16	74.19
TiO_2	0.71	0.77	0.61	0.54	0.34	0.59	0.59	0.54	0.47	0.46
Al_2O_3	16.94	15.89	15.33	14.90	12.99	15.81	15.05	14.51	14.63	12.89
Fe_2O_3	2.79	2.89	2.12	2.10	1.39	3.25	2.03	1.89	1.49	1.35
FeO	4.31	3.67	3.07	1.95	1.47	4.79	4.78	4.37	2.69	2.15
MnO	0.16	0.16	0.13	0.11	0.09	0.15	0.14	0.13	0.12	0.07
MgO	2.73	2.06	1.49	0.92	0.58	3.13	2.29	1.52	1.06	0.68
CaO	6.99	5.58	4.75	3.92	2.57	7.24	5.97	5.40	4.25	3.13
Na_2O	3.38	3.64	4.01	3.99	4.17	2.90	3.26	3.60	3.98	3.90
K_2O	0.61	0.86	0.87	1.07	1.18	0.74	0.92	0.91	1.00	1.11
P_2O_5	0.19	0.16	0.18	0.15	0.22	0.15	0.15	0.15	0.14	0.08
n	44	43	38	19	14	18	31	17	7	8

Trace elements+ (p.p.m.)

Rb	7(7)+	3.2(1)	n.d.	n.d.	n.d.	9(9)	14(19)	12(7)	10(2)	13(5)
Ba	120(1)	436(3)	287(5)	445.(2)	403(3)	180(9)	302(21)	224(7)	268(2)	289(5)
Sr	155(11)	182(4)	171(11)	285(3)	117(3)	285(9)	306(21)	291(7)	243(2)	145(5)
Zr	n.d.	n.d.	n.d.	n.d.	n.d.	49( )	61(20)	58(7)	71(2)	95(5)
Zn	83(10)	81(3)	100(7)	88(1)	82(1)	92(7)	97(16)	94(7)	76(2)	49(2)
La	3.9(1)	10(5)	6.6(4)	n.d.	6.7(2)	3.7(7)	4.0(18)	3.3(7)	4.5(2)	4(2)
Ce	11.2(1)	25(5)	20(4)	n.d.	22(2)	8.5(7)	9.8(18)	9.4(7)	12(2)	9.8(2)
Yb	2.5(1)	3.5(4)	4.3(4)	n.d.	4.9(2)	1.3(1)	2.2(3)	3.9(1)	4.5(2)	9.8(2)
Y	19(4)	19(3)	12(11)	11(4)	11(2)	25(9)	30(19)	23(7)	32(2)	34(4)
Cu	40(11)	15(4)	5(7)	1(3)	2(3)	73(9)	30(20)	16(7)	15(2)	32(4)
Ni	45(10)	26(3)	22(7)	22(1)	37(1)	6(8)	7(20)	2(7)	3(2)	2(4)
Co	29(11)	16(5)	16(8)	20(1)	7(2)	21(9)	14(18)	11(7)	7(2)	4(4)
Cr	78(10)	17(5)	6(8)	8(1)	20(2)	12(9)	25(20)	2(7)	1(2)	3(4)
V	127(4)	47(3)	23(11)	8(3)	8(2)	190(9)	101(20)	74(7)	31(2)	39(4)
Nb	n.d.	n.d.	n.d.	n.d.	n.d.	1.5(1)	3.1(2)	1.0(1)	n.d.	n.d.
Li	5(10)	7(3)	9(7)	6.5(1)	8(1)	n.d.	n.d.	n.d.	n.d.	n.d.
Pb	4(1)	6(1)	6(4)	8(2)	11(2)	2.5(5)	3.2(8)	4.1(2)	5.1(1)	2(3)
Hf	n.d.	3.5(2)	3.0(1)	n.d.	3.7(1)	0.7(1)	1.2(2)	2.2(1)	n.d.	3.4(2)

Criteria for selection of Low-K compositions after Peccerillo and Taylor (1976); see also Fig. 1.

n   Number of data used in each major element compilation

+   Numbers in brackets refer to number of data used to calculate average for each trace element

Appendix 1 - B - Compilation of mineralogical (phenocryst) data of Low-K salic volcanic rocks, corresponding to data presented in appendix 1 - A.

Phenocryst modes (volumes %)*:

Region	Japan - Kuriles - Saipan					S.W. Pacific				
SiO_2 interval	60-63	63-66	66-69	69-73	>73	60-63	63-66	66-69	69-73	>73
Sa	0	0	0	0	0	0	0	0	0	0
Pl	21.7	3.6	13.5	14.0	2.1	11.9	11.4	8.5	9.8	15.0
Qtz	0	0	0	0	1.4	0.06	0.07	0	0	3.0
Ol	0.68	0.26	4.3	1.6	0	0.18	0.02	0	0	0.67
Cpx	2.0	0.67	0.48	0.55	0	2.6	2.1	0.94	0.98	0.67
Opx	0	0.29	1.7	1.2	0	1.9	1.1	0.79	0.65	0.33
Hb	0	0	0.10	0.05	0	0.12	0.21	0	0	0
Bi	0	0	0	0	0	0	0.19	0	0	0
Sphene	0	0	0	0	0	0	0	0	0	0
Fe-Ti oxides	0.58	0.21	0.52	0.50	0	0.61	0.64	0.58	0.68	0.33
Σ	25.0	5.0	20.6	17.9	3.5	17.4	15.7	10.8	12.1	20.0
n	4	7	6	2	2	17	27	10	6	3

% Frequency occurrence of phenocryst phases

	Japan - Kuriles - Saipan					S.W. Pacific				
	60-63	63-66	66-69	69-73	>73	60-63	63-66	66-69	69-73	>73
Sa	0	0	0	0	0	0	0	0	0	0
Pl	98	88	95	94	91	94	100	100	100	100
Qtz	5	13	24	44	36	6	3	0	0	29
Ol	7	10	3	22	0	33	10	0	0	29
Cpx	86	83	92	78	73	89	94	100	100	86
Opx	88	83	90	89	73	89	97	100	100	86
Hb	19	13	24	61	0	6	13	0	0	29
Bi	0	0	0	0	0	0	3	0	0	0
Sphene	0	0	0	0	0	0	0	0	0	0
Fe-Ti oxides	88	80	92	67	73	89	100	100	100	71
n	43	40	38	18	11	18	31	16	7	7

* Abbreviations as in Table 1-B.

Appendix 2 - A - Compilation of major and trace element chemistry of calc-alkali salic volcanic rocks from selected orogenic regions. Criteria for selection of calc-alkali compositions after Peccerillo and Taylor (1976); see also Fig. 1. Major element analyses recalculated to 100% on anhydrous basis.

Region No++	2				5					6				
Region+	Middle Americas				High Cascades – Alaska – Aleutians					Japan – Taiwan – Kuriles – Kamchatka – Saipan				
SiO_2 interval	60-63	63-66	66-69	69-73	60-63	63-66	66-69	69-73	>73	60-63	63-66	66-69	69-73	>73
SiO_2	61.67	64.57	67.25	70.8	61.58	64.35	67.46	70.88	75.57	61.63	64.26	67.49	71.08	75.44
TiO_2	0.79	0.68	0.53	0.41	0.79	0.63	0.61	0.39	0.21	0.71	0.64	0.61	0.48	0.18
Al_2O_3	17.02	16.82^x	16.56	15.92	17.27	16.85	16.25	15.03	13.61	16.77	16.37	15.81	14.94	13.43
Fe_2O_3	2.50^x	2.18^x	1.92^x	1.55	2.16	2.00	2.00	1.17	0.62	2.78	2.56	2.08	1.48	0.94
FeO	2.90^x	2.35^x	1.93^x	1.32	3.53	2.63	1.74	1.59	1.03	3.76	3.12	2.37	1.67	1.16
MnO	0.11	0.10	0.11	0.07	0.11	0.10	0.10	0.06	0.06	0.12	0.13	0.12	0.09	0.07
MgO	3.19	2.18	1.35	1.04	2.71	2.34	1.48	0.82	0.36	2.99	2.25	1.45	0.85	0.43
CaO	5.69	4.63	3.81	2.75	5.92	5.15	3.40	2.52	1.49	6.19	5.16	4.22	3.17	1.92
Na_2O	4.08	4.38	4.27	3.59	4.20	4.16	4.68	4.78	4.21	3.36	3.56	3.82	3.89	3.91
K_2O	1.85	1.96	2.16	2.44	1.51	1.61	2.10	2.65	2.79	1.51	1.77	1.87	2.22	2.33
P_2O_5	0.20	0.15	0.12	0.10	0.23	0.18	0.17	0.12	0.06	0.17	0.18	0.15	0.12	0.09
n	36	33	18	5	64	51	19	27	10	120	83	49	59	43
Trace elements+ (p.p.m.)														
Rb	49(14)+	47(16)	48(6)	n.d.	35(21)	47(9)	48(3)	61(8)	44(3)	39(8)	85(2)	64(4)	n.d.	76(7)
Ba	504(7)	527(9)	474(2)	n.d.	533(17)	651(12)	443(7)	699(7)	613(4)	569(9)	934(3)	504(4)	643(4)	525(3)
Sr	480(14)	504(16)	491(6)	n.d.	651(29)	1058(18)	791(9)	467(7)	500(1)	333(10)	401(4)	233(8)	137(3)	111(9)
Zr	70(14)	172(1)	172(1)	n.d.	150(12)	152(11)	186(7)	115(5)	200(1)	120(2)	n.d.	n.d.	n.d.	125(1)
Zn	n.d.	60(15)	52(15)	n.d.	85(7)	81(1)	n.d.	n.d.	53(1)	72(4)	44(2)	37(2)	12(2)	n.d.
La	n.d.	n.d.	n.d.	n.d.	21(7)	21(2)	n.d.	26(5)	18(3)	14(8)	19(2)	11(2)	32(2)	8(2)
Ce	137(1)	137(1)	143(1)	n.d.	65(9)	62(2)	100(1)	45(2)	32(3)	36(8)	49(2)	31(2)	21(2)	21(2)
Yb	n.d.	n.d.	n.d.	n.d.	1.9(11)	1.5(9)	1.9(5)	2.5(3)	3.0(4)	2.8(8)	3.9(2)	3.5(2)	3.2(2)	2.6(2)
Y	n.d.	n.d.	n.d.	n.d.	34(9)	18(10)	30(6)	12(5)	80(1)	22(4)	15(2)	11(4)	10(4)	13(3)
Cu	17(15)	11(16)	12(5)	n.d.	33(17)	31(10)	15(7)	10(1)	21(1)	40(8)	33(2)	17(2)	n.d.	4(3)
Ni	46(15)	28(17)	21(6)	n.d.	29(17)	36(12)	27(7)	3(2)	1(1)	36(7)	14(3)	12(3)	5(1)	0.5(1)
Co	n.d.	n.d.	n.d.	n.d.	16(16)	15(12)	14(6)	5(4)	5(4)	19(13)	13(3)	7(5)	4(3)	3(1)
Cr	101(15)	67(17)	40(6)	n.d.	50(17)	50(12)	36(7)	3(4)	4(4)	43(12)	14(4)	13(3)	4(1)	4(1)
V	n.d.	n.d.	n.d.	n.d.	119(12)	109(11)	92(7)	50(2)	50(1)	149(14)	105(2)	33(4)	37(2)	18(3)
Nb	n.d.	n.d.	n.d.	n.d.	4.6(6)	3.8(5)	5(2)	n.d.	n.d.	4(2)	n.d.	n.d.	n.d.	0.5(1)
Li	n.d.	n.d.	n.d.	n.d.	35(2)	45(2)	35(2)	50(1)	10(1)	12(6)	18(2)	27(2)	n.d.	n.d.
Pb	9(15)	10(15)	8(5)	n.d.	5.6(9)	6.2(3)	8.3(2)	7(3)	10(1)	10(4)	21(2)	8(4)	8(3)	8(3)
Hf	n.d.	n.d.	n.d.	n.d.	n.d.	n.d.	n.d.	6.3(2)	4.2(3)	3.3(8)	5.3(2)	3.2(2)	5.6(1)	2.6(1)

	S.W. Pacific 8					Mediterranean 10			
Region No [++]									
Region [+]	60-63	63-66	66-69	69-73	>73	60-63	63-66	66-69	69-73
SiO_2	61.15	64.25	67.38	71.73	75.18	61.59	64.43	67.14	70.46
TiO_2	0.65	0.70	0.56	0.46	0.26	0.64	0.69	0.51	0.41
Al_2O_3	16.79	15.83	15.80	14.36	13.31	18.02	16.44	15.92	15.39
Fe_2O_3	2.71	2.19	2.06	1.66	0.89	2.47	2.27	2.03	1.16
FeO	3.49	3.37	2.14	1.52	1.00	2.58	3.04	1.95	1.44
MnO	0.12	0.12	0.10	0.09	0.07	0.11	0.12	0.10	0.08
MgO	3.28	2.38	1.47	0.70	0.30	2.19	1.87	1.46	1.02
CaO	6.39	5.07	4.04	2.74	1.57	6.46	4.69	4.29	3.12
Na_2O	3.53	3.89	4.12	4.38	4.43	3.91	4.28	4.14	4.21
K_2O	1.68	1.99	2.13	2.27	2.95	1.84	2.00	2.33	2.61
P_2O_5	0.20	0.21	0.18	0.09	0.04	0.19	0.18	0.13	0.08
n	87	45	28	14	49	20	36	12	16

Trace elements (p.p.m.)

	60-63	63-66	66-69	69-73	>73	60-63	63-66	66-69	69-73
Rb	42(51)	44(16)	37(13)	62(2)	102(13)	43(11)	61(7)	88(3)	82(4)
Ba	421(53)	563(17)	476(12)	695(3)	831(19)	838(5)	408(3)	690(1)	800(1)
Sr	432(54)	548(17)	594(13)	162(2)	114(13)	441(11)	269(8)	279(3)	185(4)
Zr	128(52)	145(17)	143(8)	163(2)	165(13)	204(7)	177(4)	129(1)	n.d.
Zn	64(7)	64(5)	76(6)	84(1)	n.d.	n.d.	63(1)	55(1)	n.d.
La	15(19)	22(11)	16(8)	15(2)	26(13)	23(3)	21(3)	19(1)	n.d.
Ce	32(19)	37(11)	35(7)	24(1)	43(3)	48(3)	45(3)	71(1)	n.d.
Yb	1.7(5)	2.2(4)	1.9(2)	n.d.	3.7(3)	2.4(3)	1.5(2)	n.d.	n.d.
Y	22(31)	29(16)	28(13)	31(2)	30(13)	23(8)	23(4)	29(1)	n.d.
Cu	38(50)	23(14)	23(11)	12(2)	6(13)	17(5)	16(3)	38(1)	n.d.
Ni	18(48)	27(12)	17(11)	5(1)	<2	3(3)	6(4)	3(2)	2(1)
Co	17(13)	12(8)	7(6)	8(1)	<2	7(3)	9(3)	8(2)	4(1)
Cr	57(52)	37(14)	18(11)	3(2)	0.7(13)	9(3)	18(4)	8(2)	0.5(1)
V	132(53)	76(14)	61(11)	16(2)	5(13)	100(3)	82(3)	90(1)	n.d.
Nb	5.2(11)	7.2(6)	6.1(1)	n.d.	6(3)	24(3)	19(3)	n.d.	n.d.
Li	16(2)	n.d.	10(1)	29(1)	37(13)	n.d.	n.d.	n.d.	n.d.
Pb	9(39)	11(12)	13(11)	7(1)	18(3)	6(4)	7(3)	n.d.	n.d.
Hf	2.5(4)	3.1(3)	4.0(2)	n.d.	4.7(3)	5.5(3)	3.4(2)	n.d.	n.d.

+   See Introduction

n   Number of data used in each major element compilation

++   Numbers in brackets refer to number of data used to calculate average for each trace element

n.d.   Insufficient data

x Fe_2O_3/FeO values adjusted according to method of Le Maitre (1976) for much of data used in compilation of these analyses

Appendix 2 - B - Compilation of mineralogical (phenocryst) data of calc-alkali salic volcanic rocks, corresponding to data presented in appendix 1 - A.

Phenocryst modes (volume %)*:

Region No.	2				5					6				
Region	Middle Americas				High Cascades - Alaska - Aleutians					Japan-Taiwan-Kuriles-Kamchatka-Saipan				
SiO_2 interval	60-63	63-66	66-69	69-73	60-63	63-66	66-69	69-73	>73	60-63	63-66	66-69	69-73	>73
Sa	0	n.d.	0	n.d.	0	0	0	0	n.d.	0	0	0	0	0
Pl	28.7	n.d.	15.6	n.d.	17.4	22.9	12.7	15.3	n.d.	15.1	16.3	18.4	14.9	12.9
Qtz	0	n.d.	0	n.d.	0.01	0.06	0	0.41	n.d.	0	2.6	5.7	1.5	4.5
Ol	0.22	n.d.	0.02	n.d.	0	0.01	0	0	n.d.	0.04	0.01	0	0	0
Cpx	2.8	n.d.	1.2	n.d.	2.0	1.9	1.0	0.58	n.d.	2.6	0.07	0.17	0.49	0.06
Opx	6.1	n.d.	0.80	n.d.	3.4	3.3	0.40	1.1	n.d.	3.7	2.2	1.5	1.5	0.48
Hb	0.50	n.d.	1.1	n.d.	0.91	0.88	2.3	1.7	n.d.	0.89	3.6	3.8	0.12	0.30
Bi	0	n.d.	0	n.d.	0	0.06	0	0.29	n.d.	0.03	0	0.03	0	0
Sphene	0	n.d.	0	n.d.	0	0	0	0	n.d.	0	0	0	0	0
Fe-Ti oxides	1.3	n.d.	0.62	n.d.	0.64	0.76	0.57	0.68	n.d.	0.51	0.86	0.98	0.62	0.25
Σ	39.6	-	19.3	-	24.4	29.9	17.0	20.1	-	22.9	25.6	30.6	19.1	18.5
n	6		4		9	8	3	10	-	8	10	6	20	10

% Frequency occurrence of phenocryst phases

SiO_2 interval	60-63	63-66	66-69	69-73	60-63	63-66	66-69	69-73	>73	60-63	63-66	66-69	69-73	>73
Sa	0	0	0	0	0	0	0	0	0	0	0	0	0	2
Pl	93	96	94	100	100	100	100	96	100	99	99	100	100	98
Qtz	0	4	6	20	11	20	39	17	38	8	20	22	28	54
Ol	43	0	6	0	14	4	11	0	0	17	12		4	2
Cpx	96	80	77	80	84	67	67	88	38	85	62	70	74	56
Opx	100	88	71	100	96	80	72	96	63	93	82	83	88	63
Hb	36	80	77	100	25	44	72	83	50	34	54	48	39	33
Bi	0	8	0	40	2	4	11	25	0	8	14	20	11	12
Sphene	0	0	0	0	0	0	6	0	0	0	0	0	0	0
Fe-Ti oxides	82	96	77	100	90	91	83	96	63	89	93	83	91	72
n	28	25	17	5	57	45	18	24	8	117	81	46	57	43

Region No.

	8					10			
Region	S.W. Pacific					Mediterranean			
SiO$_2$ interval	60-63	63-66	66-69	69-73	>73	60-63	63-66	66-69	69-73

Phenocryst modes (volume %)*:

	60-63	63-66	66-69	69-73	>73	60-63	63-66	66-69	69-73
Sa	0	0	0	0.03	<0.01	0	0	0	0
Pl	21.1	14.7	12.3	13.3	8.2	31.1	25.2	30.3	24.1
Qtz	<0.01	0.63	0.48	2.2	1.9	0.01	0.02	0.02	0.03
Ol	0.08	0.05	0	0	<0.01	0	0	0	0
Cpx	3.4	2.2	1.5	0.50	0.03	2.1	1.7	3.6	0.03
Opx	3.1	1.5	1.4	1.1	0.41	0.96	0.67	0.54	1.4
Hb	1.7	1.9	2.0	0.84	0.23	6.3	7.2	2.9	3.4
Bi	0.09	0.20	0.02	0.03	0.15	0	0.17	0.50	0.43
Sphene	0	0	0	0	0	0	0	0	0
Fe-Ti oxides	0.92	0.79	0.55	0.52	0.33	1.6	1.0	1.5	1.1
Σ	30.4	22.0	18.3	18.5	11.3	42.1	36.0	39.4	30.5
n	61	28	22	12	44	8	6	5	3

% Frequency occurrence of phenocryst phases

	60-63	63-66	66-69	69-73	>73	60-63	63-66	66-69	69-73
Sa	0	0	0	8	2	0	0	0	0
Pl	100	100	100	100	100	100	100	100	100
Qtz	5	20	29	38	50	35	17	25	31
Ol	14	9	0	0	2	0	8	0	0
Cpx	79	91	86	69	13	65	67	83	38
Opx	75	80	71	100	96	50	78	75	75
Hb	38	36	50	38	52	70	36	58	94
Bi	10	11	14	8	17	20	17	58	44
Sphene	0	0	0	0	0	0	0	0	0
Fe-Ti oxides	91	84	86	92	100	45	89	92	94
n	80	45	28	13	48	20	36	12	16

* Abbreviations as in Table 1 - B.

Appendix 3 - A - Compilation of major and trace element chemistry and High-K salic volcanic rocks from selected orogenic regions. Criteria of selection of high-K compositions after Peccerillo and Taylor (1976); see also Fig. 1. Major element analyses recalculated to 100% on anhydrous basis.

Region No.‡	1					3					4				
Region†	Western South America					Western U.S.A. - Eastern Belt					Western U.S.A. - Western Belt				
SiO_2 interval	60-63	63-66	66-69	69-63	>73	60-63	63-66	66-69	69-63	>73	60-63	63-66	66-69	69-73	>73
SiO_2	61.93	64.50	67.36	70.45	75.41	61.79	64.52	67.52	71.10	75.75	61.89	64.67	67.79	71.74	75.94
TiO_2	0.87	0.72	0.63	0.46	0.21	0.89	0.72	0.55	0.40	0.18	0.81	0.76	0.54	0.36	0.14
Al_2O_3	16.69	16.33	15.96	15.43	13.25	16.56	16.49	16.21	15.07	13.08	16.82	16.48	16.11	14.95	13.14
Fe_2O_3	3.17	2.50	2.74	1.76	1.08	3.76	3.31	2.61	1.75	1.02	3.17	2.70	2.38	1.44	0.75
FeO	2.43	2.25	1.18	0.98	0.20	1.94	1.31	0.83	0.63	0.40	2.39	1.71	1.14	0.81	0.50
MnO	0.10	0.08	0.06	0.05	0.06	0.09	0.10	0.09	0.07	0.06	0.11	0.08	0.07	0.05	0.05
MgO	2.92	2.21	1.32	0.84	0.09	2.34	1.46	0.90	0.64	0.23	2.63	1.67	1.10	0.50	0.21
CaO	5.17	4.37	3.49	2.27	1.18	4.72	3.64	2.63	1.83	0.67	5.19	3.62	3.00	1.61	0.82
Na_2O	3.61	3.61	3.27	3.72	3.66	4.03	3.97	4.07	3.81	3.67	3.50	3.86	3.71	3.61	3.58
K_2O	2.88	3.20	3.75	3.90	4.53	3.51	3.97	4.39	4.60	4.89	3.17	4.19	3.98	4.55	4.82
P_2O_5	0.24	0.21	0.23	0.14	0.05	0.36	0.27	0.19	0.11	0.04	0.32	0.24	0.16	0.09	0.04
n	25	33	22	17	27	59	57	70	83	58	26	46	24	49	142
Trace elements + (p.p.m.)															
Rb	104(16)	127(14)	180(12)	173(9)	132(7)	102(6)	125(5)	93(3)	163(6)	231(2)	143(2)	229(6)	n.d.	151(5)	192(25)
Ba	885(6)	760(3)	580(1)	570(1)	649(9)	1682(13)	1422(23)	1680(33)	1332(19)	409(13)	1730(15)	1600(16)	1620(10)	1340(16)	363(44)
Sr	578(16)	399(14)	276(13)	214(10)	126(16)	1001(18)	768(24)	538(34)	339(22)	118(15)	1082(15)	845(18)	820(10)	437(16)	79(44)
Zr	175(11)##	133(11)##	99(12)	79(6)	307(10)	331(14)	253(23)	246(33)	248(19)	172(13)	231(15)	273(16)	303(10)	180(16)	129(44)
Zn	95(4)##	97(7)##	122(10)	90(5)	56(1)	95(1)	n.d.	68(1)	n.d.	n.d.	55(1)	85(3)	n.d.	39(4)	36(9)
La	n.d.	n.d.	n.d.	n.d.	n.d.	111(10)	96(19)	88(18)	77(14)	75(8)	94(13)	83(13)	125(6)	100(14)	53(32)
Ce	47(3)	44(7)	47(2)	n.d.	n.d.	215(8)	292(11)	271(8)	174(6)	100(1)	153(13)	155(8)	208(6)	196(10)	93(13)
Yb	2.1(3)	1.4(7)	1.4(2)	n.d.	n.d.	2.3(10)	2.6(20)	2.8(24)	2.5(14)	3.0(12)	2.2(9)	2.4(12)	2.3(9)	3.8(9)	4.5(23)
Y	8(6)	6(3)	n.d.	n.d.	n.d.	25(12)	30(23)	31(32)	29(19)	29(12)	24(15)	28(16)	23(10)	30(16)	33(43)
Cu	36(11)	27(10)	31(11)	16(6)	15(9)	25(14)	25(23)	15(33)	13(18)	5(13)	35(14)	15(16)	7(10)	11(16)	6(41)
Ni	49(12)	11(18)	12(13)	13(5)	4(1)	36(11)	29(20)	5(23)	5(18)	-1(12)	32(15)	14(16)	5(9)	4(11)	2(36)
Co	21(11)	12(10)	9(11)	8(6)	5(10)	13(12)	10(21)	6(22)	3(15)	2(13)	20(14)	18(16)	18(9)	8(9)	4(36)
Cr	72(6)	25(3)	n.d.	n.d.	n.d.	61(14)	31(22)	6(31)	4(17)	2(12)	95(15)	36(16)	16(10)	6(14)	2(35)
V	141(6)	107(3)	100(1)	40(1)	32(9)	89(14)	73(20)	56(26)	26(13)	14(13)	111(15)	79(16)	49(10)	20(14)	5(35)
Nb	n.d.	n.d.	n.d.	n.d.	n.d.	18(10)	16(16)	19(14)	18(10)	36(11)	26(2)	18(11)	24(6)	18(12)	19(41)
Li	n.d.	n.d.	n.d.	n.d.	30(4)	n.d.	n.d.	n.d.	n.d.	n.d.	n.d.	14(3)	16(3)	12(1)	42(13)
Pb	n.d.	n.d.	n.d.	n.d.	57(9)	24(11)	33(20)	33(29)	30(18)	30(12)	30(14)	30(16)	23(10)	29(15)	40(42)
Hf	n.d.	n.d.	n.d.	n.d.	n.d.	n.d.	n.d.	n.d.	n.d.	n.d.	n.d.	n.d.	n.d.	n.d.	n.d.

Region No.‡	\(\leftarrow\) 6 \(\rightarrow\)					\(\leftarrow\) 8 \(\rightarrow\)					\(\leftarrow\) 10 \(\rightarrow\)				
Region‡	Japan-Taiwan-Kuriles-Kamchatka-Saipan					S.W. Pacific					Mediterranean				
SiO2 interval	60-63	63-66	66-69	69-63	>73	60-63	63-66	66-69	69-73	>73	60-63	63-66	66-69	69-63	>73
SiO_2	61.91	64.69	67.34	70.78	75.48	61.42	64.66	67.50	71.34	75.28	61.96	64.23	67.80	70.61	75.51
TiO_2	0.71	0.65	0.51	0.37	0.18	0.81	0.73	0.67	0.39	0.22	0.69	0.68	0.50	0.40	0.18
Al_2O_3	17.03	16.71	16.57	15.08	13.38	16.07	15.95	16.12	14.53	13.34	16.80	16.45	15.63	14.86	13.38
Fe_2O_3	2.54	1.84	1.43	1.01	0.74	2.02	2.18	1.66	1.27	0.78	2.98	2.76	2.28	1.96	0.96
FeO	3.44	2.86	2.07	1.42	0.83	3.87	2.47	1.63	1.59	0.79	2.02	2.01	1.52	0.88	0.43
MnO	0.12	0.09	0.11	0.09	0.05	0.11	0.14	0.07	0.07	0.05	0.10	0.09	0.08	0.07	0.05
MgO	2.60	1.93	0.95	0.67	0.39	3.15	2.10	1.01	0.49	0.23	2.50	1.80	1.15	0.76	0.33
CaO	5.25	4.23	2.21	1.62	1.14	5.38	4.05	2.79	1.70	1.15	5.42	4.36	3.49	2.50	1.01
Na_2O	3.53	3.79	4.69	4.26	3.55	3.89	4.31	4.76	4.86	4.08	3.31	3.40	3.72	3.50	3.10
K_2O	2.66	2.90	3.89	4.57	4.15	2.93	3.12	3.57	3.70	4.03	3.92	3.95	3.66	4.32	4.94
P_2O_5	0.22	0.21	0.23	0.13	0.11	0.35	0.28	0.21	0.07	0.05	0.30	0.27	0.17	0.14	0.11
n	36	18	10	18	21	40	13	9	23	43	61	49	27	28	25
Trace elements (p.p.m.)															
Rb	n.d.	n.d.	n.d.	107(2)	n.d.	70(30)	74(8)	103(5)	114(18)	131(24)	98(12)	125(8)	138(9)	194(4)	356(7)
Ba	1667(3)	n.d.	n.d.	504(1)	n.d.	783(27)	879(10)	761(5)	825(19)	834(30)	1140(9)	1052(4)	1093(2)	167(1)	26(3)
Sr	620(2)	n.d.	n.d.	182(3)	n.d.	585(35)	718(10)	326(5)	141(18)	89(24)	533(12)	437(8)	305(9)	222(4)	13(7)
Zr	n.d.	n.d.	n.d.	n.d.	n.d.	182(34)	172(9)	359(5)	404(18)	199(24)	100(1)	178(2)	n.d.	205(1)	51(3)
Zn	n.d.	n.d.	n.d.	21(1)	n.d.	75(10)	76(7)	58(4)	59(17)	37(14)	69(8)	68(8)	57(3)	51(2)	40(7)
La	33(1)	n.d.	n.d.	21(1)	n.d.	31(18)	30(7)	43(4)	56(18)	31(23)	21(1)	26(2)	n.d.	56(1)	16(3)
Ce	73(1)	n.d.	n.d.	51(1)	n.d.	55(18)	56(8)	78(4)	87(17)	63(15)	68(1)	63(2)	n.d.	132(1)	59(3)
Yb	2.5(1)	n.d.	n.d.	2.3(1)	n.d.	2.3(7)	2.1(1)	2.1(1)	7.7(5)	2.6(5)	n.d.	n.d.	n.d.	n.d.	n.d.
Y	15(2)	n.d.	n.d.	9(1)	n.d.	29(28)	21(9)	30(5)	56(18)	21(24)	23(1)	37(2)	n.d.	41(1)	97(3)
Cu	13(2)	n.d.	n.d.	1(1)	n.d.	55(27)	22(10)	5(5)	6(18)	3(24)	28(12)	23(9)	13(3)	43(2)	13(7)
Ni	n.d.	n.d.	n.d.	n.d.	n.d.	45(27)	41(10)	6(4)	3(17)	4(14)	19(8)	14(8)	11(4)	8(2)	4(7)
Co	12(2)	n.d.	n.d.	6.4(1)	n.d.	21(10)	n.d.	n.d.	n.d.	n.d.	15(8)	14(6)	8(4)	5(2)	3(7)
Cr	6(2)	n.d.	n.d.	2.2(1)	n.d.	107(27)	67(10)	5(5)	16(18)	6(24)	11(1)	12(2)	2(1)	34(1)	35(3)
V	99(2)	n.d.	n.d.	18(1)	n.d.	133(28)	77(10)	42(5)	11(18)	9(24)	109(5)	87(3)	25(2)	35(1)	n.d.
Nb	n.d.	n.d.	n.d.	n.d.	n.d.	7(12)	8(7)	12(4)	35(17)	20(14)	n.d.	25(2)	n.d.	n.d.	n.d.
Li	n.d.	n.d.	n.d.	n.d.	n.d.	n.d.	n.d.	n.d.	28(1)	32(10)	14(7)	17(6)	26(3)	18(1)	26(4)
Pb	8(2)	n.d.	n.d.	5(1)	n.d.	16(15)	29(5)	19(5)	15(17)	19(15)	n.d.	25(2)	n.d.	18(1)	n.d.
Hf	3.7(1)	n.d.	n.d.	3.3(1)	n.d.	4.0(5)	n.d.	6.7(1)	8.9(5)	5.1(5)	n.d.	n.d.	n.d.	n.d.	n.d.

‡   See introduction
\+   Numbers in brackets refer to number of data used to calculate average for each trace element
n.d.   Insufficient data
n   Number of data used in each major element compilation.

Ignoring one anomolously high Zn value in each group

Appendix 3 - B - Compilation of mineralogical (phenocryst) data of High-K salic volcanic rocks from selected orogenic regions. Data corresponds to those in appendix 3 - A.

Phenocryst modes (volume %):

Region No.	1					3					4				
Region	Western South America					Western U.S.A. - Eastern Belt					Western U.S.A. - Western Belt				
SiO₂ interval	60-63	63-66	66-69	60-73	>73	60-63	63-66	66-69	69-73	>73	60-63	63-66	66-69	69-73	>73
Sa	0.40	0	n.d.	8.1		0.98	1.8	3.5	4.2	8.4	1.8	2.2	1.9	3.7	3.3
Pl	23.6	20.6	n.d.	5.9		16.6	14.9	18.2	10.9	3.8	18.6	20.4	19.0	9.8	2.3
Qtz	0.07	0	n.d.	7.7		0.10	0.31	0.94	2.6	3.7	0.26	0.24	5.8	3.4	2.6
Ol	0.04	0.05	n.d.	0.13		0.09	0.01	<0.01	0	0	0.16	0.08	0	0	<0.01
Cpx	1.4	1.0	n.d.	0.17		2.5	0.89	0.49	0.15	0.02	2.4	1.2	0.38	0.14	0.03
Opx	2.2	2.6	n.d.	0.17		1.6	0.65	0.09	0.15	0.07	1.3	0.50	0.34	0.02	0.01
Hb	7.4	3.2	n.d.	1.8		2.5	1.5	1.1	0.24	0.83	3.3	2.7	0.49	0.84	0.04
Bi	0.44	1.5	n.d.	0		1.8	2.3	2.9	2.0	0.01	1.4	2.7	3.2	2.1	0.32
Sphene	0.06	0	n.d.			0	<0.01	0.05	0.01	0.32	0	0.04	<0.01	0.04	0.01
Fe-Ti oxides	1.9	1.1	n.d.	0.57		1.3	0.86	1.3	0.61	0.01	1.1	0.55	0.58	0.36	0.09
Σ	37.5	30.1	n.d.	24.5		27.5	23.2	28.6	20.9	17.2	30.3	30.6	31.7	20.4	8.7
n	7	11	-	3		38	47	51	53	30	14	13	16	18	67

% Frequency occurrence of phenocryst phases

	60-63	63-66	66-69	60-73	>73	60-63	63-66	66-69	69-73	>73	60-63	63-66	66-69	69-73	>73
Sa	8	3	16	54	100	17	49	76	71	93	8	16	65	60	82
Pl	92	100	100	100	100	88	93	100	96	76	100	100	96	97	80
Qtz	38	23	63	46	96	10	25	47	52	76	16	24	78	91	76
Ol	17	7	0	0	0	7	2	1	0	0	4	7	0	3	6
Cpx	79	63	53	46	4	85	65	46	33	10	88	76	78	29	13
Opx	79	87	63	38	0	49	18	6	11	0	68	29	35	17	11
Hb	71	67	42	31	52	54	61	63	50	19	68	67	87	74	34
Bi	50	63	89	77	100	44	72	97	95	90	76	82	96	86	70
Sphene	8	0	11	23	0	0	4	19	24	5	0	9	17	40	20
Fe-Ti oxides	58	73	100	100	72	73	74	93	83	62	96	93	91	83	70
n	24	30	19	13	25	59	57	70	82	58	25	45	23	35	116

Region No.

	6					8					10				
Region	Japan-Taiwan-Kuriles-Kamchatka-Saipan					S.W. Pacific					Mediterranean				
SiO₂ interval	60-63	63-66	66-69	69-73	>73	60-63	63-66	66-69	69-73	>73	60-63	63-66	66-69	69-73	>73

SiO_2 interval

Phenocryst modes (volume %)*:

	60-63	63-66	66-69	69-73	>73	60-63	63-66	66-69	69-73	>73	60-63	63-66	66-69	69-73	>73
Sa	0	0	0	0	n.d.	0.04	0	0	<0.01	0.13	4.8	3.7	0	n.d.	15.2
Pl	4.2	6.7	9.0	3.8	n.d.	13.9	6.6	8.2	5.0	5.2	17.1	20.4	18.7	n.d.	8.5
Qtz	0.04	0.04	0.03	0	n.d.	0.03	0.07	0	0.83	1.6	0	0	0.18	n.d.	14.4
Ol	0.26	0.20	0.30	0.08	n.d.	2.1	0.46	0.90	0.09	0.02	0.03	0.97	0.88	n.d.	0
Cpx	0.62	0.84	0.70	0.36	n.d.	0.75	0.10	0.97	0.23	0.23	4.2	3.2	0.30	n.d.	0
Opx	1.2	1.9	1.9	0.44	n.d.	2.6	1.4	0.17	0.47	0.07	2.0	0.01	1.6	n.d.	0
Hb	0.01	0.18	0	0	n.d.	1.1	2.1	0	0.07	0.21	6.2	6.9	0.03	n.d.	3.6
Bi	0	0	0	0	n.d.	0	0	0	0	0	0.06	0	0	n.d.	0
Sphene	0	0	0	0	n.d.	0	0	0	0	0	0	0.02	0	n.d.	0
Fe-Ti oxides	0.28	0.34	0.83	0.39	n.d.	0.68	1.1	1.0	0.20	0.20	0	0	2.7	n.d.	0
Σ	6.6	10.2	12.8	5.1	-	21.2	11.8	11.2	6.9	7.7	34.4	35.2	24.4	-	41.7
n	8	4	3	8	-	26	7	3	14	30	12	9	4	-	12

% Frequency occurrence of phenocryst phases

	60-63	63-66	66-69	69-73	>73	60-63	63-66	66-69	69-73	>73	60-63	63-66	66-69	69-73	>73
Sa	0	0	0	0	11	3	0	0	10	3	36	45	19	50	96
Pl	97	94	100	88	100	95	100	100	90	95	100	100	96	100	100
Qtz	25	22	0	6	67	3	8	22	24	50	11	20	41	64	100
Ol	14	11	10	0	33	25	75	67	5	16	10	6	7	7	0
Cpx	58	61	90	50	39	75	75	44	43	58	92	65	48	25	0
Opx	92	100	100	88	28	48	50	56	48	53	48	57	37	14	4
Hb	78	61	40	50	56	50	33	56	43	45	62	59	70	61	96
Bi	44	28	10	31	56	35	0	0	33	0	80	78	63	82	0
Sphene	0	0	0	0	0	0	0	0	0	0	0	14	19	21	0
Fe-Ti oxides	75	78	90	81	56	48	100	67	86	68	66	53	74	61	12
n	36	18	10	16	18	40	12	9	21	38	61	49	27	28	25

* Abbreviations as in Table 1 - B.

n.d. Insufficient data

SOME TRACE ELEMENTS IN TRONDHJEMITES–THEIR IMPLICATIONS TO MAGMA GENESIS AND PALEOTECTONIC SETTING

J. G. Arth

INTRODUCTION

Over the last decade trace element abundances in trondhjemitic and related rocks have been used to help delimit the fractionation histories of trondhjemitic magmas and the mineralogical nature of their source regions. In addition, trace element abundances are potentially useful in fingerprinting the paleotectonic setting of terranes in which trondhjemites are found. In this paper the utility of various trace elements as tectonic fingerprints and genetic indicators is discusssed; trace-element patterns characteristic of various trondhjemite occurrences are noted, and genetic models for several important trondhjemite suites are reviewed.

SELECTION AND RELIABILITY OF TRACE ELEMENTS

Trace element studies of trondhjemites have focused on those elements that show a large range of concentrations in silicic igneous rocks and for which analytical techniques for precise measurement are available. Genetic implications are based on elements for which data is available for the distribution coefficient of the element between basaltic to dacitic liquid and the common rock-forming and accessory minerals. Frequently studied elements which approximately satisfy the above criteria include Rb, Sr, Ba, and the rare-earth elements. A compilation of distribution coefficients for these elements is given by Arth (1976).

For a given trace element to be reliable as a genetic and tectonic indicator, the measured abundances must reflect those of unaltered magmas. Two studies in which δO^{18} values have been measured in trondhjemitic suites indicated that this assumption is probably valid for rare-earth elements, is not valid for Rb, and is suspect for Sr and Ba. In the trondhjemites of Rio Brazos, the Twighlight Gneiss (Barker and others, 1976a), and southwest Finland (Arth and others, 1978) the Rb content increases as δO^{18} increases. The trondhjemites of the Kroenke Granodiorite (Barker and others, 1976a) show a decrease in Rb as δO^{18} increases. The Rio Brazos and Twighlight occurrences have been metamorphosed so the variation may be related to changes occurring during either metamorphic or magmatic processes. For the unmetamorphosed Kroenke Granodiorite, Barker and others were uncertain as to the cause of the observed variation, but thought it might reflect crystal fractionation involving minerals of high δO^{18} value. For the southwest Finland suite Arth and others (1978) show that the variations of δO^{18} were produced prior to magma solidification and proposed that water of high δO^{18} from the metamorphic country rock was added to the intermediate to trondhjemitic magmas accompanied by introduction of Rb and Sr and removal of Ba. Rare earths were apparently unaffected. It thus appears that the concentrations of Rb, Sr, and Ba cannot be considered to represent those of the original magmas unless the δO^{18} value of the rock is measured and is in the range 5.2 to 8.9 per mil, which Barker and others (1976b) found in trondhjemites not strongly isotopically disturbed. This criteria provides necessary, but probably not sufficient, evidence that the trace-element abundances are reliable for samples which are otherwise unaltered and unmetamorphosed. In view of the limits stated above, the significance of ratios of K/Rb, Rb/Sr, K/Ba, and Sr/Ba is also questionable.

TECTONIC ENVIRONMENTS AND TRACE ELEMENT PATTERNS

Barker (this volume) notes three Cenozoic environments in which trondhjemites are found: continental margins, ophiolites, and the subvolcanic region of island arcs. Coleman and Peterman (1975) illustrated that trondhjemites in ophiolites contain markedly greater heavy rare-earth contents than tonalite of continental occurrence. Figure 1 shows examples of the chondrite-normalized rare-earth patterns for trondhjemites and chemically equivalent dacites from four known tectonic settings. Oceanic rocks are represented by a trondhjemite from the Troodos Ophiolite Complex (Kay and Senechal, 1976) and by an island-arc dacite from Saipan (Barker and others, 1976a). Both have flat or light rare-earth-depleted patterns showing whole rock/chondrite heavy rare-earth values greater than 10 and negative Eu anomalies. Continental rocks are represented by a trondhjemite from the continental-margin batholith of the Klamath Mountains, California (Arth and Hanson, 1972) and a dacite from interior New Mexico (Arth and Barker, 1976). Both have highly fractionated patterns showing whole-rock/chondrite heavy rare-earth values less than 5 and small positive Eu anomalies.

The differences between trondhjemites originating in oceanic environments and those originating in continental environments is also reflected in Al_2O_3 content. Continental trondhjemites generally contain more than 14.5 to 15 percent Al_2O_3, whereas oceanic trondhjemites generally contain less than 14.5 to 15 percent. The variation of heavy rare-earth content with Al_2O_3 content is

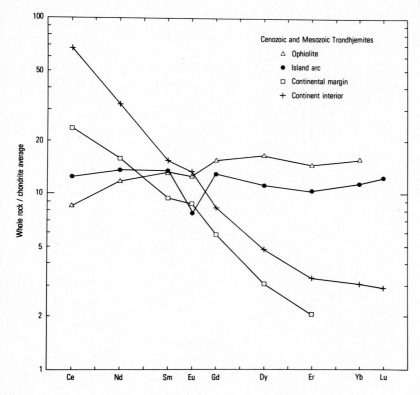

Figure 1.--Chondrite-normalized rare-earth plot for trondhjemites and
chemically equivalent dacites from various tectonic settings. Data from
Arth and Hanson, 1972; Arth and Barker, 1976; Barker and others, 1976a; Kay
and Senechal, 1976.

illustrated in Figure 2 for a large number of trondhjemites ranging in age from
early Archean to Cenozoic. For the few cases where paleotectonic setting is
known, the trondhjemites plot in the appropriate field, but further data from
known tectonic settings is clearly needed.

The boundaries in Figure 2 between continental and oceanic occurrences
should not be considered sharp ones because rocks from the mature stages of
island arc development and those in the early stages of continental margin
development should show values which are transitional between the two groups.
One example of a geographic variation from low Al_2O_3 to high Al_2O_3 type was
given by Barker and others (1976a) for the 1.7 to 1.8 b.y.-old trondhjemites of
Colorado and New Mexico. From south to north, across the general strike of the
Proterozoic continental-marginal orogenic belt and in the direction of the
Archean craton, the trondhjemites show systematic increases in Al_2O_3, Rb, Sr,

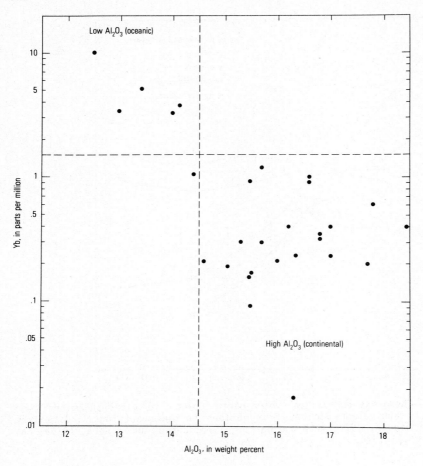

Figure 2.--Plot of Al_2O_3 vs. Yb for a large number of trondhjemites. Vertical dashed line separates low Al from high Al type at 14.5 percent Al_2O_3. Horizontal dashed line at 1.5 ppm Yb separates rocks depleted in heavy-rare-earth content from those undepleted. Data from Arth and Hanson, 1972; 1975; Arth and others, 1978; Barker and others, 1976a; Barker and others, this volume, Western U.S. studies, Trondheim region study; Hunter and others, this volume; Kay and Senechal, 1976

and Eu/Eu*, and decreases in heavy rare-earth content. Barker and others related this variation to the depth of trondhjemite generation, as discussed below. It is noteworthy that the full range of trondhjemite compositions, from low Al_2O_3 to high Al_2O_3 type are now known in every geologic era. Even some of the earth's oldest gneisses, such as the early Archean Bimodal Suite of the Ancient Gneiss Complex of Swaziland (Hunter and others, 1978), contain both types.

MODELS OF TRONDHJEMITE GENESIS

It is now generally acepted that the generation of trondhjemites is related to a basaltic source. This conclusion is based on the common association of trondhjemite with basalt, amphibolite or gabbro; the primitive initial Sr isotopic composition found in trondhjemites of all geologic eras (see Peterman, this volume); the oxygen isotope ratios of trondhjemites which are similar to those of basalts but distinct from those of other granitic rocks (Barker and others, 1976b); the suggestive results of some laboratory melting experiments (Helz, 1976); and the success of trace element models that test this hypothesis, as discussed below.

The extant models propose partial melting or fractional crystallization as the major process and differ depending on whether the trondhjemites are of high or low Al_2O_3 type. Hanson and Goldich (1972) and Arth and Hanson (1972, 1975) advanced a partial melting model to explain the origin of high Al_2O_3 tonalites, trondhjemites and dacites in the bimodal mafic-silicic suites of Archean age in northestern Minnesota. These authors argued that if Archean tholeiitic basalt was metamorphosed to amphibolite or eclogite and subsequently melted, the magma produced upon about 20 percent melting would have the trace element characteristics observed in the tonalites, trondhjemites, and dacites if the solid residue was eclogitic. The residual garnet would presumably concentrate the heavy rare earths, leaving the magmas depleted in these elements. The rare-earth patterns predicted by mathematical modeling of the melting process are shown in Figure 3, and closely resemble those of the tonalites, dacites, and trondhjemites. The melting process was thought to occur at mantle depths where the ecologitic residue would be a stable assemblage. Subsequent study of the partitioning behavior of rare earths (Nagasawa and Schnetzler, 1971; Arth and Barker, 1976) indicated that hornblende could also concentrate heavy rare earths from silicic magma. Thus Arth and Barker (1976) suggested that melting of amphibolite could occur at less than 60 km depth, leave an amphibole-rich residue, and produce liquids having trace-element characteristics similar to those which might result if eclogite were residual at high pressure.

Fractional crystallization models for high Al_2O_3 type trondhjemites were offered long ago by Goldschmidt (1922), and Hietanen (1943) for the suites of the Trondheim area in Norway and the Kalanti area of southwest Finland, respectively. These suites differ from the bimodal ones mentioned above in that they show a complete range in composition from gabbro through diorite, tonalite, and trondhjemite. Barker and Millard (this volume) restudied the suite in Norway and suggest that its geochemistry and origin may be analogous to the better preserved southwest Finland suite, which has been restudied by Arth and others (1978). Rare-earth patterns for the Finland suite (Fig. 4)

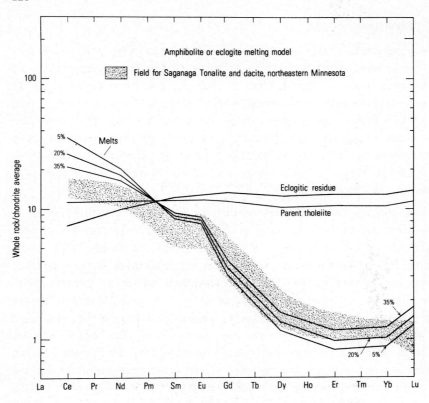

Figure 3.--Chondrite-normalized rare-earth plot showing the patterns predicted in the melting model proposed by Hanson and Goldich (1972) and Arth and Hanson (1972, 1975) to explain the origin of trondhjemites, tonalites and dacites of Archean age in northestern Minnesota.

show a smooth variation from gabbro to trondhjemite. Unlike many calc-alkaline suites, this calc-alkaline trondhjemitic suite shows a decrease in rare earth content and an increasing positive Eu anomaly from the intermediate to trondhjemitic samples. Arth and Barker (1976) illustrated that this type of variation can result through fractional crystallization of hornblende and plagioclase. They did this by measuring the rare earth content of a high-Al_2O_3 dacite (chemically equivalent to trondhjemite) and then measuring the groundmass after the phenocrysts of hornblende and plagioclase (5 percent each) were removed (see Fig. 5). Arth and others (1978) preferred to retain a fractional crystallization model for the Finland suite because hornblende-cumulate rocks were present, but they noted that partial melting of amphibolite or eclogite may also have contributed tonalitic to trondhjemitic magma.

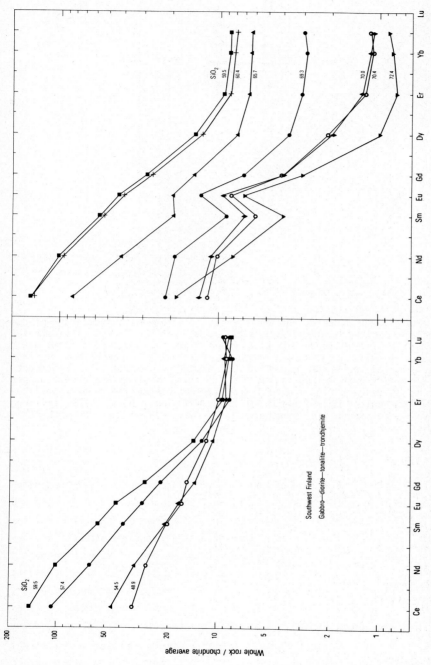

Figure 4.--Rare-earth patterns for samples from the gabbro-diorite-tonalite-trondhjemite suite of southwest Finland (Arth and others, 1978). Rare-earth contents vary sympathetically with SiO_2 content. From 48.9 to 59.5 percent SiO_2, light rare-earth contents increase whereas heavy rare-earth contents are buffered. From 59.5 to 72.4 percent SiO_2, all rare earths decrease in abundance and a positive Eu anomaly develops.

130

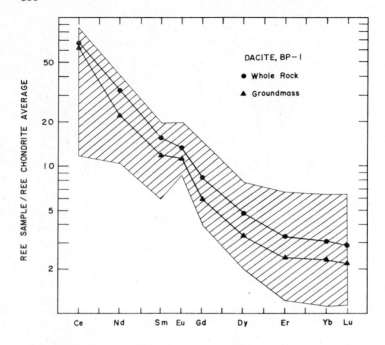

Figure 5.--Rare-earth patterns for whole rocks and groundmass from a hornblende plagioclase dacite porphyry (Arth and Barker, 1976). The plot illustrates that removal of hornblende and plagioclase from a magma (whole rock) would produce a liquid (groundmass) which is relatively impoverished in rare earths and has a larger positive Eu anomaly. Shaded area represents tonalites and trondhjemites having SiO_2 contents of from 65 percent (upper limit) to 70 percent (lower limit) from the well-preserved gabbro-tonalite-trondhjemite suite of southwest Finland (Arth and others, 1978) and from the type area south of Trondheim in Norway (Baker and Millard, this volume).

Models explaining the origin of low Al_2O_3 trondhjemites also vary depending on whether the trondhjemites occur in bimodal or continuous suites. Kay and Senechal (1976) interpreted trondhjemite from the Troodos Ophiolite Complex (rare-earth pattern in Fig. 1) as a late-stage differentiate derived by low-pressure crystal settling of plagioclase, pyroxene and olivine from basalt magma having a pattern similar in shape to that of trondhjemite, but having lower concentrations of rare earths and no Eu anomaly. Barker and others (1976a) offered a generalized model for low Al_2O_3 trondhjemites. They suggested that the low Al_2O_3 and Sr contents and negative Eu anomalies indicate that plagioclase was a residual phase in either a partial melting or fractional crystallization model. The relatively flat REE patterns suggest that garnet was not residual. They also suggested that the absence of intermediate rocks in many bimodal suites favors an origin by partial melting, but does not preclude fractional crystallization. The presence of plagioclase in either process would restrict the depth of generation to less than 60 kilometers.

CONCLUSIONS

Rare-earth elements appear to be the most reliable of the elements used in studies of trondhjemite genesis and paleotectonic setting. Low-Al_2O_3-type trondhjemites have flat or mildly fractionated rare-earth patterns that show negative Eu anomalies and high heavy-rare-earth content (Yb greater than 8 times chondritic values). High-Al_2O_3-type trondhjemites generally have positively fractionated rare-earth patterns that show positive or no Eu anomalies and low heavy-rare-earth contents (Yb less than 8 times chondritic values).

More data is needed to fully characterize paleotectonic setting, but low-Al_2O_3-, high-Yb-type trondhjemites generally originate in oceanic environments whereas the high-Al_2O_3-, low-Yb-type generally originates at continental margins or interiors.

Generation of low-Al_2O_3-type trondhjemites is thought to occur by fractional crystallization or partial melting of basalt at shallow depths where residual phases would include plagioclase. Generation of high-Al_2O_3-type trondhjemites is thought to occur by fractional crystallization of basalt at intermediate depths where residual phases include hornblende and plagioclase; or by partial melting of metabasalt at intermediate depths leaving a hornblende-rich residue; or by partial melting at mantle depths leaving an eclogitic residue.

REFERENCES

Arth, J. G., 1976. Behavior of trace elements during magmatic processes--a summary of theoretical models and their applications. U.S. Geol. Surv. J. Research, 4: 41-47.

Arth, J. G. and Barker, F., 1976. Rare-earth partitioning between hornblende and dacitic liquid and implications for the genesis of trondhjemitic-tonalitic magmas. Geology, 4: 534-536.

Arth, J. G., Barker, F., Peterman, Z. E. and Friedman, I., 1978. Geochemistry of the gabbro-diorite-tonalite-trondhjemite suite of southwest Finland and its implications for the origin of tonalitic and trondhjemitic magmas. J. Pet., 19: (in press).

Arth, J. G. and Hanson, G. N., 1972. Quartz diorites derived by partial melting of eclogite or amphibolite at mantle depths. Contrib. Miner. Pet., 37: 161-174.

Arth, J. G. and Hanson, G. N., 1975. Geochemistry and origin of the early Precambrian crust of northeastern Minnesota. Geochim. Cosmochim. Acta, 39: 325-362.

Barker, F., Arth, J. G., Peterman, Z. E. and Friedman, I., 1976a. The 1.7- to 1.8-b.y.-old trondhjemites of southwestern Colorado and northern New Mexico: Geochemistry and depths of genesis. Geol. Soc. Am. Bull., 87: 189-198.

Barker, F., Friedman, I., Hunter, D. R. and Gleason, J.D., 1976b. Oxygen isotopes of some trondhjemites, siliceous gneisses, and associated mafic rocks. Precambrian Res., 3: 547-557

Coleman, R. G. and Peterman, Z. E., 1975. Oceanic plagiogranite. J. Geophys. Res., 80: 1099-1108.

Goldschmidt, V. M., 1922. Stammestypen der eruptivgesteine. Vidensk. Skrifter, Kristiania, I. Mat. Na. Klasse, 10: 1-12.

Hanson, G. N. and Goldich, S. S., 1972. Early Precambrian rocks of the Saganaga Lake-Northern Light Lake Area, Minnesota-Ontario: Part II: Petrogenesis. Geol. Soc. Amer. Mem., 135: 179-192.

Helz, R. T., 1976. Phase relations of basalts in their melting ranges at P_{H_2O} = 5 kb. Part II. Melt compositions. J. Pet., 17: 139-193.

Hietanen, A., 1943. Uber das grundgebirge des Kalantigebietes im sudwestlichen Finnland Bull. Comm. Geol. Finlande, 130, 150 pp.

Hunter, D. R., Barker, F. and Millard, H. T., Jr., 1978. The geochemical nature of the Archean Ancient Gneiss Complex and Granodiorite Suite, Swaziland: a preliminary study. Precambrian Res. 6: (in press).

Kay, R. W. and Senechal, R. G., 1976. The rare earth geochemistry of the Troodos Ophiolite Complex. J. Geophys. Res., 81: 964-970.

Nagasawa, H. and Schnetzler, C. C., 1971. Partitioning of rare earth, alkalic and alkaline earth elements between phenocrysts and acidic igneous magma. Geochim. Cosmochim. Acta, 35: 953-968.

Chapter 4

STRONTIUM ISOTOPE GEOCHEMISTRY OF LATE ARCHEAN TO LATE CRETACEOUS TONALITES AND TRONDHJEMITES

Z. E. Peterman

ABSTRACT

Initial $^{87}Sr/^{86}Sr$ ratios for 17 tonalites and trondhjemites representing approximately 2,600 m.y. of earth history are used to define a mantle growth curve. The data define a simple linear trend between meteorites (4.5 b.y. ago) and a value of 0.7039 $\pm$ 0.0004 at the present time. The growth curve can be represented by an average present-day Rb/Sr ratio of 0.025. Rocks of tonalitic and trondhjemitic composition are characterized by low Rb/Sr ratios that range between mantle-like and upper crustal values. The distribution of ratios is strongly asymmetric; the median value is 0.075. Granites derived by partial melting of a tonalitic terrane would have mantle-like initial $^{87}Sr/^{86}Sr$ ratios even if the tonalites were several hundred million years older than the time of anatexis.

INTRODUCTION

Considerable effort has been expended in attempting to characterize the Sr-isotope evolution of the earth's mantle--that is the time dependent change in $^{87}Sr/^{86}Sr$. The pattern of Sr-isotope evolution established by Gast (1960), Hurley and others (1962), Faure and Hurley (1963), and Hedge and Walthall (1963) has been changed little by voluminous data generated since these pioneering investigations. The evolution curve is generally assumed to be constrained by two points. Data for meteorites augmented by data from lunar samples provide a $^{87}Sr/^{86}Sr$ value of 0.6990 at approximately 4.5 b.y. ago. The present-day end of the curve is limited by Sr-isotope data for volcanic rocks of the ocean basins (see summary by Hofmann and Hart, 1978). Mid-ocean ridge tholeiites are characterized by $^{87}Sr/^{86}Sr$ values in the range of 0.7022 to 0.7030 with somewhat higher values from the Indian Ocean (Subbarao and Hedge, 1973). Many values for oceanic-island basalts are in the range of 0.7030 to 0.7040 with some values up to 0.7065. These variations reflect differences in Rb/Sr ratios that were established in the past (Gast and others, 1964; Hedge, 1966, 1978; Peterman and Hedge, 1971; Hofmann and Hart, 1978). Volcanic rocks formed in magmatic arcs generally have $^{87}Sr/^{86}Sr$ ratios in the range of oceanic-island basalts. However, arc-related rocks in ensimatic environments, especially those marginal to the Pacific Basin, show an extremely restricted range in $^{87}Sr/^{86}Sr$, and Hart and Brooks (1977) reported a range in $^{87}Sr/^{86}Sr$ of 0.7034 to 0.7042 and a mean of 0.7036_3. To this array, much additional high-quality data can be added as summarized by Hedge and Peterman (1974) and Peterman and Heming (1974). Neither the range nor average is changed significantly over that reported by Hart and Brooks (1977).

In contrast to the two end points, the Sr-isotope evolution curve between the time of formation of the earth and the present day is not well defined in detail, and the problems are formidable. The differences in $^{87}Sr/^{86}Sr$ between 4,500 m.y. ago and today are small (0.004 to 0.007). Definition of the middle part of the curve must rely on data obtained mostly from Precambrian rocks. Thus, $^{87}Sr/^{86}Sr$ values are generally based on Rb-Sr isochrons with all of the inherent assumptions and uncertainties. Attempts to use Precambrian volcanic rocks have not been fruitful because of alteration and metamorphism. A notable exception is the study of fresh clinopyroxenes (Hart and Brooks, 1977) from low-grade ultramafic rocks that are 2,700 m.y. old. The $^{87}Sr/^{86}Sr$ value of 0.7011_4 is one of the few precisely determined direct measurements that can be used to define a mantle evolution curve. Efforts to obtain Sr-isotope values on Alpine-type ultamafic rocks (see summaries by Faure and Powell, 1972; Hedge and Peterman, 1974), have failed to provide convincing data on which to construct mantle-evolution curves. A number of compilations of initial Sr-isotope ratios of granitic rocks (e.g., Faure and Powell, 1972) show large variations and are not useful in establishing mantle growth in $^{87}Sr/^{86}Sr$. Selected values (Kagami and others, 1976) show less variation and may approach a probable mantle trend. Initial Sr ratios obtained on gneiss complexes, especially very ancient ones, must be used with caution because the pre-metamorphic history of these rocks rarely can be firmly established.

The present study is an attempt to characterize the Sr-isotopic character of Precambrian and Phanerozoic rocks of tonalitic and trondhjemitic composition with some latitude to include a few granodiorites. As emphasized in other chapters of this compendium, rocks of the tonalite clan are important components during early stages of crustal growth throughout geologic time. All crustal materials have ultimately been derived from the mantle but the number of intermediate stages and the residence times of the intermediate products in the crust varies. The basic premise in this investigation is that the tonalites and trondhjemites are derived directly or indirectly from the mantle. The temporal position and abundance of these rocks in the early stages of crustal evolution suggest that any intermediate stages are short lived. Thus, whether the tonalites and trondhjemites are derived directly from the mantle, through fractionation of mantle-derived magmas, or by partial melting of mantle-derived rocks, is of secondary importance in the Sr-isotope geochemistry of these rocks. Therefore, the Sr-isotope ratios of the tonalites and trondhjemites provide valuable data for defining the $^{87}Sr/^{86}Sr$ growth in the upper mantle.

SAMPLES AND CRITERIA

Most of the data were obtained specifically for this investigation or as parts of topical studies that have been published elsewhere. A few data which meet the criteria were taken from published studies by other researchers--the Saganaga Tonalite and Northern Light Gneiss (Hanson and others, 1971), the tonalite of southern Greenland (Van Breeman and others, 1974), and the Sesombi Tonalite of Rhodesia (Hawkesworth and others, 1975). The ages of most of the units are well estblished either through multiple dating methods or through geologic relations. All of the units are of igneous origin and most are plutonic rocks. Data are included for three gneiss units that were probably derived from stratified volcanic sequences--the Northern Light Gneiss,the Twilight Gneiss, and gneisses of the Wind River Range. Multiple dating methods indicate that the time span between formation and metamorphism was so short that the initial $^{87}Sr/^{86}Sr$ ratios are essentially those of the protoliths. All of the rocks are characterized by low Rb/Sr ratios so that extrapolation through the isochron systematics to the initial Sr ratios tends to minimize uncertainties.

The geologic details of the various units for which data are cited from the literature can be found in the references given in Table 1. Data for five units are here reported for the first time. Gneisses from the Wind River Range are described by Barker and Millard (this volume). The tonalites from Saudi Arabia are part of a Late Proterozoic terrane where they occur in domical-shaped plutons surrounded by metasedimentary and metavolcanic rocks (R. G. Coleman, personal commun.). The trondhjemites from Idaho are from the western part of the Idaho batholith in a gneissic border zone; rock descriptions and analyses are given by Hamilton (1962). The rocks from Alaska are trondhjemites from the Alaska Range batholith and have been described and dated by Reed and Lanphere (1969). The Trinity Alps are in the Klamath Mountains of northern California where a number of small plutons are zoned from diorite to trondhjemite (Lipman, 1963; Lanphere and others, 1968; Hotz, 1971).

DATA

Rb, Sr, and Sr-isotope data for the rocks are listed in Table 1. All of the $^{87}Sr/^{86}Sr$ ratios are relative to a value of 0.7080 for the Eimer and Amend

TABLE 1 : Rb, Sr, and $^{87}Sr/^{86}Sr$ in tonalites and trondhjemites

Unit	Age[1]	Sample No.[2]	Rock type[3]	Rb,ppm	Sr/ppm	Rb/Sr	$^{87}Sr/^{86}Sr$	$(^{87}Sr/^{86}Sr)_o$[4]	Ref.[5]
Saganaga Tonalite MN-Ont.	LA	(7)	TO-GD	32	1021	0.031	------	0.7009 ± 0.0006	(1)
Northern Light Gneiss Ont.	LA	(5)	TR	31	573	0.054	------	0.7006 ± 0.0004	(1)
Sesombi Tonalite Rhodesia	LA	(6)	TO	48	366	0.131	------	0.7008 ± 0.0004	(2)
Wind River Gneisses WY	LA	WR-1	AM	25	132	0.189	0.7233)		
		WR-2	TR	20	744	0.027	0.7046)		
		WR-5	GD	42	180	0.232	0.7296)	0.7014 ± 0.0007	(3)
		WR-6	AM	3.8	52	0.073	0.7094)		
		WR-7	QM	127	265	0.479	0.7555)		
Southwest Finland	EP	(6)	TR	57	709	0.080	------	0.7021 ± 0.0002	(4)
Anticlinal Granodiorite South Greenland	EP	(1)	TO	32	958	0.033	------	0.7022 ± 0.0010	(5)
Twilight Gneiss, CO	EP	(7)	TR	45	217	0.207	------	0.7015 ± 0.0004	(6,7)
Trondhjemite of Rio Brazos, NM	EP	(6)	TR	28	101	0.277	------	0.7026 ± 0.0004	(7,8)
Kroenke Grandodiorite CO	EP	(9)	GD	76	547	0.138	------	0.7027 ± 0.0006	(7,8)
Pitts Meadow Grano-diorite, CO	EP	(6)	GD	67	508	0.131	------	0.7017 ± 0.0010	(7,9)
Khamis Mushayt Saudi Arabia	LP	58785	TO	12	696	0.017	0.7032)		
		58893	TO	64	584	0.109	0.7062)		
		58931	TO	49	966	0.051	0.7040)		
		62046	TO	33	744	0.044	0.7046)	0.7028 ± 0.0006	(3)
		62092	GD	58	616	0.095	0.7056)		
Trondheim, Norway	EЄ	(5)	TR-GD	52	515	0.101	------	0.7039 ± 0.0002	(10)
Western Idaho Bath. ID	T	148432	TR	26	815	0.032	0.7040)		
		148429	TR	9.0	913	0.010	0.7039)		
		148431	TR	18	711	0.025	0.7037	0.7037 ± 0.0002	(3)

Location	Age	Sample	Rock type						Ref.
Trinity Alps, CA	LJ-EK	(T-1645	TR	35	393	0.089	0.7037)		(3)
		(T-392	TR	40	392	0.101	0.7040)		(3)
Canyon Creek Pluton		(T-393	TO	32	469	0.068	0.7038)		(3)
		(T-61	TO	33	591	0.055	0.7037)		(3)
		(T-394	TO	23	541	0.043	0.7036)	0.7034 ± 0.0001	(3)
		(T-1647a	TR	20	461	0.043	0.7037)		(3)
Gibson Peak Pluton		T-1049C	TO	29	609	0.048	0.7037)		(3)
Caribou Mt. Pluton		T-39	TR	14	392	0.028	0.7036)		(3)
Craggy Peak Pluton		(1)	TR	16	509	0.032	0.7035)		(11)
Western Sierra Nevada CA	EK	(1)	TR	10	482	0.022	------	0.7032 ± 0.0002	(11)
	EK	(1)	TR	57	432	0.131	------	0.7044 ± 0.0002	(11)
Alaska Range Bath. AK	LK	65AR818	TR	25	813	0.030	0.7039)		(3)
		65AR1034	TR	47	679	0.069	0.7039)	0.7037 ± 0.0002	(3)
		65AR866	TR	55	911	0.061	0.7037)		(3)

1/ The age designations for the Precambrian rocks are informal: LA (late Archean), EP (early Proterozoic), and LP (late Proterozoic). Age designations for the Phanerozoic rocks are: EC (early Cambrian), T (Triassic); LJ (late Jurassic), and EK and LK (early and late Cretaceous, respectively).

2/ Sample numbers are given for new data reported here. The numbers in brackets refer to the number of data points taken from the literature to calculate the mean Rb/Sr ratio. In some cases, more samples than indicated are represented by the published isochrons but rocks other than tonalites and trondhjemites are included.

3/ Rock types: TO = tonalite, TR = trondhjemite, GD = granodiorite, AM = amphibolite, QM = quartz monzonite.

4/ Uncertainties are at 2-sigma.

5/ References: (1) Hanson and others (1971), (2) Hawkesworth and others (1975), (3) This paper, (4) Arth and others (1978), (5) Van Breeman and others (1975), (6) Barker and others (1969), (7) Barker and others (1976), (8) Barker and others (1974), (9) Hansen and Peterman (1968), (10) Peterman and Barker (1976), (11) Kistler and Peterman (1973).

standard Sr reagant. Replicate determinations of $^{87}Sr/^{86}Sr$ in this laboratory during the period when the rocks were analyzed indicated a precision of approximately 0.03 percent (2σ). The age correction is nominal for young rocks, and the analytical precision of the measurements is an appropriate statistic to apply to the initial Sr ratios. Data for rocks from the Trinity Alps are an example as the variance in initial values for the different rock types is well within the predicted analytical uncertainty. The uncertainties in initial $^{87}Sr/^{86}Sr$ for the older rocks are determined from isochron systematics. The radiometric ages of the units have been recalculated using the recommended constants summarized by Steiger and Jager (1977). Most of the Rb and Sr data were obtained by isotope dilution techniques, but data for samples from the Wind River Range, Alaska Range, Trinity Alps, and Idaho, were determined by XRF with 2-sigma uncertainties of ± 3 percent for Rb/Sr ratios and ± 10 percent for Rb and Sr concentrations (Doering, 1968). This increased variance in Rb/Sr ratios over that of the isotope dilution ratios has negligible effect on the precision of the initial $^{87}Sr/^{86}Sr$ ratios.

RESULTS

Mantle Evolution

A plot of initial $^{87}Sr/^{86}Sr$ against age of the rocks produces a remarkably simple pattern (Fig. 1). A regression of the data, omitting both the meteorite and present-day value, results in a line that intersects the Sr-isotope axis at

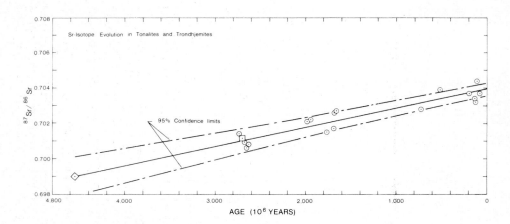

Figure 1.--$^{87}Sr/^{86}Sr$ in tonalitic and trondhjemitic rocks. The solid line is a regression fit with a zero age intercept of $0.7039_1 \pm 0.0003_8$ and a slope of -1.076 ± 0.231 ($\times 10^{-6}$); both uncertainties are at the 95-percent confidence level based upon inclusion of the scatter of data. The clinopyroxene point is from Hart and Brooks (1977) and BABI is from Papanastassiou and Wasserburg (1969).

$0.7039_1 \pm 0.0003_8$ (2σ) and the 4,550 m.y. time line at 0.6990. The latter has a large uncertainty of 0.0011 (2σ) because of the long extrapolation. The regression was made using 2σ blanket errors of ± 0.05 percent for $^{87}Sr/^{86}Sr$ and ± 5 percent for the ages. The former is approximately a median of the errors for the individual points (Table 1).

The intercept at 0.7039 ± 0.0004 is indistinguishable from the average value of 0.7037 ± 0.0002 calculated by Hart and Brooks (1977) for modern oceanic island and arc basalts, and the lower value at 4,550 m.y. is essentially the same as BABI (Papanastassiou and Wasserburg, 1969). The average $^{87}Sr/^{86}Sr$ ratio of 0.7011_4 for 2,700 m.y.-old clinopyroxenes (Hart and Brooks, 1977) is close to the regression line which has a value of 0.7010 at 2,700 m.y. ago.

The scatter of data points about the regression, although exceeding the assigned errors, is small and substantially less than variations in $^{87}Sr/^{86}Sr$ for modern mantle-derived basalts from the oceanic domain. This feature is illustrated in Figure 2 where the differences between observed values and values obtained from the regression at the same time point are plotted. The ranges for oceanic-island basalts, ocean-ridge basalts, and arc basalts are shown for comparison. The variations in $^{87}Sr/^{86}Sr$ for the tonalites and trondhjemites over 2,700 m.y. are about one-third that of oceanic island and ocean-ridge basalts but are approximately the same as the variations for island arc rocks. These data show that the source region for tonalitic and trondhjemitic rocks has been relatively uniform in Rb/Sr ratios throughout geologic time. Sr-isotope ratios can be contained within two bounding growth curves emanating from BABI and intersecting the Y-axis at 0.7030 and 0.7050 with corresponding Rb/Sr ratios of 0.021 and 0.031, respectively.

Two contemporary Sr-isotope evolution models for the mantle are compared with the curve defined by tonalitic rocks in Figure 3. There is little difference in the main trend of the evolution line of Hart and Brooks (1977) and the line defined by tonalites and trondhjemites. The evolution trend proposed by Hurst (1978) differs significantly from both. Hurst (1978) places great emphasis on initial Sr-isotope ratios of the ancient gneisses of Greenland and Labrador and argues that these are primary mantle values. As noted by Moorbath (1975) for the Greenland gneisses, only a relatively short period of geologic time (50 to 100 m.y.) would be required for a pre-metamorphic crustal residence time of the precursors to explain the slightly elevated initial $^{87}Sr/^{86}Sr$ ratios.

In developing a multistage evolution model for Sr in the mantle, Hart and Brooks (1977) suggested that the major Rb/Sr and U/Pb variations that have caused the respective Sr- and Pb-isotope variations in young mantle-derived basalts formed at 1.7 $\pm$ 0.2 b.y. ago, and Sun and Hanson (1975) estimate broader limits (2.0 $\pm$ 1.0 b.y.) for the development of these heterogeneities. Tatsumoto (1978) questions a single mantle event and suggests an early stage of differentiation concurrent with the development of a protocrust. The original compositional stratification was disrupted and rearranged into domains by convection with modern basalts being derived from these early-formed domains as well as subsequent mixtures. In this model, Tatsumoto (1978) suggests that the Sr and Pb isochrons are merely average values with no specific time significance. The model of Hart and Brooks (1977) would be consistent with the limited Sr-isotope variation for trondhjemites and tonalites in the Archean and Early Proterozoic, but the younger rocks exhibit no more scatter in $^{87}Sr/^{86}Sr$ than the older ones.

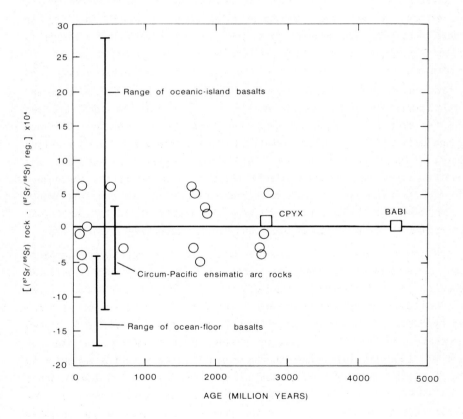

Figure 2.--Deviations of $^{87}Sr/^{86}Sr$ for tonalites and trondhjemites from regression line of Figure 1. Ranges of modern oceanic basalts (Hofmann and Hart, 1978) and circum-Pacific island arc rocks (Hart and Brooks, 1977; Hedge and Peterman, 1974; and Peterman and Heming, 1974) are shown for comparison independently of the time axis.

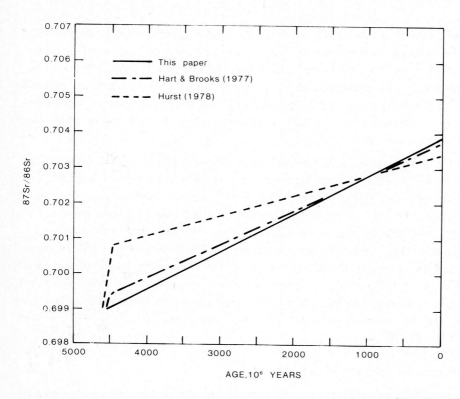

Figure 3.--Three contemporary models for the evolution of $^{87}Sr/^{86}Sr$ in the earth's mantle. The secondary trends for young basalts are omitted from the model of Hart and Brooks (1977).

The isotopic variations in Sr among ocean-ridge and oceanic-island basalts and the ensuing systematics and time connotations, whether discrete events or time-integrated averages, are unquestionably real. At the same time, the data reported here characterize the mantle source for tonalites and trondhjemites over 2,600 m.y. of earth history. The differences between these two groups of data must be rationalized in a geologic sense. The agreement between the Sr-isotope data for island-arc rocks and the tonalites and trondhjemites is impressive and may provide the key to understanding these discrepancies. The same basic premise applies in interpreting the Sr-isotope data for arc rocks as for the tonalites and trondhjemites. The former are variously interpreted as either direct mantle derivatives or the result of multiple-stage processes. Whichever is correct, the arc rocks are derived from a source that is amazingly uniform in $^{87}Sr/^{86}Sr$ just as are the tonalites and trondhjemites (and many of the oceanic-island basalts for that matter). In explaining some of the higher $^{87}Sr/^{86}Sr$ values of oceanic-island basalts, Hedge (1978) concludes that these are the product of two-stage development in the mantle. This is consistent with the observed correlation in composition as reflected in Na_2O/K_2O, Rb/Sr, and initial $^{87}Sr/^{86}Sr$ ratios for oceanic-island basalts. Either the tonalites, trondhjemites, and arc rocks have not had access to these pods of enriched mantle or the tectonomagmatic process controlling the generation of these rocks effectively rehomogenizes isotopic and compositional differences that were established in the past.

Hanson (1978) emphasizes the volume relations between parent material and extracted magma of silicic composition. His example deals with a granitic body occupying 125 km^3 that, if generated by 20 percent partial melting, would require a parent volume of 625 km^3. This is an important consideration in assessing the possibility of homogenizing isotopic and chemical variations in the source. The tonalites and trondhjemites considered here are siliceous rocks and an extremely large volume of mantle peridotite per unit volume of tonalite or trondhjemite would be required regardless of the number of intermediate stages involved. Thus, the large parent/daughter ratio offers the possibility of integrating isotopic variations that are reflected in the oceanic basalt data.

Implications for Partial Melting

Hedge (1966) emphasized the coherence of Rb and Sr through a wide range of ultramafic to intermediate rock compositions and cautioned against using initial $^{87}Sr/^{86}Sr$ as unique indicators of magma genesis. In many studies, comparisons are made between mantle-like Sr-isotope ratios and those that would evolve along growth curves controlled by upper crustal Rb/Sr ratios that are about an order of magnitude higher than mantle values. Consideration of the intermediate-composition rocks with low Rb/Sr ratios is commonly neglected. The data reported here (Table 1) further emphasize the problem.

Figure 4 shows the incremental growth rate of $^{87}Sr/^{86}Sr$ per units of 100 m.y. as a function of Rb/Sr ratios. The average Rb/Sr ratios for the rocks in Table 1 are plotted on the line with mantle and upper crustal ranges in Rb/Sr incorporated for comparison. The range in Rb/Sr ratios of the tonalites and trondhjemites is approximately an order of magnitude extending from mantle-like values to upper crustal values. The median Rb/Sr ratio is 0.075 which corresponds to a rate of $^{87}Sr/^{86}Sr$ growth of 0.00031 per 100 m.y. At the low extreme in Rb/Sr, some tonalites and trondhjemites of Precambrian age have present-day $^{87}Sr/^{86}Sr$ ratios that are within the range of values for modern oceanic basalts.

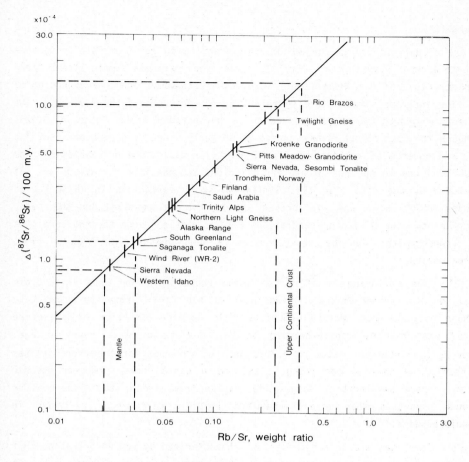

Figure 4.--Growth rate of $^{87}Sr/^{86}Sr$ (per 100 m.y.) as a function of Rb/Sr ratios. (This is a 100 m.y. isochron on a log-log plot.) The mean Rb/Sr ratios of the tonalites and trondhjemites (Table 1) are shown on the isochron. The median of these values is 0.075.

The implications are clear with regard to the petrogenesis of granitic rocks that have mantle or near-mantle values of $^{87}Sr/^{86}Sr$. In an evolving crust or one that is subjected to later periods of orogenesis, granites with low $^{87}Sr/^{86}Sr$ ratios could be derived through partial melting of earlier-formed crust dominated by rocks of tonalitic and trondhjemitic composition. For example, a 3.0 b.y.-old crust formed with a mantle $^{87}Sr/^{86}Sr$ value of 0.7007 with a mean Rb/Sr ratio of 0.075 would generate a Sr-isotope ratio of 0.7016 in 300 m.y. Thus, a granite derived from this terrane at 2,700 m.y. age could have a relatively low initial Sr ratio in spite of the fact that it was derived from significantly older crustal rocks.

CONCLUSIONS

(1)   Tonalitic and trondhjemitic rocks ranging in age from Late Cretaceous to Late Archean have initial $^{87}Sr/^{86}Sr$ ratios that define a simple linear trend between values of 0.7039 (present) to 0.7010 (2,650 m.y. ago); an extension of the line intersects the $^{87}Sr/^{86}Sr$ value for meteorites at 4,550 m.y. ago.   The Sr-isotope growth curve is defined by a present-day Rb/Sr ratio of 0.025. Although the data do not show evidence of an early stage of growth of $^{87}Sr/^{86}Sr$ as a consequence of a substantially higher Rb/Sr ratio, the extrapolation from 2,700 m.y. ago to the age of the earth is long and possible variations are not precluded by the data (Fig. 1). Similarly, small variations in Rb/Sr ratios between 2,700 m.y. ago and present would not be resolved by the data. Nevertheless, the Sr-isotope variations in the mantle source for the tonalites and trondhjemites can be described as a near-linear growth as a first approximation.

(2)   The variation in $^{87}Sr/^{86}Sr$ among Phanerozoic and Late Proterozoic tonalites and trondhjemites is the same as for Early Proterozoic and Late Archean rocks.   This feature contrasts with the wide variation in Sr-isotope ratios exhibited by mantle-derived oceanic basalts of late Cenozoic age. However, the intercept value of 0.7039 and the variance for the trondhjemites is nearly the same as for young island-arc volcanic rocks formed on oceanic crust.   These similarities suggest derivation from similar mantle sources or through processes that have homogenized isotopic differences reflected in oceanic basalts.

(3)   Tonalites and trondhjemites are characterized by low Rb/Sr ratios that range between mantle-like and upper crustal values. A median Rb/Sr value of 0.075 characterizes the asymmetric distribution of ratios.   These data show that granitic rocks (sensu stricto) could be derived through anatexis of tonalitic and trondhjemitic rocks with geologically significant crustal residence times; the granites would not necessarily have unusually high $^{87}Sr/^{86}Sr$ ratios.

ACKNOWLEDGMENTS

Samples were kindly provided by R. G. Coleman, W. Hamilton, M. A. Lanphere, and P. Lipman.   The rock samples were prepared by G. Cebula and J. Groen.   The chemical work was done by the late W. T. Henderson.   R. A. Hildreth completed the mass spectrometric analyses.   J. G. Arth, C. E. Hedge, and S. S. Goldich reviewed the manuscript and offered many valuable suggestions. The assistance of all these people is gratefully acknowledged.

REFERENCES

Arth, J. G., Barker, F., Peterman, Z. E. and Friedman, I., 1978. Geochemistry of the gabbro-diorite-tonalite-trondhjemite suite of southwest Finland and its implications for the origin of tonalitic and trondhjemitic magmas. J. Pet., in press.

Barker, F., Peterman, Z. E. and Hildreth, R. A., 1969. A rubidium-strontium study of the Twilight Gneiss, west Needle Mountains, Colorado. Contrib. Miner. Pet., 23: 271-282.

Barker, F., Arth, J. G., Peterman, Z. E. and Friedman, I., 1976. The 1.7- to 1.8-b.y.-old trondhjemites of southwestern Colorado and northern New Mexico: Geochemistry and depths of genesis. Geol. Soc. Am. Bull., 87: 189-198.

Barker, F., Peterman, Z. E., Henderson, W. T. and Hildreth, R. A., 1974. Rubidium-strontium dating of the trondhjemite of Rio Brazos, New Mexico, and of the Kroenke Granodiorite, Colorado. U.S. Geol. Surv. J. Res., 2: 705-709.

Doering, W. P., 1968. A rapid method for measuring the Rb/Sr ratio in silicate rocks. U.S. Geol. Surv. Prof. Pap., 600-C: C164-C168.

Faure, G. and Hurley, P. M., 1963. The isotopic composition of strontium in oceanic and continental basalts: application to the origin of igneous rocks. J. Pet., 4: 31-50.

Faure, G. and Powell, J. L., 1972. Strontium isotope geology. Springer-Verlag, N.Y., 188 pp.

Gast, P. W., 1960. Limitations on the composition of the upper mantle. J. Geophys. Res., 65: 1287-1297.

Gast, P. W., Tilton, G. R. and Hedge, C. E., 1964. Isotopic composition of lead and strontium from Ascension and Gough Islands. Science, 145: 1181-1185.

Hamilton, W., 1962. Trondhjemite in the Riggons quadrangle, western Idaho. U.S. Geol. Surv. Prof. Pap., 450-E: E98-E102.

Hansen, W. R. and Peterman, Z. E., 1968. Basement-rock geochronology of the Black Canyon of the Gunnison, Colorado. U.S. Geol. Surv. Prof. Pap., 600-C: C80-C90.

Hanson, G. N., 1978. The application of trace elements to the petrogenesis of igneous rocks of granitic composition. Earth Planet. Sci. Lett., 38: 26-43.

Hanson, G. N., Goldich, S. S., Arth, J. G. and Yardley, D. H., 1971. Age of the early Precambrian rocks of the Saganaga Lake-Northern Light Lake area, Ontario-Minnesota. Can. J. Earth Sci., 8: 1110-1124.

Hart, S. R. and Brooks, C., 1977. The geochemistry and evolution of early Precambrian mantle. Contrib. Miner. Pet., 61: 109-128.

Hawkesworth, C. J., Moorbath, S., O'Nions, R. K. and Wilson, J. F., 1975. Age relationships between greenstone belts and "granites" in the Rhodesian Archaean craton. Earth Planet. Sci. Lett., 25: 251-262.

Hedge, C. E., 1966. Variations in radiogenic strontium found in volcanic rocks. J. Geophys. Res., 71: 6119-6126.

Hedge, C. E., 1978. Strontium isotopes in basalts from the Pacific Ocean Basin. Earth Planet. Sci. Lett., 38: 88-94.

Hedge, C. E. and Peterman, Z. E., 1974. Strontium: 38-B isotopes in nature. In: Handbook of Geochemistry. Springer-Verlag, N.Y., II/4: 38B-1 to 38B-14.

Hedge, C. E. and Walthall, F. G., 1963. Radiogenic strontium-87 as an index of geologic processes. Science, 140: 1214-1217.

Hofmann, A. W. and Hart, S. R., 1978. An assessment of local and regional isotopic equilibrium in the mantle. Earth Planet. Sci. Lett., 38: 44-62.

Hotz, P. E., 1971. Plutonic rocks of the Klamath Mountains, California and Oregon. U.S. Geol. Surv. Prof. Pap., 684-B: B1-B20.

Hurley, P. M., Hughes, H., Faure, G., Fairbairn, H. W. and Pinson, W. H., 1962. Radiogenic strontium-87 model of continent formation. J. Geophys. Res., 67: 5315-5333.

Hurst, R. W., 1978. Sr evolution in the west Greenland-Labrador craton: a model for early Rb depletion in the mantle. Geochim. Cosmochim. Acta, 42: 39-44.

Kagami,H., Shuto, K. and Gorai, M., 1976. A consideration on the relation between rock types of acid igneous rocks and their initial Sr isotopic ratios. J. Geol. Soc. Jap., 82: 655-660.

Kistler, R. W. and Peterman, Z. E., 1973. Variations in Sr, Rb, K, Na, and initial $^{87}Sr/^{86}Sr$ in Mesozoic granitic rocks and intruded wall rocks in central California. Geol. Soc. Am. Bull., 84: 3489-3512.

Lamphere, M. A., Irwin, W. P. and Hotz, P. E., 1968. Isotopic age of the Nevadan orogeny and older plutonic and metamorphic events in the Klamath Mountains, California. Geol. Soc. Am. Bull., 79: 1027-1052.

Lipman, P. W., 1963. Gibson Peak pluton--a discordant composite intrusion in the southeastern Trinity Alps, northern California. Geol. Soc. Am. Bull., 74: 1259-1280.

Moorbath, S., 1975. Evolution of Precambrian crust from strontium isotopic evidence. Nature, 254: 395-398.

Papanastassiou, D. A. and Wasserburg, G. J., 1969. Initial strontium isotopic abundances and the resolution of small time differences in the formation of planetary objects. Earth Planet. Sci. Lett., 5: 361-376.

Peterman, Z. E. and Barker, F., 1976. Rb-Sr whole-rock age of trondhjemites and related rocks of the southwestern Trondheim region, Norway. U.S. Geol. Surv. Open-File Rept., 76-670: 17 pp.

Peterman, Z. E. and Hedge, C. E., 1971. Related strontium isotopic and chemical variations in oceanic basalts. Geol. Soc. Am. Bull., 82: 493-500.

Peterman, Z. E. and Heming, R. F., 1974. $^{87}Sr/^{86}Sr$ ratios in calc-alkali lavas from the Rabaul Caldera, Papua New Guinea. Geol. Soc. Am. Bull., 85: 1265-1268.

Reed, B. L. and Lanphere, M. A., 1969. Age and chemistry of Mesozoic and Tertiary plutonic rocks in south-central Alaska. Geol. Soc. Am. Bull., 80: 23-44.

Steiger, R. H. and Jager, E., 1977. Subcommission on geochronology: convention and use of decay constants in geo- and cosmochronology. Earth Planet. Sci. Lett., 35: 359-362.

Subbarao, K. V. and Hedge, C. E., 1973. K, Rb, Sr, and $^{87}Sr/^{86}Sr$ in rocks from the mid-Indian oceanic ridge. Earth Planet. Sci. Lett., 18: 223-228.

Sun, S. S. and Hanson, G. N., 1975. Evolution of the mantle: geochemical evidence from alkali basalt. Geology, 3: 297-302.

Tatsumoto, M., 1978. Isotopic composition of lead in oceanic basalt and its implication to mantle evolution. Earth Planet. Sci. Lett., 38: 63-87.

Van Breeman, O., Aftalion, M. and Allaart, J. H., 1974. Isotopic and geochronologic studies on granites from the Ketilidian mobile belt of South Greenland. Geol. Soc. Am. Bull., 85: 403-412.

Chapter 5

OCEANIC PLAGIOGRANITE REVISITED

R. G. Coleman and M. M. Donato

ABSTRACT

Leucocratic rocks called plagiogranites are found in the upper parts of gabbros and in sheeted complexes of ophiolites, and represent small localized differentiates of subalkaline tholeiitic basalt. These rocks are composed of quartz and plagioclase, with accessory ferromagnesian minerals. Low-temperature hydrothermal alteration is evidenced by secondary minerals including epidote, chlorite, and actinolite.

Plagiogranites are characterized by unique low K_2O contents; Na_2O and CaO values are higher, and total iron contents are lower than most granites and rhyolites of continental affinities. Plagiogranites can be distinguished from continental leucocratic rocks by these and other chemical characteristics, including K/Rb, Rb/Sr, and rare-earth element values.

Normal compositional zoning of plagioclase and compositions of granophyric intergrowths indicate that these rocks are the product of igneous processes. Their low K_2O character is not solely the result of post-crystallization hydrothermal alteration. However, strontium and oxygen isotope data show that interaction with seawater or meteoric water has taken place at some stage during the formation of plagiogranite.

INTRODUCTION

The presence of leucocratic rocks within the upper parts of cumulate gabbros and as dikes in the sheeted complexes of ophiolite suites has been reported by numerous authors (Dubertret, 1955; Wilson, 1959; Bear, 1960; Brunn, 1960; Thayer and Himmelberg, 1968; Reinhardt, 1969; Bailey et al., 1970; Coleman, 1971; Alavi-Tehrani, 1976; Beccaluva et al., 1977). It is now generally agreed that these leucocratic rocks, called plagiogranite (Coleman and Peterman, 1975), represent small localized differentiates of sub-alkaline tholeiitic basalt.

Plagiogranite is restricted to allochthonous ophiolites and never invades the juxtaposed autochthonous rocks. In many cases, the plagiogranite interdigitates with the underlying cumulate gabbro or the overlying diabase (Wilson, 1959). Only rarely does the plagiogranite intrude downward into the underlying peridotite of the ophiolite sequence, but tectonic blocks of plagio-granite are commonly found in the serpentinized peridotite. In this situation, plagio-granite becomes desilicated and forms albitite (Iwao, 1953; Coleman, 1961). Detailed mapping of ophiolite complexes shows that the volume of plagiogranite within the gabbroic parts of the ophiolite is generally less than 5 percent.

Ophiolites are generally considered to represent fragments of oceanic crust formed by submarine volcanic processes at midocean spreading ridges, marginal basins, or within island arcs (Coleman, 1977). The close spatial relation of plagiogranite to the gabbroic parts of ophiolites and their compositional gradation from tonalite through trondhjemite to albite granite are evidence for a common parent. Thus the presence of cogenetic leucocratic rocks within the upper parts of basaltic constructional piles of oceanic crust suggests that some differentiation of the basalt has taken place. Current intensive study of modern oceanic crust by dredging and drilling has revealed only a few specimens considered to be true leucocratic differentiates (Aumento, 1969). Nonetheless, careful studies in the FAMOUS area by Bryan and Moore (1977) have documented evidence for differentiation at the present day Mid-Atlantic Ridge. The rarity of plagiogranites recovered in dredge hauls or drilling parallels their paucity in ophiolites and their nominal occurrence under several kilometers of pillow lava and sheeted dikes.

Even though oceanic plagiogranite is not volumetrically important, it provides an important contrast to continental trondhjemite and tonalite. Plagiogranite formed by shallow differentiation of basaltic magma within oceanic crust is chemically and mineralogically distinct from the trondhjemite developed under thick Precambrian continental crust by partial melting or fractional crystallization. The distinction between oceanic plagiogranite and trondhjemite-tonalite formed within Phanerozoic orogenic belts is less clear.

KERATOPHYRE AND PLAGIOGRANITE

The problem of keratophyre and its possible relationship to plagiogranite must be addressed in any discussion of leucocratic rocks in ophiolite sequences. One interpretation of keratophyre (that is, a fine-grained rock composed essentially of sodic plagioclase and quartz), is that its high-Na, low-K character is the result of low-temperature hydrothermal alteration of intermediate to siliceous lava, involving interaction with seawater (Amstutz, 1974). Keratophyre occurs as small intrusive plugs or parallel dikes interspersed with basalt in the sheeted complexes of ophiolites (e.g. Oman). In many such cases, intrusive relations with the surrounding mafic rocks are unclear. However, there is textural and field evidence to suggest that the "keratophyres" are indeed magmatic, not metasomatic products, and may be thought of as the volcanic equivalents of plagiogranite.

In some ophiolites, siliceous flows and dikes of "keratophyres" composition within the upper parts of some ophiolite constructional piles may actually predominate over basaltic rocks (Bailey and Blake, 1974; Evarts, 1978. Evidently, such substantial volumes of rock cannot be accounted for solely by simple differentiation; indeed, such keratophyres are difficult to explain in terms of a mid-ocean spreading ridge ophiolite model. In such cases, great care must be taken to establish accurate field relations and to recognize ophiolites of island-arc or marginal-basin affinities. The age of the siliceous volcanic rocks with respect to the mafic-ultramafic part of the ophiolite is critical, since most ophiolites have complex and varied histories and structural settings. As with many geologic problems, semantics plays a large part; no doubt there are "keratophyres and keratophyres."

NOMENCLATURE

Available modal analyses of plagiogranites fall along the quartz-plagioclase join of a Q-A-P diagram (fig. 1). Staining of plagiogranite slabs from numerous localities has revealed only trace amounts of interstitial potassium feldspar. According to the IUGS classification of plutonic rocks (Streckeisen, 1973), leucocratic rocks with these modal abundances of quartz and plagioclase are called tonalite (ferromagnesian minerals less than 10%). When the plagioase composition is An_{10} or less, these rocks are called albite granites.

Coleman and Peterman (1975) have suggested that "oceanic plagiogranite" be employed as a general descriptive and collective term, since the leucocratic rocks from ophiolites encompass a large spectrum of plagioclase-quartz ratios. Use of this name avoids confusion with rocks called tonalite, trondhjemite, diorite, and albite granite, all of which were originally described from continental igneous complexes, and whose origins are distinct from that conceived for ophiolites. We suggest continental trondhjemite as a general all-inclusive term for those leucocratic hypabyssal rocks that have formed either at the margins of or in the interior of the continents.

PETROGRAPHY

Plagiogranites from ophiolite sequences are medium- to fine-grained hypidiomorphic-granular rocks consisting predominantly of quartz and zoned plagioclase (An_{10-60}). In contrast to granophyres found in the differentiated parts of continental mafic intrusions, plagiogranites contain little or no potassium feldspar. Ferromagnesian minerals, primarily hornblende or pyroxene, are

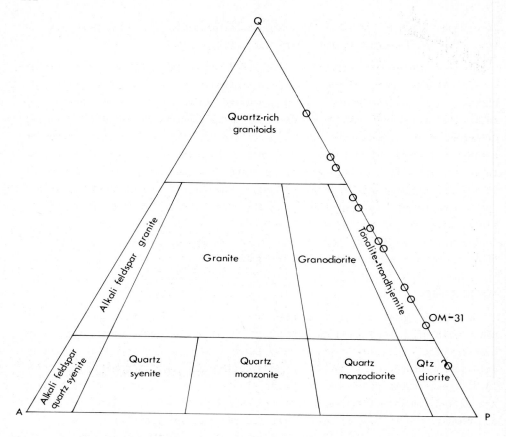

Figure 1.--Modal analyses of plagiogranites from Cyprus and Oman, after Coleman and Peterman (1975). Rock classification after Streckeisen (1973).

present in only minor amounts (less than 10%). Commonly these minerals are altered to chlorite, hence their primary compositions are difficult to establish. Although these rocks are low in iron, magnetite-ilmenite intergrowths are present as accessory minerals. Zircon is also a common accessory mineral, particularly in the quartz-rich (greater than 68% SiO_2) plagiogranites, and has provided important new U-Pb ages for ophiolite complexes (Mattinson, 1975).

Characteristically, rocks from ophiolite assemblages have undergone widespread hydrothermal metamorphism (Gass and Smewing, 1973; Spooner and Fyfe, 1973). Nearly all of the plagiogranites studied in this investigation showed some effects of this metamorphism, and contain secondary epidote, chlorite, actinolite, and albite. Metasomatism may accompany this metamorphism, and locally within the plagiogranite, the original minerals and bulk composition may have been altered. Even though metamorphism and recrystallization are common in these leucocratic rocks, the modal consistency and preservation of igneous textures indicate that these are primary igneous rocks rather than products of metasomatism. Lack of metamorphic fabric demonstrates that the metamorphism was a static hydrothermal event.

INTERGROWTHS

A typical textural feature of plagiogranite is an intimate intergrowth of plagioclase and quartz in the mesostasis. The term "myrmekite" is considered inappropriate here because most previously described myrmekites are associated with potassium feldspar, and we believe that the vermicular and graphic textures in plagiogranites have a different origin.

Three varieties of quartz-plagioclase intergrowths have been observed in plagiogranite. All three may occur in the same rock, but the latter two predominate.

1. Vermicular intergrowths in which quartz appears to embay or invade the plagioclase grain.

2. Vermicular intergrowths in which worm-like blebs of plagioclase and quartz make up much of the mesostasis between euhedral to subhedral plagioclase grains (fig. 2a). The plagioclase blebs are often visibly attached to and continuous with the rim of the adjacent euhedral grain, suggesting crystallographic continuity throughout growth. Quartz blebs are optically continuous with one another, and form discrete "domains" up to 1.5 mm in diameter. Quartz and feldspar appear to have crystallized simultaneously. This form of intergrowth is similar to Barker's (1970) "granophyres."

3. Graphic intergrowths of quartz and plagioclase in which the plagioclase host contains quartz grains having triangular or semi-regular boundaries (fig. 2b). These textures also suggest simultaneous crystallization of quartz and feldspar and may be thought of as small-scale sodic analogues of "graphic granite" (Barker, 1970).

The plagioclase-quartz intergrowths in the mesostasis of many plagiogranites provide textural and chemical evidence for the igneous origin of these rocks. As mentioned above, the intergrowths strongly resemble so-called "graphic" and "granophyric" textures generally held to be products of simultaneous growth of quartz and feldspar from a fluid (Barker, 1970). Intimate intergrowths of sodic plagioclase and quartz are not as common as potassium-feldspar-quartz intergrowths, but are reported from graphic pegmatites (Černy, 1971). It is reasonable to assume that igneous processes similar to those

Figure 2.--Photomicrographs of two types of quartz-plagioclase intergrowths in a plagiogranite from Oman (sample Om-31). Plagioclase is light; quartz is dark. (a) Irregular blebs of sodic feldspar are optically continuous with euhedral normally zoned plagioclase. (b) Graphic intergrowths of quartz and plagioclase grains and semi-regular boundaries.

called upon for the origin of potassic granophyre (simultaneous late-stage growth of quartz and plagioclase from a fluid) occur in the crystallization of plagiogranites. In the case of plagiogranites, however, there is simply insufficient K_2O in the melt to produce potassium feldspar

The compositions and modal percentages of feldspars in an unaltered plagiogranite from the Semail Ophiolite, Oman, also indicate an igneous history. Electron microprobe analyses of plagioclase phenocrysts and vermicular blebs in intergrowths are summarized in table I and figure 3.

Strong compositional zoning of plagioclase phenocrysts, evident in thin section, is confirmed by the microprobe analyses. A systematic decrease in CaO from core to rim is complemented by an increase in Na_2O and, significantly, K_2O in rims and blebs of feldspar in the mesostasis. Rim and bleb feldspar compositions are similar to those reported for sodic graphic pegmatites (Černý, 1971). Such compositional trends must reflect crystal-fluid interaction during the late stages of crystallization and cannot be accounted for by simple post crystallization hydrothermal alteration. Note that much of the K_2O rock

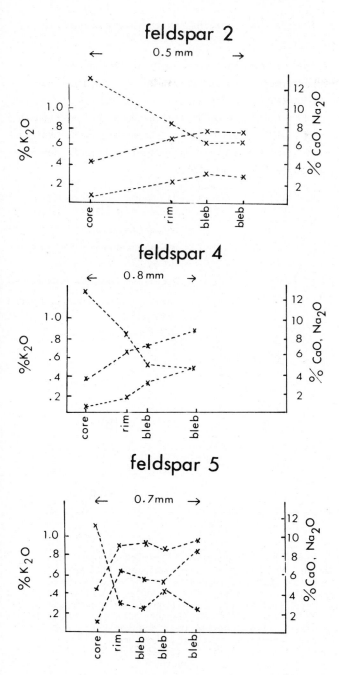

Figure 3.--K$_2$O, CaO, and Na$_2$O values for zoned feldspar grains and adjoining vermicular blebs in a plagiogranite from the Semail Ophiolite, Oman (sample OM-31). Electron microprobe determinations by Lewis Calk, USGS.

appears to be present in the feldspar intergrowths, which in some cases make up 30 to 40 percent of the rock.

The bulk compositions of the intergrowths also imply an igneous origin for these rocks. Modal analyses performed on photomicrographs of intergrowths provide an estimate of weight percentages of plagioclase and quartz in the mesostasis. This information, combined with compositional data on the intergrowth feldspars, yields an approximate bulk composition for the intergrowths that is well within the range expected for extremely differentiated liquids derived from an initially low-K magma (table I and fig. 4b).

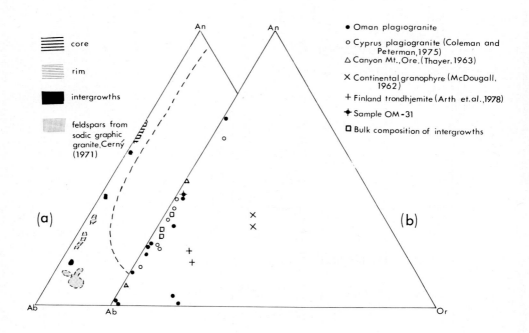

Figure 4.--Feldspar compositions (a) and normative whole-rock compositions (b) in the system An, Ab, Or. (a) Core, rim, and intergrowth plagioclase compositions for plagiogranite OM-31, as determined by microprobe analysis. Feldspars from Černý's (1971) sodic graphic pegmatite are similar to, but slightly more potassic than intergrowth feldspars. (b) Whole-rock compositions of selected plagiogranites. Two potassic Oman samples contain K-feldspar, but field relations suggest they may be later intrusive rocks unrelated to ophiolite formation. Also shown are continental trondhjemites, granophyres, and OM-31 intergrowth bulk compositions.

TABLE I.--Compositions of feldspars in quartz-plagioclase intergrowths,
estimated intergrowth bulk compositions, and host rock bulk composition
for a plagiogranite from the Semail Ophiolite, Oman.

	Feldspar 3 (Qz 49%, Plag 51%) "graphic" type	Feldspar 4 (Qz 52%, Plag 48%) "Vermicular type"	Intergrowth bulk compositions[1]		Host rock bulk composition[2]
	Average of 4 points	Average of 2 points	Feldspar 3	Feldspar 4	(OM-31)
SiO_2	60.9[3]	61.7	80.1	81.6	64.0
Al_2O_3	24.7	23.4	12.6	11.3	15.1
CaO	6.5	5.0	3.3	2.4	5.5
Na_2O	7.7	8.0	3.9	3.8	3.9
K_2O	0.30	0.40	0.15	0.19	0.18
An	31.0	25.0			
Or	2.0	2.0			
Ab	67.0	73.0			

[1] Estimated from modal analyses of intergrowths.

[2] Determined by XRF rapid rock analysis, H. Smith, U.S.G.S. analyst.

[3] Electron microprobe analyses by Lewis Calk, U.S.G.S.

CHEMISTRY

Major elements

The bulk chemical composition of plagiogranite is similar in many ways to
that of granite or rhyolite. There are, however, important chemical distinc-
tions. K_2O in plagiogranite is usually less than one percent whereas granite
and rhyolite generally contain three percent or more K_2O. Also, plagiogranite
generally has greater Na_2O, CaO, and lower total iron contents than normal
granite and rhyolite. Al_2O_3 decreases slightly with increasing SiO_2 content,
reflecting the change in the An content of the plagioclase toward albite in the
cases of extreme differentiation. Major- and trace-element compositions of
some selected plagiogranites appear in table II.

The extremely low potassium content of oceanic plagiogranite, perhaps its
most distinctive chemical characteristic, allows us to distinguish this rock
type from continental granophyres. A semilog plot of SiO_2 versus K_2O (fig. 5)
illustrates that the average oceanic plagiogranite contains less potassium than
average continental basalt and more than ten times less than continental
granophyres.

TABLE II.--Major and trace element contents of selected plagiogranites
(N.D.: not detected; --: not analyzed.)

	OM-31	OM-32	100-D	Cy-55C	Cy-52	Cy-55A	Bcm-3	UK-12	Red Sea
SiO_2	64.0	73.0	70.7	69.4	65.4	65.2	74.9	72.39	67.6
Al_2O_3	15.1	13.4	14.1	14.0	14.5	13.5	13.0	15.51	13.0
Fe_2O_3	3.2	2.8	5.6	3.2	3.4	3.5	1.3	0.22	4.2
FeO	4.2	0.92	--	2.9	2.4	4.1	2.0	1.39	2.7
MgO	3.2	1.0	0.40	0.54	1.7	2.6	0.24	0.63	0.64
CaO	5.5	3.0	4.7	4.6	7.6	2.6	1.5	2.11	2.6
Na_2O	3.9	5.3	3.7	3.8	2.0	2.4	2.9	5.00	4.3
K_2O	0.18	0.12	0.2	0.07	0.30	0.64	0.33	1.78	2.5
H_2O+	0.86	0.89	--	0.56	1.1	3.0	1.3	0.52	0.74
H_2O-	0.14	0.41	--	0.12	0.52	1.4	0.06	0.03	0.34
TiO_2	0.92	0.47	0.50	0.56	0.84	0.77	0.22	0.23	0.76
P_2O_5	0.12	0.12	--	0.15	0.10	0.11	0.06	0.06	0.22
MnO	0.13	0.02	0.08	0.06	0.04	0.06	0.10	0.02	0.17
CO_2	0.02	0.03	--	0.05	0.05	0.05	0.05	0.04	.05
	101	101	100	100	100	100	100	100	99

Trace elements (ppm)

	OM-31	OM-32	100-D	Cy-55C	Cy-52	Cy-55A	Bcm-3	UK-12	Red Sea
Ni	18	9	0	15	10	10	--	3	--
Co	17	5	--	7	7	10	1.6	--	5
Cr	14	2	--	N.D.	N.D.	N.D.	2	40	1
Cu	4	3	--	--	--	1.5	--	--	9
Zn	19	7	--	--	--	--	--	--	--
La	3	4	3.9	--	--	--	3.1	--	34
Ce	9	12	11.1	--	--	--	9.2	14.7	100
Nd	--	--	10.7	--	--	--	--	4.68	60
Sm	2.8	3.8	4.3	--	--	--	2.4	0.727	13
Eu	0.9	1.1	1.2	--	--	--	0.9	0.489	3
Gd	--	--	6.9	--	--	--	--	0.755	--
Tb	0.7	1.0	--	--	--	--	0.8	--	2.5
Dy	--	--	9.1	--	--	--	4.97	0.300	--
Tm	--	--	--	--	--	--	--	--	--
Yb	3.5	4.9	5.9	5	5	5	3.2	0.171	16
Lu	0.5	0.8	0.85	--	--	--	0.61	0.0304	2

TABLE II: continued

	OM-31	OM-32	100-D	Cy-55C	Cy-52	Cy-55A	Bcm-3	UK-12	Red Sea
Zr	86.0	108.0	83.0	70.0	70.0	70.0	102.0	--	650.0
Hf	2.4	3.9	--	--	--	--	3.7	--	16.0
Th	1.2	0.4	--	--	--	--	0.37	3.5	8.0
U	0.28	0.19	--	--	--	--	--	3.9	--
Ba	95.0	64.0	42.0	20.0	2.0	10.0	--	209.0	430.0
Rb	5.0	5.0	2.0	1.0	3.5	3.4	1.8	65.9	85.0
Sr	107.0	114.0	95.0	135.0	148.0	114.0	78.0	387.0	145.0
$(^{87}Sr/^{86}Sr)_o$	--	--	--	0.7057	0.7053	0.7059	--	--	0.7048

EXPLANATION OF SAMPLE NUMBERS

OM-31   Plagiogranite from upper part of gabbro, Falaj Ali, Rustaq.
        Semail ophiolite, Oman.

OM-32   Plagiogranite from upper part of gabbro, Falaj Ali, Rustaq.
        Semail ophiolite, Oman.

100-D   Quartz diorite from unit H Troodos ophiolite, Cyprus (Kay and
        Senechal, 1976).

Cy-55C Plagiogranite, Kykko Monastery Road about 2 km east of Pedhoulas,
        Troodos ophiolite, Cyprus (Coleman and Peterman, 1975).

Cy-52   Plagiogranite, near village of Phini, Troodos ophiolite, Cyprus
        (Coleman and Peterman, 1975).

Cy-55A Plagiogranite, Kykko Monastery Road about 2 km east of Pedhoulas,
        Troodos ophiolite, Cyprus (Coleman and Peterman, 1975).

Bcm-3   Trondhjemite, Canyon Mountain ophiolite, Grant County, Oregon
        (unpublished data from F. Barker).

UK-12   Trondhjemite, Uusikaupunki-Kalanti Archean igneous terrane,
        southwest Finland, Arth and others (1978).

Red Sea Granophyre from Miocene Tihama Asir ophiolite near Jizan, Saudi
        Arabia (Coleman and others, 1978).

The distinctive chemical properties of plagiogranites are reflected in their normative mineral contents. Plagiogranites plot in the low-pressure one-feldspar field on the normative Or-An-Ab triangular diagram (fig. 4a). In contrast, granophyres formed by differentiation of continental basaltic magmas contain more than 20 percent normative orthoclase.

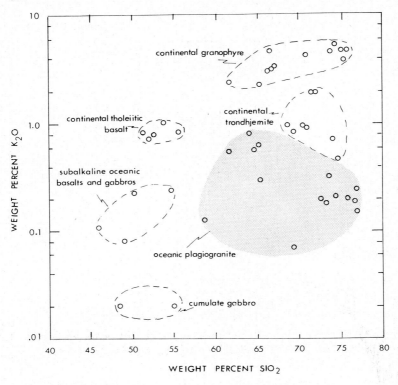

Figure 5.--Semilog plot of SiO₂ vs. K₂O, comparing oceanic plagiogranites with continental granophyres, trondhjemite, tholeiite, and subalkaline oceanic basalts and gabbros.

Differentiation trends that give rise to oceanic plagiogranites can be illustrated by the triangular AFM diagram (fig. 6). By using the average subalkaline oceanic basalt as the starting liquid, it can be shown that the ophiolite leucocratic rocks follow the tholeiitic differentiation trend rather than the calc-alkaline trend. Cumulate mafic and ultramafic rocks in ophiolites illustrate that mafic minerals separate from subalkaline basaltic magma which may eventually evolve into small amounts of a leucocratic residual differentiate. Continental granophyres also display a tholeiitic trend but contain more iron and K₂O than their oceanic counterparts.

Trace elements

Rubidium and strontium contents of plagiogranite can be used to discriminate it from other igneous rocks that have similar compositions and mineral assemblages. A Rb-Sr variation diagram (fig. 7) compares data for plagio-

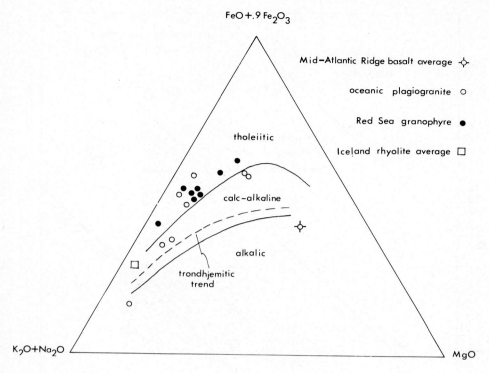

Figure 6.--AFM diagram comparing differentiation trend of plagiogranite
with other leucocratic rock types. Solid lines separate fields
of tholeiitic, calc-alkaline, and alkalic rocks. Continental
trondhjemite trend is dashed. Data from Coleman and Peterman
(1975) and Barker and Arth (1976).

granites from several different localities with tonalite-trondhjemite from
continental environments and granophyre-pitchstone derived from sub-alkaline
basaltic magmas and protected from subsequent oceanic hydrothermal alteration.
Plagiogranites characteristically contain less than 5 ppm Rb and have a Rb-Sr
ratio usually less than 0.015, whereas the more abundant trondhjemites from
continental environments characteristically contain more than 10 ppm Rb and
have Rb/Sr ratios in excess of 0.015. The consistency of this data suggests
that plagiogranite can be characterized, in part, by Rb-Sr abundance.

The very high K and Rb values of granophyre from the Miocene Red Sea ophiolite (Coleman et al., 1978) and Iceland rhyolites (Walker, 1966), both of which
were derived from sub-alkaline tholeiitic basalts of oceanic regime, are in
strong contrast to the distinctively low K and Rb contents of oceanic plagiogranite. This apparent discrepancy may reflect interaction of the rocks (or
magmas?) with external hydrothermal fluids possessing fundamentally different

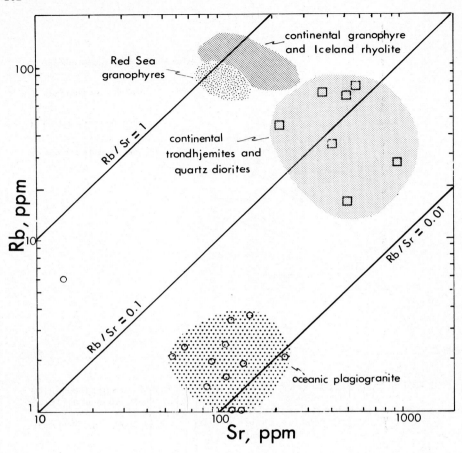

Figure 7.--Rb/Sr variation diagram.   Oceanic plagiogranites have
        compositions more akin to those of gabbro, basalt, and diabase
        than to those of continental granophyres and trondhjemites
        (after Coleman and Peterman, 1975).

chemistries. Pervasive circulation of hot ocean water through ancient oceanic
crust during the formation of plagiogranites has been verified in several well-
known ophiolite occurrences (Spooner et al., 1974). Conceivably, the low K and
Rb contents of plagiogranite are due to the hydrothermal leaching of these
elements.   Unlike the ancient ophiolites, the Red Sea granophyre and Iceland
rhyolite developed in a regime where the agent of hydrothermal alteration was
normal meteoric water, as indicated by oxygen isotope studies (Taylor and
Coleman, 1977).   Leaching of K and Rb did not occur, and the Red Sea and
Iceland leucocratic rocks therefore retain their original igneous K and Rb
concentrations.

Strontium isotope data also support this thesis. Previous determinations of initial $^{87}Sr/^{86}Sr$ for plagiogranites from ophiolites has shown that they are significantly higher than those of ocean-ridge tholeiites (Coleman and Peterman, 1975; Peterman et al., 1971). Coleman and Peterman (1975) found that apparently unaltered igneous plagioclase from gabbros associated with plagio-granites gave lower initial ratios (0.7043) than the whole-rock plagiogranites (0.7053 to 0.7059). Since seawater is enriched in ^{87}Sr (for Jurassic seawater $^{87}Sr/^{86}Sr$ = 0.7068 to 0.7075) relative to ocean-ridge basalts ($^{87}Sr/^{86}Sr$ = 0.7035), the high $^{87}Sr/^{86}Sr$ of plagiogranites may be due to contamination by hot ^{87}Sr rich seawater (Spooner et al., 1974).

The distribution of rare-earth (REE's) in plagiogranites provides addi-tional evidence as to the origin of these rocks (table II). Chondrite-normalized values for selected plagiogranites are presented in figure 8. Previous REE analyses of plagiogranite (Coleman and Peterman, 1975; Kay and Senechal, 1976; Coleman, 1977; Montigny et al., 1973) are similar, and the new data presented in this paper reconfirm the consistency of REE patterns among plagiogranites. The plagiogranite distribution is quite similar to that of average Mid-Atlantic basalts (Coleman, 1977) and low-potassium basalts in general (Tanaka, 1975). For the plagiogranites, the light REE's are depleted relative to the heavy REE's, and both are enriched approximately ten times relative to the average chondrite. The distinct negative europium anomaly is thought to reflect the early abstraction of Eu from the basaltic melt by removal of calcic plagioclase. Mafic cumulate gabbros associated with plagio-granites in ophiolites often show positive Eu anomalies, and calculated REE distributions within a fractionating basalt magma show a similar partitioning of Eu between cumulus phases and residual magma (Allegre and others, 1973). Apparently, the original igneous REE's in plagiogranite are unaffected by post-magmatic hydrothermal alteration. This is in accord with the results of Hermann et al. (1974), who concluded that low-grade metamorphism (up to 400°C) and spilitization of basaltic rocks do not affect REE contents.

The Red Sea granophyre is anomalous in its overall enrichment in REE's com-pared with other plagiogranites. In addition, it displays a strong enrichment in the light REE's. This is difficult to explain if both leucocratic rock types are derived from subalkaline tholeiite. Several factors, including con-tamination by Precambrian crust and meteoric hydrothermal fluids, may have affected the composition of the Red Sea granophyre. At any rate, it is unlikely that the consistent REE patterns observed in plagiogranites were pro-duced by hydrothermal leaching of a Red Sea-type granophyre.

The REE distribution of plagiogranite is distinctly different from intru-sive tonalite-trondhjemite plutons in Archean and Proterozoic igneous terranes

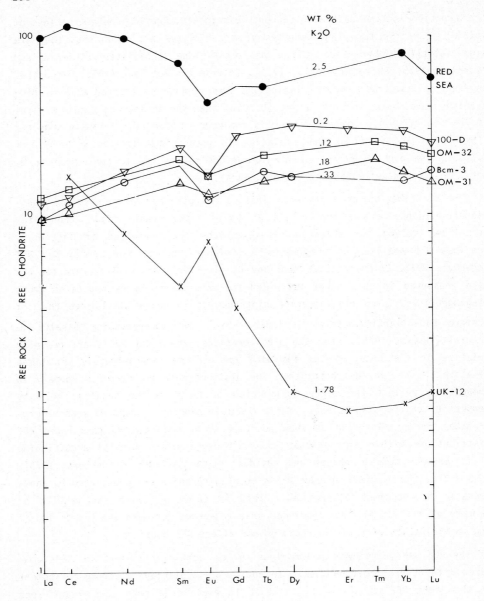

Figure 8.--Chondrite-nomalized rare-earth element distribution for selected
Oman plagiogranites and other leucocratic rocks. Sample number
explanation same as for table II.

(Arth and others, in press), whose REE distributions are characterized by relative enrichment of the light REE's and a positive Eu anomaly (fig. 8). On the basis of normalized REE contents, then, it is possible to distinguish ophiolitic plagiogranites from tonalites-trondhjemites. The trace-element compositions provide some interesting insights to their origin. REE's demonstrate an igneous history tied to differentiation of a basaltic magma; K, Rb, and ^{87}Sr concentrations suggest post-magmatic or deuteric hydrothermal alteration by oceanic brines.

SUMMARY

Plagiogranites from ophiolites have been shown to be chemically and mineralogically distinct from leucocratic rocks formed in "continental" regimes. Although local post-crystallization metasomatism has affected the chemical compositions of some plagiogranites, geochemical, textural, and mineralogical lines of evidence show that they are primarily products of igneous processes such as crystal fractionation and crystal-fluid interaction during the evolution of a basaltic magma. However, there is evidence that hydrothermal alteration by seawater has played a part in the evolution of plagiogranite, as suggested by trace-element and isotope data.

The absence in these rocks of the enrichment in potassium that characterizes leucocratic differentiates of most basaltic magmas is puzzling. Simple differentiation of a subalkaline tholeiite magma cannot account for the lack of K enrichment in these leucocratic rocks, regardless of the low initial alkali content. A more complex history involving interaction with hot circulating seawater is indicated. Iceland rhyolites and Red Sea granophyres are contradictions of the hypothesis that fractionation of "oceanic" basalts will produce K-poor differentiates. These cases may be related to interaction with meteoric water, rather than seawater, an idea also supported by oxygen isotope information.

REFERENCES

Alavi-Tehrani, 1976. Geology and petrography in the ophiolite range NW of Sabzevar (Khorassan/Iran) with special regard to metamorphism and genetic relations in an ophiolite suite. Unpub. Ph.D. dissertation: Saarland University (W. Germany).

Allegre, C. J., Montigny, R., and Bottinga, Y., 1973. Cortege ophiolitique et cortege oceanique, geochemie comparee et mode de genese. Bull. Soc. Geol. France, 15: 461-477.

166

Amstutz, G. C., 1974. Spilites and spilitic rocks, New York-Heidelberg-Berlin: Springer.

Arth, J. G., Barker, F., Peterman, Z. E., and Friedman, I., 1978. Geochemistry of the gabbro-diorite-tonalite-trondhjemite suite of southwest Finland and its implications for the origin of tonalitic and trondhjemitic magmas. J. Pet., in press.

Aumento, F., 1969. Diorites from the Mid-Atlantic Ridge at 45^0 N. Science, 165: 1112-1113.

Bailey, E. H., and Blake, M. C., 1974. Major chemical characteristics of Mesozoic Coast Range ophiolite in California. J. Res., U.S. Geol. Surv., 2: 637-656.

Bailey, E. H., Blake, J. C., Jr., and Jones, D. L., 1970. On-land Mesozoic oceanic crust in California Coast ranges. U.S. Geol. Surv. Prof. Pap., 700-C: C70-C81.

Barker, D. S., 1970. Compositions of granophyre, myrmekite, and graphic granite. Geol. Soc. Am. Bull., 81: 3339-3350.

Barker, F., and Arth, J. G., 1976. Generation of trondhjemitic-tonalitic liquids and Archean bimodal trondhjemite-basalt suites. Geology, 4: 596-600.

Bear, L. M., 1960. The geology and mineral resources of the Akaki-Lythrodonha area. Cyprus Geol. Surv. Dept. Mem., 3: 122 p.

Beccaluva, L., Ohnenstetter, D., Ohnenstetter, M., and Venturelli, G., 1977. The trace element geochemistry of Corsican ophiolites. Contrib. Miner. Pet., 64: 11-31.

Brunn, J. H., 1960. Mise en place et differenciation pluto-volcanique du cortege ophiolitique. Rev. Geogr. Phys. Dyn., 3: 115-132.

Bryan, W. B., and Moore, J. G., 1977. Compositional variations of young basalts in the Mid-Atlantic Ridge rift valley near 36 49^0 N. Geol. Soc. Am. Bull., 88: 556-570.

Černy, P., 1971. Graphic intergrowths of feldspars and quartz in some Czechoslovak pegmatites. Contrib. Miner. Pet., 30: 343-355.

Coleman, R. G., 1961. Jadeite deposits of the Clear Creek area, New Idria district, San Benito County, California. J. Pet., 2: 209-247.

Coleman, R. G., 1971. Plate tectonic emplacement of upper mantle peridotites along continental edges: Jour. Geophys. Res., 76: 1212-1222.

Coleman, R. G., 1977. Ophiolites. Springer-Verlag, New York, 229 p.

Coleman, R. G., and Peterman, Z. E., 1975. Oceanic Plagiogranite. J. Geophys. Res., 80: 1099-1108.

Coleman, R. G., Hadley, D. G., Fleck, R. G., Hedge, C. T., and Donato, M. M., 1978. The Miocene Tihama-Asir Ophiolite and its bearing on the opening of the Red Sea. In Evolution and Mineralization of the Arabian-Nubian Shield, Jeddah.

Dubertret, L., 1955. Geologie des roches vertes du Nord-Ouest de la Syrie et du Hatay. Notes et mem. Moyen-Orient, 6: 2-179.

Evarts, Russell C., 1978. The Geology and petrology of the Del Puerto ophiolite, Diablo Range, central California Coast Ranges. Oregon Dept. of Geol. and Min. Ind. Bull., 95: 121-140.

Gass, I. G., and Smewing, J. D., 1973. Intrusion, extrusion and metamorphism at constructive margins: Evidence from the Troodos Massif, Cyprus. Nature, 242: 26-29.

Hermann, A. G., Potts, M. J., and Knake, D., 1974. Geochemistry of the rare earth elements in spilites from oceanic and continental crust. Contrib. Miner. Pet., 44: 1-16.

Iwao, S., 1953. Albitite and associated jadeite rock from Kotaki district, Japan; A study in ceramic raw material. Jap. Geol. Surv. Rep., 153: 1-25.

Kay, R. W., and Senechal, R. G., 1976. The rare earth chemistry of the Troodos ophiolite complex. J. Geophy. Res., 81: 964-970.

McDougall, I., 1962. Differentiation of the Tasmanian Dolerites: Red Hill dolerite-granophyre association. Geol. Soc. Am. Bull., 73: 279-316.

Mattinson, J. M., 1975. Early Paleozoic ophiolite complexes of Newfoundland: Isotopic ages of zircons. Geology, 3: 181-183.

Montigny, R., Bougault, H., Bottinga, Y., Allegre, C. J., 1973. Trace element geochemistry and genesis of the Pindos ophiolite suite. Geochim. Cosmoschim. Acta, 37: 2135-2147.

Peterman, Z. E., Coleman, R. G., Hildreth, R. A., 1971. $^{87}Sr^{86}Sr$ in mafic rocks of the Troodos Massif, Cyprus. U.S. Geol. Surv. Prof. Pape., 750-D: D157-D161.

Reinhardt, B. M., 1969. On the genesis and emplacement in the Oman Mountain geosyncline. Schweiz. Mineral. Pet. Mitt., 49: 1-30.

Spooner, E. T. C., and Fyfe, W. S., 1973, Sub-sea-floor metamorphism, heat and mass transfer: Contrib. Miner. Pet., 42: 287-304.

Spooner, E. T. C., Beckinsale, R. D., Fyfe, W. S., Smewing, J. D., 1974. O^{18}-enriched ophiolitic metabasic rocks from E. Liguria (Italy), Pindos (Greece), and Troodos (Cyprus). Contrib. Miner. Pet., 47: 41-62.

Streckeisen, A. L., 1973. Plutonic rocks: Classification and nomenclature--Recommended by the IUGS Subcommission on the Systematics of Igneous Rocks. Geotimes, 18: 26-30.

Tanaka, T., 1975. Geological significance of rare earth elements in Japanese geosynclinal basalts. Contrib. Miner. Pet., 52: 233-246.

Taylor, H. P., and Coleman, R. G., 1977. Oxygen isotopic evidence for meteoric-hydrothermal alteration of the Jabal at Tirf igneous complex, Saudi Arabia (abs.): AGU Trans., 58: 516.

Thayer, T. P., 1963. The Canyon Mountain Complex, Oregon, and the alpine ultramafic magma stem. U.S. Geol. Surv. Prof. Pap. 475-C: C82-C85.

Thayer, T. P., and Himmelberg, G. R., 1968. Rock succession in the alpine type mafic complex at Canyon Mountain, Oregon. 23rd Int. Geol. Cong., 1: 175-186.

Walker, G. P. L., 1966. Acid volcanic rocks in Iceland. Bull. Volcanol. 29: 375-406.

Wilson, R. A. M., 1959. The geology of the Xeros-Troodos area. Cyprus Geol. Survey Dept. Mem., 1: 184 p.

Chapter 6

ARCHEAN GRAY GNEISSES AND THE ORIGIN OF THE CONTINENTAL CRUST: EVIDENCE THE GODTHÅB REGION, WEST GREENLAND

V. R. McGregor

ABSTRACT

Gray gneisses having general trondhjemitic affinities are the main components of the Greenland Archean. In the Godthåb region gray gneisses were formed during two periods of crustal development--the Amitsoq gneisses at 3800-3600 m.y. and the Nuk gneisses at 3000-2800 m.y. Each period of crustal development began with the outpouring of voluminous basaltic volcanics. During subsequent plutonic activity huge volumes of syn-tectonic tonalitic-granodioritic magmas were intruded and crystallized with primary gneissic textures. The chemistry of these gray gneisses is consistent with an origin by partial melting of basaltic rocks, but precludes an origin by re-melting of sialic rocks. The environments in which the Greenland gray gneisses were generated and intruded do not appear to have any close analogues in later Earth history. A model is suggested in which the continental crust of the Greenland Archean was built up mainly from magmas produced by partial melting of basaltic rocks above a zone of mantle downwelling.

INTRODUCTION

The rocks of the Archean Gneiss Complex of Greenland (Bridgwater et al., 1976) preserve mineral associations of amphibolite to granulite facies that crystallized at depths of 25-35 km (Wells, 1976) ca. 2800-2500 m.y. ago. This extremely well exposed terrain thus presents a moderately deep section of the late Archean crust. Gray gneisses of tonalitic to granodioritic composition, but with general trondhjemitic affinities, make up more than 80% of the Greenland Archean and hold the key to an understanding of the formation of the continental crust in this area.

The Buksefjorden-Godthåb-Isua region (Fig. 1) is unique in the Greenland Archean because gneisses of two different ages have been recognized there (McGregor, 1973). The Amitsoq gneisses have yielded isotopic ages of ca. 3700 m.y. and are dominantly gray gneisses. The younger Nuk gneisses have yielded isotopic ages of ca. 2800-2900 m.y. and are almost exclusively of gray-gneiss

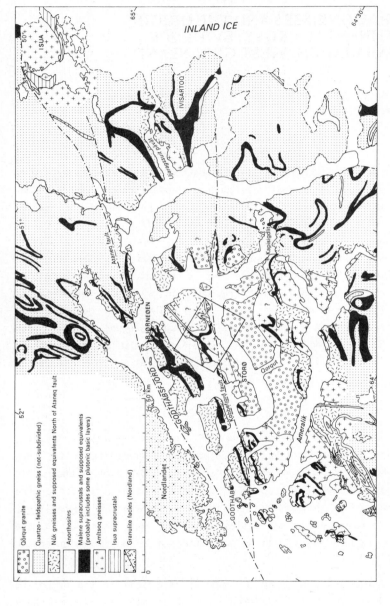

Figure 1.--Geological map of the Godthåb region. The area shown in Figure 2 is indicated. Sources of data: Ameralik and Godthåbsfjord, except for inner part--writer's own mapping; Isua area--J. Allaart; area south of outer part of Ameralik--Exeter University group; remainder of map--Itivnera mapping group, Geological Survey of Greenland, compiled by J. Allaart.

type. The Amitsoq and Nuk gray gneisses, although separated in time by 800 m.y., are so similar in chemistry and field character that it is reasonable to assume that they were formed by very similar processes. These were the processes by which the continental crust in this area was generated in two separate pulses.

This paper presents part of the results of a joint project carried out by D. Bridgwater and the writer and supported by the Geological Survey of Greenland. The aim of the project has been to obtain data on the chemistry of granitic rocks in the Godthåb region in order to elucidate the development of the Archean crust in this area. This paper presents our data on gray gneisses belonging to both the Nuk and the Amitsoq gneisses. The more voluminous and much better preserved Nuk gneisses are discussed first and conclusions regarding the origin of the Nuk gneisses are used to formulate a model for crustal development in the later part of the Archean. Evidence from the Nuk gneisses is then applied to the chemically very similar, but more strongly modified Amitsoq gray gneisses. We intend to present our data on the chemistry of the Amitsoq augen and dioritic gneisses and of the Qorqut granite elsewhere, but average compositions and our provisional conclusions regarding the origin of these rocks are included here in order to provide a more complete picture of crustal development in the area.

THE NUK GNEISSES
Definition

The term Nuk gneisses is applied to those quartzo-feldspathic gneisses in the Godthåb region which do not contain Ameralik dykes (see section on the Amitsoq gneisses) and which intrude and migmatize Amitsoq gneisses, Malene supracrustals and rocks of the leucogabbro-anorthosite complexes (McGregor, 1973).

Isotope Geology

Rb/Sr whole rock isochrons on Nuk gneisses from three areas in the Godthåb region and on similar gneisses from three areas in the Buksefjorden region and one in the Fiskenaesset region have yielded ages of 2780-2930 m.y. with initial $^{87}Sr/^{86}$ Sr ratios of 0.7015-0.7031 (Moorbath and Pankhurst, 1976). (A decay constant of 1.39 x 10^{-11} yr^{-1} for ^{87}Rb has been used in all work on Godthåb rocks.) Although there is considerable overlap in the range of errors, there are small, but significant differences in the ages and initial Sr isotope ratios.

Zircons from a late, massive body of granodioritic Nuk gneiss ca. 4 km southeast of the town of Godthåb give a U-Pb concordia-discordia age of $1824 \pm$ 50 m.y. (Baadsgaard, 1976).

Field Relations

The Nuk gneisses intrude a sequence of older rocks that comprises inter-layered units of Amitsoq gneisses, Malene supracrustals and leucogabbroic-anorthositic rocks (Table 1).

The Malene supracrustals are dominantly amphibolites with smaller amounts of metasedimentary gneisses. Pillow lava structures have been recognized in the amphibolites in a few localities, but in most places primary structures have been erased by the very intense penetrative deformation that accompanied and followed the intrusion of the Nuk magmas. It seems likely, however, that a large proportion of the Malene amphibolites are derived from submarine basic volcanic parents. Rb/Sr whole rock isochrons from Malene supracrustals give ages in the same general range as the.Nuk gneisses (S. Moorbath, pers. comm.). Zircon dates from Malene supracrustals are ambiguous, but do not suggest an age significantly older than the Nuk gneisses (Baadsgaard, 1976). Pb and Rb/Sr isotopic studies suggest that the anorthositic rocks, too, are not significantly older than the Nuk gneisses (Gancarz, 1976; S. Moorbath, pers. comm.). Lithologically similar anorthositic rocks in the Fiskenaesset region to the south are known to intrude supracrustal amphibolites of Malene type (Escher and Myers, 1975).

The Nuk gneisses were intruded as sub-concordant sheets and larger com-plexes that penetrated and disrupted the sequence of older rocks. The Nuk sheets range from thin veins to sills hundreds of metres thick. Their sub-concordant nature and great lateral extent appear to be original features accentuated by strong later deformation. Mapping of the Godthåb district has shown how Nuk gneisses penetrated into the sequence of older rocks and "exploded" it (Fig. 2; McGregor, 1973, Fig. 17). The situation produced, where the gray gneisses occupy much greater volumes than the framework of older rocks that they intruded, is typical of most of the Greenland Archean (Bridgwater et al., 1976).

The type Nuk gneisses, which crop out in a north-northeast trending com-plex that passes through the town of Godthåb (Nuuk in the Greenlandic dialect of Eskimo), include a wide variety of compositions and textures. The oldest rocks are massive, homogeneous dioritic gneisses which appear to be the disrupted fragments of a large pluton. The dominant rocks of the complex are gray tonalitic and pale granodioritic gneisses. Granodioritic gneisses are almost invariably younger than adjacent tonalitic gneisses. Inclusions of

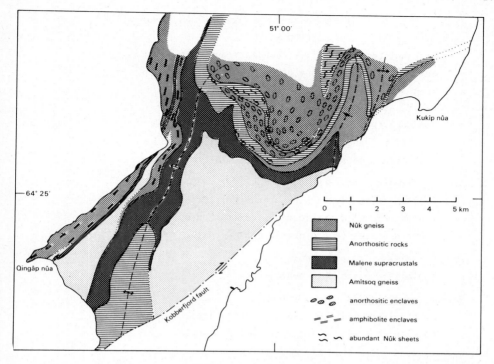

Figure 2.--Geological map of part of Storø, Godthåbsfjord, showing intrusion of sub-concordand sheets of Nuk gneisses from the north and west into a sequence of Amitsoq gneisses, Malene supracrustals and anorthositic rocks.

supracrustal rocks (mainly amphibolite), ultramafic rocks, anorthositic rocks and of dioritic gneisses and other earlier Nuk phases are common.

Most of the Nuk gneisses are inhomogeneous. Examples of different types of inhomogeneity are: (a) Poly-phase gneisses (Figs. 3, 4, 5). A number of different gneiss phases which range from dark gray to very pale cream form discrete small bodies deformed to lenses and discontinuous layers a few centimetres to several metres thick. Where the rocks are less deformed it is clear that the different phases have intruded one another and in most places the darker, more biotite-rich phases are older than and cut by paler phases. (b) Pegmatite-layered gneisses. Gneisses that can be homogeneous on the scale of an outcrop, but which have fine, sub-parallel pegmatitic layers. Sheets of pegmatite-layered gneisses have been noted in which the pegmatite layering is clearly an original feature formed as the sheet crystallized (Fig. 6). (c) Streaky gneisses (Fig. 7). Gneisses with clots, veins, and diffusely bounded bodies of pegmatite and gneiss of differing appearance which are drawn out into elongated lenses and streaks. Sheets of streaky gneiss are common in which the

Table 1.--Godthåb Archean stratigraphy

1. Isua supracrustals ca. 3800 m.y.
        Amphibolites, quartzites, banded ironstones,
        acid volcanics, carbonates, ultramafics.
        Isua area only.
        Akilia association ?ca. 3800 m.y.
        Amphibolites, pyroxenites, hornblendites, etc.
        (komatiitic and tholeiitic volcanics?), banded
        ironstones, detrital metasediments, ultramafics.

2. Amitsoq gneisses ca. 3800-3700 m.y.
        Gray gneisses (syntectonic tonalites, trondhjemites,
        granodiorites);dioritic gneisses (ferrodiorites),
        augen gneisses (basic quartz monzonites).

3. Ameralik dykes ?ca. 3600 m.y.
        Tholeiitic basic dyke swarm.

4. Malene supracrustals ?ca. 3000 m.y.
        Amphibolites (pillow lavas, pyroclastics), quartz-
        cordierite gneisses, detrital metasediments.

5. Anorthositic rocks ?ca. 3000 m.y.
        Metamorphosed layered complex(es) of leucogabbro,
        anorthosite, gabbro.

6. Nuk gneisses ca. 2950-2800 m.y.
        Dioritic gneisses (hornblende diorites), gray gneisses
        (syntectonic tonalites, trondhjemites, granodiorites).

7. Qorqut granite 2530 m.y.
        Migmatitic quartz monzonite.

fabric is clearly related to differential movement of the walls and appears to
have developed as the magma crystallized (Fig. 8).

   There is considerable evidence that intrusion of the Nuk gneisses was
accompanied by deformation. Many of the Nuk sheets, both large and small, can
be seen to have been intruded along active movement planes (Figs. 8, 9).
Earlier phases were strongly deformed before the intrusion of later phases
(McGregor, 1973, Plate 3). Most of the inhomogeneities now seen in the
gneisses appear to be primary and to be the result of movement during the
emplacement and crystallization of the magmas. The original structures have,
however, been strongly modified by intense later deformation in most places.

Figure 3.--Little deformed, poly-phase Nuk gneisses containing inclusions of supracrustal amphibolite and cut by a late dyke of quartz-monzonitic aplite. South coast of Bjørneøen, Godsthåbsfjord.

Original inhomogeneities in the gneisses have commonly been so intensely deformed and drawn out that they now form fine and often very regular compositional layering which might easily be confused with relict sedimentary bedding (Fig. 5).

Mode of Intrusion

Gray gneisses of Nuk type are by far the most abundant lithology in the Greenland Archean. Most, if not all, are intrusive in origin and most occur as sub-concordant sheets (Myers, 1976). Taken together, this intrusive suite is comparable in volume with the calc-alkaline batholiths of convergent plate margins; e.g., in western North America. Yet the form of the Nuk bodies is very different from the form of the component plutons of these batholiths.

The Mesozoic to Tertiary batholiths of western North America are characteristically made up of many plutons that vary in area from several hundred square kilometers to about a square kilometer (Bateman et al., 1963; Gastil et al., 1974). The plutons appear to have been generally globular or tadpole-

Figure 4.--Moderately deformed poly-phase Nuk gneisses. Ikarissat island.

shaped masses that, at the level now seen in the Sierra Nevada and Southern California batholiths, were emplaced diapirically by forcible upward intrusion of light magmas through denser, solid crust.

The Nuk magmas must have been less dense than the rocks into which they were intruded, being intrinsically less dense than the amphibolites and anorthositic rocks, and less dense than the compositionally similar Amitsoq gneisses because they were hotter. Yet only a few of the youngest grano-diorites appear to have been globular, diapiric masses. Most were intruded as sub-concordant sheets. The reason for this must be sought in the tectonic conditions that prevailed during the intrusion of the Nuk magmas.

Figure 6.--Part of folded sheet of pegmatite-layered Nuk gneisses. Kobbefjord.

Figure 5.--Very strongly deformed Nuk gneisses, probably originally with poly-
phase structure. Pikiutdleq island.

Figure 7.--Streaky texture in Nuk gneisses. South coast of Bjorneoen, Godthåbsfjord.

Figure 9.--Thin Nuk vein emplaced along a movement plane. Kangimut sangmissoq, south coast of Ameralik.

The Nuk magmas were intruded during a period of very intense horizontal movement (Bridgwater et al., 1974). Before (and probably during) the intrusion of the Nuk, the Amitsoq gneisses and Malene supracrustals were intercalated to form a sequence of alternating units. Several lines of evidence suggest that this sequence is a pile of thrust slices and that the contacts between units of Malenes and Amitsoqs are thrust faults that were healed by recrystallization during subsequent metamorphism (McGregor, 1975). Many Nuk sheets were emplaced along Malene-Amitsoq and Malene-anorthosite contacts (Fig. 2; McGregor, 1973, Fig. 17).

Many of the thinner Nuk sheets were clearly intruded along active movement planes (Figs. 8, 9). These sheets are commonly inhomogeneous and have primary gneissic fabrics related to differential movement of the walls. It appears that when this movement occurred the magma in the dykes was partly crystallized and that the inhomogeneity was produced by some form of filter-pressing action.

Figure 8.--Nuk gneiss dyke with inhomogeneity related to movement along the plane of the dyke. Nipinganeq, north coast of Ameralik.

The conclusions drawn from smaller Nuk sheets probably apply to the larger sills too. (1) The Nuk magmas were emplaced into active thrust planes both between and within units of older rocks. (2) Differential movement of the walls of the sills continued as the magmas solidified and this imparted primary gneissic fabrics and structures (poly-phase structure, streaky texture, pegmatite layering, etc.) to the rocks as they crystallized. (3) Deformation of the crystal-liquid mushes resulted in filter pressing and the squeezing off of late-crystallizing trondhjemitic and granitic (pegmatitic) fractions (see later).

It seems likely that the Nuk magmas did in fact tend to rise diapirically, but that they encountered and became trapped within thrust planes along which movement was substantially faster than the vertical movement of the magmas.

Chemistry

The Nuk gneisses analyzed come from a single complex that extends north-northeast through the town of Godthåb. The analyses span a considerable range of compositions, with SiO_2 ranging from 49 to 76% (Tables 2, 4; Fig. 10). There is a fairly continuous range of dioritic gneisses with SiO_2 between 51 and 56% and a very continuous range of gray gneisses with SiO_2 between 63 and 74%. Rocks with SiO_2 contents between 56 and 63% appear to be absent from this complex, although they are found among gneisses of Nuk age elsewhere in the Greenland Archean.

The Nuk gneisses have an alkali-lime index and of 50 amd can thus be classified as calc-alkaline. On an AFM diagram they lie along a typical calc-alkaline trend (Bridgwater et al., 1976, Fig. 17b). On a Na-K-Ca diagram (Fig. 11), however, they fall along a trend that is clearly different from a typical calc-alkaline trend (Southern California batholith).

The Nuk dioritic gneisses (Table 4, no. 7) are similar in most major elements to many hornblende diorites from western North America, e.g., the Klamath Mountains (Hotz, 1971), and to many basaltic andesites (Taylor, 1969).

The gray gneisses analyzed have a considerable and virtually continuous range of compositions. For convenience they have been divided rather arbitrarily on the basis of chemistry into a tonalitic group with 62-68% SiO_2 (and all except one with K_2O less than 2%), a granodioritic group with 69-74% SiO_2 and 2-3% K_2O, and a trondhjemitic group with 69-74% SiO_2 and 1-2% K_2O (Table 4). Most of the gray gneisses are generally trondhjemitic in that they are modally leucocratic quartz diorites with little or no potash feldspar and biotite as the most important mafic mineral.

Tonalitic gneisses dominate the earlier Nuk phases. The gneisses commonly have strongly developed gneissic textures and structures. The trondhjemitic gneisses characteristically form relatively small bodies, many of them late dykes of homogeneous or streaky white gneiss. The granodioritic gneisses are the youngest major Nuk phases and include some of the largest continuous bodies of Nuk rocks. Some are remarkably homogeneous and have only weak gneissic structure. Others, however, have very pronounced gneissic structure.

TABLE 2 : Representative analyses of Nuk gneisses

	131579	131565	131536	91654	131587	131582	91711
SiO_2	51.65	55.29	64.50	67.65	69.49	71.73	72.37
TiO_2	1.06	0.81	0.44	0.42	0.35	0.10	0.15
Al_2O_3	18.28	19.58	17.28	16.42	15.32	16.34	15.44
$FeO*$	8.14	5.63	3.05	2.79	2.68	0.80	0.93
MnO	0.12	0.08	0.04	0.04	0.04	0.01	0.01
MgO	4.55	2.88	1.68	1.20	1.10	0.40	0.40
CaO	7.74	7.54	4.41	3.87	3.22	3.06	2.07
Na_2O	4.4	4.7	5.0	5.3	4.8	5.9	4.9
K_2O	1.59	1.24	1.54	1.24	2.18	0.99	2.66
P_2O_5	0.75	0.36	0.18	0.17	0.15	0.04	0.05
l.o.i.	0.50	0.85	0.88	0.74	0.50	0.53	0.57
Total	98.78	98.96	99.00	99.84	99.83	99.90	99.55
Rb	40	43	51	35	42	18	71
Sr	1119	800	737	604	460	678	505
Ba	1010	480	859	440	1340	460	830
Zn	79	47	52	36	44	10	25
Y	19	7	4	1	5	-	1
Zr	113	48	139	124	108	71	86
Pb	11	17	14	17	17	12	31
Nb	6	6	3	5	2	3	3
Cr	90	80	40	30	30	23	23
Co	28	19	17	20	11	12	14
Ni	54	48	26	6	7	-	2
U	0.31	1.70	0.54	0.58	0.29	0.52	0.77

Leeds University XRF analyses (except U, by delayed neutron activation, Risø, Denmark). Major elements in weight percent, minor elements in ppm. Total Fe is reported as $FeO*$.
l.o.i. = loss on ignition.

TABLE 3 : Representative analyses of Amitsoq grey gneisses

	155766 G	155787 L	155775 G	155701 G	155764 L	155763 L	155707 G	155801 G
SiO_2	65.32	67.51	68.81	69.51	70.24	71.80	73.29	73.57
TiO_2	0.45	0.43	0.43	0.30	0.26	0.12	0.20	0.18
Al_2O_3	17.11	15.22	15.00	15.71	14.93	14.77	14.14	14.44
Fe_2O_3		1.23	0.36				0.11	0.26
FeO	2.95^t	3.48^t	2.78	1.87	2.35^t	1.13^t	1.36	1.15
MnO	0.04	0.07	0.08	0.02	0.07	0.03	0.03	0.02
MgO	1.35	1.34	1.04	0.82	0.83	0.36	0.36	0.46
CaO	4.09	3.30	3.15	3.05	2.73	1.96	1.79	2.65
Na_2O	5.2	3.6	4.30	5.04	5.3	4.8	3.58	4.55
K_2O	1.50	2.53	1.94	1.69	1.42	3.28	4.08	1.4
P_2O_5	0.16	0.15	0.11	0.15	0.09	0.05	0.04	0.06
l.o.i.	2.3	1.48	1.23	0.80	1.1	0.6	0.48	0.61
Total	100.47	99.11	100.10	99.22	99.32	98.90	99.46	99.41
	L		L				L	L
Rb	66	137	118		80	106	103	64
Sr	421	244	296		236	214	205	195
Ba	245	350	245		85	375	707	174
Zn	40	45			45	20		
Y	5	8	9		3	-	3	5
Zr	84	126	179			64	172	128
Pb	12	15	18		26	30	19	21
Nb	5	10			9	5	5	<3
Cr	40	50	45		40	25	11	13
Co	19	21	11		22	33	25	9
Ni	8	19	14		6	-	<3	<3
U	0.47	1.53			0.43	2.0		
Th	8.2	18			6.9	20		

Major elements as weight percent, minor elements as ppm. L = Leeds
University XRF analysis. G = GGU wet chemical/XRF analysis.
t = total Fe as FeO*. l.o.i. = loss on ignition. All minor elements
except U and Th by Leeds XRF analyses.

TABLE 4 : Average analyses of Godthåb granitic rocks

	1	2	3	4	5	6	7	8	9	10
	n=25	n=12	n=16	n=8	n=19	n=13	n=7	n=6	n=12	n=18
SiO_2	66.7	65.7	71.0	71.0	72.7	71.7	53.3	55.1	65.7	72.9
TiO_2	0.47	0.46	0.29	0.22	0.18	0.20	0.83	2.2	0.99	0.19
Al_2O_3	16.0	16.9	15.3	15.8	14.6	15.4	18.2	13.0	14.5	14.6
FeO*	3.6	3.2	2.1	1.5	1.4	1.4	7.1	13.2	5.8	1.5
MnO	0.06	0.05	0.04	0.02	0.03	0.02	0.11	0.19	0.09	0.02
MgO	1.5	1.7	0.8	0.7	0.4	0.5	4.5	2.8	1.1	0.5
CaO	3.9	4.1	2.9	3.0	1.9	2.2	8.0	6.9	3.6	1.4
Na_2O	4.6	5.0	4.9	5.3	4.1	5.0	4.4	3.2	3.5	3.6
K_2O	1.5	1.6	1.5	1.5	3.7	2.6	1.2	1.3	3.4	5.0
P_2O_5	0.14	0.19	0.09	0.08	0.07	0.08	0.42	0.5	0.31	0.09
Rb	71	52	69	32	122	53	32	17	86	222
Sr	343	585	380	562	252	562	804	279	220	183
Ba	298	709	232	818	607	1017	622	469	750	780
Y	7	3	4	<2	<2	<2	11	40	39	
Zr	144	139	120	124	136	107	72	218	380	196
Pb	18	14	21	13	29	24	12		18	60
Nb	6	4	7	4	4	2	6	10	13	
Cr	39	42	23	33	23	24	100	60	23	28
Co	17	16	15	12	18	11	27	37	14	15
Ni	13	18	5	6	3	<3	58	20	6	5

1. Amîtsoq tonalitic gneisses (64-68% SiO_2).
2. Nûk tonalitic gneisses (64-68% SiO_2).
3. Amîtsoq trondhjemitic gneisses (69-74% SiO_2, <2% K_2O).
4. Nûk trondhjemitic gneisses (69-74% SiO_2, <2% K_2O).
5. Amîtsoq granodioritic gneisses (69-74% SiO_2, >2% K_2O).
6. Nûk granodioritic gneisses (69-74% SiO_2, >2% K_2O).
7. Nûk dioritic gneisses.
8. Amîtsoq dioritic gneisses.
9. Amîtsoq augen gneisses.
10. Qôrqut granite.

    (Total iron as FeO*. n = number of analyses.)

The most characteristic features of Nuk gneiss chemistry are: (1) Considerable scatter of points on plots of SiO_2 against Al_2O_3, total iron, Na_2O and especially K_2O (Fig. 10). (2) High contents of Al_2O_3, Na_2O, Sr, and Ba and low contents of TiO_2 compared with many other calc-alkaline rocks with similar SiO_2 contents. (3) Very low concentrations of Y, suggesting that the rocks are depleted in heavy rare earths. (4) High Ni in the more basic rocks compared with Cenozoic calc-alkaline rocks (Taylor, 1969), but a very marked decrease in Ni with increasing SiO_2.

No rare earth element analyses are as yet available for the type Nuk gneisses, but Compton (in press) reports REE data for Nuk gneisses from the Buksefjorden region.

ORIGIN OF THE NUK MAGMAS

One of the main objectives of the joint geochemical project with Bridgwater

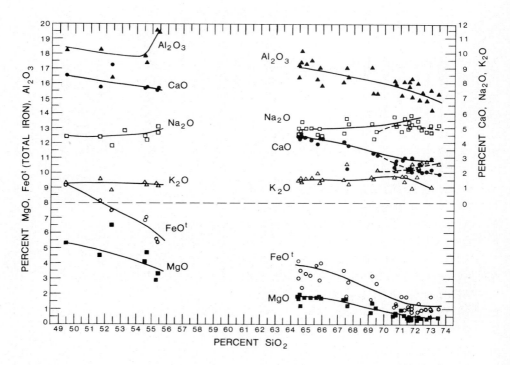

Figure 10.--Harker variation diagram for Nuk gneisses from western Godthåbsfjord. Solid lines are approximate compositional trends, not necessarily the result of differentiation, for dioritic, tonalitic and trondhjemitic gneisses. Dashed lines are compositional trends for granodioritic gneisses where they diverge from the tonalitic-trondhjemitic trends (Na_2O, CaO, K_2O).

has been to test the various modes of origin that have been suggested for the Nuk gneisses and to use the results as a model for other parts of the Archean complex in Greenland where the field control is not as well established. Several possible modes of origin for the Nuk magmas may be considered.

Re-melting of older sialic material

Bridgwater and Myers (in Bridgwater et al., 1974) suggested that the Nuk gneisses represent older sialic material equivalent to Rb-depleted Amitsoq gneisses that was taken down into the lower crust and upper mantle during thrusting, melted and then intruded higher in the crust. Moorbath (1975, 1976, 1977) and Moorbath and Pankhurst (1976) have pointed out that the low initial $^{87}Sr/^{86}Sr$ ratios of the Nuk gneisses (ca. 0.702) preclude an origin by re-melting of markedly older rocks with Rb/Sr ratios at all like those measured from Amitsoq gneisses exposed at present. Moorbath has argued that the low, upper-mantle-type initial Sr ratios of the Nuk gneisses and many other ancient gneisses indicate that their immediate precursors were predominantly juvenile additions to the crust at, or very close to the measured Rb-Sr whole rock isochron ages.

Perhaps the strongest arguments against the hypothesis that the Nuk magmas represent re-melted crustal material equivalent to the Amitsoq gneisses stem from the chemistry of the gneisses. The range of major element chemistry of the Amitsoq and Nuk gray gneisses is virtually identical (See section on the Amitsoq gneisses). Derivation of the Nuk gneisses from Amitsoq-like parents would require that the latter were completely melted. This is a most unlikely process because tonalites and granodiorites, which are the dominant compositions of the Amitsoq gneisses, melt over a considerable temperature range (Lambert and Wyllie, 1974; Wyllie, 1977), and quartz monzonitic early-melting fractions would almost certainly have been produced and separated off. Yet quartz monzonites are very uncommon in the Nuk gneisses and are usually restricted to the latest minor phases.

The expected product of partial re-melting of gray gneisses deep in the crust is in fact found in the Godthåb region in the form of the 2530 m.y. old Qorqut granite, a complex, migmatitic quartz monzonite that crops out in a relatively narrow belt more than 100 km long (McGregor, 1973).

The composition of the Qorqut granite(Table 4, no. 10, Fig. 11) corresponds to the minimum melting composition for the granite system. It has an initial Sr isotope ratio of 0.708 (Moorbath, 1977) compared with only 0.7015-0.7031 for the Nuk gneisses and equivalent rocks. Both the chemistry and the isotopic data are consistent with an origin by partial melting of rocks equivalent to a mixture of Amitsoq and Nuk gray gneisses, probably localized over a subcrustal, linear source of heat and/or water.

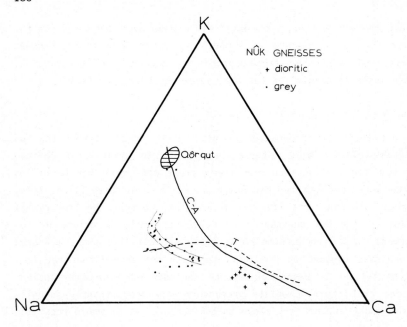

Figure 11.--Nuk gneisses from western Godthåbsfjord plotted on a Na-K-Ca diagram. The dotted lines enclose most analyses of voluminous phases of gray gneisses and define the main Nuk trend. Field of Qorqut granite analyses is shown. T = trondhjemitic calc-alkaline trend, Southwest Finland (Barker and Arth, 1976). C-a = "normal" calc-alkaline trend, Southern California batholith (data from Larsen, 1948).

Contamination of basic magmas with sialic crustal material

The low initial Sr isotope ratios of the Nuk gneisses and the small amount of coeval basic rocks makes this seem unlikely unless the sialic rocks had been heavily depleted in Rb shortly after their formation and unless most of the basic rocks crystallized at even deeper levels in the crust.

Fractional crystallization of basaltic magmas

Barker and Arth (1976) suggested that most trondhjemites and tonalites were produced either by fractionation of wet basaltic magmas with hornblende as a major cumulate phase or by partial melting of hydrous metabasalt (amphibolite) at depths of less than 60 km. Plutonic differentiation suites that include high-alumina trondhjemites (with more than 15% Al_2O_3) show complete continuity from gabbro through diorite, tonalite, and trondhjemite. One of the most complete suites of this type is that of the Uusikaupunki-Kalanti area of southwest Finland (Arth et al., in press). The differentiation trend of the

Finnish suite is compared with the Nuk gneisses on a ternary Na-K-Ca diagram in Figure 11. The Finnish trondhjemitic calc-alkaline trend is clearly different from the main trend of the Nuk gneisses. The Nuk dioritic and tonalitic gneisses are more sodic than the Finnish rocks, but show a trend towards enrichment in potash in the more silicic rocks (granodiorites), while the Finnish suite has decreasing potash with increasing silica in the same range.

Only very subordinate quantities of intrusive rocks of normal basaltic compositions are associated with the Nuk gneisses or equivalent rocks elsewhere in the Greenland Archean. The Nuk dioritic gneisses and/or the anorthositic complexes could conceivably be differentiation products of basic magmas that were also the parents of the gray gneisses. If the gray gneisses that make up more than 80% of the Greenland Archean have been produced by fractionation of basaltic magmas, then large volumes of cumulate rocks, dominantly hornblendites, must have been produced. While it is possible that such differentiation occurred entirely within the mantle or the lower crust and that the basic magmas were seldom intruded at depths of less than 35 km, such an origin is less attractive than one involving partial melting.

Partial melting of basaltic rocks

Trondhjemitic Nuk gneisses are similar in chemistry to ca. 2700 m.y. quartz dioritic rocks from the Minnesota-Ontario border (Hanson and Goldich, 1972; Arth and Hanson, 1972) for which an origin by partial melting of amphibolite or eclogite of basaltic composition at depths of greater than 30 km has been proposed. The trondhjemitic Nuk gneisses are closely similar in both minor and major elements to the Northern Light Gneiss, while the more basic tonalitic gneisses are similar in many, but not all respects to the Saganaga Tonalite, in which Rb is considerably lower and Sr higher than in the Nuk tonalites.

The Nuk granodioritic gneisses are very similar in both major and minor element chemistry to the 1700-1800 m.y. Pitts Meadow and Kroenke Granodiorites of Colorado, for which Barker et al. (1976) preferred an origin by partial melting of basaltic rocks, the Pitts Meadow Granodiorite at a depth of 50-60 km where garnet, amphibolite, plagioclase, and perhaps clinopyroxene were residual, and the Kroenke Granodiorite at a depth of greater than 60 km, where garnet and clinopyroxene were residual.

Compton (in press) considered various partial melting models for Nuk gneisses in the Buksefjorden region on the basis of REE data. He suggested that the early Nuk diorites and tonalites were produced by partial melting of garnet-bearing amphibolites or basic granulites, while the later granodiorites, which have more strongly fractionated REE patterns, were produced by small degrees of partial melting of sources rich in garnet, possibly eclogites. The high contents of lithophilic elements indicate that the granodiorites were probably derived from undepleted source rocks rather than from the refractory residues of earlier episodes of partial melting. The trondhjemitic gneisses have REE patterns that are consistent with an origin by hornblende fractionation of dioritic or tonalitic magmas, or by a large fraction of partial melting of amphibolites. Their occurrence as minor phases mainly associated with the early tonalitic gneisses favours the former possibility.

On a ternary Na-K-Ca diagram (Fig. 11) the compositions of the more voluminous phases of the Nuk gneisses lie along a relatively well-defined line, called here the main Nuk trend. The compositional range along this trend from diorite through tonalite to granodiorite may be the result of one or more of a number of possible processes: (1) Partial melting at a range of depths involving metabasaltic rocks with different mineral assemblages (Compton, in press). (2) Different degrees of partial melting. (3) Partial melting of source rocks with varying proportions of basaltic and short-lived sedimentary or tonalitic components. (4) Differentiation of the more silicic magmas towards a granitic minimum melt composition. (5) Mixing of tonalitic magmas with quartz monzonitic magmas produced by partial melting of earlier members of the same suite. Rare earth and other trace element work in progress should enable some of these possibilities to be discarded. The data available at present favours process (1).

The Nuk gneisses whose compositions lie off the main trend may be differentiation products of the main trend magmas. The deformation that is thought to have accompanied crystallization of the Nuk magmas would have facilitated the action of filter-pressing processes and the squeezing off of late-crystallizing fractions. The trondhjemitic gneisses could well have been produced by hornblende-dominated fractionation of tonalitic and dioritic magmas (Compton, in press). This would be represented on the Na-K-Ca diagram by lines sub-parallel to Arth et al.'s (in press) trondhjemitic trend. The remainder of the Nuk gneisses analyzed lie between the main trend and a minimum melt composition, typified by the Qorqut granite. Most of these more potassic rocks are minor aplitic phases. They could be the products of differentiation of granodioritic liquids involving cotectic crystallization of quartz and plagioclase. A small number of Nuk gneisses analyzed are quartz monzonites similar in composition to the Qorqut granite. These rocks might be the products of partial melting of earlier members of the Nuk suite in the actively thickening continental crust.

It seems likely, then, that the majority of the Nuk gneisses are the products of partial melting of basaltic rocks. The Malene amphibolites may well be remnants, preserved within the crust, of these parental basaltic rocks.

COMPARISON WITH YOUNGER TECTONIC ENVIRONMENTS

The environment in which the gray gneisses of the Greenland Archean were generated and intruded may not have close analogues in later Earth history. Windley and Smith (1976) suggested that high-grade Archean gneiss complexes, of which they considered the Greenland Archean to be a typical example, are ancient analogues of the Mesozoic-Tertiary batholiths of the western Americas, formed along destructive plate margins located at the contact between oceanic and continental crust.

There are some similarities between the gneisses of Nuk type in the Greenland Archean and the batholiths of western North America in that both suites are calc-alkaline and very voluminous. However, a more careful comparison reveals very significant differences. The difference in form of intrusion between the generally globular, diapiric plutons of the Sierra Nevada and Southern California batholiths and the subconcordant, presumably thrust-controlled sills of Nuk-type gneisses reflects very different tectonic conditions accompanying intrusion of the magmas.

More important, perhaps, the range of compositions found in the Nuk gneisses is very different from that found in the different sections of the western North American batholiths. The range of compositions of the western North American rocks varies systematically from west to east (Moore, 1959; Bateman and Dodge, 1970; Gastil et al., 1974; Kistler, 1974). West of the quartz diorite boundary line the plutonic rocks are dominantly quartz diorites (tonalites) associated with gabbros, trondhjemites, and basic granodiorites. East of this line the plutonic rocks are predominantly granodiorites and quartz monzonites. In north-central California, Kistler and Peterman (1973) found that initial $^{87}Sr/^{86}Sr$ values of less than 0.704, suggesting an origin directly or indirectly from the mantle, were characteristic of the quartz diorites and trondhjemites west of the quartz diorite line. Initial Sr isotope values of more than 0.706 were found to the east, where quartz monzonites become important. Quartz diorites and granodiorites with intermediate initial Sr isotope ratios occupy an intermediate zone.

The Nuk gneisses, with their low initial Sr isotope ratios, might be expected to be comparable to the plutonic rocks west of the quartz diorite line in California, and some rocks from the two suites are in fact similar in many respects. Some of the Nuk gneisses are similar to hornblende diorites, tonalites, and trondhjemites of the Klamath Mountains of northwestern California (Hotz, 1971), particularly those of the Trinity Mountains area. Compared with Klamath Mountains rocks with similar SiO_2 contents, the Nuk gneisses have lower contents of Al_2O_3 and Na_2O and higher contents of MgO and K_2O. Unlike the Nuk gneisses the Klamath Mountains tonalites and trondhjemites are associated with considerable volumes of gabbroic rocks. Tonalites with 56-64% SiO_2 are common and the associated granodiorites are more basic than the Nuk granodiorites.

The Southern California batholith is dominated by tonalites that are more basic than the tonalites in the Greenland gray gneisses. Tonalites with an average SiO_2 content of 62% make up more than 60% of the part of the batholith studied by Larsen (1948). Similarly in the Coast Plutonic Complex of British Columbia, tonalites with an average SiO_2 content of 59% are the dominant lithology (Roddick and Hutchison, 1974). Rocks with this composition, corresponding to andesites, are not represented among the Nuk and Amitsoq gray gneisses analyzed in this study. The same is true of other Archean gray gneisses (Barker and Peterman, 1974). Granodiorites associated with the tonalites in the western North American batholiths are generally considerably more basic than the Godthåb granodiorites. For example, granodiorites in the Coast Plutonic Complex of British Columbia have an average SiO_2 content of 63% (Roddick and Hutchison, 1974), while granodiorites in the Nuk gneisses all have SiO_2 contents greater than 67%, with an average of about 71%.

In addition to being considerably more silicic than corresponding rocks in the western North American batholiths, the Nuk gneisses are generally more sodic. This is clearly seen on the Na-K-Ca plot (Fig. 11) where the Nuk gneisses can be seen to lie along a trend quite distinct from the typical calc-alkaline trend of the Southern California batholith.

The Nuk gneisses are even less comparable with plutonic rocks east of the quartz diorite boundary line in western North America. In the latter, quartz monzonites become an important component, whereas they are only a very minor element in the Nuk gneisses.

The considerable differences in range of compositions between the Nuk gneisses and the western North American batholiths must reflect important differences in the source rocks or in the conditions of magma generation, or in both. The high initial Sr isotope ratios of the western North American quartz monzonites and their occurrence in a belt to the east, where the plutonic rocks intrude older sialic rocks, strongly suggest that the quartz monzonites were derived to a considerable extent by re-melting of continental crust. Quartz monzonites are relatively unimportant in the Greenland Archean, except for a few late bodies such as the Qorqut granite and the Ilivertalik granite (Kalsbeek and Myers, 1973), which post-date the gray gneisses. This suggests that the Greenland Archean was not a continent margin environment, as suggested by Windley and Smith (1976).

Myers (1976) suggested that the sheet-like granitoid intrusions of the

Greenland Archean might have been generated at a Himalayan-type convergent plate margin. This would have provided an extensive environment in which thrust tectonics were associated with the production of granitoid rocks and crustal thickening. However, the granitic rocks generated in such an environment could be expected to include a considerable proportion of quartz monzonites, which are only a minor element of the Greenland Archean.

A MODEL FOR THE GENERATION OF THE NUK GNEISSES

A model for the generation of the Nuk gneisses and equivalent rocks elsewhere in the Greenland Archean must explain the following features:

1) Over most of the Greenland Archean Nuk-type magmas were intruded into country rocks made up dominantly of basaltic volcanics, with smaller quantities of anorthositic layered complexes and of sediments. Only in the Buksefjorden-Godthåb-Isua region (which includes the area sampled in this study) have pre-Nuk rocks, the Amitsoq gneisses, been recognized. It is not clear whether the Amitsoq gneisses formed a basement on which the Malene supracrustals were lain down or whether they were interleaved tectonically with these volcanics and sediments after the latter had been lain down.

2) The generation of the very voluminous tonalites and granodiorites was preceded and accompanied by pervasive thrusting. The granitic rocks were intruded as sub-concordant sheets, probably along active thrust planes. They appear to have crystallized with primary gneissic fabrics.

3) The volume of the tonalitic-granodioritic magmas intruded at the present level of exposure is much greater than the volume of older rocks that make up the framework into which the magmas were intruded.

4) The composition of the Nuk tonalites-granodiorites is consistent with an origin by partial melting of basaltic rocks. The volumes of basic rocks which were partially melted must have been very large.

5) Emplacement of the granitic rocks was followed by very plastic recumbent folding that overlapped in time with the last phases of intrusion. Later deformation phases produced more upright folds. As deformation waned the metamorphic grade in some areas now exposed rose to granulite facies grade.

The following model appears to be consistent with the geology as it is presently understood:

About 3000 m.y. ago the Earth was probably hotter than at present. Mantle convection may have been more active and have involved smaller cells (McKenzie and Weiss, 1975). Crust made up mainly of basaltic volcanics was formed over areas of mantle upwelling. Where upwelling was particularly active and long-lived, thick accumulations of dominantly basaltic rocks were built up; these became greenstone belts. Elsewhere thinner oceanic-type crust may have been produced by processes more like those of present-day spreading ridges. The Malene supracrustals may be remnants of such oceanic-type crust.

Where there was mantle downwelling, the basaltic rocks were swept together and accumulated. Bodies of older continental rocks, such as the Amitsoq gneisses, were carried into these areas of crustal accumulation. The geothermal gradient may have been generally steeper than at present and the lithosphere thinner. It may have been much easier for the cooler, more rigid upper crust to have become detached from its hotter, more plastic substratum (Armstrong and Dick, 1974). Above zones of mantle downwelling extensive sheets of crustal rocks became detached from the down-going substratum, were thrust over one another, and piled up. Where older granitic rocks were involved, they were intercalated with basaltic rocks that were carried into the area of downwelling, perhaps from other directions or at other times (Amitsoq gneisses intercalated with Malene supracrustals). Elsewhere the accumulating piles of thrust slices were made up entirely of oceanic-type crust.

As the piles thickened the basic rocks in the lower parts were converted into amphibolites which, together with interbedded rocks of sedimentary origin, began to melt. Some of the basaltic crust that was carried into the zones of mantle downwelling may have been dragged down into the mantle and melted there. The tectonic processes involved may have been very different from those that take place at present-day convergent plate margins. Because the geothermal gradient was steeper, basaltic rocks began to melt at shallower depths than is generally the case at present. The compositions of the resultant magmas were thus rather different from those of magmas produced now at convergent plate margins.

The earlier, dominantly tonalitic magmas rose and, on encountering the thrusts in the overlying pile, moved along the thrust planes where they crystallized as sills with primary gneissic fabrics. The pile continued to thicken, both because of continuing piling-up of thrust slices and because of the intrusion of the newly-generated tonalitic magmas. At later stages partial melting occurred at greater depths, where the basaltic rocks had been converted to eclogites. The deeper parts of the pile, where partial melting occurred, may have included growing proportions of tonalitic gneisses intruded earlier. The later magmas produced were dominantly granodioritic and even included some quartz monzonites. Later pulses of granodioritic magmas rose into the pile as thrusting gave way to recumbent folding. The deformation was very plastic, the amount of strain was very large, and primary structures in most rocks were erased. As more and more granitic rocks were intruded and crystallized, a thick, continental-type crust was built up.

Later deformation was less plastic and produced more upright folds. High temperatures were maintained, water was gradually "stewed off," deformation became more brittle, and the metamorphic grade rose to granulite facies in the deeper parts of the pile. Local re-melting deep in the crust under dry conditions gave rise to charnockitic magmas (e.g., the Ilivertalik granite, Compton, in press).

According to this model the continental crust of the Greenland Archean was built up mainly from magmas produced by partial melting of basaltic material above a zone of mantle downwelling.

THE AMITSOQ GNEISSES
Definition

The term Amitsoq gneisses is applied to those quartzo-feldspathic gneisses in the Godthåb region that are cut by abundant metamorphosed basic dykes or that contain abundant fragments of amphibolite derived from basic dykes (Black et al., 1971; McGregor, 1973). As a working hypothesis it has been assumed that all the basic dykes were part of a single major swarm and they were called the Ameralik dykes (McGregor, 1968).

Isotope Geology

Rb-Sr whole rock isochrons on Amitsoq gneisses from three different areas give dates of 3700-3780 m.y. with initial $^{87}Sr/^{86}Sr$ ratios of 0.6998-0.7015 (Moorbath et al., 1972, 1975, 1977). Pb-Pb whole rock isochrons on Amitsoq gneisses from the Isua area give an age of 3800 $\pm$ 129 m.y., while four stotal dissolution analyses from south of Ameralik yield a Pb-Pb age of 3760 $\pm$ 150 m.y. (Black et al., 1971; Moorbath et al., 1975). Zircons from Amitsoq gneisses south of the mouth of Ameralik give U-Pb and Th-Pb concordia-discordia dates of 3650 $\pm$ 50 m.y. and 3648 $\pm$ 85 m.y., respectively (Baadsgaard, 1973). Gancarz and Wasserburg (1977) reported studies of U, Th, and Pb isotopes in feldspar augen from Amitsoq gneisses south of Godthab. Pankhurst et al. (1973) and Baadsgaard et al. (1976) have reported mineral age relations in Amitsoq gneisses that indicate a complex, polymetamorphic history.

Distribution

Most Amitsoq gneisses have been strongly reworked during later plutonic activity and their recognition is difficult in some areas. Isotopically confirmed Amitsoq gneisses have been recognized over a distance of 180 km from the islands on the outer coast between the mouths of Ameralik and Buksefjorden to the margin of the ice sheet at Isua (Fig. 1). Rocks containing Ameralik-dyke-like amphibolites occur within dominantly Nuk gneisses for another 20 km towards the southeast (Chadwick et al., 1974), but isotopic work has failed to confirm their identity as Amitsoq gneisses (Moorbath and Pankhurst, 1976). The area in which the presence of Amitsoq gneisses has been confirmed is bounded to the northwest by a major transcurrent fault, the Ataneq fault, that follows the western arm of Godthåbsfjord (Fig. 1).

Over most of the area in which they have been recognized, Amitsoq gneisses are interleaved on a large scale with units of Malene supra-crustals, anorthositic rocks, and Nuk gneisses. They were intensely deformed and recrystallized during the period of plutonic activity that included the intrusion of the Nuk gneisses. Amitsoq gneisses and enclosed closed supracrustal rocks at Isua, at the margin of the ice sheet 40 km north of the head of Godthåbsfjord, are not intercalated with younger rocks and have escaped much of the later reworking. The Ameralik dykes over an area of about 120 km^2 at Isua have been little deformed and only weakly metamorphosed.

Stratigraphic Relations

Throughout the area in which they have been recognized, the Amitsoq gneisses enclose and intrude large and small bodies of older supracrustal rocks. The largest and best preserved of these forms an arcuate belt 32 km long and between 0.8 and 3 km wide in the Isua area (Bridgwater et al., 1976; Allaart, 1976). The Isua supracrustals comprise (1) amphibolites of presumed volcanic origin and with Fe-rich tholeiitic chemistry; (2) finely laminated quartzites, thought to be derived from cherts, and banded quartz-magnetite ironstones; (3) ultra-mafic rocks, including large bodies of altered dunite; (4) carbonate-rich lithologies; (5) leucocratic schists of acid volcanic origin, many of them conglomeratic; (6) massive greenschists apparently derived from basic sills. The association of lithologies is comparable to that found in the upper part of many greenstone belts.

Elsewhere the inclusions of older rocks are smaller and more intensely modified. They have been termed the Akilia association (McGregor and Mason, 1977). The dominant lithologies are amphibolites and pyroxenites with the chemistry of Fe-rich tholeiites and komatiites and with these are associated small amounts of ultrabasic rocks, ironstones and gneisses of detrital sedimentary origin. Gneisses of acid volcanic origin may also be present, but are difficult to distinguish from lithologically similar Amitsoq gneisses of intrusive origin. The association of lithologies suggests that the rocks of the Akilia association are disrupted fragments of a greenstone-belt type of sequence.

Relations between Amitsoq gneisses and the very continuous and often quite thin units of Malene supracrustals that are intercalated with them have been the subject of some dispute (Chadwick and Coe, 1975; 1976). No convincing evidence has been found of a basement-cover relationship or of Amitsoq gneisses intruding Malene supracrustals. Indirect evidence suggests that the alternating units of Amitsoqs and Malenes are thrust slices and that the contacts are thrust faults strongly modified by subsequent deformation and metamorphic recrystallization (McGregor, 1975).

The relations of the Amitsoq gneisses gneisses to the anorthositic rocks are not known, but Pb isotopic studies suggest that the anorthositic rocks in the Godthab district were intruded into a sequence that included Amitsoq gneisses (Gancarz, 1976).

Lithological Characters

Intense plutonic reworking has erased the original structures and textures of most Amitsoq gneisses. Only at Isua are pre-Ameralik dyke features preserved over a larger area. The Amitsoq gneisses in the Isua area are remarkably similar in appearance to the less deformed Nuk gneisses. Poly-phase structure, pegmatite layering and streaky texture precisely comparable to those found in the Nuk gneisses are very common. This strongly suggests that the Amitsoq gneisses in this area are syn-tectonic intrusives and that deformation accompanied the crystallization of the magmas producing primary gneissic textures. Chemically these gneisses are tonalites and granodiorites of gray-gneiss type.

Outside the Isua area the Amitsoq gneisses are also dominantly tonalites and granodiorites of gray-gneiss type, but in most places primary structures have been modified beyond recognition. Over much of the area north of Ameralik the gneisses have a strong secondary pegmatite layering that appears to be the result of deformation at temperatures near the solidus of the rocks. At localities south of the mouth of Ameralik where the gneisses and enclosed Ameralik dykes are relatively little deformed, the gray gneisses generally have strong textural and compositional inhomogeneity that may well be primary.

Chemistry

The major element chemistry of the Amitsoq gray gneisses is very similar to that of the Nuk tonalites, trondhjemites and granodiorites (Tables 3, 4). Only a few Amitsoq gneisses with compositions comparable to the Nuk dioritic gneisses have been noted. No Amitsoq gray gneisses with SiO_2 contents between 54 and 62% have been found. The range of Al_2O_3 contents is ca. 1% lower in the

Amitsoq gray gneisses than in the Nuk gneisses and the range of K_2O contents is greater. The Amitsoq gray gneisses analysed include more granodiorites and several quartz monzonites, but most of these are late, minor phases that were collected to provide rocks with higher Rb/Sr ratios for isotopic work.

In view of the great similarity in major elements, the differences in some minor elements between the two groups of gray gneisses is surprising. The Amitsoq gray gneisses and especially those from Isua generally have much lower contents of Sr and Ba than corresponding Nuk gneisses and higher contents of Rb (Table 4).

O'Nions and Pankhurst(974) reported rare earth analyses for eight Amitsoq gray gneisses. Full analyses of a number of these rocks are included in Table 3. The chondrite-normalized patterns are surprisingly varied and there is little correlation with major element chemistry. All the analyzed samples from the Isua area and one from the outer part of Ameralik have moderately fractionated patterns with light REE enrichment and no or only weak Eu anomalies. These include three tonalitic, one granodioritic, and one trondhjemitic gneiss. Three samples, a tonalite from Praestefjord, a trondhjemite from Narssaq, and a granodiorite from Quilangarssuit, have more marked positive Eu anomomalies. The trondhjemitic gneiss from Narssaq (155701) has extreme depletion of heavy REE with a Ce_N/Tb_N ratio of ca. 320. However, 155764, a trondhjemitic gneiss from Isua which is chemically very similar to 155701 with respect to major elements (Table 3), has a smooth REE pattern with only moderate fractionation (Ce_N/Yb_N = 10.4) and no Eu anomaly.

Amitsoq Augen Gneisses

Augen gneisses lithologically quite distinct from the gray gneisses make up ca. 20% of the Amitsoq gneisses south of the mouth of Ameralik. They are derived from rather homogeneous, big-feldspar quartz monzonites (McGregor, 1973, Plate 2). Augen gneisses dominated the specimens collected during early work on the Amitsoq gneisses and this gave the impression that rocks with this rather special composition were typical of the Amitsoq gneisses as a whole (Krupicka, 1975; Lambert and Holland, 1976). It should be stressed that these rather basic, Fe-rich quartz monzonites make up a small proportion of the Amitsoq gneisses in one area only and that gray gneisses of tonalitic-granodioritic composition are overwhelmingly dominant over most of the Godthab region.

Relations between the augen gneisses and the gray gneisses are ambiguous. Almost all contacts are strongly deformed and therefore concordant. Paler gneisses, possibly belonging to the gray gneisses, have been seen to cut augen gneisses in several places. On the other hand, augen gneisses have nowhere been seen to cut gray gneisses.

Chemically the augen gneisses are rather basic quartz monzonites which compared with Amitsoq gray gneisses of similar SiO_2 contents have considerably higher contents of TiO_2; total iron, K_2O, Ba, Y, Zr, and Nb; higher Fe/Mg ratios; and lower contents of Na_2O, Al_2O_3 and Sr (Table 4). They are clearly unrelated chemically to the gray gneisses. This is shown, for example, by the rare earth patterns (O'Nions and Pankhurst, 1974).

The augen gneisses are chemically similar to members of the anorogenic rapakivi suite that is commonly associated with massive anorthosites (Bridgwater and Windley, 1973; Emslie, in press). Ferrodiorites, believed to be differentiation products of anorthositic bodies, are a minor, but character-istic member of this association (Emslie, in press). The Amitsoq augen gneisses, too, are associated with small bodies of dioritic gneisses (Table 4, no. 8) that are chemically comparable to these ferrodiorites and to ice-landites. On one small group of islands between the mouths of Ameralik and Buksefjorden, rocks of the Akilia association are intruded by moderately calcic leucogabbroic rocks, now deformed to gneisses. Augen gneisses crop out on adjacent islands.

Origin of the Amitsoq Gneisses

Most of the Amitsoq gneisses are much more strongly modified than the Nuk gneisses and their present form is the result of later processes (thrusting, intrusion of the Nuks). Original textures and structures, form of intrusion, relations to earlier rocks, etc., are only locally preserved. Consequently deductions regarding their origin are subject to greater uncertainties than is the case for the Nuk gneisses.

The close similarity in textures and in the range of compositions between the less modified Amitsoq gray gneisses and the Nuk gneisses implies a similar mode of origin for both suites of rocks. It seems likely that the Amitsoq gray gneisses are dominantly the products of partial melting of basaltic rocks and that the magmas were intruded under syntectonic conditions like those under which the Nuk magmas were intruded. The Isua supracrustals and the Akilia association may be remnants preserved within the crust of the dominantly basaltic parents from which the Amitsoq gray gneisses were derived.

It is not yet clear why the Amitsoq gray gneisses have different levels of Sr, Ba, and Rb compared with corresponding Nuk gneisses. Two possibilities that might be considered are: (1) Differences in composition of the parental basaltic rocks. The Akilia association includes a significant proportion of rocks with komatiitic affinities, whereas such compositions are rare in the Malene supracrustals. (2) The geothermal gradient may have been steeper around 3700 m.y. ago than it was around 2900 m.y. ago and the basaltic parents of the Amitsoq magmas may have begun to melt at shallower depths, where mineral parageneses were different from those in the rocks from which the Nuk magmas were generated.

The genetic significance of the augen gneisses and associated dioritic gneisses (ferrodiorites) is one of the main problems of Godthab geology. The chemistry of the augen gneisses implies an origin by relatively dry partial melting of sialic rocks deep in a thick crust. Yet the field relations suggest that they pre-date the Amitsoq gray gneisses which appear to have been the first voluminous sialic rocks produced in the region. Genetic considerations favour the explanation that the gneisses seen to intrude the augen gneisses are young phases associated with the parents of the augen gneiss itself rather than with the bulk of the gray gneisses, that the augen gneisses post-date the majority of the gray gneisses, and that they were generated late in the "accretion-differentiation" period, after a thick sialic crust composed mainly of gray gneisses had been built up and at a time when granulite facies conditions prevailed at deeper levels. The relations of the augen gneisses to the Amitsoq gray gneisses may thus correspond to the relations of the Ilivertalik granite to the Nuk gneisses.

CONCLUSIONS

In the Godthåb region a remarkably similar pattern of events was repeated twice during the Archean (Table 5). Each period of crustal development began with the outpouring of voluminous basaltic volcanics, at least some of them and perhaps the majority erupted under water. Sequences of supracrustal rocks were built up that at the present metamorphic grade are made up mainly of amphibolite and contain much smaller proportions of gneisses derived from detrital sediments. During subsequent periods of orogenic activity huge volumes of syn-tectonic tonalitic-granodioritic magmas with general trondhjemitic affinities were intruded and crystallized with primary gneissic textures. The chemistry of these gray gneisses is consistent with an origin by partial melting of basaltic rocks, but precludes an origin by re-melting of sialic rocks.

There is no evidence in the Amitsoq gneisses or associated supra-crustal rocks, the oldest known terrestrial rocks, that suggest the existence of a primordial granitic or anorthositic crust. Rather, the continental crust in this area appears to have been generated in two complex cycles at 3800-3600 m.y. and 3000-2700 m.y. ago. The first crustal rocks in each cycle appear to

TABLE 5 : Godthåb crust-forming periods

3850-3600 M.Y.	3000-2700 M.Y.
FORMATION OF SUPRACRUSTAL SEQUENCES DOMINATED BY BASALTIC VOLCANICS (ISUA SUPRACRUSTALS, AKILIA ASSOCIATION), ? GREENSTONE BELT(S).	FORMATION OF SUPRACRUSTAL SEQUENCES DOMINATED BY BASALTIC VOLCANICS (MALENE SUPRACRUSTALS), ? OCEAN FLOOR.
	INTRUSION OF ANORTHOSITE-LEUCOGABBRO LAYERED COMPLEX(ES).
	THRUSTING, INTERCALATION OF BASALTIC (MALENE) AND GRANITIC (AMITSOQ) ROCKS.
SYNTECTONIC INTRUSION OF VERY VOLUMINOUS TONALITES-GRANODIORITES (AMITSOQ GREY GNEISSES).	SYNTECTONIC INTRUSION OF VERY VOLUMINOUS TONALITES-GRANODIORITES (NUK GNEISSES).
AT LEAST TWO PHASES OF DEFORMATION	AT LEAST 3 FOLD PHASES, EARLIER PHASES RECUMBENT, LATER PHASES UPRIGHT.
INTRUSION OF BASIC DYKE SWARM (AMERALIK DYKES).	
METAMORPHISM CULMINATING LOCALLY IN GRANULITE FACIES; ? LOCAL INTRUSION OF BASIC QUARTZ MONZONITES (PARENTS OF AMITSOQ AUGEN GNEISSES).	METAMORPHISM CULMINATING LOCALLY IN GRANULITE FACIES; LOCAL INTRUSION OF QUARTZ MONZONITES (ILIVERTALIK GRANITE).

have been basaltic volcanics. Great volumes of basaltic rocks must have been extruded that were subsequently carried back down to depths where they were partially melted. The resultant tonalitic-granodioritic magmas crystallized under syntectonic conditions to give the gray gneisses that are the main component of the continental crust. Moorbath (1975, 1976, 1977) has argued that these major crustal "accretion-differentiation" periods, during which the continental crust has grown by a process of irreversible differentiation from the upper mantle, occurred within a time span of only 50- 100 m.y.

ACKNOWLEDGMENTS

The chemical data on which this paper is based was obtained as part of a joint project with D. Bridgwater, who undertook all the time-consuming work of arranging for the specimens to be analyzed and also arranged for the drafting of most of the figures. Without his efforts there would have been no chemical data for me to discuss. The ideas presented here have been crystallized during fruitful discussions with many friends, but especially with D. Bridgwater, J. Arth, and S. Moorbath. I wish to thank the Director of the Geological Survey of Greenland for permission to publish the paper. I acknowledge a grant from the Arthur L. Day Fund of the National Academy of Science which enabled me to spend two months at the National Museum of Science, Washington, D.C., working on the paper.

REFERENCES

Allaart, J. H., 1976. The pre-3760 m.y. old supracrustal rocks of the area, central West Greenland, and the associated occurrence of quartz-banded ironstones. In Windley, B. F., (Ed.), The early history of the Earth, 177-189, Wiley, London.

Arth, J. G. and Hanson, G. N., 1972. Quartz diorites derived by partial melting of eclogite or amphibolite at mantle depths. Contrib. Miner. Pet., 37: 161-174.

Arth, J. G., Barker, F., Peterman, Z. E. and Friedman, I., in press. Geochemistry of the gabbroiorite-tonalite-trondhjemite suite of southwest Finland and its implications for the origin of tonalitic and trondhjemitic magmas. J. Pet.

Armstrong, R. L. and Dick, H. J. B., 1974. A model for the development of thin overthrust sheets of crystalline rock. Geology, 2: 35-40.

Baadsgaard, H., 1973. U-Th-Pb dates on zircons from the early Precambrian Amitsoq gneisses, Godthaab district, West Greenland. Earth Planet. Sci. Lett., 19: 22-28.

Baadsgaard, H., 1976. Further U-Pb dates on zircons from the early Precambrian rocks of the Godthaabsfjord area, West Greenland. Earth Planet. Sci. Lett., 33: 261-267.

Baadsgaard, H., Lambert, R. St. J. and Krupicka, J., 1976. Mineral isotopic age relationships in the polymetamorphic Amitsoq gneisses, Godthaab district, West Greenland. Geochim. Cosmochim. Acta, 40: 513-527.

Barker, F. and Arth, J. G., 1976. Generation of trondhjemitic-tonalitic liquids and Archean bimodal trondhjemite-basalt suites. Geology, 4: 596-600.

Barker, F. and Peterman, Z. E., 1974. Bimodal tholeiitic-dacitic magmatism and the early Precambrian crust. Precambrian Res., 1: 1-12.

Barker, F., Arth, J. G., Peterman, Z. E. and Friedman, I., 1976. The 1.7- to 1.8-b.y.-old trondhjemites of southwestern Colorado and northern New Mexico: geochemistry and depth of genesis. Geol. Soc. Am. Bull., 87: 189-198.

Bateman, P. C. and Dodge, F. C. W., 1970. Variations of major chemical constituents across the central Sierra Nevada batholith. Geol. Soc. Am. Bull., 81: 409-420.

Bateman, P.C., Clark, L. D., Huber, N. K., Moore, J. G. and Rinehart, C. D., 1963. The Sierra Nevada batholith--a synthesis of recent work across the central part. U.S. Geol. Surv. Prof. Pap., 414-D: D1-D46.

Black, L. P., Gale, N. H., Moorbath, S., Pankhurst, R. J. and McGregor, V. R., 1971. Isotopic dating of very early Precambrian amphibolite facies gneisses from the Godthaab district, West Greenland. Earth Planet. Sci. Lett., 12: 245-259.

Bridgwater, D. and Windley, B. F., 1973. Anorthosites, post-orogenic granites, acid volcanic rocks and crustal development in the North Atlantic shield during the mid-Proterozoic. In: Lister, L. A., (Ed.), Symposium on granites, gneisses and related rocks. Geol. Soc. S. Africa Spec. Publ. 3: 307-317.

Bridgwater, D., McGregor, V. R., and Myers, J. S., 1974. A horizontal tectonic regime in the Archean of Greenland and its implications for early crustal thickening. Precambrian Res., 1: 179-197.

Bridgwater, D., Keto, L., McGregor, V. R. and Myers, J. S., 1976. Archean gneiss complex of Greenland. In: Watt, W. S. and Escher, A. E., (Eds.), Geology of Greenland, 18-75, Grønlands Geol. Unders., Copenhagen.

Chadwick, B. and Coe, K., 1975. A horizontal tectonic regime in the Archean of Greenland and its implications for early crustal thickening--a comment. Precambrian Res., 2: 397-404.

Chadwick, B. and Coe, K., 1976. New evidence relating to Archean events in southern West Greenland. In: Windley, B. F., (Ed.), The early history of the Earth, 203-211, Wiley, London.

Chadwick, B., Coe, K., Gibbs, A. D., Sharpe, M. R. and Wells, P. R. A., 1974. Field evidence relating to the origin of 3000 Myr gneisses in southern West Greenland. Nature, 249: 136-137.

Compton, P. M., in press. Rare earth evidence for the origin of the Nuk gneisses, West Greenland. Contrib. Minera. Pet.

Emslie, R. F., in press. Anorthosite massifs, rapakivi granites, and late Proterozoic rifting of North America. Precambrian Res.

Eschner, J. C. and Myers, J. S., 1975. New evidence concerning the original relationship of early Precambrian volcanics and anortho- site in the Fiskenaesset region, southern West Greenland. Rapp. Grønlands Geol. Unders., 75: 72-76.

Gancarz, A. J., 1976. 2.8 AE old anorthosites from West Greenland. Unpublished Ph. D. thesis, California Institute of Technology.

Gancarz, A. J. and Wasserburg, G. J., 1977. Initial Pb of the Amitsoq gneiss, West Greenland, and implications for the age of the Earth. Geochim. Cosmochim. Acta, 41: 1283-1301.

Gastil, R. G., Krummenacher, D., Doupont, J. and Bushee, J., 1974. The batholithic belt of southern California and western Mexico. Pacific Geol., 8: 73-78.

Hanson, G. N. and Goldich, S. S., 1972. Early Precambrian rocks in the Saganaga Lake-Northern Light Lake area, Minnesota-Ontario--Pt. 2, Petrogenesis. Geol. Soc. Am. Mem., 135: 179-192.

Hotz, P. E., 1971. Plutonic rocks of the Klamath Mountains, California and Oregon. U.S. Geol. Surv. Prof. Pap., 684-B.

Kalsbeek, F. and Myers, J. S., 1973. The geology of the Fiskenaesset region. Rapp. Grønlands Geol. Unders., 51: 5-18.

Kistler, R. W., 1974. Phanerozoic batholiths in western North America: a summary of some recent work on variations in time, space, chemistry, and isotopic compositions. Ann. Rev. Earth Planet. Sci., 2: 403-418.

Kistler, R. W. and Peterman, Z. E., 1973. Variations in Sr, Rb, K, Na and initial Sr^{87}/Sr^{86} in Mesozoic granitic rocks and intruded wall rocks in central California. Geol. Soc. Am. Bull., 84: 3489-3512.

Krupicka, J., 1975. Early Precambrian rocks of granitic composition. Can. J. Earth Sci., 12: 1307-1315.

Lambert, I. B. and Wyllie, P. J., 1974. Melting of tonalite and crystal- lization of andesite liquid with excess water to 30 kilobars. J. Geol., 82: 88-97.

Lambert, R. St. J. and Holland, J. G., 1976. Amitsoq gneiss geochemistry: preliminary observations. In: Windley, B. F.,(Ed.), The early history of the Earth, 191-201, Wiley, London.

Larsen, E. S., Jr., 1948. Batholith and associated rocks of Corona, Elsinore, and San Luis Rey quadrangles, southern California. Geol. Soc. Am. Mem., 29: 182 pp.

McGregor, V. R., 1968. Field evidence of very old Precambrian rocks in the Godthåb area, West Greenland. Rapp. Grønlands Geol. Unders., 19: 31-35.

McGregor, V. R., 1973. The early Precambrian gneisses of the Godthåb district, West Greenland. Phil. Trans. R. Soc. Lond., A273: 343-358. McGregor, V. R., 1975. A horizontal tectonic regime in the Archean of Greenland and its implications for early crustal thickening--a reply. Precambrian Res., 2: 400-404.

McGregor, V. R. and Mason, B., 1977. Petrogenesis and geochemistry of metabasaltic and metasedimentary enclaves in the Amitsoq gneisses, West Greenland. Am. Miner., 62: 887-904.

McKenzie, D. P. and Weiss, N., 1975. Speculations on the thermal and tectonic history of the Earth. Geophys. J. Roy. Astr. Soc., 42: 131-174.

Moorbath, S., 1975. Constraints for the evolution of Precambrian crust from strontium isotopic evidence. Nature, 254: 395-398.

Moorbath, S., 1976. Age and isotope constraints for the evolution of Archean crust. In: Windely, B. F., (Ed.), The early history of the Earth, 351-360, Wiley, London.

Moorbath, S., 1977. Ages, isotopes and evolution of Precambrian continental crust. Chem. Geol., 20: 151-187.

Moorbath, S. and Pankhurst, R. J., 1976. Further rubidium-strontium age and isotopic evidence for the nature of the late Archean plutonic event in West Greenland. Nature, 262: 124-126.

Moorbath, S., O'Nions, R. K., Pankhurst, R. J., Gale, N. R. and McGregor, V. R., 1972. Further rubidium-strontium age determinations on the very early Precambrian rocks of the Godthaab district, West Greenland. Nature Phys. Sci., 240: 78-82.

Moorbath, S., O'Nions, R. K. and Pankhurst, R. J., 1975. The evolution of early Precambrian crustal rocks at Isua, West Greenland--geochemical and isotopic evidence. Earth Planet. Sci. Lett., 27: 229-239.

204

Moorbath, S., Allaart, J. H., Bridgwater, D. and McGregor, V. R., 1977. Rb-Sr ages of early Archean supracrustal rocks and Amitsoq gneisses at Isua. Nature, 270: 43-45.

Moore, J. G., 1959. The quartz diorite boundary line in the western United States. J. Geol., 39: 198-210.

Myers, J. S., 1976. Granitoid sheets, thrusting and Archean crustal thickening in West Greenland. Geology, 4: 265-268.

O'Nions, R. K. and Pankhurst, R. J., 1974. Rare-earth element distribution in Archean gneisses and anorthosites, Godthåb area, West Greenland. Earth Planet. Sci. Lett., 22: 328-338.

Pankhurst, R. J., Moorbath, S., Rex, D. C. and Turner, G., 1973. Mineral age patterns in ca. 3700 m.y. old rocks from West Greenland. Earth Planet. Sci. Lett., 20: 157-170.

Roddick, J. A. and Hutchison, W. W., 1974. Setting of the Coast Plutonic Complex, British Columbia. Pacific·Geol., 8: 91-108.

Taylor, S. R., 1969. Trace element chemistry of andesites and associated calc-alkaline rocks. Oregon Dep. Geol. Miner. Ind. Bull., 65: 43-63.

Wells, P. R. A., 1976. Late Archean metamorphism in the Buksefjorden region, Southwest Greenland. Contrib. Miner. Pet., 56: 229-242.

Windley, B. F. and Smith, J. V., 1976. Archean high grade complexes and modern continental margins. Nature, 260: 671-675.

Wyllie, P. J., 1977. Crustal anatexis: an experimental review. Tectonophys., 43: 41-72.

Chapter 7

METAMORPHIC DEVELOPMENT OF EARLY ARCHEAN TONALITIC AND TRONDHJEMITIC GNEISSES: SAGLEK AREA, LABRADOR

K. D. Collerson and D. Bridgwater

ABSTRACT

Early Archean (pre-3.6 Ga) continental crust in Northern Labrador is composed predominantly of either migmatitic or porphyroclastic (augen) gneiss, containing inclusions of supracrustal lithologies, leucogabbro and anorthosite. The migmatitic and augen gneiss are subdivided into two suites (designated the Uivak I and Uivak II gneisses), which both fall on the 3622 Ma Rb/Sr isochron. The Uivak I suite, which is regarded as being derived mainly from trondhjemitic to granodioritic parents, experienced a complex structural and metamorphic history prior to the intrusion of the protoliths of the Uivak II gneisses.

The early metamorphic history of the terrain involved the formation of both granulite and amphibolite facies assemblages at different structural levels. Microstructural and paragenetic relationships in the Uivak I gray gneiss indicate that retrogression from granulite to amphibolite facies occurred after the establishment of the planar anisotropy in the suite. This retrogression involved the development of biotite and secondary hornblende from hornblende and orthopyroxene in the early granulite facies gneisses. It was also associated with an increase in modal microcline and quartz. We interpret alteration in the suite to be the result of K and Rb metasomatism associated with the emplacement and deformation of the parents of the Uivak II gneisses. The increase in Rb produced lower K/Rb and higher Rb/Sr ratios than are normally observed in trondhjemitic-tonalitic associations. The age indicated by the isochron is considered to date this allochemical event.

Highly fractionated REE patterns and variable Ce/Y ratios in the Uivak I gneisses are interpreted to be induced either by metamorphic or igneous processes. These processes involved the transport of heavy REE's and Y (as well as other LIL elements) in the form of soluble complexes with volatiles derived from the lower crust or upper mantle.

We present a model whereby the trondhjemitic and tonalitic parents of the Uivak I gneisses are generated by partial melting of mafic granulite under the influence of a high early Archean geothermal gradient and massive volatile outgassing from the mantle and lower crust. The production of early Archean sialic crust is envisaged as a cumulative, cyclic process, mafic and ultramafic volcanism occurring synchronously with the partial melting at depth of earlier formed mafic granulite facies crust. The Uivak II gneisses are considered to have formed by partial melting of granulite facies tonalitic and trondhjemitic gneisses, possibly with some fractional crystallization of the derived melt.

INTRODUCTION

Polygenetic suites of both complexly layered and homogeneous quartzo-feldspathic gneisses (gray gneisses), which chemically resemble trondhjemite, tonalite and granodiorite, are a volumetrically important element of high-grade gneiss terrains (Glikson and Sheraton, 1972; McGregor, 1973, this volume; Bridgwater et al., 1973, in press; Collerson et al., 1976). Interleaved with these gneisses are units of supracrustal rocks (metasediments and metavolcanics), as well as variably deformed basic and ultrabasic originally intrusive rocks (gabbro, leucogabbro, anorthosite, and peridotite). Basic dykes, of a variety of ages, showing differing amounts of strain, commonly exhibit intrusive relations with the quartzo-feldspathic gneisses and are therefore useful as lithostratigraphic markers (cf. McGregor, 1973; Bridgwater et al., 1975).

In some Archean gneiss terrains, for example the Ancient Gneiss Complex of Swaziland (Hunter, 1970, 1973, 1974; Hunter et al., in press) and gneisses from the Webb Canyon area of Wyoming (Barker et al., this volume), metabasic units interlayered with trondhjemitic and tonalitic gneisses are interpreted as reflecting a bimodal protolith relationship between dacitic and basaltic flows (cf. Barker and Peterman, 1974). However, in other gneiss terrains such as the Lewisian of Scotland (Sheraton et al., 1973), the Saglek area of Labrador (Collerson et al., 1976; Bridgwater and Collerson, 1976, 1977) and the Godthaab district of Greenland (McGregor, 1973) no such bimodality is observed; gross compositional differences between the dominant acid gray gneisses and subordinate intermediate and basic members of the same suite are interpreted to reflect either volcanic or plutonic protolith variation.

As vestiges of early Archean crust are commonly preserved in such gneissic complexes (Moorbath et al., 1972, 1975, 1977a,b; Baadsgaard, 1973, 1976; Baadsgaard et al., 1976; Hurst et al., 1975; Hawkesworth et al., 1975; Barton et al., 1977; Wilson et al., 1978; Goldich and Hedge, 1974; Wooden et al., 1975) an understanding of the petrological and geochemical development of these enigmatic "granitic" suites is of fundamental importance in modelling crustal development and growth during the early stages of Earth history.

A plethora of hypotheses have been proposed to explain the formation and geochemical character (in particular the heavy rare earth element depletion) of the low potash siliceous protoliths for these gneissic suites:

1)   Remobilization of primordial sialic crust (MacGregor, 1951; Hunter, 1957; Sutton, 1973);

2)   Partial melting of graywacke (Cheney and Stewart, 1975; Dougan, 1976);

3)   Fractional crystallization of wet basaltic magma (Goldschmidt, 1922; Hietanen, 1943; Arth et al., in press);

4)   Partial melting of oceanic crust (Glikson, 1970, 1971);

5)   Partial melting of eclogite (Green and Ringwood, 1968; Glikson, 1972; Arth and Hanson, 1972, 1975; Condie and Hunter, 1976);

6)   Hydrous fractionation of garnet-hornblende bearing upper mantle under reducing conditions (Lambert and Holland, 1976);

7)   Partial melting of amphibolite (Glikson, 1972; Green and Ringwood, 1968; Barker and Arth, 1976; Nicollet and Leyreloup, this volume);

8)   Fractional crystallization of garnet from basic or intermediate magma, or partial melting of a garnetiferous basic or intermediate source (O'Nions and Pankhurst, 1974); and

9)   Partial melting of mafic granulite under the influence of a high geothermal gradient and high a_{CO_2} (Collerson and Fryer, in press).

In this paper we review field, petrological and geochemical evidence regarding the origin of the 3.6 Ga old Uivak gneisses in northern Labrador. We also evaluate the extent to which high-grade metamorphic tectonities of trondhjemitic to tonalitic composition, from early Archean gneiss terrains, can be modelled using classical igneous petrological methods.

GEOLOGICAL SETTING

The Archean gneiss complex in Labrador comprises an elongate coastal terrain c. 600 km long.   It is located on the western flank of the North American craton (Bridgwater, et al., 1973) within the Nain Province of the Canadian Shield (Fig. 1).   The Archean gneisses are bounded on the west by the Churchill Province, a gneiss terrain which experienced intense deformation and granulite facies metamorphism during the Hudsonian Orogeny ca. 1.8 Ga ago (Morgan, 1974, 1975).

Unconformably overlying the Archean complex are a number of early Proterozoic (Aphebian) cover sequences. These supracrustal belts are dominated by clastic and carbonate sedimentary rocks (the Ramah and Snyder Groups, Knight

208

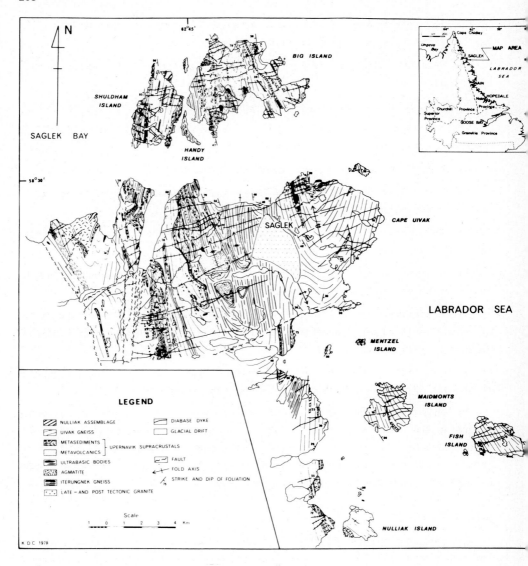

Figure 1.--Geological map of the Saglek area, Northern Labrador.

and Morgan, 1976; Speer, 1978), or by mafic volcanic rocks and diabase sills (the Mugford Group, Smith, 1976).

The Ramah Group, which crops out along the boundary between the Nain and the Churchill Provinces, west of Saglek, occupies a linear tract some 100 km long and 8 to 16 km wide. Tight to open macroscopic folds, the result of deformation during the Hudsonian Orogeny, are well developed in the sequence.

There is a marked increase in intensity of deformation along the western margin of the belt, where it is in thrust contact with granulite facies (reworked Archean) gneisses of the Churchill Province. Metamorphic grades range from amphibolite facies in the thrust zone to greenschist facies in the central and eastern portions of the belt. The underlying Archean gneisses to the east, however, show no obvious penetrative effects of this younger event, despite their proximity to the reworked zone.

The southern margin of the Archean complex and overlying Aphebian cover sequences in this region were variably deformed, metamorphosed to greenschist-amphibolite facies and intruded by a number of plutonic complexes during the Hudsonian Orogeny (Martin, 1977).

Both the Archean complex and gneisses in the Churchill Province are intruded by post-tectonic rocks of the Nain anorthosite-adamellite suite (Wheeler, 1960), which are in turn cut by a suite of alkali granites (Collerson, in prep.)

GEOLOGICAL RELATIONS IN THE SAGLEK AREA

The Archean gneiss complex in the Saglek area (Fig. 1) comprises a number of discrete lithostratigraphic units; gray orthogneisses, supracrustal metavolcanic and metasedimentary units, fractionated and layered metabasic intrusive bodies, pods of ultramafic rock and late-syntectonic to post-tectonic 'granitic' sheets and stockworks, which are interleaved on a macroscopic and mesoscopic scale as a result of tectonic and/or igneous processes.

The terrain has a general N-S trending structural grain defined by a regional schistosity, which is commonly developed parallel to the compositional layering in the different lithological units. Judging from the transposed nature of the compositional layering and from the presence of isoclinal intrafolial folds and of refolded folds, the regional structure may be the result of a number of ductile deformation events. Macroscopic folds, overturned to the east, and plunging either N or S on gentle axes, with a map pattern characterized by sheared, tight synforms and open antiforms, are interpreted to be the result of relatively late Archean strains (ca. 3.0 Ga, Hurst et al., 1975).

Within the complex, the gneisses are exposed at a number of structural levels due to block faulting, possibly associated with events that culminated in the opening of the Labrador Sea in the Mesozoic (Hyndman, 1973). Rocks with granulite facies mineral assemblages are therefore commonly juxtaposed in adjacent fault bounded blocks. Amphibolite facies enclaves are, however, locally developed in areas dominated by granulite facies assemblages indicating that metamorphism occurred under variable conditions of P_{H_2O} relative to P_{total}. In other regions, relict assemblages which formed during an earlier granulite facies event (pre- 3.6 Ga ago) are preserved in inclusions of supracrustal units in amphibolite facies gray orthogneiss.

Deformation of basement complexes such as the North Atlantic craton is typically inhomogeneous on a macroscopic and mesoscopic scale (Bridgwater et al.,, 1973; Myers, 1978). Domains of relatively high and relatively low strain may therefore be synchronously developed. As a result different stages of the structural and lithological evolution of a particlar terrain can be recognized. A relative chronology for the different major gneissic units in the Saglek area is presented in Table 1. The sequence is based in part on the relationship between a swarm of metadiabase dykes (Saglek dykes) and the different gneissic lithologies, and on rarely observed intrusive relations among the igneous protoliths of some of the gneisses, which are preserved in domains of low finite strain.

The Saglek dykes are in most cases readily recognized in the field, on the basis of their texture and mineral composition. In areas of low finite strain the dykes exhibit discordant contacts with, and apophyses into their host gneisses, which in all cases developed strong tectonite fabrics prior to the intrusion of the dykes. In highly strained areas the dykes are found as discrete layers concordant with the main gneissic layering (due to tectonic rotation), or as trains of variably rotated boudins. On the basis of their primary relationships with the country rocks the Saglek dykes cannot represent part of a bimodal suite with the gneisses.

The dykes are fine-grained and are composed principally of plagioclase (An_{34}), hornblende and rarely clinopyroxene, which develop decussate to granoblastic miocrostructures. Contained within the dykes are irregular concentrations of megacrystic plagioclase up to 2 cm in diameter, or xenoliths of anorthosite (presumably cognate concentrations of these megacrysts) ranging up to 10 cm in diameter. Some of the feldspars have relict cores of bytownite (An_{77}) which are surrounded by coronas of fine-grained granoblastic, recrystallized andesine (An_{33-36}), which is apparently in equilibrium with the groundmass metamorphic plagioclase. The megacrysts record variable amounts of extension due to later deformation and recrystallization.

The width of individual dykes is variable, ranging from less than 10 cm to greater than 10 m. The widest dykes, which occur on Mentzel Island (Fig. 1) have fine-grained metamorphosed chilled contacts containing abundant plagioclase porphyroclasts, and coarse-grained blasto-gabbroic cores.

The 'stratigraphy' of the gneiss terrain is subdivided into two groups

TABLE 1: Simplified Geological Evolution of the Archean Gneiss Complex in the Saglek Area

---

1. Early crust ?

2. Deposition of <u>Nulliak assemblage</u> (ironstones, volcanics)

3. High-grade metamorphism (granulite facies)

4. Emplacement of trondhjemitic-tonalitic granodioritic and basic to intermediate protoliths of the Uivak I gneisses

5. Deformation and metamorphism-formation of the <u>Uivak I gneisses</u>

6. Emplacement of layered diorite-gabbro-anorthosite complex (<u>Mentzel Intrusive Association</u>)

7. Emplacement of granodioritic-granitic protoliths of the Uivak II gneisses

8. Deformation-metamorphism (retrogression of early high-grade assemblages to amphibolite facies assemblages) Formation of the <u>Uivak II gneisses</u>   c. 3.62 Ga

9. Intrusion of <u>Saglek dykes</u>

10. Deposition and extrusion of <u>Upernavik supracrustals</u> (volcanics, pelites, semipelites, quartzites, ironstones)

11. Emplacement of layered ultramafic-gabbroic-anorthositic bodies

12. Intercalation of Uivak gneisses and Upernavik supracrustals
                                                          <u>pre 3 Ga</u>

13. Deformation and metamorphism-reworking of gneisses in tight linear synformal structures   <u>c. 3.0 Ga</u>

14. Emplacement of syntectonic tonalitic-granitic sheets

15. Granulite and amphibolite facies metamorphism

16. Emplacement of post-tectonic potassic granites (<u>sensu stricto</u>)
                                                            <u>2.5 Ga</u>

using these dykes; (1) lithologies which pre-date the dykes,and (2) lithologies formed from protoliths emplaced, laid down or tectonically re-foliated after emplacement of the dykes (Table 1).   The chronology presented in Table 1 resembles that established in the Godthaab area of west Greenland by McGregor (1973, this volume), although detailed isotopic studies have revealed a number of important contrasts (Baadsgaard et al., in prep.)

The following discussion deals with components of the gneiss terrain which pre-date Saglek dyke emplacement, and which are considered to be older than ca.

3.6 Ga. Details of the geological evolution of the complex after this event are presented elsewhere (Collerson et al., 1976; Bridgwater et al., in press) and will not be considered in this paper.

META-PLUTONIC ROCKS: THE UIVAK GNEISSES

The Uivak (Inuit meaning "outermost point") gneisses, a composite group of orthogneisses, are the oldest and regionally the most extensive lithological units in the Saglek area. They are subdivided on field and geochemical criteria into two discrete groups; designated the Uivak I and Uivak II gneisses, both of which define a whole rock Rb/Sr isochron of 3622 ± 72 Ma with an initial ratio of 0.7014 ± 0.0008 (Hurst et al., 1975). When compared with the ca. 3.6 Ga Amitsoq gneisses in Greenland (McGregor, 1973, this volume) the Uivak I gneisses are broadly correlative with the Amitsoq gray gneisses (the K-poor suite of Lambert and Holland, 1976) and the Uivak II gneisses resemble McGregors' 'augen' Amitsoq gneisses (Lambert and Holland's "normal suite").

The Uivak I gneisses constitute more than 80% of the exposed 3600 Ma old rocks in the area. They are a compositionally variable, polyphase suite of

Figure 2.--Uivak I tonalitic gneiss with abundant veins of pegmatite. Also shown is a boudinaged unit of meta-gabbro. Near Cape Uivak, Saglek.

intercalated fine- to medium-grained quartzofeldspathic 'gray' gneisses and migmatites. In ice-scoured coastal exposures they appear as light- to dark-gray mineralogically banded units (as a result of variation in the proportions of felsic and ferromagnesian constituents), showing a weak to strongly developed foliation. They contain prominent mesoscopic and microscopic veins of potash feldspar-rich pegmatite concordant or discordant to the gneissic layering (Fig. 2). Homogeneous portions of the gneisses are dominated by quartz-oligoclase-microcline-biotite-hornblende-bearing trondhjemitic, tonalit-

ic, and granodioritic compositions, which are interleaved with septa of more leucocratic gneiss that contains abundant microcline. Sheets of melanocratic hornblende- or biotite-rich gabbroic, dioritic and monzonitic gneiss up to 1 m wide, which are commonly more homogeneous than the pegmatitically banded quartzo-feldspathic gneiss, are present in subordinate amounts, and represent more mafic phases of the Uivak I suite.

Field evidence from areas of relatively low finite strain, such as the hinges of late antiformal macroscopic folds in the region, indicates that the

Figure 3.--Uivak I gray gneiss folded by several generations of mesoscopic isoclinal folds and cut by a Saglek dyke. Approximately 6 km SE of Saglek.

gneisses were subjected to an extremely complex structural history prior to emplacement of the Uivak II protoliths. In these domains the Uivak I gneissose structures are well preserved. The gneissic layering and parallel mineral fabric are commonly folded by several generations of mesoscopic, isoclinal folds, all of which have strong axial plane foliations in their hinge regions (Fig. 3) and lineations parallel to the different axial directions of folds (Fig. 4). In domains of high finite strain early isoclinal folds appear as rootless intrafolial closures (Figs. 5a, b).

Figure 4.--Strongly lineated Uivak I gray gneiss. Same locality as Figure 3.

Figure 5a.--Intrafolial fold in Uivak I gneiss showing a prominent axial plane fabric. The gneiss is cut by a Saglek dyke containing deformed plagioclase megacrysts. Little Island near Saglek Bight.

Figure 5b.--Uivak I gray gneiss with rootless intrafolial folds. St. John's Harbour, Saglek.

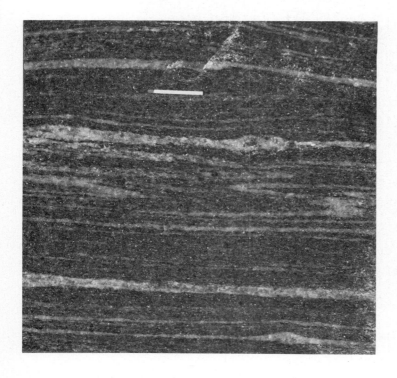

Although the gross compositional differences in the Uivak I suite are probably indicative of compositional variation among the igneous protoliths of the gneisses, we interpret the leucocratic veining and layering to be dominantly a secondary feature, related to anatexis and to high-grade metamorphic differentiations during deformation. Whether or not this layering was produced synchronously with the intrusion of the protoliths, or whether it was the result of subsequent deformation and metamorpism is still a matter for debate.

The Uivak II gneisses are a medium- to coarse-grained suite. Generally they are more potassic, and have a higher ferromagnesian content than Uivak I gneisses of equivalent silica content. In areas of low finite strain, intrusive igneous relationships with the Nulliak assemblage supracrustal lithologies and with the Uivak I suite are preserved (Figs. 6 and 7). In areal abundance they constitute less than 10% of the gneiss complex, occurring principally in an irregular belt from White Point through Mentzel Island and Maidmont Island to the coast opposite Nulliak Island. They are also well exposed along the southern shore of Saglek Bay ca. 2 km east of Saglek (Fig.

Figure 6.--Xenoliths of Nulliak assemblage supracrustal rocks in Uivak II augen gneiss. Coast oppostite Nulliak Island.

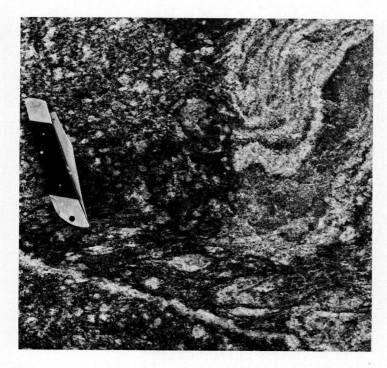

Figure 7.--Xenolith of Uivak I gray gneiss surrounded by augen gneiss. Same
locality as Figure 6.

1). In these less highly deformed structural domains outcrop widths range up
to 1 km. In other areas the Uivak II gneisses occur as narrow sheets 4 to 5 m
in width with intrusive or tectonic contacts against Uivak I migmatites.

The gneisses are characterized by strong L-S or L fabrics. The schistosity
forms augen around elongate porphyroclasts of microcline (as large as 1 x 2 cm
in size; Fig. 8). As a result of intense elongation of the porphyroclasts a
strong rodding is commonly apparent in the foliation plane with aspect ratios
of the megacrysts ranging up to 30:3:1 (Fig. 9). In some areas the L-S fabric
is deformed to produce chevron folds (Fig. 10). In zones of high finite strain
these folds are structurally transposed into a new compositional layering,
associated with a grain size reduction due to dynamic recrystallization and the
development of an anastomosing mylonitic microstructure (Fig. 11). Even in
areas of comparatively low intensity deformation, in which the megacrystic
character of the gneisses is still apparent, local inhomogeneity in the
distribution of strain results in the development of zones of banded gneisses.
Where this process occurs on an outcrop scale (Fig. 12), discrimination between

Figure 8.--Deformed augen gneiss with L-S fabric and porphyroclasts of microcline. Mentzel Island, Saglek.

highly strained Uivak II and Uivak I gray gneisses on purely structural grounds becomes extremely difficult; however, mineralogical and chemical differences persist.

Mega-xenoliths (as large as 20 x 5 m in size) of a disrupted compositionally layered meta-gabbro-leucogabbro-anorthosite-diorite plutonic body (the Mentzel Intrusive Association) are observed at several localities within the Uivak II gneisses; possibly representing an early phase of this suite.

SUPRACRUSTAL ROCKS

Interlayered with the Uivak I gneisses and occurring as xenoliths in the Uivak II suite (Fig. 6) are a group of supracrustal rocks (the Nulliak assemblage) composed of thinly layered felsic and mafic metavolcanics, green clinopyroxene-bearing hornblendites (possibly originally pyroxenites or komatiitic volcanics), banded silicate-oxide iron formation, carbonate-rich

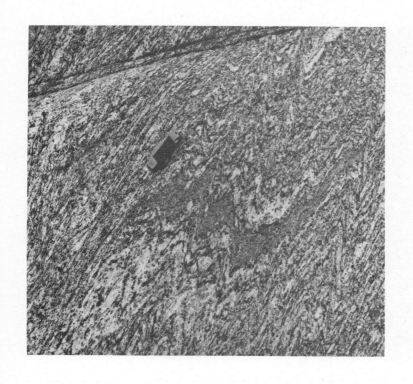

Figure 10.--Mesoscopic chevron folds deforming L-S fabric in Uivak II gneiss. Coast opposite Nulliak Island.

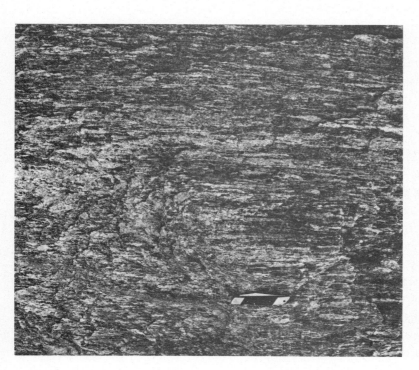

Figure 9.--Mineral elongation lineation in augen gneiss due to deformation of feldspar porphyroclasts. Mentzel Island.

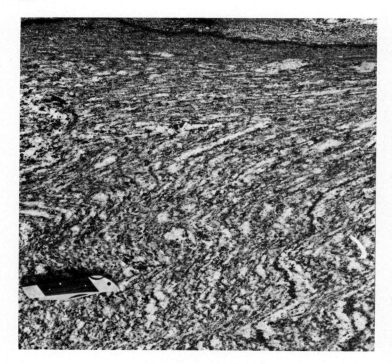

Figure 11.--Zone of high finite strain in augen gneiss showing the development of an anastomosing mylonitic mineral fabric. Coast opposite Nulliak Island.

lithologies and minor pelitic schists. Outcrops of this unit range from continuous horizons that extend as much as 2 km along strike and are as wide as 50 to 100 m to small (as large as 3 x 0.5 m) tectonically disrupted, highly attenuated fragments and boudins in size within Uivak I gneisses. Some of the mafic compositions are altered along their margins to monominerallic biotite rocks, as a result of metasomatic reaction with the surrounding gneisses.

Units of silicate-oxide iron formation commonly exhibit granulite facies mineral assemblages (ferrohypersthene-orthoferrosilite-hedenbergite-magnetite-quartz). In other lithologies, however, minerals are retrogressed to amphibolite facies assemblages, apparently in equilibrium with those in the surrounding gneisses. The presence of partially or completely retrogressed phases in the Nulliak sequence indicates that these early Archean supracrustal rocks were effected by a pre-3.6 Ga granulite facies event. This event could have occurred prior to or after the emplacement of the Uivak I protoliths.

These early Archean supracrustal lithologies are similar both in field relations and lithological character to rocks of the Akilia association described recently by McGregor and Mason (1977) from the Godthaab district of west Greenland.

Figure 12.--Outcrop of highly strained augen gneiss showing the development of a new compositional layering. Same locality as Figure 11.

PETROLOGY

The Uivak I Gneisses

On petrographic examination the Uivak I suite appears to be relatively simple. Acid to intermediate homogeneous areas of the layered gray gneisses are generally characterized by the following mineral assemblages:

Quartz-biotite-oligoclase

Quartz-biotite-hornblende-oligoclase

Quartz-biotite-oligoclase-microcline

Quartz-biotite-hornblende-oligoclase-microcline

and more mafic members of the suite by:

Andesine-labradorite-hornblende-clinopyroxene-biotite.

Wart-like growths of myrmekite along plagioclase-microcline interfaces are common in almost all of the acid to intermediate gneisses. Accessory phases include Fe-Ti oxides, apatite, zircon, allanite, epidote, and sphene. Pleochroic haloes around metamict allanite and zircon occur in both biotite and amphibolite.

Microstructures in almost all of the gray gneisses involve medium- to fine-grained xenoblastic grains of quartz, plagioclase and microcline, which form inequigranular- to equigranular-granoblastic mosaics. Grain boundaries between these phases are straight, curved, amoeboid or serrated. Triple point junctions, indicating an approach to microstructural equilibrium by annealing, are distinctive in some sections (Fig. 13). The dominant mineral fabric, which parallels the compositional layering, is defined by the aligment of subidioblastic to idioblastic flakes or decussate aggregates of biotite

Figure 13a.--Uivak I gneiss with granulite facies mineralogy (orthopyroxene, hornblende, biotite, plagioclase and quartz) with medium to fine grained granoblastic microstructure. Length of bar 0.5 cm.

Figure 13c.--Amphibolite facies Uivak I gneiss with inequigranular granoblastic microstructure. Note the variation in grain size of the quartzo-feldspathic phases from (a) to (b) to (c). Length of bar 1.0 cm.

Figure 13b.--Amphibolite facies Uivak I gray gneiss containing the assemblage
hornblende-biotite-microcline-plagioclase and quartz. The microstructure
is medium grained granoblastic. Length of bar 1.0 cm.

(averaging 1 x 0.25 mm, and up to 7 mm in length, respectively) and also by subidioblastic grains of green hornblende up to 3 x 0.5 mm in size. The fabric is also manifest in other sections by the presence of wavy lenticles of quartz up to 1 cm in length, forming granoblastic elongate microstructures (Collerson, 1974).

The more mafic members of the Uivak I suite are characterized by granoblastic (generally equigranular) microstructures. Grain boundaries between plagioclase and ferromagnesian phases are either straight or gently curved, and both rational and irrational interfaces are developed between biotite and amphibole.

In a number of specimens from the lower structural levels of the terrain, well preserved replacement relationships between green hornblende and clinopyroxene or orthopyroxene, have been found in mafic compositions. In all cases the hornblende replacement is mimetic with respect to the fabric in the rock.

In the trondhjemitic to granodioritic Uivak I gray gneisses, hornblende-biotite microstructural relations indicate that the biotite, which defines the mineral fabric, is in part a static, homoaxial replacement of hornblende. In thin section this biotite is strongly pleochroic with the following schemes:

      X - neutral to pale yellow
   Y = Z - olive green to orange brown, red brown, black brown,
           or green brown

which presumably reflect compositional differences. It has a large aspect ratio (length:width) in sections perpendicular to (001), and generally forms decussate mats composed of subidioblastic flakes showing either curved and embayed irrational interfaces or sharp rational boundaries against amphibole of a later generation (see below). Included within the biotite, or marginal to it, are fine-grained aggregates of platy or granular epidote, apparently lying in the basal plane of the host biotite. In sections normal or oblique to this plane the epidote aggregates appear to be deformed by slip along (001), resulting in the development of chevron micro-folds.

The biotite also displays a characteristic sagenitic microstructure, i.e., it contains numerous crystallographically oriented acicular needles of rutile in 110 and 010 planes (Figs. 14 and 15). There are several possible interpretations for this intergrowth. It could be the result of sub-solidus exsolution of rutile from titaniferous biotite as a result of physical conditions which destabilized titanium in the biotite structure. Or

Figure 14.--Basal orientation of biotite with crystallographically oriented needles of rutile in 110 and 010 planes. Note the replacement relationship between biotite and hornblende, as well as the coronas of granular epidote. Length of bar 1.0 mm.

alternatively it might have developed at the same time as hornblende was being replaced to form biotite (see above). Again, this implies that titaniferous biotite was not stable under the prevailing physical conditions.

In an attempt to resolve the origin of the sagenite, and the replacement of hornblende, we petrographically examined a number of Uivak I gray gneisses from a low structural level in the terrain, which retained granulite facies mineral assemblages. These gneisses are virtually devoid of alkali feldspar and are composed of medium- to fine-grained equigranular granoblastic aggregates of quartz and calcic oligoclase. They have a relatively strong mineral fabric defined by the alignment of subidioblastic orthopyroxene and clinopyroxene as well as elongate xenoblastic grains of strongly pleochroic green-brown hornblende and idioblastic flakes of reddish-brown biotite, in apparent microstructural equilibrium with the pyroxene and amphibole (Fig. 13a). Inclusion trails of very fine grained ilmenite and olive-green spinel are prominent in the amphibole.

Figure 15.--Biotite orientations oblique to the 001 plane showing the effect of crystallographic orientation on the sagenitic rutile needles. Length of bar 1.0 mm.

By examining microstructural relationships from gneisses showing signs of partial retrogression we recognized all stages of replacement of granulite facies assemblages grading to those which finally equilibrated under amphibolite facies conditions (Table 2; Fig. 13). In Figure 13 it is noticeable that the average grain size of the partially altered rocks (13a) is smaller than that of the gneisses carrying well-developed amphibolite facies assemblages (13b,c; see below).

In petrographic character the sagenitic biotite closely mimics the shape and mineral fabric orientation of the granulite facies xenoblastic hornblende. Other features observed in the paragenetic development of the amphibolite facies Uivak I gneisses include: (1) an increase in the modal content of potassium feldspar and quartz; (2) orthopyroxene replaced by Mg-amphibole (anthophyllite-cummingtonite) and clinopyroxene by actinolite in the initial stage of alteration, and subsequently as a result of an increased a_{Al} they react to form secondary green hornblende; (3) the secondary amphibole may be partially or completely replaced by a tertiary growth of reddish-brown to green

TABLE 2: Paragenetic Development of Uivak I Quartzo-Feldspathic Gneisses

Relict Assemblage

Quartz ——————————————————————— Quartz Increases

Calcic Oligoclase/Alkali Feldspar ——————— Plagioclase Decreases

Orthopyroxene —— Mg Amphibole ——————————— Non-Sagenitic Biotite

Clinopyroxene —— Actinolite —— 2° Hornblende —— Non-Sagenitic Biotite

Biotite ————— Sagenitic Biotite ——————————— Non-Sagenitic Biotite

Hornblende

Ilmenite ————⟩ Sagenitic Biotite + Epidote —— Non-Sagenitic Biotite

Spinel

Secondary Assemblage

Quartz-Microcline-Oligoclase-Myrmekite-Sagenitic Biotite-2° Hornblende-3°

Biotite-Epidote-Zircon-Allanite-Sphene

biotite, coronas of this biotite are also developed around the sagenitic biotite; and (4)accompanying the increase in the amount of potassium feldspar there is also an increase in the abundance of myrmekite.

Preliminary microprobe analyses of sagenitic biotite, primary (granulite facies) amphibole and biotite in equilibrium with this amphibole from gneisses in the Saglek area are given in Table 3. As the analysis of the sagenitic biotite was made in an area free of rutile needles, this TiO_2 value must therefore represent a minimum value (2.7%) for the overall biotite composition. Assuming an additional amount of titania in the range ca. 0.5-2.0% (estimated from the density of rutile needles), and on the assumption that the replacement principally involved the addition of potassium, the parental amphibole should have contained between ca. 3.2 and 4.7% TiO_2. This is significantly greater than the TiO_2 content of the granulite facies hornblende (1.6%). However, if the inclusions in the granulite facies hornblende are taken into account (ilmenite and Al-spinel) a mass balance can be calculated whereby biotite, epidote and rutile are produced from the hornblende; iron entering the biotite structure along with titanium, and calcium (from the breakdown of hornblende) reacting with the Al-spinel to form epidote.

TABLE 3: Microprobe analyses of sagenitic biotite, non-sagenitic primary
biotite and hornblende from Uivak 1 gneisses

Specimen Number	KC/74/32Y	-/75/67a	-/75/67a
SiO_2	35.6	38.0	42.9
TiO_2	2.7	3.8	1.6
Al_2O_3	16.5	16.0	12.1
Cr_2O_3	-	0.1	0.1
FeO	24.9	17.2	16.0
MnO	0.2	0.1	0.2
NiO	-	0.1	0.1
MgO	7.3	12.8	11.2
CaO	-	-	11.9
Na_2O	-	-	1.4
K_2O	8.1	8.6	1.1
Total	95.3	96.6	98.6
Si	5.53	5.60	6.37
Al^{iv}	2.47	2.40	1.63
Al^{vi}	0.55	0.39	0.49
Ti	0.32	0.42	0.17
Cr	-	0.01	0.01
Fe^{2+}	3.24	2.12	1.99
Mn	0.02	0.01	0.02
Ni	-	-	0.01
Mg	1.68	2.82	2.47
Ca	-	-	1.89
Na	0.01	-	0.41
K	1.61	1.61	0.21
No. of oxygens	22	22	23
mg	0.34	0.57	0.55

Analyst K. D. Collerson

Automated JEOL JXA 50A microprobe. Memorial University.

The puzzling question which remains, however, is the reason for biotite becoming unstable with respect to TiO_2, when granulite facies gneisses from the same area contain biotite as much as 3.8% TiO_2, and in other areas as much as 5.5% TiO_2 (Leelanandam, 1970). References to the formation of sagenitic biotite are scarce in the literature. Hatch et al. (1972), however, have suggested that its development may be related to pneumatolytic activity. If this is the reason for its formation in the Saglek area, the timing of the event is important. We tentatively suggest that the development of sagenitic biotite in this early Archean gneiss terrain was related to volatile fluxing (diffusion) synchronously with the addition of potassium (and other LIL elements) to lithologies previously depleted in these elements (cf. Bridgwater and Collerson, 1976, 1977; and below).

The Uivak II Gneisses

The Uivak II suite of acid to intermediate augen gneisses has a higher modal content of ferromagnesian phases (biotite and hornblende) than Uivak I gneisses and shows approximately equivalent contents of quartz and feldspar. The gneisses are characterized by medium- to coarse-grained, inequigranular to equigranular, granoblastic or granoblastic elongate microstructures. A prominent schistosity defined by anastomosing biotite intergrowths surrounding variably recrystallized porphyroclasts of potassium feldspar also is ubiquitous.

The most commonly developed mineral assemblage is quartz-oligoclase-microcline-biotite$^{\pm}$hornblende-Fe-Ti oxides. Microcline is present in amounts ranging from ca. 5 to 30%. It commonly is perthitic, shows shadowy cross-hatched twinning, and forms either large 'poikilitic' elongate porphyroclasts as large as 2.5 x 1 cm, granoblastic aggregates derived from these megacrysts by recrystallization, or small xenoblastic grains as a groundmass phase; also it commonly is closely associated with growths of myrmekite. In more highly strained gneisses the distinction between porphyroclastic and groundmass alkali feldspar becomes equivocal. The megacrysts are interpreted to be primary features of the suite, related to grain variation in the protolith. However, whether they were formed by magmatic, or by metasomatic processes, such as those suggested for the formation of potassium feldspar phenocrysts in granite by Mehnert (1968), remains to be evaluated. It is clear, however, that they are pretectonic with respect to the deformation which formed the mineral fabric in the gneisses.

Quartz and oligoclase form medium- to fine-grained inequigranular granoblastic aggregates. Grain boundaries are either curved, smoothly embayed or highly serrated. Albite and pericline twins in the plagioclase are interpreted to be the result of deformation (cf. Vance, 1961; Vernon, 1965). Relatively large elongate grains of quartz as large as 0.75 x 0.25 cm are commonly aligned with the mineral fabric. The quartz is invariably strained and exhibits a prominent substructure defined either by areas of patchy undulose extinction, or by extinction bands showing sharp sub-grain boundaries (cf., White, 1973). In some sections the quartz sub-grain boundaries may participate in triple point junctions with quartz or other phases. These microstructures are interpreted to indicate deformation by dynamic recovery, at relatively high temperatures and slow strain rates (cf. White, 1976, 1977).

Biotite, the dominant ferromagnesian phase in the Uivak II gneisses exhibits the following pleochroic schemes:

        X - pale yellow
    Y = X - reddish brown, green brown, green black

It is variably sagenitic and contains numerous fine-grained inclusions of epidote. Microstructures are characerized by decussate intergrowths composed of xenoblastic elongate flakes with a high aspect ratio (as much as 3.0 x 0.3 mm), developing ragged irrational interfaces against plagioclase, or smoothly embayed boundaries, approximately parallel to (001), against quartz. Some sections contain inclusions of idioblastic to subidioblastic zircon, or metamict allanite, surrounded by large pleochroic haloes (cf. Baadsgaard et al., 1976). Although microstructural relationships for the origin of the sagenitic biotite are not as clear in the Uivak II gneisses as they are in the Uivak I gray gneisses, it is nevertheless sufficiently similar in character to be interpreted as a probable pseudomorph after hornblende--a fact which has considerable petrogenetic significance.

Iron-rich hornblende is conspicuous in some examples of Uivak II gneiss; particularly those with lower contents of quartz and feldspar. It is pleochroic (X-yellow, Y-green brown, Z-dark olive green) and forms subidioblastic to xenoblastic grains up to 6 x 1 mm in size, apparently in microstructural equilibrium with the sagenitic biotite. Incipient alteration to fine-grained, decussate, pale-green biotite is commonly observed, particularly along cleavage traces.

Accessory phases include small idioblastic grains of zircon, monazite, apatite, allanite (rimmed by epidote) and sphene.

Petrographic Summary

In view of the widespread development of relatively simple amphibolite facies assemblages in the Saglek area, it is tempting to interpret the Uivak I and UIvak II suites as being formed simply by the prograde isochemical metamorphism of a variety of plutonic protoliths ranging in composition from gabbro, through trondhjemite and tonalite to granodiorite and granite. This concept has been suggested for the Amitsoq gneisses in Greenland by McGregor (1973; this volume). It is clear, however, from field and petrological relationships in both the Uivak I and II gneisses that the gneiss terrain experienced a complex polymetamorphic history.

Microstructural relations in both the older Uivak I gneisses and the younger Uivak II augen gneisses indicate that the metamorphic, or igneous protoliths contained hornblende, and, at least locally, those for the Uivak I gneisses contained pyroxene. This is because hornblende appears to have been homoaxially replaced by biotite, and pyroxene by secondary hornblende. In the Uivak I gneisses this replacement is considered to have occurred 'statically', or after the units had achieved their strong anisotropy, because both the biotite and the secondary hornblende mimic an earlier partially granoblastic to granoblastic elongate microstructure.

In earlier publications (Bridgwater and Collerson, 1977), we suggested that the Uivak I suite had been influenced by the metasomatic addition of a number of large ion lithophile elements, i.e., K and Rb, because the gneisses have low K/Rb and high Rb/Sr ratios, which are atypical of postulated protolith compositions (see below). As both the Uivak I and Uivak II gneisses define essentially the same Rb/Sr isochron (Hurst et al., 1975), yet obviously form discrete structural-lithological units, we consider the age indicated by the isochron to be the time of K and Rb metasomatism. This event was probably synchronous with the intrusion and deformation of the igneous protoliths of the augen gneisses (cf. McGregor, this volume)

Such large-scale diffusion of alkalis implied by this model would be facilitated by the physical conditions indicated from the microstructures in the gneisses, viz., high temperatures and slow strain rate. These conditions, during the syntectonic emplacement of the Uivak II protoliths would result in deformation by dynamic recovery. It is conceivable that this deformation mechanism would be assisted by the presence of a volatile phase which could lower activation energies thereby encouraging diffusion to occur more pervasively.

GEOCHEMISTRY

Chemical analyses and selected elemental ratios of representative amphibolite and granulite facies Uivak I gneisses, and amphibolite facies Uivak II gneisses are presented in Tables 4, 5, and 6, respectively. Average compositions of different members of both groups of gneisses, together with analyses for comparison, are listed in Table 7. Salient chemical relationships between the Uivak I and II suites are depicted in Figures 16 to 29.

Major elements were determined by a combination of X-ray fluorescence spectrometry (using lithium tetraborate fusions), and atomic absorption spectrometry. Trace element analyses were obtained by X-ray fluorescence spectrometry using pressed pellets. Details of statistical data for trace elements on a number of USGS standard rocks, analyzed in conjunction with the Uivak analyses are given in Table 9. Reconnaissance rare earth element (REE) data was obtained by X-ray fluorescence spectrometry using the method of Fryer (1977). Results are given in Table 10.

The Uivak I Suite
Major elements

The Uivak I suite is dominated by siliceous gray gneisses which are broadly similar in composition to gneisses from other Archean terrains (Tables 4, 5, 7, and 8). The presence of subordinate mafic and intermediate rocks within the suite indicates that it is not bimodal in character (cf., Barker and Peterman, 1974; Hunter et al., in press). The suite defines a linear trend on an AFM plot (Fig. 16), which is similar to that exhibited by calc alkaline igneous suites, and by the Amitsoq gray gneisses.

SiO_2 contents in the gray gneisses range from 62.0 to 76.4%, and Al_2O_3 from 8.3 to 17.3%, with a distinct node at ca. 15%. There is no obvious relationship between the alumina and alkali content (Fig. 17b). Na_2O ranges between 2.11 and 5.40%, and K_2O between 0.67 and 5.60% (Fig. 17a); resultant Na_2O/K_2O ratios varying between 0.48 and 4.66. To facilitate the comparison of analytical data, following Condie and Hunter (1976), gneisses with Na_2O/K_2O ratios less than 2.0 are classified as 'granitic' or 'granodioritic', and those with ratios greater than 2.0 are termed 'trondhjemitic' or 'tonalitic'.

In the trondhjemitic to tonalitic gray gneisses MgO concentrations range from 5.98 to 0.65%, with average values of 2.39% and 0.89% in the least- and most-silicic gneisses, respectively. Potassic members of the suite have lower magnesia contents, ranging from 1.39 to 0.16%, with an average of 0.70%. CaO varies between 5.78 and 1.98%, averaging 4.2% and 2.72% in the least-, and

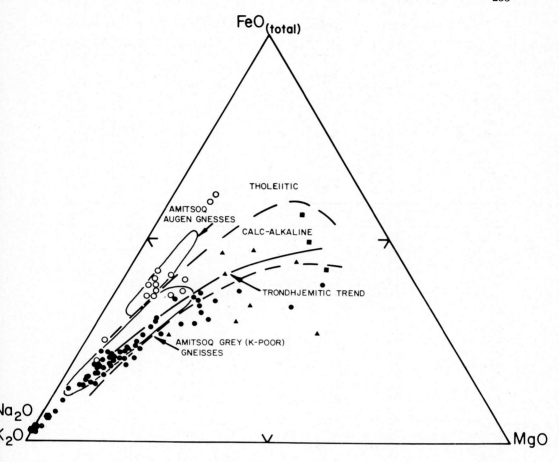

Figure 16.--Ternary AFM projection showing the Uivak I and Uivak II gneisses.
Ornamentation: Solid circles--Uivak I gneisses with greater than 60% SiO₂;
solid triangles--Uivak II gneisses with 50-60% SiO₂; solid squares--Uivak I
gneisses with less than 50% SiO₂; solid hexagons--pre-Saglek dyke
pegmatites; open circles--Uivak II augen gneisses. Also shown are the
fields for the Amitsoq augen and gray gneisses, from McGregor (1975), for
comparison. The tholeiitic and calc-alkaline fields and trondhjemite trend
are from Barker and Arth (1976).

most-silicic gray gneisses. In the potassic gneisses values range from 3.88 to
0.36% with a mean of 1.95%. Average titania contents range from a high of 0.56%
in the sodic gneisses to a low of 0.24% in the granodioritic to granitic
gneisses.

The mafic and intermediate members of the Uivak I suite have generally
higher contents of TiO_2, total Fe, MgO, and CaO than the more silicic members
of the suite. Alkali abundances, however, are extremely variable and Na_2O/K_2O

TABLE 4 : Representative analyses of amphibolite facies Uivak I gneisses

Sample	75-297B	75-248C	76-331B	75-263	75-28z	75-320	75-229D
SiO_2	48.7	53.6	55.7	56.4	56.7	59.8	62.1
TiO_2	0.84	1.24	0.48	0.52	0.66	0.77	0.52
Al_2O_3	14.0	17.4	12.8	22.0	16.8	15.8	15.6
Fe_2O_3	4.69	1.62	1.43	0.75	1.33	1.43	1.21
FeO	7.36	7.82	4.51	3.14	3.93	5.63	4.27
MnO	0.22	0.12	0.12	0.06	0.12	0.15	0.10
MgO	7.95	3.40	10.14	2.38	4.95	3.39	3.70
CaO	10.18	5.22	6.46	4.78	5.94	5.19	5.72
Na_2O	2.94	4.21	3.38	6.20	4.97	4.44	4.09
K_2O	1.06	3.01	2.40	2.18	2.35	1.99	1.37
P_2O_5	0.29	0.68	0.39	0.17	0.42	0.23	0.21
LOI	2.35	1.86	1.63	0.99	1.46	1.02	1.03
Total	100.58	100.18	99.44	99.58	99.63	99.82	99.92
Zr	69	336	121	227	179	144	116
Sr	226	713	865	431	1305	388	209
Rb	38	211	139	157	112	131	79
Zn	125	98	83	71	159	184	68
Cu	41	76	24	9	48	25	8
Ba	116	934	572.	192	680	180	125
Ce	–	270	220	24	183	101	19
La	–	140	93	18	111	53	14
Nb	–	–	5	–	9	9	8
Ga	19	26	19	25	24	29	22
Pb	12	10	14	15	17	17	11
Ni	117	20	266	19	120	42	64
Cr	277	–	350	36	117	114	72
V	245	–	111	75	107	103	76
Y	19	46	20	4	18	20	20
Na_2O/K_2O	2.77	1.40	1.41	2.84	2.12	2.23	2.99
K/Rb	232	118	143	115	174	126	144
Ba/Rb	3.05	4.43	4.12	1.22	6.07	1.37	1.58
K/Ba	75.9	26.8	34.8	94.3	28.7	9.18	90.9
Rb/Sr	0.168	0.296	0.161	0.364	0.086	0.338	0.378
Sr/Ba	1.95	0.76	1.51	2.25	1.92	2.16	1.67
Ce/Y	–	7.22	11.00	6.00	10.17	5.05	0.95

Analysts: K.D. Collerson, D. Press and G. Andrews.

ratios range from 2.84 to 0.65 in the intermediate gneisses (Na_2O varying between 2.0 and 6.49%, and K_2O between 1.86 and 3.78%). The mafic gneisses all hae Na_2O/K_2O ratios greater than 2.0 (Na_2O averaging 2.89% and K_2O, 1.04%).

In terms of SiO_2/K_2O ratios (Fig. 18), the Uivak I suite shows a general increase in K_2O with SiO_2. The gray silicic gneisses partially overlap the compositional field of continental trondhjemites and granophyre, although some

TABLE 4 : continued

75-260Bβ	75-229C	75-320/1	76-426A	74-161A	75-260Bγ	75-28Vβ	75-28Xβ
64.2	64.5	65.6	65.8	66.3	67.6	68.6	69.4
0.60	0.58	0.52	0.62	0.44	0.45	0.35	0.34
15.7	16.3	16.0	16.3	17.3	15.9	15.7	15.8
0.92	1.12	0.87	0.54	0.68	0.49	0.34	0.35
4.03	3.70	3.76	3.15	2.33	2.98	2.19	1.81
0.02	0.07	0.07	0.03	0.05	0.07	0.06	0.05
2.32	2.29	2.38	1.45	1.30	1.39	1.36	0.83
3.92	4.82	4.32	3.32	3.06	3.28	2.78	2.77
4.71	4.24	4.47	4.82	5.78	4.45	5.04	5.20
1.84	1.63	1.68	2.18	2.03	2.31	2.17	2.18
0.22	0.25	0.12	0.24	0.16	0.20	0.20	0.16
1.14	0.87	0.96	0.79	0.87	0.83	0.84	0.46
99.62	100.37	100.75	99.24	100.30	99.95	99.63	99.35
190	163	162	303	185	135	170	167
378	232	510	263	756	423	630	524
134	95	106	144	116	120	117	126
144	56	85	74	58	141	129	147
12	27	42	20	7	23	29	12
69	263	238	1084	159	372	298	222
84	34	66	90	43	61	82	40
42	13	38	56	33	32	51	21
8	7	2	10	6	9	16	13
28	23	25	20	22	25	23	24
16	11	17	20	14	12	20	23
36	25	22	9	7	4	9	-
72	35	57	21	14	43	37	14
66	76	91	57	33	47	30	20
15	19	20	3	11	9	12	9
2.56	2.60	2.66	2.21	2.85	1.93	2.32	2.39
114	143	132	126	145	160	154	144
0.52	2.77	2.25	7.53	1.37	3.10	2.55	1.76
221.4	51.5	58.6	16.7	106.0	51.6	60.5	81.5
0.354	0.409	0.208	0.548	0.153	0.284	0.186	0.240
5.48	0.88	2.14	0.24	4.76	1.14	2.11	2.36
5.60	1.79	3.30	30.00	3.91	6.78	6.83	4.44

gneisses exhibit an almost linear vertical trend of potash increasing for silica values of ca. 70.0%.

When represented on a ternary K-Na-Ca projection (Fig. 19), the Uivak I suite occupies an extensive field which partially straddles the compositional variation trend exhibited by the gabbro to trondhjemite suite from S.W. Finland (Barker and Arth, 1976), and shows a significant trend towards potassium. In

TABLE 4 : continued

Sample	74-46J	75-32P	75-32Y	76-334A	75-291F	75-252E	75-296A
SiO_2	69.7	70.4	70.5	70.7	70.7	71.2	71.4
TiO_2	0.54	0.38	0.40	0.26	0.22	0.36	0.32
Al_2O_3	8.30	16.1	14.9	15.7	15.6	15.1	15.5
Fe_2O_3	1.34	0.49	0.05	0.58	0.74	0.55	0.29
FeO	4.30	1.72	2.11	1.37	1.21	1.27	1.10
MnO	0.17	0.04	0.03	0.02	0.02	0.02	0.01
MgO	5.98	0.89	0.73	0.87	0.87	0.89	0.51
CaO	5.50	2.66	2.10	2.46	2.80	1.58	1.68
Na_2O	2.11	5.08	4.37	4.90	4.56	3.42	4.28
K_2O	0.67	1.28	2.89	2.64	2.04	4.90	3.84
P_2O_5	0.19	0.14	0.14	0.14	0.13	0.11	0.09
LOI	1.02	0.59	0.61	0.66	0.54	0.79	0.47
Total	99.82	99.77	98.83	100.30	99.43	100.19	99.49
Zr	74	157	207	136	123	282	147
Sr	124	391	509	468	356	490	400
Rb	24	102	119	110	117	254	147
Zn	57	70	58	50	46	55	35
Cu	12	18	24	7	63	27	33
Ba	66	39	354	462	619	1424	294
Ce	19	40	140	19	44	27	44
La	13	21	70	–	23	19	27
Nb	5	6	5	4	2	45	2
Ga	14	20	22	24	20	15	24
Pb	6	19	19	18	25	21	24
Ni	211	–	–	–	–	–	–
Cr	821	12	8	12	15	9	13
V	57	29	26	28	18	18	12
Y	12	12	17	7	9	7	6
Na_2O/K_2O	3.15	3.97	1.51	1.86	2.24	0.70	1.12
K/Rb	232	104	202	199	145	160	217
Ba/Rb	2.75	0.38	2.98	4.20	5.29	5.61	2.00
K-Ba	84.3	272.5	67.8	47.4	27.4	28.6	108.4
Rb/Sr	0.194	0.261	0.234	0.235	0.329	0.518	0.368
Sr/Ba	1.88	10.03	1.43	1.01	0.58	0.34	1.36
Ce/Y	1.58	3.33	8.24	2.71	4.89	3.86	7.33

some of the gneisses this increase in potassium is accompanied by a sympathetic decrease in the Ca/Na ratio; however, the most significant increase is reprsented by gneisses in which the Ca/Na ratio remains almost constant.

When plotted in terms of normative An-Ab-Or the Uivak I gray gneisses lie in the compositional fields of trondhjemite-tonalite-granodiorite-adamellite, and granite, which were outlined by O'Connor (1965), comparing closely with the

TABLE 4 : continued

74-40A	75-298	75-295A	74-32X	75-28Y∝	75-183B	75-28V∝	75-260B∝	76-421A
71.8	72.2	72.2	72.3	73.2	73.9	74.0	74.2	76.4
0.33	0.08	0.50	0.31	0.03	0.00	0.06	0.07	0.12
15.3	15.0	14.8	14.9	15.4	14.7	13.3	14.3	11.8
0.30	0.34	0.31	0.60	0.00	0.10	0.17	0.00	0.53
1.90	1.23	1.31	1.30	0.20	0.20	0.52	0.59	0.77
0.03	0.02	0.02	0.02	0.02	0.02	0.03	0.11	0.02
0.94	0.48	0.50	0.65	0.09	0.05	0.19	0.22	0.24
2.91	1.62	1.56	3.04	2.05	1.06	1.13	2.16	0.36
5.10	4.48	4.10	5.40	5.11	3.79	3.13	3.91	2.66
1.62	3.38	3.86	1.16	2.87	5.09	6.10	3.50	5.60
0.11	0.10	0.10	0.10	0.08	0.06	0.05	0.09	0.04
0.50	0.52	0.58	0.70	0.38	0.26	0.74	0.72	0.20
100.84	99.45	99.84	100.48	99.40	99.23	99.42	99.89	98.74
126	160	156	170	128	64	74	128	126
373	384	333	423	1337	318	469	509	33
92	132	165	69	100	127	147	110	285
65	53	34	54	89	23	96	105	27
19	19	21	13	28	16	22	25	8
163	263	257	153	958	527	1042	606	317
-	55	54	-	-	1	16	28	69
-	30	31	-	-	1	9	17	28
6	3	2	5	12	-	13	15	11
23	26	26	25	19	21	14	16	19
14	21	23	15	24	21	29	14	22
5	-	-	-	-	-	-	-	4
18	7	14	22	3	3	7	2	11
32	15	12	26	-	-	-	-	4
9	13	8	11	5	3	2	7	13
3.15	1.33	1.06	4.66	1.78	0.75	0.51	1.12	0.48
146	213	194	140	238	333	345	264	163
1.77	1.99	1.56	2.22	9.58	4.15	7.09	5.51	1.11
82.5	106.7	124.7	62.9	24.9	80.2	48.6	47.9	146.7
0.247	0.344	0.495	0.163	0.075	0.399	0.313	0.216	8.636
2.29	1.46	1.30	2.77	1.40	0.60	0.45	0.84	0.10
-	4.23	6.75	-	-	0.33	8.00	4.00	5.31

field for the Amitsoq gneisses (Fig. 20). Q-Or-Ab normative compositions of the Uivak I gneisses, along with the fields of the Amitsoq gray gneisses, and gneisses from the bimodal suite and granodiorite suite in the Ancient Gneiss Complex of Swaziland are plotted in Figure 21. The majority of the Uivak trondhjemitic to tonalitic gneisses occupy a relatively confined area away from the Or-apex and show a distinct spread in the Q-Ab direction, reflecting

238

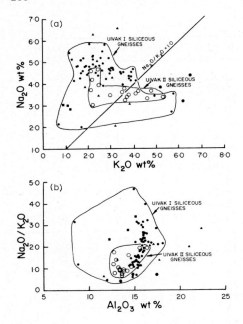

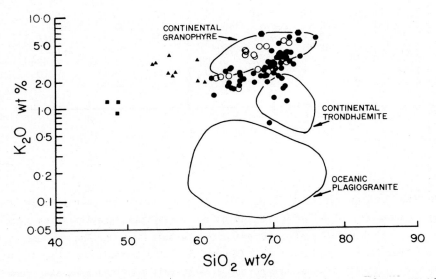

Figure 17.--(a) Plot of Na₂O against K₂O for the Uivak gneisses. Ornamentations in Figure 16. (b) Variation diagram showing the relationship between the Na₂O/K₂O ratio and alumina. Ornamentation as in Figure 16.

Figure 18.--K₂O and SiO₂ contents of the Uivak gneisses. Ornamentation as in Figure 16. The fields of other rock suites are from Coleman and Peterman (1975).

TABLE 5: Representative analyses of granulite facies Uivak gneisses

Sample	75-238B	75-238A	76-348	75-216B	74-122A
SiO_2	64.0	64.6	69.2	69.3	70.0
TiO_2	0.34	0.50	0.32	0.42	0.44
Al_2O_3	15.8	16.4	15.7	14.3	15.2
Fe_2O_3	0.56	0.96	0.31	0.24	0.26
FeO	3.38	3.52	1.79	2.64	1.92
MnO	0.07	0.06	0.04	0.04	0.02
MgO	2.97	2.51	1.08	1.61	0.84
CaO	4.58	4.60	2.86	2.74	2.72
Na_2O	4.48	4.76	5.03	3.81	4.14
K_2O	1.71	1.48	2.15	2.60	2.72
P_2O_5	0.25	0.21	0.20	0.15	0.10
LOI	0.70	0.76	0.52	0.84	0.71
Total	98.84	100.36	99.20	98.69	99.07
Zr	103	99	115	202	112
Sr	600	473	631	306	393
Rb	45	30	68	87	73
Zn	61	65	55	51	44
Cu	20	9	457	51	12
Ba	368	320	54	624	767
Ce	31	47	54	43	27
La	30	33	6	27	19
Nb	5	6	6	3	5
Ga	22	24	23	21	19
Pb	8	14	6	12	11
Ni	47	27	9	45	5
Cr	88	44	21	42	11
V	71	80	43	46	36
Y	10	11	10	9	6
Na_2O/K_2O	2.62	3.22	2.34	1.47	1.52
K/Rb	316.0	410.0	263.0	248.0	309.0
Ba/Rb	8.12	10.7	0.79	7.17	10.5
K/Ba	38.6	38.4	330.5	34.6	29.4
Rb/Sr	0.075	0.063	0.108	0.284	0.186
Sr/Ba	1.63	1.48	11.7	0.49	0.51
Ce/Y	3.10	4.27	5.40	4.78	4.50

Analysts: K. D. Collerson, D. Press and G. Andrews

TABLE 6: Representative analyses of amphibolite facies Uivak II gneisses

Sample	74-161G	76-431B	75-287	74-42A	75-291
SiO_2	62.5	66.6	66.7	66.7	67.8
TiO_2	1.29	0.88	0.70	0.58	0.81
Al_2O_3	12.6	13.2	14.4	13.5	13.6
Fe_2O_3	3.43	1.33	1.42	1.64	0.78
FeO	7.28	4.69	3.88	4.11	4.54
MnO	0.11	0.10	0.09	0.08	0.23
MgO	1.49	1.38	1.02	0.92	1.97
CaO	4.14	3.32	2.94	2.72	2.10
Na_2O	3.63	3.44	3.68	3.44	3.31
K_2O	2.09	3.73	3.54	4.01	3.67
P_2O_5	0.34	0.29	0.24	0.19	0.21
LOI	0.79	0.61	0.61	0.69	0.89
Total	99.69	99.57	99.22	98.58	99.91
Zr	231	301	285	264	288
Sr	185	319	314	248	164
Rb	101	116	140	147	252
Zn	51	76	80	98	159
Cu	34	32	44	12	28
Ba	562	1240	1375	985	1067
Ce	105	114	102	135	97
La	44	61	56	66	24
Nb	4	9	7	5	15
Ga	18	20	18	20	21
Pb	1	23	20	13	21
Ni	10	11	--	9	9
Cr	17	10	29	2	41
V	55	77	80	50	58
Y	26	38	24	27	20
Na_2O/K_2O	1.74	0.92	1.04	0.86	0.90
K/Rb	172.0	267.0	210.0	227.0	121.0
Ba/Rb	5.56	10.69	9.82	6.70	4.23
K/Ba	30.9	25.0	21.4	33.8	28.6
Rb/Sr	0.546	0.364	0.446	0.593	1.537
Sr/Ba	0.33	0.26	0.23	0.25	0.15
Ce/Y	4.04	3.00	4.25	5.00	4.85

Analysts: K. D. Collerson, D. Press and G. Andrews.

75-291D	76-448D	75-291E	75-277A	74-45B
68.3	68.5	69.5	69.7	72.7
0.78	0.80	0.84	0.50	0.44
14.0	13.5	13.1	15.4	12.7
0.10	1.14	0.61	0.30	0.10
4.18	3.82	3.92	2.15	2.80
0.07	0.08	0.07	0.06	0.04
1.43	0.98	1.02	1.27	0.47
2.34	2.60	2.02	2.56	1.57
3.80	3.26	3.16	4.58	3.60
2.40	4.55	3.54	2.40	4.73
0.22	0.10	0.17	0.26	0.13
0.95	0.52	0.79	0.96	0.20
98.57	99.85	98.74	100.14	99.48
313	249	297	210	274
166	263	183	994	165
207	167	183	168	178
85	66	82	62	67
23	24	18	50	12
590	1246	801	1687	901
120	104	157	147	--
23	40	68	82	--
8	11	9	3	11
19	19	18	21	16
19	25	25	39	17
3	8	--	--	11
27	16	48	51	21
74	51	49	46	21
23	26	25	15	24
1.58	0.72	0.89	1.91	0.76
96.3	226.0	161.0	119.0	221.0
2.85	7.46	4.38	10.0	5.06
33.8	30.3	36.7	11.8	43.6
1.247	0.635	1.000	0.169	1.079
0.28	0.21	0.23	0.59	0.18
5.22	4.00	6.28	9.80	--

242

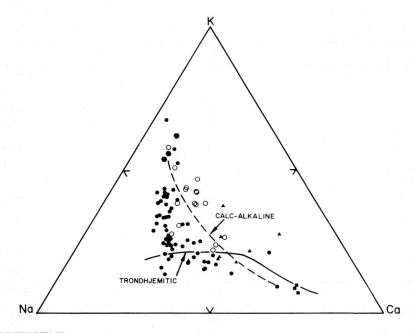

Figure 19.--Ternary K-Na-Ca projection for the Uivak gneisses showing the trends for calc-alkaline and trondhjemitic suites (from Barker and Arth, 1976).

variation in normative quartz content. A number of the potash-rich pegmatites and pegmatite-rich Uivak gneisses lie closer to the Or-apex, approximating to low melting compositions. Intermediate and mafic members of the suite lie along, or near, the Or-Ab tie-line in a field which reflects variation in normative Ab/Or, as well as degree of silica saturation. There is no clear relationship between the fields for different compositions in the suite and the calc-alkaline or gabbro-trondhjemite trends given in Barker and Arth (1976).

In view of the complex metamorphic and microstructural history of the suite, the extent to which major element variation is due to protolith compositional differences, is open to debate. Certain gross compositional differences in SiO_2, TiO_2, total Fe, MgO, and perhaps CaO are likely to reflect protolith abundance levels, to some extent, as these elements are present in amounts which compare favourably with concentrations reported from less metamorphosed Archean 'granites' (Glikson and Sheraton, 1972; Viljoen and Viljoen, 1969; Hunter, 1973; Arth and Hanson, 1975; Glikson, 1976). However, the Uivak I gneiss complex is pervaded on all scales by potassium feldspar-quartz pegmatitic veins which pre-date, or are synchronous with, the emplacement of the Uivak II augen gneisses. The Uivak I gneisses also display microstructural evidence for reactions involving the transformation of potassium-poor minerals (plagioclase, hornblende, orthopyroxene, clinopyroxene) into such potasic phases as biotite, microcline, and myrmekite. It is therefore likely that the metamorphic history of the complex involved allochemical processes.

Nevertheless, by analogy with less deformed and metamorphosed Archean granitic suits, it is probable that the protoliths of the Uivak I suite, in particular the gray gneisses, were dominantly trondhjemite and tonalite. Also the intermediate and acidic gneisses with Na_2O/K_2O ratios less than 2.0 are not necessarily isochemically metamorphosed monzonites and granites, but represent altered lithologies whose alkali ratios have been lowered by metsomatism.

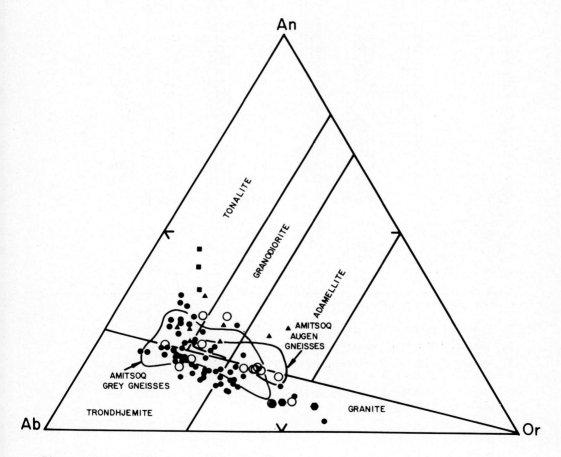

Figure 20.--Ternary plot of normative An-Ab-Or for the Uivak gneisses. Ornamentation as in Figure 16. The fields for the Amitsoq gneisses are from McGregor (1975). The classification boundaries are from O'Connor (1965).

TABLE 7 : Average analyses of early Archean gneisses from the Saglek area

	1 (n=3)		2 (n=9)		3 (n=6)		4 (n=12)	
	$\bar{x}$	s	$\bar{x}$	s	$\bar{x}$	s	$\bar{x}$	s
SiO_2	48.2	(0.8)	57.0	(2.6)	63.6	(1.3)	67.7	(1.8)
TiO_2	0.99	(0.4)	0.68	(0.2)	0.56	(0.1)	0.44	(0.1)
Al_2O_3	13.6	(1.5)	16.5	(3.4)	16.6	(0.9)	15.4	(2.3)
Fe_2O_3	3.54	(1.1)	1.42	(0.9)	1.14	(0.3)	0.63	(0.3)
FeO	8.75	(2.3)	5.43	(2.1)	3.63	(0.7)	2.65	(1.1)
MnO	0.24	(0.1)	0.12	(0.1)	0.06	(0.03)	0.07	(0.04)
MgO	8.25	(0.9)	4.80	(2.7)	2.39	(0.9)	1.81	(1.4)
CaO	10.3	(0.4)	5.35	(1.2)	4.20	(1.1)	3.33	(0.9)
Na_2O	2.89	(0.1)	4.29	(1.5)	4.76	(0.7)	4.74	(0.9)
K_2O	1.04	(0.2)	2.65	(0.7)	2.02	(0.5)	1.90	(0.5)
P_2O_5	0.33	(0.04)	0.30	(0.2)	0.19	(0.1)	0.18	(0.1)
LOI	2.01	(0.4)	1.37	(0.4)	1.02	(0.2)	0.83	(0.1)
Zr	70	(22)	178	(71)	165	(39)	168	(58)
Sr	156	(61)	549	(356)	502	(287)	478	(169)
Rb	29	(9)	138	(42)	110	(28)	113	(33)
Zn	142	(18)	118	(37)	82	(33)	91	(35)
Cu	57	(38)	36	(30)	36	(9)	29	(24)
Ba	84	(34)	445	(244)	233	(119)	303	(261)
Ce	22	(17)	117	(103)	47	(24)	52	(26)
La	17	(10)	73	(68)	25	(12)	32	(17)
Nb	6	(6)	5	(4)	5	(3)	8	(5)
Ga	21	(7)	24	(4)	25	(2)	22	(3)
Pb	18	(6)	13	(5)	14	(2)	18	(6)
Ni	147	(35)	111	(110)	31	(21)	32	(59)
Cr	240	(61)	181	(207)	46	(32)	99	(228)
V	233	(23)	88	(42)	65	(16)	44	(24)
$Na_2O/$ K_2O	2.78		1.63		2.36		2.49	
K/Rb	298		159		153		140	
Ba/Rb	2.90		3.22		2.12		2.68	
K/Ba	102.8		49.4		71.9		52.1	
Rb/Sr	0.19		0.25		0.22		0.24	
Sr/Ba	1.86		1.23		2.15		1.58	

Average composition of Uivak gneisses

1. Univak I gabbroic gneisses (SiO_2 47.2-48.7 wt %).

2. Univak I dioritic - monzonitic gneisses.

3. Univak I tonalitic - trondhjemitic gneisses (Na_2O/K_2O greater than 2.0 SiO_2 61.0-65.0 wt %).

4. Univak I tonalitic - trondhjemitic gneiss (Na_2O/K_2O greater than 2.0 SiO_2 65.0-70.0 wt %).

TABLE 7 : continued

5 (n=6)		6 (n=24)		7 (n=3)		8 (n=5)		9 (n=18)	
$\bar{x}$	s	$\bar{x}$	s	$\bar{x}$	s	$\bar{x}$	s	$\bar{x}$	s
71.2	(0.8)	71.9	(1.4)	72.2	(3.0)	66.7	(3.2)	67.71	(3.0)
0.28	(0.1)	0.24	(0.1)	0.02	(0.03)	0.37	(0.1)	0.77	(0.3)
15.5	(0.4)	14.7	(1.5)	15.1	(2.0)	15.7	(0.6)	13.7	(1.2)
0.55	(0.2)	0.41	(0.2)	0.13	(0.1)	0.67	(0.4)	1.18	(1.0)
1.49	(0.3)	1.37	(0.7)	0.32	(0.2)	2.63	(1.0)	4.12	(1.4)
0.03	(0.01)	0.03	(0.03)	0.02	(0.01)	0.05	(0.02)	0.09	(0.04)
0.89	(0.2)	0.70	(0.9)	0.14	(0.1)	1.94	(1.1)	1.18	(0.4)
2.72	(0.3)	1.95	(0.8)	1.16	(0.1)	3.86	(1.0)	2.74	(0.9)
4.94	(0.3)	4.18	(0.7)	3.77	(0.6)	4.52	(0.4)	3.67	(0.5)
1.74	(0.5)	3.52	(0.9)	5.87	(0.7)	1.80	(0.3)	3.29	(1.0)
0.13	(0.03)	0.11	(0.03)	0.06	(0.01)	0.20	(0.1)	0.22	(0.1)
0.58	(0.1)	0.58	(0.2)	0.52	(0.2)	0.71	(0.2)	0.73	(0.3)
137	(21)	166	(42)	70	(6)	108	(20)	267	(45)
392	(69)	434	(225)	398	(76)	510	(120)	299	(241)
101	(18)	138	(48)	147	(20)	49	(20)	155	(52)
57	(9)	59	(27)	47	(43)	58	(8)	89	(35)
23	(20)	23	(17)	18	(4)	103	(198)	31	(15)
305	(252)	564	(390)	791	(258)	323	(188)	866	(369)
41	(13)	44	(22)	10	(8)	37	(7)	125	(26)
23	(8)	24	(13)	6	(4)	23	(10)	57	(22)
5	(2)	7	(11)	4	(6)	5	(1)	8	(4)
22	(2)	22	(4)	20	(6)	23	(1)	20	(2)
19	(4)	23	(8)	22	(7)	10	(4)	19	(10)
10	(8)	6	(28)	0	(0)	24	(18)	6	(2)
19	(8)	35	(115)	4	(3)	44	(31)	24	(15)
26	(9)	16	(11)	0	(0)	59	(28)	56	(22)
11	(2)	9	(3)	4	(2)	10	(2)	23	(7)
2.84		1.19		0.64		2.51		1.12	
143		212		332		305		176	
3.02		4.09		5.38		6.59		5.59	
47.4		51.8		61.6		46.3		31.5	
0.26		0.32		0.37		0.10		0.52	
1.29		0.77		0.50		1.58		0.35	

5. Uivak I tonalitic - trondhjemitic gneisses (Na_2O/K_2O greater than 2.0 SiO_2 70.0-75.0 wt %).

6. Uivak I granodioritic - granitic gneisses (Na_2O/K_2O less than 2.0 SiO_2 70.0-76 wt %).

7. Pegmatite veins in Uivak I gneisses.

8. Uivak I tonalitic - trondhjemitic gneiss from region containing granulite facies assemblages.

9. Uivak II augen gneisses.

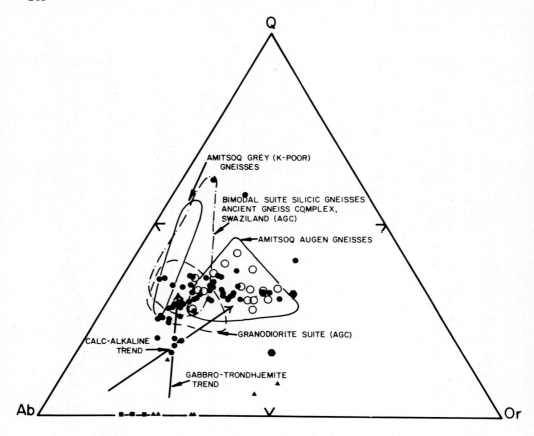

Figure 21.--Ternary normative plot of Q-Or-Ab for the Uivak gneisses. Ornamentation as in Figure 16. The fields for the Amitsoq gneisses are from Lambert and Holland (1976), and those for gneisses from the Ancient Gneiss Complex in Swaziland are from Hunter et al. (in press). The calc-alkaline and tronhjemite trends are from Barker and Arth (1976).

The increasing tendency in geochemical studies of Archean gneisses to view major element compositions as 'primary' features may not be correct, as important chemical changes, particularly in the abundances of certain of the LIL elements may have occurred during the metamorphic evolution of a particular terrain. The trace element distribution in the Uivak I suite provides further evidence in support of this suggestion.

Trace Elements

Trace element mean abundances in Uivak I gneisses of similar major element compositions have relatively large standard deviations (Table 7). This is a reflection of the migmatitic, geochemically heterogeneous nature of the suite. Important variations are shown by Rb, Ba, Sr, Ce, the heavy REE's, and Y. Other trace elements are present in abundances which are generally similar to those observed in trondhjemites, tonalites, and granodiorites (Tables 4, 5, 7, and 8).

In the trondhjemitic to tonalitic amphibolite facies Uivak gray gneisses, Rb values range from 24 to 145 ppm (Tables 4,7) and K/Rb ratios from 104 to 232 (Fig. 22), with mean values of 140, 143, and 153 in different groups of these gneisses (Table 7). Granulite facies gneisses from lower structural levels, however, have lower abundances of Rb (30 to 68 ppm) and higher K/Rb ratios (Table 5, Fig. 22), which may reflect depletion of Rb from the suite during metamorphism (cf. Lambert and Heier, 1968; Sighinolfi, 1971; Tarney and Windley, 1977). This depletion may have occurred synchronously with the metasomatism in the amphibolite facies gneisses, or alternatively, the granulite facies gneisses may represent lithologies which were not enriched in potassium, rubidium, and other LIL elements.

The average Rb values in the amphibolite facies gray gneisses are higher than those reported for similar Archean gneisses in Greenland, Swaziland, and Venezuela (Table 8), although individual analyses compare closely with averages reported from these terrains. K/Rb ratios for the Uivak gray gneisses are generally lower than averages for the Amitsoq gneiss (McGregor, this volume; Table 8), but are broadly similar to those from the Venezuelan Shield and the

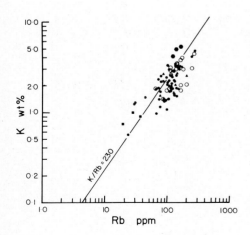

Figure 22.--Log-log plot of K against Rb for the Uivak gneisses. Ornamentation the same as in Figure 16 except that granulite facies gneisses are shown as partially closed circles.

TABLE 8 : Comparison of Archean grey gneisses from other areas with possible protolith compositions.

	1	2	3	4	5	6	7
SiO_2	66.7	71.0	72.7	55.1	65.7	71.0	74.1
TiO_2	0.47	0.29	0.18	2.20	0.99	0.31	0.12
Al_2O_3	16.0	15.3	14.6	13.0	14.5	15.4	13.9
Fe_2O_3						0.50	0.23
FeO	3.60^t	2.10^t	1.40^t	13.2^t	5.80^t	2.11	0.97
MnO	0.06	0.04	0.03	0.19	0.09	0.04	0.04
MgO	1.50	0.80	0.40	2.80	1.10	0.85	0.23
CaO	3.90	2.90	1.90	6.90	3.60	3.13	1.00
Na_2O	4.60	4.90	4.10	3.20	3.50	4.82	3.85
K_2O	1.50	1.50	3.70	1.30	3.40	1.22	4.87
P_2O_5	0.14	0.09	0.07	0.50	0.31	0.10	0.03
Zr	144	120	136	218	380	-	-
Sr	343	380	252	279	220	314	130
Rb	71	69	122	17	86	70	231
Zn	-	-	-	-	-	-	-
Cu	-	-	-	-	-	-	-
Ba	298	232	607	469	750	163#	-
Ce	-	-	-	-	-	-	-
La	-	-	-	-	-	-	-
Nb	6	7	4	10	13	-	-
Ga	-	-	-	-	-	-	-
Pb	18	21	29	-	18	-	-
Ni	13	5	3	20	6	-	-
Cr	39	23	23	60	23	-	-
V	-	-	-	-	-	-	-
Y	7	4	2	40	39	-	-
Na_2O/K_2O	3.07	3.27	1.11	2.46	1.03	3.95	0.79
K/Rb	175	180	252	635	328	145	175
Ba/Rb	4.2	3.4	5.0	27.6	8.7	2.3	-
K/Ba	41.8	53.7	50.6	23.0	37.6	62.1	-
Rb/Sr	0.21	0.18	0.48	0.06	0.39	0.22	1.78
Sr/Ba	1.2	1.6	0.4	0.6	0.3	1.9	-

8	9	10	11	12	13	14	15
57.3	68.6	69.9	71.0	69.1	67.3	70.6	68.9
0.30	0.39	0.20	0.23	0.20	0.22	0.24	0.30
17.8	13.7	16.2	15.7	17.0	17.3	15.0	17.3
0.89	4.49^t	0.30	0.40	0.69	0.84	0.39	0.76
4.65		1.40	1.20	1.12	1.14	1.26	1.58
0.13	0.03	0.02	0.00	0.03	0.04	0.03	0.03
4.21	1.00	0.88	0.59	0.69	1.39	1.06	1.22
8.47	1.76	2.70	2.40	3.60	3.45	2.37	3.69
4.11	4.50	5.12	4.06	5.69	6.05	5.37	5.16
0.60	1.38	1.60	2.40	1.31	1.08	1.55	0.62
0.05		0.07	0.06	0.21	0.13	0.06	0.09
-	182	110	140	-	-	55	55
276	464	744	443	661	1002	573	627
63	84	20	39	26.7	16.1	42.1	16.8
-	49	-	-	-	-	47	46
-	-	-	-	-	-	5	8
-	651	530	1810	489	604	290	146
-	-	17	37	108	11.4	25	15
-	-	9.4	18	-	-	13	17
-	-	-	-	-	-	6	2
-	23	-	-	-	-	-	-
-	10	-	-	-	-	-	-
-	19	-	-	-	-	21	13
-	25	12	9.3	-	-	15	24
-	50	-	-	-	-	24	36
-	17	-	-	-	-	53	34
6.85	3.26	3.20	1.69	4.34	5.60	3.46	8.32
79	136	664	510	407	557	306	306
-	7.8	26.5	46.4	18.3	37.5	6.9	8.7
-	17.6	25.1	11.0	22.2	14.8	44.4	35.3
0.23	0.18	0.03	0.09	0.04	0.02	0.07	0.03
-	0.7	1.4	0.2	1.4	1.7	2.0	4.3

TABLE 8, continued:

	16	17	18	19	20	21	22	23
SiO_2	73.4	67.5	71.3	61.3	73.3	69.4	65.1	68.4
TiO_2	0.21	0.50	0.22	0.68	0.25	0.56	0.60	0.42
Al_2O_3	14.0	16.0	13.6	17.6	13.5	14.0	14.1	14.7
Fe_2O_3	0.47	0.86	0.77	1.65	2.18	3.20		
FeO	1.26	2.44	2.11	2.52	1.37	2.90	7.80[t]	4.78[t]
MnO	0.03	0.05	0.07	0.04	0.07	0.06	0.20	
MgO	1.23	1.11	0.98	1.84	0.32	0.54	1.50	2.23
CaO	0.55	3.03	2.13	3.49	1.29	4.60	5.90	2.89
Na_2O	7.09	5.39	5.02	8.65	6.35	3.80	3.00	2.68
K_2O	0.20	1.56	0.77	0.04	0.32	0.07	1.10	3.17
P_2O_5	0.05	0.19	0.05	0.25	0.01	0.15	-	-
Zr	170	170	58	159	256	70	47	195
Sr	129	707	136	93	111	135	300	190
Rb	4.5	26.6	11.5	1	2	<1	16	121
Zn	40	100	45	30	42	-	-	-
Cu	5	10	11	12	10	-	27	22
Ba	69	540	78	131	154	20	280	500
Ce	31	63	-	-	-	-	-	-
La	18	36	-	-	-	-	-	-
Nb	9	9	6	8	7	-	-	-
Ga	-	-	13	20	21	-	-	20
Pb	-	-	3	-	-	-	4	29
Ni	19	7	0.5	7	3	15	-	15
Cr	13	10	8	-	5	-	4	34
V	20	52	44	43	12	-	93	65
Y	12	9	21	58	61	30	-	37
Na_2O/K_2O	35.5	3.46	6.52	216	19.8	54.3	2.73	0.85
K/Rb	369	487	511	332	1328	>581	571	218
Ba/Rb	15.3	20.3	6.3	131	77.0	> 20	17.5	4.1
K/Ba	24.1	23.9	81.6	2.53	17.3	29.1	32.6	52.6
Rb/Sr	0.03	0.04	0.09	0.01	0.02	< 0.01	0.05	0.64
Sr/Ba	1.9	1.3	1.74	0.71	0.72	6.75	1.07	0.38

TABLE 8, continued:

1. Average analysis of Amitsoq tonalitic gneiss (n=25), McGregor, this volume.

2. Average analysis of Amitsoq trondhjemitic gneiss (n-16), McGregor, this volume.

3. Average analysis of Amitsoq granodioritic gneiss (n=19), McGregor, this volume.

4. Average analysis of Amitsoq dioritic gneiss (n=6), McGregor, this volume.

5. Average analysis of Amitsoq augen gneiss (n-12), McGregor, this volume.

6. Average analysis of siliceous low K gneiss (n=3), Ancient Geniss Complex, Swaziland, Hunter et al., in press.

7. Analysis of quartz monzonite gneiss, Ancient Gneiss Complex, Swiziland, Hunter et al., in press.

8. Analysis of diorite gneiss, Ancient Gneiss Complex, Swaziland, Hunter et al., in press.

9. Average analysis of biotite-quartz-oligoclase gneiss (n=18), Venezuelan Shield, Dougan (1976).

10. Analysis of trondhjemitic gneiss, Wilson Creek area, Wyoming, Barker et al., (this volume).

11. Analysis of tonalitic to granodioritic gneiss, Wilson Creek area, Wyoming, Barker et al., (this volume).

12. Analysis of trondhjemitic Northern Light Gneiss, Thunder Bay, Ontario, Arth and Hanson, (1975).

13. Analysis of Saganaga Tonalite, Thunder Bay, Ontario, Arth and Hanson, (1975).

14. Analysis of Theespruit tonalite, Barberton Mountainland, South Africa Glikson (1976).

15. Analysis of Nelshoogte tonalite, Barberton Mountainland, South Africa Glikson (1976).

16. Analysis of Theespruit porphyry, Barberton Mountainland, South Africa Glikson (1976).

17. Analysis of Middle Marker porphyry, Barberton Mountainland, South Africa Glikson (1976).

18. Average analysis of trondhjemite from the Little Port Complex (n=14), Malpas (this volume).

19. Analysis of trondhjemite from the Bay of Islands Complex, No. 31, Malpas (this volume).

20. Analysis of trondhjemite from the Bay of Islands Complex, No. 41, Malpas (this volume).

21. Analysis of plagiogranite from Cyprus No. Cy 55C, Coleman and Peterman (1975).

22. Analysis of dacite from Tonga, Ewart and Bryan (1973).

23. Average analysis of granodiorite (n=20), Kolbe and Taylor (1966).

Swaziland Basement Complex (Table 8). These Rb, and K/Rb values are invariably higher or lower, respectively, than values from other low-potash siliceous Archean gneisses, granites, and porphyries (4.5 to 42 ppm and 306 to 664), and from the Phanerozoic trondhjemites, plagiogranites, and dacites (1 to 16 ppm and 332 to 1328).

In the granodioritic to granitic gneisses, Rb has a mean value of 138 ppm, and the K/Rb ratio is 212 (Table 7; Fig. 22). These values compare relatively well with values for the Amitsoq granodioritic gneisses, as well as with averages presented by Kolbe and Taylor (1966) for post-tectonic granodiorites (Table 8). However, in view of the compelling evidence for Rb mobility this similarity may have no genetic significance. Pegmatitic veins in the gneisses have similar Rb contents (147 ppm, but significantly higher average K/Rb ratios (332). This difference is related to the fact that the pegmatites are microcline-rich rather than biotite- or muscovite-rich.

The intermediate and mafic gneisses having Rb values of 138 and 29 ppm, and K/Rb ratios of 159 and 298, respectively, (Tables 4 and 7) also are considered to be influenced by the migration of K and Rb during metamorphism.

On a plot of K/Rb against K (Fig. 23), analyses of the Uivak I gneisses show a considerable spread. The amphibolite facies gneisses exhibit a weak positive slope and the granulite facies gneisses show a steep negative

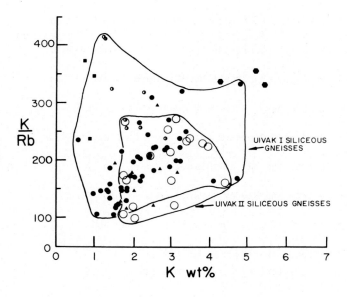

Figure 23.--Plot of K/Rb ratios against K for the Uivak gneisses. Ornamentation as in Figure 22.

TABLE 9 : Compilation of USGS standards analysed at Memorial University during 1977

		Zr	Sr	Rb	Zn	Cu	Ba	Ce	La	Nb	Ga	Pb	Ni	Cr	V	Y
G2	$\bar{x}$	290	469	164	85	14	1890	157	92	10	23	29	5	13	43	10
	s	(4)	(8)	(4)	(2)	(1)	(24)			(1)	(2)	(3)	(1)	(3)	(3)	(2)
GSP	$\bar{x}$		229	256	114						21	29				25
	s		(1)	(1)	(2)						(1)	(1)				(1)
AGV1	$\bar{x}$	229	653	68	84	63	1231	78	49	13	21	35	15	16	127	22
	s	(2)	(10)	(2)	(2)	(2)	(25)			(1)	(2)	(5)	(3)	(3)	(3)	(1)
W1	$\bar{x}$	96	188	21	85	115	167	27		9	18	5	73	90	239	24
	s	(1)	(2)		(2)	(4)	(10)			(1)	(3)	(4)	(2)	(9)	(6)	(1)
BCR1	$\bar{x}$	186	329	47	119	27	753			12	22	15	13	23	400	36
	s	(2)	(4)	(3)	(3)	(1)	(20)			(1)	(2)	(3)	(3)	(5)	(6)	(3)

TABLE 10 : Reconnaissance REE analyses of Uivak gneisses and BCR-1.

Sample	75-297B	75-248C	76-331B	75-320/1	75-295A	75-32P	75-32Y	74-32X	76-431B	75-291D	75-291E	75-183B	BCR-1	Chrondr.
La	4.40	138.5	85.7	25.2	31.0	29.8	73.5	33.16	59.7	32.6	69.4	3.05	27.1	0.315
Ce	9.73	269.9	212.7	55.2	54.2	51.9	144.4	60.79	119.2	117.2	164.1	5.67	49.7	0.813
Pr	-	32.5	24.7	5.84	5.71	4.10	14.94	6.52	13.15	7.01	15.46	-	-	0.116
Nd	6.98	119.1	98.7	28.5	24.6	19.5	65.4	25.80	53.78	27.45	59.31	1.68	26.8	0.597
Sm	2.03	20.68	13.3	5.01	4.34	3.44	11.99	4.31	9.63	5.68	9.33	0.10	6.82	0.192
Eu	0.88	2.91	2.46	1.25	1.02	1.23	2.35	0.80	1.83	1.33	1.47	-	2.11	0.072
Gd	2.16	14.25	7.10	2.96	2.73	2.45	7.34	2.45	6.83	3.77	5.99	-	6.48	0.259
Dy	2.57	5.55	2.44	4.41	1.20	1.15	2.02	1.24	4.36	2.57	4.04	-	5.81	0.325
Ho	-	-	0.11	-	-	-	-	-	-	-	-	-	-	0.073
Er	1.05	1.02	-	-	-	-	-	-	1.26	0.86	1.10	-	3.25	0.213
Σ REE	29.8	604.4	447.2	128.3	124.8	113.5	321.9	135.1	270.0	198.4	330.2	10.5	128.1	1.960
Y	18.7	46.6	20.0	19.5	8.0	12.0	17.0	11.0	38.2	23.3	25.7	2.4	25	

As reported in Fryer (1977) REE data are considered to be within ± 10% of the abundances reported.

distribution. These contrasting patterns presumably are the result of mineralogical control on the K/Rb ratio (cf. Shaw, 1968; Sighinolfi, 1971). Assuming the premise is correct that the Uivak suite is derived from genetically related igneous protoliths, the lack of a negative correlation between K and K/Rb implies that changes in the relative distribution of K and Rb must have occurred after igneous crystallization of the suite. The negative correlation displayed by the granulite facies gneisses is considered to be the result of fractionation of these elements during metamorphism of the suite.

Ba has a wide range in the gray gneisses (30 to 1084 ppm), showing mean values of 233, 303, and 305 in different groups of the gneisses (Tables 4 and 7). Although these values are comparable with Ba values in the Amitsoq gray gneisses (McGregor, this volume), and in similar gneisses from the Ancient Gneiss Complex in Swaziland (Condie and Hunter, 1976; Hunter et al., in press), they are lower than values reported from certain other Archean terrains (Table 8; 489 to 1810 ppm). However, other sodic Archean lithologies as well as Phanerozoic trondhjemites, plagiogranites, and dacites, do range to lower values of Ba (290 to 20 ppm; Table 8) due presumably to their exeedingly small content of potassium feldspar.

Barium in the granodioritic and granitic gneisses also has an extensive range (109 to 1424 ppm). Selected Ba values and averages for the intermediate and mafic gneisses are given in Tables 4 and 7, respectively. There is no significant difference currently recognized in Ba abundances from granulite and amphibolite facies gray gneisses in the Saglek area (Tables 4 and 5).

Regarding the distribution of K and Ba in the gray gneisses, K/Ba ratios range between 16.7 and 272.5, with mean values of 71.9, 52.1, and 47.4 (Table 7). These are similar to the range for the more potassic gneisses 25.2 to 270. From Figure 24, it is clear that there is no apparent relation between Ba and Rb in the suite, which might be expected if inter-element variation were related to fractional crystallization, equilibrium crystallization, or fractional melting (cf. McCarthy and Hasty, 1976). Similarly there is no obvious relationship between Sr and major element chemistry, particularly Ca (Fig. 25), which would also be expected if igneous protoliths of the suite had been metamorphosed isochemically. Sr values range between 124 and 834 ppm in the low potash gray gneisses and between 33 and 1337 ppm in the granodioritic and granitic gneisses (Tables 4 and 5).

Rb/Sr ratios in the amphibolite facies gneisses vary from 0.075 to 8,636 (with mean values between 0.22 and 0.32; Tables 4 and 7). These ratios are generally lower than Rb/Sr ratios for granulite facies gray gneises (0.063 to 0.28; mean 0.10; Tables 5 and 7). In Figure 26 the amphibolite facies gneisses

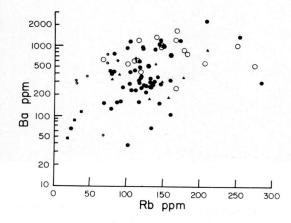

Figure 24.--Plot showing variation in Ba/Rb ratios for the Uivak gneisses. Ornamentation as in Figure 22.

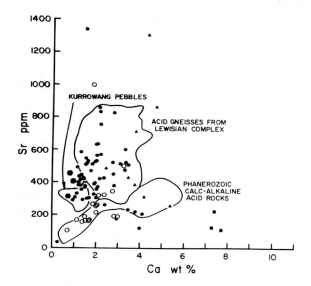

Figure 25.--Variation diagram showing relationship between Sr and Ca for the Uivak gneisses. Ornamentation as in Figure 16. A comparison is made with other suites given by Glikson and Sheraton (1972).

that the "igneous precursors of the gneisses..." must have been "...formed by a variety of different processes.....from chemically variable sources."

Such variable fractionation of REE's in Archean trondhjemitic and tonalitic gneisses generally is ascribed to the influence of garnet or hornblende in the source region of the igneous protoliths of the gneisses (Arth and Hanson, 1972, 1975; Arth and Barker, 1976;Hunter et al., in press). This is because they have distribution coefficients which facilitate the retention of HREE's. An

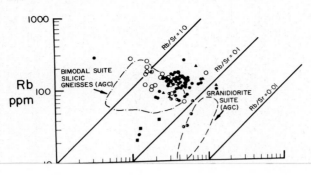

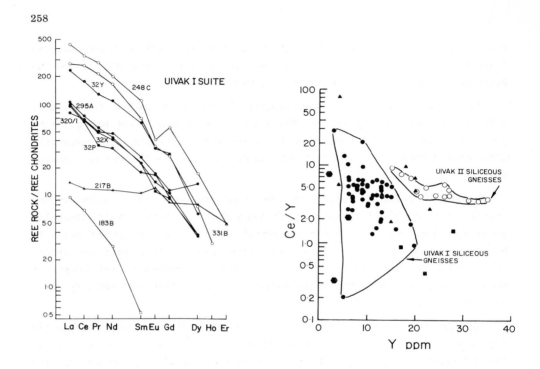

Figure 27.--Rare earth element patterns for the Uivak I gneisses.

Figure 28.--Plot of Ce/Y ratio against Y for the Uivak gneisses to show the degree of rare earth fractionation in the different suites.

alternative hypothesis is that the heavy REE's form compexes with volatiles known to be present in the lower crust (CO_2, CO, SO_2, halogens; Touret, 1974; Goldsmith, 1976) in the manner suggested by Kosterin (1959) and Collerson and Fryer (in press). The depletion might therefore be induced by metamorphic processes during the formation of early Archean gneiss complexes. Alternatively, it might be related to volatile transport during the emplacement of the protoliths into the crust (cf. Holloway, 1976; Fryer and Edgar, 1977).

The Uivak II Gneisses
Major Elements

The Uivak II augen gneisses form a relatively coherent petrological and geochemical suite. It is somewhat similar in character to acid plutonic lithologies from anorogenic environments which are commonly associated with gabbros and anorthosites (Bridgwater and Collerson, 1976; Emslie, in press). The gneisses have K_2O and Na_2O contents similar to those of the granodioritic-granitic Uivak I gneisses (Fig. 17a), with Na_2O/K_2O ratios varying between 0.72 and 1.91 (Tables 6 and 7). They are, however, distinctly less aluminous than the majority of the Uivak gray gneisses (Fig. 17b), which have a mean Al_2O_3 content of 13.7% (Table 7), and a range from 12.48 to 16.30%. On a SiO_2-K_2O plot (Fig. 18) they have a weak linear trend with a positive slope, lying in the field of continental granophyres (Coleman and Peterman, 1975). The augen gneisses also are richer in TiO_2 and total FeO (0.77 and 5.17%, respectively), than Uivak I gneisses showing similar values of SiO_2 and alkalis.

The gneisses have a distinct field on an AFM plot (Fig. 16), lying above that of the Uivak I gneisses, with an iron-enrichment trend reminiscent of that displayed by suites with tholeiitic rather than calc- alkaline affinities. This trend is similar to that of the Amitsoq augen gneisses (Bridgwater et al., 1976; Lambert and Holland, 1976; McGregor, this volume), which helps to support the conclusion that the two suites are petrologically equivalent. In terms of K-Na-Ca, the suite exhibits a trend similar to that defined by calc-alkaline plutonic rocks (Fig. 19).

In Figure 20, a ternary normative An-Ab-Or diagram, the gneisses fall in a region above the thermal valley, in a crude linear field which extends radially away from the Or apex towards the AB-An tie-line. If this is the result of igneous processes it could indicate that plagioclase fractionation has affected the genesis of the suite. On the other hand, if metamorphic redistribution of lime, alkalis and alumina has occurred, then this apparent relationship may be artificial. A similar line of reasoning maybe applied equally in Figure 21, where the Uivak augen gneisses span the field of minimum melt compositions for Ab/An ratios $= \infty$, occupying an area broadly equivalent to that of the Amitsoq augen gneisses.

Trace Elements

The augen gneisses have generally higher contents of Zr, Rb, La, Ce, and Y, and lower levels of Sr than siliceous gneisses from the Uivak I suite (Tables 6 and 7). K/Rb ratios range from 96.3 to 267 (Fig. 22), reflecting variation in modal hornblende and biotite. There is no apparent relation between potash content and K/Rb ratio in the suite (Fig. 23), which would be expected if the distribution of K and Rb were related to igneous fractionation (Shaw, 1968). The distribution of these elements therefore is interpreted to be the result of other processes, i.e., syn- or post-magmatic redistribution during deformation and metamorphism. Similarly, variation in K/Ba and Ba/Rb ratios (11.8 to 43.7 and 2.85 to 10.69; Fig. 24) are interpreted to reflect variable abundances of metamorphic biotite and potassium feldspar.

Apart from one sample containing 998 ppm Sr, the majority of the augen gneisses have between 100 and 496 ppm of this element, and show a mean value of 299 ppm (Table 7). The gneisses show a strong linear relationship between Sr and Ca, with a positive slope (Fig. 25), occupying a field quite distinct from that of the Uivak I gneisses. This relationship shows that Ca and Sr substitution in plagioclase (the principal Ca-bearing phase) has been relatively systematic. Whether it is the result of igneous or metamorphic processes remains a matter for debate. Certainly such a pattern could be established during fractional crystallization of a magma, but whether it would be preserved during deformation and recrystallization would depend on the stability of the igneous plagioclase.

Rb/Sr ratios for the suite are higher than ratios exhibited by the Uivak I siliceous gneisses, ranging from 0.169 to 1.537 (Table 6), with a mean value of 0.52 (Table 7). In Figure 26, the suite has a negative trend, distinct from that of the Uivak gray gneisses. This relation between Rb and Sr could be interpreted as an inherited igneous feature. But, in view of the compelling evidence concerning the behaviour of Rb in the suite, this is considered to be unlikely.

Sr/Ba ratios in the range from 0.15 to 2.33 (Tables 6 and 7) and are regarded as being caused by the irregular, generally low levels of Sr, and the variable distribution of Ba. These variations both appear to mirror modal plagioclase and potassium feldspar abundance levels in the suite.

The Uivak II gneisses are generally richer in REE's than the Uivak I siliceous gneisses (Tables 6, 7, and 10), which facilitates recognition of members of the suite in zones of intense deformation. Chondrite normalized REE patterns are linear, show variable Eu depletion, and appear to be less fractionated than the Uivak I gneisses. This produces straight rather than concave upward patterns (Fig. 29). These patterns are similar to those displayed by a number of other Archean granodiorites and quartz monzonites: e.g., the Dalmein granodiorite (Condie and Hunter, 1976) and the Giants Range Batholith (Arth and Hanson, 1975), which are interpreted to indicate formation of partial melting of siliceous granulite, or short-lived graywacke.

Rare-earth patterns for the Amitsoq augen gneisses presented by Lambert and Holland (1976) have a more extensive range in light REE abundances (ca. 50-150x chondrite) and variable degrees of fractionation. In contrast, the pattern for a member of the same suite analyzed by O'Nions and Pankhurst (1974) has a significantly less fractionated pattern. This is indeed surprising, if in fact these are from the same suite, and REE abundances are controlled by mineral phases in the igneous protoliths of the gneisses.

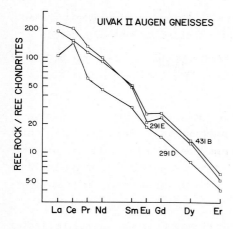

Figure 29.--Rare earth element patterns for the Uivak II gneisses.

Ce/Y ratios for the Uivak gneisses range from 3 to 9.8, which is significantly less than the range shown by the Uivak I gneisses (Fig. 28). This implies that the augen gneisses have more consistent degrees of HREE depletion than the gray gneisses, and contrasts with the REE behaviour currently recognized in the Amitsoq augen gneiss.

DISCUSSION AND ORIGIN OF THE UIVAK GNEISSES

From field evidence, and by analogy with other Archean gneiss terrains (Hunter et al., in press; McGregor, this volume), it can be surmised that the Uivak gneisses are orthogneisses derived from such protoliths as gabbros, trondhjemites, diorites, tonalites, granodiorites, and granites. The microstructural development of the gneisses and their chemical composition indicates clearly the involvement of allochemical processes during their metamorphic history. Such processes involved principally the migration of K, Rb, and Si. The alteration also may have involved elements that are considered usually to be relatively immobile during metamorphism such as Y and the heavy REE's.

As a result, discussion of the petrogenesis of chemically modified gneisses in terms of igneous processes alone must be viewed with some caution. The nature of these chemical changes is significant. They obviously reflect crustal processes which occurred during the early Archean, synchronously with, or post-dating the igneous events which formed the trondhjemitic-granitic protoliths of the gneisses.

In modelling the formation and metamorphic alteration of plutonic rocks in pre-3.6 Ga old continental crust the following factors must be considered:

(1) Probable high crustal geothermal gradients during the first 1.0 Ga of Earth history (Birch, 1965; Hanks and Anderson, 1969), most likely in excess of $100^{\circ}C/km$ (Fyfe, 1973).

(2) Widespread development of granulite facies assemblages in response to these high gradients, resulting in the formation of a crust ca. 12 km thick (the thickness is constrained by the intersection of such a geotherm with the solidi for anhydrous granitic or basaltic compositions). This crust would be composed of heterogeneous granulite facies lithologies overlain by subordinate amounts of more hydrous lithologies.

(3) Fractionation of major and trace elements during granulite facies metamorphism in response to migration of fluids (such as carbonic fluids rich in oxidized S and halogens) through the crust. These fluids would be capable of comlexing and transporting certain incompatible elements (Th, U, Y, K, Rb, heavy REE's and, under some circumstances, Ba and Sr) from lower to higher crustal levels.

If the above constraints are valid they have important implications for igneous processes in the early crust, particularly those relating to 'granite' petrogenesis. For example, eclogite would not form (Green, 1975) and would not be available to generate the heavy rare earth depletion typical of many Archean trondhjemite-granite suites (Arth and Hanson, 1972, 1975). Furthermore, under the influence of high thermal gradients (greater than $60^{\circ}C/km$), partial melting of amphibolites would not occur as granulite facies metamorphic assemblages would exist under the P, T conditions where melting could occur (Collerson and Fryer, in press). Amphibolite facies partial melting would not develop until thermal gradients had decreased to values less than ca. $60^{\circ}C/km$ (cf. Wyllie, 1977a).

As outlined above, hypotheses accounting for the formation of Archean tonalites and tronhjemites or the protoliths of their metamorphic products are many and varied. Nevertheless, they can be simplified into four contrasting models:

(1) Partial melting of tholeiitic compositions at mantle depths, leaving an eclogitic (garnet-clinopyroxene) residue (Hanson and Goldich, 1972; Arth and Hanson, 1972).

(2) Partial melting or fractional crystallization of wet basalt or amphibolite (Goldschmidt, 1922; Arth and Barker, 1976; Arth et al., in press).

(3)   Fractional crystallization of basalt (Coleman and Peterman, 1975; Coleman, 1977).

(4)   Melting of sialic and/or simatic crust previously depleted in incompatible elements (Sutton, 1973; Bridgwater and Fyfe, 1974; Collerson and Fryer, in press), which all have merit in specific cases.

However, in view of the constraints on crustal processes discussed above, the first two models may not be applicable to early Archean crustal development. Similarly, the volumes of 'granitic' material generated are, by analogy with present day regions of basaltic volcanism and high geothermal gradients, considered to be too small and, therefore, unrealistic for the Archean (model 3).

Under the influence of high early Archean geothermal gradients, partial melting of basaltic compositions and the geochemical behaviour of certain elements would be controlled by physical conditions and processes typical of granulite facies environments. Melting of mafic granulite (pyribolite) would be expected to occur at temperatures approaching $1100^{\circ}C$, producing trondhjemitic and tonalitic magmas (cf. Wyllie, 1977a, 1977b). Partial melting of mafic compositions at crustal levels would be facilitated by the presence in the crust of mantle derived komatiitic ultramafic and mafic magmas with liquidus temperatures greater than $1200^{\circ}C$ (Green et al., 1975). Deformation of the crust (controlled by the spacing of convection cells in the mantle and by the speed of convection) would be occurring at the same time as this igneous activity. Contemporaneous melting of pre-existing mafic crustal material would occur to produce sodic granitic rocks. These would be emplaced to higher crustal levels during or after deformation, either in the form of sheet-like intrusions (cf. Myers, 1976)or as late syntectonic or post-tectonic plutons. The melts generated in this fashion would exhibit 'mantle-like' isotopic abundances as these are characteristic of depleted, lower continental crust (Spooner and Fairbairn, 1970; Gray and Oversby, 1972).

Volatiles in the lower crust rich in CO_2, CO, oxidizing S, and halogens, could form complexes or soluble compounds with Y, Rb, Th, U, K, and the heavy REE's. Their movement from the lower crust to higher crustal levels is possible by several mechanisms; volume- or grain boundary-diffusion, or within magmas (Holloway, 1976). This volatile migration provides a viable mechanism to account for the depletion of these elements from the lower continental crust. This accounts for anomalous geochemistry and partially explains the microstructural history of the Uivak and other early Archean tonalitic gneisses (McGregor, this volume; Wooden et al., 1975).

The formation of minerals capable of partitioning particular elements from the volatile phase would control the chemical character of the gneisses through which it passed. For example, from microstructural evidence it is obvious that biotite formed at the expense of hornblende in the Uivak I gray gneisses. This resulted in the lower K/Rb ratios discussed above. The lack of significant increases in other trace elements in the Uivak gneisses, which was questioned by Moorbath (1977), might be due to the fact that these elements were transported as more stable complexes. For example, the low U abundances reported from Archean gneiss terrains by Sighinolfi and Sakai (1977) could be the result of complexing of uranium with CO_2 or CO to form highly soluble uranyl carbonate (Naumov, 1959). Under the influence of a chemical potential gradient the volatile phase containing this complex would probably migrate to higher structural levels before it was precipitated. Similarly the varying degrees of heavy REE depletion and Ce/Y fractionation recorded in the Uivak and other gneisses from the North Atlantic craton could be due to differential complexing and removal of heavy REE's in a volatile phase. Alternatively, it may be due to variable precipitation of the heavy REE's and Y from this volatile phase.

The more potassic members of the Uivak suite are interpreted to be derived in a number of ways. Some compositions particularly in the Uivak I suite could be the result of severe metasomatic addition of K and Rb from deeper levels in the crust. However others, especially the Uivak II augen gneisses, are interpreted to have been formed by partial melting of tonalite and trondhjemite under granulite facies conditions, possibly with some subsequent fractional crystallization. Melts derived in this way would show variable fractionation in heavy REE's. This would depend on the concentration of REE's in the source, the composition of the volatile phase, and on the extent to which the volatile phase was entrapped in the crystallizing magma. The melts derived by this mechanism would have lower Sr contents, higher Th, U, Rb, and Pb concentrations, and larger Rb/Sr ratios than their tonalitic protoliths because these elements would be selectively removed in the syn-melting volatile phase. Elemental abundances would also be influenced by metamorphic processes. Small quantities of residual anorthosite and leuco-gabbro would be expected to develop as a cumulate residue during or after removal of the potassic melt (Frith and Currie, 1976). In the Saglek area the Mentzel intrusive association may be a residue of this type.

IMPLICATIONS FOR ARCHEAN CRUSTAL DEVELOPMENT

On present evidence it appears that a substantial amount of the continental crust had separated from the mantle/lithosphere by ca. 2800 $\pm$ 200 Ma (Patterson and Tatsumoto, 1964; Armstrong, 1968; Jahn and Nyquist, 1976). Moorbath (1975,

1977) considers that crustal growth is episodic and recognizes a number of events throughout geological time during which 'irreversible chemical differentiation of...the upper mantle....produced new continental crust.' One of these events at ca. 2900 to 2600 Ma he regards as being 'undoubtedly one of the major rock-forming episodes in earth history.'

Assuming that the rate of separation of sial is governed by the total energy of the system (both thermal and gravitational; Elder, 1977), one should expect more rapid mantle convection in numerous small cells to be related to faster and more efficient separation of the continental crust. If the sial forming event at ca. 2800 Ma is, in fact, contributing new crustal material, rather than recycling pre-existing crust, one would be forced to invoke the existence of a curious thermal event ca 1800 Ma after accretions of the Earth to facilitate the production of this volume of sialic crust. When one considers the fact that cratons were stabilizing during the period 2800 to 2500 Ma, presumably because of a lowering of thermal gradients and cessation of small-scale convective processes in the mantle, the existence of such a thermal event becomes even more unlikely.

An alternative explanation is that continental crust was forming continually throughout the Archean. However, its rate of separation was, in fact, decreasing as thermal gradients were lowered.

ACKNOWLEDGMENTS

This research was supported by the National Research Council of Canada (Grant A-8694 to Collerson) during 1974-1977 and by a research grant from the Department of Indian and Northern Affairs to Memorial University in 1977. Bridgwater received financial support for field expenses in 1974 and 1975 from the Geological Survey of Canada.

We are grateful to T. Calon, B. J. Fryer, and J. Malpas for constructive comments on the manuscript.

REFERENCES

Armstrong, R. L., 1968. A model for Sr and Pb isotope evolution in a dynamic earth. Rev. Geophys., 6: 175-199.

Arth, J. G., and Barker, F., 1976. Rare-earth partitioning between hornblende and dacitic liquid and implication for the genesis of trondhjemitic-tonalitic magmas. Geology, 4: 534-536.

Arth, J. G., Barker, F., Peterman, Z. E. and Friedman, I., in press. Geochemistry of the gabbro-diorite-tonalite-trondhjemite suite of southwest Finland and its implications for the origin of trondhjemitic-tonalitic magmas. J. Pet.

Arth, J. G. and Hanson, G. N., 1972. Quartz diorites derived by partial melting of eclogite or amphibolite at mantle depths. Contrib. Miner. Pet., 37: 161-174.

Arth, J. G. and Hanson, G. N., 1975. Geochemistry and origin of the early Precambrian crust of northeastern Minnesota. Geochim. Cosmochim. Acta, 39: 325-362.

Baadsgaard, H., 1973. U-Th-Pb dates on zircons from the very early Precambrian Amitsoq gneisses, Godthaab district, West Greenland. Earth Planet. Sci. Lett., 19: 22-28.

Baadsgaard, H., 1976. Further U-Pb dates on zircons from the early Precambrian rocks of the Godthaabsfjord area, West Greenland. Earth Planet. Sci. Lett., 33: 261-267.

Baadsgaard, H., Lambert, R. St. J. and Krupicka, J., 1976. Mineral isotopic age relationships in the polymetamorphic Amitsoq gneisses, Godthaab District, West Greenland. Geochim. Cosmochim. Acta, 40: 513-527.

Barker, F. and Arth, J.G., 1976. Generation of trondhjemitic-tonalitic liquids and Archean bimodal tronhjemite-basalt suits. Geology, 4: 596-600.

Barker, F., Arth, J. G., Peterman, Z. E. and Friedman, I., 1976. The 1.7- to 1.8-b.y.-old trondhjemites of southwestern Colorado and northern New Mexico: Geochemistry and depths of genesis. Geol. Soc. Am. Bull., 87: 189-198.

Barker, F. and Peterman, Z. E., 1974. Bimodal tholeiitic-dacitic magmatism and the early Precambrian crust. Precambrian Res., 1: 1-12.

Barton, J. M., Jr., Fripp, R.E.P. and Ryan, B., 1977. Rb/Sr ages and geological setting of ancient dykes in the Sand River area, Limpopo Mobile Belt, South Africa. Nature, 267: 487-490.

Birch, F., 1965. Speculations on the Earth's thermal history. Geol. Soc. Am. Bull., 76: 133-154.

Bridgwater, D. and Colleson, K. D., 1976. The major petrological and geochemical characters of the 3600 m.y. Uivak gneisses from Labrador. Contrib.Miner. Pet., 54: 43-59.

Bridgwater, D. and Collerson, K. D., 1977. On the origin of early Archean gneisses: a reply. Contrib.Miner. Pet., 62: 179-191.

Bridgwater, D., Collerson, K. D., Hurst, R. W. and Jesseau, C. W., 1975. Field characters of the early Precambrian rocks from Saglek, coast of Labrador. Pap.Geol. Surv. Canada, 74-1a: 287-296.

Bridgwater, D., Collerson, K. D. and Myers, J. S. (in press). The development of the Archean Gneiss complex of the North Atlantic region. In: D. H. Tarling (Editor), Evolution of the Earth's Crust, pp. 19-69. London Academic Press.

Bridgwater, D. and Fyfe, W. S., 1974. The pre-3 b.y. crust: fact-fiction-fantasy. Geoscience Canada, 1: 7-11.

Bridgwater, D., Watson, J. and Windley, B. F., 1973. The Archean craton of the North Atlantic region. Phil. Trans. R. Soc. Lond., A273: 493-512.

Cheney, E. C. and Stewart, R. J., 1975. Subducted graywacke in the Olympic Mountains, USA--implications for the origin of Archaean sodic gneisses. Nature, 258: 60-61.

Coleman, R. G., 1977. Ophiolites Ancient Oceanic Lithosphere? Berlin: Springer-Verlag, pp. 229.

Coleman, R. G. and Peterman, Z. E., 1975. Oceanic plagiogranite. J. Geophys. Res., 80: 1099-1108.

Collerson, K. D., 1975. Contrasting patterns of K/Rb distribution in Precambrian high grade metamorphic rocks from central Australia. J. Geol. Soc. Aust., 22: 145-158.

Collerson, K. D., 1974. Descriptive microstructural terminology for high-grade metamorphic tectonites. Geol. Mag., 111: 313-318.

Collerson, K. D. and Fryer, B. J., 1978, in press. Role of fluids in the formation and subsequent development of the early Continental crust. Contrib. Miner. Pet.

Collerson, K. D., Jesseau, C. W. and Brigwater, D., 1976. Crustal development of the Archean gneiss complex: estern Labrador. In: B. F. Windley (Editor), The Early History of the Earth, pp. 237-253. New York: Wiley.

Condie, K. C. and Hunter, D. R., 1976. Trace element geochemistry of Archean granitic rocks from the Barberton region, South Africa. Earth Planet. Sci. Lett., 29: 389-400.

Dougan, T. W., 1976. Origin of trondhjemitic biotite-quartz-olioclase gneisses from the Venezuelan Guyana Shield. Precambrian Res., 3: 317-342.

Drury, S. A., 1973. The geochemistry of Precambrian granulite facies rocks from the Lewisian complex of Tiree, Inner Hebrides. Chem. Geol., 11: 167-188.

Elder, J. W., 1977. Thermal convection. J. Geol. Soc. Lond., 133: 293-309.

Emslie, R. F., in press. Anorthosite mossifs, rapikivi granites and late Proterozoic rifting of North America. Precambrian Res.

Ewart, A. and Bryan, W. B., 1973. The petrology and geochemistry of the Tongan Islands. In, P. J. Coleman (Editor), the Western Pacific Island arcs, marginal seas, geochemistry: Perth, Univ. Western Australia Press, pp. 503-522.

Frith, R. A. and Currie, K. L., 1976. A model for the origin of the Lac St. Jean anorthosite massif. Can. J. Earth Sci., 13: 389-399.

Fryer, B. J., 1977. Rare earth evidence in iron-formations for changing Precambrian oxidation states. Geochim. Cosmochim. Acta, 41: 361-367.

Glikson, A. Y. and Sheraton, J. W., 1972. Early Precambrian evidence of a primitive ocean crust and island nuclei of sodic granite. Geol. Soc. Am. Bull., 83: 3323-3344.

Glikson, A. Y., 1976. Trace element geochemistry and origin of early Precambrian acid igneous series, Barberton Mountainland, Transvaal. Geochim. Cosmochim. Acta, 40: 1261-1280.

Glikson, A. Y. and Sheraton, J. W., 1972. Early Precambrian trondhjemitic suites in Western Australia and northwestern Scotland, and the geochemical evolution of shields. Earth Planet. Sci. Lett., 17: 227-242.

Glikson, A. Y., 1971. Primitive Archaean element distribution patterns: chemical evidence and geotectonic significance. Earth and Planetary Sci. Letters,12: 309-320.

Glikson, A. Y., 1970. Geosynclinal evolution and geochemical affinities of early Precambrian systems. Tectonophysics, 9: 397-433.

Goldich, S. S. and Hedge, C. E., 1974. 3,800 Myr granitic gneiss in southwestern Minnesota. Nature, 252: 467-468.

Goldschmidt,V. M., 1922. Stammestypen der eruptivgesteine. Vid. Skr. 1. Ma., 10: 3-12.

Goldsmith, J. R., 1976. Scapolites, granulites and volatiles in the lower crust. Geol. Soc. Am. Bull., 87: 161-168.

Gray, C. M. and Oversby, V. M., 1972. The behaviour of lead isotopes during granulite facies metamorphism. Geochim. Cosmochim. Acta, 26: 939-952.

Green,D. H., 1975. Genesis of Archean peridotitic magmas and constraints on Archean geothermal gradients and tectonics. Geology, 3: 15-18.

Green, D. H., Nicholls, I. A., Viljoen, M. and Viljoen, R., 1975. Experimental demonstration of the existence of peridotitic liquids in earliest Archean magmatism. Geology, 3: 11-14.

Green, T. H. and Ringwood, A. E., 1968. Genesis of the calc alkaline igneous rock suite. Contrib. Miner. Pet., 18: 105-162.

Hanks, T. C. and Anderson, D. L., 1969. The early thermal history of the Earth. Phys. Chem. Earth Planetary Int., 2: 19-29.

Hanson, G. N., 1978. The application of trace elements to the petrogenesis of igneous rocks of granitic composition. Earth Planet. Sci. Lett., 38: 26-43.

Hanson, G. N. and Goldich, S. S., 1972. Early Precambrian rocks in the Saganaga Lake-Northern Light area, Minnesota-Ontario, Part II: petrogenesis. Geol. Soc. Am. Mem., 135: 179-192.

Hatch, F. H., Wells, A. K. and Wells, M. K., 1972. Petrology of the igneous rocks. Murby, London.

Hawkesworth, C. J., Moorbath, S., O'Nions, R. K. and Wilson, J. F., 1975. Age relationships between greenstone belts and "granites" in the Rhodesian Archaean craton. Earth Planet. Sci. Lett., 25: 251-262.

Hietanen, A., 1943. Über das grundgebirge des Kalantigebietes im südwestlich. Bull. Comm. Geol. Finlande, 130: 105 pp.

Holloway, J. R., 1976. Fluids in the evolution of granitic magmas: consequences of finite CO_2 solubility. Geol. Soc. Am. Bull., 87: 1513-1518.

Hunter, D. R., 1974. Crustal development in the Kaapvaal craton, 1. The Archean. Precambrian Res., 1: 259-294.

Hunter, D. R., 1973. The granitic rocks of the Precambrian of Swaziland. Geol. Soc. S. Afr., Spec. Publ., 3: 131-147.

Hunter, D. R., 1970. The Ancient Gneiss Complex in Swaziland. Trans. Geol. Soc. S. Afr., 73: 107-150.

Hunter, D. R., Barker, F. and Millard, H. T., Jr., in press. The geochemical nature of the Archean Ancient Gneiss Complex and granodiorite suite, Swaziland: a preliminary study. Precambrian Res.

Hurst, R. W., Bridgwater, D., Collerson, K. D. and Wetherill, G. W., 1975. 3,600 m.y. Rb-Sr ages from very early Archean gneisses from Saglek Bay, Labrador. Earth Planet. Sci. Lett., 27: 393-403.

Hyndman, R. D., 1973. Evolution of the Labrador Sea. Can. J. Earth Sci., 10: 673-644.

Jahn, B. M. and Nyquist, L. E., 1976. Crustal evolution in the Early Earth-Moon system: constraints from Rb-Sr studies. In, B. F. Windley (Editor) The Early History of the Earth. Wiley, London, pp. 55-76.

Jakes, P. and Gill, J., 1970. Rare earth elements and the island arc tholeiite series. Earth. Planet. Sci. Lett., 9: 17-28.

Knight, I. and Morgan, W. C., 1976. Stratigraphic subdivision of the Aphebian Ramah Group, Northern Labrador. Geol. Surv. Can. Pap., 77-15: 31 pp.

Kolbe, P. and Taylor, S. R., 1966. Major and trace element relationships in granodiorites and granites from Australia and South Africa. Contrib. Miner. Pet., 12: 202-222.

Kosterin, A. V., 1959., The possible modes of transport of the rare earths by hydrothermal solutions. Geochem., 4: 381-387.

Lambert, I. B. and Heier, K. S., 1968. Geochemical investigations of deep-seated rocks in the Australian shield. Lithos, 1: 30-53.

Lambert, R. St. J. and Holland, J. G., 1976. Amitsoq gneiss geochemistry: preliminary observations. In: B. F. Windley (Editor), The Early History of the Earth, pp. 191-201. New York: Wiley.

Leelanandam, C., 1970. Chemical mineralogy of hornblendes and biotites from the charnockitic rocks of Kondapalli, India. J. Pet., 11: 475-505.

MacGregor, A. M., 1951. Some milestones in the Precambrian of southern Rhodesia. Geol. Soc. S. Africa Proc., 54: xxvii-lxxi.

Marten, B., 2977. The relationship between the Aillik Group and the Hopedale Complex Kaipokok Bay, Labrador. Ph. D. thesis. Memorial University of Newfoundland, St. John's. Nfld., Canada.

McCarthy, T. S. and Hasty, R. A., 1976. Trace element distribution patterns with reference to the crystallization of granitic melts. Geochim. Cosmochim. Acta, 40: 1351-1358.

McGregor, V. R., 1975. The earliest granites: evidence from the Godthaab district, West Greenland. In: The Early History of the Earth. Nato Advanced Studies Institute. Progr. with Abstr.

McGregor, V. R., 1973. The early Precambrian gneisses of the Godthaab district, West Greenland. Phil. Trans. R. Soc. Lond., A273: 343-358.

McGregor, V. R. and Mason, B., 1977. Petrogenesis and geochemistry of metabasaltic and metsedimentary enclaves in the Amitsoq gneisses, West Greenland. Am. Miner., 62: 887-904.

Mehnert, K. R., 1968. Migmatites and the origin of granitic rocks. Elsevier, Amsterdam, 393 pp.

Moorbath, S., 1975. The geological significance of early Precambrian rocks. Proc. Geol. Assoc., 86: 259-279.

Moorbath, S., 1977. Ages, isotopes and evolution of Precambrian continental crust. Chem. Geol., 20: 151-187.

Moorbath, S., Allaart, J. H., Bridgwater, D. and McGregor, V. R., 1977a. Rb-Sr ages of early Archaean supracrustal rocks and Amitsoq gneisses at Isua. Nature, 270: 43-45.

Moorbath, S., O'Nions, R. K. and Pankhurst, R. J., 1975. The evolution of early Precambrian crustal rocks at Isua, West Greenland--geochemical and isotopic evidence. Earth Planet. Sci. Lett., 27: 229-239.

Moorbath, S., O'Nions, R. K., Pankhurst, R. J., Gale, N. H. and McGregor, V. R., 1972. Further rubidium-strontium age determinations on very early Precambrian rocks of the Godthaab district, West Greenland. Nature Phys. Scik., 240: 78-82.

Morgan, W. C., 1975. Geology of the Precambrian Ramah Group and basement rocks in the Nachvak Fiord-Saglek Fiord area, North Labrador. Geol. Surv. Can. Pap., 74-54: 42 pp.

Morgan, W. C., 1974. The Nain-Churchill boundary in the Torngat Mountains, northern Labrador: an Archean-Proterozoic structural province contact in the Canadian Precambrian shield. Geol. Soc. Am. Abstr., 6: 876-877.

Myers, J. S., 1978. Formation of banded gneisses by deformation of igneous rocks. Tectonophysics, 6: 43-64.

Myers, J. S., 1976. Granitoid sheets, thrusting, and Archean crustal thickening in West Greenland. Geology, 4: 265-268.

Naumov, G. B., 1959. Transportation of uranium in hydrothermal solutions as a carbonate. Geochem., 4: 5-20.

O'Connor, J. T., 1965. A classification of quartz-rich igneous rocks based on feldspar ratios. U.S. Geol. Surv. Prof. Pap., 525B.

O'Nions, R. K. and Pankhurst, R. J., 1974. Rare-earth element distribution in Archaean gneisses and anorthosites, Godthaab area, west Greenland. Earth Planet. Sci. Lett., 22: 328-338.

Patterson, C. and Tatsumoto, M., 1964. The significance of lead isotopes in detrital feldspar with respect to chemical differentiation of the Earth's mantle. Geochim. Cosmochim. Acta, 28: 1-22.

Price, R. C. and Taylor, S. R., 1977. The rare earth geochemistry of granite, gneiss and migmatite from the Western Metamorphic Belt of South-Eastern Australia. Contrib. Miner. Pet., 62: 249-263.

Shaw, D. M., 1968. A review of K-Rb fractionation trends by covariance analysis. Geochim. Cosmochim. Acta, 32: 573-601.

Sheraton, J. W., Skiner, A. C. and Tarney, J., 1973. The geochemistry of the Scourian gneisses of the Assynt district. In: R. G. Park and J. Tarney (Editors), The Early Precambrian of Scotland and related rocks of Greenland. Univ. Keele, pp. 13-30.

Sighinolf, F. P., 1971. Investigations into deep crustal levels: fractionating effects and geochemical trends related to high-grade metamorphism. Geochim. Cosmochim. Acta, 35: 1005-1021.

Sighinolfi, G. P. and Sakai, T., 1977. Uranium and thorium in Archaean granulite facies terrains of Bahia (Brazil). Geochim. J., 11: 33-39.

Smyth, W. R., 1976. Geology of the Mugford Group, Northern Labrador. Nfld. Dept. Mines and Energy, Min. Dev. Div. Report of Activities for 1975: 72-79.

Speer, J. A., 1978. The stratigraphy and depositional environment of the Aphebian. Snyder Group, Labrador. Can. J. Earth Sci., 15: 52-68.

Spooner, C. M. and Fairbairn, H. W., 1970. Strontium 87/Strontium 86 initial ratios in pyroxene granulite terrains. J. Geophys. Res., 75: 6706-6713.

Sun, S. S. and Nesbitt, R. W., 1978. Petrogenesis of Archaean ultrabasic and basic volcanics: evidence from rare earth elements. Contrib. Miner. Pet., 65: 301-325.

Sutton, J., 1973. Stages in the evolution of the granitic crust. Geol. Soc. S. Africa Spec. Publ., 3: 1-6.

Tarney, J., 1976. Geochemistry of Archaean high-grade gneisses, with implications as to the origin and evolution of the Precambrian crust. In: B. F. Windley (Editor), The Early History of the Earth, pp. 405-417. New York: Wiley.

Tarney, J. and Windley, B. F., 1977. Chemistry, thermal gradients and evolution of the lower continental crust. J. Geol. Soc. Lond., 134: 153-172.

Touret, J., 1974. Facies granulite et inclusions carboniques. In: J. Belliere and J. C. Duchesne (Editors), Geologie des Domaines Cristallins: Leige. Ann. Soc. Geol. Belgique, Vol. Spec. P. Michot, pp. 267-287.

Vance, J. A., 1961. Plagioclase twins in some mafic gneisses from Broken Hill, Australia. Min. Mag., 35: 488-507.

Viljoen, M. J. and Viljoen, R. P., 1969. The geochemical evolution of the granitic rocks of the Barberton region. Geol. Soc. S. Africa Spec. Publ., 2: 189-220.

Wheeler, R. P., 2d, 1960. Anorthosite-adamellite complex of Nain, Labrador. Geol. Soc. Am. Bull., 71: 1755-1762.

White, S., 1977. Geological significance of recovery and recrystallization processes in quartz. Tectonophysics, 39: 143-170.

White, S., 1976. The effects of strain on the microstructures, fabrics and deformation mechanisms in quartzite. Phil. Trans. R. Soc. Lond., A282: 69-86.

White, S., 1973. The dislocation structures responsible for the optical effects in some naturally-deformed quartzes. J. Materials Sci., 8: 490-499.

Wilson, J. F., Bickle, M. J., Hawkesworth, C. J., Martin, A., Nisbet, E. G. and Orpen, J. L., 1978. Granite-greenstone terrains of the Rhodesian Archaean craton. Nature, 271: 23-27.

Wooden, J. L., Goldich, S. S. and Ankenbauer, G. N., 1975. 3,600-m.y. old tonalitic gneiss near Delhi, Minnesota. Geol. Soc. Am. Abstr., p. 1322.

Wyllie, P. J., 1977a. Crustal anataexis: an experimental review. Tectonophys., 43: 41-71.

Wyllie, P. J., 1977b. Effects of H_2O and CO_2 on magma genesis in the crust and mantle. J. Geol. Soc. Lond., 134: 215-234.

Chapter 8

GEOCHEMISTRY OF ARCHAEAN TRONDHJEMITIC AND TONALITIC GNEISSES FROM SCOTLAND AND EAST GREENLAND

J. Tarney, B. Weaver and S. A. Drury

ABSTRACT

High Na/K gneisses of tonalitic-trondhjemitic composition dominate the Archaean high-grade terrain of Scotland and East Greenland. Gneiss compositions range from ultramafic to trondhjemite, but the compositional distribution is bimodal, particularly in the amphibolite facies gneiss zones. The tonalitic gneisses have moderately high Al_2O_3 (mean >15%) and high CaO, but SiO_2 is mostly below 70 percent except in the minor trondhjemitic bodies and veins. The levels of Ba and Sr are high, and Sr concentrations remain high even in siliceous gneisses.

There are marked negative correlations between Y and SiO_2 and between TiO_2 and SiO_2. Ce_N/Y_N ratios increase with SiO_2, primarily as a result of strong depletion of heavy rare earth elements in the more siliceous gneisses, and may reach values in excess of 100. However, total rare earth levels and Ce/Yb ratios are lower in some trondhjemitic rocks. Many of the siliceous gneisses have prominent positive Eu anomalies, though the magnitude of the Eu anomaly is related to total REE content, and some trondhjemitic rocks have slight negative Eu anomalies.

The geochemical relationships suggest strongly that if the range of gneiss compositions are related by fractional crystallization, then hornblende has been a major controlling mineral phase, and the whole gneiss complex may have evolved under high P_{H_2O} conditions deep in the crust. However, partial melting models involving amphibolite and particularly garnet amphibolite as the primary source material seem best able to explain the geochemical features and field relationships. The deeper parts of the gneiss complex inverted to dry granulite facies assemblages during or shortly after the phase of crustal generation, probably in response to changing fluid composition (CO_2-rich). Expulsion of hydrous fluids was accompanied by loss of K, Rb, Th and U, thus enhancing the tonalitic/trondhjemitic characteristics of the gneiss complex.

INTRODUCTION

The Archaean gneiss terrain of Scotland and East Greenland has similar characteristics to other high grade gneiss granulite regions in other parts of the world. Both amphibolite and granulite facies areas are represented, but have been variably affected by later Proterozoic activity. Available isotopic evidence on the Lewisian gneisses of Scotland (summarised in Moorbath, 1976, suggests that the majority of the gneisses were generated about 2.9 b.y. ago.

The dominant component is a tonalitic grey gneiss composed of quartz, plagioclase, hornblende and biotite, but with varying proportions of hornblende and biotite. The equivalent granulite facies assemblage is quartz-plagioclase-hypersthene, with minor clinopyroxene. Small amounts of microcline may be present in the assemblages of the amphibolite-facies gneiss terrains but K-feldspar is uncommon in the granulite-facies gneisses (even in the retrogressed granulites) but does occur as an antiperthitic component in the plagioclases, and in minor late-stage trondhjemitic pegmatoid veins.

Throughout the gneiss terrain the rocks are extensively deformed, and the complex is heterogeneous on a scale of metres. Many of the gneisses are strongly banded, so that the original plutonic (? or volcanic) form and nature of the gneisses is largely obscured. This strong deformation probably coincided with the emplacement of the rocks and certainly pre-dated the granulite-facies metamorphism (ca 2.8 b.y.). It is important to bear in mind this strong deformation since there are a few means of assessing the degree of chemical interchange between layers and bands which may perhaps have suffered continual deformation over a period in excess of 100 m.y. In addition, there is later Proterozoic reworking and retrogressive activity to contend with: this has also been shown to involve considerable chemical mobility (Beach and Tarney, 1978).

The amphibolite-facies gneiss terrain, in both Scotland and Greenland, is bimodal (cf Barker and Peterman, 1974), there being abundant amphibolite (mafic) and hornblendite (ultramafic) balls and lenses scattered throughout the host tonalitic gneisses. The granulite-facies zones in Scotland and Greenland have a mean composition which is distinctly more basic (Tarney et al., 1972), but in Scotland at least the acid tonalite component is dominant. Moreover, the compositional distribution in these granulite areas is not so clearly bimodal, there being a continuum of gneiss compositions between ultramafic and silicic tonalites and trondhjemites. As many of the intermediate gneiss types are finely banded, it is not known to what extent the continuum is a feature of strong tectonic intermixing of original bimodal components, or whether there was an original compositional gradation in the gneiss precursors. We suspect both possibilities may be valid. Differences between the granulites and amphibolite zones have been intepreted in terms of differing crustal levels, now juxtaposed as a result of early Proterozoic tectonic activity (Sheraton et al., 1973). P-T conditions as high as 15 kb and 1200°C have been postulated for Lewisian granulite-facies rocks (O'Hara, 1977),though these values are rather higher than the normal range of P-T conditions (ca 9 kb,800°C) reported for granulites (Tarney and Windley, 1977).

Three other points may be made concerning the gneisses. First, there is a third, if minor, component associated with the bimodal suite: the supracrustal metasedimentary quartzites, marbles, garnet-kyanite pelites and iron formations, often associated with peridotite-metagabbro-anorthosite and amphibolite. These may have been imbricated with the gneiss precursors early in the history of the complexes (Bridgwater et al., 1974). Second, although the compositions of the granulite-facies gneisses broadly correspond with those in the amphibolite-facies zones, the granulites are notably low in Rb, K_2O, Th and U--a feature which has been attributed to granulite-facies metamorphism (Tarney et al., 1972, Drury, 1973). Thirdly, those rocks falling within the strict definition of trondhjemite constitute only a small proportion of the complex, and are mainly restricted to small bodies, late-stage veins and segregations. Nevertheless, there are many gneisses which are transitional between tonalite and trondhjemite.

GEOCHEMISTRY

A considerable amount of major and minor element geochemical data is available on the Archaean and Proterozoic rocks of Scotland and (to a lesser extent) East Greenland, much of it produced a decade or so ago at a time when comparable geochemical data on other Archaean terrains were scarce. Hence many of the results were directed to solving internal Lewisian problems. For the present purpose we will draw mainly on the data of Sheraton (1970), Tarney et al. (1972), Sheraton et al (1973), Drury (1972, 1973, 1974), Tarney (1976) and Drury (1978), together with some unpublished data.

The granulites and retrogressed granulites from the central zone of the Lewisian of the Scottish mainland give a smooth calc-alkaline trend on the AFM diagram (Tarney et al., 1972; Sheraton et al., 1973), although the granulites from E. Greenland and from Madras, India (Weaver et al., in press) have a more tholeiitic trend partly as a result of the tholeiitic nature of the mafic component of the bimodal suite. We suspect that the calc-alkaline trend may result in part from metasomatic smoothing during the retrogressive episode (Beach and Tarney, in press). Such a trend is more difficult to discern in the bimodal amphibolite-facies terrains.

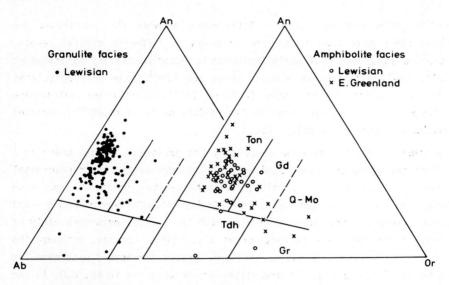

Figure 1.--Normative compositions of Scottish Lewisian and East Greenland gneisses with more than 60% SiO$_2$, classified according to O'Connor (1965).

On an O'Connor's (1965) diagram (Fig. 1) most of the silicic gneisses classify as tonalites, with few actually plotting in the trondhjemite field (sensu stricty) on account of the relatively high Ca contents. This applies to the amphibolite as well as the granulite-facies gneisses. Related to this, few of the gneisses have more than 70% SiO$_2$ (Fig. 3); those which do exceed this value tend to be trondhjemitic. This feature also applies to amphibolite-facies and granulite-facies gneisses. An exception are the early Proterozoic migmatites emplaced between the major granulite- and amphibolite-facies zones in the Lewisian and in East Greenland (Tarney et al., 1972; Drury, 1974) which have higher K$_2$O and SiO$_2$ and lower CaO and Al$_2$O$_3$. On the Q-Ab-Or and Q-Pl-Or diagrams therefore (Fig. 2) the Archaean tonalites plot towards the plagioclase corner and well away from the low-pressure cotectic in this system.

The tonalites are surprisingly uniform geochemically over the large area examined. Table I lists the mean compositions of the gray gneiss component of the bimodal suite from the Scottish mainland, the Outer Hebrides, East Greenland and the Fiskenaesset area of West Greenland (data from Tarney, 1976). The mean gray gneiss from the central granulite zone on the Scottish mainland is also included: it differs only in having lower K, Rb and Th levels, which seems to be a feature of the granulite terrain. The tonalites have relatively high Ba and Sr, but moderate K$_2$O and Rb, with Ba>Sr, Na/K ~ 2, CaO = 3-3.5%. K/Rb ratios are around the crustal average in the amphibolite-facies terrains, but much higher in the granulite terrains. Ce is between 50 and 100 times chondrite abundance, but Y is much less than 10 times chondrite abundance, except in the West Greenland samples where there are two populations (see O'Nions and Pankhurst, 1974).

The general pattern of rare earth element (REE) distributions in the gneisses can be explored by using Y as an indicator of HREE behaviour. Figure 3 shows the distinct negetive correlation of Y with SiO_2 in the Lewisian

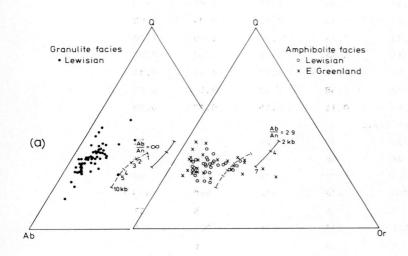

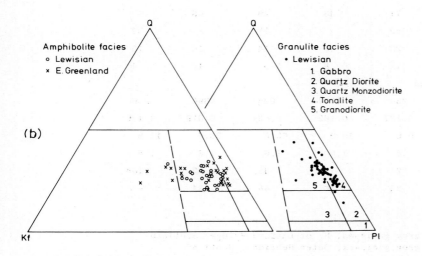

Figure 2.--(a) Normative Q-Ab-Or for Lewisian and East Greenland gneisses with more than 60% SiO_2. Loci of minimum melt compositions with varying H_2O and An/Ab from Tuttle and Bowen (1958), Luth et al. (1964) and Winkler (1967); (b) Normative Q-Or-Pl ternary plot.

Table I
Mean compositions of tonalitic grey gneisses from the North
Atlantic craton

	A	B	C	D	E
SiO_2	66.7	67.6	67.62	67.17	68.15
TiO_2	0.34	0.33	0.38	0.31	0.39
Al_2O_3	16.04	15.19	15.61	15.79	16.32
Fe_2O_3	1.49	1.75	1.89	1.68	3.60
FeO	1.47	1.28	1.05	1.41	-
MnO	0.04	0.05	0.04	0.04	0.03
MgO	1.44	1.28	1.46	1.09	1.00
CaO	3.18	3.22	3.42	3.54	3.98
Na_2O	4.90	4.15	4.97	4.74	4.45
K_2O	2.09	2.58	1.13	2.10	2.07
P_2O_5	0.14	0.11	0.15	0.12	0.20

Trace elements in p.p.m.

Cr	32	30	26	23	21
Ni	20	18	40	13	13
Rb	74	77	15	44	60
Sr	580	475	615	580	460
Y	7	6	3	8	17
Zr	193	182	278	207	215
Nb	6	5	6	6	-
Ba	713	840	984	1040	673
Ce	71	43	49	68	-
La	32	-	25	-	28
Pb	22	16	14	16	15
Th	11	8	1.5	10	4

Element ratios

K/Rb	234	278	625	396	286
Rb/Sr	0.127	0.162	0.024	0.076	0.130
Ba/Rb	9.6	10.9	65.6	23.6	11.2
Ba/Sr	1.2	1.8	1.6	1.8	1.5
Ce_N/Y_N	24	17	38	22	10*
Zr/Nb	32	36	46	34	-

* La_N/Y_N

A Av. of 39 grey gneisses, N. of Laxford Bridge, Scotland.
B Av. of 22 grey gneisses, Outer Hebrides, Scotland
C Av. of 36 retrogressed granulite-facies grey gneisses, Assynt, Scotland
D Av. of 41 grey gneisses, Angmagssalik, East Greenland
E Av. of 21 grey gneisses, Fiskanaesset, West Greenland

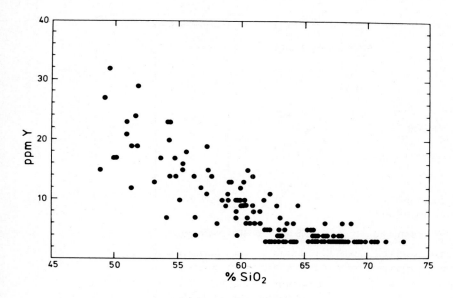

Figure 3.--Plot of Y v. SiO$_2$ for Lewisian gneisses: granulite facies zone, Assynt.

gneisses. Many silicic gneisses (>60% SiO$_2$) have Y values at or below 3 ppm, the lower limit of detection by XRF methods a decade ago. More recent measurements suggest Y is below 1 ppm in many of these rocks. Almost all rocks with more than 55% SiO$_2$ have less than 20 ppm Y (<10 times chondrite abundance). A plot of Y$_N$ v. Ce$_N$/Y$_N$ (Figure 4) also shows a good negative correlation, indicating that the more siliceous gneisses have highly fractionated REE patterns.

It is interesting to note too that TiO$_2$ shows a negative correlation with SiO$_2$ (Tarney, 1976) and a good positive correlation with Y (Figure 5). The mean ratio between Y and TiO$_2$ is almost the same as that in oceanic basalts, but whereas Y and TiO$_2$ increase linearly with crystal fractionation in basaltic systems, the reverse is true in the gneisses, and both apparently decrease in the more fractionated siliceous rocks. In Andean magmas, Y tends to increase while TiO$_2$ decreases with fractionation. The relationship suggests that there may be two mineral phases, such as garnet and ilmenite or rutile, removing Y and Ti respectively during fractionation (or retaining them during partial melting). Alternatively there may be one phase holding both these elements-- and hornblende is the most likely candidate. Note, however, that the Y-TiO$_2$ trend (Fig. 5) does not pass through the origin but intercepts the TiO$_2$ axis. This suggests that another mineral phase holding Y, but not Ti, could be

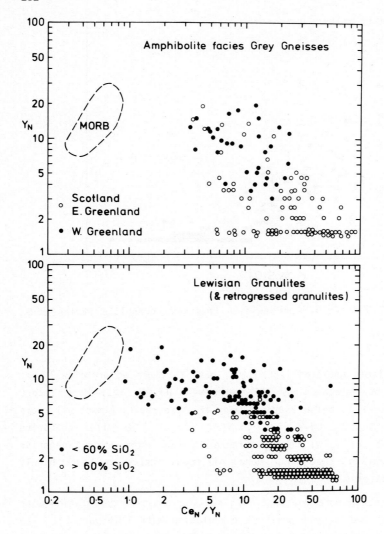

Figure 4.--Chondrite-normalised Y v. Ce/Y plot for amphibolite-facies and granulite-facies gneisses, showing increase in Ce/Y as Y decreases in the more siliceous gneisses. Most tonalitic-trondhjemitic gneisses have very high Ce/Y ratios. Field for depleted mid-ocean ridge basalts shown for reference.

involved, perhaps garnet. The influence of garnet is more likely during partial melting processes of course. Biotite fractionation would remove Ti but not Y.

Rare earth patterns of 9 tonalitic to granodioritic Lewisian gneisses from the Inner Hebrides are shown in Figure 6. All have high Ce_N/Yb_N ratios (mean

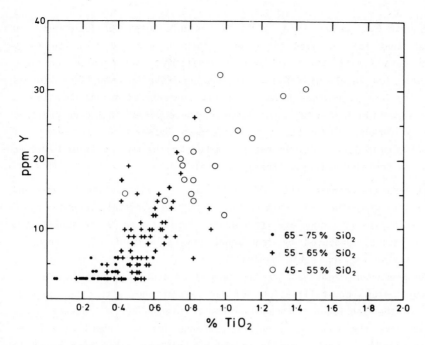

Figure 5.—Y v. TiO$_2$ for Lewisian gneisses.

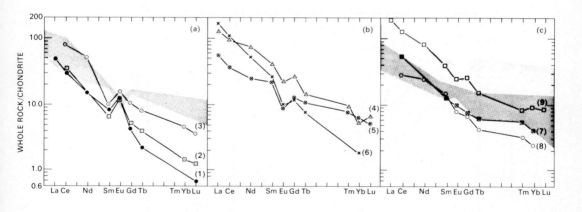

Figure 6.—Chondrite-normalised REE Plots for (a) three granulite-facies Lewisian gneisses from Coll and Tiree, with fields for gneisses from West Greenland (O'Nions and Pankhurst, 1974), N.W. Norway (Green et al., 1972) and Swaziland (Condie and Hunter, 1976) shown in light stipple, and fields for granitic rocks from South California batholith (Towell et al., 1975) shown in medium stipple. (b) three amphibolite-facies Lewisian gneisses with envelope for Archaean tonalite-granodiorite plutons (Arth and Hanson, 1975; Condie and Hunter, 1976). (c) two andesites (Condie, 1976) in medium stipple. After Drury (1978).

284

29, range 5.6 to 5.8) primarily a result of variable heavy REE depletion.   In this respect they fall in with the general pattern observed from the X-ray fluorescence data for Ce and Y in Lewisian gneisses.   The pyroxene gneisses (Fig. 6a) have low levels of REE and distinct positive Eu anomalies, whereas the amphibolite-facies gneisses have higher REE concentrations and negative Eu anomalies.   Strontium levels are also lower in the amphibolite-facies gneisses in this area (Drury, 1974) but this difference between the Sr levels of granulite and amphibolite zones is not so marked in the main bulk of Lewisian gneisses on the Scottish mainland (Sheraton et al. 1973).

This difference between the REE patterns of amphibolite-facies and granulite-facies gneisses, if related to different crustal levels, could suggest a feldspar-rich cumulate (granulite facies) and a residual melt (amphibolite facies) produced by fractional crystallisation of a precursor magma with similar Ce_N/Yb_N ratio to both.   This is illustrated in Figure 7. Assuming the precursor magma had the REE pattern of a dacitic melt (A) then 30 percent equilibrium crystallisation of an assemblage with the average mineralogy of the Hebridean pyroxene gneisses ($plag_{60}$ ksp_{10} $opyx_{10}$ qtz_{15} $opaq_5$) would give the two complementary patterns for the cumulate (C) and residual liquid (B).   Similar complementary REE patterns have been found in Proterozoic charnockites from Norway (Green et al. 1972; Ormaasen, 1977; Drury

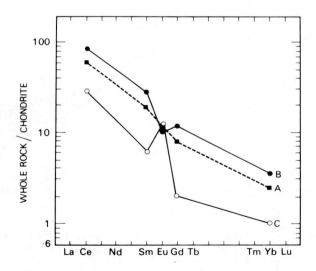

Figure 7.--Plots of chondrite-normalised Ce, Sm, Eu, Gd and Yb for: (A) 5 per cent equilibrium modal melting of garnet granulite with flat 25 times chondritic REE: (B) residual melt after extraction of 30 per cent of assemblage (pl_{60}, ksp_{10}, opx_{10}, qz_{15}, $opaq_5$) from (A); (C) accumulated solids from model (B). Compare (B) and (C) with Figures 6a and 6b.

and Field, in preparation). The mechanics of this suggested fractionation may have involved some form of filter pressing, rather than fractional crystallisation in the normal sense, in order to derive cumulate with the observed mineralogy of the granulites.

While this is a possible mechanism for explaining some of the geochemical differences between granulite facies gneiss terrains, the rare earth patterns of the more silicic members of the Lewisian granulite facies gneisses (those closest to the trondhjemite in composition) suggest a rather different story (Fig. 8). From their field relationships and from their major and trace element chemistry (Table II) they must be regarded as the residual liquids of the gneiss terrain. Instead of the negative Eu anomalies which might be expected following the extraction of a dry granulite-facies mineral assemblage, most have marked positive Eu anomalies. Patterns 6E and 16V encompass the maximum and minimum ranges in total REE content of the silicic trondhjemitic-tonalitic gneisses, but most such gneisses fall in the lower part of the range.

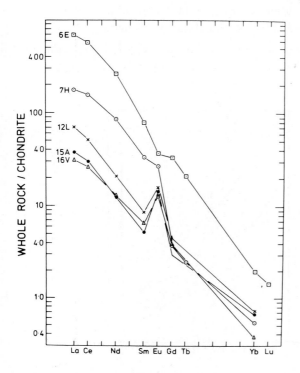

Figure 8.—Chondrite-normalised REE plots of two trondhjemitic gneisses (6E and 16V) from the granulite facies zone, Drumbeg, Assynt, and three microcline-bearing trondhjemitic gneisses (7H, 12L and 15A).

The remaining three patterns (7H, 12L and 15A) are of microcline-bearing gneisses, regarded by Sheraton et al. (1973) as either the last residual liquids during consolidation of the plutonic gneiss complex, or as pegmatitic remelts of the gneisses. They have high K/Rb ratios, unlike the later Proterozoic pegmatites, and were emplaced either just before, or during the granulite-facies metamorphism. All these rocks have high Ce_N/Y_N ratios (~300 in sample 6E) and show extreme HREE depletion. There is a broad correspondence between the total REE content and the size of the Eu anomaly. Sample 6E, with the highest REE levels, has a small negative Eu anomaly, while samples 15A and 16V, with the lowest total REE contents have marked positive Eu anomalies. There is also a broad correspondence between Eu levels and Sr levels (if so, it is likely from the XRF data for Sr, Ce and Y that most of the siliceous gneisses have positive Eu anomalies).

The very high REE concentration and high Ce_N/Yb_N ratio of sample 6E is unusual. It is possible that this rock represents a partial melting product of the associated tonalitic gneisses .(i.e. ca 5% melting of a tonalitic hornblende-poor granulite) at granulite-facies with plagioclase and pyroxene as residual phases rather than hornblende. This would permit higher HREE levels and the development of a slight negative Eu anomaly in the liquid.

Additional REE and other trace element data (Table II) are available for trondhjemitic rocks from the Lewisian of the Inner Hebrides (Fig. 9). These

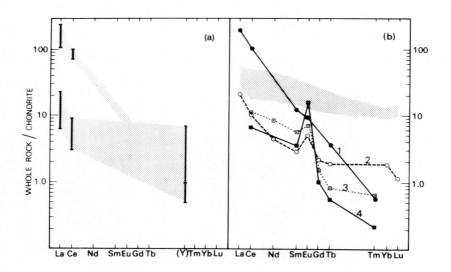

Figure 9.--REE data for trondhjemitic sheets from Coll and Tiree: (a) envelopes of chondrite-normalised values for La, Ce and Y for 14 trondhjemite bodies, (b) chondrite-normalised plots of REE in 4 trondhjemite sheets.

Table II
Major and trace element analyses of Lewisian trondhjemitic rocks

	16V	6E	7H	12L	15A	1	2	3	4	5
SiO_2	68.38	72.24	69.48	69.85	71.85	73.1	73.2	69.0	76.1	73.3
TiO_2	0.227	0.305	0.203	0.173	0.149	0.21	0.02	0.42	0.03	0.09
Al_2O_3	16.39	14.52	15.07	15.63	15.56	15.1	16.6	14.1	15.4	15.4
Fe_2O_3	1.46	1.72	1.61	1.61	1.39	1.25	0.15	2.15	0.40	1.56
FeO	0.61	0.39	0.86	0.57	0.32	0.78	0.46	1.54	0.32	
MnO	0.026	0.021	0.025	0.034	0.033	0.02	0.01	0.03	0.01	0.05
MgO	1.00	0.46	1.35	1.42	0.94	0.8	0.2	1.2	0.2	0.4
CaO	1.75	2.11	1.28	0.76	0.55	3.54	4.45	4.18	1.45	3.28
Na_2O	7.09	6.24	4.34	5.72	5.95	4.9	4.7	3.7	4.5	4.7
K_2O	0.78	0.41	2.34	2.43	2.35	0.48	0.55	0.86	2.76	1.14
P_2O_5	0.078	0.050	0.346	0.080	0.037	-	-	-	-	-

Trace elements in p.p.m.

	16V	6E	7H	12L	15A	1	2	3	4	5
Cr	13	3	6	21	11	8	23	12	6	19
Ni	26	11	33	9	3	6	11	10	-	8
Rb	11	5	22	31	23	4	13	15	47	28
Sr	554	512	341	248	290	260	170	163	277	277
Ba	609	170	1816	1248	1009	244	115	399	564	269
Zr	127	1158	195	127	70	189	71	27	12	103
Nb	5	22	4	2	5	-	-	-	-	-
Pb	21	10	7	7	21	14	29	7	13	35
Th	5	33	5	5	5	21	1.6	-	7	6
La	10	227	58	23	12	63.8	7.1	-	-	11
Ce	21	462	126	41	24	83.9	8.2	9.8	6.2	22
Nd	7.2	150	49	12	7.1	22.6	2.9	-	-	-
Sm	1.2	14.7	6.1	1.6	1.0	2.4	0.6	1.28	0.71	-
Eu	0.90	2.5	2.2	1.1	1.0	0.72	0.39	0.53	1.25	-
Gd	0.88	7.5	1.0	1.9	1.1	-	-	0.50	-	-
Tb	-	0.98	0.12	0.06	-	0.19	0.09	0.04	0.05	-
Yb	0.08	0.41	0.11	0.14	0.10	0.13	0.42	0.14	0.05	-
Lu	-	0.05	-	-	-	-	0.04	-	-	-
Y	3	13	3	3	3	-	5	-	-	4

Element ratios

	16V	6E	7H	12L	15A	1	2	3	4	5
Ce_N/Yb_N	69	295	300	77	63	143	5.0	16.0	29.0	-
Eu/Eu*	2.4	0.7	2.4	3.3	4.5	1.0	2.0	1.5	6.4	-
K/Rb	589	681	883	651	848	996	351	476	487	338
Rb/Sr	0.020	0.010	0.065	0.125	0.079	0.015	0.076	0.092	0.207	0.123

16V and 6E: trondhjemitic gneisses, Drumbeg, Assynt. Retrogessed granulites
7H, 12L and 15A: microcline-bearing trondhjemites, Drumbeg, Assynt.
1. trondhjemite sheet in garnet-hornblende granulite, Balephetrish Hill, Tiree.
2. trondhjemite sheet in hornblende granulite, Portna Luing, Coll.
3. trondhjemite sheet in hornblende granulite, Scarinish, Tiree.
4. trondhjemite sheet in garnet-hornblende granulite, Eilean Ghressamuill, Tiree.
5. average of 14 trondhjemite sheets from Coll and Tiree, Scotland.

trondhjemites are found as thin concordant veins and bands within the gneisses. They are thickest (up to 10 m) and most voluminous (up to 40 percent at outcrop) within thick sheets of basic and intermediate rocks in supracrustal belts. Both veins and host rocks show the same strutural sequence and have suffered the same metamorphism. The relationships suggest that the veins segregated from their host rocks during imbrication of supracrustals with the tonalitic gneisses and before the early granulite-facies metamorphism (Drury, 1972). Due to extensive late deformation and retrogression, both granulite- and amphibolite-facies varieties are found. Granulite-facies veins are trondhjemitic with a quartz-plagioclase-garnet (-orthopyroxene-K-feldspar) assemblage. With increasing deformation there is a parallel increase in potash feldspar. This has been regarded as evidence for potash metasomatism during retrogressive metamorphism (Drury, 1972).

The anhydrous veins are high-Ca trondhjemites, and like most of the tonalitic/trondhjemitic Lewisian gneisses, plot close to the Q-Ab and An-Ab joins on Q-Ab-Or and An-Ab-Or ternary diagrams and remote from the dry minimum melting point locus and thermal trough in these systems. The majority of the trondhjemite veins show abundances of La, Ce and Y that are extremely low for granitic rocks (Fig. 9a), but two samples show higher values for La and Ce, and have very low Y values. Rare earth patterns for four of these trondhjemitic veins, located in granulite-facies mafic host rocks, are shown in Figure 9b. Three of the samples (Nos. 2, 3 and 4) have very low total REE abundances, Ce_N/Yb_N ratios ranging from 5 to 29 and very prominent positive Eu anomalies. The remaining sample (No. 1) has a slightly fractionated REE pattern (Ce_N/Yb_N = 140) and no Eu anomaly and is similar to sample 6E from Assynt. In terms of REE there is therefore a clear division amongst the trondhjemites, but this is not apparent from other aspects of their major and trace element geochemistry, mineralogy or field association. This duality is also present within deformed and K-metasomatised veins at amphibolite facies, though the LREE-enriched variety predominates amongst the group of samples analyzed. The relationship between total REE content, Ce_N/Yb_N ratio and magnitude of the Eu anomaly is broadly similar to that in the mainland Lewisian samples (Fig. 8) and clearly implies some systematic mineralogical control over REE behaviour.

Petrogenesis of trondhjemitic bodies

The field relations of the trondhjemitic veins suggests a genetic relationship with the basic to intermediate rocks which enclose them. The light-REE enriched pattern of sample 1 can be approximated by a model involving 1 percent equilibrium modal melting of a basaltic source rock with the mineralogy of its host rock (ga_{20} cpx_{25} opx_{20} pla_{35}) and the average REE

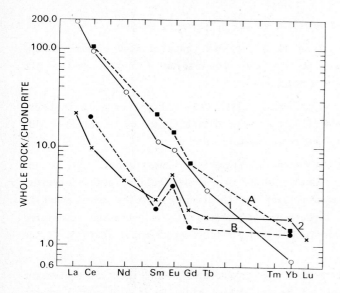

Figure 10.--Plots of chondrite-normalised Ce, Sm, Eu, Gd and Yb for: (A) 1 per cent equilibrium modal melting of source rock with garnet granulite mineralogy and average REE of basic hosts to trondhjemites. (B) 1 per cent equilibrium modal melting of hornblendite with average REE of basic hosts. Models compared with samples 1 and 2 of Figure 9b.

content of local granulite facies basic rocks (Fig. 10). This suggests that at least some of the trondhjemite bodies could be products of partial melting at granulite-facies. The rare earth patterns of the REE-depleted trondhjemites most resemble those expected in feldspathic cumulates: indeed they are similar to the REE patterns of some Proterozoic anorthosites (Green et al., 1972). Compared with their host rocks they are depleted in all REE, particularly HREE (Fig. 9b). Partial melting of the mafic host rocks at granulite facies with their present mineralogy (opx-cpx-ga-hb-pla) could not produce these patterns, nor could fractional crystallisation of a 'dry' basaltic magma produce trondhjemitic residual liquids with these characteristics. In both cases some enrichment in at least LREE would be expected. For source material with the REE patterns of the host rocks, the only feasible partial melting mechanism is one involving a hornblende-rich mafic source (see Fig. 10), for which there is no petrographic evidence. Thus either it must be accepted that the veins were externally derived and that the mafic rocks merely acted as a locus during emplacement, or that they were generated at high P_{H_2O} before stabilization of granulite-facies assemblages, or, less likely, that they represent silicified anorthosites or some complex metamorphic segregation phenomenon.

Summary: geochemical characteristics of the gray gneiss complex

1.   Taken as a whole there is a complete range between ultramafic and
trondhjemite   compositions,   but   in   the   amphibolite   facies   terrains   the
compositional distribution is bimodal.

2. Al_2O_3 is generally high (mean >15%). CaO is high, even in the most
siliceous rocks, with the result that the plagioclases are quite calcic. SiO_2
rarely exceeds 70% except in the trondhjemitic veins.

3.   Na/K ratios are high, except in migmatised gneiss zones. K_2O, Rb and
K/Rb ratios are near mean crustal values in the amphibolite facies terrains,
but K_2O, Rb, Th and U are much lower in the granulite facies zones and K/Rb
ratios much higher.   This appears to be related to the processes associated
with granulite facies metamorphism, but may reflect geochemical features of the
gneissic precursors.

4.   Cr and Ni tend to be higher than in Andean plutonic rocks of equivalent
bulk composition.   The levels of Ba and Sr are high. Ba is high and increases
with % SiO_2. Sr also increases with SiO_2, and is still at the 500 ppm level
at 70% SiO_2, thereafter decreasing.

5.   There is marked negative correlation between Y and SiO_2 and between
TiO_2 and SiO_2. Ce levels do not change significantly with SiO_2 (except they
are lower in the high SiO_2 rocks). Ce/Y ratios correlate positively with SiO_2.
Few silicic gneisses have more than 10 times chondrite abundance of Y, and many
have less than 1 times chondrite abundance.

6.   Ce /Yb   ratios increase with increasing SiO_2 and reach values of more
than 100 in some tonalitic/trondhjemitic gneisses.   Many siliceous gneisses
have distinct positive Eu anomalies. Some trondhjemitic veins have lower total
REE levels and rather less fractionated REE patterns, but enhanced positive Eu
anomalies.

DISCUSSION

The   origin   of   tonalitic-trondhjemitic   gneisses   with   the   geochemical
characteristics   described   above   must   be   considered   in   relation   to   the
geochemical features of other high-grade gneiss terrains, and in relation to
modern tonalitic rocks in cordilleran batholiths.   However, compared with
Archaean greenstone belts there is still very limited data for REE on high-
grade gneisses.

In the 3.7 b.y. Amitsoq Gneisses of West Greenland, O'Nions and Pankhurst
(1974) and Lambert and Holland (1976) have noted two distinct types of
gneisses: one group with moderately fractionated REE patterns (HREE >10 times

chondrites), negative Eu anomalies and generally more potassic; and a more dominant tonalitic group with highly fractionated REE patterns and low HREE (<4 times chondrites) abundances, positive Eu anomalies and high Sr. The latter type is similar to the tonalitic gneisses discussed here.

The bimodal suite of the Ancient Gneiss Complex of Swaziland (Hunter et al., 1978) also comprises two distinct types of siliceous gneisses: one group with high SiO_2, low Al_2O_3 (<14%), high Rb/Sr, relatively abundant REE's and patterns with negative Eu anomalies; the other group has lower SiO_2, Al_2O_3 <14%, low Rb/Sr and more fractionated REE patterns showing significant HREE depletion but no Eu anomalies.

Plutonic rock suites with the closest geochemical affinities to those described here are found in the Proterozoic gabbro-diorite-tonalite-trondhjemite suite of S.W. Finland (Arth et al., 1978) and in the similar Granodiorite Suite intruding the Ancient Gneiss Complex of Swaziland (Hunter et al., 1978). Other occurrences have been noted by Barker and Arth (1976). Andean granitic batholiths in general have REE patterns without HREE depletion, but with negative Eu anomalies (Saunders et al., 1978)--REE characteristics which are similar to Andean volcanics (Thorpe et al., 1975; Lopez-Escobar et al., 1976). However, in the more deeply eroded cordillera of S. Chile, the tonalitic batholiths have steeper REE patterns and no Eu anomalies (Stern et al., in prep.)

It seems that the mechanism of generation of tonalitic-trondhjemitic magmas (with positive Eu anomalies in the residual (liquids) is different from that in high level Andean magmas (with negative Eu anomalies in the residual liquids). The former type is clearly much more common in Archaean high-grade terrains, but this could relate either to fundamental differences in the processes of Archaean crustal generation or to differences in crustal level.

We may consider briefly the potential of fractional crystallisation and partial melting mechanism in explaining these differences, though more data on high-grade gneiss terrains is needed before models can be tested rigorously.

Fractional Crystallisation

Although crystallisation of hornblende is a possible mechanism for generating tonalites and trondhjemites with steep REE patterns and positive Eu anomalies from a basic magma (Arth et al., 1978), in practise there are several apparent difficulties: (a) the gneiss complex is largely bimodal and there are few intermediate members except in the banded gneisses of the granulite-facies zones; (b) very few of the gneisses, even in the supposed deeper-seated granulite-facies belts, have the geochemical characteristics (e.g., low Ba,

Zr, Ce, La) expected of cumulates from basic to intermediate magmas (Tarney and Windley, 1977); (c) strontium remains high, even in gneisses with ca 70% SiO_2, yet fractional crystallisation processes yielding silicic compositions from a basic magma must involve plagioclase separation, which should reduce the Sr content of the liquid. Plagioclase separation would also tend to negate (to some extent) the effect of hornblende separation in the development of positive Eu anomalies in the residual liquids.

In defense of the hornblende fractionation model, however, it may be noted that few of the gneisses have more than 70% SiO_2 (Fig. 3) and still have high CaO and Al_2O_3 (relative to normal calc-alkaline igneous rocks). It is well known that high water pressures suppress plagioclase crystallisation in mafic to intermediate magmas (Yoder and Tiller, 1962; Holloway and Burnham, 1972; Eggler and Burnham, 1973), and moreover that the minimum in the Q-Ab-Or system is displaced away from quartz and toward the plagioclase corner at progressively higher water pressures (Tuttle and Bowen, 1958; Luth et al., 1964). Thus the gneiss compositions are at least consistent with crystallisation at depth under high water pressures. Suppression of plagioclase crystallisation, relative to that of hornblende would leave the residual liquids rich in CaO and Al_2O_3. This would ensure that any plagioclase which did crystallise would be more calcic, and since calcic plagioclase has lower partition coefficients for Sr and Eu than intermediate plagioclase (Philpotts, 1970) this would enable high Sr levels to be maintained in the liquid and a positive Eu anomaly to develop in response to hornblende fractionation. Igneous hornblendes, being both less silicic and less sodic than plagioclase + pyroxene, would ensure a more rapid transition toward tonalitic-trondhjemitic residual liquids than with more normal tholeiitic differentiation. Such liquids would show heavy REE depletion as a result of the increased partitioning of HREE into hornblende in equilibrium with silicic liquids (Arth and Barker, 1976).

It is important to note that extensive hornblende fractionation is most likely to take place deep in the crust under high maintained water pressures. At higher crustal levels (and lower water pressures) pyroxenes and plagioclase would be the dominant liquidus phases. This would give rise to residual liquids with higher REE levels (since both pyroxenes and plagioclase have much lower partition coefficients for REE than hornblende), flatter patterns, and significant negative Eu anomalies due to separation of intermediate plagioclases. These textures characterise high level Andean plutons and volcanics (Saunders et al., in press; Thorpe et al., 1975). It is significant too that it is mainly Archaean gneisses or deep level plutons which have positive Eu anomalies. Compositionally equivalent extrusive dacites in Archaean greenstone belts have steep REE patterns but, with some exceptions, most seem not to have positive Eu anomalies (Arth and Hanson, 1975; Condie, 1976; Glikson, 1976; Hawkesworth and O'Nions, 1977). Many in fact are superficially similar to modern arc volcanics. The plutonic intrusions bordering greenstone belts, presumably mostly high level intrusions, may have slight positive Eu anomalies, but many have negative Eu anomalies (Arth and Hanson, 1975; Glikson, 1976; Condie and Hunter, 1976). The reason for this difference may be that silicic magmas, which have evolved at depth through hornblende fractionation at high water pressures, cannot rise to higher levels without solidifying as water pressures fall (Harris et al., 1970).

An interesting consequence of such a model is that the upper crust must be dominated by silicic rocks with negative Eu anomalies--a feature clearly evident from sedimentary REE patterns (Nance and Taylor, 1976). Silicic rocks with positive Eu anomalies may be common at greater depth, but the complementary cumulates of both might be expected in the lowermost crust.

Partial Melting

The data on the Lewisian and E. Greenland gneisses provide some constraints on possible mechanisms of generation. Note that the levels of Ba and Sr in the gneisses are high. Considering the vast areas of gneisses with these characteristics, and the different crustal levels exposed, the volume of crust with high Ba and Sr must be very large. Since much of this gneiss terrain appears from isotopic evidence to have been generated about 2.9 b.y. ago, it must have been generated at a rather high rate. It is unlikely therefore that the mantle could have been the direct source since the degree of partial melting required to attain such high Ba and Sr levels would be very small, a requirement that conflicts with the large volume of material (Tarney, 1976). A more evolved mafic source would be more appropriate, and a subduction zone environment feeding a large amount of hydrated mafic oceanic crust to the zone of crustal generation would seem to be a preferable tectonic situation, though not necessarily a mandatory one.

Partial melting processes in subduction zones have been reviewed by Ringwood (1977), who stressed the importance of water in generating more siliceous magma compositions either from the mafic crust of the subducting slab and/or from the overlying mantle wedge. The experimental work of Stern (1974) on the hydrous melting of basalt and andesite at 30 kb indicated that the liquids produced by equilibrium partial fusion of garnet-bearing assemblages would be systematically more calcic than normal calc-alkaline magma compositions owing to the low Ca content of residual garnet. The Lewisian and

Greenland tonalitic gneisses are indeed calcic, but not to the same degree as predicted by Stern's calculations. These liquid compositions might be more appropriate for melts in equilibrium with residual hornblende. Helz (1973, 1976) in fact found that melting of tholeiite at P_{H_2O} = 5 kb, with residual hornblende, produced quartzofeldspathic liquids broadly similar to tonalites and trondhjemites in composition. Residual garnet would retain Y and the heavy REE, but not titanium whereas residual hornblende would retain both Ti and Y. As we have noted, there is a linear correlation between TiO_2 and Y in Lewisian gneisses, and both elements show a strong negative correlation with SiO_2 (Figs. 3 and 5). If, as Arth et al. (1978) have argued, hornblende liquid partition coefficients for rare-earths (especially HREE) increase as the melt becomes more silicic, the negative SiO_2 - Y trend is explicable. Titanium may behave similarly. Residual hornblendes would hold less Al_2O_3 than residual garnet, hence the corresponding liquids in equilibrium with hornblende would be more alumina-rich, which seems to be a characteristic of Archaean tonalites. There is no reason why both garnet and hornblende should not be residual of course: garnet is considerably more efficient in the retention of HREE than hornblende, and very high Ce/Yb ratios of some tonalitic/trondhjemitic gneisses may be more easily explained if garnet is involved.

The critical feature of the REE patterns of these deep-seated tonalitic/trondhjemitic gneisses is the development of significant positive Eu anomalies. This could be attributable to negative Eu anomalies in residual hornblende. However, garnets in equilibrium with dacitic liquids also have appreciable negative Eu anomalies (see Arth and Barker, 1976), a feature seen also in garnets in andesites and rhyolites from the English Lake District (Millward, personal communication). These garnets are of course rather iron-rich, and it is not known whether more Mg-rich garnets would show the same feature. Watson's (1976) experimental data on element partitioning between immiscible acid and basic liquids suggests also that the compositional and structural characteristics of the melt itself may be an important factor. Watson found that cations of high field strength (including Ti and trivalent REE) were strongly partitioned into the basic melt but that alkaline-earth cations, such as Ba and Sr, were more equally distributed. Although data are not available for divalent Eu it is likely that its behaviour would closely parallel that of Sr. An important implication of these data is that solid-liquid partitioning of trivalent REE will change significantly with liquid composition, but that of Sr (and Eu^{2+}) will not, and that the effects will become more apparent where solid-liquid partition coefficients are greater than one. Thus minerals such as garnet and hornblende, which have high partition coefficients for middle-to-heavy REE, should develop significant negative Eu anomalies in equilibrium with silicic melts, but not with more basic melts. This effect will not be apparent with minerals such as olivine and pyroxenes which have low partition coefficients for these elements.

The flatter rare-earth patterns of Andean volcanics and batholiths with their higher HREE levels and more usual negative Eu anomalies (Thorpe et al., 1975; Saunders et al., in press) would be more compatible with partial melting of a mafic source with residual pyroxene and plagioclase. Andean rocks tend to have lower Sr and Ba contents than Archaean tonalitic gneisses, which would also agree with residual plagioclase, whereas residual hornblende would retain little Sr or Ba. One consequence of this is that with lower degrees of partial melting (or more subsequent crystal fractionation) Rb-Sr ratios would be higher with a dry pyroxene-plagioclase residue. In theory these differences could simply be due to higher P_{H_2O} conditions attending the generation of Archaean tonalites. With a subduction model the source of the water is ultimately the hydrothermal activity at mid-ocean ridges, the resulting partially hydrated mafic crust dehydrating during subduction and producing the necessary fluid flux for magma generation. One obvious difference between modern and Archaean oceanic crust is that the latter may have had (by analogy with greenstone belts) a high proportion of high-Mg tholeiites and peridotitic komatiites. These would have hydrated to serpentine, thus holding as much as ten times more water than equivalent modern ocean crust. Dehydration of serpentine, probably over a considerable depth range (Ringwood, 1977), would provide the necessary high P_{H_2O} conditions for magma generation involving residual hornblende (+ garnet). Depending on the state of hydration, therefore, a whole range of rare earth characteristics are possible, ranging from HREE-depleted with positive Eu anomalies to normal Andean type with negative Eu anomalies. Clearly the first type dominates in the Archaean, but the second type is possible within a subduction environment too providing eclogite is not stable in the subducting slab in an Archaean geothermal regime (as argued by Green, 1975). However, theoretical models of present-day subduction zones do propose eclogite at depths to Benioff Zones under modern calc-alkaline volcanoes. Hence it is more usual to erect hypotheses deriving modern calc-alkaline magmas from a mantle source above the subducting slab (with or without a magma component from the slab itself) where residual garnet is minor or non-existent (Ringwood, 1977).

Finally, it is necessary to incorporate into any model provision for the granulite facies event, which occurred penecontemporaneously with the emplacement of the plutonic gneiss complex. This led to removal of K, Rb, Th and U, but not to other elements such as Zr, Nb and Ba which are normally 'incompatible' in magmatic systems, and resulted in some tonalitic-trondhjemitic gneisses with very high Na/K ratios. It has been suggested that the inversion to dry granulite facies assemblages may be more a response to a change in fluid composition (CO_2 rich) rather than a temperature increase (Tarney and Windley, 1977) since fluid inclusions in granulite facies terrains tend to be CO_2-rich. K, Rb, Th and U may have been removed along with the hydrous fluids. Alternatively it is possible, if the source of the tonalitic magmas was subducting oceanic crust, that these elements may have been removed by hydrothermal activity either at the spreading ridge or during the early stages of subduction, before the tonalitic magmas were generated.

REFERENCES

Arth, J.G. and Barker, F., 1976. Rare-earth partitioning between hornblende and dacitic liquid and implications for the genesis of trondhjemitic-tonalitic magmas. Geology, 4: 534-536.

Arth, J.G., Barker, F., Peterman, Z.E. and Friedman, I., 1978. Geochemistry of the gabbro-diorite-tonalite-trondhjemite suite of southwest Finland and its implications for the origin of tonalitic and trondhjemitic magmas. J. Pet. (in press).

Arth, J.G. and Hanson, G.N., 1975. Geochemistry and origin of the early Precambrian crust of northeastern Minnesota. Geochim. Cosmochim. Acta, 39: 325-362.

Barker, F. and Arth, J.G., 1976. Generation of trondhjemitic-tonalitic liquids and Archean bimodal trondhjemite-basalt suites. Geology, 4: 596-600.

Barker, F. and Peterman, Z.E., 1974. Bimodal tholeiitic-dacitic magmatism and the early Precambrian crust. Precambrian Res., 1: 1-12.

Beach, A. and Tarney, J., 1978. Major and trace element patterns established during retrogressive metamorphism of granulite facies gneisses, N.W. Scotland. Precambrian Res., (in press).

Bridgwater, D., McGregor, V.R. and Myers, J.S., 1974. A horizontal tectonic regime in the Archaean of Greenland and its implications for early crustal thickening. Precambrian Res., 1: 179-197.

Condie, K.C., 1976. Trace element geochemistry of Archean greenstone belts. Earth Sci. Rev., 12: 393-417.

Condie, K.C. and Hunter, D.R., 1976. Trace element geochemistry of Archean granitic rocks from the Barberton region, South Africa. Earth Planet. Sci. Lett., 29: 389-400.

Drury, S.A., 1972. The chemistry of some granitic veins from the Lewisian of Coll and Tiree, Argyllshire, Scotland. Chem. Geol., 9: 175-193.

Drury, S.A., 1973. The geochemistry of Precambrian granulite facies rocks from the Lewisian complex of Tiree, Inner Hebrides, Scotland. Chem. Geol., 11: 167-188.

Drury, S.A., 1974. Chemical changes during retrogressive metamorphism of Lewisian granulite facies rocks from Coll and Tiree. Scott. J. Geol., 10: 237-256.

Drury, S.A., 1978. REE distributions in a high grade Archaean gneiss complex in Scotland: Implications for the genesis of ancient crust. Precambrian Res., 6: (in press).

Eggler, D.H. and Burnham, C.W., 1973. Crystallisation and fractionation trends in the system andesite - H_2O - CO_2 - O_2 at pressures to 10kb. Geol. Soc. Am. Bull., 84: 2517-2532.

Glikson, A.Y., 1976. Trace element geochemistry and origin of early Precambrian acid igneous series, Barberton Mountain Land, Transvaal. Geochim. Cosmochim. Acta, 40: 1261-1280.

Green, D.H., 1975. Genesis of Archean peridotitic magmas and constraints on Archean geothermal gradients and tectonics. Geology, 3: 15-18.

Green, T.H., Brunfelt, A.O. and Heier, K.S., 1972. Rare-earth element distribution and K/Rb ratios in granulites, mangerites and anorthosites, Lofoten-Vesteraalen, Norway. Geochim. Cosmochim. Acta, 36: 241-257.

Harris, P.G., Kennedy, W.Q. and Scarfe, C.M., 1970. Volcanism versus plutonism - the effect of chemical composition. In G. Newall and N. Rast (eds). Mechanism of Igneous Intrusion. Geol. Jour. Liverpool. Spec. Issue No. 2; 187-200.

Hawkesworth, C.H. and O'Nions, R.K., 1977. The petrogenesis of some Archaean volcanic rocks from Southern Africa. J. Pet. 18: 487-520.

Helz, R.T., 1973. Phase relations of basalts in their melting range at P_{H_2O} = 5Kb as a function of oxygen fugacity. J. Pet., 14: 249-302.

Helz, R.T., 1976. Phase relations of basalts in their melting ranges at P_{H_2O} = 5Kb, Part II. Melt compositions. J. Pet., 17: 139; 193.

Holloway, J.R. and Burnham, C.W., 1972. Melting relations of basalts with equilibrium water pressures less than total pressure. J. Pet., 13: 1-29.

Hunter, D.R., Barker, F. and Millard, H.T., 1978. The geochemical nature of the Archean Ancient Gneiss Complex and Granodiorite Suite, Swaziland: a preliminary study. Precambrian Res., (in press).

298

Lambert, I.B. and Wyllie, P.J., 1974. Melting of tonalite and crystallization of andesite liquid with excess water to 30 kilobars. J. Geol., 82: 88-97.

Lambert, R. St. J. and Holland, J.G., 1976. Amitsoq Gneiss Geochemistry: preliminary observations. In B. F. Windley (ed), The Early History of the Earth. Wiley, London, pp. 191-201.

Lopez-Escobar, L., Frey, F. A. and Vergara, M., 1976. Andesites from Central-South Chile: trace element abundances and petrogenesis. In Gonzaliz-Ferran, O. (ed). Symposium on Andean and Antarctic volcanology problems. Proc. IAVCEI Spec. Ser., pp. 725-761.

Luth, W. C., Jahns, R. H. and Tuttle, O. F., 1964. The granite system at pressures of 4 to 10 kilobars. J. Geophys. Res., 69: 759-773.

Moorbath, S., 1976. Age and isotope constraints for the evolution of Archaean crust. In B. F. Windley (ed), The Early History of the Earth. Wiley, London, pp. 351-360.

Nance, W.B. and Taylor, S.R., 1976. Rare earth element patterns and crustal evolution. I. Australian Post-Archaean sedimentary rocks. Geochim. Cosmochim. Acta, 40: 1539-1555.

O'Connor, J.T., 1965. A classification for quartz-rich igneous rocks based on feldspar ratios. U.S. Geol. Surv. Prof. Pap., 525-B.

O'Hara, M.J., 1977. Thermal history of excavation of Archaean gneisses from the base of the continental crust. J. Geol. Soc. Lond., 134: 185-200.

O'Nions, R.K. and Pankhurst, R.J., 1974. Rare earth element distributions in Archaean gneisses and anorthosites, Godthab area, West Greenland. Earth Planet. Sci. Lett., 22: 328-338.

Ormaason, D.E., 1977. Petrology of the Hopen mangerite-charnockite intrusion, Lofoten, North Norway. Lithos, 10: 291-310.

Philpotts, J.A., 1970. Redox estimation from a calculation of Eu^{2+} and Eu^{3+} concentrations in natural phases. Earth Planet Sci. Lett., 9: 257-268.

Ringwood, A.E., 1977. Petrogenesis in island arc systems. Am. Geophys. Union. Maurice Ewing Series, 1: 311-324.

Saunders, A.D., Weaver, S.D. and Tarney, J., (in press). The pattern of Antarctic Peninsula Plutonism. In C. Craddock (ed), Proc. Third Symposium on Antarctic Geology and Geophysics, Madison, Wisconsin.

Sheraton, J.W., 1970. The origin of the Lewisian gneisses of northwest Scotland, with particular reference to the Drumbeg area, Sutherland. Earth Planet. Sci. Lett., 8: 301-310.

Sheraton, J.W., Skinner, A.C. and Tarney, J., 1973. The geochemistry of the Scourian gneisses of the Assynt district. In R.G. Park and J. Tarney (ed), The Early Precambrian of Scotland and Related Rocks of Greenland. University of Keele, pp.13-30.

Stern, C.R., 1974. Melting products of olivine tholeiite basalt in subduction zones. Geology, 2: 227-230.

Stern, C.R., Stroup, J.B. and Tarney, J. (in preparation). Geochemistry of the Patagonian Batholith between $51^{o}S$ and $52^{o}S$ latitude.

Tarney, J., 1976. Geochemistry of Archaean high grade gneisses, with implications as to the origin and evolution of the Precambrian crust. In B.F. Windley (ed), The Early History of the Earth. Wiley, London, pp.405-417.

Tarney, J., Skinner, A.C. and Sheraton, J.W., 1972. A geochemical comparison of major Archaean gneiss units from Northwest Scotland and East Greenland. Rept. 24th Int. geol. Congress, Montreal., 1: 162-174.

Tarney, J. and Windley, B.F., 1977. Chemistry, thermal gradients and evolution of the lower continental crust. J. Geol. Soc. Lond., 134: 153-172.

Thorpe, R.S., Potts, P.J. and Francis, P.W., 1976. Rare-earth data and petrogenesis of andesite from the North Chilean Andes. Contrib. Miner. Pet., 54: 65-78.

Towell, D.G., Winchester, J.W. and Spirn, R.W., 1965. Rare-earth distributions in some rocks and associated minerals of the batholith of Southern California. J. Geophys. Res., 10: 3485-3496.

Tuttle, O.F. and Bowen, N.L., 1958. Origin of granite in the light of experimental studies in the system $NaAlSi_3O_8$ - $KAlSi_3O_8$ - SiO_2-H_2O. Geol. Soc. Am. Mem., 74: 153pp.

Yoder, H.S. and Tilley, C.E., 1962. Origin of basalt magmas: an experimental study of natural and synthetic rock systems. J. Pet., 3: 342-532.

Watson, E.B., 1976. Two-liquid partition coefficients: experimental data and geochemical implications. Contrib. Miner. Pet., 56: 119-134.

Weaver, B. L., Tarney, J., Windley, B. F., Sugavanam, E. B. and Venkata Rao, V., (in press). Madras granulites: geochemistry and P-T conditions of crystallisation. In B. F. Windley and S.M. Naqvi (eds), Archaean Geochemistry, Elsevier, Amsterdam.

Winkler, H.G.F., 1967. Petrogenesis of metamorphic rocks. 2nd Ed. Springer Verlag, Berlin. 237 pp.

Chapter 9

THE ROLE OF TONALITIC AND TRONDHJEMITIC ROCKS IN THE CRUSTAL DEVELOPMENT OF SWAZILAND AND THE EASTERN TRANSVAAL, SOUTH AFRICA

D. R. Hunter

INTRODUCTION

Rocks of tonalitic and trondhjemitic compositions constitute the most abundant salic component of the pre-3.1 b.y.-old crust in Swaziland and the adjacent areas of the Transvaal province of South Africa (Fig. 1). Similarities in major element chemistry and mineralogy led Viljoen and Viljoen (1969a) to propose that these rocks were co-genetic. Based on this assumption and the fact that some of the tonalitic rocks clearly intrude the lower formations of the Onverwacht Group, Viljoen and Viljoen (1969a) further concluded that all the tonalitic and trondhjemitic rocks post-date the 3.5 b.y.-old Swaziland Supergroup of which the Onverwacht Group is the lowest unit and which constitutes the Barberton greenstone belt (Fig. 1). Hunter (1968, 1973) considers the tonalitic and trondhjemitic rocks to constitute a number of separate igneous and/or metamorphic events in the geologic evolution of the area. On the basis of field relationships in Swaziland and metamorphic and structural studies, Hunter (1968, 1973) has argued that these rocks were formed during events pre-dating and post-dating the Swaziland Supergroup.

The purpose of this paper is to review the available geochemical and other data to demonstrate that the tonalitic and trondhjemitic rocks are not co-genetic and that the generation of rock types of these compositions in different environments was fundamental to the development of the early sialic crust. Comparisons with similar areas in Rhodesia suggest that there is a cyclic repetition of the development of banded gneisses, greenstones, and both sodic and potassic granites.

GENERAL GEOLOGIC SETTING OF SWAZILAND AND EASTERN TRANSVAAL

Various granitoid rocks ranging in age from >3.4 b.y. to 2.6 b.y.-old surround an approximately triangular area underlain by the volcanic and sedimentary rocks of the Swaziland Supergroup, which forms the Barberton greenstone belt (Fig. 1). The Swaziland Supergroup consists of a lower

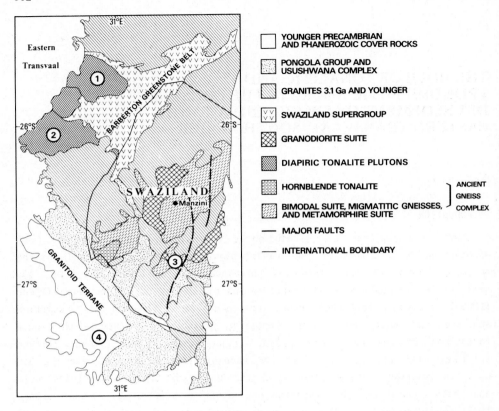

Figure 1.--Generalized geologic map of the granitic terrane in Swaziland and the eastern Transvaal. (1) Kaap Valley "granite" diapiric pluton; (2) this area consists of Stolzberg and Theespruit diapiric tonalite plutons together with bimodal gneisses, the limits of which have not been defined. The Nelshoogte diapiric tonalite pluton is between (1) and (2); (3) the Mkhondo valley area of the Ancient Gneiss Complex which is represented mainly by members of the metamorphite suite; (4) unmapped granitoid terrane that includes areas of bimodal gneisses and more homogeneous granitoids.

volcanic unit (the Onverwacht Group) characterized by cyclic repetition of ultramafic and mafic or mafic and felsic flows, and an upper sedimentary unit (Anhaeusser, 1973). The latter consists of an assemblage of turbidites (the Fig Tree Group) overlain by the dominantly quartzitic Moodies Group. Although the broad structure of the Swaziland Supergroup is that of a synform of pronounced northeasterly trend, also present are a series of tight or isoclinal synclines, generally overturned to the northwest, separated by major faults. A consequence of this structural arrangement is that rocks of the Onverwacht Group are preserved around the periphery of the greenstone belt. Although regional metamorphism of low greenschist grade is characteristic of most of the greenstone belt, the core of the synform barely reaches this grade while a narrow auerole of upper greenschist to amphibolite grade is developed around the periphery adjacent to intrusive granitoids.

Widespread intrusion of quartz monzonite occurred at 3.1 b.y. causing metamorphism and deformation of the Swaziland Supergroup. Overlying this quartz monzonite are substantial remnants of the younger volcanic and sedimentary Pongola Group in southern Swaziland. This group has been intruded by the mafic Usushwana Complex at 2.8 b.y. (Davies and others, 1970) and by quartz monzonite and granite at 2.6 b.y.

Rocks of tonalitic and trondhjemitic compositions in the eastern Transvaal and Swaziland have been subdivided as follows (Hunter, 1973):

(i)   the Ancient Gneiss Complex

(ii)   the Granodiorite Suite, and

(iii) the diapiric tonalite plutons.

The Ancient Gneiss Complex is best preserved in the central areas of Swaziland. The complex has suffered polyphase deformation (Hunter, 1970) and metamorphism with the result that the age relationships of the various lithologic units within the complex are uncertain. Geochronologic data are not yet sufficient to resolve all of these relationships. The following units, arranged in an assumed order of decreasing geologic age, have been recognized:

(i)   bimodal gneiss suite consisting of complexly interlayered gneisses of trondhjemitic and tonalitic compositions and amphibolites. No reliable radiometric age.

(ii)   hornblende tonalite gneisses that are found in a discrete area of southwestern Swaziland. The gneisses are homogeneous in composition and only rarely display layering. Age: $3395^{+}_{-}86$ m y.,R_o = 0.7006 $^{+}_{-}$ 0.0012 (Davies and Allsopp, 1976).

(iii) migmatitic gneisses that crop out in a belt approximately 12 km wide immediately east of the largest intrusion of the Granodiorite Suite in central Swaziland. No radiometric dating.

(iv)   metamorphite suite which consists of interlayered quartzofeldspathic gneisses of quartz monzonite composition, amphibolites, various cordierite- and/or garnet-bearing gneisses, quartz-hornblende-biotite gneisses and iron formation. No radiometric dating.

(v)   quartz monzonite that is medium-grained and forms small, homogeneous lenses, the longer axes of which are aligned parallel to the ENE foliation of the bimodal gneisses. Age: $3203^{+}_{-}0.0011$ m.y. (Davies and Allsopp, 1976).

Preliminary structural analysis shows that units 1 and 2 above have suffered at least three phases of deformation, the earliest of which apparently pre-dates the metamorphite suite. The plots of s-surfaces from the migmatitic gneisses show a considerable scatter when a distinction is drawn between plots of migmatitic gneisses with well-defined layering and those with a more nebulitic migmatitic appearance; the latter are found to contribute mainly to the departure from regularity of the s-surfaces and lineations (Hepworth, 1971). The fact that a large proportion of the plots of the migmatitic gneisses with the well-defined layering conforms to the tectonic axes recognized in the bimodal gneisses suggests that the generation of the migmatitic textures post-dates the imposition of the tectonic fabrics seen in the bimodal gneisses and the hornblende tonalite gneisses.

The quartz monzonite lenses that are approximately 2 km long and 1/2 km wide, are devoid of a prominent fabric and are elongated parallel to the axial traces of the third and last deformation in the bimodal gneisses. This suggests that the quartz monzonite lenses were generated at a late stage in the geologic evolution of the Ancient Gneiss Complex, and by inference, after the deformation of the metamorphite suite.

The Ancient Gneiss Complex is found in juxtaposition to the Barberton greenstone belt in Swaziland at only one locality but no conclusions regarding relative ages can be determined as the contact is faulted. Elsewhere in the area younger intrusive granitoids intervene between the rocks of the greenstone belt and the Ancient Gneiss Complex.

The Granodiorite Suite consists of coarse-grained rocks ranging in composition from hornblendite and gabbro through quartz diorite to tonalite and trondhjemite. Rocks of this suite form three discrete intrusions elongated in a northeasterly direction parallel to the main structural trend of the Barberton greenstone belt (Fig. 1). Nowhere are the Granodiorite Suite and the rocks of the greenstone belt in juxtaposition and it is not possible to establish their relative ages.

The Granodiorite Suite is intrusive into the bimodal and migmatitic gneisses of the Ancient Gneiss Complex. Good examples of this relationship are exposed north and southwest of Manzini.

The diapiric tonalite plutons are found around the southern and western periphery of the Barberton greenstone belt into which they are intrusive (Fig. 1). The plutons consist of coarse-grained, light-colored trondhjemite and tonalite, the foliation of which is parallel to the contacts of individual plutons. One pluton, known as the Kaap Valley "granite," is distinguished from the other plutons by the presence of hornblende in addition to biotite (Fig.

1). Individual plutons vary in diameter from 40 km (Kaap Valley "granite") to 1.6 km (Viljoen and Viljoen, 1969a). These plutons are intrusive into the lower formations of the Onverwacht Group and include Onverwacht xenoliths that are aligned parallel to the foliation in the plutons.

GEOLOGY OF THE TONALITIC-TRONDHJEMITIC SUITES

Rocks of trondhjemitic composition are found in four distinct settings, namely:

(i) bimodal gneissic association of trondhjemitic or tonalitic gneisses and amphibolites in the Ancient Gneiss Complex.

(ii) hornblende tonalite gneisses within the Ancient Gneiss Complex.

(iii) diapiric tonalite plutons intrusive into the lower formations of the Onverwacht Group and having the appearance of gneissic domes, and

(iv) the differentiated Granodiorite Suite that intrudes the bimodal and migmatitic gneisses of the Ancient Gneiss Complex in central Swaziland.

The lighter colored, siliceous layers in the bimodal gneisses are medium-grained, strongly foliated and may display compositional banding due to variations in the proportions of the dark minerals. Biotite is the most common mafic mineral, accounting for up to 10 percent by volume of the darkest layers. The aligned laths of partially chloritized biotite define the foliation. Hornblende is atypical in the siliceous layers but may be present in small amounts (<3 percent) in the darker layers. In the only gneiss of dioritic composition yet found in the bimodal gneisses, hornblende is a more abundant constituent ($\pm$8 percent). Typical siliceous layers in the bimodal gneisses are composed predominantly of complexly interlocking, inequigranular grains of plagioclase and quartz, with plagioclase (An_{25}) forming as much as 55 volume percent. Minor amounts of interstitial microcline are found in some layers. Accessory minerals include apatite and zircon.

The amphibolitic layers are foliated, medium-grained, and composed of plagioclase (An_{35-45}), hornblende and minor amounts of quartz (<5 percent by volume). Some amphibolites display fine-scale layering in which bands containing diopside alternate with those containing hornblende. Some amphibolites are composed entirely of hornblende.

Individual layers of both tonalitic and amphibolitic compositions vary in width from 1 to 2 cm to over a meter. Amphibolite layers up to 1/2 km wide are found sparingly, the thicker layers being traceable along strike for distances as great as 8 km. The thinner amphibolite bands frequently have biotite-rich margins formed as a result of the alteration of the hornblende.

Several generations of pegmatitic stringers, composed of quartz and feldspar, are common throughout the bimodal gneisses and are arranged parallel to, or crosscutting the foliation.

The hornblende tonalite gneisses are coarse-grained and lack the conspicuous banding of the bimodal gneisses. They are confined to a roughly triangular-shaped area in southwestern Swaziland (Fig. 1) and can be shown to be intrusive into the bimodal gneisses. The hornblende tonalite gneisses are composed of quartz, plagioclase (An_{30}), biotite and hornblende. The two latter minerals constitute up to 15 volume percent and are present either in approximately equal amounts or in variable proportions with biotite usually exceeding hornblende. Accessory minerals include apatite, zircon, sphene, and epidote.

The migmatic gneisses of tonalitic, trondhjemitic, and granodioritic compositions crop out in a 12-km wide belt in central Swaziland immediately to the east of the Granodiorite Suite intrusion near Manzini. The migmatitic gneisses are characterized by the presence of prominent quartz-feldspar veinlets developed parallel to the compositional banding that locally becomes nebulitic and ill-defined. The Granodiorite Suite post-dates the migmatitic gneisses, but their absolute age is unknown. The migmatitic gneisses are medium-grained rocks which display contorted compositional layers. Mineralogically the gneisses have a similar composition to the siliceous bimodal gneisses except that interstitial microcline is more abundant in some samples. Thin bands of amphibolitic composition are interlayered with the siliceous migmatitic gneisses, much of the hornblende being altered to biotite.

The diapiric tonalite plutons are coarse-grained rocks that form gneissic domes intrusive into the lower formations of the Onverwacht Group. Age relationships with the bimodal gneisses have not been established unequivocally. Diapiric tonalite plutons are not found in the Ancient Gneiss Complex in Swaziland. Banded gneisses, similar to the bimodal gneisses in Swaziland, cropping out in the Transvaal at the southern end of the Barberton greenstone belt have not been mapped in detail. Viljoen and Viljoen (1969a) consider that the banded gneisses in this locality are derived from a diapiric tonalite pluton by metamorphic differentiation accompanying a thermal event. It seems more likely from the style of deformation that the banded gneisses were subjected to polyphase deformation prior to the intrusion of the diapiric tonalite pluton. The light colored tonalites building the plutons are strongly foliated due to the presence of aligned biotite laths ($\pm$15 percent by volume). In addition to biotite, the tonalites consist of oligoclase, often as large and slightly sericitized grains, and quartz forming a finer grained aggregate.

Sphene and apatite are common accessory minerals and minor amounts of microcline, zoisite, and chlorite are present interstitially.

The dark colored Kaap Valley "granite" differs from the other tonalite plutons by virtue of the presence of green hornblende, frequently altered to chlorite, and a lower content of quartz. Accessory minerals include sphene, apatite, zircon, and magnetite. Like the other tonalite plutons, the Kaap Valley "granite" is lithologically homogeneous, coarse-grained, and well-foliated. This "granite" is not found in contact with the Ancient Gneiss Complex and is separated from the light colored tonalite plutons by a narrow septa of strongly deformed rocks of the Onverwacht Group, so that its age relative to these plutons cannot be established. A radiometric date of $3310^{\pm}40$ m.y. has been reported for the Kaap Valley "granite" whereas the light colored tonalite plutons have yielded ages of $3250^{\pm}40$ m.y. and $3220^{\pm}40$ m.y. (U/Pb method; Oosthuyzen, 1970). Proof is lacking that these plutons post-date the upper sedimentary formations of the Swaziland Supergroup.

The Granodiorite Suite consists of coarse-grained rocks ranging in composition from hornblendite and gabbro through quartz diorite and granodiorite to trondhjemite. Rocks of this suite build three discrete intrusions elongated in a northeasterly direction that intrude the bimodal and migmatitic gneisses of the Ancient Gneiss Complex in central Swaziland. An imperfect foliation is developed in the more mafic varieties, and is aligned parallel to the long axes of these intrusions. Ultramafic rocks constitute 0.6 percent, gabbro and quartz diorite 29.0 percent, and granodiorite and trondhjemite 70.4 percent of the surface area underlain by the Granodiorite Suite. The more leucocratic members of the suite are composed of an inequigranular intergrowth of quartz, plagioclase (An_{24}) and minor amounts of biotite or, more rarely, hornblende. Compositionally these rocks are similar to the diapiric tonalite plutons and to the siliceous gneisses of the bimodal suite. They differ from the former in having only a poor or no foliation and from the latter in their coarser grain size. The quartz dioritic and gabbroic members consist of plagioclase, relict pyroxene and minor amounts of quartz.

The Granodiorite Suite and the Swaziland Supergroup are not in juxtaposition, nor has radiometric dating of the suite been undertaken. Intrusive relationships of this suite with the bimodal gneisses indicate that it post-dates part, at least, of the Ancient Gneiss Complex.

GEOCHEMISTRY OF THE TONALITE-TRONDHJEMITE SUITES

Major-element chemistry is available for 29 samples of the Ancient Gneiss Complex and 12 samples of the Granodiorite Suite. Thirty of these samples (25 from the Ancient Gneiss Complex and 5 from the Granodiorite Suite) have been analyzed for Rb, Sr, and rare earth elements (REE'S) (Hunter and others, in press). Additional major- and trace-element data for the diapiric tonalite plutons and of the hornblende tonalite gneisses have been reported by Viljoen and Viljoen (1969b) and Condie and Hunter (1976).

Normative Qz-Ab-Or ratios

On a normative Qz-Ab-Or diagram the plots of the siliceous bimodal gneisses containing >65% SiO_2 occupy an elongate field approximately parallel to the Qz-Ab-Or tie-line close to a mean normative Or-content of 10 percent (for details, see Hunter and others, in press). The associated amphibolites plot as quartz-normative metabasalt near the Ab apex or as olivine-normative metabasalt along the Ab-Or tie-line (Hunter and others, in press). The plots of the hornblende tonalite gneiss, migmatitic gneisses and the diapiric tonalitic plutons lie close to or overlap the field of the siliceous bimodal gneisses in the general tonalite-trondhjemite region of the Qz-Ab-Or diagram (Hunter and others, in press).

The plots of the Granodiorite Suite extend from the Ab-Or tie-line towards the Qz-apex in a field similar to that of the differentiation suite of the Uusikaupunki-Kalanti area of Finland (Arth and others, in press), except that a complete range of intermediate compositions has not yet been recognized in Swaziland.

K-Ca-Na ternary diagram and K versus Rb diagram

The plots of the bimodal gneisses, hornblende tonalite gneisses, the diapiric plutons and the Granodiorite Suite on the K-Ca-Na ternary diagram (Fig. 2) define a trend towards the Na-apex, which distinguishes them from the metamorphite suite and quartz monzonite of the Ancient Gneiss Complex and the calc-alkaline granitoids emplaced at 3.1 and 2.6 b.y. in Swaziland and the eastern Transvaal.

A further distinction between these two trends is illustrated in the K versus Rb diagram (Fig. 3). Trends of the bimodal suite and tonalitic rocks are at a rather sharp angle to that of the metamorphite suite, and the migmatitic gneisses have a wide scatter which may reflect gain or loss of K and/or Rb during migmatization. The more siliceous samples (>54% SiO_2) of the Granodiorite Suite, despite their characteristic sodic trend on the K-Ca-Na diagram, do not conform with the other rock units showing this trend.

Comparison of the Swaziland and eastern Transvaal granitoids with those from Rhodesia show similar trends on the K-Ca-Na diagram. Siliceous gneisses in Rhodesia, lithologically similar to the Swaziland bimodal gneisses, dated at

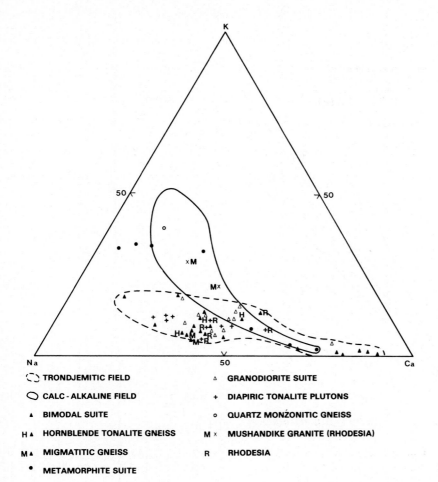

Figure 2.--K-Na-C ternary plots of the Ancient Gneiss Complex (bimodal suite, hornblende tonalite gneisses, migmatitic gneisses, and metamorphite suite), Granodiorite Suite and Rhodesian gneisses and granites. The unbroken line encloses the field of the granitic rocks of 3.1 Ga and younger in Swaziland.

3.5 b.y. and 2.8 b.y. together with Rhodesian 2.7 b.y.-old, post-greenstone tonalite plutons overlap the Swaziland and eastern Transvaal Na-trend but other 3.5 and 2.6 b.y. granitoides from Rhodesia lie within the potassic trend (Fig. 2). This suggests the possibility that there may be cyclic repetition of tonalitic/trondhjemitic and potassic magmatism during the first billion years of recorded geologic history.

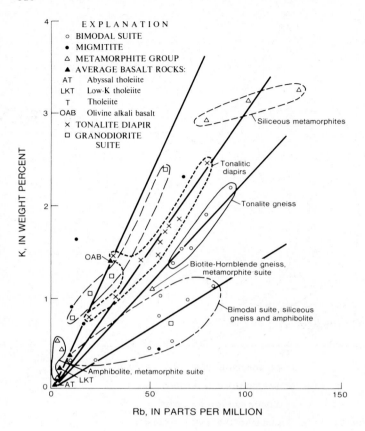

Figure 3.--K versus Rb plot of various units of the Ancient Gneiss Complex, Granodiorite Suite and a tonalite diapir, as contrasted with modern basalts (after Hunter et al., in press).

Trace-element data

Siliceous gneisses of the bimodal suite typically show 50-100 ppm of Rb and 50-500 ppm of Sr, and intermediate to high Rb/Sr ratios of 0.19 to 1.31. The interlayered amphibolites have a rather wide scatter of Rb content (8 to 49 ppm) that is perhaps due to gain during diagenesis or metamorphism from the enclosing gneisses. The hornblende tonalite gneisses have Rb- and Sr-contents within the range of the siliceous bimodal gneisses but have higher and more consistent K/Rb ratios. The migmatitic gneisses contain less Rb (10-70 ppm) and more Sr (140-620 ppm), and have lower Rb/Sr ratios (0.02-0.11) than the siliceous bimodal gneisses (Hunter and others, in press).

The diapiric tonalite plutons show 30-80 ppm of Rb and 300-750 ppm of Sr, and low Rb/Sr ratios. K/Rb ratios are generally consistent between 200 and 300 (Condie and Hunter, 1976; Viljoen and Viljoen, 1969b).

Rb contents of the Granodiorite Suite are low (10-61) ppm and show an erratic decrease with increasing SiO_2. Sr contents are high (414-1249 ppm) and also show an erratic decrease with increasing SiO_2. K/Rb ratios show a wide range and Rb/Sr ratios are less than 0.09 with a narrow range (Hunter and others, in press).

Two distinct types of REE patterns that can be correlated with major element abundances are recognized in the siliceous gneisses of the bimodal suite (Hunter and others, in press). The first type contains less than about 75 percent SiO_2, more than 14 percent Al_2O_3, Rb/Sr ratios of 0.1 to 0.3, La-Ce less than 100 times chondrites, heavy REE's less than 10 times chondrites and small positive or negative Eu anomalies. The second type is highly siliceous (>75 percent SiO_2), and has less than 14 percent Al_2O_3, Rb/Sr ratios of 0.5-1.3, La-Ce 100-300 times chondrites, heavy REE's 20-50 times chondrites, and pronounced negative Eu anomalies (Hunter and others, in press).

These high SiO_2-type gneisses in the bimodal suite are rare in Archean gneiss complexes, having been reported, to our knowledge, only in the Webb Canyon Gneiss of Wyoming where metarhyodacites are interlayered with metatholeiite (Reed and Zartman, 1973; Barker and Millard, this volume). The REE patterns of the highly siliceous bimodal gneisses are similar to those of the Proterozoic Twilight Gneiss of Colorado (Barker and others, 1976a), but with much enhanced abundances of total REE's.

The interlayered amphibolites in the bimodal gneisses have flat REE patterns (less than 10 times chondrite), some showing slight depletion in La and Ce, and small positive Eu anomalies (Hunter and others, in press).

The hornblende tonalite gneisses have REE patterns similar to the siliceous bimodal gneisses with normal SiO_2 contents (type 1 above) except for gentler slopes of the heavy REE's (Ce_N/Yb_N = 6.2; type 1 gneisses 8.7).

The migmatitic gneisses have steep REE patterns (Ce_N/Yb_N = 59.0) (Hunter and others, in press). In spite of their migmatitic character the tonalitic to trondhjemitic migmatites have REE patterns like those of non-migmatitic rocks of these compositions (Hunter and others, in press). The migmatites have high K/Rb ratios between 300 and 1000, but there is no correspondence of LILE with REE abundances.

The diapiric tonalite plutons show two distinct REE patterns. The hornblende-bearing Kaap Valley "granite" with SiO_2 contents between 62.5 and 68.4% SiO_2 has a moderately steep slope of the light REE's and a flat slope for the heavy REE's, similar to the patterns of the hornblende tonalite gneisses from the Ancient Gneiss Complex in Swaziland (Condie and Hunter, 1976; Hunter and others, in press). The light colored tonalites and trondhjemites of the other diapiric tonalite plutons have Ce abundances 20 to 45 times chondrite and Yb-contents of about 1.4 times chondrite with Eu showing slight negative to slight positive anomalies (Eu/Eu* values range from 0.94 to 1.2) (Condie and Hunter, 1976). These patterns are similar to those of the Saganaga tonalite of Minnesota (Arth and Hanson, 1975) except that total REE abundances are greater in the eastern Transvaal rocks. The slope of the REE patterns of the diapiric tonalite plutons is slightly steeper than those of the type 1 gneisses of the bimodal suite described above.

The Granodiorite Suite samples show an increase in total REE content from gabbro with 51.2% SiO_2, thereafter decreasing with increasing SiO_2 content. The REE pattern of the gabbro is moderately steep and typical of alkali basalts. Patterns for rocks of SiO_2 contents greater than 54.7 percent are steep and progressively depleted in all REE's except Eu (Hunter and others, in press).

ORIGIN OF THE TONALITE-TRONDHJEMITE SUITES

Reconnaissance geological data show that the various tonalitic and trondhjemitic rocks in the eastern Transvaal and Swaziland have distinctive characteristics that vary according to the environments in which they are found. Tonalitic and trondhjemitic rocks are found in the eastern Transvaal and Swaziland as:

(i) components of the Ancient Gneiss Complex forming (a) part of a bimodal gneiss suite; (b) essentially homogeneous hornblende tonalite gneisses; and (c) migmatitic gneisses;

(ii) discrete homogeneous intrusions (the diapiric tonalite plutons); and

(iii) end-members of a differentiation suite (the Granodiorite Suite).

Ancient Gneiss Complex

Characteristic of Archean shields are gray gneiss complexes in which trondhjemitic and tonalitic gneisses are intimately interlayered with amphibolites. The distinctive feature of these gneiss complexes is their marked bimodality of composition. The light colored layers contain 70 percent SiO_2 and the amphibolites less than 55 percent SiO_2, rocks of intermediate SiO_2 content being absent or rare. The bimodal gneisses in Swaziland are typical of these gray gneiss complexes. Such intimate interlayering of rock types of contrasting chemistry can be attributed to a number of processes:

(i)   lit-par-lit intrusion either of siliceous magma into basic rocks or of basic magma into siliceous rocks;

(ii)   metamorphic differentiation;

(iii) in situ metasomatism by either wet or dry diffusion of an original sedimentary and/or sedimentary-volcanic layered sequence;

(iv) intense deformation of trondhjemitic and tonalitic intrusives or extrusives that contain mafic dykes;

(v)   intense deformation of a bimodal dacitic-basaltic volcanic suite;

(vi) intense deformation of basaltic volcanics intruded by tonalitic and trondhjemitic plutonic rocks.

In the case of the Swaziland bimodal gneisses, field and/or geochemical evidence appears to exclude the probability that processes (i), (ii), or (iii) could provide satisfactory modes of origin.   Initial $^{87}Sr/^{86}Sr$ ratios of geochemically and lithologically similar gneisses in other parts of the world appear to discount an origin by reworking of older sialic crust (Moorbath, 1976).   Although data of this kind are lacking for the Swaziland rocks, their REE patterns and low $\delta^{18}O$ values (Barker and others, 1976b) suggest that they were derived from mantle sources. However, the data are inadaequate to permit discrimination between processes (iv), (v), and (vi).

As has been emphasized elsewhere (Barker and Arth, 1976) the gray gneiss-amphibolite terranes contain few rocks of original andesitic composition. These authors pointed out that the apparent absence of andesites is a result of either their non-existence in Archean times or, if such liquids were generated, that they were not emplaced at levels presently exposed. Barker and Arth (1976) conclude that had andesitic liquids been generated they should be represented in gray gneiss complexes at least as frequently as tonalites and trondhjemites. It would appear, therefore, that andesitic liquids did not form during much of Archean time and that the close spatial association of tonalite/trondhjemite and metabasalt is not accidental but reflects specific conditions under which the two liquids were generated.

Two major types of tonalitic/trondhjemitic gneiss are represented in the bimodal suite, each closely interlayered with amphibolite.   The type that is most common in this and other gray gneiss complexes contains less than about 75 percent SiO_2, has low Rb/Sr ratios and is strongly depleted in the heavy REE's. Models for the generation of such magmas include fractionation of wet basaltic magma (Arth and others, in press), partial melting of quartz eclogite (Arth and Hanson, 1972, 1975), and partial melting of amphibolite (Barker and Arth, 1976).   The last-named is the preferred model, because early Archean terranes

partial melting of eclogite of average Archean tholeiite composition (Arth and Hanson, 1972, 1975; Condie and Hunter, 1976); and (iii) partial melting of amphibolite (Hunter and others, in press).   The diapiric tonalite plutons are

apparently contain no eclogite whereas amphibolites are common. The amphibolites of the bimodal suite in Swaziland contain small percentages of quartz but garnet is rare. On partial melting of such amphibolite, quartz, plagioclase, and some hornblende would enter the melt and the excess anorthite

confined to the periphery of the Barberton greenstone belt where basalts are common. If these basalts were metamorphosed to amphibolite and depressed during deformation to depths where partial melting could occur, it would account for the close spatial association of the diapiric tonalite plutons with the Barberton greenstone belt. It is not possible to discriminate between this model and that involving partial melting of eclogite, produced as a result of the sinking of the cooling mantle plume that may initially have been the source of the mafic volcanics of the Onverwacht Group (Hunter, 1974). The lower REE abundances in the leucocratic diapiric tonalite plutons could be accounted for by either (i) accumulation of quartz and feldspar diluting the liquid in all REE's except Eu, or (ii) fractionation of the liquid by removal of hornblende which can be a liquidus phase at low (<70 percent) SiO_2 contents. The lack of pronounced Eu anomalies implies that feldspar fractionation did not play a major role in the genesis of these rocks.

Granodiorite Suite

The Granodiorite Suite is plutonic, post-dating the Ancient Gneiss Complex, and displays a range of compositions from gabbro to high-Al_2O_3 trondhjemite. The trend of the REE patterns (Hunter and others, in press) is like that shown by the gabbro-trondhjemite suite of the Uusikaupunki-Kalanti area, Finland (Arth and others, in press), except that abundances of light REE's are several times higher in the Granodiorite Suite. The Uusikaupunki suite contains a more complete range of intermediate compositions than the Granodiorite Suite. Goldschmidt (1922) and Hietanen (1943) suggested that the trondhjemitic and tonalitic magmas were generated by differentiation of wet basaltic liquid, a model which is supported by new isotopic and chemical studies (Arth and others, in press). Hunter (1973) proposed that the Granodiorite Suite was a differentiation suite but invoked incorporation of country rock to account for the large volume of trondhjemitic and tonalitic rocks. The new chemical studies (Hunter and others, in press) support differentiation but not incorporation of country rock. It is concluded that the Granodiorite Suite was generated by differentiation of relatively wet, mildly alkaline basaltic liquid in which hornblende and some biotite were major precipitating phases. The structural features of the Granodiorite Suite suggest that it was emplaced synkinematically with the ENE-oriented folding of the Swaziland Supergroup.

SUMMARY AND DISCUSSION

Tonalitic and trondhjemitic rocks constitute the most salic component of the pre-3.1 b.y. crust in Swaziland and the adjacent areas of the eastern Transvaal. Some of the liquids from which these rocks crystallized could have been derived either by hornblende-controlled fractionation of more mafic magma or by partial melting of amphibolite or eclogite with hornblende and/or garnet as residual phases.

The geochemical data (Hunter and others, in press) apparently preclude direct analogy between the Archean tonalite/trondhjemite suites and Cenozoic island areas or active continental margins. The siliceous bimodal gneisses have steep REE patterns in contrast to the flat patterns for dacitic rocks from modern island arcs. The interlayered amphibolites have REE patterns similar to those of modern oceanic tholeiites but have lower contents of Ti and lower K/Rb ratios than modern oceanic tholeiites. The latter feature may be a reflection of gain of Rb during diagenesis or metamorphism from the enclosing siliceous gneisses.

Isotopic data for the bimodal gneisses in Swaziland are lacking but similar gneiss terranes elsewhere are distinguished by their low initial $^{87}Sr/^{86}Sr$ ratios (Moorbath, 1976). The low mean $\delta^{18}O$ values of 5.9 to 7.2 $^{o}/oo$ obtained from the siliceous bimodal gneisses are interpreted to mean that these rocks were derived from the mantle by igneous and metamorphic processes without involvement of a weathering stage (Barker and others, 1976b; Hunter and others, in press). It is suggested, therefore, that no older continental crust existed in the eastern Transvaal and Swaziland prior to the formation of the bimodal suite. The preferred model, then, for the generation of this suite envisages an early stage involving the development of a hydrous lithosphere and a crust in a highly metastable condition. Partial melting of mantle material, possibly initiated by local concentrations of high heat flow, generated basaltic liquids whose crystallization products were ultimately preserved in relatively thick accumulations as the stability of the lithosphere and crust increased. The lower parts of these basaltic piles were metamorphosed to amphibolite at relatively shallow depths as a consequence of the steep Archean geothermal gradient and the abundance of H_2O. Further depression resulted in partial melting of the amphibolites at the base of the pile with the generation of tonalitic and trondhjemitic liquids which rose, as a result of their lower density, into the overlying basalts. Some of these liquids could be extrusive whereas others could be intrusive into the basaltic pile. Following deformation of this early crust, resurgence of heat flow would cause renewed melting of the now less hydrous mantle to give the mafic and ultramafic volcanics typical of greenstone belts. As heat flow waned, again, partial melting of either the metabasalts of the now deformed greenstone belt or eclogite produced as a result of the sinking of a cooling mantle plume would produce more tonalitic and trondhjemitic liquids that rose and intruded the greenstone belt. At approximately the same time the older bimodal gneiss suite was further deformed, metamorphosed, and partially melted to yield small amounts of quartz monzonite liquid which coalesced to form small lensoid masses. The alignment of these lenses parallel to the ENE foliation of the bimodal gneisses into which they intrude supports this time sequence.

Although the stratigraphic position of the metamorphite suite of the Ancient Gneiss Complex is uncertain, it seems likely that the quartz monzonite gneisses in this suite could also have formed from liquids generated by partial melting of the bimodal gneisses. However, the trace element geochemistry of the quartz monzonite gneisses of the metamorphite suite requires their parental rocks to have contained little or no residual hornblende or garnet, and plagioclase must have been in residuum. The low-Al_2O_3 gneisses interlayered with amphibolite in the bimodal suite would, when metamorphosed to granulite grade, consist largely of feldspar, pyroxene and quartz, the low Al_2O_3 content precluding the formation of garnet. Partial melting of a granulite of this composition could produce liquids having trace element characteristics similar to those of the quartz monzonite gneisses of the metamorphite suite. An anhydrous environment is implied by the requirement that hornblende should be absent. The presence of rocks with Na/K ratios approaching unity in old gneiss terranes does not necessarily imply or require, therefore, the prior existence of a sedimentary cycle of deposition of graywackes, shales, or other suitable parental material. Initial continental crust could thus have been formed without addition of sedimentary material on a large scale. Continental growth in the early stages could have been achieved by igneous and metamorphic processes alone.

There is increasing evidence from southern Africa that crustal development up to 2.6 b.y. involved major and repetitive tectonothermal events (Wilson and others, 1978), during which the generation of basaltic, tonalitic/trondhjemitic and quartz monzonitic liquids was a prime factor in the growth of continents. In the eastern Transvaal and Swaziland a cycle consists of (i) the development of a bimodal gneiss complex, (ii) greenstone belt volcanism, (iii) diapiric tonalite plutonism, and (iv) quartz monzonitic plutonism. The evidence from Rhodesia supports this concept. In Rhodesia an older bimodal gneiss sequence is associated with relics of mafic volcanics and is intruded by the Mushandike "granite" at 3.5 b.y. A further development of bimodal gneisses at 2.9 b.y. with low initial $^{87}Sr/^{86}Sr$ ratios is probably related in time to volcanism of greenstone type and intrusions of diapiric tonalite plutons. A clear unconformity separates these greenstones and granitoids from the third cycle of greenstone volcanism, diapiric tonalite plutonism and quartz monzonite intrusion that terminated at 2.6 b.y. (Wilson and others, 1978). Hawkesworth and others (1975) have emphasized with respect to the third event that the development of bimodal gneisses, greenstone belts, and post-greenstone tonalite plutons occurred within a period of 200 m.y. or less. If future geochronologic studies confirm the relatively brief time-span required for the completion of this and other tectonothermal cycles, it would suggest that new crust was being developed at rates that could result in successive cycles overlapping each other, being telescoped or being incomplete. The separate identities of individual cycles may then be indistinguishable.

A complete tectonic model to account for the evolution of the Archean crust in Swaziland and the eastern Transvaal is constrained by gaps in geochronologic and other geologic information, but analogies with other early Archean terranes in southern Africa suggest that significant development of continental crust occurred during the period from 3.7 to 2.6 b.y. in a series of repetitive cycles which commenced with bimodal volcanism and/or basaltic volcanism and tonalitic plutonism in a hydrous environment, and was followed by deformation to give gray gneiss complexes, greenstone belt volcanism, tonalitic and trondhjemitic plutonism confined to the greenstone belts and terminated with quartz monzonite intrusions. It is still uncertain how the Granodiorite Suite can be accommodated in this sequence of events because the only occurrence yet described is that found in Swaziland and which has not been dated radiometrically.

It is not yet possible to identify how many cycles are represented in Swaziland but taking the broader view the following three major cycles appear to be identifiable in Rhodesia, Swaziland, and the eastern Transvaal:

Cycle I   Bimodal gneisses and relicts of mafic volcanics in Rhodesia intruded and terminated by the Mushandike granite at 3.5 b.y.

Cycle II   Bimodal gneisses of Ancient Gneiss Complex in Swaziland, Barberton greenstone belt, tonalitic plutonism terminated at 3.2 b.y.

Cycle III Bimodal gneisses, greenstone belts (of two ages?), tonalitic plutonism terminated at 2.7 b.y. This cycle may have occupied 200 m.y. or less.

This outline of cycles is tentative at this stage as geochronologic data are insufficient to date the full sequence of events listed in the first two cycles. What is more certain is that tonalitic and trondhjemitic rocks derived from mantle sources played a major role in early Archean crustal development in southern Africa.

320

REFERENCES

Anhaeusser, C. R., 1973. The evolution of the early Precambrian crust of southern Africa. Phil. Trans. R. Soc. Lond., A273: 359-388.

Arth, J. G. and Hanson, G. N., 1972. Quartz diorites derived by partial melting of eclogite or amphibolite at mantle depths. Contrib. Miner. Pet., 37: 161-174.

Arth, J. G. and Hanson, G. N., 1975. Geochemistry and origin of the early Precambrian crust of northeastern Minnesota. Geochim. Cosmochim. Acta, 39: 325-362.

Arth, J. G., Barker, F., Peterman, Z. E. and Friedman, I. (in press). Geochemistry of the gabbro-diorite-tonalite-trondhjemite suite of southwest Finland and its implications for the origin of tonalitic and trondhjemitic magmas.

Barker, F. and Arth, J. G., 1976. Generation of trondhjemitic-tonalitic liquids and Archean bimodal trondhjemite-basalt suites. Geology, 4: 596-600.

Barker, F., Arth, J. G., Peterman, Z. E. and Friedman, I., 1976a. The 1.7-1.8-b.y.-old trondhjemites of southwestern Colorado and northern New Mexico: geochemistry and depths of genesis. Geol. Soc. Am. Bull., 87: 189-198.

Barker, F., Friedman, I., Hunter, D. R. and Gleason,J. D., 1976b. Oxygen isotopes of some trondhjemites, siliceous gneisses and associated mafic rocks. Precambrian Res., 3: 547-557.

Condie, K. C. and Hunter, D. R., 1976. Trace element geochemistry of Archean granitic rocks from the Barberton region, South Africa. Earth Planet Sci. Lett., 29: 389-400.

Davies, R. D. and Allsopp, H. L., 1976. Strontium isotopic evidence relating to the evolution of the lower Precambrian crust in Swaziland. Geology, 4: 553-556.

Davies, R. D., Allsopp, H. L., Erlank, A. J. and Manton, W. I., 1970. Sr-isotope studies on various layered mafic intrusions in southern Africa. Geol. Soc. S. Afr., Spec. Publ., 1: 576-593.

Goldschmidt, V. M., 1922. Stammestypen der eruptivgesteine. Norske Vid. Skr. Krist. I Mat.-Nat. Kl., 10: 1-12.

Hawkesworth,C. J., Moorbath, S., O'Nions, R. K. and Wilson, J. F., 1975. Age relationships between greenstone belts and "granites" in the Rhodesian Archaean craton. Earth Planet. Sci. Lett., 25: 251-262.

Helz, R. T, 1973. Phase relations of basalts in their melting range at P_{H_2O} = 5 kb as a function of oxygen fugacity. Pt. I Mafic phases. J. Pet., 14: 249-302.

Helz, R. T., 1976. Phase relations of basalts in their melting range at P_{H_2O} = 5 kb. Pt. II Melt compositions. J. Pet., 17: 139-193.

Hepworth, J. V., 1971. Report on Swaziland Project, 1970. Inst. Geol. Sci. Lond. Photogeological Unit Report, 48 (unpub.)

Hietanen, Anna, 1943. Uber das Grundgebirge des Kalantigebietes im sudwestlichen Finnland. Finlande Comm. Geol. Bull., 130: 105 pp.

Holloway, J. R. and Burnham, C. W., 1972. Melting relations of basalt with equilibrium water pressure less than total pressure. J. Pet., 13: 1-29.

Hunter, D. R., 1968. The Precambrian terrane in Swaziland with particular reference to the granitic rocks. Unpublished Ph. D. thesis, Univ. of the Witwatersrand, Johannesburg.

Hunter, D. R., 1970. The Ancient Gneiss Complex in Swaziland. Trans. Geol. Soc. S. Afr., 73: 107-150.

Hunter, D. R., 1973. Granitic rocks of the Precambrian in Swaziland, in Lister, L. A. (ed.), Symposium on granites, gneisses and related rocks. Geol. Soc. S. Afr., Spec. Publ., 3: 131-145.

Hunter, D. R., 1974. Crustal development in the Kaapvaal craton. Pt. I, The Archean. Precambrian Res., 1: 259-294.

Hunter, D. R., Barker, F. and Millard, H. T., Jr. (in press). The geochemical nature of the Archean Ancient Gneiss Complex and Granodiorite Suite, Swaziland: a preliminary study. Precambrian Res.

Luth, W. C., Jahns, R. H. and Tuttle, O. F., 1964. The granite system at pressures of 4 to 10 kilobars. J. Geophys. Res., 69: 759-773.

Moorbath, S., 1976. Age and isotope constraints for the evolution of Archean crust, in Windley, B. F. (ed.). The early history of the Earth. (John Wiley and Sons, Ltd., London): 351-360.

Oosthuyzen, E. J., 1970. The geochronology of a suite of rocks from the granitic terrane surrounding the Barberton Mountain Land. Unpublished Ph. D. thesis, Univ. of Witwaterstrand, Johannesburg.

Reed, J. C., Jr. and Zartman, R. E., 1973. Geochronology of Precambrian rocks of the Teton Range, Wyoming. Geol. Soc. Am. Bull., 84: 561-582.

Tuttle, O. F. and Bowen, N. L., 1958. Origin of granite in the light of experimental studies in the system. $NaAlSi_3O_8-KAlSi_3O_8-SiO_2-H_2O$. Geol. Soc. Am. Mem., 74: 153 pp.

Viljoen, M. J. and Viljoen, R. P., 1969a. A proposed new classification of the granitic rocks of the Barberton region. Geol. Soc. S. Afr. Spec. Pub., 2: 152-180.

Viljoen, M. J. and Viljoen, R. P., 1969b. The geochemical evolution of the granitic rocks of the Barberton region. Geol. Soc. S. Afr. Spec. Pub., 2: 189-218.

Wilson, J. F., Bickle, M. J., Hawkesworth, C. J., Martin, A., Nisbet, E. G. and Orpen, J. L., 1978. Granite-greenstone terrains of the Rhodesian Archaean craton. Nature, 271: 23-27.

Chapter 10

PETROCHEMISTRY AND TECTONIC SETTING OF PLUTONIC ROCKS OF THE SUPERIOR PROVINCE IN MANITOBA

I. F. Ermanovics, W. D. McRitchie and W. N. Houston

ABSTRACT

The variation of major elements in approximately 850 samples of plutonic and volcanic rocks from the Superior Province in Manitoba is related to their tectonic setting in the English River, Uchi, Berens, and Sachigo provinces. The study distinguishes between an older (pre-Kenoran and early Kenoran) suite of tonalitic rocks spatially related to greenstone belt development, and a younger (Kenoran), unmetamorphosed suite of potassic rocks that characterizes large regions between volcanic belts. AFM, KNaCa, and QAbOr diagrams are utilized to demonstrate trondhjemitic (sodic) or calc-alkaline (potassic) differentiation trends for rock suites from the different subprovinces.

Strong trondhjemitic (Na) differentiation trends are developed in most igneous rocks of the Uchi subprovince, in metaplutonic rocks of the Berens subprovince, and in plutonic and metaplutonic rocks of the Sachigo subprovince. Calc-alkaline trends are defined by volcanic and massive plutonic rocks of the Berens and Sachigo subprovinces. Metamorphic alteration is ruled out as a cause of Na-enrichment except in rocks of the English River subprovince. Supracrustal rocks of the northern portion of this subprovince are related to eugeosynclinal tectonics and the bulk of these rocks may have been the source rock from which both potassic and sodic magmas were derived during metamorphism.

Within the tectonic setting of the western Superior Province, plutonic rocks, characterized by trondhjemitic trends, are seen as high temperature magma varieties related to a thicker 'granitic' crust overlying 'basaltic' crust. In general, the plutonic rocks of the western Superior Province display secular evolution from Na-rich tonalites and granodiorites to tonalites and granite.

INTRODUCTION

In the present work we attempt to distinguish between an early gneissic suite of tonalitic rocks spatially related to greenstone belts, and a later, gregarious, unmetamorphosed suite of calc-alkaline potassic rocks that characterizes large areas of intervolcanic-belt terrain in the Superior Province. However, English River gneisses present a unique setting in which magma generation may be related to a regional pattern of metamorphic zonation within a eugeosynclinal framework. The data was derived from an area in Manitoba between latitudes 50° and $54^{\circ}N$ which includes (from south to north) the following subprovinces: English River gneiss belt, Uchi volcanic belt, Berens batholithic belt, and Sachigo volcanic belt. Although all of our data are from Manitoba, recent work (e.g., Breaks and Bond, 1977a and b; Goodwin, 1977; Beakhouse, 1977; Ayres, 1974) shows that most of our observations probably also apply in Ontario immediately east of Manitoba.

Data were assembled from two sources which are appropriately acknowledged throughout the text. One source is Publication 71-1 of the Manitoba Mines Branch (McRitchie and Weber, editors, 1971) which includes considerable detail on the geology of the Uchi volcanic and English River gneiss belts in Manitoba. The second source of data is the area bounded by latitudes 51° to $54^{\circ}N$ in Manitoba which was mapped for publication at 1:250,000 scale by Ermanovics and summarized in Ermanovics and Davison (1976). Samples for analysis were collected routinely for purposes of solving local problems of petrology and for regional syntheses. For example, chemical data for volcanogenic tonalites in Uchi volcanic rocks were originally utilized to demonstrate alteration zones in gold deposits (e.g., Stephenson, 1971), whereas samples collected between latitudes 51° and $52^{\circ}N$, which includes the Uchi and Berens subprovinces, were the subject of an analysis of variance study based on a randomized sampling scheme covering 12,950 km^2.

Analyses were made in the laboratories of the Geological Survey of Canada, Department of Earth Sciences of the University of Manitoba, and the Manitoba Department of Mines and Natural Resources during the period of 1970-1974. Various 'best method' rapid analytical techniques were used for major and trace elements, and included X-ray fluorescence, atomic absorption and optical emission spectrometry. The specific methods employed may be found in the cited references.

TERMINOLOGY

Rocks are named according to the recommendations of the IUGS Subcommission on the Systematics of Igneous Rocks (Streckeison, 1976). Trondhjemite is a leucocratic tonalite with colour index 10 percent or less. Chemically the 10 percent mafic mode expresses itself as $FeO + 0.9\ Fe_2O_3 + MgO \simeq 3\%$ (Barker, this volume). Similarly, the boundary between granodiorite and tonalite, placed modally at 90 percent plagioclase of total feldspar, is approximately represented by 2 percent K_2O. Diorite is distinguished from gabbro in that the 'An' proportion of plagioclase in diorite is less than 50 percent. This criterion is difficult to apply in orthogneisses and consequently normative criteria are used. Modal rock names throughout the present work are field terms.

Broadly speaking, normative proportions of 'An' and 'colour index' of Irvine and Baragar (1971) are used as follows: basalt = gabbro, andesite = quartz diorite and diorite, dacite = tonalite and granodiorite, and rhyolite = granite. Nickolds' (1954) averages of some rocks are superimposed on the normative scheme in Figure 1. In the present study, tonalites tend to be distributed from the mid-normative dacite to andesite fields.

No attempt is made to align the normative data with the QAP modal classification except for one example to show that a reasonable fit can be obtained (Fig. 1).

The term batholith is used as a non-generic term denoting a large area of moderately homogeneous granitic rock. Such areas are tectonically distinct from belts of supracrustal rocks and include massive and metamorphosed phases which in the present study area have been intruded over a time span of 400 million years.

REGIONAL GEOLOGY

Archean rocks of the western Superior Province have been subdivided into east-west trending belts on the basis of variable tectonic styles (Douglas, 1973; Wilson, 1971). The divisions used in this paper follow those of Douglas (1973), and the terms 'subprovince' and 'belt' are used interchangeably (Fig. 2). A uniformitarian and causal approach has been used to link the development of some subprovinces to each other (e.g., Goodwin, 1977; Ermanovics and Davison, 1976). In Manitoba, for example, McRitchie (1971a) has postulated that the Uchi subprovince occupies a zone of dislocation along the northern edge of the English River eugeosyncline. Volcanic and subsequent plutonic activity of the Uchi subprovince are thought to be a response to tectonic activity in the English River subprovince. Boundaries between subprovinces are controversial, but in a general way serve to delineate domains of varying lithology, metamorphism, and structural style in Manitoba (McRitchie and Weber, 1971; Ermanovics and Davison, 1976).

English River subprovince

The English River subprovince comprises a pronounced linear and belt-like crustal structure 1,200 km in length and ranging from 32 to 130 km in width.

ROSS RIVER PLUTON

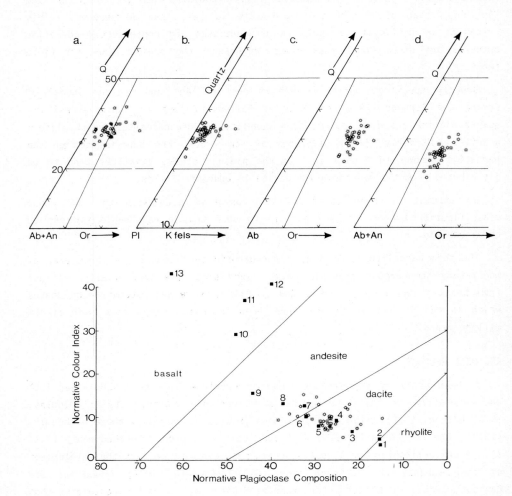

Figure 1.--Modal (Fig. 1b; Quartz, pl - plagioclase, K-fels - microcline) and normative (Fig. 1a, c, and d; Q + Ab + Or and Q + (Ab + An) + Or) plots of the Ross River Pluton of the Rice Lake volcanic belt. The data in Figure 1a is derived from a mesonorm which calculates biotite and hornblende (also present in the rock) and shows a shift of the data into the tonalite field in keeping with the mode of Figure 1b. Date and modal plot (Fig. 1b) from Paulus and Turnock (1971, Fig. 3, p. 217 and Table 1, p. 223). Nockolds' (1954) averages: 1 - biotite granite; 2 - average alkali granite; 3 - biotite adamellite; 4 - biotite tonalite; 5 - biotite granodiorite; 6 - average granodiorite; 7 - hornblende-biotite granodiorite; 8 - average tonalite; 9 - hornblende-biotite tonalite; 10 - hornblende-biotite diorite; 11 - average diorite; 12 - average tholeiitic andesite; 13 - average gabbro.

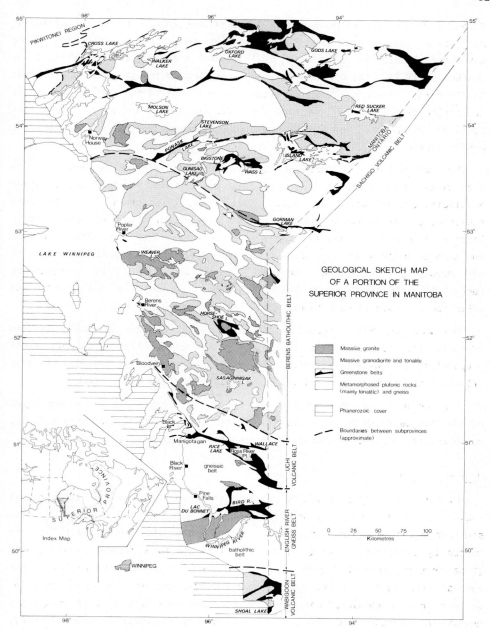

Figure 2.--Geological sketch map and index of names used in text.

Recent work has confirmed a two-fold subdivision into a northern, Ear Falls-Manigotagan supracrustal gneiss belt (mobile belt), and a southern Winnipeg River batholithic belt (McRitchie, 1971b; Breaks and Bond, 1977a; Harris, 1976; Beakhouse, 1977). The boundary between these two domains is marked in the west by the Bird River-Separation Lake greenstone belt and in the east by the abrupt transition from catazonal gneisses and intrusive stocks and batholiths in the south to the metasedimentary and associated migmatitic rocks of the northern mobile domain.

Paragneisses of the northern domain (Ear Falls-Manigotagan gneiss belt) show zones of metamorphic facies ranging north to south from lower to upper amphibolite, culminating in anatexis (McRitchie, 1971a and b). Low pressure subfacies of the pyroxene granulite facies are characteristic of some rocks in Ontario (Breaks and Bond, 1977b). These rocks have been subjected to a long and complex history of metasomatism and deformation. Four periods of folding of gradually decreasing intensity were accompanied by metamorphic recrystallization and rheid remobilization. Episodes of deformation and metamorphism produced characteristic suites of granitic rocks.

The Winnipeg River batholithic domain contains older diffusely layered granodiorite, tonalite, and trondhjemite gneisses (20%) and nearly equal proportions of syn-late tectonic intrusive tonalite (38%) and syn-post tectonic intrusive quartz monzonite and granite (39%) (Breaks and Bond, 1976b).

The southern boundary of the English River subprovince (Winnipeg River batholithic belt) with the Wabigoon volcanic subprovince "is variably a fault, an intrusive contact, or a gradational contact" (Beakhouse, 1977, p. 1483).

Uchi subprovince

In Manitoba this subprovince contains the Rice Lake group of supracrustal rocks in the south and amphibolite-gneissic tonalite in the north. The southern boundary of the Uchi belt against the English River gneiss belt is marked by cataclastic rocks, inferred faults, and by a change of metamorphic grade from greenschist facies in the Uchi belt to amphibolite facies in the English River belt. The northern bondary of the Uchi belt is marked by a low Bouguer gravity anomaly, steep aeromagnetic gradients, and by both abrupt and gradational lithological contacts. Here, layered and foliated tonalitic rocks and amphibolite remnants of the Uchi subprovince give way to the acidic plutons and migmatite of the Berens subprovince.

The Rice Lake group of rocks of the Uchi subprovince extends from Black Island on Lake Winnipeg as a narrow belt south-southeast beyond the Manitoba border to Red Lake in Ontario. Locally, the succession has been subdivided (e.g., Weber, 1971; Church and Wilson, 1971) into an older bimodal basalt-dacite sequence and a younger completed basalt-andesite-dacite-rhyolite sequence. Both volcanic cycles have associated sediments comprising conglomerate, arkose, feldspathic graywackes, siltstone, sandstone, chert, black shale, and oxide iron-formation (Campbell, 1971). A younger formation of rhythmically interlayered argillite and graywacke overlies both volcanic regimes and its facies has been interpreted as eugeosynclinal, (Weber, 1971).

Gabbroic rocks intrude the volcanic rocks. Sills may have been intruded contemporaneously with basalt, and one sill with an anorthositic core is interpreted as demonstrating consanguinity with ultrabasic and ultramafic rocks (Scoates, 1971).

Tonalite, trondhjemite, and quartz diorite occur as intravolcanic belt plutons, conformable lensoid masses, and as irregular masses on the north side adjacent to the supracrustal succession. The Ross River intravolcanic belt pluton occupies a well developed volcanic area (Campbell, 1971) and hence may be inferred to be co-magmatic with the dacitic phases of volcanism. However, all phases of the volcanic rocks are intruded by tonalitic rocks of the Ross River type and hence most are younger than the effusive phases of the magma.

The tonalite suite ranges from phases that show primary igneous textures to phases competely recrystallized. Judging from isotopic age determinations, rocks of almost exclusively tonalitic composition were emplaced over a period of 400 Ma.

Berens subprovince

The Berens subprovince in Manitoba is characterized by an abundance of granitic plutonic rocks (96% by area) and a dearth of supracrustal rocks (4%). Salient features of the belt have been summarized by Ermanovics and Davison (1976) and the rock types are present in the following proportions:

a : b : c :: 4 : 6 : 9 where

a = granite (massive)

b = granodiorite, minor tonalite and trondhjemite (massive)

c = granodioritic gneiss (migmatite gneiss)

The massive suite of rocks (51% of the area in Manitoba) represents late Kenoran plutonic rocks that were probably intruded into terrain of the type represented by the Sachigo or Uchi subprovinces. The Horseshoe Lake succession of supracrustal rocks is likely related to this late Kenoran plutonic event and may represent a direct relationship between acid plutonism and concomitant acid volcanism.

Migmatitic gneiss is characterized by foliated tonalitic and trondhjemitic rocks which are altered, generally by lit-par-lit injection of massive granitic rock, to an average granodioritic composition. Relicts of amphibolitic material are locally abundant, but metasedimentary inclusions are rare. The present erosion surface probably exposes the mesozone and low pressure metamorphism has altered the supracrustal rocks to amphibolite facies.

The Berens subprovince extends beyond the Manitoba border for 400 km into Ontario where it pinches out. Excluding the portion that extends westward beneath Lake Winnipeg, the belt has an exposed outcrop area of 110,334 km^2. More than half of this area is probably underlain by massive granite, granodiorite, and minor tonalite-trondhjemite emplaced at the culmination of the Kenoran orogeny. Nearly all of this area may have been molten or mobile (as in the formation of migmatite of early gneissic tonalite) at that time (ca. 2500 Ma ago). Large tonalitic plutons that are characteristically spatially related to greenstone development in the Uchi or Sachigo belts do not occur in late Kenoran time in the Berens belt.

The boundary between the Berens and Sachigo subprovinces is not distinct, and is a subjective function of the parameters used. Regionally the boundary can be placed where the percentage of K-rich, massive, plutonic rocks decreases to 35 percent. This coincides roughly with the -30 mgal Bouguer gravity anomaly in the region. Additional criteria are steep aeromagnetic gradients coincident with lithological change and localized zones of cataclastic rocks.

Sachigo subprovince

The Sachigo subprovince comprises supracrustal rocks that are typically distributed east-west as thin curvilinear, bifurcating belts which may constitute 10 to 15% of the region. The supracrustal rocks are generally characterized by a lower succession of volcanogenic rocks and a disconformable upper group of mainly sedimentary rocks. Emplacement of plutons is seen as ranging from early synkinematic (diapiric) to late synkinematic (Park and Ermanovics, in press; Fyson et al., in press).

Plutonic rocks occur as oval-shaped masses between volcanic belts. Two main suites are present. The earliest is layered and foliated augen gneiss which includes tonalite, trondhjemite, and granodiorite with flattened skialiths and amphibolite lenses. Parts of this suite may represent basement to the supracrustal rocks. This early suite constitutes 40 to 45% of all the rocks. The second and younger suite comprises massive to weakly foliated rocks ranging in composition from quartz diorite to granite, constituting 24 to 30% of the rocks of the southern Sachigo subprovince, of which only 5% is granite. Massive and foliated migmatite and agmatite are transitional rock types between areas of supracrustal and batholithic rocks and constitute about 10 percent of the belt. The plutonic rocks exhibit a full range of recrystallization from unmetamorphosed granitoid to completely recrystallized orthogneiss.

The difference between the younger suites of the Berens and Sachigo belts lies in the lower proportion of granites in the Sachigo belt. Furthermore, the late massive suite of the Sachigo belt has developed a foliation, usually weak but locally pronounced. Another distinctive feature in the Sachigo belt is that in two localities an unmetamorphosed diorite ($\pm$ gabbro)-quartz diorite-tonalite-trondhjemite-granite series was observed.

REGIONAL GEOPHYSICS

Seismic profiles (Hall and Hajnal, 1973) show that the intermediate discontinuity is depressed while the Mohorovicic discontinuity is warped up beneath the northern gneissic portion to the English River subprovince and the Uchi subprovince relative to the adjacent Berens and Winnipeg River batholiths (southern portion of English River subprovince, Figs. 2 and 11). Thus the areas of regular zonation of low to high metamorphic grade (including anatexis) underlain by supracrustal rocks and associated tonalitic plutons are characterized by a relatively thin crust with respect to the dominantly batholithic domains.

Gravity maps of the area show relatively positive Bouguer anomalies reflecting more dense rock, (-15 to -30 milligals) over the English River gneiss belt compared to the Uchi and Wabigoon volcanic belts (-3 to -50 milligals). The Berens belt, like the English River belt, is also characterized by high Bouguer anomalies, ranging from -35 to 20 milligals. North of the Berens belt Bouguer values again decrease to -50 milligals. A gravity 'low' lies along a series of tonalite and orthogneiss bodies situated on the south side of the narrow Ponask-Stevenson-Island Lake volcanic belt of the Sachigo subprovince, finally coinciding with a thick succession of supracrustal rocks at Island Lake. Another gravity low straddles the lithological boundary between the potassic Berens and sodic Uchi subprovinces.

The reason for the Bouguer gravity anomalies is not clear. A thin crust can explain the gravity high for the northern gneissic terrain of the English River gneiss belt, but not for the southern batholithic area where the crust thickens again. Nor can a thin crust be the explanation of high gravity anomalies in the Berens belt, since it is not present. One explanation may be that the Berens batholithic belt and the English River gneiss belt are underlain by denser rocks. Such dense rock could possibly be pyroxene-bearing, as is exposed north of the Sachigo subprovince (Pikwitonei granulite belt).

Magmatic intensities and surface lithologies correlate well (see also Beakhouse, 1977). Aeromagnetic intensities are highest over unmetamorphosed igneous rocks and lowest over greenstone belts lacking magnetite formations. Since most tonalitic rocks associated with greenstone belts are metamorphosed, these early plutonic rocks show low magnetic intensities even though their total iron content is higher relative to the massive phases (Table 1). Tonalitic plutons within supracrustal rocks are well defined magnetically and steep magnetic gradients along their borders may suggest steep or vertical contacts of the plutons. Massive rocks of the Berens and Winnipeg River batholithic belts show the highest magnetic intensities except where they include migmatized remnants of greenstone belts, and where the rocks are deformed by late cataclasis. Migmatized remnants and cataclasis generally coincide to form linear bands of low magnetic intensities.

Aeromagnetic data filtered to highlight long regional wavelengths and regional anomalies at depths of 6-12 km show a general correspondence to the surface geology (Beakhouse, 1977). For this reason it is thought that surface lithologies can be extrapolated to considerable depth. Preliminary data (P. McGrath, Geological Survey of Canada, personal comm., 1978) suggest that surface lithologies extend to greater depths (8 to 10 km) in metatonalite and supracrustal belts than in potassic batholithic belts (5 to 7 km).

AGE OF PLUTONISM

The main geological events affecting the Archean rocks of the western Superior Province have recently been grouped into two geotectonic cycles based on U-Pb and Rb/Sr ages (Goodwin, 1977). Each tectonic cycle, modelled after "accretion superevents" of Moorbath (1976), comprises deposition of volcanics and sediments followed by regional metamorphism and emplacement of plutons, followed once more by late or post-tectonic granite. U-Pb zircon and Rb/Sr (using the decay constant for $Rb^{87} = 1.42 \times 10^{-11}y^{-1}$) age data show events surrounding the Kenoran orogeny from 2760 to 2500 Ma. The regional peak of metamorphism was attained ca. 2680 Ma. ago (see also Turek, 1971). At least one tonalitic pluton of the Uchi belt slightly predates (2750 Ma., U-Pb zircon age, Krogh et al., 1974) this metamorphic event and is coeval with the proposed regional volcanic activity (Goodwin, 1977). Two unmetamorphosed granites from the Berens belt yielded Rb/Sr whole rock ages of $2677^{\pm}$ 160 Ma and 2557 $^{\pm}$ 44 Ma. A U-Pb zircon determination on a similar granite yielded 2715 Ma (Krogh et al., 1975). Turek (1971) recorded a persistent Rb/Sr metamorphic event for the Uchi and English River gneiss belts to have occurred ca. 2500 Ma ago. Coincident with this last metamorphism are potassic mobilizates yielding U-Pb zircon ages of 2560 Ma in Ontario (Krogh et al., 1975) and Rb/Sr mineral ages of 2340 $\pm$ 100 Ma in Manitoba (Turek, 1971, p. 319). Based on U-Pb zircon data alone, Krogh et al. (1975) have made a convincing argument that the main metamorphism is younger than 2688 Ma in the English River subprovince, but older than 2715 Ma in the Uchi-Berens subprovince. Regardless of which isotopic system is used, it is evident that potassic plutonic activity in the Berens belt overlapped and closely followed plutonic activity in the Uchi and English River provinces.

The above range of tectonic activity pertains to the Kenoran orogeny that peaked 2660-2680 Ma ago (Goodwin, 1977, p. 2741). There exists yet an older rock regime based on U-Pb zircon ages in Manitoba and Ontario which range from ca 2900 to 3100 Ma (see Krogh et al., 1975; Goodwin, 1977). These older ages derive from tonalitic plutons and gneisses. In the Sen Bay (Lac Seul) batholithic complex of Ontario, Breaks and Bond (1977a) describe seven plutonic phases, one of whose U-Pb zircon ages is 3080 Ma. They report this age from homogeneous fine-grained biotite-hornblende diorite as inclusions in foliated inequigranular diorite-quartz diorite and trondhjemite. In Manitoba, a variously foliated porphyroclastic tonalitic and trondhjemitic gneiss at Black Island on Lake Winnipeg (Uchi belt) yielded U-Pb zircon ages of ca. 3000 and 2900 Ma, respectively (Krogh et al., 1974). A U-Pb zircon age of 2950 Ma was reported by Krogh and Davis (1971) from a gneissic trondhjemite along the northern edge of the Berens belt at Favourable Lake in Ontario (Sachigo subprovince).

In the Lac Seul area evidence for the existence of an early supracrustal succession is afforded by amphibolitic skialiths in the old plutonic rocks. However, in the Black Island area of Manitoba, the evidence is ambiguous and shows tonalites tectonically intercalated with an early volcaniclastic sequence (Brown and Ermanovics, in preparation). A rhyolite from the younger volcaniclastic succession yielded a U-Pb zircon age of 2728 Ma (Wanless, personal comm.).

The factor common to all three regimes in which the 3000 Ma event is recorded is that substantial potassic plutonic rocks are not recognized from this early plutonic cycle. The reasons for this are not clear; however it is likely that large quantities of granite were not produced from the base of the crust until Kenoran times.

Initial $^{87}Sr/^{86}Sr$ compositions have not helped to subdivide or classify the plutonic rocks. For example, two massive granites from the Berens belt yielded $^{87}Sr/^{86}Sr$ ratios equal to 0.7024 $\pm$ 0.0010 and 0.7010 $\pm$ 0.0020. A layered

334

tonalite gneiss on Lake Winnipeg, yielding a U-Pb zircon age of 2900 Ma, also has a Rb/Sr whole rock age of 2674 ± 126 Ma with initial $^{87}Sr/^{86}Sr$ of 0.7010 ± 0.0006.

PETROCHEMISTRY

   The sections to follow deal essentially with three populations of rocks in their tectonic setting: metavolcanic, intrusive (plutonic), and metaintrusive (metaplutonic).   The data are plotted on AFM (FeO + 0.9 Fe_2O_3, Na_2O + K_2O, MgO), QAbOr (normative quartz, albite and orthoclase) and KNaCa (potassium, sodium and calcium diagrams to demonstrate the degree of coincidence elements of each population indicate to one another. Additionally, the data are used to test in a qualitative sense the degree to which their distribution describes a normal calc-alkaline trend or trondhjemitic trend.   For the purpose of the present work a trondhjemitic trend is calc-alkaline in which a Na-rich rather than K-rich rock composition·is the end result of magmatic or anatectic differentiation. These trends are depicted in QAbOr and KNaCa diagrams (Fig. 3). By analogy, a trondhjemitic trend (gabbro to trondhjemite) may be similar to a discontinuous or incomplete series of basalt to dacite. In keeping with this scheme a normal calc-alkaline trend in plutonic rocks (gabbro to granite) could give rise to the continuous or complete series of basalt to rhyolite. The distinction of whether a suite of rocks is 'tholeiitic' or 'calc-alkaline' is based on the criteria developed by Irvine and Baragar (1971, Figs. 2 and 6, p. 528, 536).   In the present study, most plutonic rocks describe a calc-alkaline series.

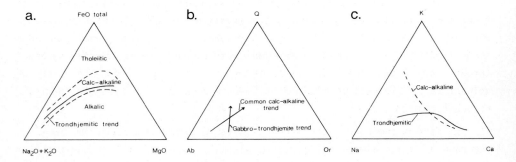

Figure 3.--Calc-alkaline and trondhjemitic trends (from Barker and Arth, 1976).
   a. Ternary AFM (FeO + 0.9 Fe_2O_3, Na_2 + K_2O,MgO) diagram showing trend of gabbro-trondhjemite suite (solid line) and fields distinguishing alkalic, calc-alkalic, and tholeiitic suites (broken lines). b. Generalized paths of calc-alkaline and trondhjemitic trends with respect to Q, Ab, and Or (normative quartz, albite and orthoclase). c. Ternary KNaCa (potassium, sodium and calcium) plot showing the common calc-alkalic trend (Nickolds and Allen, 1953) and a distinctly sodic trend of a trondhjemite suite, in this case from southwest Finland.

Metatonalite suite from the Black Island succession of the Uchi subprovince

Porphyroclastic tonalite and layered trondhjemite are field terms applied to a suite of problematical rocks in the Black Island area on Lake Winnipeg (Ermanovics, 1970a). The porphyroclastic member is thought to be orthogneiss (possibly hypabyssal) whereas the layered trondhjemite has affinities to

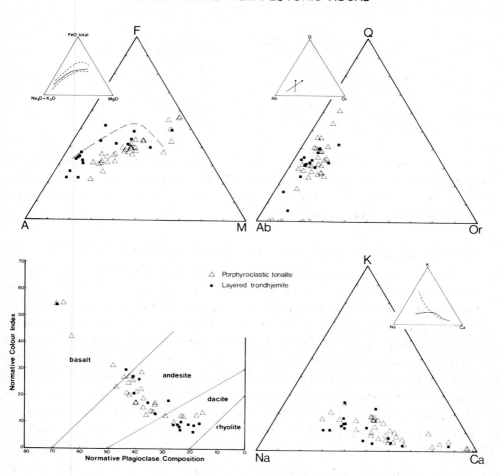

BLACK ISLAND METAPLUTONIC ROCKS

Figure 4.--Tonalite and trondhjemite from the Black Island area (Uchi belt) whose U-Pb zircon age is ca. 3.0 Ga. The rocks include porphyroclastic and problematical layered varieties associated with the succession of supracrustal rocks. Broken line in AFM separates the tholeiitic from the calc-alkaline field. Calculation of normative colour index and normative plagioclase composition after Irvine and Baragar (1971).

paragneiss in outcrop. Although the relationship of these rocks to the supracrustal rocks is not clear, it is considered (Brown and Ermanovics, in preparation) that they either intrude or are interfolded with the lower supracrustal succession of the Black Island group of rocks.

Figure 4 demonstrates that both units have sodic (trondhjemitic) trends and that the bulk of compositions ranges from dacite to andesite. Granitic rocks of the younger Kenoran regime intrude these gneisses and this may be reflected in those scattered analyses that seem quartz and K-rich. Both members of the suite are further characterized as follows:

	Porphyroclastic tonalite	Layered trondhjemite
SiO_2	61%	67%
Al_2O_3	15%	15%
TiO_2	0.61%	0.4%
K_2O/Na_2O	0.35	0.25

In the normative scheme for volcanic rocks of Irvine and Baragar (1971) both members of the suite are calc-alkaline. Metagabbro and meta-ultramafic rocks (mainly peridotites and dunite, not plotted) intrude the porphyroclastic tonalite and are likely comagmatic.

Rice Lake and Ross River (Pluton) group of rocks of the Uchi subprovince

The data here are presented to reflect the relationship between intrusive and extrusive rocks. It is apparent from the diagrams (Figs. 5 and 6) that both suites are sodic with respect to the Lac du Bonnet granite, which occurs in the batholithic portion of the southern English River subprovince and which is here used as a K-rich (calc-alkaline) reference. The tonalitic rocks are variously metamorphosed and some of the massive varieties (Fig. 5) collected from the margin of the Rice Lake supracrustal succession have been correlated with the peripherally weakly metamorphosed intravolcanic Ross River Pluton (e.g., Marr, 1971). Large bodies of granite are absent in this environment, although potassic mobilizate in the form of pegmatite and clots are common in some rocks.

Ages of volcanic and plutonic activity have not been firmly established but it is likely that rocks of both the 3.0 Ga and younger Kenoran ages are present.

Intrusive rocks

Gabbroic rocks which in the field are associated with volcanic rocks show a
greater affinity with normative basaltic rocks of ordinary Na contents rather
than with the tonalitic suite (Fig. 5). Compared to the Ross River Pluton (Fig.
6) regional tonalites show a great deal of scatter which probably reflects
their diverse histories. Their compositions plot as normative, calc-alkaline

RICE LAKE VOLCANIC AND INTRUSIVE ROCKS

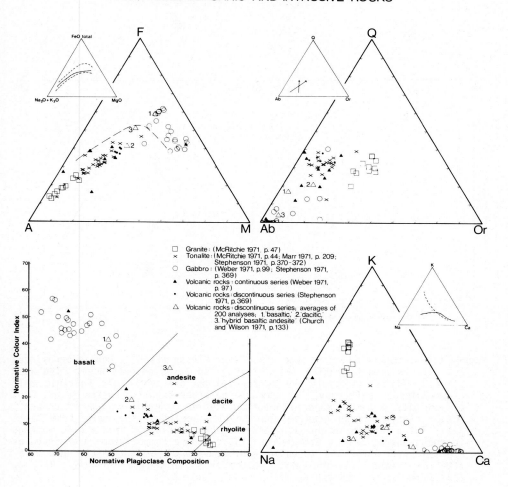

Figure 5.--Comparative display of intrusive and volcanic rocks of the Rice Lake
group of rocks of the Uchi belt. The unmetamorphosed Lac du Bonnet granite
of the English River gneiss belt is shown as a reference state of potassic,
calc-alkaline differentiation. The QAbOr and KNaCa plots show that this
granite is well removed from the trondhjemitic affinities exhibited by all
other rocks.

ROSS RIVER TONALITE AND LAC DU BONNET GRANITE

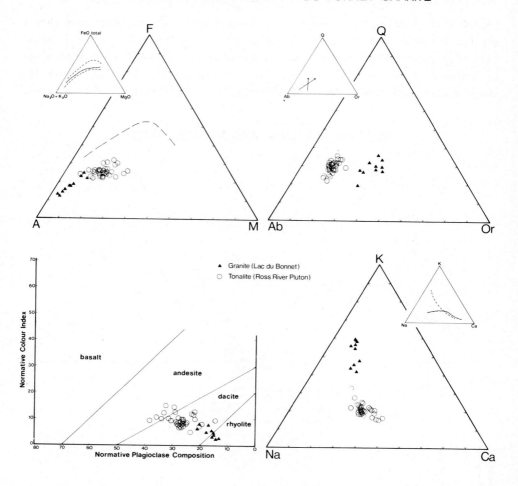

Figure 6.--Normative plots of the Ross River Pluton (Fig. 2, Uchi subprovince) and Lac du Bonnet granite (Fig. 2, English River subprovince). The Ross River tonalite is completely surrounded by the Rice Lake volcanic belt (intravolcanic belt body) and compared to other tonalite masses (e.g., Fig. 4) exhibits a small major element variation. Normative quartz contents (QAbOr plot) of both granite and tonalite are equal and range from 20 to 38%. The differentiation path described by tonalite is Na:K = 6:4, whereas in the granite, Na:K = 2.8 (KNaCa plot). These compositions are viewed as representing sodic and potassic end members of trondhjemitic and calc-alkaline trends, respectively. (Data from Paulus and Turnock, 1971, p. 223, Table 1; and McRitchie, 1971, p. 47, Table 6.)

dacite and andesite, and the majority of compositions cluster within the dacite field. Four groups of rocks (A to D) mapped as tonalitic (McRitchie, 1971; Marr, 1971; Stephenson, 1971) have the following chemical characteristics:

	A	B	C	D	Ross River Pluton
SiO_2	64%	65%	68%	69%	69%
Al_2O_3	17%	16%	17%	15%	16%
TiO_2	0.52%	0.52%	0.32%	0.40%	0.32%
K_2O/Na_2O	0.44	0.34	0.40	0.26	0.40

The late synkinematic Ross River Pluton is characterized by a remarkably homogeneous composition (Fig. 6). Paulus and Turnock (1971) report slight quartz enrichment toward the centre of the batholith and slight mafic enrichment (CaO and total iron) near the margins. The rocks are calc-alkaline normative dacite and andesite. In Figure 6 the Lac du Bonnet granite is used as a K-rich reference, and it is apparent that the Ross River Pluton fits a trondhjemitic trend as distinct from the granite. The QAbOr diagram shows that the normative quartz content of granite and tonalite is the same.

Extrusive rocks

Volcanic rocks of the continuous series (Weber, 1971) show weak affinities with a calc-alkaline trend (Fig. 5). Again using the Lac du Bonnet granite as a reference state, the alkalic end-member of the volcanic suite is more sodic than the granite. The amount of material for the continuous and discontinuous volcanic successions removed by erosion and the extent to which this erosion may have modified the present succession are not known. However, Church and Wilson (1971) point out that the continuous series is much more common than the discontinuous series in the Superior Province.

The discontinuous volcanic suite is represented by rocks reported by Church and Wilson (1971) to consist of a bimodal suite of 'basalt-dacite.' In their scheme of analysis the composition of the basaltic rocks is near the end point of the Icelandic trend, whereas that of the 'dacitic' rocks is midway on the Cascade differentiation trend. In the present scheme, their three class averages (labelled 1, 2, 3, Fig. 5) of over 200 analyses calculate as tholeiitic basalt and calc-alkaline andesite. However, the distinctiveness of the three populations is still reflected in the present plots (Fig. 5). Basalt (class 1) plots at the edge of the gabbro cluster of analyses. Andesite (class 2) shows a normal shift toward the alkali-quartz fields. The andesite of class 3 ('hybrid basaltic andesite'), however, shows extraordinary enrichment of Na (5.15 wt.% Na_2O; Table 3, Church and Wilson, 1971) with respect to normative colour index. This composition may represent either sodic magma or basaltic magma contaminated by soda-rich rocks. By way of comparison with this 'Na-lava' the tonalitic rocks average 4.5 wt.% Na_2O with remarkably small standard deviations of mean. The porphyroclastic tonalite at Black Island, however, reflects a somewhat smaller Na_2O content of 3.4 wt.% which is more in keeping with a dacite-andesite mode.

In summary, both volcanic and intrusive rocks appear to stem from tholeiitic roots and branch to sodic rather than potassic end-members. Tonalitic rock compositions tend to cluster about the normative andesite-dacite boundary (Fig. 5). The exception to this lies in rocks of the older age regime at Black Island where normative andesite compositions are well represented (Fig. 4). Gabbroic rocks intrusive or coeval with basalts appear to have greater chemical similarity with basaltic volcanic rocks than with tonalitic rocks (basalt 1, Fig. 5). The exception to this observation also is found in the older age regime of the Black Island group of rocks, where tonalites appear to vary smoothly within the normative dacite, andesite and basalt fields (Fig. 4).

It should be noted that areas of tonalitic rock within the Uchi subprovince are locally potassic (granodioritic). However, this secondary K-enrichment is commonly found in hybrid rocks demonstrably related to late Kenoran tectonic activity (e.g., Rb/Sr K-feldspar age of ca. 2.3 to 2.5 Ga; Turek, 1971, p. 319) as exemplified by the Berens batholithic belt.

Comparison of plutonic rocks from the northern Uchi subprovince and Berens subprovince

The chemical data of Figure 7 and Table 1 derive from an area of 12,950 square kilometers (Hecla-Carroll Lake, Ermanovics, 1970a) which was sampled using a six-stage, nested (hierarchical) analysis of variance design (E. M. Cameron, I. Ermanovics and T. Goss, in preparation). The data are weighted by area and thus provide an estimate of the overall plutonic rock composition of the Berens versus the Uchi subprovinces in Manitoba.

With the exception of the Rice Lake succession rocks of the area are metamorphosed as high as middle amphibolite facies. In the Uchi belt the intrusive rocks are variably metamorphosed, and variably migmatized remnants similar to them are found throughout the Berens belt (Fig. 8). The Berens batholithic belt is characterized by large volumes of post-metamorphic, massive plutonic rocks.

Table 1 contains weight averages of six groups of rocks, as displayed on Figure 7, and shows that the most discriminating criterion between the Uchi and

PLUTONIC ROCKS OF THE BERENS BATHOLITHIC AND UCHI VOLCANIC BELTS

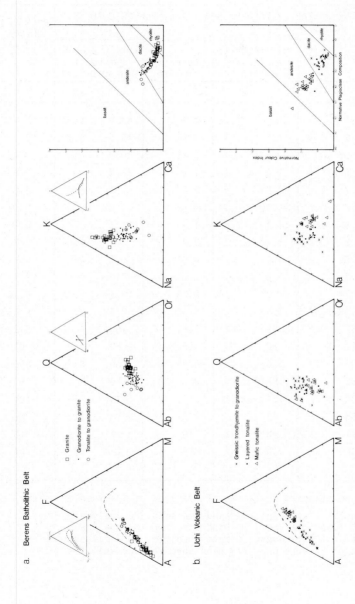

Figure 7.--A comparison of plutonic rocks from the Berens (series "a", unmetamorphosed) and the Uchi (series "b", metamorphosed) subprovinces. The samples from which these analyses derive were areally weighted over an area of 12,950 sq. km. between latitudes 51° and 52°. (See Table 1 for class averages and Figure 2 for location.) The Uchi suite exhibits trondhjemitic trend characteristics and ranges in composition from normative dacite to andesite. The Berens suite shows calc-alkaline trends and ranges in composition from normative rhyolite to dacitic andesite.

TABLE 1 : Averages of chemical analyses (major elements in weight per cent
and trace elements in ppm) of two major suites of plutonic rocks
and greywacke from the Uchi volcanic belt and Berens batholithic
belt in the Superior Province of Manitoba. Rock names are field
terms and map units after Ermanovics (1970)

| | SUPRACRUSTAL ROCKS | | METAMORPHOSED, EARLY PLUTONIC ROCKS | | | | | | AVERAGE OF COLUMNS 2, 3 AND 4 | |
| | Greywacke | | Mafic Quartz Diorite and Tonalite | | Layered Tonalite | | Gneissic Trondh- jemite and Granodiorite | | | |
	1	1S	2	2S	3	3S	4	4S		S
SiO_2	64.2	3.1	60.8	2.5	67.2	2.1	68.9	2.5	65.7	4.4
Al_2O_3	17.2	1.0	17.7	0.6	16.9	0.6	17.0	0.8	17.2	0.3
TiO_2	0.57	0.10	0.64	0.11	0.43	0.08	0.3	0.11	0.47	0.17
Fe_2O_3	1.5	0.5	2.4	0.5	1.6	0.4	1.0	0.4	1.6	0.8
FeO	3.7	1.3	3.8	0.8	2.4	0.8	1.7	0.6	2.6	1.2
MnO	0.08	0.02	0.10	0.02	.0.06	0.02	0.05	0.02	0.07	0.03
MgO	2.9	1.2	3.1	0.6	1.4	0.5	1.1	0.6	1.9	1.1
CaO	3.3	1.3	5.1	0.7	3.4	0.7	2.7	0.6	3.7	1.8
Na_2O	4.6	1.6	4.1	0.3	4.6	0.7	4.7	0.7	4.5	0.6
K_2O	1.9	1.0	1.9	0.8	2.0	0.7	2.4	0.8	2.1	0.8
P_2O_5	0.14	0.03	0.24	0.13	0.13	0.0	0.11	0.05	0.16	0.11
K_2O/Na_2O	0.50	0.36	0.47	0.19	0.43	0.14	0.52	0.22	0.48	0.20
Sr	487	185	629	201	416	133	460	124	512	178
Rb	51	32	60	45	55	37	63	30	61	37
Ba	435	247	566	272	526	174	560	224	556	230
Zr	168	33	196	71	227	73	170	52	190	66
V	135	30	151	26	75	29	73	82	101	69
Cr	105	68	43	16	17	14	14	19	25	22
Ni	51	23	26	21	10	8	8	9	15	16
Cu	40	15	36	39	32	23	18	11	27	28

2S = one standard deviation of averages of analyses of column 2.

Column 1: 6 stations, 44 hand specimen, 22 analyses.
Column 2: 10 stations, 76 hand specimen, 38 analyses.
Column 3: 10 stations, 80 hand specimen, 40 analyses.
Column 4: 24 stations, 172 hand specimen, 86 analyses.

UNMETAMORPHOSED LATE PLUTONIC ROCKS						AVERAGE OF COLUMNS 5, 6 and 7	
Tonalite, Trondh-jemite and Granodiorite		Granodiorite and Granite		Granite			
5	5S	6	6S	7	7S		S
65.7	2.9	67.7	2.7	71.1	2.0	68.6	3.1
17.4	0.9	16.8	0.7	15.9	0.9	16.6	0.9
0.50	0.18	0.42	0.20	0.25	0.08	0.37	0.19
1.9	0.8	1.5	0.6	0.9	0.5	1.4	0.7
2.2	0.6	1.8	0.7	1.1	0.5	1.6	0.7
0.07	0.02	0.06	0.02	0.05	0.03	0.06	0.03
1.7	0.6	1.3	0.5	0.7	0.3	1.1	0.6
3.6	0.6	2.7	0.6	1.6	0.6	2.4	0.9
4.5	0.5	4.3	0.3	3.8	0.8	4.1	0.6
2.3	0.7	3.2	0.5	4.5	0.6	3.5	0.9
0.20	0.15	0.17	0.10	0.09	0.04	0.14	0.10
0.52	0.17	0.75	0.14	1.23	0.31	0.89	0.33
563	266	574	126	386	149	510	191
69	28	99	28	140	45	110	41
642	229	839	482	883	334	832	417
215	88	214	93	183	71	204	86
92	29	74	29	39	20	64	32
2	27	13	9	7	5	12	12
14	15	7	6	5	2	7	7
18	9	22	29	10	6	18	23

Column 5: 9 stations, 64 hand specimen, 32 analyses.
Column 6: 45 stations, 296 hand specimen, 148 analyses.
Column 7: 27 stations, 160 hand specimen, 80 analyses.

Berens plutonic rocks is the K_2O/Na_2O ratio (0.48 versus 0.89). The Sr/Rb ratio varies from 7.3 in the Uchi to 4.6 in the Berens. K/Rb ratios, calculated from Table 1 are 263, 302, and 316 for columns 2, 3, and 4, respectively (average of columns is 285) in the early plutonic population. K/Rb ratios of late plutonic rocks are 277, 269, and 267 for columns 5, 6, and 7, respectively (average of columns is 264). The proportion of normative andesite in the Uchi belt to that of the Berens belt is 3:1.

Uchi subprovince

Compositions of the Uchi subprovince are distributed in the normative calc-alkaline dacite and andesite field (Fig. 7b). A curious lack of data points characterizes the dacite-andesite boundary and centroid of data points in the KNaCa diagram. Rhyolitic compositions are absent and the normative colour index is generally higher than for similar compositions in the Berens belt (Fig. 7a).

The KNaCa plot shows a scatter of data (Fig. 7b). The rocks show affinities with both trondhjemitic and calc-alkaline trends which overlap the KNaCa data of the Berens belt. The QAbOr lot also shows a scatter of data points (Fig. 7b). In a general way the rocks define a trondhjemitic trend; however, some rocks, noted in the field as being affected by K-metasomatism, overlap the calc-alkaline trend of the Berens subprovince (Fig. 7a.)

Berens subprovince

Compositions are well distributed from the normative rhyolite to dacite fields. A small part of the population lies at the edge of the andesite field (Fig. 7a). The KNaCa plot shows a well defined enrichment in K_2O (felsic portion of calc-alkaline trend) and confirmation of the field nomenclature of the three classes of rock types. Curiously enough, the lower portion of the trend coincides with the area of the KNaCa plot of the Uchi belt in which a dearth of data points exists. The QAbOr plot (Fig. 7a) shows good data cluster and defines a well established upper limit of normative quartz (ca. 35%) and K-differentiation.

Test of the hypothesis:sodic skialiths in the Berens subprovince

Figure 8 displays data collected from the Berens subprovince (Berens River-Deer Lake; Ermanovics, 1970b), north of the statistically based study area of the previous section. Variously hybridized 'tonalitic gneiss' in this area is considered to have been derived from a sodic substrate similar to that which constitutes the Uchi subprovince. From those gneisses in which no mesoscopic

PLUTONIC ROCKS OF THE BERENS BATHOLITHIC BELT

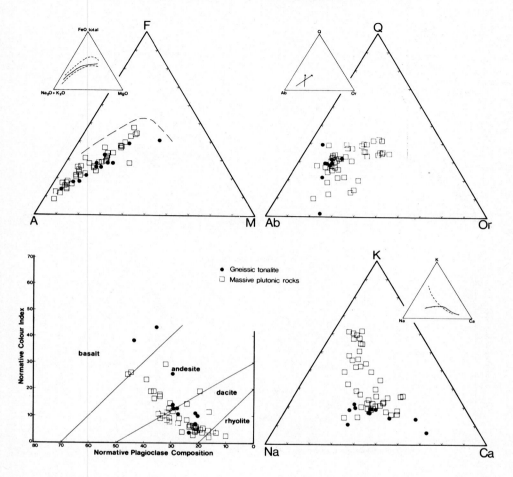

Figure 8.--A comparison of massive plutonic (Kenoran) rocks (quartz diorite, tonalite, granodiorite and granite) and gneissic tonalite relics interpreted as remnants of a pre-Kenoran or early Kenoran crust of the Berens belt north of latitude 52°. The tonalitic rocks describe a trondhjemitic trend.

metasomatism could be demonstrated the data confirm the findings of the previous sections, namely that metaplutonic rocks likely to be the early expression of plutonism exhibit trondhjemitic trends.

Horseshoe Lake volcanic belt

The Horseshoe Lake volcanic belt (Fig. 2) is thought to be related to the late Kenoran plutonism of the subprovince. The supracrustal rocks (mainly

HORSESHOE LAKE VOLCANIC AND PLUTONIC ROCKS

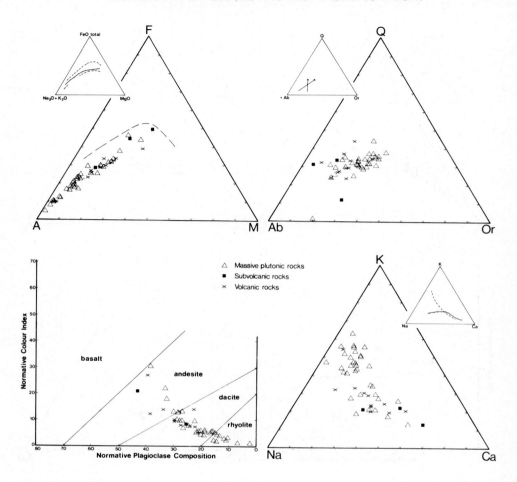

Figure 9.--Calc-alkaline differentiation trend exhibited by rocks from the Horseshoe Lake group of rocks of the Berens subprovince. The volcanic rocks are metamorphosed to amphibolite facies, and are intruded by the plutonic rocks. The subvolcanic rocks (see text) appear to show trondhjemitic affinities.

porphyritic dacite, quartzo-feldspathic pelite and calc-silicate gneiss) are metamorphosed to amphibolite facies and are intruded by post metamorphic (massive) plutonic rocks ranging from granite to tonalite (Ermanovics, 1970b). In some dacites phenocrysts are so abundant that rock modes assume dioritic compositions and are here termed subvolcanic (Fig. 9). This succession is thought to be very shallow and underlain by massive granite, and it is therefore likely that its metamorphism is related to the emplacement of these granites. Figure 9 shows that volcanic and massive plutonic rocks describe a continuous and overlapping calc-alkaline trend.

The interpretation of these data is that calc-alkaline volcanism of the Horseshoe Lake succession is genetically related to potassic plutonism of the Berens belt. In contrast, in the Uchi belt the plutonism is not as readily related to volcanism, although both plutonism and volcanism show variations of trodhjemitic trends.

In summary, the Berens belt and Uchi belt are characterized by distinctive chemical populations of rocks. The Berens subprovince shows strong late potassic calc-alkaline affinities, whereas the Uchi belt and old lithologic relicts in the Berens belt exhibit trondhjemitic affinities. Some overlap of trends occurs and may be related to Kenoran K-metasomatism affecting the early sodic plutonic rocks.

Relationship of plutonic rocks to volcanic rocks of the Gunisao and Stevenson Lakes area of the Sachigo subprovince

The Sachigo subprovince is set apart from the Uchi and Berens subprovinces by different tectonic characteristics and it does not display the clearcut chemical distinction between sodic and potassic suites previously demonstrated. Each ovoid plutonic complex, defined and bounded by infolded supracrustal rocks, contains a heterogeneous assemblage of plutonic phases of variable ages. This melange of multiple compositional and textural phases causes difficulties in categorizing plutonic events. For example, Ayres (1974) describes a portion of the batholithic terrain in the Trout Lake area of Ontario as follows: "The northern, North Trout Lake batholith, is composed of 20 discrete intrusive phases that range in composition from diorite to granite and form stocks, sills, dikes, and dike swarms; each phase has sharp, intrusive contacts with older phases. The general sequence of intrusion is toward increasing K_2O, Na_2O, and SiO_2 and decreasing CaO, MgO, and total iron, although interruptions and reversals of this trend are common. The earliest phase, a biotite trondhjemite, has an age of 2.950 million years and may be pre-volcanism basement."

The data in Figure 10 include volcanic, plutonic, and metaplutonic rocks. Unmetamorposed plutonic rocks range from well within the normative rhyolite field to well within the normative basalt fields. In the map areas involved two small bodies show rather complete magmatic differentiation ranging from gabbro to granite. Metaplutonic rocks range from the mid-normative dacite field to basalt. The volcanic rocks range from andesite to basalt and this chemical range reflects an observation made in the field that the upper silicic volcanic

GUNISAO–STEVENSON LAKES VOLCANIC AND INTRUSIVE ROCKS

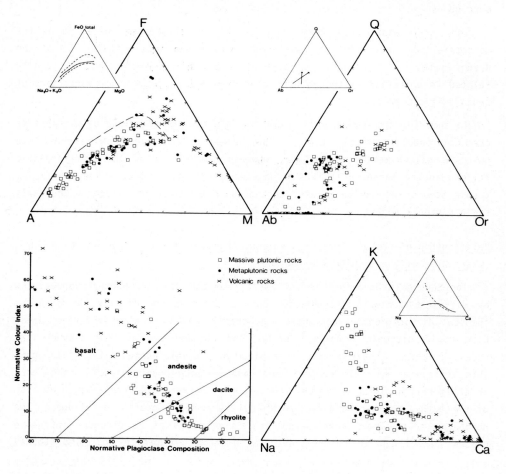

Figure 10.--Igneous rocks of the Sachigo subprovince north of latitude 53°, but south of 54° (Gunisao and Stevenson Lakes, Fig. 2). Volcanic rocks exhibit a calc-alkaline trend; metaplutonic rocks exhibit a trondhjemitic trend; unmetamorphosed plutonic rocks show affinities to both types of trends.

succession is missing from the present sample area (Ponask-Stevenson Lakes belts).

The QAbOr plot (Fig. 10) shows that massive plutonic and metaplutonic rocks have a calc-alkaline trend. Metaplutonic rocks show affinities to a trondhjemitic trend. The KNaCa plot (Fig. 10) may be used to draw similar conclusions; however, interpretation is hindered because the data do not extend over a great enough compositional range.

In summary, generalizations regarding the Sachigo subprovince cannot be based on the limited data of the present study. The data demonstrate the rather wide range of massive plutonic rocks (normative basalt to rhyolite) of the Sachigo subprovince absent in the Berens and Uchi subprovinces. However, in keeping with earlier observations, metaplutonic rock compositions still only range from mid-dacite to more cafemic compositions. Volcanic rocks show a weak calc-alkaline trend (KNaCa plot).

English River subprovince

Normative and modal data of granitic rocks, as well as P-T conditions of metamorphism in the English River subprovince of Manitoba may be found in McRitchie (1971a and b; McRitchie and Weber, 1971). The present discussion, therefore, deals with temporal and spatial variations of granitic rocks in the light of new geochronological data made available since 1971.

In Manitoba the highest grade paragneisses and migmatites of the Manigotagan gneissic belt display an overall conformity and are interfolded with diffusely layered granitoid gneisses more typical of the Pine Falls and Winnipeg River batholithic complexes. This has been interpreted as a basement cover relationship between pre-Kenoran orthogneisses and younger supracrustal sediments (Breaks and Bond, 1977b; Beakhouse, 1977). McRitchie (1971a) interpreted this relationship as a metamorphic boundary between metasedimentary migmatites containing autochthonous-allochthonous mobilizates and an autochthonous, catazonal 'degranitized' tonalitic and trondhjemitic residuum representing deeper levels of the same sedimentary pile (McRitchie, 1971a). The prolonged deformational and metamorphic reworking precludes a definitive interpretation of this relationship; however, the basement-cover concept is possibly more valid in view of the abrupt contact of the Pine Falls plutonic complex with the Bird River greenstone belt and the scattered occurrence (4%) of both metavolcanic and metasedimentary supracrustal relics throughout the southern Winnipeg River batholithic complex.

Ear Falls-Manigotagan gneiss belt

The oldest rocks recognized here are a gray granodioritic, tonalitic and trondhjemite gneissic suite which is generally hornblende and biotite-bearing, diffusely layered and ubiquitously transected by thin lenticular pink potassium feldspar enriched veinlets. Amphibolite lenses and boudins are generally conformable yet locally can be shown to cut across the major mineralogical and textural layering. The Black River suite (Fig. 2) represents one of the most variable derivatives of the older gneisses and exhibits regional variations in composition and texture which have been attributed to regional potassium metasomatism. A gradational increase for over 12 km in the proportion of microcline porphyroblasts is accompanied by an attendant change in the host phase from gray hornblende and biotite-bearing tonalitic gneisses to a coarse massive equigranular biotite granite. This culminates at the extreme eastern end of the suite in a locally intrusive inequigranular granite showing plagioclase and microcline poikiloblasts.

The composition of the tonalitic and granodioritic gneisses though characterized by low standard cell volumes (Marmo, 1967) is similar to analyses of the graywacke-derived migmatites and metasediments. The mean level of sodium in the gneissic suite increases slightly and antipathetically with potassium from metasediment, through migmatite to higher grade gneiss and was originally thought to support the concept of 'granodioritizing' the sediments by driving off the initial partial melts and effectively degranitizing them (Marmo, 1967). An extension of the concept has been used to infer a crustal zonation with increasing temperature and depth from metasediment through migmatite and tectothermally degranitized tonalitic gneiss into a zone in which the tonalitic residuum might ultimately give rise to trondhjemite magma generation (McRitchie, 1971).

Winnipeg River batholithic belt

The rock suites of the batholithic belt trend approximately parallel to the main trend of the English River subprovince. The older granitoid gneisses make up only a minor portion of the batholithic belt, 8% of which comprises discrete plutons, batholiths and stocks of younger intrusive tonalite and granite. The granitoid gneisses are restricted to the western portion of the belt and are referred to as a hybrid catazonal granitoid complex of trondhjemite, tonalite, and granodiorite which has been subjected to severe deformation and recrystallization during or prior to the emplacement of the younger intrusions. In this context they are considered to be orthogneisses emplaced over a long period of time, and now represent the eventual product of repeated magma injection, metsomatism and partial anatexis (Breaks and Bond, 1977b). Chemically the older gneisses resemble the tonalitic and granodioritic intrusions which cut them; however, an overall enrichment in potassium is apparent from one suite to another and culminates in the emplacement of late- to post-tectonic granites as, for example, at Lac du Bonnet (Figs. 2 and 11).

Tonalitic, granodioritic and trondhjemitic intrusions occur as dykes, stocks, and elliptical bodies of batholithic proportions. Fresh ideomorphic textures near their cores commonly give way to foliated and recrystallized margins indicating minor deformation after their emplacement. Hornblende and biotite are typical constituents whereas garnet is absent. This contrasts with

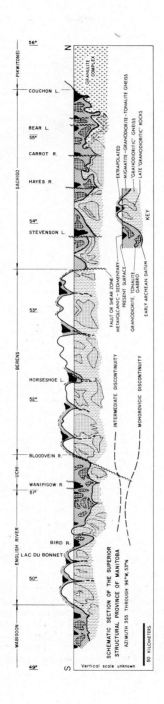

Figure 11.--Schematic north-south section of the Superior Province in Manitoba (after Ermanovics and Davidson, 1976, Fig. 6, p. 342). The model shows two main periods of plutonism (pre- and early Kenoran, and Kenoran) separated by a line labelled "Early Archean Datum." The depth of the discontinuities is schematic and is derived from the data of Wilson (1971) and Hall and Hajnal (1973). The Wanipigow River is coincident with the Rice Lake group of rocks in the cross section.

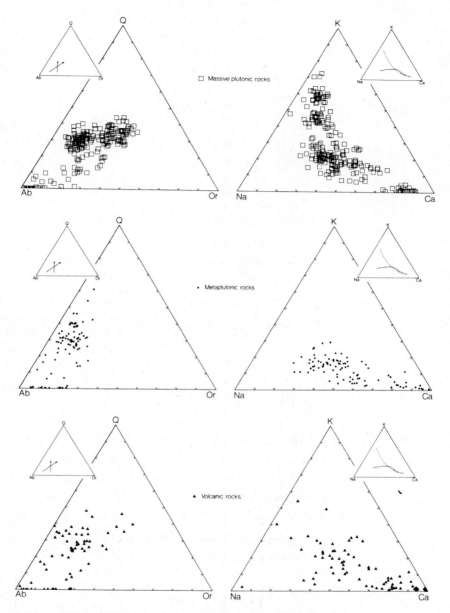

Figure 12.--QAbOr and KNaCa summary plots of all analyses (Figs. 4 to 10). Metaplutonic rocks show distinct trondhjemitic trend characteristics. Massive plutonic rocks show affinities to both calc-alkaline and trondhjemitic trends and the data for these rocks is greatly weighted toward trends observed in the Sachigo subprovince (Fig. 10, KNaCa plot). Volcanic rocks appear to exhibit a straight line trend defined approximately by Na:K = 13:7 in terms of KNaCa; however, both calc-alkaline and trondhjemitic similarities may be present.

the typical anatectic phases of the Ear Falls-Manigotagan gneiss belt in which garnet and biotites are ubiquitous.

The younger intrusions are compositionally and texturally homogeneous pink granodiorite to granite batholiths (Lac du Bonnet, Tetu and Launt Lake) and intrusive complexes that are generally surrounded by vein and dyke swarms of pegmatite and aplite. The intrusions are either equigranular or porphyritic and display fresh textures with little or no evidence of metamorphic recrystallization or deformation.

In most of these respects the Berens subprovince contains suites of rocks (Figs. 7 and 8) and parageneses like those described above.

TECTONIC SETTING

Preceding sections demonstrate that trondhjemitic (Na) differentiation trends were developed in all igneous rocks of the Uchi subprovince, in metaplutonic rocks of the Berens subprovince, and in plutonic and metaplutonic rocks of the Sachigo subprovince. These observations seem to preclude that metamorphism was the cause of Na enrichment in these subprovinces, because both massive and metaplutonic rocks show trondhjemitic trends. However, where tonalite suites are metamorphosed they are early synkinematic and some, as in the case of the Black Island suite (Uchi subprovince) or the Favourable Lake tonalites (Ayres, 1974, Sachigo subprovince), may belong to a pre-Kenoran tectono-thermal event ca. 3.0 Ga old (e.g., Lac Seul event, Goodwin, 1977, p. 2741).

Early tonalites may have been robbed of their potassium (they presently contain ca. 1% in the Black Island suite and 1 to 2% in presumed younger suites) during subsequent amphibolite facies metamorphism. On the other hand, we do not expect all of the massive Berens plutonic phases to have formed by anatexis of a parent rock such as tonalite. Possible potassic anatectic fractionation to form the massive Kenoran plutonic rocks is contraindicated by the observation that tonalite-granite suites in the Berens belt appear to be cogenetic and nearly coeval. Earlier metatonalite remnants are granitized by the Kenoran suite, rather than giving rise to it. The evidence in the Ear Falls-Manigotagan gneiss belt of the English River subprovince is contrary to this. Here the bulk of the original gneisses is viewed as the source rock from which both potassic magma and sodic magma were derived. The gneisses now have an intermediate K and Na content between these magmatic end-members. The original graywacke and shale sedimentation in the Manigotagan belt and the volcanism now represented by the greenstones of the Uchi and Bird River belts probably were contemporaneous (Weber, 1971; McRitchie, 1971; Harris, 1976).

This evolutionary link was maintained during the subsequent Kenoran orogeny when early syntectonic gradational metamorphic zonations were developed from greenshist facies in the Rice Lake and Bird River volcanic rocks to uppermost amphibolite and local granulite facies conditions in the intervening gneissic belt (McRitchie, 1971; Butrenchuk, 1970; D. L. Trueman, University of Manitoba, personal comm.). The higher temperatures in the metsedimentary belt led to the development of widespread metatexites and diatexites having medium-grained to pegmatitic leucosomes ranging in composition from tonalite to granite (Breaks and Bond, 1977b). Pelitic gneisses are associated with potassium-enriched neosomes whereas the feldspathic wackes apparently yielded either granodioritic, tonalitic, or trondhjemitic segregations (Breaks and Bond, 1977b; Kilinc, 1972).

Vis a vis the northern belts the style of deformation in the English River gneiss belt is unique and can be likened to a mobile belt (McRitchie, 1971, p. 38) in that deformational strains are high and complex (but not uniformly so), the grade of metamorphism is high and progressive, tectono-plutonic activity probably lasted over a long time span, and deformation generally kept pace with metamorphic recrystallization. The present age data in Manitoba and Ontario suggest continued mobility of the English River subprovince coeval with sodic igneous activity in the Uchi belt. The argument that potassic compositions may be found in upper sections of the Uchi belt but have been removed by erosion does not apply because, as previously discussed, the evidence pertaining to the Berens belt seems to suggest granite emplacement beneath a sodic layer during uplift.

It has been suggested (Goodwin, 1977) that the Berens block represents an uplifted early sedimentary-volcanic basin. Such a basin may have been dominantly metasedimentary. Granitic rocks of the Berens subprovince probably are isostatically balanced with supracrustal-plutonic rocks of the Sachigo subprovince (Fig. 11). A similar observation may be made between the southern and northern portions of the English River subprovince (Fig. 11). The model envisaged is one of an older sodic and granitic substrate that was raised above its erosion level by enormous masses of K-rich plutonic rocks. There is little evidence within the Berens belt itself to suggest what may have caused this plutonism, but regional aeromagnetic values and Bouguer gravity anomalies suggest that denser rocks than than presently exposed exist at depths of about 7 to 10 km.

Wilson (1971, p. 42) estimates that total crustal thicknesses in the Berens, Uchi (Red Lake of Wilson), and English River subprovinces are 36 km, 34 km, and 30 km, respectively; the proportions of 'granitic' to'basaltic' crust is estimated by him to be 18 and 18 km, 20 and 14 km, and 22 and 8 km, respectively. This implies that the potassic Berens and Winnipeg River batholithic belts are underlain by more immediate and greater thicknesses of 'basaltic' rock than either of the sodic Uchi or mobile English River gneiss belts. The latter, however, was subjected to Abukuma-type metamorphism in response to high heat flows associated with proximity of the mantle source.

Crustal thicknesses for the Sachigo subprovince are not known; however, the repetitious granite-greenstone configurations of east-west trending elliptical granitic domes and intervening, bifurcating supracrustal belts is absent in the Berens, Uchi and English River subprovinces. The tectonics of this belt are readily rationalized by structural analysis of the Ramberg (1967) type. In this scheme the differential uplift between the Greenstone and plutonic domains is seen as the product of a static stress field in which the maximum compressive stress axis was horizonal. As the plutonic domes developed they mutually interfered and produced relatively straight intervening greenstone belts (Brown, 1973). In the Trout Lake area of Ontario, Ayres (1974) describes 'passive' emplacement of a batholith into an existing anticlinal supracrustal succession. In such a model, volcanism, plutonism, sedimentation and deformation are all very closely linked in time, and rocks of such activity are subjected to the same, continuous stress field throughout their formative stages (Park and Ermanovics, in press; Fyson et al., in press). This process of deformation, contemporaneous with plutonic development, is reflected in the observed complexity of gradational metamorphic fabrics and polyphase magmatic intrusions. The stress model also provides long periods of time within which uninterrupted magmatic differentiation may proceed without separation of the resulting fractions.

Discrete K-rich stocks in the southern Sachigo belt are few and small. However, large areas of gneissic granodiorite are characterized by aureoles of late microcline surrounding small stocks of granite (Ermanovics, 1973). Extending such K-metasomatism in time in a uniformitarian sense and under a continuous stress field, it is possible to conceive of granite formation in the Sachigo belt on a scale observed in the Berens belt. Vertical fault displacements of blocks within the large Sachigo subprovince (e.g., Wilson, 1971) should should make it possible to observe this potassic plutonism at various levels of development.

SUMMARY AND CONCLUSIONS

1) Tonalitic rocks, especially metamorphosed ones, tend to be spatially related to volcanic belts or volcanic belt relics. In some instances this probably is a function of the synclinal folding of greenstones in which

underlying rocks are transported adjacent to greenstone boundaries. However, the Rice Lake supracrustal rocks may occupy a graben interpreted as a fundamental dislocation in the crust (Wilson, 1971) along which initial basic lava, and subsequent tonalitic magma was emplaced (McRitchie, 1971a). Ultramafic and gabbroic rocks intrude volcanic successions, and metatonalitic rocks. This spatial relationship may imply that all three rock groups are linked to a common origin in the lower crust or upper mantle.

2) Normative compositions of metatonalite suites (early plutonic regimes) range from mid-dacite to basalt, and andesitic compositions are well developed (e.g., Figs. 4, 5, and 7). Normative compositions of the massive later plutonic regimes range from rhyolite to andesite, but rocks of andesitic composition are few (e.g., Figs. 6, 7, and 9).

3) The oldest rocks recognized in all four subprovinces under discussion here are metatonalites, generally biotite-bearing.

4) Metatonalites exhibit greater major element variations than do unmetamorphosed tonalites (e.g., Figs. 6 and 7). The explanation for this may lie in metamorphic differentiation but more likely may reflect the composite origin of some of these rocks (e.g., paragneiss versus orthogneiss). Graywackes derived from basaltic rocks may have compositions similar to mafic tonalite (Table 1), and in their metamorphosed state (paragneiss) may become indistinguishable from orthogneiss in their major element content.

5) The granitoid gneisses and intrusive rocks of the English River subprovince comprise three discrete and genetically distinct suites. The older granodioritic, tonalitic, and trondhjemitic gneisses have yielded 3.0 + Ga ages (Krogh, 1975) and are thought to represent a pre-Kenoran complex rather than an ultrametamorphic product of the paragneisses in the Ear Falls-Manigotagan gneiss belt, as was previously suggested (McRitchie, 1971a,b). Their paragenesis and crustal setting is such that a direct association with volcanic rocks appears to have been precluded. Their conformable and intimate association with the sediments is taken to indicate a pre-tectonic juxtaposition which may have been primary. The later intrusive suite of tonalites and granodiorites occurs within the Winnipeg River batholithic belt and Uchi subprovince but appears to be absent from the Pine Falls and Ear Falls-Manigotagan gneiss belts. The occurrence of volcanic rocks in the former group and predominantly sedimentary relics in the latter is taken to indicate a significant paragenetic association between the supracrustals and their respective intrusions. The third and youngest intrusions are late to post-tectonic granite batholiths (e.g., Lac du Bonnet, Tetu, and Launt Lakes granites), and stocks of the Turtle-Tooth Lakes suite.

6) The Uchi volcanic belt exhibits both sodic volcanism and plutonism; both prekinematic (pre-Kenoran) and late synkinematic plutons reflect trondhjemitic trends. The conclusion drawn from this observation is that the Uchi belt was inherently a sodic igneous subprovince of the Superior Province in Manitoba, possibly linked to the high heat flow of the mobile English River gneiss belt.

7) The best major element discriminator between the Uchi and Berens belts is the K_2O/Na_2O ratio, which is larger in the Berens belt by a factor of two. The Sr/Rb ratio probably reflects major element content of the rocks and is larger in the Uchi belt by a factor of 2. Andesitic compositions are more common in the Uchi than the Berens belt by a factor of 3.

8) The massive plutonic rocks that define the Berens subprovince, in which granites are areally numerous and well developed, are viewed as invading a sodic plutonic precursor (substrate). The youngest volcanic and plutonic rocks show well developed calc-alkaline trends leading to potassic compositions (Figs. 7, 8, and 9).

9) In the southern Sachigo subprovince volcanic rocks show calc-alkaline trends, whereas metaplutonic rocks have trondhjemitic affinities. Non-metamorphosed plutonic rocks, however, exhibit both potassic and sodic trends (Fig. 10). The chemical similarity and trends exhibited by the plutonic and metaplutonic rocks of the Sachigo subprovince may have an explanation in the thesis of a static stress field in which compositional and textural characteristics of the plutonic rocks were permitted to develop passively over a long period of time. This would allow magmas to differentiate without separation of resulting fractions, and consequently could result in complete gabbro-granite stocks as observed in at least two localities. In relating surface compositions to known crustal composition and thickness as in the other belts, the crust of the Sachigo belt may be inferred to be thinner but more 'basaltic' than that of the Berens block. The implication of this is that magmatic differentiation to greater volumes of granites (as in the Berens belt) has not been completed in the Sachigo belt, probably as a result of the cessation of tectonic stresses.

10) If depth and composition of crust are utilized as an explanation of the observed characteristics of the plutonic rock regimes, the Berens belt is underlain by a thicker crust and a thicker 'basalt' layer than either the Uchi or English River subprovinces. The English River subprovince with its 'mobile belt' characteristics is underlain by shallower crust and least 'basalt.' The Uchi belt occupies an intermediate position geographically, as well as in terms of crustal thickness and composition.

11) In its most simplistic conception the model envisaged here for plutonic

rocks is one in which potassic end-member compositions, resulting from differentiation of basaltic magmas via calc-alkaline differentiation trends, follow the development and emplacement of a sodic plutonic precursor. Rocks characterized by trondhjemitic trends appear to be among the earliest rocks developed (implying as yet undiscovered early volcanism) and may be related to a thicker 'granitic' crust. A thicker 'granitic' crust must mean higher temperatures and pressures in underlying 'basaltic' layers which in turn must yield higher temperature magmas represented by tonalite. It must be emphasized that large plutons do not invade the northern mobile sector of the English River gneiss belt despite its proximity to the mantle. Tectonic activity within the belt may thus be linked only indirectly to Kenoran batholith emplacement north and south of it.

In general, the plutonic rocks of the western Superior Province display secular evolution from Na-rich, mafic tonalites and granodiorites to tonalites and leucocratic granite. Normative andesite (plutonic) is more voluminous in the earlier regime of plutonic activity. This is in keeping with observations made in other Archean terrains (e.g., Glikson, 1978). Additionally, in a bipartite or tripartite scheme of Archean greenstone-pluton development (e.g., Goodwin, 1977; Glikson, 1976; Moorbath, 1976) and given the present sparse state of geochronological information, it is likely that some of the supracrustal rocks "developed in partly cratonized regions where primary greenstones were earlier intruded by sodic granites" (Glikson, 1976, p. 257).

ACKNOWLEDGMENTS

Jane Murray prepared all figures and helped in the organization of the manuscript in its early stages. W. N. Houston was responsible for converting the chemical data to its normative state and for providing computer-based plots from which the figures could be traced. W. R. A. Baragar and A. Davidson read the manuscript critically. All errors in fact or in interpretation which may exist are of course our own.

REFERENCES

Ayres, L. D., 1974. Geology of the Trout Lakes area, District of Kenora (Patricia Portion). Ontario Div. Mines, GR 113, 197 pp.

Barker, F. and Arth, J. G., 1976. Generation of trondhjemitic-tonalitic liquids and Archean bimodal trondhjemite-basalt suites. Geology, 4: 596-600.

Beakhouse, G. P., 1972. A subdivision of the western English River subprovince. Canadian Jour. Earth. Sci., 14: 1481-1489.

Breaks, F. W. and Bond, W. D., 1977a. English River subprovince (Marchington Lake area), District of Kenora. In Summary of Field Work, 1977, by the Geological Branch. Edited by V. G. Milne, O. L. White, R. B. Barlow, and J. A. Robertson. Ontario Geol. Surv., Misc. Paper, 75: 18-28.

Breaks, F. W. and Bond, W. D., 1977b. Manifestations of recent reconnaissance investigations in the English River subprovince, Northern Ontario Geotraverse Conf., 1977.

Brown, A., 1973. Vertical tectonics in the Superior Province. In Volcanism and Volcanic Rocks. Edited by I. F. Ermanovics. Geol. Surv. Canada, Open-File, 165: 153.

Butrenchuck, S., 1970. Metamorphic petrology of the Bird Lake area, southestern Manitoba. Unpub. MSc Thesis, Univ. Manitoba.

Campbell, F. H. A., 1971. Stratigraphy and sedimentation of part of the Rice Lake Group. In Geology and Geophysics of the Rice Lake Region, Southeastern Manitoba (Project Pioneer). Edited by W. D. McRitchie and W. Weber. Manitoba Mines Branch, Publ. 71-1: 135-188.

Church, N. and Wilson, H. D. B., 1971. Volcanology of the Wanipigow Lake-Beresford Lake area. In Geology and Geophysics of the Rice Lake Region, southeastern Manitoba (Project Pioneer). Edited by W. D. McRitchie and W. Weber. Manitoba Mines Branch, Publ. 71-1: 127-134.

Douglas, R. J. W., 1973. Geological provinces. In The National Atlas of Canada. Geol. Surv. Canada, Map 27-28.

Ermanovics, I. F., 1970a. Precambrian geology of Hecla-Carroll Lake map-area, Manitoba-Ontario. Geol. Surv. Canada Paper, 69-42, 33 pp.

Ermanovics, I. F., 1970b. Geology of Berens River-Deer Lake map-area, Manitoba and Ontario, and a preliminary analysis of tectonic variations in the area. Geol. Surv. Canada Paper, 70-29, 24 pp.

Ermanovics, I. F., 1971. "Granites," "granite gneiss" and tectonic variation of the Superior Province of southeastern Manitoba. In Geoscience Studies in Manitoba. Edited by A. C. Turnock. Geol. Assoc. Canada Spec. Paper, 91: 77-82.

Ermanovics, I. F., 1973. Precambrian geology of the Norway House and Grand Rapids map area. Geol. Surv. Canada Paper, 72-29, 27 pp.

Ermanovics, I. F. and Davison, W. L., 1976. The Pikwitonei granulites in relation to the northwestern Superior Province of the Canadian Shield. In The Early History of the Earth. Edited by F. B. Windley. John Wiley & Sons, London, England: 331-347.

360

Ermanovics, I. F. and Froese, E., in press. Metamorphism in the Superior Province of Manitoba. In Metamorphism in the Canadian Shield. Edited by J. A. Fraser and W. W. Heywood. Geol. Surv. Canada, Paper.

Fyson, W. K., Herd, R. K. and Ermanovics, I. F., in press. Diapiric structures and regional compression in an Archean greenstone belt, Island Lake, Manitoba. Canadian Jour. Earth Sci.

Glikson, A. Y., 1976. Stratigraphy and evolution of primary and secondary greenstones: significance of data from shields of the southern hemispere. In The Early History of the Earth. Edited by B. F. Windley. John Wiley & Sons, London, England: 257.

Glikson, A. Y., 1978. On the basement of Canadian greenstone belts. Geoscience Canada, 5: 3-17.

Goodwin, A. M., 1977. Archean basin-craton complexes and the growth of Precambrian shields. Canadian Jour. Earth Sci., 14: 2737-2759.

Hall, D. H. and Hajnal, Z., 1973. Deep seismic crustal studies in Manitoba. Seismological Soc. America Bull., 63: 885-910.

Harris, N., 1976. Evolution of the eastern Lac Seul region of the English River gneiss belt. Geotraverse Conference 1976, Report 18-1: 65-73.

Irvine, T. N. and Baragar, W. R. A., 1971. A guide to the chemical classification of the common volcanic rocks. Canadian Jour. Earth Sci., 8: 523-548.

Kilinc, I. A., 1972. Experimental study of partial melting of crustal rocks and formation of migmatites. 24th Internatl. Geol. Cong., Sec. 2, Petrology; 109-113.

Krogh, T. E. and Davis, G. L., 1971. Zircon U-Pb ages of Archean metavolcanic rocks of the Canadian Shield. In Annual Report of the Director, Geophysical Laboratory Yearbook, 70: 241-242.

Krogh, T. E., Davis, G. L., Harris, N. B. W. and Ermanovics, I. F., 1975. Isotopic ages in the estern Lac Seul region of the English River gneiss belt. In Annual Report of the Director, Geophysical Laboratory Yearbook, 74: 623-625.

Krogh, T. E., Ermanovics, I. F. and Davis, G. L., 1974. Two episodes of metamorphism and deformation in the Archean rocks of the Canadian Shield. In Annual Report of the Director, Geophysical Laboratory Yearbook, 73: 573-575.

Marmo, V., 1967. On the granite problem. Earth Science Reviews, 3: 7-29

Marr, J. M., 1971. Petrology of the Wannipigow River suite. In Geology and Geophysics of the Rice Lake Region, Southeastern Manitoba (Project Pioneer). Edited by W. D. McRitchie and W. Weber. Manitoba Mines Branch Pub., 71-1: 203-214.

McRitchie, W. D., 1971a. Petrology and environment of the acidic plutonic rocks of the Wanipigow-Winnipeg Rivers region, Southeastern Manitoba. In Geology and Geophysics of the Rice Lake Region, Southeastern Manitoba (Project Pioneer). Edited by W. D. McRitchie and W. Weber. Manitoba Mines Branch Pub. 71-1: 7-62.

McRitchie, W. D., 1971b. Metamorphism in the Precambrian of Manitoba; an outline. In Geoscience Studies in Manitoba. Edited by A.C. Turnock. Geol. Assoc. Canada Spec. Pap., 91, pp. 69.

McRitchie, W. D. and Weber, W., 1971. Metamorphism and deformation of the Manigotagan gneissic belt, Southeastern Manitoba. In Geology and Geophysics of the Rice Lake Region, Southestern Manitoba (Project Pioneer). Edited by W. D. McRitchie and W. Weber. Manitoba Mines Branch Pub., 71-1: 235-284.

Moorbath, S., 1976. Age and isotope constraints for the evolution of Archean crust. In The Early History of the Earth. Edited by B. F. Windley. John Wiley & Sons, London, England: 351-360.

Nockolds, S. R., 1954. Average chemical composition of some igneous rocks. Geol. Soc. Amer. Bull., 65: 1007-1032.

Nockolds, S. R. and Allen R., 1953. The geochemistry of some igneous rock series. Geochim. Cosmochim. Acta, 4: 105-142.

Park, R. G. and Ermanovics, I. F., in press. Tectonic evolution of two greenstone belts from the Superior Province in Manitoba. Canadian Jour. Earth Sci.

Paulus, G. E. and Turnock, A. C., 1971. Petrology of the Ross River Pluton, Manitoba. In Geology and Geophysics of the Rice Lake Region, Southeastern Manitoba (Project Pioneer). Edited by W. D. McRitchie and W. Weber. Manitoba Mines Branch Publ., 71-1: 215-226.

Ramberg, H., 1967. Gravity, deformation and the Earth's crust; as studied by centrifuged models. Academic Press, London, England, 214 pp.

Scoates, R. F. J., 1971. A description and classification of Manitoba ultramafic rocks. InGeology and Geophysics of the Rice Lake Region, Southeastern Manitoba (Project Pioneer). Edited by W. D. McRitchie and W. Weber. Manitoba Mines Branch Publ., 71-1: 89-96.

362

Stephenson, J. F., 1971.   Gold deposits of the Rice Lake-Beresford Lake greenstone belt.   In Geology and Geophysics of the Rice Lake Region, Southeastern Manitoba (Project Pioneer).   Edited by W. D. McRitchie and W. Weber. Manitoba Mines Branch Publ., 71-1: 337-374.

Streckeisen, A., 1976.   To each plutonic rock its proper name. Earth Science Reviews, 12: 1-33.

Turek, A., 1971.   Geochronology of the Rice Lake-Beresford Lake area.   In Geology and Geophysics of the Rice Lake Region, Southeastern Manitoba (Project Pioneer).   Edited by W. D. McRitchie and W. Weber.   Manitoba Mines Branch Publ., 71-1: 313-324.

Weber, W., 1971.   Geology of the Long Lake-Gem Lake area.   In Geology and Geophysics of the Rice Lake Region, Southeastern Manitoba (Project Pioneer).   Edited by W. D.McRitchie and W. Weber.   Manitoba Mines Branch Publ., 71-1: 63-106.

Weber, W. and Scoates, R. F. J., in press.   Archean and Proterozoic metamorphism in the northwestern Superior Province and the Churchill-Superior boundary, Manitoba.   In Metamorphism in theCanadian Shield. Edited by J. A. Fraser and W. W. Heywood. Geol. Surv. Canada, Paper.

Wilson, H. D. B., 1971.   The Superior Province in the Precambrian of Manitoba. In Geoscience Studies in Manitoba.   Edited by A. C. Turnock.   Geol. Assoc. Canada Spec. Pap., 91:L 41-50.

Chapter 11

THE OXYGEN-ISOTOPE GEOCHEMISTRY OF ARCHEAN GRANITOIDS

F. J. Longstaffe

ABSTRACT

The $\delta^{18}O$ values of Archean granitoids from northwestern Ontario range from 3.2 to 11.7 $^o/oo$, and reflect a myriad of magmatic, metamorphic, sedimentary, and alteration processes.

The Pakwash and Footprint gneisses contain some samples with $\delta^{18}O$ values of 6 to 7 $^o/oo$, much lower than measured for other portions of these rocks. The low $\delta^{18}O$ values probably reflect isotopic exchange with a low ^{18}O external reservoir (basalt?) during partial melting accompanying upper amphibolite facies metamorphism. The metasedimentary Group A Twilight gneiss, which has been metamorphosed to granulite facies, appears to have isotopically exchanged with the surrounding volumetrically more important metaigneous granitoids. Other less metamorphosed parts of these and other gneisses retain oxygen isotope compositions diagnostic of their clastic sedimentary (Pakwash gneiss) or metaigneous (and probably metaplutonic) protoliths (Footprint, Cedar Lake, and Kenora area gneisses).

Some Archean granitoids of lower metamorphic grades have also been depleted in ^{18}O but such occurrences are localized. Greenschist facies felsic metavolcanic rocks in the vicinity of the Burditt Lake granodiorite pluton have been chemically altered and depleted in ^{18}O, by interaction action with stock-derived magmatic fluids. Portions of the Jackfish Lake Complex granodiorites also have low $\delta^{18}O$ values due to exchange with low ^{18}O fluids (probably ground waters). The chemical composition of these rocks, including their LREE abundances also have been affected by this activity.

Unaltered portions of the plutonic Jackfish Lake Complex range in $\delta^{18}O$ from 6.4 to 9.2 $^o/oo$, higher values accompanying the progressive differentiation of the Complex from dioritic to granodioritic compositons.

The unaltered Archean metaplutonic granitoids of tonalitic to granitic composition have $\delta^{18}O$ values of 7.3 to 9.3 $^o/oo$, somewhat lower than Phanerozoic analogues. Such results probably reflect the more juvenile nature of the sialic material added to the continental crust during this period of Archean crustal evolution.

Most Archean granitoids while not grossly disturbed, are nevertheless out of oxygen isotopic equilibrium. This disequilibrium is indicated by variable and usually large quartz-microcline fractionations, large quartz-biotite fractionations, and, for many of the gneisses, low $\delta^{18}O$ values for biotite (less than 3 $^O/oo$). Quartz-magnetite temperatures calculated for the Kenora area gneisses provide a reasonably good minimum estimate of the real temperatures achieved near the culmination of metamorphism; the low ($400^{O}C$) quartz-biotite "temperatures" calculated for the gneisses, however, reflect only the preferential isotopic exchange of biotite (relative to quartz and magnetite), most likely with low ^{18}O fluids.

INTRODUCTION

The purpose of this contribution is to interpret oxygen isotope data obtained for Archean granitoids ('granitoid' is used in a broad sense to refer to holocrystalline quartz-bearing rocks. Specific plutonic rock names used herein conform to the recommendations of the IUGS (1973) commission on rock nomenclature) from northwestern Ontario in terms of various magmatic, sedimentary, metamorphic and/or alteration processes by which these rocks have been affected.

Special attention is afforded to Archean granitoid gneisses. The hypothesis that oxygen isotope ratios, in conjunction with other geological and chemical data, can provide information concerning the protolith of these gneisses, is developed and constrained.

Interpretation of the oxygen isotope variations observed for Archean granitoids requires consideration of the following problems:

1. What is the observed range of $\delta^{18}O$ values for Archean granitoids?

2. To what extent are the $\delta^{18}O$ values of Archean granitoids a function of magmatic differentiation at high temperature, sedimentary processes (during the formation of a paragneiss protolith, for example), metamorphism, and/or alteration?

3. Are Archean granitoids in oxygen isotopic equilibrium: What importance can be attached to oxygen isotope temperatures derived from mineral pairs for such rocks?

Some preliminary replies to these questions are attempted to the pages that follow.

ANALYTICAL METHODS

Oxygen isotope analyses were performed on 12 to 25 mg rock and mineral powders. Oxygen extractions were performed using BrF_5 (Clayton and Mayeda, 1963). O_2 was converted to CO_2 by reaction with a hot graphite rod (Taylor and Epstein, 1962). Mass spectrometric analyses of CO_2 were performed using a dual inlet, collecting Nier-type mass spectrometer. Yields obtained for mineral samples and standards were $100\pm2\%$

The experimental results are reported in the usual δ notation relative to Standard Mean Ocean Water (SMOW) (Craig, 1961):

$$(\text{per mil}) = \frac{R(\text{sample}) - R(\text{standard})}{R(\text{standard})} \; 1000; \quad R = {}^{18}O/{}^{16}O.$$

$\delta^{18}O$ values have been calculated relative to an internal calcite standard (GCS), which has been calibrated relative to NBS-20 assuming $\delta^{18}O$ of NBS-20 = -4.14 $^o/oo$ on the PDB scale, $^{18}CO_2$ of PDB = 0.22 $^o/oo$ relative to SMOW (Craig, 1957, 1961), and an $^{18}CO_2$ fractionation factor between CO_2 and H_2O at 25^oC of 1.0412 (O'Neil et al., 1975). Many of the unknowns have been analyzed in duplicate; reproductibility is about ±0.1-0.2 $^o/oo$.

The oxygen isotope fractionation between two mineral phases A and B is given by

$$\triangle_{AB} = \delta_A - \delta_B = 1000 \ \text{in}\, \alpha_{AB}\% \quad \text{for } \triangle < 10$$

where α is the oxygen isotope fractionation factor between A and B.

Chemical analyses were performed by x-ray fluorescence using a Phillips PW 1450 automatic sequential machine. Agreement with accepted rock standard values (Abbey, 1975) is good (Longstaffe, 1978).

LOCATIONS OF STUDY AREAS

Most of this discussion will be focused upon four groups of gneisses (Fig. 1). These are:

A. The Footprint gneiss, a quartz dioritic to granitic gneiss located at the western margin of the Rainy Lake batholith, within the Wabigoon granite-greenstone belt.

B. The Cedar Lake-Clay Lake area gneiss, tonalitic to granodioritic rocks from the predominantly plutonic southern portion of the English River gneiss belt.

C. The Kenora area gneisses and associated metamorphosed plutonic granitoids, also located within the southern portion of the English River gneiss belt.

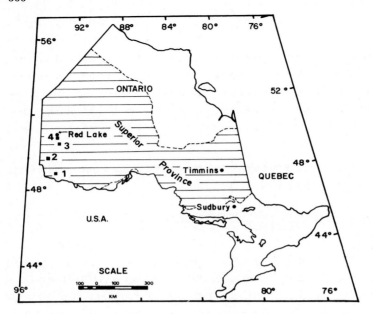

Figure 1.--Locations of study areas: 1. Burditt Lake-Lake Despair area, Wabigoon granite-greenstone belt (Footprint gneiss, Jackfish Lake Complex, Northwest Bay Complex, Burditt Lake pluton, Burditt Lake felsic metavolcanic rocks, Manomin Lake felsic schists); 2. Kenora area; 3. Cedar Lake-Clay Lake area; 4. Pakwash Lake area.

D.   The Pakwash gneiss, a banded paragneiss and migmatite associated with a major supracrustal sequence located in the northern portion of the English River gneiss belt.

Plutonic granitoids and felsic metavolcanic rocks from the Wabigoon granite-greenstone belt were also analyzed; these include the Burditt Lake-Lake Despair area samples (Jackfish Lake Complex, Northwest Bay Complex, Burditt Lake pluton, the Burditt Lake felsic metavolcanics, and the Manomin Lake felsic schists) (Fig. 1).

THE OXYGEN ISOTOPIC COMPOSITION OF ARCHEAN GRANITOIDS--A REVIEW

Oxygen isotope studies of Archean granitoids have been reported by Fourcade (1972), Fourcade and Javoy (1973), Viswanathan (1974a, b), Taylor and Magaritz (1975), Barker et al. (1976a, b), Perry et al. (1976), Shieh and Schwarcz (1977), and Taylor (1977).   In addition, some of the results presented in this paper have been cursorily discussed by Longstaffe et al. (1976a, b; 1977a, b, c), and Longstaffe and Schwarcz (1977).   Shieh and Schwarcz (1974) and Shieh et al. (1976) have analyzed somewhat similar rocks of Proterozoic age.   Wilson et al. (1970) and Wilson and Green (1971) measured the oxygen isotope ratios of some Archean and Proterozoic mafic granulites. Some of these studies provide information concerning the effects of magmatism, metamorphism, and alteration upon the oxygen isotope compositions of Archean granitoids.

Fourcade and Javoy (1973) reported $\delta^{18}O$ values of 5.5 to 7.8 ^{o}/oo for pelitic to granitic Archean granulites of detrital origin from the Algerian Sahara. Such values are lower than observed for most plutonic granitoids (7-10 ^{o}/oo; Taylor, 1977), and far lower than usual for paragneisses such as those described by Garlick and Epstein (1967).

Fourcade and Javoy (1973) developed two end member hypotheses of their results. The first model required the granulites to isotopically exchange with low ^{18}O rocks of the upper mantle during high-grade metamorphism. Because of both the absence of large-scale partial melting of the In Ouzzal rocks and the preservation of high and concordant oxygen isotope temperatures, the exchange medium was suggested to be CO_2 outgassing from the mantle rather than water. According to the second model, the sedimentary protolith of the granulites was derived from acid rocks with $\delta^{18}O$ values near that of basalt. Such compositions presumably could be attained by differentiation of the acid rocks from basalt at high temperatures. The erosion and sedimentation of the rocks then occurred too rapidly to affect the isotopic composition of the detritus.

Variations of these two hypotheses have been used to explain other occurrences of Archean and Proterozoic low ^{18}O granitoids. Shieh and Schwarcz (1974) analyzed two groups of Proterozoic Grenville rocks from Ontario. Group A contained upper amphibolite to granulite facies migmatites, paragneisses and concordantly emplaced granitic gneisses, and ranged in $\delta^{18}O$ from 5 to 9 ^{o}/oo. Group B was composed of lower-grade metasedimentary rocks and high level plutons that ranged in $\delta^{18}O$ from 9 to 17 ^{o}/oo. Shieh and Schwarcz (1974) proposed that large-scale isotopic exchange with a mafic reservoir located in the lower crust or upper mantle had depleted the Group A rocks in ^{18}O during migmatization. Other examples of ^{18}O depletion accompanying the metaigneous and metasedimentary rocks have also been reported by Hoernes and Friedrichsen (1974), Black (1974), Dontsova (1970), and Taylor and Coleman (1968), although not all of these studies link the exchange episode specifically to migmatization.

Barker et al. (1976a, b) reported $\delta^{18}O$ values for Proterozoic and Archean granitoids and their metamorphosed equivalents. The $\delta^{18}O$ values of apparently undisturbed (unaltered) samples ranged from 4.9 to 8.6 ^{o}/oo (recalculated from Barker et al., 1976b, to SMOW = 0 ^{o}/oo). Specifically, tonalitic gneisses from South Africa had $\delta^{18}O$ values of 5.8 to 7.7 ^{o}/oo. Barker and his co-workers have proposed high temperature origins for tonalitic Archean rocks by differentiation from hydrous primitive rocks of basaltic composition; Barker et al. (1976b) suggested that $\delta^{18}O$ values of 5 to 7 $^{o}/oo$, such as observed for most of the South African gneisses, support such an interpretation.

Taylor (1977) and Taylor and Magaritz (1975) found that some South African Archean granitoids had oxygen isotope ratios that were somewhat lower than measured for most granitoids associated with Phanerozoic batholiths. Except for a few Archean gneisses of sedimentary origin, no samples had $\delta^{18}O$ values greater than 9.0 $^{o}/oo$. Taylor (1977), suggested that these $^{18}O/^{16}O$ ratios reflected formation of the granitoids from primitive low ^{18}O crust, or else directly from the mantle.

The difference process envisaged by Taylor (1977) to produce granitoids of 7 to 9 $^{o}/oo$ must differ in some aspect from that pictured by Barker et al. (1976b) to produce similar rocks with $\delta^{18}O$ values of 5 to 7 $^{o}/oo$. One possible solution to this dilemma may have been provided by Perry et al. (1976; in press); they reported $\delta^{18}O$ values of 7.9-9.0 $^{o}/oo$ for tonalitic to granodioritic gneisses from Greenland. Perry et al. (in press) suggest that basaltic rocks enriched in ^{18}O by submarine weathering were subsequently buried (subducted?) and then partially melted to produce an equally enriched sialic protolith. This parent rock was subsequently metamorphosed to form the gneiss. Thus the initial isotopic composition of the basaltic source rocks possibly melted to produce Archean siliceous liquids may have varied.

The lowest $^{18}O/^{16}O$ ratios observed for Archean granitoids (less than 3 $^{o}/oo$) appear unrelated to magmatic or metamorphic processes. Taylor and Magaritz (1975) and Taylor (1977) have attributed such results for some South African granitoids to interaction with meteoric waters. Longstaffe et al. (1977b) have reported a few similar results, discussed in more detail elsewhere in this report.

$\delta^{18}O$ RESULTS FOR GRANITOIDS FROM NORTHWESTERN ONTARIO

The $\delta^{18}O$ rock results for Archean granitoid gneisses from northwestern Ontario are given in Table 1 and illustrated by Figure 2. The oxygen isotope ratios of these rocks range from 5.9 to 11.7 $^{o}/oo$; however, only samples from the Pakwash gneiss have $\delta^{18}O$ values higher than those measured for unaltered Archean plutonic granitoids, also from northwestern Ontario.

Most of the $\delta^{18}O$ values for the Footprint, Clay Lake, Cedar Lake, Twilight (not to be confused with the Proterozoic Twilight Gneiss of Colorado, Barker et al., 1976a) and Kenora area gneisses lie within the I to H_2 categories defined by Taylor (1968) for granitic rocks (see Fig. 2). The $\delta^{18}O$ values measured for

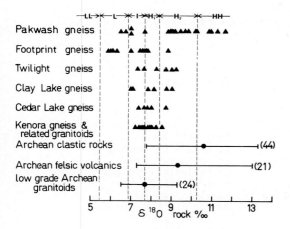

Figure 2.--Oxygen isotope whole-rock values for Archean gneisses from northwestern Ontario. The mean and range of $\delta^{18}O$ values for Archean greenschist facies clastic metasedimentary rocks and felsic metavolcanic rocks (Longstaffe and Schwarcz, 1977) also are shown as well as results for unaltered Archean plutonic granitoids (Jackfish Lake Complex dioritic rocks not included). Values in parentheses indicate the number of samples. The oxygen isotope classification scheme (LL, L, I, H_1, H_2, HH) is from Taylor (1968).

the least metamorphosed plutonic rocks are also no higher than 9.3 ^{o}/oo (Table 2, Fig. 3). Thus these Archean granitoids are generally less enriched in ^{18}O than similar rocks from the Phanerozoic batholiths of the western U.S.A., which have oxygen isotopic composition concentrated in the H_2 group (Taylor, 1968, 1977).

$^{18}O/^{16}O$ ratios that lie in the LL-L groups of Taylor (1968) include some diorites and granodiorites from the Jackfish Lake Complex and some samples from the Pakwash and Footprint gneisses (Figs. 2 and 3). The low values of the diorites are not surprising given the mafic composition of these rocks (Longstaffe et al., 1977a); the low ^{18}O granodiorites of the Jackfish Lake Complex have been produced by exchange with ground waters. Of immediate interest are the low ^{18}O rocks from the Pakwash (6.53-6.99 ^{o}/oo) and Footprint (5.93-7.00 ^{o}/oo) gneisses; such values are similar to those reported by Fourcade and Javoy (1973), Shieh and Schwarcz (1974) and Barker et al. (1977b).

The Oxygen Isotope Geochemistry of the Pakwash gneiss

The migmatized metasedimentary gneisses (including the Pakwash gneiss) located within the northern portion of the English River gneiss belt have been recently discussed by Beakhouse (1974a, b; 1977) and Breaks and Bond (1977). The Pakwash gneiss is composed of plagioclase, quartz, biotite, garnet and

TABLE 1 : $\delta^{18}O$ whole-rock values, Archean gneisses, northwestern Ontario

Locality	$\delta^{18}O^{o}/oo$	Rock Type

LAKE DESPAIR, WABIGOON GRANITE-GREENSTONE BELT

Footprint Gneiss

F110	8.85	granitic gneiss
F103	7.79	tonalitic gneiss
F10	7.59	trondhjemitic gneiss
F73	7.72	granodioritic gneiss
F152	7.45	trondhjemitic gneiss
F98	7.57	granodioritic gneiss
F99	7.00±0.16 (2)	tonalitic gneiss
F150	6.31	quartz dioritic gneiss
F7	6.09	tonalitic gneiss
F151	6.05	trondhjemitic gneiss
F149	5.93	granodioritic gneiss

CEDAR LAKE-CLAY LAKE, SOUTHERN PORTION, ENGLISH RIVER GNEISS BELT

1. Twilight Gneiss

309 Group A	7.33±0.32 (2)	granulite facies paragniess
377 Group A	8.29±0.09 (2)	granulite facies paragneiss
535 Group A	8.73	granulite facies paragneiss (?)
448 Group B	9.03	granulite facies paragneiss (?)
538 Group B	9.25	granulite facies paragneiss (?)

2. Clay Lake Gneiss

513A	7.02	granulite facies enderbite
433	7.06	granulite facies enderbite
553	7.87	granulite facies enderbite
516	9.03	granulite facies alaskite
458	8.15	granulite facies alaskite
367	8.76	granulite facies alaskite

3. Cedar Lake Gneiss

432	8.72	amphibolite facies granitoid gneiss
24	7.37	amphibolite facies granitoid gneiss
62	7.63	amphibolite facies granitoid gneiss
350	8.01	amphibolite facies granitoid gneiss
560	7.81	amphibolite facies granitoid gneiss

*Estimated from mineral $\delta^{18}O$ and modal data

The following persons provided samples:

Cedar Lake-Clay Lake area:		C. Westerman
Kenora area	:	C. Gower
Pakwash Lake (P-series samples)	:	G. Beakhouse

TABLE 1, continued

Locality	$\delta^{18}O$ $^o/oo$	Rock Type

KENORA AREA, SOUTHERN PORTION, ENGLISH RIVER GNEISS BELT

G106B	7.59	biotite tonalitic gneiss
G110A	7.39	leucogranitoid associated with tonalitic gneiss
G350A	7.96	biotite tonalitic gneiss
G350B	8.02	granitic pegmatoid gneiss
G886	8.26	granitic pegmatoid gneiss
G715	7.51	Melick tonalite
G596A	7.85	Melick tonalite
G135	7.54	Dalles grey granodiorite
G145	7.26	Dalles pink granite
G835B	8.56	leucogranitoid associated with amphibolite

PAKWASH LAKE, NORTHERN PORTION, ENGLISH RIVER GNEISS BELT

L37	8.97	plagioclase-quartz-biotite-garnet layered metagreywacke
P178	10.95	plagioclase-quartz-biotite-layered metagreywacke
P249A	9.18	plagioclase-quartz-biotite-garnet layered metagreywacke
P61A	11.31	plagioclase-quartz-biotite-garnet layered metagreywacke
P164	9.04	plagioclase-quartz-biotite-garnet layered metagreywacke
P205B	9.83	plagioclase-quartz-biotite-garnet layered metagreywacke
P202A	11.69	plagioclase-quartz-biotite-garnet layered metagreywacke
P306A	10.93	plagioclase-quartz-biotite-garnet layered metagreywacke
P1097	8.83	plagioclase-quartz-biotite-garnet layered metagreywacke (?)
P52B	10.21	plagioclase-quartz-biotite-layered metagreywacke
P181	9.11	plagioclase-quartz-biotote-garnet layered metagreywacke
P80	10.23	plagioclase-quartz-biotite-garnet layered metagreywacke
L42	9.46	plagioclase-quartz-biotite-garnet layered metagreywacke
L40	6.75	migmatized metagreywacke
L44A	6.99	migmatized metagreywacke
L44B	6.53	migmatized metagreywacke
L43	7.68	leucosome: quartz-plagioclase microcline-muscovite pegmatoid
L45B	6.99	migmatized metagreywacke
L45A	9.70	migmatized metapelite
L41	10.0*	pink pegmatite dike

TABLE 2 : $\delta^{18}O$ whole rock values, Archean plutonic rocks, Burditt Lake-Lake
Despair area, northwestern Ontario

Locality		$\delta^{18}O^O/_{OO}$	Rock Type
Burditt Lake Pluton			
G53	(south lobe)	8.23	muscovite-biotite granodiorite
G56	(south lobe)	8.34	muscovite-biotite granodiorite
442-10	(south lobe)	7.76	biotite-hornblende granodiorite
441-2	(south lobe)	8.04	muscovite-biotite granodiorite
G21	(north lobe)	8.55	biotite-hornblende granodiorite
G22	(north lobe)	8.91	biotite-hornblende granodiorite
G8	(north lobe)	9.17	biotite-hornblende granodiorite
G51	(south lobe)	9.27	fine-grained granodiorite
G78	(south lobe)	8.84	massive aplite
Northwest Bay Complex			
F129		7.50 ± 0.24 (3)	granite
Jackfish Lake Complex			
F139		6.37	meladiorite
F146		6.68	meladiorite
F84		6.99	diorite
F21		6.86 ± 0.17 (2)	diorite
D8		6.96	diorite
F131		7.19	diorite
F144		7.33 ± 0.06 (2)	diorite
F135		7.54	monzodiorite
F82		7.72	monzodiorite
F133		7.26	quartz monzodiorite
F94		7.54	leucodiorite
F24		8.08 ± 0.16 (2)	leuco quartz diorite
F113		7.61	granodiorite
F118		7.77	granodiorite
F26		7.48	granodiorite
D1		8.17	granodiorite
F3		8.24	granodiorite
F40		6.58*	granodiorite
F37		5.41*	granodiorite
F67		3.16*	granodiorite
F46		7.10	Na-syenite
F28		6.49	Na-syenite
F86		7.21	albitite dike
F23		9.23	quartz-plagioclase dike

* altered

Samples from the Burditt Lake pluton were provided by D. Birk.

sometimes muscovite, sillimanite, magnetite, and cordierite. Variations in biotite and garnet contents help to define a primary layering which Beakhouse (1974b) has interpreted as an interlayered sequence of metagraywacke, shaly metagraywacke and metaargillite. Sedimentary structures are not well preserved, but Beakhouse (1977) has observed slump structures, graded bedding, and small-scale cross-laminations.

The Pakwash gneiss has been metamorphosed to middle to upper amphibolite facies and partially melted. Breaks and Bond (1977) have classified similar rocks from the area according to their leucosome/paleosome ratios; the two groups examined in this study are the 'protometatexites' (leucosome/paleosome <0.1), for which the leucosome is confined to lenses and pods within the peletic layers of the gneiss (L37, L42, and the P-series; Table 1), and the 'metatexites' (leucosome/paleosome = 0.1 to 0.6), which are characterized by stromatic banding of metagraywacke paleosomes with continuous bands of leucosome (L40, L44A, L44B, L45A, L45B). In this latter group, some leucosome is also discordantly injected into the metagraywacke paleosome.

The $\delta^{18}O$ rock results for the metagraywacke paleosome of the Pakwash gneiss range from 6.5 to 11.7 ^{O}/oo (Table 1, Fig. 2). The protometatexites (8.8-11.7 ^{O}/oo) have the highest oxygen isotope ratios reported for Archean gneisses. These values overlap the range reported by Longstaffe and Schwarcz (1977) for

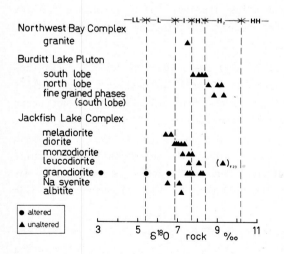

Figure 3.-- $\delta^{18}O$ whole-rock values, plutonic rocks from the Burditt Lake-Lake Despair area, Wabigoon granite-greenstone belt. The low $\delta^{18}O$ values of some of the Jackfish Lake Complex granodiorites are due to alteration. The somewhat lower values of the Na-syenite from the Complex may reflect magmatic processes or isotopic exchange with adjacent mafic metavolcanic country rocks.

Archean greenschist facies clastic metasedimentary rocks, and therefore support a sedimentary origin for this unit. However, an altered metavolcanic protolith cannot be ruled on the basis of the isotopic data alone.

The metagraywacke layers analyzed from both groups of the Pakwash gneiss have compositions similar to many chemically mature clastic sediments. Moore and Dennen (1970) and Dennen and Moore (1971) pointed out that chemically mature clastic sediments have Al/Fe ratios of about 1.9±0.4; the Si contents

$$\text{(expressed as Si}' = \frac{Si}{Si + Al + Fe} \text{ X 100)}$$

vary because of hydraulic sorting processes. The Pakwash metagraywacke paleosomes have compositions that plot within this field (Fig. 4), unlike most of the other gneisses investigated. More mature Archean clastic metasedimentary rocks from northern Ontario also have Al/Fe of about 1.9, and are enriched in ^{18}O (Longstaffe, 1978). However, very immature Archean metagraywackes, such as those from Kakagi Lake, can have higher values; the upper limit observed by Longstaffe (1978) is indicated on Figure 4.

Shaw (1972) proposed a major element discriminant function (D.F.) for gneisses of igneous and sedimentary origins. Values of D.F. less than zero indicated a sedimentary protolith and values greater than zero an igneous parent. Values of this function for many of the gneisses analyzed are plotted versus their $\delta^{18}O$ values, after the fashion of Shieh et al. (1976), on Figure 5. Unlike most of the other granitoids studied, the data points for the Pakwash metagraywacke layers cluster near or within the sedimentary field, regardless of their isotopic composition.

It is clear, therefore, at least in this case, that the low ^{18}O rocks from the Pakwash gneiss have not been formed by magmatic processes. The high $\delta^{18}O$ values of the protometatexites indicate that enrichment in ^{18}O did not occur during sedimentary processes (Longstaffe and Schwarcz, 1977), contrary to the second hypothesis of Fourcade and Javoy (1973). I suggest that the Pakwash metatexites were depleted in ^{18}O during high-grade metamorphism and partial melting. The presence of a silicate melt and/or fluids in the metatexites may have facilitated isotopic exchange with some external low ^{18}O reservoir at high temperatures.

Oxygen isotope results for minerals from the Pakwash gneiss reflect the isotopic variations observed in the rock samples (Table 3, Fig. 6). Excepting the (unexplained) $\delta^{18}O$ quartz value of L37, the two samples of unmigmatized (protometatexite) metagraywacke paleosome (L42, L37) have much higher $^{18}O/^{16}O$ ratios than comparable minerals from the metatexites (L40, L44A, L44B). The leucosome (L43), associated with the migmatized metagraywackes, has similar $\delta^{18}O$ mineral values. However, the mineral phases are not grossly out of oxygen

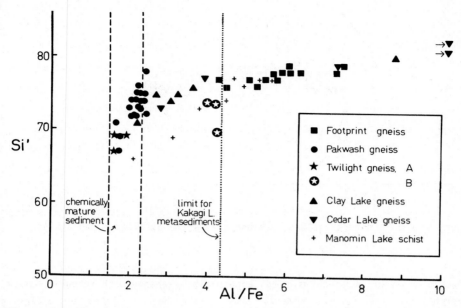

Figure 4.--Normalized Si (Si') versus Al/Fe diagram (Dennen and Moore, 1971) for some Archean gneisses. The field for chemically mature clastic rocks is from Dennen and Moore (1971); Al/Fe>10.

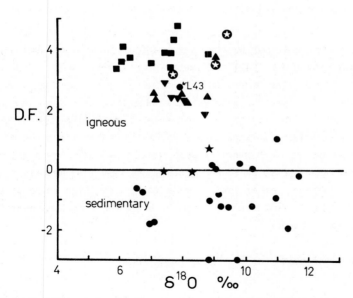

Figure 5.--Discriminant function (D.F.) versus $\delta^{18}O$ for some Archean gneisses. The discriminant function is from Shaw (1972):

$$D.F. = 10.44 - 0.21\ SiO_2 - 0.32\ Fe_2O_3\ t - 0.98\ MgO + 0.55\ CaO + 1.46\ Na_2O + 0.54\ K_2O$$

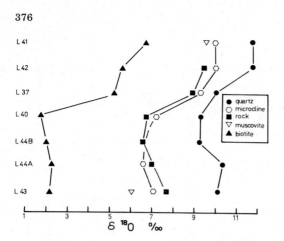

Figure 6.-- $\delta^{18}O$ mineral values, Pakwash gneiss and associated pegmatoids.

isotopic equilibrium, such as often accompanies exchange with meteoric waters. Nevertheless, the various mineral phases have been depleted by differing amounts; the micas have experienced the greatest average loss of ^{18}O (3.9%/oo), followed by the feldspars (2.8 %/oo) and then by quartz (1.5 %/oo). O'Neil and Chappell (1977) and Cole and Ohmoto (1976) have indicated that the relative exchange rates of biotite and feldspar can depend upon the composition of the exchange medium.

High $\delta^{18}O$ values were measured for two samples from an area of dominantly low ^{18}O rocks, pink pegmatite (L41) and metapelite (L45A), with which the pegmatite is in contact. The high $^{18}O/^{18}O$ ratio of the pegmatite, which discordantly intrudes the low ^{18}O metatexites, suggests that this rock was formed by partial melting of isotopically undepleted metasedimentary rocks. Perhaps isotopically undepleted paragneiss was partially melted after the major period of migmatization at a higher crustal level than the metatexites. Because this melting occurred at shallower depths, the resulting magma did not re-equilibrate with a deeper seated low ^{18}O reservoir. The high value of the metapelitic rock probably resulted from isotopic exchange with the pegmatite during the latter's emplacement.

The Oxygen Isotope Geochemistry of the Footprint gneiss

The tonalitic to granitic Footprint gneiss, like the Pakwash gneiss, contains granitoids with low $\delta^{18}O$ values (5.9-7.0 %/oo), as well as rocks of isotopically more normal compositions. As is the case for the Packwash gneiss, there are no significant chemical differences between the two groups of

TABLE 3 : Oxygen isotope mineral results for Pakwash gneiss and
associated pegmatoids

	Quartz	Microcline	$\delta^{18}O\ ^o/oo$ Plagioclase	Muscovite	Biotite
L41[1]	11.79±0.05	10.02±0.01		9.54	6.69±0.07
L42	11.81±0.07	10.02±0.08			5.57±0.17
L37	10.05		9.32±0.007 An20		5.20
L40[3]	9.30±0.03		7.28±0.01 An20		1.63±0.19
L44B[3]	9.22±0.06				1.95±0.26
L44A[3]	10.33±0.02	6.52±0.13			2.17±0.19
L43[2]	10.11±0.02	7.09±0.25		5.59	2.10±0.37

Errors given as deviation from mean of duplicate analyses

[1]   discordant pink pegmatite
[2]   leucosome, white pegmatoid
[3]   migmatized

TABLE 4 : Oxygen isotope mineral results, Footprint Gneiss

	Quartz	Microcline	$\delta^{18}O\ ^o/oo$ Epidote	Muscovite	Magnetite
F110	10.59±0.10	7.99±0.17	5.74	2.52±0.08	0.18±0.29
F73	10.64±0.13	6.63±0.13		2.50±0.26	±
F98	9.76±0.17	7.08±0.27	3.91±0.10	1.36±0.12	0.00±0.07
F103	9.65±0.12	7.57±0.25	4.66±0.16	2.04±0.25	0.24±0.49
F10	9.74±0.15	7.65±0.11	4.45±0.01	2.34	
F152	8.86	8.14		4.49	
F99[1]	8.84±0.12	8.55		1.69±0.09	
F150[1]	8.66±0.03	5.59±0.02	3.63	0.20±0.23	0.61
F7[1]	8.97±0.02	6.65		2.70	
F151[1]	9.62±0.25	7.30±0.20	2.87	2.18	-1.81±0.10
F149[1]	8.86±0.00	7.05±0.10	4.59	1.89±0.03	-0.09±0.02

[1]   'migmatized'
[2]   plagioclase (An24)
Errors given as deviation from mean of duplicate analyses

samples. The metaigneous nature of the Footprint gneiss is beyond doubt (Figs. 4 and 5; Longstaffe, 1978; Longstaffe et al., 1977a).

The $^{18}O/^{16}O$ ratios of minerals from the Footprint gneiss also decrease in a parallel fashion to the rock ratios (Table 4), although admittedly there is some scatter in the data. Again, however, with the exception of magnetite from F150, all of the phases from a given sample have oxygen isotope compositions that decrease in the expected order for unaltered granitoids--quartz, feldspar, biotite, magnetite (Taylor, 1968; Taylor and Epstein, 1962).

The Footprint gneiss is deformed, contains migmatized mafic ampibolite enclaves, and has locally developed stromatic, phlebitic, and ptygmatic structures. These features suggest that the rocks have undergone metamorphism to middle to upper amphibolite facies, a conclusion that cannot be reached from the relatively uninformative quartz-plagioclase-microcline-biotite mineralogy.

A quantitative division between the gneiss and migmatite is extremely difficult to make for individual samples. However, re-examination of those localities containing low ^{18}O rocks indicates that such areas contain abundant quartz-microcline-plagioclase bands. These 1-5 cm wide bands occur concordantly interlayered with narrower (0.5-2.0 cm) biotite-rich melanosomes and quartz-plagioclase-biotite paleosomes. The 'unmigmatized' gneiss is also laminated, but its layering is less well defined. Unlike the 'migmatites,' the contacts between the layers are quite diffuse. An increase in grain size and the emergence of distinct layering is characteristic of other areas where tonalitic gneisses are transformed into migmatites (Kays, 1976).

Because of these features, it seems likely that the low ^{18}O rocks within the Footprint gneiss are also the product of isotopic exchange accompanying migmatization, rather than primary magmatic processes.

The Nature of the Low ^{18}O Reservoir

If the isotopic depletion of the Pakwash and Footprint gneisses is caused by exchange during partial melting associated with high-grade metamorphism, some limits can be placed upon the nature of the hypothetical exchange reservoir.

Firstly, the exchange should occur at temperatures of at least 650 to $700^{o}C$, the minimum melting temperature for rocks similar in composition to the Footprint and Pakwash gneisses.

Secondly, the exchange reservoir should be capable of producing similar final isotopic compositions in both groups of gneisses (5.9 to $7.0^{o}/oo$), despite the initial differences in isotopic composition between the Pakwash ($8.83-11.69^{o}/oo$) and Footprint ($7.45-8.85^{o}/oo$) units. The specific nature of the isotopic exchange medium is unknown; fluid (mostly water?) associated with partial melting is a likely candidate.

These conditions require that the exchange medium be in high temperature isotopic equilibrium with an oxygen isotope reservoir that is large compared to the gneisses (reservoir/gneiss ratio must be greater than about 2) and that the reservoir have a $\delta^{18}O$ value of about $6^{o}/oo$ (Longstaffe, 1978). The only common rock types with such $\delta^{18}O$ values are mafic and ultramafic rocks. The most ubiquitous of these in Archean terrains is basalt. One might speculate, therefore, that the gneisses have re-equilibrted during partial melting with fluids whose isotopic composition is controlled by (underlying) basalt.

Other Possibilities for ^{18}O Depletion.

Two other possible origins for the low ^{18}O gneisses merit consideration; these are exchange with meteoric waters and interaction with sea-water.

Taylor and his co-investigators (see summary by Taylor, 1974, 1977) have documented the depletion of ^{18}O and D in granitoids by interaction with heated ground waters. Magaritz and Taylor (1976) showed that meteoric water can affect granitic rocks on a batholith size scale; however, Taylor (1976, 1977) concluded that while meteoric water circulatory systems had been established in most batholiths, the bulk of such rocks, except perhaps for the D/H ratios of hydrous minerals, were isotopically undisturbed by such processes.

Because of recrystallization, petrographic data is of little use in the detection of meteoric water-related alteration of gneisses that occurred prior to the last period of metamorphism. However, other factors suggest that such activity has not significantly affected the $^{18}O/^{16}O$ rock ratios of the Footprint and Pakwash gneisses. Firstly, no $\delta^{18}O$ values less than 5.9 $^{o}/oo$ have been measured; secondly, the admittedly small sample population shows no systematic geographical distribution such as is characteristic of meteoric water-rock interaction zones (Taylor, 1977; Forester and Taylor, 1977); finally, almost all of the mineral phases have oxygen isotope fractionations (Δ) that are of the normal sense.

The juvenile and unstable nature of the Archean crust makes it impossible to exclude, a priori, the possibility that seawater may have percolated through portions of the Footprint and Pakwash gneisses at some stage in their history. This seems unlikely, however, for the major, minor, and trade element compositions of these rocks do not indicate any differences between the depleted and undepleted samples. Chemical changes would be expected had seawater alteration occurred.

The Oxygen Isotope Geochemistry of the Cedar Lake-Clay Lake area: Possible ^{18}O Depletion in a Granulite Facies Terrain

The geology and geochemistry of the Cedar Lake-Clay Lake area have been studied by Westerman (1975, 1978), Breaks et al. (1975), and Breaks and Bond (1977). Westerman (1975, 1978) defined three major units of interest to us-- the amphibolite facies Cedar Lake gneiss and the granulite facies Clay Lake and Twilight gneisses.

The Cedar Lake gneiss is an interlaminated assemblage of deformed amphibolitic to granitic rocks; Westerman (1975, 1978) suggests that the protolith of the felsic units was an intrusive granitoid. The felsic rocks follow a normal calcalkaline differentiation trend, rather than one purely of Na enrichment.

The Clay Lake gneiss is a calcalkaline suite of metaintrusive rocks that range in composition from tonalite to granite. Retrograded enderbites occur interlayered with garnetiferous alaskites; Westerman (1975, 1978) suggested that the present concordance of these somewhat chemically different layers resulted either from emplacement as as sheets or from strong flattening during deformation.

Westerman (1975, 1978) has subdivided the Twilight gneiss into two groups. Group A is believed to have a clastic metasedimentary protolith. Group B is coarser grained, more massive, and less voluminous than Group A, and Westerman (1975, 1978) has proposed a pyroclastic parent, possibly reworked, for these rocks.

Figure 4 shows that the Cedar Lake, Clay Lake, and Group B Twilight gneisses lie outside the field observed by Dennen and Moore (1971) for chemically mature clastic sediments. Only Group A rocks plot along with the Pakwash metagraywacke layers. Nevertheless, Group B has Al/Fe ratios within the limit observed for the immature Kakagi Lake metagraywackes. Shaw's (1972) discriminant function (Fig. 5) also clusters the Group A rocks within or near the sedimentary field, unlike Group B which plot with the other gneisses of igneous origins. Again, however, very immature Archean metagraywackes can also have discriminant function values much greater than zero (Longstaffe, 1978). Thus, while the sedimentary nature of Group A is supported by these chemical tests, the igneous or sedimentary nature of Group B remains uncertain.

The Twilight gneiss has been severely deformed and metamorphosed to the granulite facies (Westerman, 1975, 1978); however, only limited amounts of partial melting have occurred.

Oxygen Isotope Results

All of the gneisses from the Cedar Lake-Clay Lake area have $\delta^{18}O$ values of 7.0-9.3 $^O/oo$, despite their varied protoliths (Table 1, F Fig. 7). Specifically, the Group A and B rocks of the Twilight gneiss have similar ranges of $^{18}O/^{16}O$ ratios. If the Group A rocks were derived from chemically mature clastic sedimentary rocks, they almost certainly have been depleted in ^{18}O by 1-3 $^O/oo$ (Longstaffe and Schwarcz, 1977). The $\delta^{18}O$ values are notably lower than most of the undepleted samples from the chemically similar Pakwash gneiss (Fig. 2). Group B has $\delta^{18}O$ values that suggest a metaigneous origin for these rocks; however, if Group A has been depleted in ^{18}O, the interbedded Group B rocks should have been similarly affected along with the granulite facies Clay Lake gneiss.

I suggest that the Twilight and Clay Lake gneisses did isotopically re-equilibrate, but that the Group B and Clay Lake rocks were already similar in isotopic composition to the exchange reservoir. It is unlikely that the Group A rocks exchanged with an unaltered mafic reservoir, such as basalt, as no $\delta^{18}O$ values less than 7 $^O/oo$ were measured. An alternative and simpler explanation is that the granulite facies rocks underwent isotopic exchange with the surrounding volumetrically more important amphibolite facies metaigneous rocks (such as the Cedar Lake gneiss).

The isotopic results for the Twilight Group A gneiss show that Archean gneisses of sedimentary origin can have $\delta^{18}O$ values similar to those of unaltered Archean plutonic granitoids. Care, therefore, must be excercised when interpreting the $^{18}O/^{16}O$ ratios of upper amphibolite to granulite facies gneisses in terms of their presumed protoliths.

The Oxygen Isotope Alteration of the Burditt Lake Felsic Metavolcanics and the Jackfish Lake Complex Granodiorite: Interaction with Magmatic and Meteoric Fluids

The preceding sections have shown that some portions of Archean gneisses have retained $^{18}O/^{16}O$ ratios diagnostic of their original protoliths, but that high-grade metamorphism can cause such records to be disturbed. In this section, two other types of alteration that can affect the oxygen isotopic compositions of Archean granitoids are described. In these examples, both occur in rocks that have not been metamorphosed above greenschist facies.

A. Burditt Lake felsic metavolcanic rocks

Longstaffe and Schwarcz (1977) reported $\delta^{18}O$ values for the Burditt Lake greenschist facies felsic metavolcanic rocks of 7.9 to 11.4 $^O/oo$ and suggested

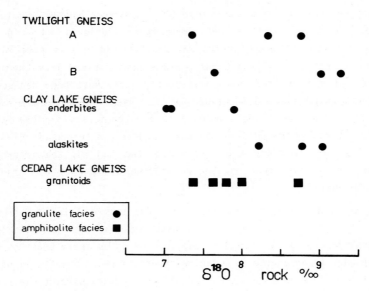

Figure 7.-- $\delta^{18}O$ whole-rock values, Cedar Lake-Clay Lake area gneisses.

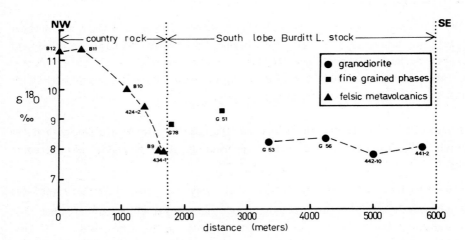

Figure 8.-- $\delta^{18}O$ whole-rock values for a northwest-southeast traverse across the Burditt Lake felsic metavolcanic rocks and the south lobe of the Burditt Lake granodiorite pluton. Felsic metavolcanic samples 424-2 and 434-1 lie southwest of the traverse line, but at the distances from the pluton-country rock contact that are indicated; they fit the depletion pattern shown by samples B9, B10, B11, and B12. Fine-grained phases G51 and G78 are also on the traverse line; they are enriched in ^{18}O relative to the medium-grained granodiorite of the south lobe. $\delta^{18}O$ values of the felsic metavolcanic rocks are given in Longstaffe and Schwarcz (1977), p. 1305.

that the more ^{18}O-rich samples located in this area had been subjected to some type of low temperature alteration and enrichment in ^{18}O. Greenschist facies mafic metavolcanic rocks from the same area are also enriched in ^{18}O (Longstaffe et al., 1977a).

Closer examination of the Burditt Lake greenschist facies felsic metavolcanic rocks has revealed that their isotopic history is even more complex than previously recognized. Those samples located less than 1,000 meters from the Burditt Lake granodiorite pluton have $\delta^{18}O$ values within the normal range for unaltered felsic volcanic rocks (Taylor, 1968), but appear to have obtained such compositions during alteration related to the intrusion of the Burditt Lake pluton rather than from igneous processes.

Oxygen isotope results for a northwest-southeast trending traverse across the Burditt Lake pluton and its felsic metavolcanic country rocks are shown by Figure 8. $\delta^{18}O$ values of the muscovite-biotite and biotite-hornblende granodiorites from the south lobe of the Burditt Lake stock do not differ notably from the pluton's center to its southeastern margin, but are about 1 $^o/oo$ lower than both the microcline megacrysts-bearing granodiorites of the smaller north lobe and the fine-grained phases (G51, G78) that crop out in parts of the south lobe (Table 2). The $\delta^{18}O$ values of the felsic metavolcanic country rocks decrease from 11.4 $^o/oo$ 1,700 meters from the pluton to 7.9 $^o/oo$ within 50 meters of the country rock-pluton contact.

The similarity of $\delta^{18}O$ values between the felsic metavolcanic rocks at the contact (7.9 $^o/oo$) and the muscovite-biotite and biotite-hornblende granodiorites that comprise most of the south lobe (mean $\delta^{18}O$ of 8.0 $^o/oo$) suggests that the felsic metavolcanic rocks have isotopically re-equilibrated to varying degrees with the south lobe granodiorites. The most viable exchange mechanism is magmatic fluid initially in high temperature isotopic equilibrium with muscovite-biotite and biotite-hornblende granodiorites of the south lobe.

Turi and Taylor (1971a, b) showed that depletion in ^{18}O can occur in relatively dry country rocks about the roof zones of plutons; in such areas, the host rocks are able to exchange with magmatic fluids moving upwards through the granitoid. Birk and McNutt (1976, 1977) have emphasized the importance of fluids during the latter stages of crystallization of the Burditt Lake pluton; the higher $\delta^{18}O$ values of the north lobe granodiorites and the fine-grained granodiorites of the south lobe may be related to this autometasomatic Birk and McNutt (1977) have also indicated the presence of sharply brecciated contacts, evidence for high level exposure of the pluton.

Thus, providing that the felsic metavolcanic country rocks were relatively dry, all of the necessary conditions for magmatic water-country rock interaction were probably satisfied in this area.

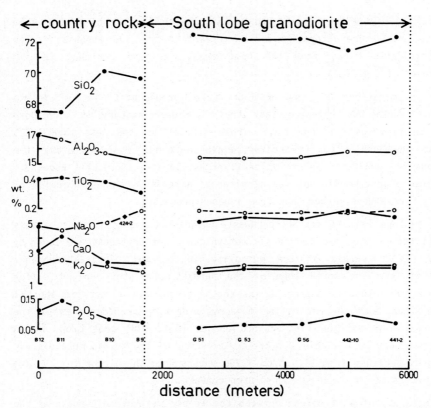

Figure 9.--Chemical variation of the Burditt Lake felsic metavolcanic rocks in the vicinity of the Burditt Lake pluton. Na_2O for 424-2 and chemical analyses for the main phase granodiorite were provided by D. Birk.

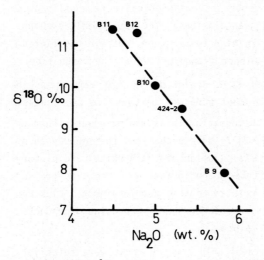

Figure 10.-- $\delta^{18}O$ versus Na_2O for the Burditt Lake felsic metavolcanic rocks near the Burditt Lake pluton.

Chemical alteration of the felsic metavolcanic rocks in the contact zone would be expected to accompany fluid transfer from the pluton into the country rocks. The chemical composition of the country rocks has indeed been altered (Fig. 9); mineralogical evidence of alteration is provided by the albitization of the affected country rocks. The correlation observed for the country rocks between Na_2O and $\delta^{18}O$ (Fig. 10) emphasizes the importance of somewhat Na-rich magmatic fluids in this modification.

B.   The Jackfish Lake Complex granodiorite

The Northwest Bay Fault forms the southern boundary of the Jackfish Lake Complex granodiorite (Blackburn, 1976).   The Jackfish Lake Complex rocks located near the fault are visibly altered; plagioclase has a clouded appearance and the rocks themselves have a reddish hue due to iron staining.

Systematic chemical variations in the rocks occur as the fault is approached (Fig. 11).   Of particular interest is a comparison of chondrite normalized rare earth element patterns for altered (F37, granodiorite) and unaltered samples (F118, granodiorite and F135, monzodiorite). The latter two samples bracket the compositional range of unaltered portions of the Jackfish Lake Complex granodiorite suite.   Compared to the unaltered samples, F37 is very much enriched in the light rare earth elements (Fig. 12; Longstaffe and Crocket, in preparation).

The altered samples also have unusual $\delta^{18}O$ values (Table 2). $^{18}O/^{16}O$ ratios decrease from 7.9 $^o/oo$ 2,300 m from the fault to 3.2 $^o/oo$ within 220 m (Fig. 13).   The $\delta^{18}O$ values of minerals from the altered granodiorite (F37; Table 5) are also grossly out of oxygen isotopic equilibrium.   For example, microcline has an $^{18}O/^{16}O$ ratio lower than that of coexisting hornblende.

These features suggest that the granodiorites located near the fault have been affected by interaction with meteoric water, such as has been described by Taylor (1974).

One anomalous feature of the isotopic and chemical alteration pattern remains to be described.   The $\delta^{18}O$ values of two granitoids (F31, F129), located within 300 m of the fault, but on its south side (within the Northwest Bay Complex), are perfectly normal (Tables 2 and 6). These rocks are chemically unaltered and contain mineral phases that are in isotopic equilibrium.   This suggests that either the Northwest Bay Complex rocks were faulted into their present position after the cessation of meteoric water activity, or else these rocks were faulted up from depths unaffected by meteoric water-rock inter-actions.   Nonetheless, the fault itself seems to have served as a conduit for low ^{18}O fluids.

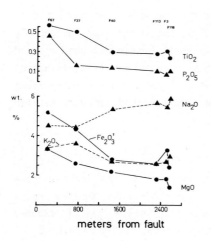

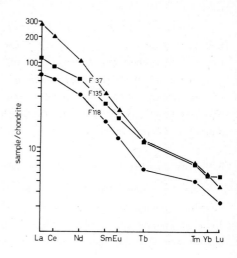

Figure 11.--Some chemical variations of the Jackfish Lake Complex granodiorite near the Northwest Bay Fault. F113, F3, and F118 are unaltered.

Figure 12.--Chondrite normalized rare earth element patterns of some Jackfish Lake Complex rocks: F37, altered granodiorite; F135, monzodiorite; F118, granodiorite.

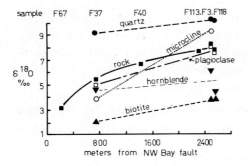

Figure 13.-- $\delta^{18}O$ results for rocks and minerals from the Jackfish Lake Complex in the vicinity of the Northwest Bay Fault.

The Jackfish Lake Complex: Oxygen Isotope Evolution During Differentiation

While the preceding examples have dealt with oxygen isotope variation that can be attributed to sedimentary, metamorphic and alteration processes, the $\delta^{18}O$ values observed for unaltered portions of the Jackfish Lake Complex can be discussed in terms of magmatic evolution.

The geology and geochemistry of a portion of the Jackfish Lake plutonic Complex has been investigated by Longstaffe (1978), Longstaffe et al. (1976a, 1977a), and Blackburn (1976). By volume, most of the Complex rocks outside the immediate study area are diorites and monzodiorites. Within the area of interest, however, progressively smaller volumes of (quartz) monzodiorites, leuco (quartz) diorites, tonalites, granodiorites and Na-syenites also occur. Longstaffe (1978) has suggested that the bulk of the Complex formed by partial melting of basaltic rocks at depth; this melt was then emplaced to its present position where most of the magma crystallized to form the diorites. A small volume of magma, however, was progressively differentiated. This differentiation was controlled initially by the crystallization of amphibole, but later the crystallization of sodic plagioclase and microcline became quite important. The modal content of amphibole, for example, ranges from 70 ^{o}/o for the most mafic diorite to 5 ^{o}/o in the most felsic rocks.

The $\delta^{18}O$ rock values measured for unaltered samples range from 6.4-9.2 ^{o}/oo (Fig. 3 and Table 2), and usually increase as the rocks become more leucocratic: meladiorites, 6.4-6.7 ^{o}/oo; diorites, 6.9-7.3-8.1 ^{o}/oo; (quartz) monzodiorites, 7.3-7.7 ^{o}/oo; leuco (quartz) diorites, 7.5-8.1 ^{o}/oo; granodiorites, 7.5-8.2 ^{o}/oo. The Na-syenite and albitite, however, which are the volumetrically least important rocks but among the most leucocratic, do not follow this pattern. These rocks have lower $\delta^{18}O$ values (6.5-7.2 ^{o}/oo) than the granodiorites with which they are closely associated.

These isotopic variations can be explained in terms of the mineralogical evolution of the suite. The initial crystallization of large quantities of amphibole (and, perhaps, some pyroxene), which have low $\delta^{18}O$ values (4-6 ^{o}/oo) would create rocks with low $\delta^{18}O$ values. Once ^{18}O-rich phases such as quartz and feldspar began dominating the crystallization, resulting rocks would have progressively higher $\delta^{18}O$ values. Once large quantities of the ^{18}O-rich phases had crystallized from the residual magma, however, the very last remaining liquids (Na-syenite and albitite) probably could become somewhat depleted in ^{18}O relative to earlier phases such as the granodiorites. Notably, the Na-syenite and albitite are very feldspar-rich (>95 modal ^{o}/o), but contain very little quartz which is the most ^{18}O-rich of the felsic mineral phases). Alternatively, the Na-syenites, being the roof-zone portion of the Jackfish Lake Complex, may have isotopically exchanged with the host mafic metavolcanic rocks ($\delta^{18}O \approx 5.5$ ^{o}/oo; Longstaffe, 1978).

Oxygen Isotope Equilibrium and Disequilibrium in Archean Granitoids

The final question posed in the introduction to this paper was "Are Archean granitoids in oxygen isotopic equilibrium?" The preceding discussions have

TABLE 5 : Oxygen isotope mineral results, Jackfish Lake Complex

$\delta^{18}O/oo$

	Quartz	Microcline	Plagioclase	Hornblende	Biotite	Magnetite
F146			8.79±0.00	6.17±0.00	4.53	
F135	10.36	8.04	8.67±0.15	6.54	5.15±0.03	
F21		8.10±0.20	8.25	6.12±0.01	4.15±0.15	
F24		7.83±0.22	8.08	5.42±0.01		
D1	10.51±0.01	7.61±0.36	7.51±0.13	5.37±0.22	4.24±0.15	
F3	10.16	9.17±0.23	8.14±0.01	6.01±0.11	3.70±0.22	
F26	10.41±0.10	9.12	7.29	6.35±0.10	5.70±0.18	0.56
F118	10.06	7.12±0.07	7.36±0.02	4.37±0.22	3.70±0.07	
F37*	9.19±0.29	3.93±0.00	5.02±0.29	4.70	2.00±0.33	
F46		7.47±0.10	7.70±0.11	4.92		-1.89

Error shown is difference from mean of duplicate analyses

* altered

TABLE 6 : Oxygen isotope mineral results, Northwest Bay Complex and
Manomin Lake felsic schists

$$\delta^{18}O \quad °/oo$$

Sample	Quartz	Microcline	Biotite
F124 - felsic schist	12.52±0.05	10.00±0.11	5.04±0.11
F121 - felsic schist	11.79	8.59±0.00	4.56±0.31
F31 - N.W. Bay granodiorite	9.65±0.22	8.40	3.92±0.16

Errors given as deviation from mean of duplicate analyses.

TABLE 7 : Oxygen isotope mineral results, Kenora area

	Quartz	Microcline	$\delta^{18}O°/oo$ Hornblende	Biotite	Magnetite
G106B	10.13±0.25			2.73±0.06	
G110A	10.29±0.08	6.97±0.07		1.59	
G350A	10.50±0.10		5.18±0.12	3.09	
G350B	9.65±0.10	8.42		2.29	
G886	10.46±0.06	7.63		2.20±0.06	
G715	9.94			2.24	3.26
G596A	9.31±0.09	7.54±0.03		2.70±0.25	1.71±0.06
G135	9.73±0.03	7.07		2.70±0.03	1.35±0.19
G145	9.70±0.10	7.07		2.29	3.33
G835B	9.96±0.14			3.12	

Errors given as deviation from mean of duplicate analyses.
Mineral separates provided by C. Gower.

shown that they are not. The purpose of this section is to briefly examine the
extent of the disequilibrium; a detailed discussion will be presented in a
separate paper.

The first indication of isotopic disequilibrium in these rocks is the wide
range of quartz-microcline isotopic fractionations (Δquartz-microcline). Most
igneous rocks in oxygen isotopic equilibrium have quartz-microcline values of
0.8-2.0 $°/oo$ (O'Neil and Taylor, 1967). Δquartz-microcline values for the
least metamorphosed Jackfish Lake Complex rocks range from 0.9-2.9 $°/oo$, and
the calculated isotopic isotopic temperatures from this mineral pair are
usually discordant when compared to those obtained from quartz-hornblende and
quartz-biotite pairs. Nor are the latter two temperature estimates always in

agreement! The microcline from the Jackfish Lake Complex granodiorites occurs as megacrysts (Longstaffe et al. 1977a); its occurrence and isotopic composition appear related to autometasomatic activity (Longstaffe et al., in preparation).

$\triangle$quartz-microcline values of the gneisses also indicate a lack a lack of isotopic equilibrium. Values for both 'migmatized' and 'unmigmatized' portions of the Footprint gneiss range from 0.3-4.0 ^{o}/oo and there are no significant differences in the fractionations between the two groups. $\triangle$Quartz-microcline values for the Kenora area gneisses (Table 7) (1.2-3.3 ^{o}/oo) and the 'migmatized' Pakwash gneisses (3.0-3.8 ^{o}/oo) are also generally larger than expected for high-grade metamorphic rocks. In all of these cases, the quartz-microcline temperatures do not usually agree with those obtained from other mineral pairs, and, more often as not, are lower. Similar comments can also be made for quartz-plagiclase pairs.

A second indication of isotopic disequilibrium is provided by the low $\delta^{18}O$ biotite values and the associated large quartz-biotite fractionations of the Footprint, Kenora, and 'migmatized' Pakwash gneisses (Tables 3, 4, and 7). Most biotites from plutonic granitoids have higher $\delta^{18}O$ values (3-7 ^{o}/oo; see summary of literature in Longstaffe, 1978), such as have been measured for the Jackfish Lake and Northwest Bay Complexes (Tables 5 and 6). Because of the large quartz-biotite fractionations of the gneisses, calculated quartz-biotite temperatures are low (mean values of 340-410°C; Table 8); all temperatures reported have been calculated according to Bottinga and Javoy (1975). The amphibolite facies Manomin Lake felsic schists, while they have normal $\delta^{18}O$ biotite values, also have larger than expected $\triangle$quartz-biotite values and correspondingly lower quartz-biotite temperatures (Table 8).

On the other hand, the Jackfish Lake Complex rocks, along with unmigmatized (lower grade) portions of the Pakwash gneiss, have mean quartz-biotite temperatures of 490 to 515° C (Table 8), higher than those of the gneisses. Quartz-amphibole temperatures for the Jackfish Lake Complex are higher still, ranging from 450-600° C. Hornblende, therefore, seems less susceptible than biotite to the subsolidus exchange that occurred in the Jackfish Lake Complex.

Some of the $\delta^{18}O$ values of biotites from the gneisses have been lowered during the bulk depletions of ^{18}O described previously. This is most true for the 'migmatized' portions of the Pakwash gneiss, where the $^{18}O^{16}O$ ratios of biotite have decreased from 5.2-6.7 ^{o}/oo to 1.6-2.2 ^{o}/oo. However, this effect is less pronounced for the Footprint gneiss (see Table 4) and does not apply at all to the rocks from the Kenora area, which have $\delta^{18}O$ biotite values of 1.59-3.2 ^{o}/oo. It is also worth noting that because of the low modal abundance of

TABLE 8 : Summary of oxygen isotope temperatures[1]

	Δ quartz-biotite		Δ quartz-amphibole		Δ quartz-magmetite	
	Range	Mean	Range	Mean	Range	Mean
Footprint gneiss[2]	365-460	400 (10)			425-560	490 (6)
Kenora Area gneiss	360-435	405 (10)		475 (1)	550-660	610 (4)
Migmatized Pakwash gneiss	375-410	390 (4)				
Manomin Lake felsic schists	405-415	410 (2)				
Jackfish Lake complex3	440-560	490 (5)	450-600	540 (5)		480 (1)
Northwest Bay Complex		490 (1)				
Unmigmatized Pakwash gneiss	460-550	515 (3)				

1. calculated using equations of Bottinga and Javoy (1975).
2. F152 excluded: $T^{o}C$ (quartz-biotite) = 590°C.
3. Altered granodiorite F37 excluded

Values in parentheses indicate number of mineral pairs.

biotite in these rocks, its $\delta^{18}O$ value has little influence upon the $\delta^{18}O$ rock composition.

Garlick and Epstein (1967) recognized that biotite usually undergoes isotopic re-equilibration during retrograde metamorphism, obliterating the initial isotopic fractionations established at the peak of metamorphism. Bottinga and Javoy (1975) noted that rocks formed at less than 700°C (igneous or metamorphic) usually end up with discordant isotopic temperatures, as equilibrium is not frozen into each mineral phase at the same temperatures; biotite and microcline are especially susceptible to continued exchange. O'Neil et al (1977) and O'Neil and Chappell (1977) have reported large quartz-biotite fractionations for granitic rocks that seem to have resulted from the preferential depletion of biotite in ^{18}O relative to other mineral phases; they suggest that preferential interaction of the biotite with ground waters on a very small scale is one possible explanation of such behaviour.

It seems likely that preferential isotopic exchange of biotite during retrograde metamorphism has caused the low quartz-biotite temperatures observed for the gneisses. However, whether the fluids involved were meteoric or of some other source is difficult to determine from the existing data.

The quartz-magnetite temperatures obtained for the Footprint and Kenora area gneisses (425-660°C; Table 8) provide the final indication of isotopic disequilibrium that I wish to discuss. These temperatures are higher than the quartz-biotite temperatures obtained for the same rocks.

The quartz-magnetite temperatures calculated for the Kenora area rocks (550-660°C) are similar to those estimated by Gower and Clifford (1977) for the M_1 metamorphism of these rocks (650 $\pm$ 40°C). Since magnetite is much more resistant to isotopic exchange than biotite, such temperatures probably provide useful minimum estimates of the rock temperatures existing shortly after the culmination of the main period of metamorphism.

While the quartz-biotite 'temperatures' preserved for the Kenora area and Footprint rocks are similar, the quartz-magnetite temperatures for the former area (mean of 610°C) are higher than the mean quartz-magnetite temperature calculated for the latter (490°C). The cause of this variation is unknown; however, the bulk ^{18}O depletion of the Footprint Gneiss may be, at least in part, responsible.

In conclusion, while Archean granitoids are not usually grossly out of isotopic equilibrium, neither do they closely approach a state of equilibrium. This is best reflected in the hierarchy of isotopic quenching temperatures observed for the granitoids, both plutonic and metamorphic. The highest, and most useful temperatures are preserved by quartz-magnetite pairs, followed by quartz-hornblende pairs and then by quartz-biotite pairs. The quartz-biotite temperatures are probably of little use, especially if they reflect preferential exchange of the biotite with some as yet unidentified fluid reservoir.

CONCLUSIONS

The following replies can now be made to the questions posed in the introduction to this paper:

1. The $\delta^{18}O$ values of Archean granitoids from northwestern Ontario range from 3.2 to 11.7 $^{\circ}$/oo.

2. The $\delta^{18}O$ values of isotopically undepleted Archean metaigneous gneisses (7.3-9.0 $^{\circ}$/oo) are similar to those of unaltered Archean plutonic granitoids of similar chemical composition (7.3-9.3 $^{\circ}$/oo, Jackfish Lake Complex diorites not included). The $\delta^{18}O$ values of isotopically undepleted gneisses of clastic sedimentary origins (8.8-11.7 $^{\circ}$/oo) also resemble those of their protoliths; Archean felsic metavolcanic rocks have a similar range of oxygen isotope values (Longstaffe and Schwarcz, 1977) but if the isotope data are used in conjunction with chemical information (such as Al/Fe, D.F., for example)

chemically mature clastic sedimentary protoliths can usually be distinguished from igneous parent rocks. At least up to the onset of partial melting during metamorphism, Archean gneisses have $\delta^{18}O$ values diagnostic of their protoliths.

3. The range of $\delta^{18}O$ values observed for many unaltered Archean igneous and metaigneous granitoids is somewhat lower than that of Phanerozoic batholiths (Taylor, 1968, 1977). The lower values are compatible with other geochemical arguments that require much of the Archean sialic crust to be new material differentiated from mafic rocks of the upper mantle or lower crust. The lower $\delta^{18}O$ values of these granitoids suggest that pre-existing ^{18}O-enriched crustal material was not a major component of most granitoid magmas, and/or that these magmas did not isotopically re-equilibrate with pre-existing sialic rocks during emplacement.

4. Open-system oxygen isotope exchange with a low ^{18}O reservoir (6 $^o/oo$) such as basalt seems to have accompanied upper amphibolite facies metamorphism and partial melting of the Pakwash and Footprint gneisses. The low oxygen isotope ratios in these areas, therefore, are due to metamorphic processes rather than primary magma generation from basaltic rocks.

5. Granulite facies metamorphism of the Twilight gneiss appears to have been accompanied by oxygen isotopic re-equilibration of the presumed sedimentary protolith with the surrounding metaigneous granitoids, some of which are also in the granulite facies of metamorphism.

6. Archean granitoids of much lower metamorphic grades are not immune to the alteration of their original oxygen isotope compositions. Greenschist facies felsic metavolcanic rocks located near the Burditt Lake granodiorite pluton have been depleted in ^{18}O by as much as 3.5 $^o/oo$ by magmatic fluids emanating from the stock. The felsic metavolcanic rocks unaffected by this depletion are themselves unusually enriched in ^{18}O relative to unaltered felsic volcanics, thus reflecting another, earlier alteration episode during which the ^{18}O contents of the rocks were enriched. Portions of the Jackfish Lake Complex granodiorite have been depleted in ^{18}O by exchange with low ^{18}O fluids (probably meteoric water); the chemical composition of these rocks, including their LREE contents, has been affected by this alteration.

7. Most Archean granitoids are not completely in oxygen isotopic equilibrium. In the case of the gneisses, quartz-magnetite temperatures may be frozen in near the thermal peak of metamorphism, but the quartz-biotite 'temperatures' are much lower, reflecting preferential exchange of biotite to lower $\delta^{18}O$ values.

ACKNOWLEDGMENTS

The supervision of Drs. R. H. McNutt and H. P. Schwarcz during the course of this investigation is gratefully acknowledged. G. Beakhouse, D. Birk, C. Gower, and C. Westerman provided many of the samples and gave free access to their pertinent unpublished data.

The research has been funded by various grants and scholarships from the National Research Council and the Department of Energy, Mines and Resources of the Government of Canada. The manuscript was prepared during the tenure of a Killam Post-Doctoral Fellowship at the University of Alberta and the analytical work performed in the Department of Geology at McMaster University.

REFERENCES

Abbey, S., 1975. Studies in "standard samples" of silicate rocks and minerals. Part 4: 1974 edition of "usable" values. Geol. Surv. Can., Paper 74-41, 23 pp.

Barker, F., Arth., J. G., Peterman, Z. E. and Friedman, I., 1976a. The 1.7-1.8 b.y. old trondhjemites of southwestern Colorado and northern New Mexico: Geochemistry and depths of genesis. Bull. Geol. Soc. Am., 87: 189-198.

Barker, F., Friedman, I., Hunter, D. R. and Gleason, J. D., 1976b. Oxygen isotopes of some trondhjemites, siliceous gneisses and associated mafic rocks. Precambrian Res., 3: 547-557.

Beakhouse, G. P., 1974a. A preliminary appraisal of the geology and geophysics of the English River gneiss belt. Centre for Precambrian Studies, University of Manitoba, Ann. Rept., part 2: 233-239.

Beakhouse, G. P., 1974b. Geology of the Pakwash Lake area, northwestern Ontario. Centre for Precambrian Studies, University of Manitoba, Ann. Rept., part 2: 240-245.

Beakhouse, G. P., 1977. A subdivision of the western English River sub-province. Can. J. Earth Sci., 14: 1481-1489.

Birk, D. and McNutt, R. H., 1976. Autometasomatism as a mechanism of differentiation in Archean granitoid diapirs (abstract). Abst. Program, 1976 Ann. Meetings, Geol. Assoc. Can., 1: 74.

Birk, D. and McNutt, R. H., 1977. Rb/Sr isochrons for Archean granitoid plutons within the Wabigoon greenstone belt, northwestern Ontario: a preliminary evaluation. Geol. Surv. Can., Paper 77-1A, rep. 33.

Black, P. M., 1974.   Oxygen isotope study of metamorphic rocks from the Ouegoa District, New Caledonia. Contrib. Miner. Pet., 47: 197-206.

Blackburn, C. E., 1976.   Geology of the Off Lake-Burditt Lake area, District of Rainy River.   Ont. Div. Mines, GR 140, 62 p.   Accompanied by Map 2325, scale 1 inch to 1 mile (1:63,360).

Bottinga, Y.   and Javoy, M., 1975.   Oxygen isotope partitioning among the minerals in igneous and metamorphic rocks.   Rev. Geophys. Space Phys. 12: 403-418.

Breaks, F. W.   and Bond, W. D., 1977.   Manifestations of recent reconnaissance investigations   in   the   English   River   subprovince.   1977   Geotraverse Conference Rept. 27, University of Toronto: 170-211.

Breaks, F. W., Bond, W. D., Harris, N.   and Westerman, C., 1975. Operation Kenora-Ear Falls, District of Kenora. Summary of field work, 1975.   Ont. Div. Mines, M.P. 63: 19-33.

Clayton, R. N.   and Mayeda, T. K., 1963.   The use of bromine pentafluoride in the extraction of oxygen from oxides and silicates for isotopic analysis. Geochim. Cosmochim. Acta, 27: 43-52.

Cole, D. R.   and Ohmoto, H., 1976.   Effect of NaCl on the rate of oxygen isotopic exchange reactions between rocks and water (abstract). 1976 Ann. Meetings, Geol. Soc. Am., Abst. Programs, 8: 817.

Craig, H., 1957.   Isotopic standards for carbon and oxygen and correction factors   for   mass-spectrometric   analysis   of   carbon   dioxide.   Geochim. Cosmochim. Acta, 12: 133-149.

Craig, H., 1961.   Standard for reporting concentrations of deuterium and oxygen-18 in natural waters. Science, 133: 1833-1834.

Dennen, W. H. and Moore, B. R., 1971.   Chemical definition of mature detrital sedimentary rocks.   Nat. Phys. Science, 234: 127-128.

Dontsova, Ye. I., 1970.   Oxygen isotope exchange in rock-forming processes. Geochem. Int. 8, 624-635; trans. from Geokhimiya, 8: 903-916.

Forester, R. W. and Taylor, H. P., Jr., 1977. $^{18}O/^{16}O$, D/H and $^{13}C/^{12}C$ studies of the Tertiary igneous complex of Skye, Scotland.   Am. J. Sci., 277: 136-177.

Fourcade, A., 1972.   Etude   des   fractionnements   isotopiques $^{18}O/^{16}O$ dans quelques   séries   métamorphiques   et   massifs   granitiques   précambriens   de l'Ahagaar algérien.   Thèse 3e cycle, Université Paris VI, 102 pp.

Fourcade, S. and Javoy, M., 1973. Rapports $^{18}O/^{16}O$ dans les roches du vieux socle catazonal d'In Ouzzal (Sahara algerien). Contrib. Miner. Pet., 42: 235-244.

Garlick, G. D. and Epstein, S., 1967. Oxygen isotope ratios in coexisting minerals of regionally metamorphosed rocks. Geochim. Cosmochim. Acta, 31: 181-214.

Gower, C. F. and Clifford, P. M., 1977. Metamorphism in the English River subprovince near Kenora, northwest Ontario (abstract). Proceedings 23rd. Meeting, Institute on Lake Superior Geology, May 1977, 19.

Hoernes, S. and Friedrichsen, H., 1974. Oxygen isotope studies on metamorphic rocks of the Western Hohe Tauern area (Austria). Schweiz. Min. Pet. Mitt., 54: 769-788.

IUGS Subcommission on the Systematics of Igneous Rocks, 1973. Classification and nomenclature of plutonic rocks, recommendations. N. Jahrb. Miner. Mh.: 149-164.

Kays, M. A., 1976. Comparative geochemistry of migmatized, interlayered quartzofeldspathic and pelitic gneisses: a contribution from rocks of southern Finland and northeastern Saskatchewan. Precambrian Res., 3: 433-462.

Longstaffe, F. J., 1978. Oxygen isotope and elemental geochemistry of Archean silicate rocks from northern Ontario. Unpub. Ph.D. thesis, McMaster University, Hamilton, Ontario, 564 pp.

Longstaff, F. J. and Schwarcz, H. P., 1977. $^{18}O^{16}O$ of Archean clastic meta-sedimentary rocks: a petrogenetic indicator for Archean gneisses? Geochim. Cosmochim. Acta, 41: 1303-1312.

Longstaffe, F. J., McNutt, R. H. and Schwarcz, H. P., 1976a. Geochemistry of the Lake Despair area, northwestern Ontario (abstract). Abst. Program, 1976 Ann. Meetings, Geol. Assoc. Can., 1: 48.

Longstaffe, F. J., Schwarcz, H. P. and McNutt, R. H., 1976b. Whole rock oxygen isotope results for Archean clastic metasediments (abstract). Abst. Program, 1976 Ann. Meetings, Geol. Assoc. Can., 1: 46.

Longstaffe, F. J., McNutt, R. H. and Schwarcz, H. P., 1977a. Geochemistry of the Archean Lake Despair area, a preliminary report. Geol. Surv. Can., Paper 77-1A: 169-178.

Longstaffe, F. J., McNutt, R. H. and Schwarcz, H. P., 1977b. $^{18}O/^{16}O$ results for Archean plutonic rocks, Lake Despair area, northwestern Ontario (abstract). Proceedings 23rd. Meeting, Institute on Lake Superior Geology, May 1977, 24.

Longstaffe, F. J., Schwarcz, H. P. and McNutt, R. H., 1977c. $^{18}O/^{16}O$ in Archean gneisses: primary and metamorphic variations (abstract). Abst. Program, 1977 Ann. Meetings, Geol. Assoc. Can. 2: 33.

Magaritz, M. and Taylor, H. P., Jr., 1976. $^{18}O/^{16}O$ and D/H studies along a 500 km traverse across the Coast Range batholith and its country rocks, central British Columbia. Can. J. Earth Sci., 13: 1514-1536.

Moore, B. R. and Dennen, W. H., 1970. A geochemical trend in silicon-aluminum-iron ratios and the classification of clastic sediments. J. Sed. Petrol., 40: 1147-1152.

O'Neil, J. R. and Chappell, B. W., 1977. Oxygen and hydrogen isotope relations in the Berridale batholith. J. Geol. Soc. Lond., 133: 559-571.

O'Neil, J. R. and Taylor, H. P., Jr., 1967. The oxygen isotope and cation exchange chemistry of feldspars. Am. Miner., 52: 1414-1437.

O'Neil, J. R., Adami, L. H. and Epstein, S., 1975. Revised value for the O^{18} fractionation between CO_2 and H_2O at $25^{\circ}C$. J. Res. U.S. Geol. Surv., 3: 623-624.

O'Neil, J. R., Shaw, S. E. and Flood, R. H., 1977. Oxygen and hydrogen isotope compositions as indicators of granite genesis in the New England batholith, Australia. Contrib. Miner., Pet., 62: 313-328.

Perry, E. C., Jr., Ahmad, S. N., Read, D. L. and Swulius, T. M., 1976. Oxygen and carbon isotope geochemistry of the 3.7 AE Isua supracrustal belt, West Greenland (abstract). 1976 Ann. Meetings, Geol. Soc. Am., Abst. Programs, 8: 1047-1048.

Perry, E. C., Jr., Ahmad, S. N. and Swulius, T. M., in press. The oxygen isotope composition of 3800 m.y. old metamorphosed chert and iron formation from Isukasia, West Greenland. J. Pet.

Shaw, D. M., 1972. The origin of the Apsley gneiss, Ontario. Can. J. Earth Sci., 9: 18-35.

Shieh, Y. N. and Schwarcz, H. P., 1974. Oxygen isotope studies of granite and migmatite, Grenville province of Ontario, Canada. Geochim. Cosmochim. Acta, 38: 21-45.

Shieh, Y. N. and Schwarcz, H. P., 1977. An estimate of the oxygen isostope composition of a large segment of the Canadian Shield in northwestern Ontario. Can. J. Earth Sci., 14: 927-931.

Shieh, Y. N., Schwarcz, H. P. and Shaw, D. M., 1976. An oxygen isotope study of the Loon Lake Pluton and the Apsley gneiss, Ontario. Contrib. Miner. Pet., 54: 1-16.

Taylor, H. P., Jr., 1968. The oxygen isotope geochemistry of igneous rocks. Contrib. Miner. Pet., 19: 1-71.

Taylor, H. P., Jr., 1974. The application of oxygen and hydrogen isotope studies to problems of hydrothermal alteration and ore deposition. Econ. Geol., 69: 834-883.

Taylor, H. P., Jr., 1976. Water-rock interactions and the origin of H_2O in granitic batholiths (abstract). William Smith Lecture, Geol. Soc. Newsletter, 5: 14-15.

Taylor, H. P., Jr., 1977. Water/rock interactions and the origin of H_2O in granitic batholiths. J. Geol. Soc. Lond., 133: 509-558.

Taylor, H. P., Jr. and Coleman, R. G., 168. $^{18}O^{16}O$ ratios of co-existing minerals in glaucophane-bearing metamorphic rocks. Bull. Geol. Soc. Am., 79: 1727-1756.

Taylor, H. P., Jr. and Epstein, S., 1962. Relationship between $O^{18}/^{16}O$ ratio in co-existing minerals of igneous and metamorphic rocks, parts 1 and 2. Bull. Geol. Soc. Am., 73: 461-480; 675-694.

Taylor, H. P., Jr. and Magaritz, M., 1975. Oxygen and hydrogen isotope studies of 2.6-3.4 b.y. old granites from the Barberton Mountain Land, Swaziland and the Rhodesian craton, South Africa (abstract). 1975 Ann. Meetings, Geol. Soc. Am., Abst. Programs, 7: 1293.

Turi, B. and Taylor, H. P., Jr., 1971a. An oxygen and hydrogen isotope study of a granodiorite pluton from the Southern California bathlith. Geochim. Cosmochim. Acta, 35: 383-406.

Turi, B. and Taylor, H. P., Jr., 1971b. O^{18}/O^{16} ratios of the Johnny Lyon granodiorite and Texas Canyon quartz-monzonite plutons, Arizona and their contact aureoles. Contrib. Miner. Pet., 32: 138-146.

Viswanathan, S., 1974a. Oxygen isotope studies of Early Precambrian granitic rocks from the Giants Range batholith, northeastern Minn., U.S.A. Lithos, 7: 29-34.

Viswanathan, S., 1974b. Oxygen isotope ratios of quartz in granitic rocks of magmatic and metasomatic origins. Indian J. Earth Sci., 1: 12-21.

Westerman, C. J., 1975. Tectonic evolution of the Archean English River gneissic belt at Cedar Lake, N.W. Ontario (N.T.S. 52K). Unpublished progress report, Dept. Geol., McMaster University, Hamilton, Canada.

Westerman, C. J., 1978. Unpublished Ph.D. thesis, McMaster University, Hamilton, Ontario, Canada.

Wilson, A. F. and Green, D. C., 1971. The use of oxygen isotopes for geothermometry of Proterozoic and Archean granulites. Spec. Publs. Geol. Soc. Aust., 3: 389-400.

Wilson, A. F., Green, D. C., and Davidson, L. R., 1970. The use of oxygen isotope geothermometry on the granulites and related intrusives, Musgrave Ranges, central Australia. Contrib. Mineral. Pet., 27: 166-178.

Chapter 12

ARCHEAN TRONDHJEMITES OF THE SOUTHWESTERN BIG HORN MOUNTAINS, WYOMING: A PRELIMINARY REPORT

F. Barker, J. G. Arth and H. T. Millard, Jr.

ABSTRACT

The Archean terrane of the southwestern Big Horn Mountains includes two generations of trondhjemitic rocks. The older generation (E-1) consists of trondhjemitic-tonalitic gneiss that shows irregular banding, was twice metamorphosed to upper amphibolite facies, and contains 5-10 percent of irregularly dispersed pegmatite stringers and 1-5 percent of lenses of metabasalt. Geochronology of these rocks by the methods of U-Pb in zircon and whole-rock Rb-Sr gives respective ages of 2,972 $\pm$ 180 (2σ) and 3,007 $\pm$ 68 (2σ) m.y. (T. W. Stern, J. G. Arth and M. F. Newell, unpub. results, 1978).

The younger generation (E-2) is found as a pluton of 45 km^2 area that consists of synkinematically intruded trondhjemite and minor tonalite and granodiorite of probable 2,800-m.y.-age (Arth, unpub. results, 1978).

Major-element and minor-element contents of the E-2 pluton mostly are identical to those of the E-1 trondhjemitic-tonalitic gneiss: 14 samples range from 69.5-72.5 percent SiO_2, 14.6-16.3 percent Al_2O_3, and 1.20-1.65 percent K_2O (one sample showed 2.64 percent K_2O). Six samples analyzed show 45-55 ppm Rb and 299-527 ppm Sr. Thus the trondhjemitic rocks of both E-1 and E-2 events are of the common high-Al_2O_3 type ($Al_2O_3 \geq 15$ percent). The trondhjemitic rocks of both events also are markedly depleted in heavy REE's (rare-earth elements): La ranges from 27-97 times chondrites and Lu 1-3.3 times. The E-2 trondhjemite, however, is slightly enriched in light REE's relative to the E-1 type.

Amphibolite lenses in the E-1 gneiss have the compositions of tholeiitic basalts and basaltic andesite. Thin dikes of hornblende-biotite gneiss of late E-1 age show major-element composition of andesite, but are anomalously high in light REE's (La = 249-485 times chondrites).

INTRODUCTION

The Big Horn Mountains, north-central Wyoming (Fig. 1a), are one of the major uplifts of the Rocky Mountains. The core of this range consists largely

111°	109°	107°	105°

| Deformation, second foliation, and metamorphism to middle amphibolite facies | → | BASALTIC DIKES (NOW METAGABBRO) late kinematic, subplanar, boudinaged *SHARPLY CROSSCUTTING* MAJOR SYNKINEMATIC INTRUSIVES OF BIOTITE-HORNBLENDE QUARTZ DIORITE, BIOTITE TONALITE, | SECOND EVENT E-2 2740-2860 m.y. ago |

TABLE I : Major-element analyses of trondhjemitic=tonalitic gneiss of event 1 (E-1), Lake Helen quadrangle, southwestern Big Horn Mountains

	LH-37	LH-32	LH-38	LH-39	LH-16	LH-40	LH-43	LH-15	LH-5	average
SiO_2	69.58	69.88	70.37	70.64	71.28	71.32	71.50	71.76	72.06	70.93
Al_2O_3	15.84	16.00	15.12	15.95	15.64	14.80	15.22	15.61	15.89	15.56
Fe_2O_3	.52	1.15	.82	.44	.46	.84	.75	.48	.21	.63
FeO	1.98	1.79	2.01	1.49	1.44	1.85	1.23	1.45	.92	1.57
MgO	1.02	1.04	.75	.76	.62	.77	.67	.65	.62	.77
CaO	3.38	2.82	2.80	3.14	2.92	2.85	2.72	3.04	3.36	3.00
Na_2O	4.94	5.22	5.06	5.46	5.26	4.92	5.48	5.18	4.38	5.10
K_2O	1.20	1.57	1.64	1.28	1.47	1.45	1.32	1.15	1.65	1.41
H_2O	.63	.42	.44	.30	.30	.39	.40	.29	.36	.39
TiO_2	.40	.35	.46	.25	.24	.30	.26	.26	.20	.30
P_2O_5	.09	.11	.15	.08	.09	.09	.07	.08	.06	.09
MnO	.04	.04	.03	.03	.03	.05	.03	.03	.02	.03
Total	99.62	100.39	99.65	99.82	99.75	99.63	99.65	99.98	99.73	

Analyses by x-ray fluorescence, except FeO determined volumetrically and H_2O by Penfield method. N. H. Elsheimer, L. Espos and J. H. Tillman, analysts.

Thirteen samples of the E-2 quartz diorite-granite suite yield a whole-rock isochron of 2,801 $\pm$ 31 (1σ) m.y. having an initial $^{87}Sr/^{86}Sr$ ratio of 0.7015 $\pm$ 0.0002. This result is similar to the age of 2,805 $\pm$ 37 (1σ) m.y. (as recalculated using the 1.42 x 10^{-11} decay constant) determined on eight whole-rock samples of gneiss from the southern Big Horn Mountains by Stueber and Heimlich (1977). The E-2 trondhjemite thus was emplaced in the interval 3,000-2,800 m.y., and probably closer to the younger limit than the older.

MAJOR- AND MINOR-ELEMENT ABUNDANCES

Major-element analyses of nine samples of E-1 trondhjemitic-tonalitic gneiss are given in Table I, of five E-1 amphibolites in Table II, of three samples of the late E-1 dikes of hornblende-biotite gneiss in Table III, and of five samples of the E-2 trondhjemite pluton in Table III. Al_2O_3, MgO, FeO*

Table II: Major-element analyses of amphibolite of event 1 (E-1), Lake Helen quandrangle, southwestern Big Horn Mountains.

	LH-45	LH-44	LH-14	LH-34	LH-35	average
SiO_2	47.68	47.90	49.58	50.99	54.94	50.22
Al_2O_3	15.80	14.87	14.32	13.98	14.46	14.69
Fe_2O_3	2.75	3.03	3.23	1.58	2.29	2.58
FeO	9.93	10.05	8.56	7.89	9.06	9.10
MgO	6.20	6.84	7.52	9.56	5.12	7.05
CaO	10.04	9.50	10.52	12.48	8.68	10.24
Na_2O	3.15	2.81	2.54	1.47	2.41	2.48
K_2O	.86	1.22	.75	.28	.66	.75
H_2O	1.45	1.58	1.47	1.59	1.22	1.46
TiO_2	1.22	1.24	.92	.36	.78	.90
P_2O_5	.09	.11	.08	.01	.06	.07
MnO	.18	.25	.20	.19	.19	.20
CO_2	.20	.01	n.d.	n.d.	n.d.	n.d.
Total	99.35	99.40	100.27	100.38	99.87	

Analyses by x-ray fluorescence, except FeO volumetrically and H_2O by Penfield method.
N.H. Elsheimer, L. Espos and J.H. Tillman, analysts.
n.d. : not determined

Table III: Major-element analyses of dikes of hornblende-biotite gneiss that were injected late in event 1 (E-1), and trondhjemite of event 2 (E-2), Lake Helen quandrangle southwestern Big Horn Mountains.

| | Hornblende-biotite gneiss | | | | E-2 Trondhjemite | | | | | |
	LH-33	LH-19	LH-41	average	LH-24	LH-26	LH-28	LH-27	LH-9	average
SiO_2	56.83	58.41	59.04	58.09	69.51	70.10	70.36	70.69	72.55	70.64
Al_2O_3	15.58	15.17	15.06	15.27	16.34	15.56	15.70	15.58	14.98	15.63
Fe_2O_3	4.34	4.20	4.09	4.21	.82	.96	.93	.87	.54	.82
FeO	5.17	5.81	4.58	5.19	1.66	1.73	1.68	1.79	1.26	1.62
MgO	2.62	2.71	2.38	2.57	.92	.86	.91	.90	.61	.84
CaO	5.77	5.76	5.56	5.70	3.52	3.12	3.30	3.31	2.74	3.20
Na_2O	3.97	3.78	4.08	3.94	5.22	5.17·	4.92	4.96	3.69	4.79
K_2O	1.78	1.36	1.43	1.52	1.20	1.56	1.62	1.46	2.64	1.69
H_2O	.89	.92	.78	.86	.18	.00	.09	.11	.40	.16
TiO_2	1.35	1.20	1.20	1.25	.31	.34	.32	.35	.25	.31
P_2O_5	.54	.34	.40	.43	.09	.12	.10	.12	.08	.10
MnO	.10	.11	.11	.11	.03	.04	.03	.04	.04	.05
Total	98.84	99.77	98.71		99.80	99.56	99.96	100.18	99.76	

Analyses by x-ray fluorescence, except FeO volumetrically and H_2O by Penfield method.
N. H. Elsheimer, L. Espos and J. H. Tillman, analysts.

(FeO + 0.9 Fe_2O_3), CaO, Na_2O, and K_2O of these four rock units are plotted against SiO_2 in Figure 3.

The salient features of Figure 3 are that:

1. abundances of major elements of the E-1 trondhjemitic-tonalitic gneiss and of the E-2 trondhjemite are identical, and are of the common high-Al_2O_3 type (i.e., they contain more than 15 percent Al_2O_3 at 70 percent SiO_2, Barker et al., 1976).

2. the amphibolites have major elements like those of mafic igneous rocks; they are of three types: LH-14, LH-44 and LH-45 are sodic (2.54-3.15 percent Na_2O) olivine- and olivine-nepheline-normative tholeiites of rather high FeO*/(FeO* + MgO) ratio (1.52-2.0); LH-34 is a calcic, low-K olivine-normative tholeiite of low FeO*/(FeO* + MgO) ratio; and LH-35 is quartz-normative basaltic andesite; and

3. the hornblende-biotite gneiss is andesitic in composition; these dikes apparently formed in a minor magmatic event that was not related to the more mafic and more silicic magmatic events.

An Alk-F-M plot (Fig. 4) shows the E-1 amphibolites to be tholeiitic, the late E-1 hornblende-biotite gneisses of andesitic composition to lie near the tholeiitic-calc-alkaline boundary of Irvine and Baragar (1971), and the E-1 and E-2 trondhjemitic-tonalitic rocks to be calc-alkaline. As in Figure 3, points for the E-2 trondhjemite largely overlap those of the E-1 trondhjemitic gneisses.

Rb-Sr abundances (in ppm, as determined by the isotope-dilution technique) are:

E-1 trondhjemitic-tonalitic gneiss: 45-54 Rb, 299-527 Sr;

E-1 E-1 amphibolites: 3.6-8.1 Rb, 65-104 Sr; and

E-2 trondhjemite pluton: 47-55 Rb, 385-416 Sr.

(The late E-1 dikes of hornblende-biotite gneiss have not yet been analyzed.) The Rb/Sr ratios of the trondhjemitic-tonalitic rocks range from 0.09 to 0.16. These low values are typical of trondhjemitic rocks (see Peterman, this volume).

Rare earth elements have been determined by instrumental neutron activation analysis for 17 samples (Figs. 5 and 6). The field given by seven E-1 trondhjemitic gneisses (Fig. 5) shows strong depletion of heavy REE's--five of the seven samples showing Lu less than 1.4 times chondrites. Only one sample, LH-43, shows a moderate positive Eu anomaly; the remainder do not show

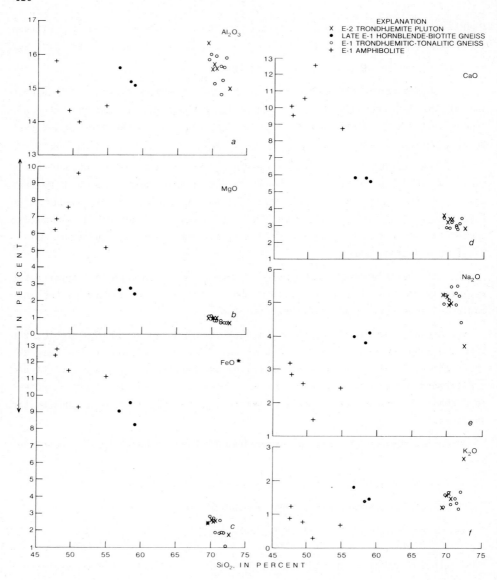

Figure 3.--Silica variation diagrams of E-1 amphibolite, E-1 trondhjemitic-tonalitic gneiss, late E-1 hornblende-biotite gneiss, and E-2 trondhjemite pluton.

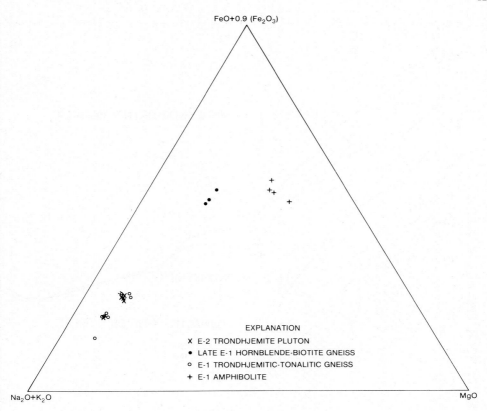

Figure 4.--Alk-F-M plot.

anomalies. The E-1 tonalite gneiss, LH-32, shows depletion of the heavy REE's like the trondhjemitic gneisses (Fig. 5), but about twice the light REE's, with La 160 times chondrites. Generation by partial melting of a hornblende- or garnet-bearing parental rock of basaltic composition is indicated.

The five amphibolites analyzed for REE's show types of patterns (Fig. 6): the moderately Fe-enriched tholeiites (LH-14, 44 and 45) show flat patterns at 10-20 times chondrites and thus resemble most of Arth and Hanson's (1975) Archean tholeiites of northeastern Minnesota; the calcic, low $Fe/(Fe + Mg)$ tholeiite (LH-34) gives a light-REE-depleted pattern at only 5-8 times chondrites; and the amphibolite (LH-35) of basaltic andesitic composition has enriched light REE's, with La 50 times chondrites. The heterogeneity of both major and minor elements of these five metabasaltic samples also is borne out by Th and U concentrations: LH-14, 44 and 45 show 0.35-0.77 ppm Th and 0.62-

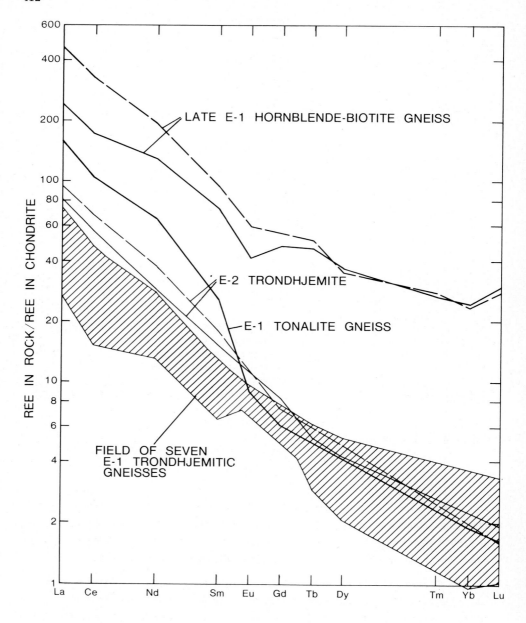

Figure 5.--Chondrite-normalized REE plots of the field of seven samples (LH-15, 16, 37, 38, 39, 40 and 43) of E-1 trondhjemitic gneiss, of E-1 tonalitic gneiss (LH-32), of late E-1 hornblende-biotite gneiss (LH-33 and 41), and of E-2 trondhjemite (LH-24 and 28).

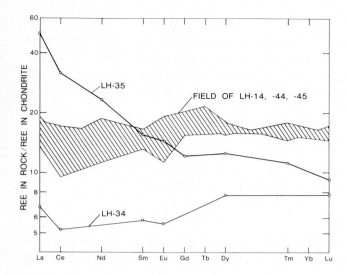

Figure 6.--Chondrite-normalized REE plots of E-1 amphibolites.

0.79 ppm U; LH-34 shows only 0.21 ppm Th and 0.20 ppm U; and LH-35 shows 5.2 ppm Th and 0.93 ppm U. The REE patterns of these five samples are not sufficiently precise for modelling studies. The REE-depleted sample LH-34, which shows affinities to basaltic komatiite of Munro Township, Ontario (Arth et al., 1977), stands by itself as a distinct geochemical type. LH-35, which shows such pronounced light REE enrichment, probably is not related to the other two types.

Two samples of the late E-1 hornblende-biotite gneiss were analyzed for REE's (Fig. 5). Both show marked enrichment in light REE's, small negative Eu anomalies, and heavy REE's at 25-50 times chondrites. The abundances of light REE's are much larger than those of most andesite, yet these dikes of hornblende-biotite gneiss have major elements like those of modern andesite. Further work is needed.

One aspect of the composition of the E-1 trondhjemitic-tonalitic gneiss deserving comment concerns the ubiquitous pegmatite stringers. These stringers consist of subequal amounts of microcline, sodic plagioclase and quartz. If they formed by uniform partial melting of 5-10 percent of the banded gneiss-- and not simply by melting of hypothetical potassic layers of the gneiss--we estimate that the average K_2O composition of the gneiss before metamorphism and partial melting was 0.2 to 0.5 percent higher than the 1.41 percent given in Table I. These pegmatite stringers contain little biotite, and so the correction for Rb would be fractionally smaller than that for K_2O.

414

Our results to date suggest that more than 99 percent of the E-1 banded trondhjemitic gneiss, amphibolite and hornblende-biotite gneiss of the southern part of the Lake Helen quadrangle are derived from igneous rocks. This is at variance with Heimlich and Banks' working hypothesis (1968) that the gneisses and associated rocks were derived from "a largely sedimentary rock sequence that was folded and recrystallized."

ACKNOWLEDGMENTS

We thank Roy J. Knight for assistance with the INAA analyses, and Wallace M. Cady and Malcolm D. Hill for their reviews of the manuscript.

REFERENCES

Arth, J. G. and Hanson, G. N., 1975. Geochemistry and origin of the Early Precambrian crust of northeastern Minnesota. Geochim. Cosmochim. Acta, 39: 325-362.

Arth, J. G., Arndt, N. T. and Naldrett, A. J., 1977. Genesis of Archean komatiites from Munro Township, Ontario: trace-element evidence. Geology, 5: 590-594.

Barker, F., Arth, J. G., Peterman, Z. E. and Friedman, I., 1976. The 1.7-to 1.8-b.y. old trondhjemites of southwestern Colorado and northern New Mexico: geochemistry and depths of genesis. Geol. Soc. Am. Bull., 87: 189-198.

Heimlich, R. A., 1969. Reconnaissance petrology of Precambrian rocks in the Bighorn Mountains, Wyoming. Contr. Geol., 8: 47-61.

Heimlich, R. A., 1971. Chemical data for major Precambrian rock types, Bighorn Mountains, Wyoming. Contr. Geol., 10: 131-140.

Heimlich, R. A. and Banks, P.O., 1968. Radiometric age determinations, Bighorn Mountains, Wyoming. Am. J. Sci., 266: 180-192.

Heimlich, R. A. and Armstrong, R. L., 1972. Variance of Precambrian K-Ar biotite dates. Earth Planet. Sci. Lett., 14: 74-78.

Irvine, T. N. and Baragar, W. R. A., 1971. A guide to the chemical classification of the common volcanic rocks. Can. J. Earth Sci., 8: 523-548.

Osterwald, F. W., 1955. Petrology of Pre-Cambrian granites in the Northern Bighorn Mountains, Wyoming. J. Geol., 63: 310-327.

Stueber, A. M. and Heimlich, R. A., 1977. Rb-Sr isochron age of the Precambrian basement complex, Bighorn Mountains, Wyoming. Geol. Soc. Am. Bull., 88: 441-444.

Chapter 13

FOUR LOW-K SILICEOUS ROCKS OF THE WESTERN U.S.A.

F. Barker, H. T. Millard, Jr., with P. W. Lipman (Trinity Alps)

INTRODUCTION

This paper describes four unrelated suites or bodies of low-K ($K_2O \leqq 2.5$ percent) siliceous igneous and metaigneous rocks of the Rocky Mountains and Klamath Mountains, U.S.A. These rocks include (Fig. 1) the Archean Webb Canyon Gneiss of the Teton Range, western Wyoming, a metavolcanic unit consisting of interlayered metarhyodacite and metabasalt; Archean tonalitic and trondhjemitic gneiss and amphibolite of the Wilson Creek area, Wind River Mountains, Wyoming; the Mesozoic trondhjemitic intrusives of the Riggins area, western Idaho; and three of the composite Jurassic intrusives of the Trinity Alps, Klamath Mountains, northern California.

This study is part of a reconnaissance investigation made by the authors. Major- and minor-element analyses of 24 rocks are given. Detailed hypotheses of generation of the rocks from Wyoming and Idaho cannot be made and so the data are presented for their own sake. We do give, however, a hypothesis for the origin of the concentrically zoned intrusives of the Trinity Alps.

WEBB CANYON GNEISS

The Archean Webb Canyon Gneiss was named and described from the northern part of the Teton Range, Wyoming (Fig. 1) by Reed and Zartman (1973). This formation consists of conformably and grossly interlayered quartzofeldspathic gneiss and amphibolite. Several bodies of the Webb Canyon occur; the largest is about 3 by 15 km. This unit shows concordant contacts with the enclosing layered biotite gneiss, hornblende gneiss, amphibolite and migmatite.

The quartzofeldspathic layers of the Webb Canyon Gneiss range in thickness from a few meters to about 100 m and they consist of foliated, light gray, homogeneous, fine- to medium-grained plagioclase-quartz-microcline-hornblende gneiss (minerals listed in order of decreasing abundance) and plagioclase-quartz-microcline-biotite gneiss. Amphibolite, as layers a few centimeters to about 100 m thick, forms 10 to 25 percent of the Webb Canyon and shows sharp, conformable contacts with the interlayered quartzofeldspathic gneiss. The

416

Figure 1.--Index map showing locations of rock suites.

amphibolite is homogeneous, fine- to medium-grained green hornblende-andesine-quartz rock. Retrograde albite, sericite, chlorite and epidote locally are present.

The Webb Canyon Gneiss shows two generations of folds (Reed, 1963)--early rootless isoclines and superposed open folds. Reed and Zartman (1973) suggested that this formation is volcanic in origin and was deposited as interlayered silicic and basaltic flows or tuffs.

An Rb-Sr study by Reed and Zartman (1973) of five whole-rock samples of the quartzofeldspathic gneiss layers of the Webb Canyon showed $^{87}Rb/^{86}Sr$ ratios from 1.35 to 5.03. These five points give an isochron of 2,790 m.y. and an initial $^{87}Sr/^{86}Sr$ ratio of 0.703 $\pm$ 0.017. For purposes of more meaningful age determination, Reed and Zartman combined data for the Webb Canyon Gneiss with that obtained from one sample of layered gneiss of the enclosing rocks and from three samples of the Rendezvous Metagabbro. The metagabbro lies in the southern part of the Teton Range; it has a metamorphic history like that of the Webb Canyon Gneiss. The $^{87}Rb/^{86}Sr$ ratios of the layered gneiss and metagabbro range from 0.140 to 0.675. All nine points yield an isochron age of 2,875 $\pm$ 150 m.y. and a primitive initial $^{87}Sr/^{86}Sr$ ratio of 0.700 $\pm$ 0.002. Reed and Zartman (1973) concluded--assuming no post-Archean disturbance of Rb/Sr ratios--that the Webb Canyon and Rendezvous parental magmas were derived from the mantle not long before high-rank metamorphism and folding about 2,875 m.y. ago.

Abundances of major and minor elements of the Webb Canyon Gneiss are given in Tables I and II. The amphibolite is basaltic in composition, olivine-normative and tholeiitic (Jakes and Gill, 1970). WC-3 and WC-2B show relatively high K_2O, Rb and Ba contents: 1.01-1.16 percent, 49-41 ppm and 146-222 ppm, respectively. Rare earth elements (REE's) of the amphibolite or metabasalt show flat patterns at 10-20 times chondrites.

The quartzofeldspathic gneiss layers of the Webb Canyon are highly siliceous but low in Al_2O_3, relatively ferruginous but low in MgO, and of moderate Na_2O/K_2O ratio. The original volcanic rock probably was siliceous, normal to leucocratic rhyodacite. This gneiss also shows moderate Rb contents, ranging from 36 to 78 ppm and averaging 57 ppm, and low Sr contents, ranging from 52 to 128 ppm and averaging 79 ppm (Reed and Zartman, 1973). The average Rb/Sr ratio is 0.72, Ba contents are about 1,000 ppm, Th contents are moderate to high at 20-25 ppm, U contents are 4.4-4.9 ppm, and Zr contents are high at about 500 ppm. Light REE's are anomalously high at about 200 to 370 times chondrites (Fig. 2), the negative Eu anomalies are pronounced (Eu/Eu*~0.45), and heavy REE's are relatively abundant (Yb and Lu are about 75-110 times chondrites). The patterns show moderate slopes, with Ce/Yb ratios about 4 to 5. The gently sloping REE patterns of WC-1A and WC-2A are almost unique among Archean siliceous, low-K gneisses; the only similar ones known to us are two measured from the Ancient Gneiss Complex of Swaziland (Hunter, et al., in press. The two samples from Swaziland also have similar major and other minor elements. Thus the quartzofeldspathic gneiss of the Webb Canyon and the gneiss of Swaziland apparently represent a special, albeit rate, Archean REE-enriched siliceous rhyodacite or dacite. The high REE abundances apparently prohibit direct analogies of the origin of the Webb Canyon with similar rocks of plate-tectonic environments. The general environment of the Teton Range 2.8-2.9 b.y. ago may have been at or near a continental margin, where the landmass lay to the north and west--as now exposed in the Beartooth uplift and Big Horn Mountains--and the ocean basin lay to the south.

ROCKS OF WILSON CREEK AREA, WIND RIVER MOUNTAINS

Wilson Creek lies in the eastern Wind River Mountains, Wyoming (Fig. 1). The rocks along Wilson Creek, first mapped and studied by Perry (1964), are Archean in age and consist consist mostly of gray quartzofeldspathic gneisses and of minor interlayered amphibolite. North of Wilson Creek and at higher elevations lenticular to irregularly shaped bodies of foliated granite and

TABLE I : Major-element analyses of Webb Canyon Gneiss, Teton Range, Wyoming

	METABASALT[a/]			QUARTZO-FELDSPATHIC GNEISS (METARHYODACITE)	
	WC-1B	WC-3	WC-2B	WC-1A[a/]	WC-2A[a/]
SiO_2	47.75	48.12	48.27	76.95	79.06
Al_2O_3	12.68	15.64	13.94	11.04	10.74
Fe_2O_3	2.17	1.81	2.30	.98	.28
FeO	12.47	9.39	11.46	2.27	2.13
MgO	7.18	6.35	6.34	.16	.05
CaO	10.44	10.64	10.06	1.41	1.07
Na_2O	2.04	2.41	2.56	3.87	3.13
K_2O	.59	1.01	1.16	2.17	2.50
H_2O^+	1.90	2.19	1.61	.34	.34
H_2O^-	.08	.12	.27	.06	.05
TiO_2	1.42	.96	.97	.18	.14
P_2O_5	.11	.07	.07	.03	.02
MnO	.23	.18	.21	.06	.04
Total	99.52	98.89	99.25	99.52	99.55

a/ Analyses by L.F. Espos and S.T. Neil: FeO by volumentric, H_2O by gravimetric, other elements by XRF methods.

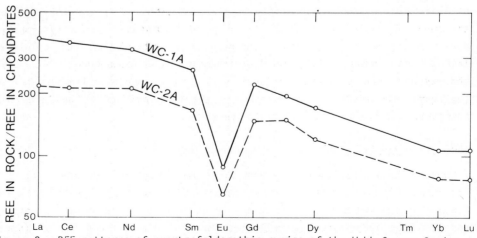

Figure 2.--REE patterns of quartzofeldspathic gneiss of the Webb Canyon Gneiss. Teton Range, Wyoming.

TABLE II: Minor-element analyses of Webb Canyon Gneiss, Teton Range, Wyoming[a]. All values are in parts per million.

	METABASALT			SILICEOUS GNEISS	
	WC-1B	WC-3	WC-2B	WC-1A	WC-2A
Rb	23	49	41	43	44
Sr	--	--	--	--	--
Ba	84	146	222	970	1060
Th	0.6	0.4	0.4	25	20
U	0.2	0.2	0.3	4.9	4.4
La	5.0	3.8	3.7	121	71
Ce	11	9	8.3	284	171
Nd	11	7	7.1	189	121
Sm	3.1	2	3.4	49	31
Eu	1.1	1.0	1.3	6.2	4.5
Gd	4.0	3.3	4.9	57	38
Tb	--	--	--	9.3	7.1
Dy	--	3.7	6.5	52	37
Tm	0.5	0.5	0.7	23	
Yb	3.1	2.3	5.5	3.8	17
Lu	0.5	0.4	0.9	0.9	2.7
Zr	84	72	69	535	454
Hf	2	1.6	1.6	11	13
Zn	480	417	477	52	36
Sc	43		41	1.3	0.8
Cr	269	283	205	7.7	4.1
Co	60	47	52	1.1	0.7

a/ U by delayed neutron analysis, all other elements by instrumental neutron activation analysis (INAA). Coefficients of variation of INAA for values given generally fall within the following ranges:
1 - 5%: La, Sm, Eu; 1 - 10%: Th, Ce, Nd, Dy, Lu, Hf, Zn;
5 - 15%: Gd, Tb, Yb, Zr, Sc, Cr; 10 - 20%: Ba, Tm, Ta, Co.

420

amphibolite or metagabbro have intruded the gneisses. Perry described two
generations of folds, an early recumbent type, and a later cross folding that
he related to intrusion of the granite and metagabbro. Metamorphic rank along
Wilson Creek is amphibolite facies; to the north it increases and part of the
metagabbro is at granulite facies (Perry, 1964). Access to this area is
severely restricted, so the first author was able to collect only eight samples
of a size suitable for geochemical study. Two of these proved to be affected by
retrograde metamorphism or shearing, so only the six remaining samples were
analyzed. A preliminary study of these six samples by Z. E. Peterman (unpub.
results, 1974) gives an approximate age either of igneous crystallization or of
metamorphism of the quartzofeldspathic gneiss of 2.8-3.0 b.y.

Major- and minor-element analyses of these rocks are given in Tables III
and IV. Both the amphibolite that is interlayered with gray quartzofeldspathic
gneiss along Wilson Creek, WR-1, and the metagabbro or amphibolite to the
north, WR-6, have major-element compositions like olivine-normative tholeiite.
As shown in Figure 3, however, these two metabasalts are rather different
geochemically. The amphibolite is relatively enriched in K_2O, Rb, Sr, Ba, and
light REE's. The metagabbro, in contrast, is depleted in these elements and is
similar to modern abyssal tholeiite.

The gray gneisses WR-2, WR-5 and WR-8, collected from a mappable layer

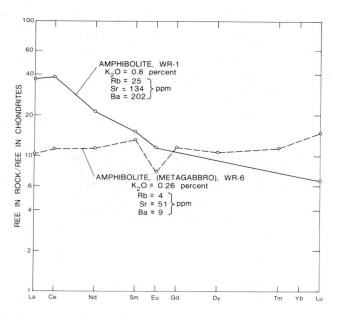

Figure 3.--REE patterns of amphibolite and metagabbro, Wind River Mountains,
Wyoming.

TABLE III: Major-element analyses of amphibolite, plagioclase-quartz-biotite gneiss and quartz monzonite of the Wilson Creek area, Wind River Mountains, Wyoming[a]

	AMPHIBOLITE		PLAGIOCLASE-QUARTZ GNEISS			QUARTZ MONZONITE
	WR-1	WR-6	WR-2	WR-5	WR-8	WR-7
SiO_2	50.5	50.1	69.9	68.3	71.0	70.8
Al_2O_3	10.4	12.2	16.2	15.5	15.7	15.4
Fe_2O_3	2.1	1.6	.30	1.2	.40	1.2
FeO	9.5	9.2	1.4	2.0	1.2	.64
MgO	12.5	12.1	.88	.87	.59	.59
CaO	9.2	12.0	2.7	3.0	2.4	1.6
Na_2O	1.96	.92	5.12	4.02	4.06	3.82
K_2O	.85	.26	1.60	2.40	2.40	4.20
H_2O^+	1.8	.89	.76	1.1	.73	.57
H_2O^-	.01	.00	.04	.03	.02	.07
TiO_2	.72	.50	.20	.33	.23	.28
P_2O_5	.05	.03	.07	.00	.06	.07
MnO	.18	.26	.02	.02	.00	.03
CO_2	.02	.02	.02	.02	.02	.02
Total	100	100	99	99	99	99

a/ Alkalies analyzed by V.M. Merritt by atomic absorption method, other elements by L. Artis by rapid techniques.

several hundred meters thick (Perry, 1964), are tonalitic to trondhjemitic. WR-2 and WR-8 are foliated plagioclase-quartz-biotite gneisses. WR-5 is plagioclase-quartz-biotite-epidote gneiss in which the biotite and epidote may have formed from early hornblende. All three samples are homogeneous in hand specimen. Major elements of these three samples (Table III) are similar except for slightly more FeO^* ($FeO^* = FeO + 0.9 Fe_2O_3$) in WR-5 and more Na_2O and less K_2O in WR-2 than in the other samples. Their minor elements, in contrast, show consistent differences from WR-2 to WR-8 to WR-5 (Table IV and Fig. 4). The light REE's differ by a factor of 3; Rb by a factor of 2; and Ba, U, Th and Sr by a factor of 4. WR-8 and WR-5 show progressively higher concentrations of REE's, Rb, Th, Zr, and Hf, but lower Sr. Ba, U, Sc, Cr, and Co do not show serial changes. We have no ready explanation of these differences. Magmatic fractionation is not feasible, at least in any simple way, because all samples have about the same SiO_2 contents.

The spatially related cross-cutting granite found north of Wilson Creek

TABLE IV : Minor-element analyses of rocks of the Wilson Creek area, Wind River Mountains[a]. All values are in parts per million.

	AMPHIBOLITE		PLAGIOCLASE-QUARTZ GNEISS			QUARTZ MONZONITE
	WR-1	WR-6	WR-2	WR-5	WR-8	WR-7
Rb	25	3.8	20	42	39	127
Sr	132	51	744	180	443	265
Ba	202	9	530	975	1810	1328
Th	5.3	2.1	1.4	6.1	3.3	30
U	.6	0.2	0.3	1.6	1.7	3.2
La	12	3.3	9.4	29	18	65
Ce	30	8.9	17	58	37	122
Nd	12	6.5	7.2	27	14	46
Sm	2.8	2.4	1.6	4.5	2.4	6.9
Eu	0.8	0.5	0.5	1.0	0.9	1.3
Gd	1.5	3.0	1.3	4.4	--	3.5
Tb	--	--	0.2	0.7	0.2	0.5
Dy	--	3.3	1.5	2.0	1.4	1.1
Tm	--	0.4	--	--	--	--
Yb	1.4	1.6	0.4	1.1	0.3	0.6
Lu	0.2	0.5	0.07	0.09	0.06	--
Zr	--	--	110	226	140	222
Hf	1.7	0.7	2.5	4.8	3.2	5.2
Sc	30	39	3.3	7.6	2.7	3.0
Cr	1160	880	12	11	9.3	26
Co	65	54	4.9	5.2	3.3	2.7

shows moderate enrichment in light rare earths and strong depletion in heavy rare earths (Fig. 4). K_2O is 4.2%, Na_2O 3.8%, and SiO_2 71% (Table III). This granite is remarkably similar in both major and minor elements to the Paleozoic Westerly Granite of Rhode Island, or G2, as reported by Buma, Frey, and Wones (1971). It also is not unlike Archean quartz monzonite of NE Minnesota, as described by Arth and Hanson (1975). Following these authors, we suggest that this Wind River granite also formed by the partial melting of quartzo-feldspathic gneisses, here probably only a few kilometers below the present level of exposure. Patial melting presumably occurred as the source rocks were being dewatered at the boundary between upper amphibolite and granulite facies.

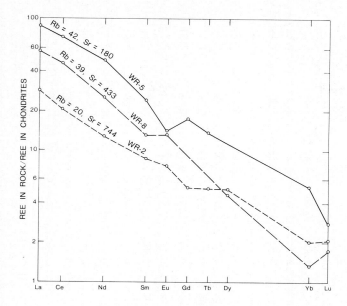

Figure 4.--REE patterns of quartzofeldsapthic gneiss, Wind River Mountains, Wyoming.

TRONDHJEMITE, RIGGINS AREA, IDAHO

Hamilton (1963a, 1963b, 1969a) has described the field occurrence, petrography and major-element chemistry of trondhjemite of the Riggins area, Idaho (Fig. 1). He found that trondhjemite occurs as two large and several small plutons and as abundant dikes on the west flank of the Idaho batholith. The batholith has a border zone of tonalitic gneiss and other rocks that is about 50 km wide. All trend north-south. This border zone lies west of the granodioritic to granitic core of the batholith. The trondhjemite bodies lie in the western half of the border zone.

The trondhjemite is light gray, foliated, medium grained, commonly contains biotite schlieren, and consists largely of oligoclase, quartz and biotite. Epidote, a reaction product of late magmatic origin (Hamilton, 1963a), typically is associated with biotite. Several percent of untwinned potassic feldspar is present in most samples of strongly gneissic trondhjemite, but this mineral is rare or absent otherwise. Small amounts of hornblende are present in tonalitic varieties, which also contain about 10 percent of biotite. Muscovite and garnet also are present in some varieties.

Hamilton (unpub. data, 1960) provided us with powders and major-element

424

TABLE V: Major-element analyses of trondhjemite and associated rocks of the Riggins area, Idaho; and the Trinity Alps, Klamath Mountains, California.

| | Riggins area [a] | | | | | Trinity Alps [b] | | | | | | | |
| | trondhjemite | | | | pegmatite | Canyon Creek pluton, mafic tonalite to trondhjemite | | | | | | Gibson Peak pluton | Caribou Mountain pluton |
	R1	R2	R3	R4	R5	T394	T61	T393	T1647a	T392	T1645	T1049C	T39
SiO_2	66.1	68.1	69.6	71.2	75.7	61.5	64.9	65.4	66.9	68.6	73.2	64.1	67.8
Al_2O_3	18.1	17.7	17.8	17.0	15.5	16.9	16.5	16.2	16.6	15.7	14.7	17.2	16.7
Fe_2O_3	1.3	1.1	1.3	0.6	0.48	1.9	0.62	1.4	1.4	0.66	0.48	1.3	1.5
FeO	1.4	1.5	0.95	0.64	0.13	3.6	3.8	2.4	2.1	2.4	1.2	2.9	1.7
MgO	0.94	0.95	0.52	0.36	0.27	3.2	2.1	2.4	1.6	1.7	0.88	2.2	1.4
CaO	4.9	4.3	5.0	3.0	1.2	5.9	5.1	5.1	4.5	3.6	3.1	4.2	4.5
Na_2O	4.7	4.6	4.7	5.5	5.1	4.00	4.59	4.11	4.20	4.11	4.01	4.60	3.95
K_2O	0.96	1.2	0.50	0.95	1.5	1.07	1.16	1.16	0.98	1.85	1.52	1.44	0.66
H_2O	0.88	0.52	0.30	0.48	0.62	0.88	1.5	0.89	1.0	0.63	0.52	1.0	1.1
TiO_2	0.33	0.34	0.23	0.18	0.02	0.67	0.48	0.44	0.34	0.36	0.17	0.49	0.31
P_2O_5	0.14	0.09	0.01	n.d.	n.d.	0.17	0.16	0.14	0.12	0.11	0.07	0.16	0.12
MnO	0.06	0.10	0.04	0.02	0.09	0.11	0.12	0.09	0.10	0.05	0.06	0.09	n.d.
CO_2	n.d.	0.06	n.d.	n.d.	n.d.	n.d.	n.d.	n.d.	n.d.	n.d.	n.d.	n.d.	n.d.
Total	100	101	101	101	101	100	100	100	100	100	100	100	100

a/ Analyses by P. Elsmore, I.D. Barlow, S.D. Botts, G. Chloe, P.W. Scott and K.E. White by rapid methods.
b/ Analyses by P. Elmore, H. Smith, J. Kelsey and J. Glenn by rapid methods, except Na_2O and K_2O by V. Merritt by flame photometry.
n.d. = not detected

analyses (Table V) of three trondhjemites and one tonalite of the Riggins area. Major elements of a trondhjemite pegmatite, sample R5, already have been reported by Hamilton (1963a, Table V).   These rocks of the Riggins area, as emphasized by Hamilton, are unusually aluminous, relatively calcic and sodic, and deficient in MgO. These are the only trondhjemites known to the authors to contain more than 17 percent Al_2O_3 at 70 percent SiO_2.   Also, the Riggins intrusives resemble the trondhjemite of the type area (Barker and Millard, this volume) and those of the Uusikaupunki-Kalanti area, Finland (Arth et al., in press), more than any others in North America.

Minor elements of the Riggins area tonalite and trondhjemites are listed in Table VI and REE patterns are shown in Figure 5. Rb contents of the three trondhjemite samples, R2, R3, and R4, are very low--9 to 26 ppm--and Sr contents are high--711 to 913 ppm; the Rb/Sr ratios of 0.01 to 0.03 are as low as those of any trondhjemites (see Peterman, this volume). The trondhjemite pegmatite, R5, shows low Rb, 23 ppm, but its Sr content of 92 ppm is an order of magnitude less than that of the associated trondhjemite. REE patterns of the three trondhjemites are heavy REE-depleted and show no Eu anomalies. Having La 22 to 63 times chondrites and Lu 0.9 to 2.3 times chondrites, these

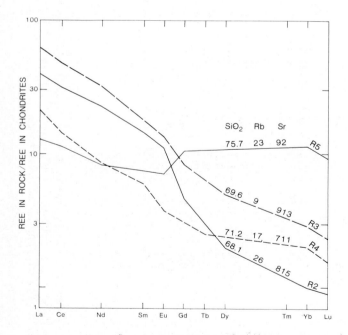

Figure 5.--REE patterns of trondhjemite and trondhjemite pegmatite (R5) of Riggins area, Idaho.

TABLE VI: Minor-element analyses of trondhjemite and associated rocks of the Riggins area, Idaho; and the Trinity Alps, Klamath Mountains, California.

| | Riggins area | | | | Trinity Alps | | | | | | | |
| | trondhjemite | | | pegmatite | Canyon Creek pluton, mafic tonalite to trondhjemite | | | | | | Gibson Peak pluton | Caribou Mountain pluton |
	R2	R3	R4	R5	T394	T61	T393	T1647a	T392	T1645	T1049c	T39
Rb	26	9	17	23	23	32	32	20	39	35	29	14
Sr	815	113	711	92	541	591	469	461	392	393	609	492
Ba	798	262	477	713	351	490	350	335	388	350	463	244
Th	1.2	1.1	0.8	0.7	1.5	3.5	3.3	2.0	7.1	5.3	3.3	1.6
U	0.45	0.44	0.36	2.0	0.56	1.4	1.3	0.9	2.5	1.4	1.8	0.4
La	13	20	7	4	15	14	14	10	18	21	15	9
Ce	27	38	11	9	26	26	29	21	31	36	29	18
Nd	13	18	5	5	15	14	14	13	13	14	14	7
Sm	2.7	3.4	1.1	n.d.	3.6	3.3	3.5	2.9	3.0	2.2	2.8	1.6
Eu	0.8	0.9	0.3	0.5	1.0	0.8	n.d.	0.8	0.7	0.6	0.9	0.7
Gd	1.2	2.1	0.5	2.7	n.d.	2.2	3.1	1.1	1.8	n.d.	2.2	n.d.
Tb	n.d.	n.d.	0.1	n.d.	n.d.	0.3	n.d.	n.d.	n.d.	0.2	n.d.	n.d.
Dy	0.6	1.1	n.d.	n.d.	2.3	2.1	2.5	1.4	1.9	1.0	1.4	1.0
Tm	n.d.	n.d.	n.d.	n.d.	n.d.	n.d.	0.2	n.d.	0.3	0.1	n.d.	n.d.
Yb	0.2	0.6	0.4	2.4	1.6	1.6	1.5	1.0	1.2	0.8	1.0	0.7
Lu	0.03	0.08	0.05	0.3	0.2	0.3	0.2	0.2	0.2	0.1	0.2	0.1
Zr	107	156	87	64	138	135	n.d.	122	147	92	145	88
Hf	2.9	3.8	2.2	1.1	3.2	3.0	n.d.	0.5	3.0	2.5	3.2	2.2
Sc	1.9	4.6	2.1	10	14	9	12	9	8	5	8	6
Cr	4.4	7.0	n.d.	3	81	18	82	24	65	23	28	32
Co	3.4	3.3	1.2	0.1	16	10	n.d.	7	8	8	12	6

a/ Rb and Sr by x-ray fluorescence, analyses by W.P. Doering. U by delayed analysis, all other elements by instrumental neutron activation analysis (INAA). Coefficients of variation of INAA values given generally fall within the following ranges: 1 - 5%: La, Sm, Eu; - 10%: Th, Ce, Nd, Dy, Lu, Hf, Zn; 5 - 15%: Gd, Tb, Yb, Sc, Cr; 10 - 20%: Ba, Tm, Ta, Co. n.d. = not determined

rocks show additional similarity to trondhjemites of Norway, southwest Finland and the Saganaga intrusive of Minnesota (Arth and Hanson, 1975). However, we cannot deduce much about the origin of the Riggins intrusives with our data. The lack of regularity of minor-element content with SiO_2, which is in direct contrast to results obtained from the Finnish suite (Arth et al., in press), may mean that generation was by partial melting of source rocks that were heterogeneous in REE content or of differing mineralogy.

JURASSIC PLUTONS, TRINITY ALPS, KLAMATH MOUNTAINS

The Trinity Alps of the south-central Klamath Moutains, northern California (Fig. 1), contain more than ten plutons of tonalite, trondhjemite, diorite and gabbro. These intrusives were emplaced in Paleozoic to Jurassic metavolcanic and metasedimentary rocks of the central metamorphic belt of the Klamath Mountains, which lies between the eastern Paleozoic belt and the western Paleozoic and Triassic belts. Intrusion took place in Late Jurassic time and may have continued into the earliest Cretaceous. The general geology of this area has been presented by Davis et al. (1965). Davis (1963) and Lipman (1963) described the structure and petrology of the Caribou Mountain and Gibson Peak plutons, respectively; Lipman (1964) briefly described the Canyon Creek pluton; and Hotz (1971) tabulated major-element analyses of many of these plutons. Lanphere et al. (1968) summarized earlier radiometric and geologic age determinations and presented many new isotopic results and major-element analyses.

This report presents data for six samples of the Canyon Creek pluton and for one sample each of the Caribou Mountain and Gibson Peak plutons (Tables V and VI). In addition, the Rb-Sr geochemistry of these rocks is presented by Peterman elsewhere in this volume. All three intrusives are roughly oval in plan, show a domical or cylindroidal pattern of foliations, and forcefully intruded their wallrocks (see Davis et al., 1965). The Canyon Creek pluton has major and minor diameters of 22 and 8.5 km, the Caribou Mountain pluton 7 and 3 km, and the Gibson Peak pluton 5 and 2 km. Compositional zoning is variable: except for a small mass of gabbro at its southeastern margin, the Canyon Creek body ranges from mafic tonalite at its borders (color index: 30) to central trondhjemite (color index: 10); the Caribou Mountain body ranges from calcic trondhjemite to trondhjemite (Davis, 1963); and the Gibson Peak body ranges from hypersthene gabbro to tonalite (Lipman, 1963).

The compositional zonation of the Canyon Creek pluton is everywhere smoothly gradational, without internal intrusive contacts. The tonalites and trondhjemites are uniformly medium grained and have hypidiomorphic granular textures. The mineralogy is biotite-hornblende-plagioclase-quartz-(K-feldspar).

Plagioclase shows striking normal oscillatory zoning and is intricately twinned. Interstices between euhedral-subhedral plagioclase and hornblende are occupied by large poikilitic quartz grains that commonly show undulatory extinction. Biotite is euhedral in outer parts of the pluton but is poikolitic in the interior. A few percent of interstitial microcline accompanies biotite in the center interior but is absent from border rocks. Opaque minerals, sphene, apatite, and minor zircon are common accessory minerals. Traces of chlorite, sericite, and epidote probably formed deuterically.

Structural features indicate that the Canyon Creek pluton was emplaced during regional deformation, at a stage of crystallization when hornblende and plagioclase were liquidus phases throughout the pluton. Biotite crystals were present in margins of the intrusion but not in the interior. Foliation, defined by these minerals, dips outward around margins of the pluton but is inward-dipping to horizontal in the interior. This central foliation basin is interpreted as related to ring fracture formation and caldera collapse at the time the pluton was consolidating; the relations are very similar to those described by Duffield (1968) for a pluton in northern Mexico.

Analyzed samples of the Canyon Creek pluton include mafic quartz diorite (T-394 of Tables V and VI) and tonalite (T61) from near the border, transitional tonalite (T393), trondhjemites of the interior (T392 and T1645), and a late dike of porphyritic dacite (T1647a). Samples of the main pluton show generally systematic compositional changes of most constituents from border to interior: these include SiO_2 (61.5 to 73.2 percent), Al_2O_3 (16.9 to 14.7 percent), FeO* (5.3 to 1.6 percent), MgO (3.2 to 0.9 percent), CaO (5.9 to 3.1 percent) TiO_2 (0.67 to 0.17 percent), Sr (541 to 393 ppm), Sc (14 to 5 ppm), Co (16 to 4 ppm), K_2O (1.1 to 1.8 percent), and Rb (23-39 ppm). Na_2O, Ba, Zr, Hf, and Cr do not show systematic changes from margin to center. The K/Rb ratios of all samples best fit a line of about 380. REE patterns of the six samples (Fig. 6) show an overall increase of La and Ce and a decrease of heavy REE's from border to interior of the pluton and also with increasing SiO_2. The patterns pivot about the region of Nd. The REE patterns also show very small or no Eu anomalies.

The change of REE patterns with increasing SiO_2 content and the absence of Eu anomalies probably result from separation of hornblende and plagioclase from the liquid; these were the major liquidus phases in the Canyon Creek pluton during emplacement. The REE partition coefficients for hornblende-dacitic liquid (SiO_2 = 67 percent) were given by Arth and Barker (1976) and for hornblende-rhyodacitic liquid (SiO_2 = 64 percent) by Zielinski and Lipman (1976). The dacitic set of coefficients may be more applicable to the Canyon Creek pluton, but the rhyodacitic set is not appreciably different. The

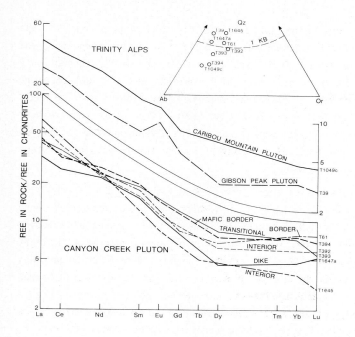

Figure 6.--REE patterns and normative Qz-Ab-Or plot of tonalite and trondhjemite of Jurassic plutons of the Trinity Alps, Klamath Mountains, California.

coefficients for Nd through Lu for hornblende-dacitic liquid are 2.8 or higher, whereas that for Ce is 0.9. La was not determined by Arth and Barker, but comparison with Zielinski and Lipman's results suggest a coefficient of about 0.6. Subtraction of hornblende alone thus should cause the REE's from Nd through Lu to be depleted in the fractionated liquid. Ce would be increased very slightly and La slightly. The pivot point of the REE patterns with increasing fraction of melting would be slightly to the right of Ce. Also, the partition coefficient for Eu is slightly less than those of Sm and Gd, so Eu of the liquid should increase during fractionation. The separation of a modest amount of plagioclase along with the hornblende would push the pivot point to the right--i.e., toward the observed pivot point near Nd--and the preference of plagioclase for Eu would tend to offset any positive Eu anomaly of the liquid caused by separation of hornblende. Eu anomalies, we recognize, are difficult to assess here because we do not know Eu* of the starting liquid, and because the precision of our INAA analyses is not high. Separation of either clinopyroxene or orthopyroxene from the liquid would tend to raise REE patterns of the liquid, but this effect would not be large and cannot be evaluated.

The significant increase of Rb from margins to interior of the Canyon Creek pluton indicates that only minor amounts of biotite settled out of the tonalitic liquid. The partition coefficients for Rb of biotite, hornblende and plagioclase versus rhyodacitic liquid are 7.1, 0.07 and 0.02, respectively (Zielinski and Lipman, 1976). Separation of hornblende and plagioclase alone would enrich the liquid in Rb, as observed, whereas separation of biotite would have the opposite effect. Zeilinski and Lipman (1976) also report that removal of hornblende from their siliceous magmas has little effect on K/Rb ratios, so the consistent value of about 380 of the Canyon Creek rocks is not inconsistent with hornblende-liquid fractionation.

The changes in REE patterns of the Canyon Creek pluton could be a result of increasing fraction of partial melting of amphibolite or quartz eclogite. Arth and Hanson (1975) calculated REE patterns for the partial melting of eclogite at 5, 20, and 35 percent of melting. Their curves show a decrease in light REE's and an increase in heavy REE's as melting increases from 5 to 35 percent. Their pivot point is between Nd and Sm. A similar set of changes would happen with the partial melting of amphibolite--either garnet-bearing or not--because the partition coefficients of REE's between tonalitic liquid and hornblende are similar to those of garnet-liquid, although not as large (Arth and Barker, 1976). This possibility would involve partial melting of the source eclogite at perhaps 30 to 50 km below the present level. Magma would accrete in an expanding chamber in or above the source rock. The smallest fraction of melt would collect in the chamber first. Successive melting of less siliceous and dense compositions would collect in the chamber below the initial trondhjemitic liquid. In this way a vertically zoned magma pod might collect--a pod whose lowest region might be dioritic or gabbroic. We cannot envision how such a pod would develop horizontal compositional zoning, however, and suggest the following model involving formation of a magma pod at depth by partial melting and fractionation of that pod during ascent:

(1) Partial melting of metabasalt in a plate-convergent environment (Hamilton, 1969b) at 15-50 km below the present surface and at 850-950°C. If amphibolite is parental, hornblende, calcic plagioclase, pyroxene, and perhaps garnet are residual; if quartz ecologite is parental, garnet and pyroxene are residual. Rocks such as pelite, graywacke, and siliceous metavolcanic rocks that would partially melt to produce granite under these circumstances apparently were absent.

(2) As the ratio of melt/residue increases and the composition of the liquid passes from trondhjemitic to tonalitic or even dioritic the melt collects as a large pod or bubble.

(3)   The magma pod reaches a critical size and mean density contrast with its wallrocks at which its buoyancy forces it through the roofrocks and a diapir is formed; this critical size would not be directly related to SiO_2 composition of the liquid, or course, but typically occurs at 25-50 percent of melting and when the liquid contains 60-65 percent SiO_2.

(4)   As the diapir rises, it loses heat to its wallrocks; hornblende, plagioclase and in some instances pyroxene or other phases crystallize; toroidal convective flow, crystal setting, and crystallization at the walls produce both a pronounced vertical zonation of the diapir into a lower, mafic cumulate, an intermediate zone and a siliceous upper zone, and a horizontal zonation as seen in the Canyon Creek pluton.

(5)   As the diapir rises, cools, fractionates, feeds volcanic eruptions during caldera collapse and becomes more viscous, it reaches conditions where upward movement ceases and any remaining liquid crystallizes.

In this model, fractionation need not occur largely at the final or present position of the diapir, although geochemical evidence is compelling for high-level differentiation in many Tertiary caldera-related igneous systems. The model is presented for plutons like the Canyon Creek, which were emplaced as single masses (Lipman, 1964; Davis et al., 1965). A composite model, involving coalescence of diapirs that are at different stages of development or involving other complications, would be necessary to rationalize the complex intrusive relations of some of the plutons of the Trinity Alps. Whether the few associated gabbroic masses are cogenetic or are merely spatially associated rocks that were generated by partial melting of peridotite remains to be determined.

The first stage of this model--partial melting of rock of basaltic composition--follows the model of Larsen and Poldervaart (1961) for generation of the Bald Rock batholith. The Bald Rock body (Compton, 1955; Hietanen, 1976), which lies about 210 km southeast of the Trinity Alps and 30 km west of the Sierra Nevada batholith, is similar to the trondhjemitic and tonalitic plutons of the Trinity Alps. Larsen and Poldervaart's model, however, differs from ours in that it ascribes all the compositional variation to fractionation between partial melt and mafic residue. We question whether the mafic residue would be able to rise gravitationally, and the zoning and twinning of the plagioclase crystals are more compatible with an origin by fractionation--as in (4) and (5) above.

The REE patterns of single samples of the Caribou Mountain and Gibson Peak plutons are similar to those of the Canyon Creek body. They do, however, show positive Eu anomalies (Fig. 6). Whether these anomalies are a result of accumulation of plagioclase, of separation of hornblende or are due to other causes cannot be evaluated.

ACKNOWLEDGMENTS

We are very grateful to Warren Hamilton and John C. Reed, Jr., for providing their samples, to Zell E. Peterman for many unpublished Rb and Sr analyses (see his chapter of this volume), to Joseph G. Arth for many stimulating discussions, and to W. Hamilton and M. H. Beeson for their reviews of the manuscript.

REFERENCES

Arth, J. G. and Hanson, G. N., 1975. Geochemistry and origin of the Early Precambrian crust of northeastern Minnesota. Geochim. Cosmochim. Acta, 39: 325-362.

Arth, J. G. and Barker, F., 1976. Rare-earth partitioning between hornblende and dacitic liquid and implications for the genesis of trondhjemitic-tonalitic magmas. Geology, 4: 534-536.

Arth, J. G., Barker, F., Peterman, Z. E. and Friedman, I., in press. Geochemistry of the gabbro-diorite-tonalite-trondhjemite suite of southwest Finland and its implications for the origin of tonalitic and trondhjemitic magmas. J. Pet.,

Buma, G., Frey, F. A. and Wones, D. R., 1971. New England granites: trace element evidence regarding their origin and differentiation. Contr. Miner. Pet., 31: 300-320.

Compton, R. R., 1955. Trondhjemite batholith near Bidwell Bar. Geol. Soc. Am. Bull., 66: 9-44.

Davis, G. A., 1963. Structure and mode of emplacement of Caribou Mountain pluton, Klamath Mountains, California. Geol. Soc. Am. Bull., 74: 331-348.

Davis, G.A., Holdaway, M. J., Lipman, P. W. and Romey, W. D., 1965. Structure, metamorphism, and plutonism in the south-central Klamath Mountains, California. Geol. Soc. Am. Bull., 76: 933-966.

Duffield, W. A., 1968. The petrology and structure of the El Pinal Tonalite, Baja California, Mexico. Geol. Soc. Am. Bull., 79: 1351-1374.

Hamilton, W., 1963a. Trondhjemite in the Riggins quadrangle, western Idaho. U.S. Geol. Surv. Prof. Pap., 450-E: E98-E102.

Hamilton, W., 1963b. Metamorphism in the Riggins region, western Idaho. U.S. Geol. Surv., Prof. Pap., 436: 95 pp.

Hamilton, W., 1969a.   Reconnaissance geologic map of the Riggins quadrangle, west-central Idaho. U.S. Geol. Surv., Map I-579.

Hamilton, W., 1969b.   Mesozoic California and the underflow of Pacific mantle. Geol. Soc. Am. Bull., 80: 2409-2430.

Hietanen, A., 1976.   Metamorphism and plutonism around the Middle and South Forks of the Feather River, California.   U.S. Geol. Surv. Prof. Pap., 920: 30 pp.

Hotz, P. E., 1971.   Plutonic rocks of the Klamath Mountains, California and Oregon. U.S. Geol. Surv. Prof. Pap., 684-B: 20 pp.

Hunter, D. R., Barker, F. and Millard, H. T., Jr., in press. The geochemical nature of the Archean Ancient Gneiss Complex and Granodiorite Suite, Swaziland: a preliminary study. Precambrian Res.,

Jakes, P. and Gill, J., 1970.   Rare earth elements and the island arc tholeiitic series. Earth Planet. Sci. Lett., 9: 17-28.

Lanphere, M. A., Irwin, W. P. and Hotz, P. E., 1968.   Isotopic age of the Nevadan orogeny and metamorphic events in the Klamath Mountains, California. Geol. Soc. Am. Bull., 79: 1027-1052.

Larsen, L. H. and Poldervaart, A., 1961.   Petrologic study of Bald Rock batholith, near Bidwell Bar, California. Geol. Soc. Am. Bull., 72: 69-92.

Lipman, P. W., 1963.   Gibson Peak pluton: a discordant composite intrusion in the southeastern Trinity Alps, northern California.   Geol. Soc. Am. Bull., 74: 1259-1280.

Lipman, P.W., 1964.   Structure and petrology of Canyon Creek pluton, Trinity Alps, northern California. Geol. Soc. Am., Spec. Pap., 76: 342 (abstr.)

Perry, K., Jr., 1964. High-grade regional metamorphism of Precambrian gneisses and associated rocks, Paradise Basin quadrangle, Wind River Mountains, Wyoming. Thesis, Yale Univ.

Reed, J. C., Jr., 1963.   Structure of Precambrian crystalline rocks in the northern part of Grand Teton National Park, Wyoming. U.S. Geol. Surv. Prof. Pap., 475-C: C1-C6.

Reed, J. C., Jr. and Zartman, R. E., 1973. Geochronology of Precambrian rocks of the Teton Range, Wyoming. Geol. Soc. Am. Bull., 84: 561-582.

Zielinski, R. A. and Lipman, P. W., 1976. Trace-element variations at Summer Coon volcano, San Juan Mountains, Colorado, and the origin of continental-interior andesite. Geol. Soc. Am. Bull., 87: 1477-1485.

Chapter 14

PETROGENESIS OF HIGH PRESSURE TRONDHJEMITIC LAYERS IN ECLOGITES AND AMPHIBOLITES FROM SOUTHERN MASSIF CENTRAL, FRANCE

C. Nicollet, A. Leyreloup, and C. Dupuy

ABSTRACT

Layers of trondhjemite occur in eclogites and high pressure amphibolites belonging to the leptyno-amphibolitic complex of Rouergue (Southern Massif Central). These trondhjemites are low in Al and depleted in K, Rb, Cs, but they have high content of other lithophile elements compared to oceanic plagiogranites and granites. Trace element data imply at least two stages in the genesis of these rocks. The textures and initial mineral assemblage (quartz, plagioclase, kyanite, zoisite, garnet) suggest that these rocks crystallized from a melt under high pressure granulite facies conditions ($P \simeq 12.5 - 20$ kb; $T \simeq 750$-840°C). Solid-solid reactions, such as zoisite→Al-epidote, indicate a subsequent retrogression under conditions of the amphibolite facies.

(Abbreviations for phases in text and figures: qz = quartz, pl = plagioclase, Ab = albite, ol = oligoclase, an = anorthite, ky = kyanite, sill = sillimanite, ga = garnet, stl = staurolite, zo = zoisite, al ep = Al epidote, cpx = clinopyroxene, amph = amphibole, hb = green hornblende, mus = muscovite, bi = biotite, co = corundum, sp = green spinel, rt = prismatic rutile, il = ilmenite, sph = sphene, V = H_2O vapor, L = liquid.)

INTRODUCTION

A distinctive association of rock types known as the leptyno-amphibolitic complex occurs in the highly deformed and metamorphosed part of the Variscan belt of Europe (e.g., in the Granulitgebirge, Munchberg, Bohemian Massif, Brittany Massif, NW Iberic peninsula, french Massif Central).

The distinctive characteristics of the association includes bimodal association of acidic and basic rocks, tholeiitic affinities of the basic rocks, presence of metagraywackes, pyroclastic rocks, carbonaceous rocks, quartzites and ultramafic rocks (Behr, 1961; Forestier, 1963; Scharbert, 1963; Lange, 1965; Matejowska, 1967; Vogel, 1967; Losert, 1971; Zoubek, 1971; Briand, 1973; Marchand, 1974; Lasnier, 1977; Piboule, 1977; Piboule and Pontier, 1977).

436

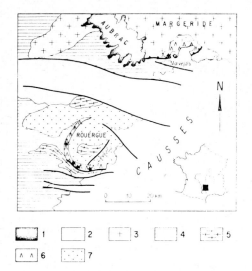

Figure 1a.--Sketch map of the studied zone (SW Massif Central). Stars: location of trondhjemites layers. (1) Plio-Quaternary basalts, (2) Post Variscan rocks, (3) Variscan granite, (4) quartz-pelitic series, (5) orthogneiss, (6) leptyno-amphibolic complex, (7) migmatites.

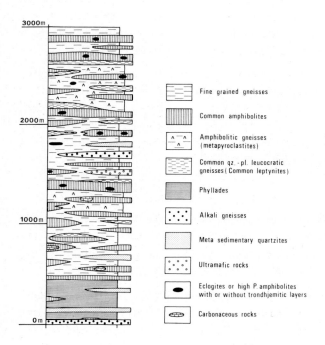

Figure 1b.--Stratigraphic sequence of the leptyno-amphibolic complex of Lévezou.

In the studied area (Fig. 1), the leptyno-amphibolitic complex has been subjected to high and low pressure metamorphism (Briand, 1973; Nicollet, 1978). We are presently concerned with the leucocratic (acidic) layers with trondhjemitic composition in the high pressure rocks. The petrogenesis of these rocks imposes constraints on the formation and evolution of the leptyno-amphibolitic complex and provides information about the origin of trondhjemites in a metamorphic context.

GEOLOGICAL SETTING AND FIELD RELATION

Such leucocratic layers have been described in various metamorphic belts (Lange, 1965; Vogel, 1967; Mottana et al., 1968; Bryhni et al., 1970; Green and Mysen, 1972; Lasnier, 1977). They were first recognized in the leptyno-amphibolitic complex of the Rouergue by Collomb (1964), where the leucocratic layers (2-10 cm thick) are intercalated with eclogites or garnet-clinopyroxene amphibolites. In some cases the interlayering is on a millimeter scale with sharp contact between basic and leucocratic layers. Where the layers are thicker (centimeters), quartz appears along the margin of basic rocks.

The complex rock system (leucocratic layers + eclogites or garnet-clinopy-roxene amphibolites) is always surrounded by the low P amphibolites which are themselves included in low P fine-grained pelitic or volcano-detrital gneisses. No direct contact between leucocratic layers and low P surrounding rocks is observed.

A systematic sampling of the acidic layers has been carried out for petro-graphical study in Lévezou and Marvejols regions (Fig. 1). The analyzed samples were taken from two outcrops 3.5 km (far apart from each other) in the Levezou area (X = 633.4; y = 3197.2; X = 637; Y = 3196.6).

PETROGRAPHY

The characteristic observed mineral association of these trondhjemitic rocks may be subdivided into quartz-rich and plagioclase-rich leucocratic layers. In the following list of mineral assemblages, the minerals in brackets form corona around the preceding mineral (e.g., ky(ol): oligoclase corona on kyanite). Successive coronas are designated by two or more brackets. Apatite, magnetite, pyrite, and zircon are present in all rocks.

Quartz-rich leucocratic layers
(a) qz-ky(ol)-zo(ol)-ga-rt-il
(b) qz-ky(co+qz$^{\pm}$sp(ol))-zo(ep(ol))-ga(hb+ol)-stl-rt(sph)-il(sph)
(c) qz-ky(sill(ol))-zo(ep(ol))-ga-rt(sph)-il(sph)
(d) qz-ky(ga(ol))-zo(ol)-ga-rt-il

(e) qz-ky(sp + pl(ga(ol)))-zo(ep(ol))-ga(hb + ol)-rt(sph)-il(sph)

(f) qz-ky(musc(ol(fk)))-zo(ol)-ga-rt-il

(g) qz-ky(musc(biot + pl(ol(fk))))-zo(ep(ol))-ga-rt(sph)-il(sph)

(h) qz-zo(ol)-ga-rt-il

(i) qz-zo(ep(ol))-ga(hb + ol)-rt(sph)-il(sph)-

Plagioclase rich leucocratic layers

(j) qz-ol-ky(ol)-zo(ol)-ga-hb-rt-il-

(k) qz-ol-ky(co+qz$^{\pm}$sp(ol))-zo(ep(ol))-ga(hb + ol)-hb-rt(sph)-il(sph)

(l) qz-ol-ky + stl(ol)-ga-hb-rt-il-ap-mg-pt,zr

(m) qz-ol-ky + stl(ol)-ga(hb + ol)-hb-rt(sph)-il(sph)-ap-mg-pt-zr

The most frequent parageneses are (a), (b), (d), (j), and (k).

Figures 2-6 illustrate the complex textures of the rocks. The detailed mineralogy has been recently described (Nicollet and Leyreloup, 1978); only a few important points are included here: The unzoned oligoclase (An_{10}-An_{25}) (Table 1) appears as polycrystalline coronas of thin crystals arranged radially around kyanite (Fig. 2), zoisite (Fig. 3) and muscovite (where it has replaced kyanite) when in contact with quartz or matrix oligoclase. Such a corona is lacking when these minerals are in contact with or included in another mineral (e.g., kyanite in garnet). The kyanite may be partially (Fig. 4) or completely rimmed by garnet. A peculiar association: kyanite, staurolite, plagioclase is found forming polycrystalline dendriform aggregates (Fig. 5a). Crystals of the

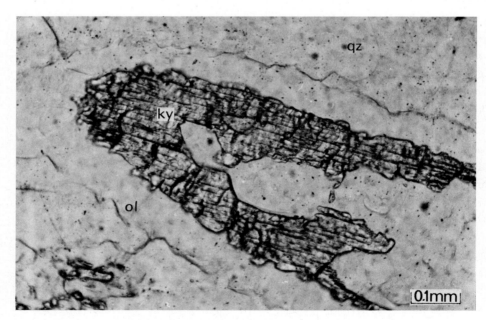

Figure 2.--Oligoclase corona surrounding kyanite.

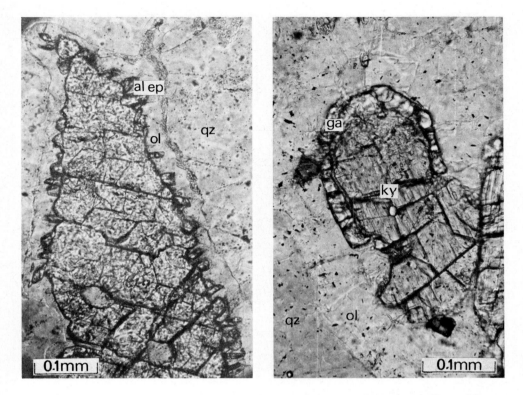

Figure 3.--Oligoclase corona surrounding zoisite.   Secondary Al epidote radially arranged at the oligoclase boundary.

Figure 4.--Rim of garnet around kyanite within the oligoclase corona.

same nature display a unique optical orientation and are limited by curved boundary (Fig. 5b).

The mineralogical features suggest a complex petrogenetic history for these rocks which includes at least a high pressure granulite metamorphism followed by sub-solidus retrogression in the amphibolite facies.

High Pressure Parageneses

The assemblages (a) (d) (h) and (j) (l) represent the most common high pressure parageneses, in quartz and plagioclase-rich rocks, respectively. The association quartz, kyanite, zoisite suggests high pressure and temperature (Boettcher, 1970), consistent with that indicated by the surrounding eclogites (omphacite, almandin-pyrope, quartz, zoisite, kyanite and exceptionally corundum (Nicollet, 1977)) and garnet-clinopyroxene amphibolites (andesine,

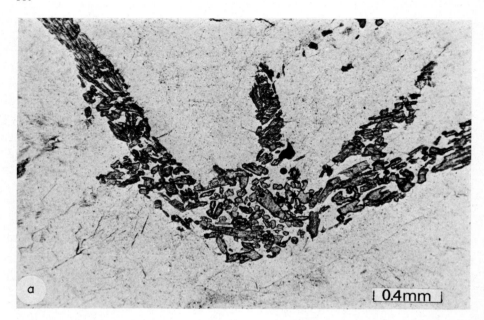

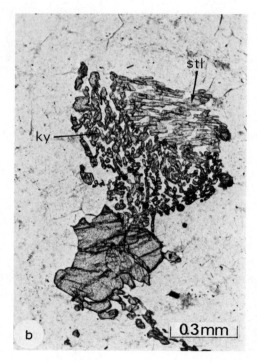

Figure 5.--Dendrites with kyanite, staurolite, oligoclase.
(a) Trifid Texture. (b) Texture showing a curved
boundary between aggregate of kyanite and staurolite.
Oligoclase represents the interdendritic phase.

TABLE 1 : Microprobe analyses of some minerals of trondhjemites.

	Plagioclases[(*)]			Zoisite 1	Al Epidote[2]	Garnet	Muscovite
	(ky)	(zo)	(mus)				
SiO_2				38.15	38.5	39.42	52.61
TiO_2				0.11	-	0.16	0.48
Al_2O_3				32.06	27.51	21.89	30.41
Fe_2O_3				1.45	7.03		2.46
FeO						20.56	
MnO				-	-	0.67	-
MgO				-	0.8	6.58	2.17
CaO	3.27	3.03	3.38	25.75	24.68	11.51	-
Na_2O	9.39	8.48	8.22	0.05	0.08	0.01	.38
K_2O	0.03	0.05	0.9	0.04	0.05	-	9.78

* : Oligoclase corona surrounding kyanite, zoisite, muscovite.

TABLE 2 : Averaged compositions of the trondhjemites and surrounding metabasites.

	Quartz-rich Leucocratic layers	Plagioclase-rich Leucocratic layers	Eclogites	*ga-cpx*	amhibolites
N	6	10	9	1	1
SiO_2	76.77(4.52)	76.87(2.79)	48.86(2.02)	54.14	54.82
TiO_2	0.33(0.13)	0.20(0.09)	1.01(0.57)	0.95	0.78
Al_2O_3	12.10(1.79)	12.35(0.90)	17.32(2.51)	15.15	16.22
Fe_2O_3	1.99(1.50)	0.72(0.44)	2.86(1.39)	4.37	4.19
FeO	2.10(1.34)	1.04(0.44)	6.68(2.00)	6.61	4.31
MnO	0.05(0.02)	0.03(0.01)	0.18(0.04)	0.21	0.11
MgO	1.06(0.58)	0.57(0.31)	7.91(1.50)	4.68	4.86
CaO	2.17(0.68)	1.64(1.07)	10.16(1.48)	3.90	7.26
Na_2O	1.86(0.81)	4.91(0.52)	2.50(0.95)	3.65	5.79
K_2O	0.48(0.51)	0.23(0.25)	0.39(0.39)	0.38	0.10
P_2O_5	-	-	-	0.40	-
H_2O^+	0.07(0.02)	0.07(0.02)	0.12(0.10)	0.18	0.15
H_2O^-	0.53(0.23)	0.47(0.19)	1.32(0.56)	1.58	0.82

( ) : Standard deviation; N : Number of samples.

442

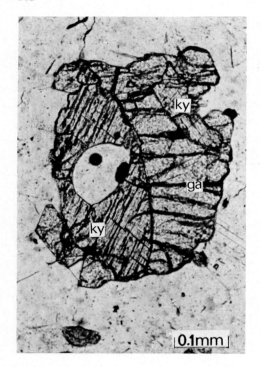

Figure 6.--Early composite garnet kyanite megacryst.

hornblende, almandine, clinopyroxene, quartz, zoisite, rutile, ilmenite).
After the work of Storre and Karotke (1972), the occasional presence of
muscovite may indicate a lower temperature for some samples. The occurrence of
plagioclase associated with kyanite and zoisite (Boettcher, 1970) approximately
established the minimum pressure these rocks were subjected to.

Sub-solidus Retrogressive Evolution.

The initial parageneses of trondhjemitic rocks and those of eclogites
suffered the same static retrogressive evolution. It is noteworthy that the
garnet-clinopyroxene amphibolites are not significantly affected by this
secondary process, since their primary paragenesis may remain stable at
intermediate pressure. The eclogites are generally retromorphosed according to
the scheme described by Lasnier (1977).

The observed sub-solidus reactions involved in the static retrogression of
the trondhjemitic primary assemblages (a, d, g, h, f, h and j, l) may be
summarized as follows:

(1) $ky \rightarrow co + qz \pm sp$

(2) $ky \rightarrow sill$

(3) $ky + ga \rightarrow sp + pl \pm qz$

(4) $ky + ga + H_2O \rightarrow stl + qz \pm sp$

(5) $zo + pl \rightarrow Al \quad ep$

(6) $ga + qz \rightarrow hb + ol$

(7) $mus + Fe, Mg \rightarrow bi + pl$

(8) $rt \rightarrow ilm \rightarrow sph$

    $rt \rightarrow sph$

(9) $ilm \rightarrow sph$

Kyanite is surrounded either by very fine symplectitic intergrowths of corundum + quartz or green spinel + quartz (1); the plagioclase in contact with spinel and quartz symplectite is zoned and may be involved in the reaction. Such reactions, already known in eclogites (Lappin, 1966; Lasnier, 1977; Nicollet, 1977) are similar to that observed in alloys during a eutectoid decomposition (Nicholson and Davies, 1971; Fridberg and Hillert, 1977). As a garnet rim sometimes exists around the green spinel-quartz symplectite it is possible to explain the formation of the symplectite by a reaction involving kyanite and garnet: garnet + kyanite → spinel + quartz $\pm$ plagioclase (3). This reaction has been described in khondalito-kinzigitic metapelites (Kornprobst, 1971; Leyreloup, 1973; Marchand, 1974; Loomis, 1976) and in metabasic rocks (Lasnier, 1977; Nicollet, 1977). A second reaction similar to one studied by Ganguly (1972) can be inferred from some textural relations between kyanite and garnet: kyanite + garnet + H_2O → staurolite + quartz $\pm$ biotite (4). Locally, kyanite is replaced by prismatic needles of sillimanite (2) and it alters in a later stage to a white mica mosaic.

Within the plagioclasic corona, small secondary Al-rich epidotes arranged radially around the primary zoisite (Fig. 3) can be explained by reaction (5). The Al-epidote becomes enriched in Fe^{3+} and may completely replace the zoisite in more retromorphosed rocks with pistacite as ultimate product. At the end of the retrogression process, Na-plagioclase and sometimes allanite formed at the expense of the epidote solid solution minerals. After Holdaway (1972), the position of the destabilization curve for the zoisite-Al-epidote transition in the P.T. grid depends on the respective iron (Fe^{3+}) contents of these two mineral species. Such a reaction is not pressure dependent and, for the composition given in Table 1, takes place at approximately $750°C$. The transformation zoisite→Al-epidote indicates a decrease of temperature. The change in the chemistry of secondary epidote has been related to a decrease in pressure-temperature and/or to an increase in $f(O_2)$ by Raith (1976). In the present case, it can be related to the retrogressive metamorphism.

Garnet has reacted not only with kyanite, as described above, but also with quartz to produce a corona of oligoclase and green hornblende (reaction 6). This reaction may be the equivalent, in the stability field of amphibole, to the classical reaction: garnet + quartz → orthopyroxene + plagioclase, which separates the intermediate and high pressure granulite facies (Green and Ringwood, 1967).

Muscovite is replaced by biotite or by a symplectitic intergrowth of biotite + plagioclase (reaction 7). Such textural relationships are commonly observed in eclogites during the kelyphytization processes (Briere, 1920; De Wit and Strong, 1975; etc.).

Rutile is altered to ilmenite and/or sphene (reaction 8).

Thus, all these retrogressive transformations have produced low pressure mineralogical assemblages typical of the amphibolite facies which are similar to those commonly found in the leptynites of the leptyno-amphibolitic complex in Europe. The main retrograde transformations associated with the various primary assemblages are summarized as follows:

Initial assemblages	Retrogressive assemblages	Involved reactions
a	b, c	1, 3, 4, 5, 6, 8, 9
d	e	3, 5, 6, 8, 9
f	g	5, 7, 8, 9
h	i	5, 6, 8, 9
j	k	1, 5, 6, 8, 9
l	m	4, 6, 8, 9

CHEMISTRY

Chemical analyses carried out by Coffrant and Piboule (1975), Piboule (1977), Piboule and Pontier (1977), have shown that the basic rocks of the leptyno-amphibolitic complex have both calc-alkaline and tholeiitic (oceanic) affinities. Our analyses (Table 2) on some eclogites and amphibolites are in agreement with their conclusions. This paper, however, concerns only the chemistsry of the leucocratic layers.

Major Elements

Sixteen samples of acidic rocks have been analyzed for major elements. Average contents are reported on Table 2. These rocks present high silica (71-83%) and relatively low Al_2O_3 content (8.7-13%). They are usually depleted in K_2O(<0.64%). In contrast, the concentration of femic elements, Ca and Na, are in the range generally registered for common acidic rocks. These chemical characteristics are quite different from those of metasediments but close to those of continental trondhjemites and more specifically the oceanic plagiogranites studied by Coleman (1977). One of these characteristics appears by plotting SiO_2 against K_2O. The high silica associated with relatively low total alkalis explains the presence of normative corundum. Normative orthoclase is less than 4 mol % (muscovite rich layer excepted) and the normative An content of the plagioclase ranges from An_4 to An_{56}. This wide range contrasts with the relative homogeneity of the bulk chemical analyses (Tables 2 and 3) and favours the hypothesis of a complex petrogenetic history for these leucocratic layers.

On the graph Ab-Or-An-normative (Fig. 7), these rocks plot within the low pressure one feldspar field (trondhjemite and tonalites; O'Connor, 1965). But the high silica content excludes any affinity with tonalites. No differentiation trend toward a ternary minimum is observed. The evolution displayed in the AFM diagram (Fig. 8) is similar to that reported for trondhjemites by Coleman (1977, fig. 18). The leucocratic layers can be considered as low Al trondhjemites. They have affinities with oceanic plagiogranites (Moores and Vines, 1971; Barker et al., 1976; Parrot, 1976; Payne and Strong, this volume; etc.) and differ from continental granophyres (Coleman, 1977) by a lower K content.

Trace Elements

Alkali, alkali-earth, Th, Hf.--The rocks studied are depleted in Rb and Cs as in K (Table 3). Their low Rb/Sr ratios (0.001-0.04) are similar to those reported by Coleman and Peterman (1975) for oceanic plagiogranites. In contrast, their Ba, Th, Hf content is quite high and in the same range as the concentrations published for leucogranites and rhyolites (Taylor et al., 1968).

Some Sr values are similar to those of Barker et al. (1976) for the low Al_2O_3 trondhjemites; others are higher. All these elements vary and generally display a good correlation between themselves (Sr excepted). A correlation also appears between K-Rb with moderately high K/Rb ratio ranging between 350-700. Then values are comparable to those of Ishizaka and Yanagi (1977) for the plagiogranites.

Sc-Co-Cr.--The content of transition elements is low and similar to those encountered in common acidic rocks (e.g., granite and leucogranites, Kolbe and Taylor, 1966; dacite and rhyolite, Taylor et al., 1969), and in plagiogranites (Coleman and Peterman, 1975). A correlation appears between Cr and Co but not between these elements and Sc. Sc is nicely correlated with La/Yb ratio (sample 6 excepted) (Fig. 9). Furthermore, Cr and Co are correlated with some incompatible elements and more especially with Ba. This anomalous correlation is not common in magmatic processes.

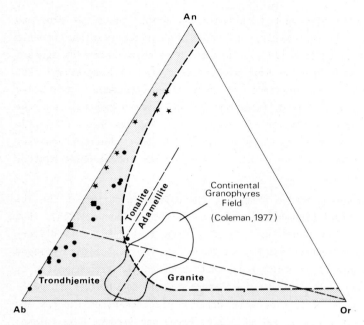

Figure 7.--An-Ab-Or normative triangular plot. Shaded area, low pressure feldspar field (<5 Kb). Separate various rock types according to O'Connor (1965). Stars: eclogites; squares, garnet-clinopyroxene amphibolites; spots, trondhjemitic layers.

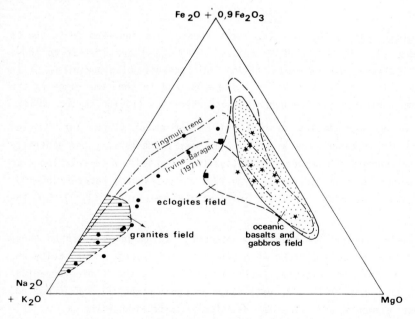

Figure 8.--A.F.M. triangular plot. Eclogitic field after Wager and Brown (1968). Oceanic rocks after Mottana et al. (1968). Symbols as on Figure 7.

TABLE 3 : Major and trace element contents of selected trondhjemitic samples.

Major elements (%)	1	2	3	4	5	6
SiO_2	83.55	78.38	74.15	73.24	80.09	78.79
TiO_2	0.22	0.25	0.25	0.55	0.10	0.37
Al_2O_3	8.73	12.16	13.49	13.70	11.73	13.47
Fe_2O_3	0.91	1.75	1.59	2.51	0.00	1.08
FeO	0.89	1.29	1.29	2.21	0.66	1.81
MnO	0.02	0.05	0.02	0.07	0.02	0.06
MgO	0.47	0.60	0.48	1.45	0.19	0.97
CaO	2.25	3.01	2.04	1.91	0.38	1.09
Na_2O	1.49	1.41	5.16	2.43	5.16	0.75
K_2O	0.34	0.17	0.07	0.36	0.03	0.17
H_2O^+	0.08	0.09	0.06	0.07	0.03	0.04
H_2O-	0.90	0.57	0.31	0.60	0.30	0.44

Trace elements (p.p.m.)	1	2	3	4	5	6
Li	21	6	5	9	5	6
Rb	8	4	1	5	1	2
Cs	0.5	0.3	0.2	0.27	0.16	0.25
Sr	445	455	710	80	225	55
Ba	785	333	129	140	77	550
Hf	16.8	8.4	5.0	5.2	3.1	4.5
Th	22.5	13.4	6.3	8.9	10.3	6.3
La	87.9	36.5	21.9	10.1	11.5	2.7
Ce	178.1	74.5	47.6	24.1	32.4	4.8
Nd	115	44.9	28.0	10.3	13.8	2.9
Sm	24.0	10.2	5.4	2.4	3.5	1.1
Eu	2.83	1.46	1.16	0.46	0.13	0.32
Tb	3.6	1.7	0.98	0.55	0.63	0.74
Yb	11.7	8.60	5.11	3.68	1.85	3.92
Lu	1.73	1.36	0.84	0.66	0.31	0.70
Sc	4.8	11.8	10.8	14.5	7	14.9
Co	12.1	6.8	3.2	6.3	1	4.3
Cr	10.7	9.2	2.8	5.9	2.6	7.1

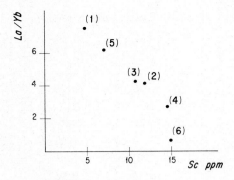

Figure 9.--Variations of La/Yb ratios against Sc in trondhjemites. The numbers are the reference samples reported in Table 3.

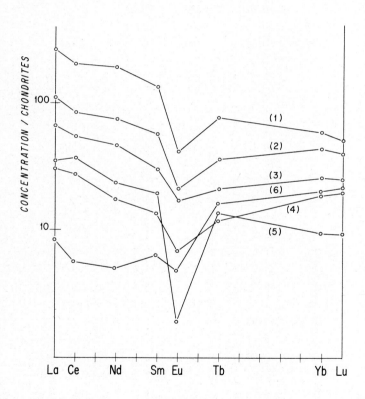

Figure 10.--Rare earth element abundances in trondhjemites normalized to a chondritic average (Frey et al., 1968). Numbers 1 to 6 refer to samples of Table 3.

R.E.E.--The R.E.E. patterns (Fig. 10) are characterized by a negative Eu anomaly and generally light RE enrichment relative to the chondrite average. These features are commonly observed in granites (s.l.) (Haskin et al., 1966; Nagasawa, 1970; Taylor et al., 1968; etc.) and differ markedly from the trend displayed either by dacite and rhyolites related to orogenic calc-alkali magmatism (Gill, 1974; Lopez-Escobar et al., 1977; Ewart et al., 1973; Dostal et al., 1977) or by oceanic plagiogranites (Kay and Senechal, 1976).

According to their La/Yb ratios, the analyzed rocks may be subdivided:

-The two samples (nos. 1 and 5) with the highest La/Yb ratios (6) are the most siliceous and display a slight heavy RE fractionation; their pattern is quite similar to those of the granophyre from Ardnamurchan (Walsh and Henderson, 1977).

-The three samples (nos. 2, 3, 4) with lower La/Yb (4.5) show very similar patterns to those reported by Barker et al. (1976) for the trondhjemites of Rio Brazos.

-Sample no. 6-- its trend is characterized by a depletion of light R.E.E. Such a pattern is generally registered by the albitized riebeckite granites in relation to secondary alteration process (Mineyev, 1963). Sample 6 has the lowest Na_2O content and does not display any trace of albitization. Metasomatic processes advocated for the generation of trondhjemites (e.g., Hughes, 1973) cannot produce such a trend (Floyd, 1977). Furthermore, it has been demonstrated (Nicollet and Leyreloup, 1978) that this alteration process is unlikely in the present case.

ORIGIN

The three main processes that have been proposed for the origin of trondhjemites are considered here. The particular chemical trend of the Rouergue trondhjemites, however, requires a fourth hypothesis implying a two-stage evolution model.

Fractional crystallization--The origin of trondhjemites by low pressure fractional crystallization from a basic magma is the most frequently suggested hypothesis (Kay and Senechal, 1976); Coleman, 1977; Erickson, 1977). A low K andesitic magma (Barker and Arth, 1976) cannot be a source for our trondhjemites because dacites and rhyolites produced from such a source(Yajima et al., 1972; Ewart et al., 1973) have a very different REE pattern and different absolute trace element contents.

A basic magma source such as those generating oceanic plagiogranites (Coleman and Peterman, 1975) and trondhjemites associated with ophiolites (Kay and Senechal, 1976; Coleman, 1977) produces a residual liquid with a lithophile element content much lower (K, Rb, Cs excepted) than those reported in Table 3. Furthermore, no low pressure fractionation process from a unique source rock may explain the geochemical characteristics of the studied trondhjemites (e.g., correlation La/Yb-Sc or Cr-Ba). This hypothesis is definitely unacceptable since four trondhjemite samples with large REE range are collected in a very small area (few square meters).

Anatexis of metasediments (Barth, 1962).--Contrary to the observations of Bryhni et al. (1970) and Green and Mysen (1972) in the Caledonian of Norway, the trondhjemites layers are exclusively located among basic rocks which are surrounded by fine-grained pelitic gneisses devoid of any trace of mobilization. Consequently, it is most unlikely that the trondhjemites were derived from the metasediments. Furthermore, the partial fusion of these gneisses cannot generate a liquid with such trace element content.

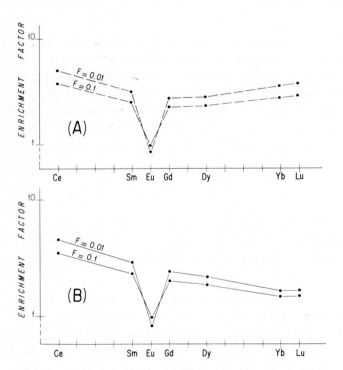

Figure 11.--Enrichment factor Cl/Co for REE in melts produced by partial melting of amphibolites. Using equation is of Shaw (1970) and the partition coefficient values compilated by Arth and Hanson (1975). Two mineralogical assemblages are considered: (A) Parent: 0.5 hb; 0.4 pl, 0.1 cpx. melt; 0.2 nb, 0.8 pl. (B) Parent: 0.5 hb; 0.4 pl, 0.05 cpx, 0.05 ga melt; 0.2 hb; 0.8 pl. The calculation has been done for variable degrees of partial melting (F). Only those for F = 1% and F = 10% are reported. The incongruent fusion of hornblende does not disturb the REE pattern in the resulting liquid.

Partial melting of the metabasic rocks (Arth and Hanson, 1972; Barker et al., 1976; Barker and Arth, 1976; Payne, 1973).--The partial fusion of eclogites or garnet granulites produces a strong RE fractionation in the resulting liquid with pattern very different from those shown by the trondhjemites (Gill, 1974; Arth and Hanson, 1975). On the other hand, the surrounding amphibolitic rocks with the mineralogical assemblages--hornblende + plagioclase $\pm$ clinopyroxene $\pm$ garnet--could be a source of the trondhjemites. The calculation of the partial fusion model of such a mineralogical assemblage (Fig. 11) explains the REE pattern of the trondhjemites (Fig. 10). It implies plagioclase as a residual phase since the trondhjemites display negative Eu anomalies and no correlation between Sr and other incompatible elements such as Ba and K. According to the partition coefficient value used for the calculation, the samples with the highest La/Yb ratio and with a slight H.R.E.E. fractionation (samples 1 and 5) imply also garnet as residuum.

The large range of R.E.E. content cannot be explained only by a variable degree of partial melting. This large range of variation implies a source rock with variable chemical and mineralogical composition. The variable mineralogical assemblage in the source rocks may easily explain the negative correlation between Sc and La/Yb ratio as shown by the calculations reported graphically in Figure 12. Samples 1 and 5 with the lowest Sc content and highest La/Yb ratio imply in agreement with the previous observation that garnet would occur in the residuum mineral assemblage. This hypothesis explains all the geochemical characteristics of the trondhjemites if quartz is present in the source rocks, in order to explain the high silica content. However, the distinctive REE pattern of sample no. 6 and the positive correlation between Cr and Ba put some constraint on this model. In sample no. 6, devoid of zoisite, a consecutive fractionation of this mineral may justify its R.E.E. trend (if we accept relative light R.E.E. enrichment in zoisite similar to those published for allanite; e.g., Adams and Sharp, 1972). But this fact cannot explain the content of other elements (for instance, the low Na_2O concentration).

Two-stage evolution model.--The partial fusion of an igneous acidic parent (Fig. 13), with a trondhjemitic mineral assemblage (quartz-oligoclase-biotite), accounts for most of the geochemical observations, even the correlation Cr-Ba and the peculiar trend of the sample (Fig. 10) The calculations reported on Figure 13 suggest that the studied rocks are partly refractory residuum and partly differentiated product. This hypothesis is sustained by the observation of thin sections; the squelettic kyanite in sample no. 6 represents remelting textures similar to those described by Busch et al. (1974). But this conclusion raises the question of the parental material of these trondhjemites. If lithophile element enrichment by some alteration process is excluded, the

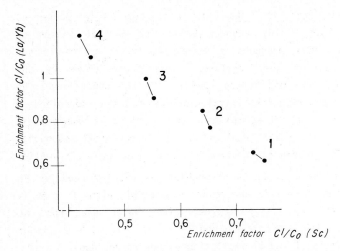

Figure 12.--Variations of La/Yb ratios against Sc (expressed as Cl/Co during partial melting of the amphibolites using equation 15 of Shaw (1970). Four mineral assemblages are considered:
1. 0.4 pl; 0.5 hb; 0.1 cpx
2. 0.3 pl; 0.6 hb; 0.1 cpx
3. 0.25 pl; 0.65 hb; 0.07 cpx; 0.03 ga
4. 0.20 pl; 0.70 hb; 0.03 cpx; 0.07 ga
In every case the fractional melt was formed from 0.8 pl and 0.2 hb. The calculation is done for F comprised between 5% and 10% with partition coefficient values of Arth and Hanson (1975) for REE and of Lopez-Escobar et al. (1977) for Sc.

plagiogranite with the composition reported by several authors (e.g., Coleman, 1977) cannot generate the acidic rocks during anatexis because of their high REE, Ba, etc., content. Continental granophyres or various acid volcanics (Barker, pers. comm.) may be in this respect a preferred source material but they imply an escape of alkali (K, Rb, Cs) during prograde metamorphism. The parental acidic rock may have been a trondhjemite produced by partial fusion of amphibolite. This last hypothesis excludes an escape of alkali but implies two successive phases of anatexis.

In any case, whatever the nature of the acidic parent rock, the trace element chemistry of the studied trondhjemites suggests a final stage of anatexis.

ORIGIN OF THE KYANITE-ZOISITE-GARNET-QUARTZ-OLIGOCLASE (MATRIX AND CORONA) ASSEMBLAGE

The P.T. stability conditions of the high pressure assemblage (Kyanite, zoisite, garnet, quartz) are bounded towards low temperature and pressure by the transition zoisite to Al-epidote, appearance of plagioclase and by the inversion kyanite-sillimanite. Consequently, this assemblage was formed at

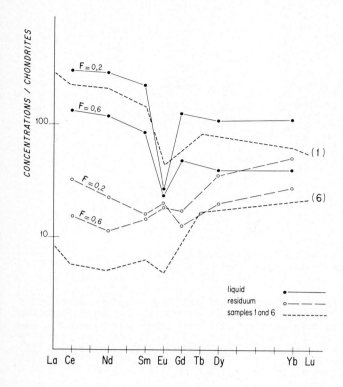

Figure 13.--Chondrite normalized rare earth abundances in theoretical liquid and corresponding residuum derived by melting of a trondhjemitic parent rock (0.5 qz; 0.44 pl; 0.6 bi) assuming incongruent fusion of biotite (1 bi   0.25 ga + 0.75 L).   The calculations have been done for F = 20% and F = 60% using partition coefficients of Arth and Hanson (1975) and incongruent melting equation of Shaw (1977).   Samples 1 and 6 are reported for comparison.   Initial rare earth element concentrations (Co) are those of sample 2.

12.5-20 Kb and 750°-840°C(Fig. 14) and is consistent with the stability field of amphibole-quartz-kyanite assemblage of Green and Vernon (1974) although the compositions of the amphiboles are not similar. Furthermore, the corona texture involving oligoclase cannot be satisfactorily explained by the sub-solidus reaction: kyanite + zoisite + quartz→anorthite + H_2O vap (Boettcher, 1970) because the three reacting minerals have to be in contact and their reaction products formed at the boundary between them. Our rocks do not show this situation: when kyanite and zoisite are in contact, the oligoclase is found at the boundary between these minerals. Furthermore, this corona appears around kyanite and zoisite when the two minerals are involved in both a quartzose or a plagioclase-rich matrix.

These observations negate a sub-solidus metamorphic transformation in high pressure conditions but favour a direct crystallization of the high pressure

454

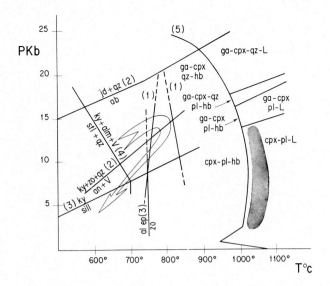

Figure 14.--P.T. crystallization conditions of the high pressure paragenesis
(gray shaded area). The dark shaded area delineates the crystallization
field of the assumed primary trondhjemitic melt. The arrow indicates the
metamorphic evolution of the trondhjemites. (1) Delineates the stability
field of the qz + ky + amph assemblage (Green and Vernon, 1974). (2)
According to Boettcher (1970, 1971). (3) Holdaway (1971, 1972). (4)
Ganguly (1972). (5) Gabbro solidus at 0.5% H_2O (Wyllie, 1971).

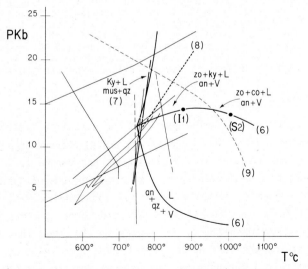

Figure 15.--P.T. crystallization conditions assuming direct crystallization
from the trondhjemitic melt (shaded area); arrow, sub-solidus state
retrogressive evolution. Fine lines refer to the reaction reported on
Figure 14. Invariant point I1, singular point S2, reactions (6): Boettcher
(1970, 1971), (7): Storre and Karotke (1972), (8) Gabbro solidus at 7 Kb P
H_2O and (9) amphibole stability limit at same P H_2O extrapolated from
Bryhni et al. (1970).

assemblage from the trondhjemitic melt. Indeed, in the simplified $SiO_2-Al_2O_3-CaO-H_2O$ system (Boettcher, 1970), the trondhjemitic melt, under P.T. conditions defined previously, may crystallize first kyanite and zoisite which is in accord with our observations (presence of early corroded kyanite and assymetrically zoned and truncated zoisite megacrysts). Then both minerals react with the liquid by peritectic reaction (kyanite + zoisite + liquid→ anorthite + H_2O vap., Boettcher, 1970) to form plagioclase (Fig. 15). In practice, kyanite and zoisite quickly become encapsulated by plagioclase which forms reaction rings (Yeh, 1970; Ehlers, 1972). The reaction is stifled by the need for diffusion through this solid layer (Nicholson and Davies, 1971; St. John and Hogan, 1977). The armoured kyanite and zoisite are then not completely reabsorbed; with decreasing P.T. the residual liquid crosses its solidus curve with secondary precipitation of quartz and plagioclase, their relative proportion and composition dependent on the composition of the residual liquid. Green hornblende forms only in rocks with Na_2O >3% in agreement with the results of Cawthorn and O'Hara(1976). At this stage, the sub-solidus reactions described above may appear with decreasing P and T conditions (Fig. 15).

The presence of primary garnet in our rocks (e.g., early composite garnet-kyanite megacrysts: Fig. 6, inclusions of garnet in kyanite) cannot be explained by the simplified system of Boettcher (1970). However, the addition of MgO and FeO in this system (Hensen, 1976) increase the stability field of garnet and may reconcile the observations. Furthermore, it has been demonstrated (Green and Ringwood, 1968a, b) that the almandine pyrope is a near liquidus phase and may coexist with kyanite in rhyodacitic liquid. The presence of garnet may also result from the incongruent melting of biotite during the hypothetical high pressure fusion of early trondhjemites as suggested from geochemical considerations (previous section).

Further observations support high pressure crystallization from a liquid. The presence of kyanite in muscovite may imply a peritectic reaction: kyanite + liquid→muscovite + quartz (Storre and Karotke, 1972). The bi- or trifid textures (Fig. 5) are compatible with those observed during the solidification of an alloy (Bouchy and Gobin, 1971; Figs. 4-15) and similar to the dendrites commonly found in peritectic reactions (Titchener and Spittle, 1975).

CONCLUSION

The metamorphic evolution of the trondhjemitic layers is indubitably associated with that of the metabasites. However, the successive metamorphic episodes which took place in this region (Nicollet, 1978) strongly complicate the petrogenetic interpretations. The geochemical data on trondhjemites suggest one step of partial fusion from an initial acidic material. In order to conciliate the analytical data and those established from the calculations, the theoretical model implies a partial fusion under high pressure conditions (appearance of garnet by incongruent fusion of biotite).

Although several hypotheses have been excluded, the problem of primary origin of the trondhjemitic material remains unsolved. Partial fusion of amphibolite or altered plagiogranite associated with an old ophiolitic complex now dismembered are the most plausible source for the acidic layers. But it is impossible to choose, at the present, between the two possibilities. The intimate field association of the trondhjemites and eclogites contrasts with the geochemical considerations which indicate they are not genetically related. Their intimate association may be explained by a process of dehydration of amphibolite during local partial fusion process under high pressure conditions (Fry and Fyfe, 1969; Essene et al., 1970; Bryhni et al., 1970; Green and Mysen, 1972).

The P.T. path of the trondhjemites indicated in Figures 14 and 15 is similar to what might be expected in a subduction zone (Raheim and Green, 1975; Miller, 1977; Reinsch, 1977). The hypothetical prograde course of this path (Fig. 14) may have been generated during burial in a subduction zone, prior to the emplacement of an orogenic belt (Bryhni et al., 1977; O'Hara, personal comm.), while decompression following uplift would be reflected in the quasi-adiabatic retrograde path (Leyreloup et al., 1975; Ernst, 1977).

ACKNOWLEDGMENTS

The research presented here represents part of the Senior author's doctoral dissertation. D. E. Strong (Memorial University of Newfoundland, Canada), P. H. Thompson (Geological Survey, Ottawa Canada) and Ph. Matte are gratefully acknowledged for critically reading and improving the English text. We extend thanks to Miss M. Serre for typing the manuscript and Mr. P. Viela for his assistance in the preparation of figures.

Financial support was provided by "Laboratoire Associe au C.N.R.S. n⁰ 266" and "A.T.P. Geodynamique."

REFERENCES

Adams, J. W. and Sharp, W. N., 1972. Thalenite and allanite derived from yttrofluorite in the white cloud pegmatite, south Platte area, Colorado. U.S. Geol. Surv. Prof. Pap., 800-C: C63-C69.

Anhaeusser, C. R., 1971. Cyclic volcanicity and sedimentation in the evolutionary development of Archean greenstone belts of shield areas. Geol. Soc. Aust. Spec. Publ., 3: 57-70.

Anhauesser, C. R., 1973. The evolution of the early Precambrian crust of Southern Africa. Phil. Trans. r. Soc. London, A-273: 359-388.

Arth, J. G. and Hanson, G. N., 1972. Quartz diorites derived by partial melting of eclogite or amphibolite at mantle depths. Contrib. Miner. Pet., 37: 161-174.

Arth, J. G. and Hanson, G. N., 1975. Geochemistry and origin of the early Precambrian crust of Northeastern Minnesota. Geochim. Cosmochim. Acta, 39: 325-362.

Barker, F. and Peterman, Z. E., 1974. Bimodal tholeiitic-dacitic magmatism and the early Precambrian crust. Precambrian Res., 1: 1-12.

Barker, F. and Arth, J. G., 1976. Generation of trondhjemitic-tonalitic liquids and Archean bimodal trondhjemite-basalt suites. Geology, 4: 96-600.

Barker, F., Arth, J. G., Peterman, Z. E. and Friedman, I., 1976. The 1.7 to 1.8 b.y. old trondhjemites of Southwestern Colorado and Northern New Mexico: Geochemistry and depths of genesis. Bull. Geol. Soc. Am., 87: 189-198.

Barth, T. F. W., 1962. A final proposal for calculating the mesonorm of metamorphic rocks. J. Geol., 70: 497-498.

Behr, H. J., 1961. Beiträge zur petrographischen und tectonischen analyse des sächsischen Granulitgebirges (mit Anlagenmappen)--Freibergen Forschttft., C119, Akademie Verlag, Berlin.

Boettcher, A. L., 1970. The system $CaO-Al_2O_3-SiO_2-H_2O$ at high pressures and temperatures. J. Pet., 11: 337-379.

Boettcher, A. L., 1971. The nature of the crust of the earth with special emphasis on the role of plagioclase. Am. Geophys. Union Geophys. Mon., 14: 261-277.

Bouchy, Ch. et Gobin, G., 1971. Métallurgie, I métallurgie structurale, Armand Colin, ed., 157 pp.

Briand, B., 1973. Lithostratigraphie et métamorphisme de la série cristallophyllienne de Marvejols. Bull. Rech. geol. min. (II serie) section I, n°. 4: 183-198.

Briere, Y., 1920. Les éclogites francaises, leur composition minéralogique et chimique, leur origine. Bull. Soc. Franç. Mineral. Crist., 43: 77-222.

Bryhni, I., Krogh, E. and Griffin, W. L., 1977. Crustal derivation of Norvegian eclogites: a review. Neues Jahrb. Mineral. Abhandl., 130: 49-68.

458

Burg, J. P. et Matte, Ph., 1977. A cross section through the Massif Central francais and its variscan evolution. Geotagung '77. Geol. Gesselshaft Göttingen.

Busch, W., Schneider, G. and Mehnert, K. R., 1974. Initial melting at grain boundaries. Part II: Melting in rocks of granodioritic, quartz dioritic and tonalitic composition. Neues Jahrb. Miner. Monatsh., 8: 345-370.

Cawthorn, R. G. and O'Hara, M. J., 1976. Amphibole fractionation in calc-alkaline magma genesis. Am. J. Sci., 276: 309-329.

Coffrant, D. et Piboule, M., 1975. Les métavulcanites basiques du Bas-Limousin (Massif Central francais); étude géochimique des éclogites et des dolerites. Bull. Soc. Géol. France, 7, 17: 620-628.

Coleman, R. G., 1977. Ophiolites in Minerals and Rocks, 12, Springer Verlag-Berlin, Heidelberg, New York, 229 pp.

Coleman, R. G. and Peterman, Z. E., 1975. Oceanic plagiogranite. J. Geophys. Res., 80: 1099-1108.

Collomb, P., 1964. Etude géologique du Rouergue cristallin. Thèse d'Etat, Paris, 5 tomes ronéotypés.

Dostal, J., Dupuy, C. and LeFevre, C., 1977. Rare earth element distribution in Plio-Quaternary volcanic rocks from Southern Peru. Lithos, 16: 173-183.

DeWit, J. and Strong, D. F., 1975. Eclogite bearing amphibolites from the Appalachian mobile belt, N.W. Newfoundland: Dry versus wet metamorphism. J. Geol., 83: 609-627.

Ehlers, E. G., 1972. The interpretation of geological phase diagrams. W. H. Freeman and Company, ed., 280 pp.

Erickson, E. H., 1977. Petrology and petrogenesis of the Mount Stuart batholith. Plutonic equivalent of the high-alumina basalt association? Contrib. Miner. Pet. 60: 183-107.

Ernst, W. G., 1977. Mineralogic study of eclogitic rocks from Alpe Arami, Lepontine Alps, Southern Switzerland. J. Pet., 18: 371-398.

Essene, E. J., Hensen, B. J. and Green, D. H., 1970. Experimental study of amphibolite and eclogite stability. Phys. Earth Planet. Interiors, 3: 378-384.

Ewart, A., Bryan, W. B. and Gill, J. B., 1973. Mineralogy and geochemistry of the younger volcanic islands of Tonga. S.W. Pacific J. Pet., 14: 465-492.

Floyd, P. A., 1977. Rare earth element mobility and geochemical characterisation of spilitic rocks. Nature, 269: 134-137.

Forestier, F. H., 1963. Métamorphisme hercynien et anté-hercynien dans le bassin du Haut-Allier (Massif Central francais). Bull. Serv. Carte geol. France, 271, 59: 294 pp.

Frey, F. A., Haskin, M. A., Poetz, J. and Haskin, L. A., 1968. Rare earth abundances in some basic rocks. J. Geophys. Res., 70: 6085-6098.

Fridberg, J. and Hillert, M., 1977. On the eutectoid transformation of Ferrite in Fe-Mo-C alloys. Acta met., 25: 19-24.

Fry, N. and Fyfe, W. S., 1969. Eclogites and water pressure. Contr. Miner. Pet., 24: 1-6.

Ganguly, J., 1972. Staurolite stability and related parageneses: Theory, experiments and applications. J. Pet., 13: 335-365.

Gill, J. G., 1974. Role of underthrust oceanic crust in the genesis of a Fijian calc-alkaline suite. Contrib. Miner. Pet., 43: 29-45.

Glikson, A. Y., 1965. Stratigraphy and evolution of primary and secondary greenstones: significance of data from shields of the Southern hemisphere, in F. B. Windley, ed., The early history of the Earth, John Wiley and Sons: 257-277.

Green, D. H. and Mysen, B. O., 1972. Genetic relationship between eclogite and hornblende + plagioclase pegmatite in Western Norway. Lithos, 5: 147-161.

Green, D. H. and Ringwood, A. E., 1967. An experimental investigation of the gabbro to eclogite transformation and its petrological applications. Geochim. Cosmochim. Acta, 31: 767-833.

Green, D. H. and Vernon, K. H., 1974. Cordierite breakdown under high pressure hydrous conditions. Contrib. Miner. Pet., 46: 215-222.

Green, T. H. and Ringwood, A. E., 1968a. Genesis of the calc-alkaline igneous rocks suite. Contrib. Miner. Pet., 18: 105-162.

Green, T. H. and Ringwood, A. E., 1968b. Origin of garnet phenocrysts in calc-alkaline rocks. Contrib. Miner. Pet., 18: 162-174.

Haskin, L. A., Haskin, M. A., Frey, F. A. and Wildeman, T. R., 1968. Relative and absolute terrestrial abundances of the rare earths, in Ahrens, L. H., ed. Origin and distribution of the elements: 889-912.

Hensen, B. J., 1976. The stability of pyrope-grossular garnet with excess silica. Contrib. Miner. Pet., 55: 279-292.

Holdaway, M. J., 1971. The aluminium silicate triple-point. Am. J. Sci., 269: 97-131.

Holdaway, M. J., 1972. Thermal stability of Al-Fe epidote as a function of $f(O_2)$ and Fe content. Contrib. Miner. Pet., 37: 307-340.

Hughes, C. J., 1973. Spilites, keratophyres and the igneous spectrum. Geol. Mag., 109: 513-527.

Irvine, T. N. and Baragar, W. R. A., 1971. A guide to the chemical classification of the common volcanic rocks. Can. J. Earth Sci., 8: 523-548.

Ishizaka, K. and Yanagi, T., 1977. K, Rb and Sr abundances and Sr isotopic composition of the Tanzawa granitic and associated gabbroic rocks, Japan: Low potash island arc plutonic complex. Earth Planet. Sci. Lett., 33: 345-352.

Kay, R. W. and Senechal, R. G., 1976. The rare earth geochemistry of the Troodos Ophiolite complex. J. Geophys. Res., 81: 964-970.

Kolbe, P. and Taylor, S. R., 1966. Major and trace element relationships in granodiorites and granites from Australia and South Africa. Contrib. Miner. Pet., 12: 202-222.

Kornprobst, J., 1971. Contribution à l'étude pétrographique et structurale de la zone interne du Rif. Thèse d'Etat, Paris, 376 pp.

Kuno, H., 1959. Origin of Cenozoic petrographic provinces of Japan and surrounding areas. Bull. Volcanol., 20: 37-76.

Lasnier, B., 1977. Persistance d'une série granulitique au coeur du Massif Central français (Haut-Allier). Les termes basiques, ultrabasiques et carbonates. Thèse d'Etat, Nantes, 351 pp.

Leyreloup, A., 1973. Le socle profond en Velay d'apres les enclaves remontées par les volcans néogènes. Son thermométamorphisme et sa lithologie: granites et série charnockitique (Massif Central francais). Thèse 3e cycle, Nantes, 356 pp.

Leyreloup, A., Lasnier, B. and Marchand, J., 1975. Retrograde corona-forming reactions in high pressure granulite facies rocks. Petrologie, I: 43-55.

Loomis, T. P., 1976. Irreversible reactions in high-grade metapelitic rocks. J. Pet., 17: 559-588.

Lopez-Escobar, L., Frey, F. A. and Vergara, M., 1977. Andesites and high Al basalts from the Central South Chili High Andes: geochemical evidence bearing on their petrogenesis. Contrib. Miner. Pet., 63: 199-288.

Losert, J., 1971. On the volcagenous origin of some Moldanubian lepytnites. Krystalinikum, 7: 61-84.

Marchand, J., 1974. Persistance d'une série granulitique au coeur du Massif Central français. Les termes acides. Thèse 3e cycle, Nantes, 207 pp.

Matejovska, O., 1967. Petrogenesis of the Moldanubian granulites near Namest nad Oslavov, Krystalinikum 5: 85-103.

Miller, C., 1977. Mineral parageneses recording the P.T. history of Alpine eclogites in the Tauern window. Austria. Neues Jahrb. Mineral. Abhandl., 130: 69-77.

Mineyev, D. A., 1963. Geochemical differentiation of the rare earths. Geochem. Intern., 12: 1129-1149.

Moores, E. M. and Vine, F. J., 1971. The Troodos massif Cypress and other ophiolites as oceanic crust: evaluation and implications. Phil. Trans. r. Soc. London, 268: 443-466.

Mottana, A., Church, W. R. and Edgar, A. D., 1968. Chemistry, mineralogy and petrology of an eclogite from the type locality (Saualpe, Austria). Contrib. Miner. Pet., 18: 338-346.

Mottana, A. and Bocchio, R., 1975. Superferric eclogites of the Voltri group Peennidic Belt, Apennines). Contrib. Miner. Pet., 49: 201-210.

Nagasawa, H., 1970. R.E. concentrations in zircon and apatite and their host dacites and granites. Earth Planet. Sci. Lett., 9: 359-364.

Nicholson, R. B. and Davies, G. J., 1971. Development of microstructure, in Finniston, H. M., ed., Structural characteristics of material. Elsevier, Amsterdam: 199-289.

Nicollet, C., 1977. Une nouvelle éclogite à disthène et corindon primaires dans les complexes leptyno-amphiboliques du Massif Central francais (Lévezou, Rouergue). Bull. Soc. Franc. Miner. Crist., 100: 334-337.

Nicollet, C., 1978. Etude pétrologique, géochimique et structurale des terrains cristallins antépermiens du versant Sud du Lévezou (Massif Central français) origine des groupes leptyno-amphiboliques. Thèse 3e cycle, Montpellier (in press).

Nicollet, C. et Leyreloup, A., 1978. Pétrologie des niveaux trondhjémitiques de haute pression associés aux éclogites et amphibolites des complexes leptyno-amphiboliques du Massif Central français. Can. J. Earth Sci. (in press).

O'Connor, J. T., 1965. A classification of quartz-rich igneous rocks based on feldspar ratios. U.S. Geol. Surv. Prof. Pap., 525-B: B79-B84.

Parrot, J. F., 1977. Assemblage ophiolitique du Baër-Bassit. Travaux et documents de l'O.R.S.T.O.M., N° 72.

Payne, J. C., 1973. Geology of the Twillingate area, Newfoundland. Unpubl. M. Sc. thesis, Memorial University, St. John's, Newfoundland, 159 pp.

Piboule, M., 1977. Mise en evidence par les méthodes statistiques multivariées de deux séries magmatiques à l'origine des ortho-amphibolites rutènes 5e Reun. Ann. Sc. Terre, Rennes: 377.

Piboule, M. et Pontier, J., 1977. Géochimie comparée des amphibolites en bancs et des métagabbros associés; application des méthodes statistiques multivariées à l'étude des métabasites rutènes et conséquences sédimentologiques 5e Reun. Ann. Sc. Terre, Rennes: 379.

Raheim, A. and Green, D. H., 1975. P.T. paths of natural eclogites during metamorphism--a record of subduction. Lithos, 8: 317-328.

Raith, M., 1976. The Al-Fe (III) epidote miscibility gap in a metamorphic profile through the penninic series of the Tauern Window, Austria. Contrib. Miner. Pet., 57: 99-117.

Reinsch, D., 1977. High pressure rocks from Val Chuisella (Sesia-Lanzo zone, Italian Alps). Neues Jahrb. Miner. Abhandl., 130: 89-102.

Scharbert, H. G., 1963. Die granulite der Südlichin niederösterreich-ischen Moldanubikums. I Teil. Neues Jahrb. Miner. Abhandl., 100: 59-86.

Shaw, D. M., 1970. Trace element fractionation during anatexis. Geochim. Cosmochim. Acta, 34: 237-243.

Shaw, D. M., 1977. Trace element melting models. IAGC Symposium Paris.

St. John, D. H. and Hogan, L. M., 1977. The peritectic transformation, Acta Met. 25: 77-81.

Storre, B. and Karotke, E., 1972. Experimental data on melting reactions of muscovite + quartz in the system $K_2O-Al_2O_3-SiO_2-H_2O$ to 20 kb water pressure. Contrib. Miner. Pet., 36: 343-345.

Taylor, S. R., Ewart, A. and Capp, A. C., 1968. Leucogranites and rhyolites. Trace elements evidence of fractional crystallization and partial melting. Lithos, 1: 179-186.

Taylor, S. R., Capp, A. C., Graham, A. L. and Blake, D. H., 1969. Trace element abundances in andesites. Contrib. Miner. Pet., 23: 1-26.

Titchener, A. P. and Spittle, J. A., 1975. The microstructures of directionally solidified alloys that undergo a peritectic transformation. Acta Met., 23: 497-502.

Vogel, D. E., 1967. Petrology of an eclogite and pyrigarnite-bearing polymetamorphic rock complex at Cabo Ortegal, N.W. Spain. Leidse geol. Meded., D40: 121-213.

Wager, L. R. and Brown, G. M., 1968. Layered igneous rocks. Oliver and Boyd, ed. Edinburgh and London.

Walsh, J. N. and Henderson, P., 1977. Rare earth element patterns of rocks from the Centre 3 igneous complex, Ardnamurchan, Argyllshire. Contrib. Miner. Pet., 60: 31-38.

Wyllie, P. J., 1971. Experimental limits for melting in the earth's crust and upper mantle. Am. Geophys. Union, Geophys. Mon. 14: 279-301.

Yajima, T., Higuchi, H. and Nagasawa, H., 1972. Variation of rare earth concentrations in pigeonitic and hypersthenic rocks series from Izu. Hakone region, Japan. Contrib. Miner. Pet., 35: 235-244.

Yeh, H. C., 1970. Interpretation of phase diagrams, in Phase diagrams-- Material Science and Technology. Vol. I, Theory, principles, and techniques of phase diagrams. Ed.: A. M. Alper: 167-197.

Zoubek, V., 1971. Upper mantle project programme in Czechoslovakia 1962-1970. Geology Final Report--Prague, 128 pp.

Chapter 15

TWO CONTRASTING TRONDHJEMITE ASSOCIATIONS FROM TRANSPORTED OPHIOLITES IN WESTERN NEWFOUNDLAND: INITIAL REPORT

J. Malpas

ABSTRACT

Trondhjemitic rocks are recognized in two ophiolitic assemblages in western Newfoundland. Regional geological considerations suggest that one of these assemblages, the Little Port Complex, represents the basement of an island arc assemblage, whilst the other, the Bay of Islands Complex, is an undeformed ophiolite and represents oceanic lithosphere. The origin of trondhjemites differs in these two complexes. In one it appears that the trondhjemites are a result of partial fusion of amphibolites; in the other a result of differentiation of basaltic magma. Chemical differences are recorded and might be used in other instances to determine the origin of trondhjemitic liquids.

INTRODUCTION

Leucocratic rocks have been described from a number of ophiolite assemblages of which they form an integral although not voluminous part. Coleman and Peterman (1975) attempted to reconcile differences of opinion on their origin and presented data consistent with the idea of low-pressure differentiation of sub-alkaline basaltic magma to form potassium-poor leuco-cratic rocks. Rocks of the ophiolite suite and of ophiolitic affinity are well preserved and exposed in western Newfoundland in the Bay of Islands area (Fig. 1). The geology of this area has been largely reinterpreted in the last six years and detailed mapping programmes have led to the recognition of a number of superposed thrust slices of igneous, metamorphic, and sedimentary rocks. These slices were displaced from an oceanic environment and emplaced onto the North American continental margin during middle Ordovician time (Williams, 1971; Williams and Malpas, 1972; Malpas, 1976).

The Upper Thrust Slices (Malpas, 1976) of the allochthonous series are a number of individual sheets constituting the "ophiolite sequences" described by Stevens (1970). These slices are made up of lower Ordovician or possibly older igneous and metamorphic rocks, only some of which are clearly ophiolitic. Four

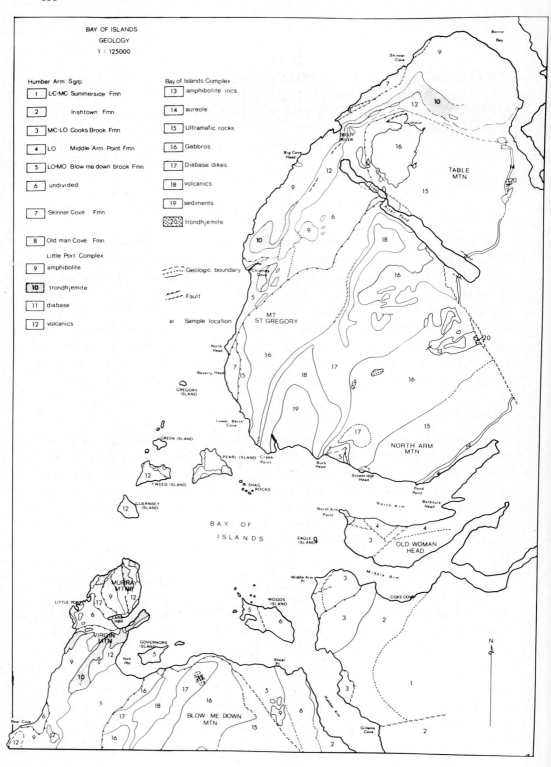

BAY OF ISLANDS
GEOLOGY
1 : 125000

Humber Arm Sgrp

1	LC-MC Summerside Fmn
2	Irishtown Fmn
3	MC-LO Cooks Brook Fmn
4	LO Middle Arm Point Fmn
5	LO-MO Blow me down brook Fmn
6	undivided
7	Skinner Cove Fmn
8	Old man Cove Fmn

Little Port Complex

9	amphibolite
10	trondhjemite
11	diabase
12	volcanics

Bay of Islands Complex

13	amphibolite incs
14	aureole
15	Ultramafic rocks
16	Gabbros
17	Diabase dikes
18	volcanics
19	sediments
20	trondhjemite

- - - - Geologic boundary

∼∼∼ Fault

21 Sample location

main slice assemblages have been recognized (Williams, 1973). These are: (i) the Skinner Cove Formation, (ii) the Old Man Cove Formation, (iii) the Little Port Complex, and (iv) the Bay of Islands Complex. These slice assemblages are always found in the same stacking order:

TOP   Bay of Islands Complex
       Little Port Complex
       Old Man Cove Formation
       Skinner Cove Formation

The two uppermost slices have clear ophiolitic affinities (Malpas, 1976) and it is within these that trondhjemites and related rocks are found (Fig. 1).

Generally rocks of two different, although not necessarily widely separated ages are represented in the Little Port Complex. The first group consists of ultramafic rocks, gabbros, amphibolites, and trondhjemites or "quartz-diorites" (Smith, 1958), which are all deformed and variably metamorphosed. These are cut by dikes which feed volcanics, both relatively unmetamorphosed and undeformed.

The gabbros and amphibolites have a well developed foliation. This fabric, although generally parallel to original layering in the gabbros, does not obliterate it. Indeed some gabbros still display pseudosedimentary structures associated with their cumulate origin. The gabbros grade into the more common amphibolites which in places are polydeformed. However, no regular pattern in the intensity of the deformation has been observed.

Leucocratic rocks are found cutting the amphibolites and intrusion breccias are often developed along their contacts. These acid rocks are deformed together with the rocks they intrude and form large bodies with lensoid shapes, their long axes parallel to the regional strike of the Complex and to the orientation of the main fabric in the amphibolites, i.e., NNE-SSW. The bodies are intensely brecciated in places, some zones resembling protomylonites or possibly tuffisite veins (Hughes, 1971).

The younger dikes are locally 'sheeted,' and may show chilled margins against neighbouring dikes. They appear as post-tectonic intrusions cutting foliated gabbro and foliated trondhjemites and the volcanics with which they are associated. However, they are almost always internally brecciated (Williams and Malpas, 1972). The dikes feed pillow lavas and breccias which

Figure 1.--Geological map of the Bay of Islands Region showing trondhjemite locations.

are juxtaposed with the deformed rocks. Although the volcanics are generally mafic, some quartz-porphyritic rhyolites are exposed in the northern part of the area.

INTERPRETATION OF THE GEOLOGY

Smith (1958) considered the igneous and metamorphic rocks of the Little Port Complex and Bay of Islands Complex together as part of one intrusive assemblage. With such an interpretation it was difficult to reconcile the large variations in metamorphic and structural style from one part of the assemblage to another. This obstacle in the interpretation of the whole assemblage as oceanic lithosphere was only overcome with the recognition of the distinct slice assemblages of igneous and metamorphic rocks. The definition of the Little Port Complex as a polygenetic assemblage distinct from the Bay of Islands ophiolite suite both resolves this problem and further eases the interpretation of the Bay of Islands Complex as oceanic crust and mantle (Williams, 1971, and see below).

Williams and Malpas (1972) drew attention to the fact that the Little Port Complex itself could not be considered as a typical ophiolite suite since the dikes and volcanics are younger and bear no genetic relationship to the deformed igneous rocks that they cut. The development of the relatively large volumes of leucocratic rocks also seems unusual in comparison with ophiolite suites elsewhere. Strong (1974), however, concluded that the rocks of the Little Port Complex represented oceanic lithosphere formed and deformed at or close to an oceanic ridge. He suggested that perhaps the younger dikes and volcanics within the Complex represented off-axis volcanism. The leucocratic rocks were considered products of partial melting of the amphibolites under conditions of high heat-flow. That such conditions might exist beneath spreading centres is exemplified by phenomena such as the high temperature Flaser gabbro of the Lizard Complex, S.W. England, which has been interpreted as oceanic lithosphere by Thayer (1972), Mitchell (1974), and Strong et al. (1975).

Several workers (Comeau, 1972; Williams and Malpas, 1972; Kennedy, 1975) considered that the deformed rocks of the Little Port Complex represent older continental crustal remnants caught up in the formation of the ophiolites during which the younger dikes and volcanics of the Complex were produced. All of these workers pointed out the similarities in lithology, structure and age with the rocks of Twillingate. The analogy is so strong that Williams and Payne (1975) suggested that the Little Port Complex could represent a sampling of the geology of the Twillingate area. Both the Little Port Complex and the Twillingate sequence have since been reinterpreted by Malpas et al. (1973),

Strong and Payne (1973), Williams and Payne (1975), and Payne and Strong (this volume) and the juxtaposition of intensely deformed amphibolites with fresh volcanic rocks compared with situations in present-day island arcs where undeformed volcanics overlie amphibolitic basement (Shiraki, 1971; Coleman, 1970; Hutchinson and Dhonau, 1969; Tobisch, 1968). This interpretation is at present adhered to, although further petrologic and structural studies are required to refine it.

LEUCOCRATIC ROCKS IN THE LITTLE PORT COMPLEX

Leucocratic rocks occur in two major forms in the Little Port Complex. Most are clearly intrusive into the amphibolites and gabbros and form large bodies, up to one and one half kilometers maximum dimensions; others are found in small local patches and vein-like bodies sitting in an amphibolite host. Taken together the leucocratic rocks make up to 35% of the Complex.

Along contacts of the larger bodies, where intrusion breccias are developed, amphibolite xenoliths appear as ghosts where they have been variably resorbed by the acidic rocks (Fig. 2). In central parts of the intrusions the rocks vary from fine-grained to coarse-grained, often with large quartz crystals up to 1 cm in size (Fig. 3). These make the rock quite distinctive especially where highlighted by differential weathering. In hand specimen the characteristic rock is a pale-gray to light-pink plagiogranite with a mottled

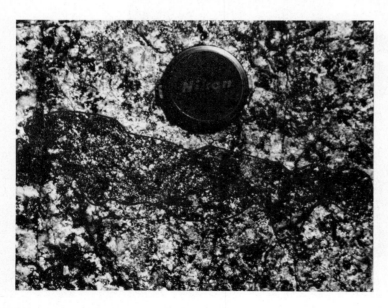

Figure 2.--Ghost of amphibolite xenolith in Little Port Complex trondhjemite.

Figure 3.--Large quartz crystals in Little Port Complex trondhjemite.

Figure 4.--Extensive cataclasis observed in thin section of Little Port Complex
trondhjemite. X15.

appearance resulting from distribution of minor mafic minerals. The rock consists of about 55% vitreous quartz, 35-40% soda-plagioclase and between 5 and 10% chloritized hornblende with minor pyrite and accessory sphene and magnetite. Extensive cataclasis is observed in thin section. Although there are some obvious recovery textures, many rocks might easily be mistaken for clastic sediments (Fig. 4). Quartz crystals invariably show undulose extinction and fractured grain boundaries. Plagioclase shows parting along cleavage, kinked twin lamellae and granulated boundaries. Where measurable the plagioclase has an average composition of Ab 85, but it is generally highly saussuritized.

The ferromagnesian minerals are commonly altered to chlorite, but remnant hornblende, and very rare biotite have been observed.

Small pockets and veinlets of trondhjemite are found throughout the amphibolites (Fig. 5). These do not show clear-cut relationships with the amphibolite, in some places being deformed with them, whilst in other places often quite close by, they are clearly cross-cutting. Such small pockets and networks have been interpreted by Payne (1974) in the Twillingate area as indicating partial melting of the amphibolites and local accumulation of the trondhjemitic melt. The features differ from the marginal intrusion breccias

Figure 5.--Small partial melts of trondhjemite (white) in amphibolite host.

of the large plutons in the amount of fine network veining with poorly defined vein margins. The pockets are also blind and cannot be traced to larger bodies of trondhjemite. The trondhjemites that occur in this form are usually fine grained and rarely contain significant amounts of ferromagnesian minerals. The brecciation that is observed in the larger bodies is also absent.

GEOLOGY OF THE BAY OF ISLANDS COMPLEX

A diagrammatic stratigraphic columnar section of three of the ophiolite massifs is presented in Figure 6. Two of the massifs, Blow Me Down Mountain and North Arm Mountain, display a completely developed ophiolite sequence. Each of the massifs has a basal portion composed of ultramafic rocks, ranging from approximately 2.5 km thick on North Arm Mountain to nearly 5 km thick on Table Mountain, which are immediately underlain by a dynamothermal aureole

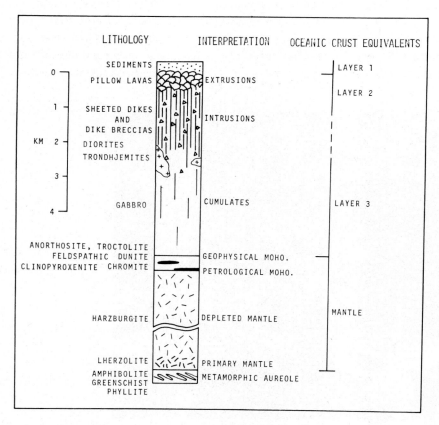

Figure 6.--Diagrammatic section through the northernmost massifs of the Bay of Islands Complex.

produced during displacement of the thrust slices (Malpas et al., 1973; Williams and Smyth, 1973). These ultramafic rocks are dominantly harzburgitic although a considerable thickness of spinel lherzolite occurs at the base of Table Mountain. Both types clearly display tectonite fabrics (Nicolas et al., 1971) thought to have developed by solid state deformation in the mantle. The tectonite fabrics both cut and are cut by numerous pyroxenite and dunite veins and dikes which were clearly intruded as liquids during the deformation of the host ultramafics. Immediately overlying the harzburgites are dunites and feldspathic dunites displaying cumulate rather than tectonite fabrics. Gabbroic rocks lie above the ultramafics and an interbanded zone separates the two rock types. This zone has been called the 'Critical Zone' by Smith (1958) and Irvine and Findlay (1972) and reaches thicknesses of the order of 400 meters. On Table Mountain the gabbros are not complete but where a full sequence is developed on North Arm and Blow Me Down Mountains, they reach an approximate thickness of 4 km. On these two massifs, diabase dikes increase in quantity at the top of the gabbros and higher up become sheeted and feed overlying pillow lavas. The diabases and pillow lavas reach a total thickness of about 2.5 km where they are overlain by siltstone and sandstone.

LEUCOCRATIC ROCKS IN THE BAY OF ISLANDS COMPLEX

Leucocratic rocks occur in association with hornblende gabbros and diorites on North Arm Mountain and Blow Me Down Mountain. In most cases rocks of this association cut massive gabbros and diabase dikes. Some basic dikes, however, intrude the acid rocks (Fig. 7). The leucocratic intrusions have never been found cutting ultramafic rocks.

The leucocratic rocks range from quartz-diorites to trondhjemites and appear to be associated with the diorites and hornblende gabbros as a complete differentiation series. The hornblende gabbros occur in blind pockets or lenses at the top of the gabbro zone. The hornblende gabbro itself is comprised of a number of phases which show intrusive relations with one another so that blocks of coarse pegmatite are often found floating in a matrix of finer grained gabbro or diorite. Typically the pegmatite contains up to 50% brown pleochroic hornblende, 40% to 45% plagioclase and accessory opaques, normally magnetite. Rocks of trondhjemitic and quartz-dioritic composition cut the basal parts of the sheeted diabase unit on Blow Me Down Mountain and occur near the Gregory Copper deposits of North Arm Mountain as small stocks. Inclusions of diabase and amphibiolite are partially resorbed and contaminate the leucocratic rocks. Outcrop areas rarely exceed 1 square km and the acid rocks volumetrically form an insignificant part of the Complex.

Plagioclase and quartz together form up to 90% of the rocks as interlocking

Figure 7.--Medium-grained trondhjemite cut by basic dike, Blow Me Down Mountain.

Figure 8.--Trondhjemite from North Arm Mountain showing good igneous textures in thin section. X15.

grains as much as 2.5 mm in size. The plagioclase varies from andesine to albite in composition and is generally greatly altered. The most common type is zoned, untwinned albite in which the rims are relatively fresh whilst the cores are highly saussuritized. Plagioclase laths are sometimes enclosed in poikilitic quartz. The quartz has undulose extinction and forms up to 45% of the rock. Crystals are equidimensional, and vary in size from 0.25 mm to 2.5 mm (Fig. 8).

Amphibolite may form up to 10% of the rock. It is green-brown pleochroic and optical properties suggest it is hornblende. Chlorite often forms alteration rims around the amphibole. In the quartz-diorites which intrude amphibolites, resorption of xenoliths may lead to apparently higher quantities of amphibole closer to the contact.

Epidote, zircon, and apatite are common accessories and in some areas the leucocratic rocks are cut by late stage prehnite veins.

CHEMISTRY OF THE TRONDHJEMITES

Little chemical data is generally available for trondhjemitic rocks associated with ophiolite suites. In this paper a total of 17 samples have been analyzed as part of a study of the upper thrust slices of the Humber Arm Allochthon. Seven of these are from the Bay of Islands Complex and ten from the Little Port Complex. Major elements were determined by atomic absorption spectrophotometry and trace elements by X-ray fluorescence spectrometry. Details of the analytical methods and precision and accuracy of the results are given in Malpas (1976).

Results of the analyses are given in Table I and diagrammatically in a series of variation plots (Figs. 9-16). At first glance it is apparent that all the rocks are characterized by relatively high, although variable, SiO_2 and Na_2O, and are impoverished in K_2O and Rb. This results in a trend on the CaO-Na_2O-K_2O plot (Fig. 9) which shows a definite Na_2O enrichment when compared to the S. W. Finland trondhjemites of Barker and Arth (1976). The chemistry is also reflected in the normative feldspar plot (Fig. 10) where strong albite enrichment is evident and all rocks fall into the trondhjemite and tonalite fields of O'Connor (1965). From this diagram a distinction can be made between the Little Port Complex and Bay of Islands Complex trondhjemites, the latter showing a closer correlation with the oceanic plagiogranites of Coleman and Peterman (1975). When plotted on the SiO_2 vs. K_2O wt % diagram (Fig. 11), however, this correlation is no longer valid, and few of the trondhjemites from either complex plot as distinctly oceanic. The Little Port Complex rocks are similar to those of Twillingate (Payne and Strong, this volume) and straddle both the oceanic plagiogranite and continental trondhjemite fields. The separation of the Bay of Islands rocks into two distinct groups is not easily explained. This separation is also apparent on the Al_2O_3 type (Barker et al., 1976), whilst the Bay of Islands rocks are divided into high SiO_2-low Al_2O_3 and

TABLE I : Chemical analyses of Little Port Complex and Bay of Islands Complex trondhjemites.

% wt.	02	03	04	05	Little Port Complex 06	15	18	19	20₁	20₂
SiO_2	72.80	76.40	72.60	67.40	72.60	69.10	73.30	68.10	69.50	72.40
TiO_2	0.26	0.22	0.14	0.28	0.26	0.32	0.26	0.24	0.16	0.16
Al_2O_3	13.10	11.80	13.40	15.30	13.40	14.30	13.70	14.00	14.60	12.00
Fe_2O_3	1.19	0.98	0.44	1.22	0.86	0.73	0.56	1.42	0.36	0.35
FeO	1.40	1.13	2.16	2.59	1.95	3.06	1.61	2.81	2.10	2.11
MnO	0.06	0.50	0.10	0.09	0.06	0.08	0.06	0.09	0.06	0.06
MgO	0.84	0.41	0.67	1.16	0.94	1.16	0.66	1.58	1.01	1.05
CaO	1.72	1.58	2.09	4.21	1.80	3.14	1.45	2.52	1.72	1.95
Na_2O	5.53	4.97	4.93	4.12	5.26	4.29	5.00	5.17	5.33	5.06
K_2O	0.25	0.33	0.47	0.81	0.49	0.91	1.25	0.55	1.22	0.74
P_2O_5	0.09	0.01	0.01	0.13	0.02	0.09	0.05	0.02	0.07	0.02
L.O.I.	1.18	1.04	1.56	1.82	1.35	1.75	1.42	2.14	1.94	2.21
Total	98.42	98.92	98.57	99.13	98.99	98.93	99.32	98.64	98.07	98.11
ppm										
Zr	67	69	83	88	51	35	32	46	73	61
Sr	95	73	119	137	99	158	119	92	274	123
Rb	5	6	10	16	9	13	20	10	20	8
Zn	32	41	61	56	35	58	41	56	41	38
Cu	11	10	6	10	9	15	7	22	8	7
Ba	34	21	27	60	47	78	130	71	81	133
Nb	7	5	4	5	6	8	6	6	6	5
Ga	12	13	13	16	11	17	12	14	15	11
Pb	nd	3	nd	1	1	1	3	5	12	nd
Ni	nd	nd	nd	1	nd	2	nd	2	nd	nd
Cr	9	9	13	12	3	8	8	6	10	6
V	25	6	32	74	39	76	23	82	39	38
Ag	40	42	39	36	40	36	40	36	40	40
Y	22	26	12	22	23	23	18	26	19	18

nd = not detected

TABLE I : continued

Bay of Islands Complex

% wt.	28	31	32	33	40	41	43
SiO_2	62.20	61.30	59.30	58.40	75.50	73.30	76.40
TiO_2	0.22	0.68	0.66	0.60	0.18	0.25	0.18
Al_2O_3	19.00	17.60	18.10	17.50	12.80	13.50	13.00
Fe_2O_3	1.30	1.65	0.75	0.53	0.81	2.18	0.93
FeO	0.91	2.52	1.38	1.26	1.35	1.37	1.29
MnO	0.03	0.04	0.03	0.03	0.06	0.07	0.06
MgO	0.51	1.84	1.87	1.72	0.13	0.32	0.12
CaO	5.49	3.49	7.00	6.87	0.86	1.29	0.93
Na_2O	8.25	8.65	7.82	8.30	6.00	6.35	5.88
K_2O	0.00	0.04	0.07	0.09	0.92	0.32	0.93
P_2O_5	0.01	0.25	0.22	0.18	0.00	0.01	0.01
L.O.I.	1.80	1.86	3.36	3.12	0.99	0.68	0.95
Total	99.72	99.92	100.56	98.60	99.60	99.64	100.68

ppm

	28	31	32	33	40	41	43
Zr	219	159	158	152	217	256	203
Sr	20	93	174	170	62	111	67
Rb	5	1	nd	1	12	2	11
Zn	23	30	24	27	71	42	70
Cu	42	12	6	7	8	10	9
Ba	208	131	144	170	204	154	206
Nb	8	8	7	9	11	7	7
Ga	22	20	21	18	22	21	21
Pb	4	nd	nd	nd	nd	nd	3
Ni	1	7	8	7	5	3	1
Cr	3	nd	14	18	6	5	9
V	20	43	52	48	4	12	4
Ag	38	36	38	38	41	38	41
Y	34	58	66	65	94	61	73

nd = not detected

478

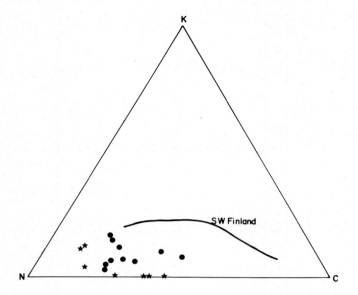

Figure 9.--CaO-Na$_2$O-K$_2$O (C.N.K.) plot for Little Port Complex (solid circles) and Bay of Islands Complex (stars) trondhjemites.

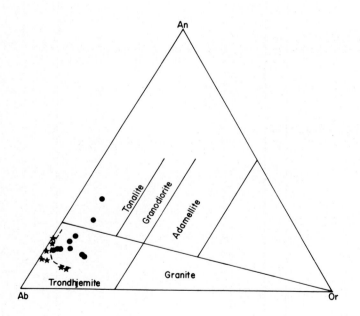

Figure 10.--Normative feldspar compositions. Symbols as for Figure 9.

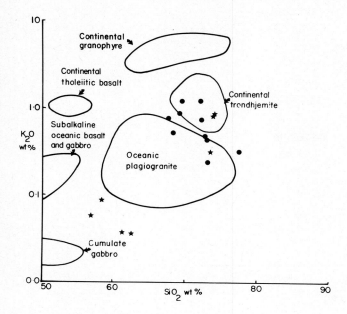

Figure 11.--K$_2$O wt % vs. SiO$_2$ wt %. Symbols as for Figure 9.

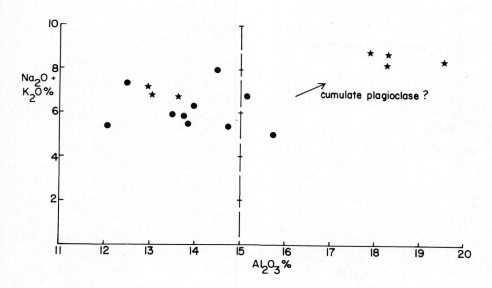

Figure 12.--Na$_2$O + K$_2$O wt % vs. Al$_2$O$_3$. Symbols as for Figure 9. Dashed line separates fields of high and low Al$_2$O$_3$ trondhjemites (Barker et al., 1976).

480

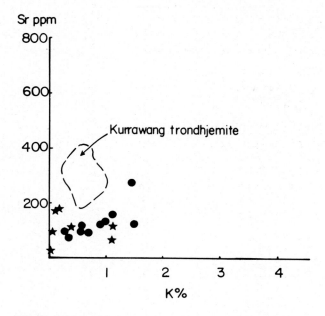

Figure 13.--K wt % vs. Sr ppm. Symbols as for Figure 9.

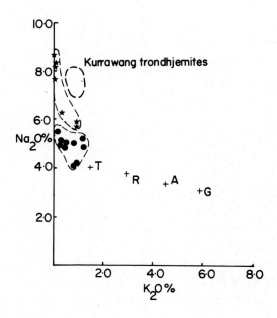

Figure 14.--K$_2$O wt % vs. Na$_2$O wt %. Symbols as for Figure 9. T = Average
Tonalite; R = Average Rhyolite; A = Average Adamellite; G = Average calc-
alkaline Granite. (After Nockolds, 1954).

low SiO_2-high Al_2O_3 groups. It is possible that the separation might be due to variable amounts of cumulate plagioclase; i.e., some high alumina compositions are not simply liquid compositions. Trace element data neither confirms nor disproves this, and REE data is not as yet available.

Plots of K vs. Sr (Fig. 13) and K_2O vs. Na_2O (Fig. 14) again show the trondhjemitic nature of the rocks from both complexes. The Na_2O vs. K_2O plot further shows a distinct separation of the rocks from each complex, the Little Port rocks being similar to those from the Twillingate area (Payne and Strong, this volume) and the Bay of Islands Complex rocks once again showing the sodium enrichment typical of oceanic plagiogranite (Coleman and Peterman, 1975).

Chemical differences between the two groups show up in a number of trace element variation diagrams. Apart from two samples, the Bay of Islands Complex rocks have low Rb/Sr ratios in the order of 0.01 which agrees with values from other oceanic plagiogranites (Fig. 15). The Little Port Complex rocks have Rb/Sr values up to ten times as large and closely resemble the Twillingate Granite. Incompatible elements, Zr and Ba, and Y which may be taken as an indication of HREE concentrations, are consistently enriched in the Bay of Islands rocks compared with those from the Little Port Complex. Plots of these elements against Ca % appear to be the most ideal for separating the two groups (Fig. 16).

ORIGIN OF THE TRONDHJEMITES AND RELATED ROCKS

The major differences between the trondhjemites and related rocks of the Little Port and Bay of Islands Complexes are summarized in Table II.

There is little doubt that the initial tectonic settings of these two complexes were quite different. Regional and structural geological considerations suggest that the Little Port Complex represents the basement of an island arc assemblage, essentially composed of deformed ophiolitic rocks and their later derivatives. The Bay of Islands Complex, however, seems to be an example of an undeformed ophiolite suite representing a sampling of oceanic lithosphere. The occurrences of trondhjemite and related rocks in the ophiolitic rocks of western Newfoundland therefore essentially depict two major processes for trondhjemite production · suggested in the literature. These processes are: (i) Fractional crystallization of basaltic magma, and (ii) Partial melting of eclogite or amphibolite.

The first process, argued by a number of workers (Goldschmidt, 1922; Coleman, 1971; Coleman and Peterman, 1975; Thayer, 1976; Barker and Arth, 1976) seems the most logical to explain the features exhibited by the Bay of Islands Complex ophiolites. The second process (Arth and Hanson, 1972; Glikson, 1972,

482

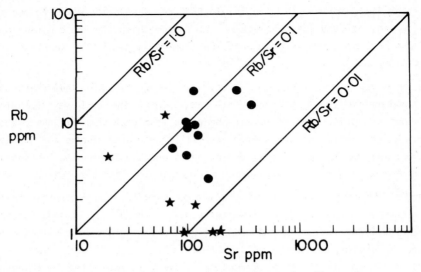

Figure 15.--Rb vs. Sr ppm (log sale). Symbols as for Figure 9.

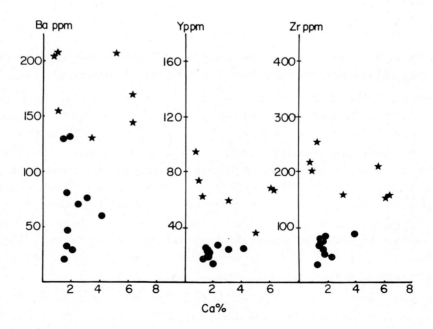

Figure 16.--Trace elements, Ba, Y, Zr plotted against Ca %. Symbols as for
  Figure 9.

TABLE II : Comparison of features for the trondhjemites of the Little Port
Complex (LPC) and Bay of Islands Complex (BIC)

LPC	BIC
1. Trondhjemites are not associated with diorites and grandiorites as part of a differentiation suite.	Trondhjemites for the end members of a differentiation suite; gabbro- diorite- granodiorite-trondhjemite.
2. Trondhjemitic rocks form large intrusive bodies or small anatectic patches within amphibolites.	Trondhjemites are invariably associated with pegmatitic hornblende gabbros in small pockets towards the tops of the ophiolite gabbro zone. They both intrude and are cut by basic rocks.
3. Trondhjemites are deformed together with the host amphibolites and gabbros and cataclastic textures are often developed.	Trondhjemites and associated differentiates are not deformed.
4. Trondhjemites have Na_2O 5%; Rb/Sr 0.1, are relatively enriched in K_2O; have low Y, Ba, Zr and Al_2O_3 and plot as trondhjemites and tonalites on An, Ab, Or. (cf. Payne and Strong, this volume).	Trondhjemites have Na_2O 6-9¢; Rb-Sr 0.01; are poorer on K_2O; have higher Y, Zr, Ba and compare with oceanic plagiogranites of Coleman and Peterman (1975).

1976; Glikson and Sheraton, 1972; Glikson and Lambert, 1976) seems most suited
to explain the features observed in the Little Port Complex. The similarity of
features observed in the Twillingate area further supports this and reference
should be made to the petrogenetic arguments of Payne and Strong (this volume).

In a note of caution, a third factor in the genesis of trondhjemites should
not be completely overlooked. Oftedahl (1959) suggested that the extreme sodic
nature of these rocks was of metasomatic rather than magmatic origin. In
ophiolite suites the metasomatic introduction of sodium and other elements by
sea water is a possibility especially in areas where the sea water is able to
percolate along deep fracture zones in the oceanic crust. Sea water might even
mix with magmas at depth, and fractionation would then lead to the crystallization of hydrous phases. It has been suggested that the hornblende gabbros
and diorites of the Bay of Islands Complex are possibly a result of such a
mechanism (Malpas, 1978).

484

It is difficult, however, to prove such a hypothesis since post magmatic metasomatism might be expected to produce similar chemical results as sea water mixing with magma. Nevertheless, it is not unlikely that some of the major chemical differences between trondhjemitic rocks of the two complexes is a result, at least in part, of sea water interaction with the ophiolitic rocks. Collerson and Fryer (1978) and Collerson and Bridgwater (this volume) have also pointed out the importance of the volatile phase in redistributing some major and trace elements. The release of elements such as Y, Ba and Na into a volatile phase during partial melting of, for example, amphibolite should result in lower concentrations of these elements in the melt phase, and might explain the chemical differences delineated above.

SUMMARY

Trondhjemites and related rocks occur in two major ophiolitic assemblages juxtaposed in the alochthonous sequences of western Newfoundland. One ophiolite assemblage consists of deformed and metamorphosed rocks forming the basement of an island arc. The other appears as a completely undeformed ophiolite suite representing oceanic lithosphere. Trondhjemites and related rocks in each complex are distinguished both by field appearance and chemistry. The chemical differences reflect two different origins (i) by partial melting of amphibolites, and (ii) by fractional crystallization of wet gabbroic magma, although introduction and loss of volatiles may have produced some chemical differences through metasomatism. It is possible that such chemical signatures might be used to differentiate these two major mechanisms of production of sodium-rich acid magmas in other areas.

ACKNOWLEDGMENTS

Investigations of western Newfoundland ophiolites are supported by N.R.C. Grant #85-666. I thank K. Goodyear for drafting assistance and G. Woodland for typing.

REFERENCES

Arth, J. G. and Hanson, G. N., 1972. Quartz-diorites derived by partial melting of eclogite or amphibolite to mantle depths. Contr. Miner. Pet., 37, 161-174.

Barker, F. and Arth, J. G., 1976. Generation of trondhjemitic-tonalitic liquids and Archean bimodal trondhjemite-basalt suites. Geology, 4: 596-600.

Barker, F., Arth, J. G., Peterman, Z. E. and Friedman, I., 1976. The 1.7- to 1.8-b.y.-old trondhjemites of southwestern Colorado and northern New Mexico. Geochemistry and depths of genesis. Geol. Soc. Am. Bull., 87: 189-198.

Coleman, P. J., 1970. Geology of the Solomon and New Hebrides Islands as part of the Melanesian Re-entrant, S.W. Pacific. Pacific Sci., 34: 289-314.

Coleman, R. G., 1971. Plate tectonic emplacement of upper mantle peridotites along continental edges. J. Gephys. Res., 76: 1212-1222.

Coleman, R. G. and Peterman, Z. E., 1975. Oceanic plagiogranite. J. Geophys. Res., 80: 1099-1108.

Collerson, K. D. and Fryer, B. J., 1978. The role of fluids in the formation and subsequent development of early continental crust. Contrib. Miner. Pet. (in press).

Comeau, R. L., 1972. Transported slices of the coastal complex, W. Newfoundland. M. Sc. thesis, Memorial University of Newfoundland, 105 p.

Glikson, A. Y., 1972. Early Precambrian evidence of a primitive ocean crust and island nuclei of sodic granite. Geol. Soc. Am. Bull., 83: 3323-3344.

Glikson, A. Y., 1976. Archean to early Proterozoic shield elements: Relevance of plate tectonics: In Metallogeny and Plate Tectonics, D. F. Strong (ed.). Geol. Assoc. Can. Sp. Paper, 14: 489-516.

Glikson, A. Y. and Lambert, I. B., 1976. Vertical zonation and petrogenesis of the early Precambrian crust in western Australia. Tectonophysics, 30: 55-89.

Glikson, A. Y. and Sheraton, J. W., 1972. Early Precambrian trondhjemitic suites in western Australia and northwestern Scotland, and the geochemical evolution of shields. Earth Planet. Sci. Lett., 17: 227-242.

Goldschmidt, V. M., 1922. Stammestypen der Eruptivgesteine. Nor. Vidensk.-Akad. Skr., Math-Natur., 10: 6.

Hughes, C. J., 1971. Anatomy of a granophyre intrusion. Lithos, 4: 403-415.

Hutchinson, C. S. and Dhonau, T. J., 1969. Deformation of an Alpine ultramafic association in Darvel Bay, east Sabah, Malaysia. Geol. Mijnbouw, 48: 481-493.

Irvine, T. N. and Findlay, T. C., 1972. Alpine peridotite with particular reference to the Bay of Islands Igneous Complex. In The Ancient Oceanic Lithosphere, E.Irving (ed.). Pub. Earth Physics Branch, E.M.R., Ottawa, 42: 97-128.

486

Kennedy, M. J., 1975. Repetitive orogeny in the Northeastern Appalachians; new plate models based upon Newfoundland examples. Tectonophysics, 28: 39-87.

Malpas, J., 1976. The petrology and petrogenesis of the Bay of Islands ophiolite suite, W. Newfoundland (2 parts). Ph. D. thesis, Memorial University of Newfoundland, 435 p.

Malpas, J., 1978. Magma generation in the Upper Mantle, Field evidence from ophiolite suites and application to the generation of oceanic lithosphere. Phil. Trans. Roy. Soc. Ser. A (in press).

Malpas, J., Stevens, R. K. and Strong, D. F., 1973. Amphibolite associated with Newfoundland ophiolite: its classification and tectonic significance. Geology, 1:45-47

Mitchell, A. H. G., 1974. Southwest England granites: magmatism and tin mineralization in a post-tectonic setting. Trans. Inst. Miner. Metall. Sec. B., 11: 219-272.

Nicolas, A., Bouchez, J. L., Boudier, F., Mercier, J. C., 1971. Textures, structures, and fabrics due to solid state flow in some European lherzolites. Tectonophysics, 12: 55-86.

Nockolds, S. R., 1954. Average chemical composition of some igneous rocks. Geol. Soc. Am. Bull., 65: 1007-1032.

O'Connor, J. T., 1965. A classification of quartz-rich igneous rocks based on feldspar ratios. U.S. Geol. Surv. Prof. Paper, 525-B.

Oftedahl, C., 1959. Om vulkanittene i den Kaledowske Ijellkjede i Norge. Norg. Geol. Unders., 39: 263-265.

Payne, J. G., 1974. The Twillingate Granite and its relationships to surrounding country rocks. M. Sc. thesis, Memorial University of Newfoundland, 159 p.

Shiraki, K., 1971. Metamorphic basement rocks of Yap Islands, western Pacific; possible oceanic crust beneath an island arc. Earth and Planet. Sci. Lett., 13: 167-174.

Smith, C. H., 1958. Bay of islands igneous complex, western Newfoundland. Geol. Surv. Can. Mem., 290, 132 p.

Stevens, R. K., 1970. Cambro-Ordovician flysch sedimentation and tectonics in W. Newfoundland and their possible bearing on a proto-Atlantic Ocean. Geol. Assoc. Can. Spec. Paper, 7: 165-177.

Strong, D. F. and Payne, J. G., 1973. Early Palaeozoic volcanism and metamorphism of the Moreton's Harbour-Twillingate area, Newfoundland. Can. J. Earth Sci., 10: 1363-1379.

Strong, D. F., 1974. An off-axis volcanic suite associated with the Bay of Islands ophiolites, Newfoundland. Earth and Planet. Sci. Lett., 21: 301-309.

Strong, D. F., Stevens, R. K., Malpas, J. and Badham, J. P. N., 1975. A new tale for the Lizard. Proc. Usher Soc., 3: 252.

Thayer, T. P., 1972. Gabbro and epidiorite versus granulite and amphibolite: a problem of the ophiolite assemblage: Caribb. Geol. Conf. Trans., 6: 315-320.

Tobish, O. T., 1968. Gneissic amphibolite at Las Palmas, Puerto Rico and its significance in the early history of the Greater Antilles Island Arc. Geol. Soc. Am. Bull., 79: 557-574.

Williams, H., 1971. Mafic-ultramafic complexes in western Newfoundland Appalachians and the evidence for their transportation: A review and interim report. Geol. Assoc. Can. Proc., 24: 9-25.

Williams, H., 1973. Bay of Islands map-area, Newfoundland. Geol. Surv. Can. Paper, 72-34.

Williams, H. and Malpas, J., 1972. Sheeted dikes and brecciated dike rocks within transported igneous complexes, Bay of Islands, W. Newfoundland. Can. J. Earth Sci., 9: 1216-1229.

Williams, H. and Smyth, W. R., 1973. Metamorphic aureoles beneath ophiolite suites and Alpine peridotites: tectonic implications with west Newfoundland examples. Am. J. Sci., 273: 594-621.

Williams, H. and Payne, J. G., 1975. The Twillingate Granite and nearby volcanic groups: an island arc complex in N.E. Newfoundland. Can. J. Earth Sci., 12: 982-995.

Chapter 16

ORIGIN OF THE TWILLINGATE TRONDHJEMITE, NORTH-CENTRAL NEWFOUNDLAND: PARTIAL MELTING IN THE ROOTS OF AN ISLAND ARC

J. G. Payne and D. F. Strong

ABSTRACT

The Twillingate pluton of north-central Newfoundland occupies an elliptical area of about 350 sq. km, with quartz-porphyry dikes extending at least 10 km away from the main body. It intrudes and has been deformed with metavolcanic rocks of greenschist to amphibolite facies, believed to represent the lowermost parts of an island arc sequence up to 12 km thick. The pluton is a remarkably homogeneous trondhjemitic composition, and similar to cotectic compositions at 4 kb P_{H_2O} and around $700^{\circ}C$ in the plagioclase-quartz-(H_2O) system. We suggest that it formed under these conditions, i.e., upper amphibolite facies, by partial melting of low-K tholeiites forming the base of the island arc sequence.

INTRODUCTION

Igneous rocks of trondjemitic composition, as reviewed in this volume, appear to have four main patterns of occurrence: (1) associated with tonalites in Archean batholiths and gneissic complexes; (2) associated with amphibolites in the earliest rocks of orogenic belts (such as the type area and including the "basements" of island arcs; e.g., Yap); (3) as plutonic and volcanic members of calc-alkaline suites of island arcs; and (4) in ophiolite suites (plagiogranites in the sense of Coleman and Peterman, 1975). Their volumetric importance appears to decrease in the order cited, with Archean trondhjemites being abundant and those of ophiolites being relatively minor.

There appear to be at least two ways of forming trondhjemites, namely by partial melting under amphibolite facies conditions (e.g., Arth and Barker, 1976; Glikson and Sheraton, 1972 -- types 1 and 2) and by various types of magmatic differentiation (e.g., Yajima et al., 1972; Arth et al., 1974; Coleman and Peterman, 1974; types 3 and 4).

This paper shows that the Twillingate pluton of central Newfoundland, in a similar geological setting to that of the type area in Norway (cf. Vokes and Gale, 1976), is of the second type, and was probably formed by amphibolite facies partial melting of low-K basalt.

490

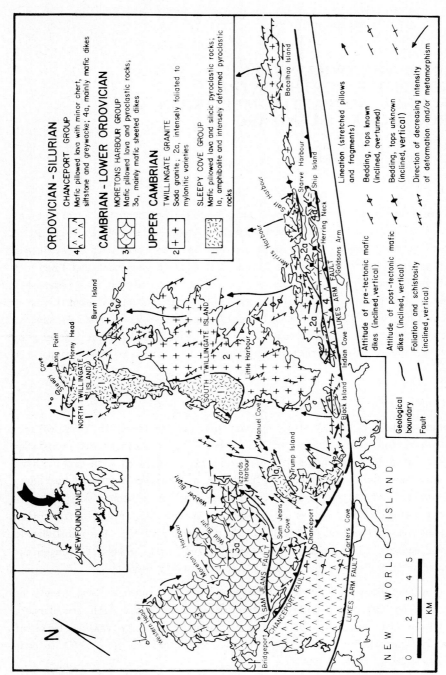

Figure 1.--Geological map of the Twillingate area (after Williams and Payne (1975)).

GEOLOGICAL SETTING

Regional Geology

The Twillingate pluton lies at the northern extremity of the Appalachian Orogen, with exposures encompassing an area of about 180 sq. km along the coast and islands in eastern Notre Dame Bay, Newfoundland (Fig. 1). Geophysical evidence (Miller and Deutsch, 1973) suggests that the pluton is shallow with an oval shape and extends northeastwards beneath the sea, approximately doubling the area exposed on land. It occurs as dikes up to 10 km from the main contact, intruding metavolcanic rocks which exhibit amphibolite and greenschist facies assemblages.

The volcanic rocks of central Newfoundland are now generally accepted as a dominantly island arc sequence constructed upon oceanic crust (see review by Strong, 1977). The Twillingate pluton occurs in the base of the island arc sequence, or possibly at the transition zone between it and oceanic crust. The volcanic rocks surrounding the pluton are defined as three groups, namely, the Moretons Harbour and Chanceport (Strong and Payne, 1973) and the Sleepy Cove Groups with a measurable thickness of 8 km, and probably in excess of 12 km (Payne, 1974; Williams and Payne, 1975). The Moretons Harbour and Sleepy Cove Groups are the oldest, and only they are intruded by the Twillingate trondhjemite. The age of the Chanceport Group is not definitely known, but Dean and Strong (1975, 1976) have suggested an upper Ordovician-Silurian age on the basis of general geological relations. Williams et al. (1976) have shown that zircons from the pluton provide an age of $510 \pm 17\text{-}16$ Ma, while $^{40}Ar^{39}Ar$ hornblende ages of dikes cutting it and mafic xenoliths within it range from 473 ± 9 to 438 ± 9 Ma. They interpret these ages (p. 1591) as indicating "prolonged metamorphism and/or slower post-metamorphic cooling for central portions of the pluton compared to its southern margin."

Local Geology

Around the margins of the Twillingate pluton there are numerous dikes of quartz porphyry of similar composition to the trondhjemite. They show the same intensity and orientation of deformation fabrics as the volcanic rocks, undeformed where the pillow lavas are undeformed (Fig. 2), and intensely flattened in the amphibolites (Fig. 3). On the other hand, there are locally areas (e.g., Sam Jeans Cove, Fig. 1) where trondhjemitic melts are clearly produced from amphibolitized pillow lavas (Fig. 4), and it is in this same region where the greatest degree of dehydration is indicated by metamorphic granular diopside greatly dominant over amphibole in strongly stretched pillow lavas. The pluton also contains numerous mafic inclusions showing all degrees

Figure 2.--Dike of Twillingate trondhjemite cutting undeformed pillow lavas of the Sleepy Cove Group.

of deformation and resorption (Figs. 5 and 6). It is cut by diabase dikes showing variations in deformation and alteration which indicate that they were intruded at various stages before, during, and after metamorphism (Figs. 7 and 8). No contact metamorphism has been detected in the undeformed volcanics intruded by the pluton.

The above features led Strong and Payne (1973) to suggest that "mafic and felsic magmatism continued during and after the intense deformation and metamorphism in the area." Such prolonged magmatic activity would presumably maintain a high heat-flow, accounting for the prolonged metamorphism and cooling suggested by Williams et al. (1976).

The rocks of the Moretons Harbour and Sleepy Cove Groups show an irregular increase in intensity of deformation and degree of metamorphism towards the contacts, and the deformation continues into the pluton. The irregularity of this change, along with the features described above, show that this change is not a simple contact aureole effect, although it must reflect the indirect influence of the pluton, e.g., as a residual heat source or as a buttress during deformation.

The pluton itself is most intensely deformed along its southern contacts

Figure 3.--Dike of Twillingate trondhjemite cutting volcanic rocks of the Sleepy Cove Group, both strongly flattened by the same deformation.

and tends to be more massive in its central and northern parts. The rock is commonly foliated, with a dominant strong S-fabric, or locally an L-S-fabric, emphasized by quartz tablets or rods, with intense mylonitization on the southern contact. This main fabric is locally kinked and tightly folded, but it is essentially parallel or sub-parallel to the margins of the pluton. Its origins are poorly understood, although it must be related to regional tectonics rather than emplacement of the pluton.

PETROGRAPHY

The Twillingate pluton is remarkably homogeneous in both mineralogy and chemistry, with variations mainly resulting from variable xenolith resorption

494

Figure 4.--Partial melting texture with trondhjemite veinlet produced from pillow lava.

Figure 5.--Mafic inclusions in Twillingate trondhjemite.

or secondary alteration and deformation. The typical Twillingate trondhjemite is gray to pink, with quartz phenocrysts up to 1 cm in diameter, and a mottling caused by irregular distribution of mafic minerals (Figs. 5 and 6). It generally consists of about 45% clear vitreous quartz locally with a bluish hue, about 45% sodic plagioclase, and about 10% mafic minerals (chlorite after biotite, chloritized hornblende) and accessory garnet, zircon, epidote, and opaques (pyrite and magnetite).

In thin section it is typically holocrystalline with an equigranular granitic texture, although recrystallization is common, resulting in the development of a mosaic texture. Typical features of deformation, such as undulose extinction in quartz, cracks in plagioclase and elongation of crystals, are abundant.

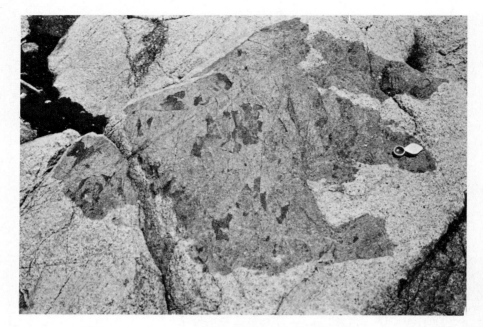

Figure 6.--Partially resorbed mafic inclusions in Twillingate trondhjemite.(CF,2)

Figure 7.--Undeformed diabase dike cutting deformed and amphibolitized dike and Twillingate trondhjemite.

Figure 8.--Deformed diabase dikes cutting Twillingate trondhjemite.

Quartz commonly occurs as large anhedral crystals with crenulated and sutured edges and inclusions of all the other minerals. The feldspar is typically anhedral oligoclase-albite, although the alteration and deformation prevent accurate compositional determinations. Most crystals are clotted with secondary sericite and epidote, although fresher albite rims are locally seen. Zoning is otherwise rare. Very minor amounts of K-feldspar are locally observed, as interstitial microcline and antiperthite, on the rims of plagioclase and as inclusions in quartz.

Ferromagnesian minerals are minor constituents, with secondary chlorite being most common, replacing hornblende and minor biotite. Hornblende is most abundant in "hybrid" rocks, as a residuum of mafic xenoliths. Where fresh it is strongly pleochroic from yellow to dark green. Garnet also occurs as a refractory phase of resorbed xenoliths, forming patchy crystals up to 1 cm in diameter.

These petrographic features classify the rocks as trondhjemite according to the definition of Goldschmidt (1916) as translated by Johannsen (1939, p. 387), "leucocratic acid plutonic rocks, whose essential constituents are soda-rich plagioclase and quartz. Potash feldspar is entirely wanting or is present only in subordinate amounts. Biotite is the most important of the mafic constituents, although it is present in small quantity."

CHEMISTRY

Introduction

One hundred and ten samples were originally analyzed as part of a reconnaissance geochemical study of eastern Newfoundland graintoid rocks (Strong et al., 1974). They were collected as closely as possible to points on a one-mile square grid, with three of these squares sampled in greater detail (Payne, 1974). Although these data served to demonstrate the homogeneity of the Twillingate pluton, for present purposes we have omitted those samples with major element totals outside the 98-101% range. Only thirty-two analyses satisfy this criterion (Table 1), but we believe them to adequately represent the pluton composition. A further 10 analyses of the pluton and dikes are available from Coish (1973), all having a similar chemical composition to those considered here.

Both major and trace elements were determined by X-ray fluorescence spectrometry, using lithium-tetraborate fusions for the former and rock powders for the latter. Na_2O and MnO were determined by Atomic Absorption spectrometry. Details of the methods and precision and accuracy are given by Payne (1974).

General Observations

The most striking features of the chemical data (Table 1) are the small variation in composition, the consistently high SiO_2 and Na_2O, and low K_2O, Al_2O_3, Sr and Ba. These rocks would be classed as low- Al_2O_3 type trondhjemite in the terminology of Barker et al. (1976), although they are almost all corundum-normative.

The normative feldspar proportions (Fig. 9) show a typical trondhjemite-tonalite composition according to the classification of O'Connor (1965). In terms of weight proportions of $CaO-Na_2O-K_2O$ (Fig. 10) they parallel the trondhjemite trend (of the SW Finland suite) shown by Barker and Arth (1976), although they are even lower in K_2O and CaO.

The average composition of Twillingate trondhjemite is presented in Table 2, along with compositions of other granites and trondhjemites for comparison.

Table 2 shows that average SiO_2 in the Twillingate trondhjemite is higher than in other trondhjemites and is significantly higher than average Cyprus plagiogranites. Glikson and Sheraton (1972) show a similar average SiO_2 value for the Kurrowang and Twillingate trondhjemite, while Larsen and Poldervaart (1961) and Hotz (1971) show lower values than Twillingate. In terms of the SiO_2/K_2O ratios (Fig. 11), the Twillingate analyses overlap the fields of both continental trondhjemite and oceanic plagiogranite shown by Coleman and

TABLE 1. Chemical Analyses of Twillingate Trondhjemites.

Sample No.	JP 5	JP 12	JP 13	JP 15	JP 24	JP 26	JP 27	JP 30	JP 34	JP 36	JP 37	JP 39
SiO_2	72.00	78.40	77.20	77.40	75.90	71.90	77.40	79.10	73.80	73.80	70.90	72.00
TiO_2	0.24	0.16	0.19	0.13	0.17	0.33	0.18	0.10	0.22	0.23	0.25	0.21
Al_2O_3	13.50	11.70	13.10	12.00	12.50	13.30	11.80	12.00	13.10	13.00	13.00	14.10
Fe_2O_3*	2.79	2.07	2.29	1.53	2.28	3.64	1.42	1.13	2.71	1.18	4.32	3.00
MnO	0.06	0.02	0.05	0.01	0.06	0.05	0.02	0.02	0.09	0.02	0.06	0.02
MgO	1.60	0.0	0.0	0.0	0.0	0.0	0.0	0.0	0.0	0.20	0.10	0.50
CaO	1.91	0.33	2.06	0.93	0.78	2.21	1.43	0.18	2.40	2.63	3.56	2.39
Na_2O	4.86	6.12	4.70	5.62	5.09	5.91	5.47	5.25	3.59	5.39	5.07	4.90
K_2O	0.86	0.14	0.40	0.35	0.19	0.32	0.26	0.74	0.81	0.33	0.74	0.16
P_2O_5	0.01	0.0	0.0	0.0	0.0	0.0	0.26	0.0	0.10	0.0	0.0	0.0
L.O.I.	1.41	0.68	0.76	0.88	1.82	0.87	0.86	0.68	1.36	1.08	1.28	0.81
TOTAL	99.24	99.62	100.75	98.85	98.79	98.53	99.10	99.20	98.18	98.86	99.28	98.09
ppm												
Zr	107	62	137	188	110	111	109	90	93	57	56	90
Sr	93	37	76	46	85	8	57	18	110	166	135	131
Rb	12	2	7	6	5	11	4	31	12	9	14	2
Zn	34	42	33	23	43	53	21	26	53	15	63	16
Cu	7	5	6	7	20	18	9	11	9	7	12	7
Ba	104	13	111	67	57	16	30	172	90	51	67	83
Nb	5	5	6	8	5	6	7	6	4	3	4	4
Ga	14	12	16	14	15	13	13	15	15	13	16	14
Pb	5	3	4	2	1	--	2	9	--	2	--	7

* Total Iron as Fe_2O_3

TABLE 1, continued

Sample No.	JP 40	JP 43	JP 44	JP 45	JP 46	JP 47	JP 48	JP 49	JP 51	JP 52	JP 57	JP 58
SiO_2	76.60	74.20	74.20	75.50	74.30	74.80	76.40	75.00	73.10	72.30	75.30	72.90
TiO_2	0.12	0.24	0.22	0.22	0.22	0.16	0.23	0.19	0.22	0.21	0.20	0.22
Al_2O_3	11.50	12.90	12.90	13.20	13.00	12.20	13.30	12.90	13.60	13.40	13.00	12.70
$Fe_2O_3^*$	1.81	2.75	2.65	2.12	2.30	2.56	1.92	2.36	2.89	2.80	2.52	2.63
MnO	0.03	0.06	0.06	0.02	0.03	0.04	0.03	0.06	0.08	0.08	0.05	0.07
MgO	0.0	0.0	0.30	0.0	0.10	1.50	0.0	1.40	0.09	1.40	0.50	0.0
CaO	0.77	2.37	1.51	2.34	2.00	0.92	3.14	2.22	1.63	2.93	0.75	2.08
Na_2O	5.62	4.24	4.97	5.58	5.30	5.73	4.61	4.64	5.38	4.67	5.50	5.47
K_2O	0.34	0.48	0.48	0.16	0.47	0.16	0.40	1.01	0.30	0.71	0.10	0.59
P_2O_5	0.0	0.0	0.0	0.0	0.0	0.0	0.0	0.0	0.0	0.0	0.0	0.0
L.O.I.	1.86	0.88	1.07	0.39	0.98	0.82	0.51	0.58	0.95	1.36	1.26	1.69
TOTAL	98.65	98.12	98.36	99.53	98.70	98.89	100.54	100.36	99.05	99.86	99.18	98.35
ppm												
Zr	90	55	59	75	83	80	90	72	105	71	88	85
Sr	40	126	100	151	113	91	156	82	109	100	83	50
Rb	7	9	8	3	8	4	9	20	7	8	2	9
Zn	44	39	46	18	17	29	49	43	51	36	39	42
Cu	16	12	58	10	9	13	9	7	7	8	10	10
Ba	16	101	121	48	42	39	78	134	70	61	13	54
Nb	6	6	5	5	5	5	6	6	5	4	6	6
Ga	12	13	13	12	13	14	15	12	15	14	12	13
Pb	7	--	1	--	--	1	3	--	7	--	--	5

TABLE 1, continued

Sample No.	JP 66	JP 67	JP 76	JP 101	JP 102	JP 106	JP 109	JP 110
SiO_2	74.90	71.00	69.40	71.40	75.30	73.10	76.10	75.70
TiO_2	0.25	0.30	0.35	0.29	0.25	0.27	0.23	0.28
Al_2O_3	12.90	13.90	15.30	14.80	12.80	13.20	12.90	13.30
$Fe_2O_3^*$	2.96	4.06	4.65	3.51	2.60	3.52	2.47	2.35
MnO	0.08	0.09	0.06	0.07	0.05	0.05	0.57	0.25
MgO	0.0	0.0	0.0	0.0	0.0	0.0	0.0	0.50
CaO	1.60	2.92	3.19	2.49	1.79	0.93	1.69	1.15
Na_2O	5.00	4.20	3.21	4.16	4.73	5.80	4.73	5.42
K_2O	0.88	0.50	0.53	0.55	0.91	0.22	0.64	0.27
P_2O_5	0.0	0.0	0.06	0.0	0.0	0.0	0.0	0.0
L.O.I.	1.02	1.37	1.84	0.90	0.82	1.61	0.83	0.92
TOTAL	99.59	98.34	98.59	98.17	99.25	98.70	100.16	100.14
ppm								
Zr	90	53	72	61	57	104	112	88
Sr	132	135	132	129	106	50	117	112
Rb	14	8	9	8	20	3	55	5
Zn	46	57	49	55	45	43	48	25
Cu	7	7	27	14	31	146	7	15
Ba	128	82	61	88	143	26	101	104
Nb	5	5	5	5	4	6	6	5
Ga	14	15	13	17	13	14	13	11
Pb	1	7	4	5	5	2	7	5

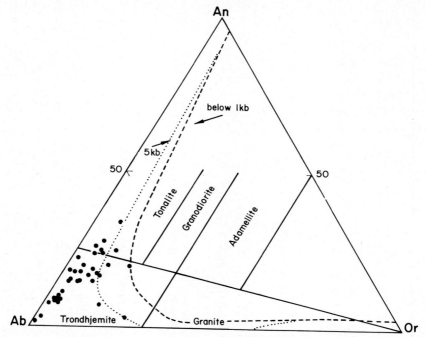

Figure 9.--CIPW normative proportions of Ab-An-Or (wt %) in rocks of the Twillingate trondhjemite. The solid lines are classification boundaries of O'Connor (1965), and the dashedlines are plagioclase boundaries as reported by Glikson and Sheraton (1972).

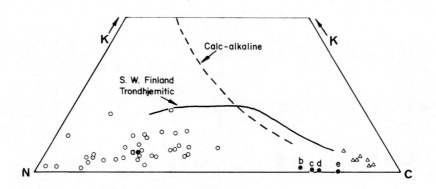

Figure 10.--Weight proportions of CaO(C):Na$_2$O(N):K$_2$O(K) in rocks of the Twillingate Trondhjemite. The trend lines are after Barker and Arth (1976). The letters refer to average Twillingate trondhjemite (a), average Sleepy Cove Group basalt (b), and the residue left after subtraction of 5% (c), 10% (d), and 20% (e) of (a) from (b). The triangles show compositions of amphiboles in amphibolites from Sam Jean's Cove.

TABLE 2.   Comparison of the average of 33 Twillingate analyses with other trondhjemites.

	1	2	3	4	5	6	7	8
SiO_2	74.45	70.8	72.8	74.60	70.2	68.58	66.7	73.6
TiO_2	0.22	0.18	0.1	0.15	.22	0.29	.72	.33
Al_2O_3	13.02	15.8	15.5	13.96	17.2	17.10	14.0	12.3
Fe_2O_3	2.62[a]	0.9	0.4	1.02[a]	.71	0.76	3.4	3.7
FeO	---	1.3	0.6	---	1.0	1.44	3.1	1.6
MnO	0.07	---	---	0.03	.06	0.23	---	.03
MgO	0.28	0.8	0.2	0.31	.66	1.18	1.6	.44
CaO	1.85	3.1	2.5	1.20	3.5	4.40	4.9	2.1
Na_2O	5.03	4.8	5.4	7.40	4.7	4.69	2.7	4.1
K_2O	0.47	1.8	2.0	0.49	.91	0.96	.34	.33
H_2O[d]	1.07[b]	0.4[c]	0.2[c]	1.19	.62	0.58	2.2[c]	1.35[b]
P_2O_5	0.01	0.1	0.2	0.03	.05	0.32	.12	---
Zr	88	---	---	100	85	---	70	70
Sr	97	---	---	298	1000	---	132	109
Rb	10	---	---	10-30	---	---	<3.4	1.6
Zn	39	---	---	---	---	---	---	---
Cu	17	---	---	7	13	---	<1.5	1.5
Ba	74	---	---	371	300	---	11	7
Nb	5							
Ga	14							
Pb	3							

1. Twillingate

2. Bald Rock batholith; average of nine trondhjemite samples (Larsen and Poldervaart, 1961).

3. Bald Rock batholith; average of three leucotrondhjemite samples (Larsen and Poldervaart, 1961).

4. Average of seven trondhjemite pebbles from the Kurrawang Conglomerate, Western Australia (Glikson and Sheraton, 1972).

5. Trondhjemite, Craggy Peak (Hotz, 1971)
    Trondhjemite, White Rock No. 54 (Hotz, 1971) } Average of all three
    Trondhjemite, White Rock No. 55 (Hotz, 1971)

6. Calcic trondhjemite, Caribou Mountain (Hotz, 1971)

7. Average of three Cyprus plagiogranites Cy 55C, 55A, and 52 (Coleman and Peterman, 1975).

8. Cyprus Keratophyre Cy 55B (Coleman and Peterman, 1975).

a = Total Fe as Fe_2O_3; b = H_2O and CO_2; c = H_2O^+ only; d = H_2O^+ + H_2O^-.

504

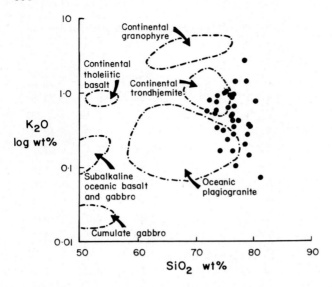

Figure 11.--K_2O and SiO_2 contents of Twillingate trondhjemite compared to other rock suites shown by Coleman and Peterman (1975).

Peterman (1975). TiO_2 and MnO are fairly consistent throughout all the trondhjemites. MgO is similarly consistent except that it is higher in the more calcic rocks. CaO in Twillingate trondhjemite is lower than all except the Kurrowang trondhjemite. Na_2O is similar to most trondhjemites, except that it is significantly higher than the Cyprus plagiogranite and granophyre. Al_2O_3 is lower in Twillingate trondhjemite than all others except the Cyprus granophyres.

Comparison of trace elements is difficult because of lack of published analyses, but the available data suggest that in the Twillingate trondhjemites compared with others, Ba and Sr are strongly depleted, and Zr, Rb, and Cu are comparable. The Rb/Sr (Fig. 12a) and Ca/Sr ratios (Fig. 12b) are approximately within the fields of modern calc-alkaline suites.

PETROGENESIS

Current Views on the Origin of Trondhjemites

Trondhjemites and sodic granites are not common rocks, but they have been the subject of many diverse interpretations. Goldschmidt (1922) suggested the possibility that sodic differentiates were produced by the fractional crystallization of basaltic magma. Battey (1956) and Kuno (1968) both stressed the importance of water in the development of soda-dominant acid rocks. Battey suggested that this process occurred in the post-magmatic stage, as

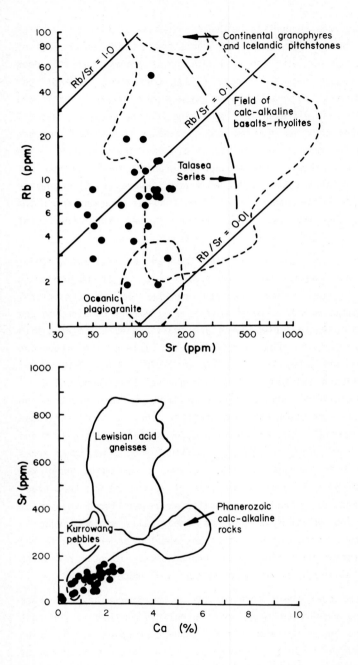

Figure 12. (Top).--Rb/Sr ratios in Twillingate trondhjemite compared to other
suites outlined by Coleman and Peterman (1975).   (Bottom) Sr/Ca ratios
compared to other suites outlined by Glikson and Sheraton (1972).

albitization of feldspars was thought to be due to a redistribution of alkalies during the subsequent burial of rhyolites. Kuno thought the enrichment of water may occur in connection with the assimilation of granitic or siliceous sedimentary rocks by basalt magma. Foslie (1922) considered amphibolites, serpentinites, trondhjemites and granites from Norway as comagmatic and formed by differentiation due to differential squeezing during crystallization. Oftedahl (1959) suggested that the extreme soda dominance of keratophyres was not magmatic in origin but more likely metasomatic, resulting from the action of sea water on rhyolitic ashes or the passage of granitic magma through wet geosynclinal sediments. Barth (1962) and Cheney and Stewart (1975) suggested the formation of trondhjemitic magmas by the melting of graywackes during metamorphism and deep burial, assuming anatexis rather than fractional crystallization.

Some recent papers (e.g., Coleman, 1971; Coleman and Peterman, 1975; Thayer, 1976) stress the relationship of small pods of trondhjemite to ophiolite suites and suggest they are the residue of the fractional crystallization of basaltic magma. Trondhjemites are commonly compared to the Norwegian Lower Paleozoic type-examples which are small bodies associated with amphibolites, probably derived from ophiolites and island arc sequences (Gustavson, 1969; Vokes and Gale, 1976). Glikson (1972, 1976), Glikson and Sheraton (1972), and Glikson and Lambert (1976) suggested that large bodies of sodic granite and trondhjemite intrude primitive Archean ocean crust at an early stage, followed by later stage potassic granite. They proposed for these a model involving a primordial crust of stratiform, oceanic-type ultrabasic and basic assemblages that were subjected to 'mega-rippling' producing linear zones of subsidence. Below these troughs partial melting of eclogite under wet conditions at about 100-150 km, or of amphibolite at around 30 km, took place to produce the sodic granites. The sodic granites represent large volumes of little differentiated, low volatile, acid melts diapirically emplaced under a steep geothermal gradient. Arth and Hanson (1972) and Barker and Arth (1976) among others have suggested the production of trondhjemite and quartz diorite by similar petrological although not necessarily tectonic processes.

Hotz (1971) suggested that the trondhjemites in the Sierra Nevada arose from an eastward dipping subduction zone, with batholiths further to the east being more potassic, in agreement with similar models proposed by Dickinson (1970), Bateman and Dodge (1970), and others. Fractional separation of plagioclase under crustal conditions could subsequently lead to the K enrichment. Late kinematic potassic granites may also have been derived through anatexis of earlier sodic granites (e.g., see Glikson and Sheraton, 1972). As reviewed by Wyllie et al., (1976), however, it appears from the experimental evidence that granitic rocks do not form from partial melting under upper mantle conditions.

In summary, four main processes have been proposed for the origin of trondhjemites: (1) fractional crystallization of basaltic magma, (2) metasomatic introduction of Na, usually by water, (3) anatexis of sediments during metamorphism, and (4) Partial melting of eclogite or amphibolite. In attempting to outline the possible origin of the Twillingate trondhjemite, it is necessary to evaluate the characteristics of the geochemical data, plus their relationship to experimental work and the general geological setting, in terms of the above processes.

Trace Elements

The low large ion lithophile (LIL) trace-element concentrations of the Twillingate trondhjemite are a striking feature which do not indicate a sedimentary parent or metasomatic origin, leaving the two other alternatives, crystal fractionation or partial melting of igneous protoliths.

If crystal fractionation is the dominant mechanism there should be a trend from basic to residual acidic rocks, but there is no evidence for this in the area, where there is a distinct lack of intermediate composition. This process would also tend to produce a concentration of LIL trace elements, especially in such siliceous rocks, for which there is no evidence.

Major Elements

In considering the field evidence described above, e.g., Fig. 4, it might be suggested that the trondhjemite veinlets and agmatites reflect vapour phase transport, without indicating partial melting. However, Holloway (1971) showed that such fluids (at least under amphibolite facies conditions) are strongly depleted in Ca and Fe, with compositions unlike those of the Twillingate trondhjemite (Fig. 13) Although the latter do approximate the igneous field shown by Holloway (Fig. 13), this implies only a crystal-silicate liquid equilibrium which could be due to either partial melting or crystal fractionation.

The Twillingate trondhjemite compositions are plotted in the An-Ab-Q (H_2O) system in Figure 14, in relation to the phase boundaries inferred by Hoffman (1976) from melting experiments with natural rocks. Although the data do plot within the Or-bearing system (because of K_2O contributed by mica and plagioclase), K-feldspar is only very rarely a free phase in these rocks, and their phase relations thus cannot be considered with respect to Or-bearing cotectic compositions because all but three rock compositions plot within the

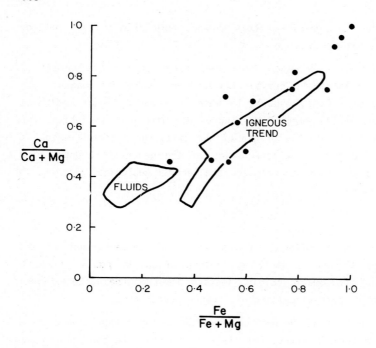

Figure 13.--Compositions of Twillingate trondhjemites compared to experimentally determined compositions of silicate liquids (igneous trend) and vapours (fluids) in the "basalt-H_2O-CO_2" system (after Holloway, 1971).

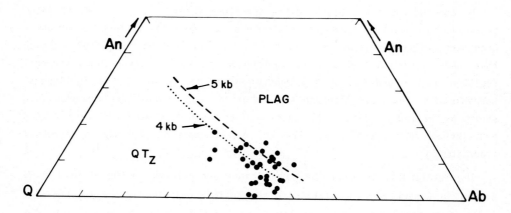

Figure 14.--An:Ab:Q (wt %) proportion of Twillingate trondhjemites compared to quartz-plagioclase cotectics suggested by Hoffman (1976).

plagioclase solid solution field, at least up to 5 kb (Fig. 9). Thus the data
are discussed only with regard to the plagioclase-quartz (-H_2O) phase relations
in Figure 14, as recently determined by Hoffmann (1976).   Note that the
projections in Figure 14 are the Barth (1959) mesonormative proportions, not
CIPW norms, as they more closely approach Hoffmann's projection method.   The
projection methods are still not precisely the same as Hoffmann's, but
insufficient modal data are available to follow his approach.   Given this
(probably minor) inconsistency, there is a correspondence of Twillingate compositions to those experimentally inferred compositions $P_{H_2O} = P_T = 4kb$
(Hoffmann's most trondhjemitic sample (no. 27 m) begins melting at 660°C, at
700°C it consists of about 70 vol. % melt, and at 712°C about 90 vol. % melt
(H. Hoffmann, pers. comm., 1977)), and we consider this to be a reasonable
equilibration pressure for the Twillingate pluton.

These conditions are compared to other relevant data in the P-T plot of
Figure 15, which shows them to be within the upper amphibolite facies of
metamorphism.   Although experimental data are not available for the low-K
basalt compositions of the Sleepy Cove and Moretons Harbour Groups, the solidus
curve for 1921 Kilauea tholeiite (Holloway and Burnham, 1972) closely
approaches the inferred conditions for equilibration of Twillingate
trondhjemite. We take this to indicate that the Twillingate rocks could have
been produced by partial melting of low-K basalt under conditions close to

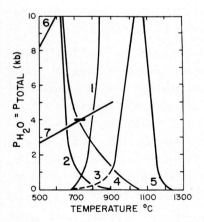

Figure 15.--Possible pressure-temperature conditions for the formation of
   Twillingate trondhjemite, shown by horizontal bar at 4 kb. The curves are
   as follows: 1 - approximate amphibolite-granulite facies boundary; 2 -
   minimum melting of granite (Tuttle and Bowen, 1958); 3 - amphibole upper
   stability limit(Yoder and Tilley, 1962); 4 - 1921 Kilauea Basalt solidus
   (Holloway and Burnham, 1972); 5 - basalt liquidus (Yoder and Tilley, 1962);
   6 - oceanic geotherm; and 7 - geotherm at 60°C/km.

those at which it equilibrated; i.e., almost in situ under upper amphibolite facies conditions. We note that this requires a high geothermal gradient, of the order of $60^{\circ}C/km$ as shown, but we suggest that such a gradient would obtain due to heat input from the basaltic magma continuously produced during formation of the Twillingate trondhjemite.

If the Twillingate trondhjemite were produced by partial melting of the mafic rocks in the region, extraction of such a composition should leave a residuum approximating the observed mineral assemblages, and also in accord with those predicted from the experimental data. Table 3 shows the average compositions of Twillingate trondhjemite (a), mafic rocks of the Sleepy Cove Group, the lowermost volcanic unit in the area (b), and the residuum left after subtraction of (a) from (b), at 5% (c), 10% (d), and 20% (e) intervals.

Because of the very high SiO_2 content of Twillingate trondhjemite, the residuum is rapidly depleted in SiO_2, with relatively smaller effects on the other elements (Table 3). These strongly undersaturated compositions, with such normative minerals as larnite and kaliophyllite, trend towards the composition of amphiboles (Fig. 16), which is in fact the dominant residual phase observed in xenoliths. These relations are shown schematically in Figure 16, with phase relations as suggested by Cawthorn and Brown (1976) for water pressures above 2 kb. This diagram clearly shows the trend from the Sleepy Cove average basalt composition towards a mixture dominated by amphibole. Although the nature of the phase boundaries is generally in agreement with observed phases, except for pyroxene not being shown, we suggest that the conditions may have been such that the garnet field was larger, with the garnet-feldspar-amphibole peritectic as shown by the dashed lines.

We note that the conditions required for formation of Twillingate trondhjemite are not those which would obtain along subduction zones, at least in current models (e.g., Toksoz et al., 1971). On the contrary, these would be precisely the conditions prevailing at the base of a volcanic sequence about 12 km thick with heat input from voluminous basaltic magmatism. The volcanic sequence at Twillingate is about 12 km thick, and basaltic magmatism was certainly common before, during and after formation of the Twillingate trondhjemite. It might thus be suggested that tectonic models for formation of the trondhjemite along any subduction zone require some reassessment.

The similarity of both the trondhjemitic and mafic rocks of the Twillingate area to those of most other trondhjemite-amphibolite terrains may support suggestions that partial melting during upper amphibolite facies metamorphism is generally responsible for the production of trondhjemites.

TABLE 3

Average compositions of Twillingate trondhjemite (a), Sleepy Cove basalt (b), and the residuum left after subtraction of (a) from (b), at 5% (c), 10% (d), and 20% (e) intervals

	Average Twillingate Trondhjemite (a)	Average Sleepy Cove Basalt (b)	5% (c)	10% (d)	20% (e)
SiO_2	75.96	49.28	45.47	41.66	34.05
TiO_2	0.22	.91	1.00	1.10	1.30
Al_2O_3	13.59	16.09	16.45	16.85	17.60
Fe_2O_3	0.50	2.63	3.00	3.30	3.90
FeO	2.01	7.47	8.25	9.00	10.55
MnO	0.07	.20	.21	0.25	0.30
MgO	0.29	8.20	9.25	10.35	12.60
CaO	2.00	10.35	11.50	12.20	15.05
Na_2O	5.25	3.83	3.65	3.50	3.10
K_2O	0.49	.13	0.09	0.05	0.00

C I P W NORMS

Q	38.51	---	---	---	---
Or	2.84	0.78	0.54	0.30	Lc -14.89
Ab	43.56	29.50	15.50	2.83	Kpl 10.97
An	9.37	26.57	28.56	30.65	37.01
Ne	---	1.74	8.52	14.80	15.42
Cor	0.89	---	---	---	Lar 6.81
Di	---	20.45	23.59	25.03	---
Hy	3.70	---	---	---	---
Ol	---	15.37	16.96	19.40	42.87
Mt	0.71	3.85	4.40	4.87	6.13
Il	0.42	1.74	1.92	2.83	2.68

Barth (1961) Mesonorms

Q	40.60	---	---		
Ab	43.83	22.80	13.17		
An	8.66	27.14	29.23		
Cor	1.18	---	---		
Edenite	---	33.78	39.32		
Ne	---	---	3.49	Insufficient SiO_2 for Mesonorm calculation	Insufficient SiO_2 for Mesonorm calculation
Bio	4.28	1.19	0.83		
Hy	0.20	8.03	---		
Di	---	---	---		
Ol	---	0.83	6.92		
Mt	0.71	3.93	4.50		
Sphene	0.54	2.30	2.54		

512

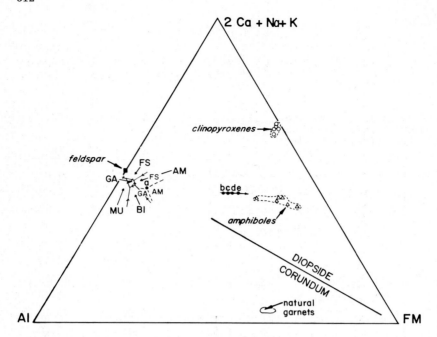

Figure 16.--Possible phase relations for formation of Twillingate trondhjemite. The solid lines show phase boundaries as suggested by Cawthorn and Brown (1976) for water pressures above 2 kb. Dashed lines are for phase relations postulated for formation of Twillingate trondhjemite, essentially with garnet and feldspar fields expanded at the expense of amphibole. The letters a, b, c, d, e, are as for Figure 10. The clinopyroxene and amphibole compositions are from the Sam Jeans Cove area, but the "natural garnets" field is taken from Cawthorn and Brown (1976). Abbreviations are as follows: GA = garnet; FS = feldspar; AM = amphibole; BI = biotite; MU = muscovite. The line from FM to feldspar separates diopside- normative from corundum-normative compositions.

ACKNOWLEDGMENTS

This study was financed by research grants from the National Research Council of Canada to H. Williams (No. A5548) and D. F. Strong (No. A7975), Canada Energy Mines and Resources Research Agreement Nos. 1135-D13-4-193/72 (with H. Williams) and 1135-D13-4-18/72 (with D. F. Strong), and the Newfoundland Department of Mines and Energy, DREE Program Project 4-3. We are grateful to G. L. Andrews, D. E. Press and J. Vahtra for chemical analyses, and to K. D. Collerson, B. Doolan, B. J. Fryer, C. Hoffman, R. A. Jamieson, and H. Williams for critical reading of the mansucript.

REFERENCES

Arth, J. G. and Barker, F., 1976. Rare-earth partitioning between Hornblende and dacitic liquid and implications for the genesis of trondhjemitic-tonalitic magmas. Geology, 4: 534-536.

Arth, J. G., Barker, F., Friedman, I. and Desborough, G. A., 1974. Geochemistry of the gabbro, diorite, tonalite, trondhjemite suite of the Kalanti area, southwest Finland. Geol. Soc. Am. Abstr. with Programs, 6: 637-638.

Arth, J. G. and Hanson, G. N., 1972. Quartz diorites derived by partial melting of eclogite or amphibolite at mantle depths. Contrib. Miner. Pet., 37: 161-174.

Barker, F. and Arth, J. G., 1976. Generation of trondhjemitic-tonalitic liquids and Archean bimodal trondhjemite-basalt suites. Geology, 4: 596-600.

Barker, F., Arth, J. G., Peterman, Z. E. and Friedman, I., 1976. The 1.7- to 1.8-b.y.-old trondhjemites of southwestern Colorado and northern New Mexico. Geochemistry and depths of genesis. Geol. Soc. Am. Bull., 87: 189-198.

Barth, T. F. W., 1959. Principles of classification and norm calculations of metamorphic rocks. J. Geol., 67: 135-152.

Barth, T. F. W., 1962. A final proposal for calculating the mesonorm of metamorphic rocks. J. Geol., 70: 497-498.

Bateman, P. C. and Dodge, F. C. W., 1970. Variations of major chemical constituents across the central Sierra Nevada Batholith. Geol. Soc. Am. Bull., 81: 409-420.

Battey, M. H., 1956. The petrogenesis of spilitic rock series from New Zealand. Geol. Mag., 93: 83-110.

Binns, R. A., 1968. Experimental studies of metamorphism of Broken Hill. In: "Broken Hill Mines-1968." Aust. Inst. Min. Metall. Melbourne, pp. 199-204.

Cheney, E. S. and Stewart, R. J., 1975. Subducted graywacke in the Olympic Mountains, U.S.A.--implications for the origin of Archean sodic gneisses. Nature, 258: 60-61.

Coish, R. A., 1973. Geology and petrochemistry of Trump Island, Notre Dame Bay, Newfoundland. Unpubl. B.Sc. thesis, Memorial University of Newfoundland, St. John's, Newfoundland, 68 pp.

Coleman, R. G., 1971. Plate tectonic emplacement of upper mantle peridotites along continental edges. J. Geophys. Res., 76: 1212-1222.

514

Coleman, R. G. and Peterman, Z. E., 1975. Oceanic plagiogranite. J. Geophys. Res., 80: 1099-1108.

Dean, P. L., 1977. Stratigraphy and Metallogeny of the Notre Dame Bay Region, Central Newfoundland. Unpubl. M.Sc. thesis, Memorial University, St. John's, Newfoundland.

Dean, P. L. and Strong, D. F., 1975. The volcanic stratigraphy, geochemistry and metallogeny of the central Newfoundland Appalachians. Ann. Mtg. Geol. Assoc. Canada, Waterloo, Ontario (Abstr. with Programs): 745-746.

Dean, P. L. and Strong, D. F., 1976. 1:50,000 scale geological maps of Notre Dame Bay. Open file release by Geol. Surv. Canada and Newfoundland Dept. of Mines and Energy.

Dickinson, W. R., 1970. Relations of andesites, granites and derivative sandstones to arc-trench tectonics. Rev. Geophys. Space Phys., 8: 813-860.

Foslie, S., 1922. Field observations in northern Norway bearing on magmatic differentiation. J. Geol., 29: 701-709.

Glikson, A. Y., 1972. Early Precambrian evidence of a primitive ocean crust and island nuclei of sodic granite. Geol. Soc. Am. Bull., 83: 3323-3344.

Glikson, A. Y., 1976. Archean to early Proterozoic shield elements: Relevance of plate tectonics. In: Metallogeny and Plate Tectonics, D. F. Strong (Ed.). Geol. Assoc. Can. Sp. Paper 14: 489-516.

Glikson, A. Y. and Lambert, I. B., 1976. Vertical zonation and petrogenesis of the early Precambrian crust in Western Australia. Tectonophysics, 30: 55-89.

Glikson, A. Y. and Sheraton, J. W., 1972. Early Precambrian trondhjemitic suites in western Australia and northwestern Scotland, and the geochemical evolution of shields: Earth Planet. Sci. Lett., 17: 227-242.

Goldschmidt, V. M., 1916. Geologische-petrographische Studien im hochebirge des südlichen Norwegens. IV. Übersicht der Eruptivgesteine im kaledonischen Gebirge zwischen Stavanger und Trondhjem: Vidensk., Skr. Kristiana, 2: 76 pp.

Gustavson, M., 1969. The Caledonian Mountain chain of the southern Troms and Lofoten area, Part II, Caledonian rocks of igneous origin: Norsk. Geol. Unders., 261 pp.

Hoffman, C., 1976. Natural granitic rocks and the granite systems Qz-Or-Ab-An(H$_2$O) and Qz-Ab-An(H$_2$O): N. Jahrbuch f. Mineralogie, Monatshefte, 289-306.

Holloway, J. R., 1971.   Composition of fluid phase solutes in a Basalt-H_2O-CO_2 System.   Geol. Soc. Am. Bull., 82: 233-238.

Holloway, J. R. and Burnham, C. W., 1972.   Melting relations of basalt with equilibrium water pressure less than total pressure: J. Pet., 13: 1-29.

Hotz, P. E., 1971.   Plutonic rocks of the Klamath Mountains, California and Oregon: U.S. Geol. Surv. Prof. Pap., 684-B.

Johannsen, A., 1939.   A descriptive petrography of the igneous rocks, Vol. 12, The quartz-bearing rocks: Chicago Press, Chicago, 428 pp.

Kuno, H., 1968.   Origin of andesite and its bearing on the island arc structure: Bull. Volcanol., 32: 141-173.

Larsen, L. H. and Poldervaart, Arie, 1961.   Petrologic study of Bald Rock batholith, near Bidwell Bar, California: Geol. Soc. Am. Bull., 79, no. 1: 69-92.

Miller, H. G. and Deutsch, E. R., 1973.   A gravity survey of eastern Notre Dame Bay, Newfoundland: In: Earth Science Symposium on Offshore Eastern Canada, P. J. Hood (Ed.): Geol. Surv. Can. Paper, 71-23.

O'Connor, J. T., 1965.   A classification of quartz-rich igneous rocks based on feldspar ratios: U.S. Geol. Surv. Prof. Pap., 525-B.

Oftedahl, C., 1959.   Om vulkanittene i den kaledonske Ijellkjede i Norge: Norg. Geol. Unders., 39: 263-265.

Payne, J. G., 1974.   The Twillingate Granite and its relationships to surrounding country rocks.   Unpubl. M.Sc. thesis, Memorial University of Newfoundland, St. John's, Newfoundland, 159 pp.

Strong, D. F., 1977.   Volcanic regimes of the Newfoundland Appalachians. In: Volcanic Regimes of Canada, W. R. A. Baragar (Ed.), Geol. Assoc. Canada Sp. Paper No. 16: 61-90.

Strong, D. F. and Payne, J. G., 1973.   Early Paleozoic volcanism and metamorphism of the Moretons Harbour area, Newfoundland: Can. J. Earth Sci., 10: 1363-1379.

Strong, D. F., Dickson, W. L., O'Driscoll, C. F. and Kean, B. F., 1974. Geochemistry of eastern Newfoundland granitoid rocks: Nfld. Dept. Mines and Energy, Min. Res. Div., Report 74-3, 140 pp.

Taylor, S. R., 1965.   The application of trace element data to problems in petrology.   Phys. and Chem. of the Earth, 6: 133-213.

516

Thayer, T. P., 1976. Metallogenic contrasts in the plutonic and volcanic rocks of the opiolite assemblage. In: Metallogeny and Plate Tectonics, D. F. Strong (Ed.), Geol. Assoc. Can. Sp. Paper 14: 211-220.

Toksoz, M. N., Minear, J. W. and Julien, B. R., 1971. Temperature field and geophysical effects of a downgoing slab: J. Geophys. Res., 76: 1113-1138.

Turner, F. J., 1968. Metamorphic petrology. Mineralogical and Field Aspects. McGraw-Hill, N.Y.

Vokes, F. M. and Gale, G. H., 1976. Metallogeny relatable to global tectonics in southern Scandinavia. In: Metallogeny and Plate Tec- Tonics, D. F. Strong (Ed.), Geol. Assoc. Canada Sp. Paper 14: 411-440.

Williams, H. and Payne, J. G., 1975. The Twillingate Granite and nearby volcanic groups: an island arc complex in Northeast Newfoundland: Can. J. Earth Sci., 12: 982-995.

Williams, H., Dallmeyer, R. D. and Wanless, R. K., 1976. Geochronology of the Twillingate granite and Herring Neck Group, Notre Dame Bay, Newfoundland: Can. J. Earth Sci., 13: 1591-1601.

Wyllie, P. J., Wuu-Liang Huang, Stern, C. R. and Maaløe S., 1976. Granitic magmas: possible and impossible sources, water contents and crystallization sequences: Can. J. Earth Sci., 13: 1007-1019.

Yajima, T., Higuchi, H., and Nagasama, H., 1972. Variations of rare earth concentrations in pigeonitic and hypersthene rocks series from Izu-Hakone region, Japan: Contrib. Miner. Pet., 35: 235-244.

Chapter 17

GEOCHEMISTRY OF THE TYPE TRONDHJEMITE AND THREE ASSOCIATED ROCKS, NORWAY

F. Barker and H. T. Millard, Jr.

ABSTRACT

New major- and minor-element analyses are given for three trondhjemites, a biotite diorite, and leucogranodiorite from the southwestern Trondheim region. The type trondhjemites are of the high-Al_2O_3 type; they show average Al_2O_3 = 16.5 percent and K_2O = 1.34 percent, and Rb = 23-35 ppm, Sr = 581-645 ppm, and Ba = 323-333 ppm. Rare earths (REE) are low: La and Ce are 15-25 times chondrites, Yb and Lu are 1-2 times, and there are no Eu anomalies. The biotite diorite has 2.2 percent K_2O, 93 ppm Rb, 338 ppm Sr, and 297 ppm Ba. REE's are moderate: La is 80 times and Lu 7 times chondrites. Whether the trondhjemites are fractionates of dioritic liquid, as suggested by Goldschmidt, or were independently generated by partial melting of eclogite or amphibolite cannot be determined by these data. A pillow greenstone from the Stören Group is an abyssal tholeiite, enriched in the light REE's.

INTRODUCTION AND AGE RELATIONS

The type trondhjemite, associated biotite diorite and other intrusives of the Trondheim-Oppdal region were described by Goldschmidt in his classic memoir of 1916. This chapter presents data on major and minor elements recently obtained on three samples of trondhjemite, and on one each of biotite diorite and leucogranodiorite. Data on pillow greenstone of the Stören Group also are given.

Trondhjemite and associated intrusives are found in a large area to the south and east of Trondheim (see, e.g., Wolff, 1976). These rocks were emplaced in sedimentary and volcanic rocks of eugeosynclinal type that collectively are called the Trondheim Supergroup (Gale and Roberts, 1974). The sequence consists of, in ascending order, the Gula Group, Stören Group, Lower and Upper Hovin Groups, and Horg Group. The Gula Group is assumed to be of Cambrian age, and the Stören Group is assigned to the lowermost Ordovician by lithologic correlation with fossiliferous slates in other areas (Gale and Roberts, 1974). The geology of this area is complex, and the rocks have been subjected both to low to intermediate rank metamorphism and to polyphase deformation that culminated in the Silurian.

Peterman and Barker (1976) made an Rb-Sr study of these rocks. Their brief summary of age relations and previous radiometric dating of these rock is as follows:

"Several ages of trondhjemites are postulated on the basis of indirect geologic evidence. Some trondhjemites intrude only the Gula Group. A conglomerate in the Lower Hovin Group contains clasts of trondhjemite (C. W. Carstens, 1951; H. Carstens, 1960; Strand and Kulling, 1972). Pegmatites of trondhjemitic composition occur in the Gula Group but are assigned to the Silurian on the basis of structural relationships (Wilson et al., 1973). In mapping and interpreting the complex structure around the Innset pluton, Rohr-Torp (1972-1974) correlated the enclosing Krokstad sediments with those of the Hovin Group. Rohr-Torp (1974) concluded that the Innset pluton was emplaced between Llandeillian and late Silurian.

"The dating of periods of trondhjemite intrusion in relation to folding events is somewhat confusing. Rohr-Torp (1974) places the intrusion of the Innset pluton well before the F_1 deformation. Wilson et al. (1973) interpret the trondhjemitic pegmatites to have been emplaced concomitantly with the F_1 folding in the area east of Trondheim whereas the Follstad trondhjemite, south of Storen, is thought to be younger than F_1 (M. R. Wilson, personal communication, 1975). Of course, the F_1 events may not be regionally contemporaneous.

"Some radiometric dating has been completed in the region. K-Ar ages determined on biotite, hornblende, muscovite, and whole-rock samples of phyllite from the metamorphic terrane and from trondhjemites of the Trondheim region are in the range from 402 to 570 m.y. (Wilson et al., 1973). Most of the ages, however, are in the range from 402 to 438 m.y., and Wilson et al. (1973) dismiss the older ages as being the result of excess argon. These authors suggest that the upper limit-- 438 m.y.--of the main group of ages provides a minimum time for the major metamorphic episode in the area. Berthomier et al. (1972) report Rb-Sr isochron ages on biotite of 475 and 470 m.y. (recalculated to the 1.39×10^{-11} decay constant) for the Kaupanger and Hog-Gia plutons, respectively. From the scatter shown by their data on microcline and whole-rock samples, one must conclude that the Rb-Sr systems have been disturbed by some post-crystallization event. If ages are calculated on the basis of appropriate whole rock and biotite pairs, the ages range

from 416 to 495 m.y.   An alternative interpretation to that of
Berthomier et al. (1972) is that the 495 m.y. biotite-whole rock age is
a minimum for the Kaupanger pluton and the spread in these ages reflects
variable response of the biotite systems to some event that occurred at
ca. 420 m.y. or later.

Rb-Sr isotopic ratios obtained by Peterman and Barker (1976), as given in
Figure 1, give an apparent age for the trondhjemite, biotite diorite and
leucogranodiorite of $548^{\pm}35$ m.y. and an initial $^{87}Sr/^{86}Sr$ ratio of $0.7039^{\pm}$
0.0002.   This Cambrian age is not at all acceptable to geologists working in
this area, yet it was obtained on fresh samples by carefully controlled
chemical and mass-spectrometric techniques.

Peterman and Barker (1976) conclude:

"Although all of the samples are low in their content of radiogenic
^{87}Sr, the analytical precision is sufficiently good to resolve time
differences at well below 100 m.y. provided that the basic assumptions
inherent in the isochron approach are met.   If the age is valid, an
important period of Cambrian or perhaps lowermost Ordovician plutonism
has been identified--uncertainties in the half life of ^{87}Rb preclude a
more precise definition of this event even though the statistical
uncertainty on the isochron is only $^{\pm}35$ m.y. Acceptance of this
interpretation implies that the structural and stratigraphic arguments
which place some of these trondhjemites in the late Ordovician or
Silurian are in need of refinement."

These workers then consider that:

"The geologic arguments are correct and the seemingly precise
isochron is merely an artifact of sampling.   This interpretation implies
that we are seeing segments of parallel isochrons representing different
plutons each with different initial $^{87}Sr^{86}Sr$ ratios and ages
significantly younger than 548 m.y.")

Much geologic and isotopic work is needed here.

PETROGRAPHY

Three trondhjemities, one biotite diorite, and a leucogranodiorite were
collected.   A pillow greenstone of the Stolen Group was also taken, in the hope
that its chemistry might tell something of the paleoenvironment.   Sample
localities are given in Table I.   Fabrics (as seen in thin section) of all

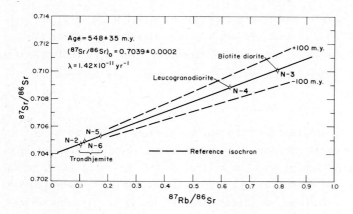

Figure 1.--Rb-Sr isotopic plot (from Peterman and Barker, 1976).

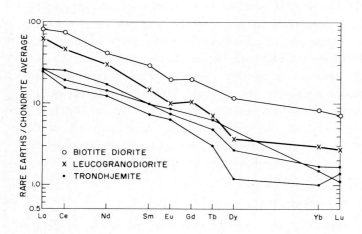

Figure 2a.--Chondrite-normalized rare-earth plots of biotite diorite, leucogranodiorite, and trondhjemite.

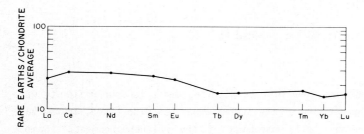

Figure 2b.--Chondrite-normalized rare-earth plot of pillow greenstone.

three compositional intrusive types are those of plutonic rocks, but reactions involving some of the original liquidus minerals--especially plagioclase--show that these rocks have been subjected to metamorphism of the upper greenschist facies.   All contain much blocky, subhedral sodic plagioclase that shows neither fracturing nor shearing and that has been heavily altered to felted masses of epidote and muscovite (as described by Goldschmidt, 1916); the grain size in the trondhjemite and diorite is 1-4 mm and in the leucogranodiorite, 1/2-2 mm.   The remaining plagioclase has been transformed to albite, much of which is compositionally zoned.   All rock types contain a few percent of disseminated, coarse epidote of problematical origin. TiO_2 apparently was expelled from biotite during metamorphism, for aggregates of tiny sphene crystals form rims around and lie along wavy internal surfaces in that mineral. Quartz has been recrystallized to mosaics of smaller grains and shows pronounced undulatory extinction.   The original K-feldspar of the leucogranodiorite now is grid-twinned microcline, which is poikilitic and forms the matrix for the blocky plagioclase subhedra.   Colorless to pale-green amphibole in the biotite diorite probably formed from original hornblende and clinopyroxene; a few pale-green relicts of the latter are present.

Modal analyses are given in Table I.   Before metamorphism the trondhjemite contained about 65-70 percent plagioclase--most of the epidote and muscovite of the modes are alteration products of the plagioclase.   The magmatic plagioclase probably was calcic oligoclase, and as it reacted to albite its anorthite component was fixed in epidote.   Potassium for the muscovite presumably came partly from original K-feldspar and partly from magmatic plagioclase.

Major elements

Major-element analyses and CIPW norms are given in Table II.   Those of the trondhjemites are very similar to Goldschmidt's old analysis (1916) of typical trondhjemite.   His analysis, however, shows a lower ratio of Fe_2O_3:FeO and 0.5 percent more Na_2O than ours, and so is not judged as wholly reliable.

The three trondhjemites contain an average of 16.5 percent of Al_2O_3 and thus are of the high-Al_2O_3 type; this average is appreciably more than the 15 percent at 70 percent SiO_2 that divides the low-Al_2O_3 and high-Al_2O_3 types (Barker, this volume).   Their K_2O content is 1.34 percent, which is typical of "primitive" trondhjemites, or ones that have not differentiated to leucogranodiorite and leucoquartz monzonite by the settling of plagioclase at relatively shallow crustal levels.   However, their FeO and Fe_2O_3 contents are relatively low, their Fe_2O_3/FeO ratios are high, and their total iron/Mg ratios also are low as compared to other trondhjemites (Arth et al., in press).

TABLE 1 : Modes of rocks. Locations are given below.

   (tr = trace; hyphen = not observed)

Rock Type	Trondhjemite	Biotite Diorite	Granodiorite	Trondhjemite	
Field No.	N-2	N-3	N-4	N-5	N-6
plagioclase	49	38	34	42	42
quartz	29	15	28	23	23
microcline	tr	-	7	tr	-
biotite	3	24	3	4	6
muscovite	9	-	11	8	9
chlorite	-	4	tr	tr	tr
epidote	9	7	16	22	19
amphibole	-	12	-	-	-
clinopyroxene	-	tr·	-	-	-
sphene	tr	tr	tr	tr	tr
apatite	tr	tr	tr	tr	tr
Fe-Ti oxides	-	tr	-	-	-

Locations: N-1: roadcut just E of Haga bridge, 1 km N of Støren.

   N-2: quarry 2 km E of Støren.

   N-3: roadcut 450 m N of Ulsberg bridge.

   N-4: roadcut opposite Donali Farm, 11 km NE of Oppdal.

   N-5: roadcut 9 km S of Meldal.

   N-6: roadcut 8 km S of Meldal.

The biotite diorite is a relatively rare rock type. Another well-known occurrence is the hornblende gabbro-trondhjemite suite of the Uusikaupunki-Kalanti area, southwestern Finland (Hietanen, 1943; Arth et al., in press). Its K_2O content is 2.2 percent, or markedly greater than that of the associated trondhjemites. This diorite, as discussed later, may be an intermediate member of a differentiation suite in which basaltic liquid was parental and trondhjemite was the terminal liquid.

The leucogranodiorite generally is similar to the trondhjemites in major-element composition (Table II), except for lower Na_2O and Al_2O_3 and higher K_2O. Its origin is not known; it may be a differentiate of a dioritic

TABLE II: Major-element analyses (by standard methods) and CIPW normative
minerals. Analyst: E.E. Engleman. Locations given in Table I.

Rock Type	Metabasalt	Biotite Diorite	Trondhjemite		Trondhjemite	Leuco-Granodiorite
Field No.	N-1	N-3	N-5	N-6	N-2	N-4
SiO_2	48.37	58.13	69.27	69.22	71.72	71.03
Al_2O_3	15.59	15.83	16.82	16.82	15.98	15.56
Fe_2O_3	3.24	1.26	0.59	0.69	0.49	0.68
FeO	6.35	4.93	0.86	0.90	0.88	0.99
MgO	6.40	5.48	0.88	0.99	0.53	0.86
CaO	12.17	5.94	3.18	3.42	2.83	2.58
Na_2O	2.95	3.33	5.53	5.42	5.56	4.74
K_2O	0.09	2.24	1.52	1.30	1.21	2.46
H_2O^+	2.53	1.63	0.68	0.64	0.53	0.71
H_2O^-	0.04	0.02	0.01	0.01	0.01	0.01
TiO_2	1.80	0.99	0.22	0.25	0.22	0.26
P_2O_5	0.21	0.23	0.08	0.09	0.06	0.08
MnO	0.15	0.11	0.03	0.03	0.03	0.04
CO_2	0.29	0.09	0.04	0.01	0.02	0.06
Cl	0.00	0.01	0.00	0.00	0.00	0.00
F	0.03	0.05	0.03	0.03	0.02	0.03
Subtotal	100.21	100.27	99.74	99.82	100.09	100.09
Less O	0.01	0.02	0.01	0.01	0.01	0.01
Total	100.20	100.25	99.73	99.81	100.08	100.08

CIPW Normative Minerals						
Q		8.5	23.2	23.9	27.7	27.2
C			0.6	0.5	0.6	0.8
OR	0.5	13.2	9.0	7.6	7.1	14.5
AB	24.9	28.0	46.9	45.9	47.0	40.0
AN	28.9	21.6	14.8	16.1	13.4	11.7
HL		0.0				
WO	11.6	2.2				
EN	15.5	13.6	2.1	2.4	1.3	2.1
FS	6.1	6.5	0.7	0.7	0.9	0.9
FO	0.2					
FA	0.1					
MT	4.6	1.8	0.8	1.0	0.7	0.9
IL	3.4	1.8	0.4	0.4	0.4	0.4
AP	0.4	0.5	0.1	0.2	0.1	0.1
FR	0.0	0.0	0.0	0.0	0.0	0.0
CC	0.6	0.2	0.0	0.0	0.0	0.1
Total	97.4	98.3	99.3	99.3	99.4	99.2
Salic	54.4	71.3	94.7	94.3	95.8	94.3
Femic	43.0	26.9	4.5	4.9	3.5	4.8

liquid. This rock is poorly exposed, and its field relations to the nearby trondhjemite are not known.

The pillow greenstone has a major-element composition (Table II), except for H_2O, rather like that of many low-K or abyssal tholeiites (Jakes and Gill, 1970). If the one analysis is representative, its 0.09 percent of K_2O and 1.8 percent of TiO_2 suggest that it is of the abyssal type. In addition, plots of SiO_2 versus FeO*/MgO (total iron as FeO is denoted as FeO*), FeO* vs FeO*/MgO, and TiO_2 vs FeO*/MgO fall near Miyashiro's curves (1975) for abyssal tholeiites. Gale and Roberts' (1974) classification of greenstone of the lower part of the Støren Group as ocean-floor type thus is supported.

MINOR ELEMENTS AND OXYGEN AND STRONTIUM ISOTOPES

Concentrations of Ba, Rb, and Sr; O^{18} values; and initial $Sr^{87/86}$ ratios are given in Table III. Concentrations of rare earths are given in Table IV.

The three trondhjemite samples show narrow ranges of Ba, Rb, and Sr contents (Table III). These are Ba, 323-333 ppm; Rb, 23.1-35 ppm; and Sr, 581-645 ppm. Similarly, the ratios of K/Rb, Rb/Sr, and Sr/Ba are consistent from one sample to another and probably imply (1) that each of the three intrusives formed from a similar or common source by a similar process, and (2) that there was little or no transfer of elements during metamorphism, except perhaps for hydrogen. Oxygen isotopes of the three samples show low fractionations, of

TABLE III: Minor-element abundances (in ppm), oxygen isotopic values (per mil), and initial strontium isotopic ratios. Ba analyses are by W.P. Doering by X-ray fluorescence.

Field No.	N-1	N-3	N-5	N-6	N-2	N-4
Ba	8	297	333	323	329	371
Rb*	1.3	93.0	35.0	25.8	23.1	83.8
Sr*	210	338	581	625	634	386
K/Rb	692	241	434	504	524	294
Rb/Sr	0.006	0.275	0.060	0.041	0.036	0.217
Sr/Ba	26.2	1.14	1.74	1.93	1.96	1.04
δO^{18}**		7.7	8.0	7.4	7.1	9.1
$(Sr^{87}/Sr^{86})_0$*0.7038(?)	(- - - - 0.7039±0.0002 - - - - - - - - - - - - - -)					

* Data from Peterman and Barker (this volume).

** Data from Barker et al. (1976).

TABLE IV: Rare-earth element analyses (in ppm) by instrumental-neutron-activation analysis. (n.d. = not determined) Coefficients of variation are generally less than 5 percent for Sm, Eu, and Dy; are in the range of 1 to 10 percent for La, Ce, and Gd; and range from 5 to 15 percent for Nd, Tb, Yb, and Lu.

Field No.	La	Ce	Nd	Sm	Eu	Gd	Tb	Dy	Tm	Yb	Lu
N-1	7.6	22.9	16.0	4.8	1.6	n.d.	0.75	5.19	0.59	2.9	0.54
N-2	8.2	12.4	7.0	1.4	0.44	n.d.	0.15	0.38	n.d.	0.21	0.05
N-3	26.4	59.3	23.4	5.4	1.4	5.1	n.d.	3.79	n.d.	1.7	0.25
N-4	20.3	36.7	16.9	2.7	0.69	2.6	0.33	1.2	n.d.	0.63	0.10
N-5	8.2	20.5	9.8	1.9	0.52	n.d.	0.22	0.89	n.d.	0.35	0.06
N-6	8.1	15.7	8.2	1.8	0.60	n.d.	0.30	n.d.	n.d.	0.32	0.04

7.1-8.0 per mil (Barker et al., 1976). Their initial $Sr^{87/86}$ ratio is relatively low, 0.7039 (Peterman, this volume), and indicates an origin (either directly or indirectly) largely from a mantle source.

Rare-earth patterns of the trondhjemites are shown in Figure 2. These show low abundances for all REE, fractionated patterns with La about 25 times chondrites and heavy rare earths 1 to 3 times chondrites, and small or no Eu anomalies. As discussed below, these patterns are very similar to those obtained from trondhjemites of southwestern Finland (Arth et al., in press).

The biotite diorite contains slightly less Ba and Sr than the trondhjemites but more Rb (Table III). Its rare-earth pattern (Figure 2) is significant, in that its slope is similar to that of the trondhjemites but the abundances are several times greater. This feature probably is due to a change in the distribution coefficients of hornblende settling out of the liquid. (See discussion below.)

The leucogranodiorite shows greater Rb and rare-earth abundances and less Sr than the trondhjemites. The Rb and Sr apparently reflect K_2O and Al_2O_3 abundances, respectively. The rare-earth abundances cannot be explained with our data. (See comments below.)

The pillow metabasalt apparently is an abyssal tholeiite. Minor-element concentrations confirm the abyssal nature of this sample: Ba = 8 ppm, Rb = 1.3 ppm, Sr = 210 ppm (Table III); and Cr = 256 ppm, Co = 38 ppm, and Sc = 39 ppm (instrumental-neutron-activation analyses by H. T. M.). However, Th = 1.25 ppm and U = 0.76 ppm (respective instrumental- and delayed-neutron analyses by H. T. M.). These are higher values than those of typical abyssal tholeiite (Jakes and Gill, 1970). This sample also is enriched in the light rare earths (Figure 2) compared to most ocean-ridge basalts. (See, e.g., Frey et al., 1974.) Recent work by Frey et al. (1974) and Schilling (1975) indicates that there are two types of abyssal or ocean-ridge tholeiite--one depleted in light rare earths and probably the more common type and another that is slightly enriched in light rare earths. The enriched type is postulated by these workers to be derived from less depleted and more "primitive" mantle than the more abundant type. Schilling (1975) also suggests that its genesis is related to a "blob" or plume of upwelling mantle material. However, a possibility remains that some "primitive" island-arc tholeiites may be compositionally similar to abyssal tholeiites. Evaluation of this idea must await future studies of modern rocks.

Our REE data apparently do not support the intermediate to siliceous part of Goldschmidt's fraction scheme (1922) for these rocks--his mica diorite stem. In this scheme biotite norite liquid differentiated first to biotite diorite and then trondhjemite. Phases subtracted from the liquid are plagioclase, biotite, pyroxenes, and minor olivine and Fe-Ti oxides. The biotite diorite as analyzed here could well be a differentiate of noritic or basaltic liquid. The lower REE abundances of trondhjemite relative to the biotite diorite, however, necessitate that phases removed from a dioritic liquid have an average partition coefficient greater than one. Neither of the phases--plagioclase and biotite-given by Goldschmidt for this part of his mica diorite stem meet this requirement, and we conclude that the trondhjemite was not generated by fractionation of dioritic liquid. A variation of Goldschmidt's stem involving hornblende in addition to plagioclase and biotite is feasible (Arth et al., in press). Hornblende has partition coefficients for all but the lightest REE's in this compositional range (Arth and Barker, 1976), and fractionation of dioritic liquid by removal of this phase could produce trondhjemite depleted in heavy REE's.

On the other hand, the trondhjemite and perhaps even the biotite diorite could have been produced by moderate to high fractions of partial melting of quartz eclogite or amphibolite (see, e.g., Arth and Hanson, 1975).

The tectonic environment in which the gabbro-diorite-trondhjemite suite forms is poorly known but may be either in a buckled trench or back-arc basin. Hietanen recently has suggested (1975) that the hornblende gabbro-trondhjemite suite of the Uusikaupunki-Kalanti area formed in an island-arc and back-arc-basin environment adjacent to the Archean craton. We definitely can say that these Norwegian trondhjemites are different from those that form at ocean ridges and in ophiolites (Coleman and Peterman, 1975), and so we must be dealing with an arc or continental-marginal environment, even though island-arc analogs are difficult to establish.

However, in the Trondheim-Oppdal region, the origin of the leuco-granodiorite remains a problem, as do the relations between the various norites, hypersthene-biotite diorite, opdalite, and other rocks discussed by Goldschmidt (1916, 1922). Perhaps differences in P_{H_2O} in some of the gabbroic and dioritic liquids were sufficient to drive hydration-dehydration reactions between hornblende and biotite on the one hand and pyroxenes and feldspars on the other.

One may speculate that extrusion of abyssal tholeiite as pillow lava in the Early Cambrian or perhaps late Precambrian (prior to about 550 m.y.) prior to intrusion of the diorite and trondhjemite, was related to development of the so-called Proto-Atlantic ocean. (See discussion of Gale and Roberts, 1974.) The enriched light rare earths of this tholeiite and its apparent derivation from relatively undepleted mantle are topics for further research.

528

ACKNOWLEDGMENTS

We are pleased to acknowledge the assistance of Dr. Harald Carstens in collecting the samples, discussions with Dr. J. G. Arth, reviews of the manuscript by Drs. Robert G. Coleman, J. G. Arth, and David Roberts, and correspondence with Dr. W. B. Size concerning his work in progress on trondhjemites of this area. We also thank the National Geographic Society for a travel grant.

REFERENCES

Arth, J. G., and Hanson, G. N., 1975. Geochemistry and origin of the Early Precambrian crust of northeastern Minnesota. Geochim. et Cosmochim. Acta, 39: 325-362.

Arth, J. G., and Barker, F., 1976. Rare-earth partitioning between hornblende and dacitic liquid and implications for the genesis of trondhjemitic-tonalitic magmas. Geology, 4: 534-536.

Arth, J. G., Barker, F., Peterman, Z. E., and Friedman, I., in press. Geochemistry of the gabbro-diorite-tonalite-trondhjemite suite of southwest Finland and its implications for the origin of tonalitic and trondhjemitic magmas. J. Pet.

Barker, F., Friedman, I., Hunter, D. R., and Gleason, J. D., 1976. Oxygen isotopes of some trondhjemites, siliceous gneisses, and associated mafic rocks. Precambrian Res., 3: 547-557.

Berthomier, C., Lacour, A., Leutwein, F., Maillot, J., and Sonet, J., 1972. Sur quelques trondhjemites de Norvege: etude geochronologique et geochemique. Sci. de la Terre, 17: 341-351.

Carstens, C. W., 1951. Lokkenfeltets geologi. Norsk Geol. Tids., 29: 9-25.

Carstens, H., 1960. Stratigraphy and volcanism of the Trondheimsfjord area, Norway. Norges Geol. Und., 212b.

Coleman, R. G., and Peterman, Z. E., 1975. Oceanic plagiogranite. J. Geophys. Res., 80: 1099-1108.

Frey, F. A., Bryan, W. B., and Thompson, G., 1974. Atlantic Ocean floor geochemistry and petrology of basalts from Legs 2 and 3 of the Deep-Sea Drilling Project. Jour. Geophys. Res., 79: 5507-5527.

Gale, G. H., and Roberts, D., 1974. Trace element geochemistry of Norwegian lower Palaeozoic basic volcanics and its tectonic implications. Earth Planet. Sci. Lett., 22: 380-390.

Goldschmidt, V. M., 1916. Geologisch-petrographische studien im hochgebirge des südlichen Norwegens, IV. Übersicht der eruptivegesteine im Kaledonischen Gebirge zwischen Stavanger und Trondjem. Skr. Norske Vidensk.-Akad. i Oslo Mat.-naturv. Kl., 2: 75-112.

Goldschmidt, V. M., 1922. Stammestypen der eruptivgesteine. Skr. Norske Vidensk.-Akad. i Oslo, Mat.-naturv. Kl., 10: 3-12.

Hietanen, A., 1943. Über das grundgebirge des Kalantigebietes im südwestlichen Finnland. Bull. Comm. Geol. Fin., 130: 105 pp.

Hietanen, A., 1975. Generation of potassium-poor magmas in the northern Sierra Nevada and the Svecofennian of Finland. U.S. Geol. Surv. J. Res., 3: 631-645.

Jakes, P., and Gill, J., 1970. Rare earth elements and the island arc tholeiitic series. Earth Planet. Sci. Lett., 9: 17-28.

Miyashiro, A., 1975. Classification, characteristics, and origin of ophiolites. J. Geol., 83: 249-281.

Peterman, Z. E., and Barker, F., 1976. Rb-Sr age of trondhjemite and diorite of the southwestern Trondheim region. U.S. Geological Survey Open-File Report 76-760: 17 pp.

Rohr-Torp, E., 1972. A major inversion of the western part of the Trondheim nappe. Norsk Geol. Tidsskr., 52: 453-458.

Rohr-Torp, E., 1974. Contact metamorphism around the Innset massif. Norsk Geol. Tidsskr., 54: 13-33.

Schilling, J. G., 1975. Azores mantle blob: rare earth evidence. Earth Planet. Sci. Lett., 25: 103-115.

Strand, T., and Kulling, O., 1972. Scandinavian Caledonides. Wiley-Interscience, London: 52-54.

Wilson, M. R., Roberts, D., and Wolff, F. C., 1973. Age determinations from the Trondheim region Caledonides, Norway: a preliminary report. Norges Geol. Und., 288: 53-63.

Wolff, F. C., 1976. Geologisk kart over Norge, berggrunnskart Trondheim, 1:250,000. Norges Geol. Und.

Chapter 18

RECONNAISSANCE GEOCHEMISTRY OF DEVONIAN ISLAND-ARC VOLCANIC AND INTRUSIVE ROCKS, WEST SHASTA DISTRICT, CALIFORNIA

F. Barker, H. T. Millard, Jr. and R. J. Knight

ABSTRACT

Major- and minor-element geochemistry of Middle Devonian Copley Greenstone and Balaklala Rhyolite of the West Shasta district, eastern Klamath Mountains, California, confirms earlier worker's conclusions that these rocks formed in an island-arc environment.

Four greenstones have 54.2-62.7 percent SiO_2 (as recalculated H_2O-free); 0.07-0.86 percent K_2O; 0-3.7 ppm Rb; 48-124 ppm Sr, 5-11 times chondrites La; 8-17.5 times chondrite Lu, and moderate depletion of light rare earth elements (REE's). These rocks are metabasaltic andesite and metaandesite, probably formed by fractionation of low-K or arc-type tholeiite. Four high-silica dacites (defined as having SiO_2 >70 percent and K_2O <2 percent) of the Balaklala Rhyolite have 76.4-79.7 percent SiO_2; low values of K, Rb, and Sr, which in part are not primary but were produced by alteration during emplacement, diagenesis, and metamorphism; 7-8 times chondrites La; 13-23 times chondrites Tb-Lu, and pronounced negative Eu anomalies. Light and intermediate REE's decrease with increasing SiO_2, perhaps by fractionation involving plagioclase, sphene, and quartz. The high—silica dacites are similar to modern arc dacites. The absence of rocks of intermediate composition is problematic and may be due to inadequate sampling.

Trondhjemite of the Mule Mountain stock is nearly identical in composition to the Balaklala high-silica dacite: two samples contain 74.0-75.2 percent SiO_2; 0.76-1.22 percent K_2O; 7-32 ppm Rb; 53-57 ppm Sr; and REE's about 10 percent greater than values of the Balaklala sample of 76.4 percent SiO_2. This trondhjemite, which was metamorphosed with the Balaklala Rhyolite to greenschist facies, probably is cogenetic with the Balaklala extrusives. It approaches some ophiolite-related plagiogranites in composition.

INTRODUCTION

The West Shasta district of northern California lies in the eastern

532

Paleozoic belt of the Klamath Mountains. This terrane is west to southwest of Shasta Lake (Fig. 1). Andesitic and highly siliceous metavolcanic rocks and a closely associated stock or small batholith of trondhjemite are the major rock units of the West Shasta district. A detailed geologic investigation of these rocks, of the Kuroko-type(?) ore deposits found in them, and of the associated, younger stratified and intrusive rocks of the district has been made by Kinkel et al. (1956).

The Devonian metavolcanic rocks consist of the stratigraphically lower Copley Greenstone, whose base is not exposed in this part of the Klamath Mountains, and the overlying Balaklala Rhyolite. Both formations have been assigned an age of early Middle Devonian (Kinkel et al., 1956; Boucot et al., 1974). There is a possibility, however, that deposition of the Copley commenced in Early Devonian time (A. W. Potter, written comm., 1976).

The trondhjemitic intrusive, which intrudes only the Copley and Balaklala units, was named the Mule Mountain stock by Hinds (1933). Like the enclosing metavolcanic rocks, the Mule Mountain intrusive was metamorphosed to

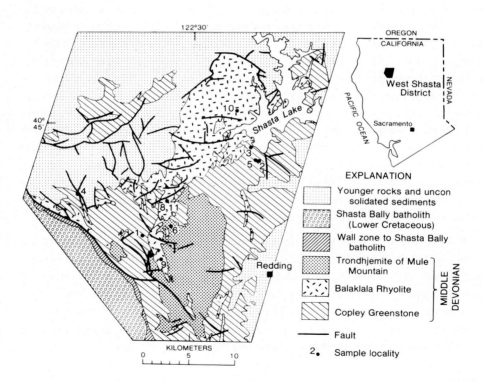

Figure 1.--Geologic sketch map of the West Shasta District, adapted from Strand (1962). Locations of samples are listed in the appendix.

greenschist facies and locally to zeolite or amphibolite facies. In addition, 20-35 percent of the stock underwent mild hydrothermal activity prior to metamorphism and now is albite-quartz-epidote rock.

Numerous earlier workers (Roberts, 1968; Hamilton, 1969; Condie and Snansieng, 1971; Burchfiel and Davis, 1972; Murray and Condie, 1973; Boucot et al., 1974; and Poole et al., 1977) proposed and presented evidence that these Devonian rocks of the Klamath Mountains formed in an island-arc environment. A major study by Potter and coworkers (Potter et al., 1975, 1976) substantiates these earlier conclusions. Our study, begun in 1973, was prompted by similarity of major element content of Balaklala Rhyolite to that of early Tertiary, high-silica dacite of Saipan, Mariana Islands (Schmidt, 1957; Barker et al., 1976). This investigation has been made primarily to obtain data on high-silica dacite of island-arc type that could be used in evaluating the origin of compositionally similar Precambrian gneisses. (We define high-silica dacite as containing more than 70 percent SiO_2 and less than 2 percent K_2O.)

DESCRIPTIONS OF ROCK UNITS

The Copley Greenstone, as described by Kinkel et al. (1976), consists of about 1,800 m of flows, tuffs, and agglomerate that are largely of andesitic composition. Keratophyre, spilite, albite diabase, and metagabbro also are present; the Copley thus ranges from basalt to dacite, although its precise chemical limits are not yet known. Minor lenses of tuffaceous shale and black shale also are present. The lower and middle parts of this formation are mostly green, keratophyric lava and tuff. Amygdaloidal varieties are common. Pillow lava forms much of the upper 300 m of the Copley. Pyroclastic breccias also are present throughout the Copley, but are most common in the upper part. These rocks were deposited under marine or near-marine conditions.

Sodic plagioclase, chlorite, epidote, quartz, green biotite, calcite, and actinolitic amphibole are the common minerals of the Copley Greenstone (see Kinkel et al., 1956). Our samples, of basaltic andesitic and andesitic compositions, show the assemblages (with minerals listed in order of decreasing abundance): albite-chlorite-epidote-quartz, chlorite-epidote-paragonite(?)-quartz, and chlorite-epidote-albite-actinolite-quartz.

The Copley Greenstone grades upward into the Balaklala Rhyolite through a breccia 45 m thick that consists of clasts of silicified greenstone and of high-silica dacite set in a matrix of chlorite schist (Kinkel et al., 1956).

The Balaklala Rhyolite (Kinkel et al., 1956) has a maximum thickness of about 1,100 m and consists largely of tuffs and flows of high-silica dacite. The Balaklala forms a broad structural dome having a northeast-southwest trending major axis 30 km long (Fig. 1). The formation is thickest along this axis. Kinkel et al. (1956) found that the early and most extensive flows of the Balaklala are nonporphyritic, that the intermediate part of the formation typically contains phenocrysts of quartz and albite 1-4 mm in size, and that the upper flows are coarsely porphyritic and contain quartz and albite phenocrysts larger than 4 mm. Fine-to coarse-grained pyroclastic beds are present throughout the Balaklala and comprise about one-fourth of the formation. Most of the flows are lenticular and less than 1 km in extent, but one flow of the upper, coarse-phenocrystic dacite was traced 10 km by Kinkel et al. (1956). This extensive flow is uniform, massive, and has a maximum thickness of about 400 m. The uppermost layers of the Balaklala are fine-grained tuff, tuffaceous shale, gray shale, and sandstone, which grade into the siliceous black shale of the Middle Devonian Kennett Formation. The Balaklala is partly of shallow marine origin. Some of the thicker flows, however, may have formed above sea level. A plate from a Devonian marine fish collected by A. R. Kinkel, Jr., from crystal tuff of the upper Balaklala has been described in detail by Boucot et al. (1974). These authors also list the marine fossils of Eifelian Age found in the Kennett Formation.

Detailed petrographic description of the Balaklala Rhyolite by Kinkel et al. (1956) is summarized as follows: The stratigraphically low, nonporphyritic to sparsely and finely porphyritic high-silica dacite typically is dense and white, light-bluish-green, or buff in color. Igneous flow banding is not uncommon. Sedimentary banding may be seen in associated water-laid tuffs. Sparsely disseminated phenocrysts of subhedral quartz and lath-like albite smaller than 1 mm are present in many of the lower layers. The groundmass may be either a massive felted aggregate or a schistose array predominantly of albite and quartz and of minor chlorite, epidote, muscovite and paragonite(?), apatite, magnetite, biotite, and sphene. Clay minerals and hydromica also are reported by Kinkel et al. (1956). The matrix of much of the nonporphyritic or finely porphyritic dacite originally was glassy, for microspherulitic structures are common. Our sample 10 contains clinoptilolite-heulandite zeolite co-existing with albite, quartz, epidote, and rutile. However, most of the Balaklala apparently is greenschist facies. The porphyritic varieties of high-silica dacite contain 5-20 percent each of phenocrysts of quartz and albite. Quartz phenocrysts are stubby bipyramids of a 2-10 mm maximum dimension. Resorbed margins are common. Phenocrysts of plagioclase are mostly euhedral, tabular, 3-6 mm in length, and contain tiny flakes of metamorphic white mica and chlorite. Plagioclase and quartz, as in many high-silica dacites, crystallized cotectically prior to extrusion.

The Mule Mountain stock is about 8 km by 16 km in plan (Fig. 1), with its major axis oriented north-south. Almost all of the stock, as described by Kinkel et al. (1956), is trondhjemite, but 20-35 percent of the stock has been altered to a massive albite-quartz-epidote rock. Altered regions are irregular in plan, are scattered through the stock and show gradational margins with the unaltered trondhjemite. Whether alteration was caused by convective motion of meteoric waters shortly after emplacement of the stock, or by waters circulating during the metamorphic event in Jurassic time is unknown. Irregular regions of intrusive breccia containing clasts of both Copley Greenstone and Balaklala Rhyolite occur in the northern part of the stock. Kinkel et al. (1956) also describe a body of hornblende-quartz diorite about 100 m in diameter associated with breccia and ascribe its origin to assimilation of greenstone by trondhjemitic magma.

All of the Mule Mountain stock has been metamorphosed, largely to greenschist facies. During metamorphism most of the An component of the primary plagioclase was incorporated in epidote, the K_2O of original biotite and feldspar in ubiquitous fine white mica, and most of the primary biotite was transformed to chlorite. The white mica and chlorite are so finely dispersed that accurate modal analyses of the rock cannot be made. Typical trondhjemite of the stock is visually estimated to consist of approximately 35-40 percent sodic oligoclase and calcic albite, 30-35 percent quartz, 10 percent epidote, 10 percent white mica, and 5-10 percent chlorite. Magnetite, sphene, and apatite are accessory. Quartz occurs both as subhedral to rounded grains as large as 10 mm--which we interpret as derived from phenocrysts--and as 1-3 mm anhedral grains. Plagioclase occurs as subhedra 1-3 mm in maximum dimension. Myrmekitic intergrowths of quartz and albite are common in the trondhjemite.

MAJOR AND MINOR ELEMENTS

Major-element contents of five samples of Copley Greenstone, two of trondhjemite of the Mule Mountain stock, and four of Balaklala Rhyolite are given in Table I. Rb and Sr abundances of all but one of these are given in Table II. Analyses of rare earth elements (REE's) and other minor elements of seven of these samples also are given in Table II.

The Copley and Balaklala Formations, having been deposited largely under marine conditions and metamorphosed, have been hydrated and have gained or lost several elements. The analytical data were recalculated to $H_2O = 0$ for plotting on Figures 2-7. Other constituents, however, cannot be treated systematically, for we have no rocks of unaltered magmatic compositions for reference. Because there is no evidence of gain or loss of SiO_2, though, and because SiO_2 is the most abundant constituent--and thus the most difficult to perturb--we have plotted major elements, Rb, and Sr, against SiO_2 on Figures 2

TABLE 1 : Major-element analyses of Copley Greenstone, trondhjemite of Mule Mountain, Balaklala Rhyolite and high-silica dacite of Saipan. Locations of samples are given in the appendix. (n.d. indicates not determined)

	Copley			Greenstone		trondhjemite of Mule Mountain		Balaklala Rhyolite				Saipan, high-SiO$_2$ dacite[d]
	1[a]	2[b]	3[a]	4[a]	5[a]	6[c]	7[a]	8[a]	9[c]	10[a]	11[a]	
SiO$_2$	51.77	52.56	57.68	60.69	60.78	72.74	74.59	75.05	77.01	77.11	77.48	78.71
Al$_2$O$_3$	14.89	17.00	17.25	15.84	15.38	14.14	13.46	12.84	12.04	11.47	11.60	10.59
Fe$_2$O$_3$	1.49	.91	2.00	2.24	1.51	1.26	1.00	1.20	.67	0.27	0.23	0.70
FeO	6.49	6.12	5.39	5.42	6.21	1.82	1.13	0.81	1.51	1.00	2.09	0.61
MgO	10.31	7.11	4.39	2.39	4.00	.63	0.34	1.42	1.29	0.22	1.93	0.60
CaO	5.95	5.55	3.35	4.59	2.63	2.12	2.34	1.22	.86	4.69	0.00	1.23
Na$_2$O	2.98	5.28	5.77	4.80	4.63	4.12	4.23	2.37	4.58	2.89	2.11	3.61
K$_2$O	0.24	.84	0.34	0.07	0.34	.75	1.22	1.99	.59	0.12	1.19	1.61
H$_2$O$^+$	4.41	3.15	2.76	2.29	3.03	1.53	0.75	1.77	1.19	1.59	2.56	2.09
H$_2$O$^-$	0.05	.10	0.03	0.01	0.04	.13	0.01	0.03	.13	0.06	0.22	0.21
TiO$_2$	0.49	.40	0.67	0.76	0.90	.26	0.18	0.21	.18	0.23	0.18	0.15
P$_2$O$_5$	0.05	.86	0.06	0.05	0.10	.05	0.02	0.04	.03	0.03	0.02	0.09
MnO	0.11	.05	0.15	0.11	0.16	n.d.	0.04	0.05	n.d.	0.03	0.04	0.04
CO$_2$	0.66	.16	0.02	0.47	0.06	n.d.	0.05	0.78	n.d.	0.01	0.01	n.d.
TOTAL	99.89	100.09	99.86	99.73	99.77	99.55	99.36	99.78	100.08	99.72	99.66	

a/ Analysis by G.O. Riddle
b/ Analysis by J. F. Fairchild (Kinkel et al., 1956).
c/ Analysis by M. K. Carron (Kinkel et al., 1956).
d/ Average of three analyses of Schmidt (1956) and one of Barker et al. (1976).

TABLE II : Minor-element analyses of Copley Greenstone, trondhjemite of Mule Mountain, Balaklala Rhyolite, and high-silica dacite of Saipan. All values in parts per million by weight. Sample localities are given in the appendix. (n.d., not determined.)

	COPLEY GREENSTONE				TRONDHJEMITE OF MULE MOUNTAIN			BALAKLALA RHYOLITE			SAIPAN, high-SiO_2 dacite[a]
	1	3	4	5	6	7	8	9	10	11	
Rb	3.7	2.5	0	2.9	7.5	32	27	16	2.5	13	20
Sr	95	124	48	100	52	58	37	76	31	24	75
Ba	76	69	n.d.	86	225	n.d.	260	n.d.	n.d.	462	135
Th	n.d.	0.21	n.d.	0.86	0.60	n.d.	0.34	0.53	n.d.	0.39	n.d.
U	.33	0.48	n.d.	0.29	0.60	n.d.	0.43	0.70	n.d.	0.49	n.d.
La	1.7	1.6	n.d.	3.5	3.1	n.d.	2.6	2.5	n.d.	2.3	n.d.
Ce	4.6	4.5	n.d.	10.4	9.9	n.d.	7.9	7.7	n.d.	6.4	9.96
Nd	5.4	5.1	n.d.	9.3	8.2	n.d.	7.9	5.5	n.d.	5.8	7.71
Sm	1.3	1.7	n.d.	2.7	3.5	n.d.	2.9	2.7	n.d.	2.2	2.48
Eu	0.56	0.90	n.d.	1.2	0.66	n.d.	0.58	0.54	n.d.	0.48	0.54
Gd	n.d.	2.6	n.d.	4.3	5.1	n.d.	5.7	n.d.	n.d.	n.d.	3.31
Tb	n.d.	n.d.	n.d.	n.d.	n.d.	n.d.	0.9	0.8	n.d.	0.6	n.d.
Dy	2.2	n.d.	n.d.	5.2	5.2	n.d.	6.0	4.8	n.d.	3.9	3.42
Tm	n.d.	0.4	n.d.	n.d.	n.d.	n.d.	n.d.	n.d.	n.d.	n.d.	n.d.
Yb	1.4	2.4	n.d.	3.1	3.8	n.d.	3.8	3.8	n.d.	3.5	2.40
Lu	0.3	0.5	n.d.	0.6	0.7	n.d.	0.8	0.7	n.d.	0.7	0.43
Zr	57	79	n.d.	91	176	n.d.	119	143	n.d.	118	n.d.
Sc	37	33	n.d.	29	11	n.d.	10	11	n.d.	9.9	n.d.
Cr	490	20	n.d.	2.5	13	n.d.	2.2	11	n.d.	6.1	n.d.
Co	37	23	n.d.	.20	4.3	n.d.	1.5	2.0	n.d.	0.7	n.d.

(Rb and Sr analyses by X-ray fluorescence by W. P. Doering; U by delayed neutron analysis; all other elements by instrumental neutron activation analysis (INAA). Coefficients of variation of INAA for values given generally fall within the following ranges: 1-5%, La, Sm, Eu; 1-10%, Th, Ce, Nd, Dy, Lu, Hf; 5-15%, Gd, Tb, Yb, Sr, Sc, Cr; 10-20%, Ba, Tm, Ta, Co)

a/ Values from Barker et al. (1976)

538

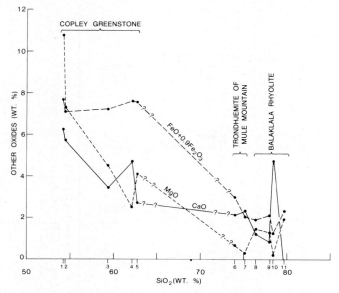

Figure 2.--Plot of MgO, FeO+0.9 Fe_2O_3, and CaO versus SiO_2 . Sample numbers are included along abscissa.

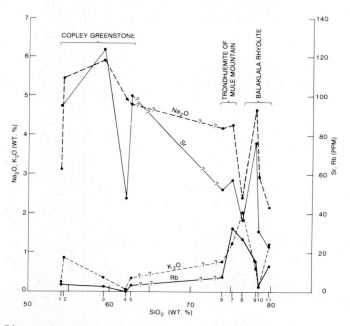

Figure 3.--Plot of Na_2O, K_2O, Sr, and Rb versus SiO_2. Sample numbers are included along abscissa.

and 3. The pronounced deviations from smooth curves in these two diagrams probably indicate local migrations of elements. Inspection of Figures 2 and 3 shows probable addition of Ca to sample 4 and the zeolitized sample 10, and loss of Ca from sample 11. Abundances of Mg are erratic from one sample to another, whereas FeO* (FeO + $0.9Fe_2O_3$) is more regular. Na is depleted in sample 8, but enriched in sample 9. Sr abundances generally reflect those of Na, except in sample 4. K is enriched in sample 8 and depleted in samples 9 and 10. Rb abundances reflect those of K. Abundances of Na and K in part are antithetic. We presume that most of these compositional disturbances are a result of interaction of these rocks with sea water or connate waters derived from sea water, and that much of this interaction occurred while the rocks retained much of their magmatic heat.

Our data are not sufficient to determine if the gap in SiO_2 of about 12 percent that separates samples 5 and 6 is significant, or if it is merely an artifact of incomplete sampling. Kinkel et al. (1956) give petrographic descriptions of dacite that may lie in this gap.

The disturbances involving Mg and alkalies affect locations of points in the Alk-F-M and normative quartz-albite-orthoclase plots (figs. 4 and 5, respectively). In the Alk-F-M diagram, values of the Copley and Balaklala plot over such a wide range of FeO*/MgO ratios and of Na_2O+K_2O contents that we cannot use this diagram to determine if these rocks are calc-alkaline or tholeiitic. In the quartz-albite- orthoclase diagram the Copley samples lie close to the quartz-albite sideline--in keeping with their low contents of K, but the Balaklala samples scatter widely--reflecting changes of K/Na ratios and loss of alkalies for the three points showing quartz >60 percent. The Balaklala Rhyolite plots well into the experimentally determined quartz (±tridymite) field, as does the compositionally similar high-silica of Saipan (data of Schmidt, 1956; and Barker et al., 1976).

Plots of REE data (Table II), normalized to values for chondrites, are given on Figures 6 and 7. The patterns for the basaltic andesite (sample 1) and two andesites (samples 3 and 5) of the Copley Greenstone (Fig. 6) show depletion in light REE's, flat slopes of intermediate and heavy REE's, small to moderate positive Eu anomalies and a general increase of REE's with increasing SiO_2 content. The moderate Eu anomaly of sample 3 may be a result of accumulation of plagioclase, for this sample shows higher modal and normative plagioclase than either samples 1 or 5. The stacking of REE patterns with SiO_2 content may indicate derivation of these andesites by fractionation of basaltic liquid, but three analyses probably are not sufficient to warrant such a conclusion.

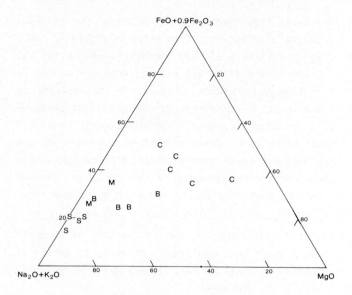

Figure 4.--Alk-F-M plot. C, Copley Greenstone; B, Balaklala Rhyolite; M, trondhjemite of Mule Mountain; S, dacite of Saipan.

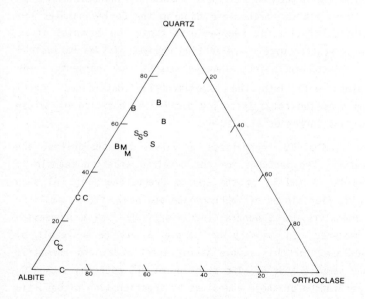

Figure 5.--Normative quartz-albite-orthoclase plot. C, Copley Greenstone; B, Balaklala Rhyolite; M, trondhjemite of Mule Mountain; S, dacite of Saipan.

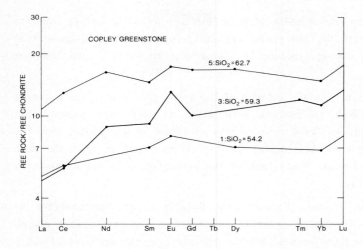

Figure 6.--REE patterns of three samples of Copley Greenstone, showing sample numbers and (recalculated anhydrous) SiO_2 values.

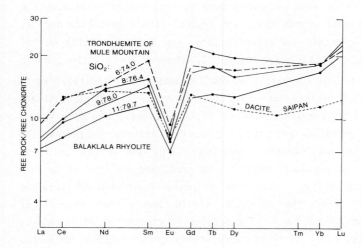

Figure 7.--REE patterns of trondhjemite of Mule Mountain stock and of three samples of Balaklala Rhyolite, showing sample numbers and (recalculated anhydrous) SiO_2 values.

REE patterns of the trondhjemite of Mule Mountain and of Balaklala Rhyolite (Fig. 7) are self-consistent and almost certainly indicate that REE abundances are remarkably stable during exposure to sea water, diagenesis, and low-rank metamorphism.

The correspondence of the REE pattern of the trondhjemite with the patterns of the Balaklala, taken in context with other chemical and petrographic similarities, and with the field observations of Kinkel et al. (1956) that the trondhjemite intruded only the Copley and Balaklala, implies that the Mule Mountain stock is a plutonic equivalent of the extrusive Balaklala high-silica dacitic flows and tuffs.

The four patterns of Mule Mountain and Balaklala are characterized by light-REE depletion, pronounced negative Eu anomalies, concave-upward shapes from Gd to Lu, and low abundances of REE's. Furthermore, the decrease of REE's with increasing SiO_2 is notable and best developed for light and intermediate REE's. We infer that these four rocks are comagmatic and related by fractionation. The disposition of the REE patterns--especially the nearly pivotal motion of Gd, Tb, and Dy about Yb--with respect to SiO_2 cannot be explained by simple removal of plagioclase from or/and addition of quartz (as a dilutent) to a parental liquid of SiO_2 content less than 72 percent. Removal of a phase having greater partition coefficients (defined as REE_{solid}/REE_{liquid}) for the elements Ce to Dy than for Yb and Lu is required. The only phase known to us that possesses such partition coefficients, occurs as a liquidus phase in both trondhjemite and crystal-rich high-silica dacite, and probably grows as crystals sufficiently large and dense to settle out of such liquids is sphene. C. E. Hedge and E. C. Simmons (pers. comm., March 1977) report newly determined REE partition coefficients for sphene relative to granodioritic liquid that satisfy the above requirements. In addition, Staatz et al. (1977) report high concentrations of light and heavy REE's in sphene from holocrystalline granitic and syenitic rocks. Apatite possesses the necessary REE partition coefficients (Nagasawa, 1970) and occurs in these rocks, but is present in such small crystals and small amounts that it may not be able to fractionate REE's. Thus the proposed fractionation involves subtraction of sphene from the parental liquid and either removal of plagioclase or addition of quartz. The scatter of abundances of Na and Ca with SiO_2 content (Figs. 2 and 3) precludes determination of relative movements of plagioclase and quartz.

The REE patterns of the Copley Greenstone, Mule Mountain stock, and Balaklala Rhyolite are like those of tholeiite-derived andesite and dacite of the Izu-Hakone arc (Yajima et al., 1972) and of dacite of Saipan (Fig. 7), except that aphyric dacite of Hakone volcano shows only a small negative Eu anomaly. The Shastan rocks definitely do not show the mild enrichment of light REE's of the calc-alkaline series of Kuno (1950), reported by Yajima et al. (1972). REE patterns of the Mule Mountain and Balaklala samples also resemble those of plagiogranites derived from ophiolites--for example, the trondhjemite of the Canyon Mountain ophiolite complex, Oregon, and and trondhjemite near Sparta, Oregon (Coleman and Donato, this volume; Phelps, this volume).

CONCLUSIONS

The metaandesite of the Copley Greenstone, trondhjemite of the Mule Mountain stock, and high-silica metadacite of the Balaklala Rhyolite are of island-arc affinity, rather than of ocean-ridge or normal calc-alkaline types. Elemental abundances of the Copley--including K_2O at 0.25-0.35 percent, Rb <4 ppm, Sr at 60-100 ppm, Ba at 68-86 ppm, TiO_2 at 0.49-0.90 percent, Th and U each <1 ppm and REE's of low abundances and flat light-REE-depleted patterns-- correspond to Jakes' and Gill's (1970) characterization of island-arc tholeiitic rocks. The close correspondence of many geochemical parameters of the Mule Mountain and Balaklala to siliceous dacites of the Izu-Mariana arc also substantiates earlier workers' designation of an island-arc environment in the eastern Klamath Mountains in Middle Devonian time.

ACKNOWLEDGMENTS

We express our thanks to J. N. Batchelder for collecting samples, to W. E. Hall for discussions of geology of the West Shasta district, to A. W. Potter for his unpublished data, and to F. C. Dodge and R. W. Kistler for reviewing the manuscript.

REFERENCES

Barker, F., Arth, J. G., Peterman, Z. E., and Friedman, I., 1976. The 1.7- to 1.8-b.y. old trondhjemites of southwestern Colorado and northern New Mexico: geochemistry and depths of genesis. Bull. Soc. Am., 87: 189-198.

Boucot, A. J., Dunkle, D. H., Potter, A., Savage, N. M. and Rohr, D., 1974. Middle Devonian orogeny in western North America?: a fish and other fossils. J. Geol., 82: 91-708.

Burchfiel, B. C. and Davis, G. A., 1972. Structural framework and evolution of the southern part of the Cordilleran orogen, western United States. Am. J. Sci., 272: 97-118.

Condie, K. C. and Snansieng, S., 1971. Petrology and geochemistry of the Duzel (Ordovician) and Gazelle (Silurian) Formations, Northern California. J. Sed. Pet., 41: 741-751.

Hamilton, W., 1969. Mesozoic California and the underflow of Pacific mantle. Bull. Geol. Soc. Am., 80: 2409-2430.

Hinds, N. E. A., 1933. Geologic formations of the Redding-Weaverville districts, northern California. Calif. Jour. Mines and Geol., 29: 77-122.

Jakes, P. and Gill, J., 1970. Rare earth elements and the island arc tholeiite series. Earth Planet Sci. Lett., 9: 17-28.

Kinkel, A. R., Jr., Hall, W. E. and Albers, J. P., 1956. Geology and base-metal deposits of West Shasta copper-zinc district, Shasta County, California. U.S. Geol. Surv., Prof. Pap., 285: 156 pp.

Kuno, H., 1950. Petrology of Hakone Volcano and adjacent areas, Japan. Bull. Geol. Soc. Am., 61: 957-1020.

Murray, M. and Condie, K. C., 1973. Post-Ordovician to early Mesozoic history of the Eastern Klamath subprovince, northern California. J. Sed. Pet., 43: 505-515.

Nagasawa, H., 1970. Rare earth concentrations in zircons and apatites and their host dacites and granites. Earth Planet. Sci. Lett., 9: 359-364.

Poole, F. G., Sandberg, C. A. and Boucot, A. J., 1977. Silurian and Devonian paleogeography of western United States, in J. H. Stewart, C. H. Stevens and A. E. Fritsche (Editors), Paleozoic paleogeography of the western United States. Soc. Ed. Pal. Min., Pacific Sec., Pacific Coast Paleogeog. Symp. 1: 39-65.

Potter, A. W., Scheidegger, K. F., Corliss, J. B. and Dasch, E. ᴶ., 1975. Magma types present in Paleozoic keratophyres and spilites from the Gazelle area, eastern Klamath Mountains, northern California. Geol. Soc. Am., Abstr. with Programs, 7: 1231-1232 (abstr.).

Potter, A. W., Scheidegger, K. F. and Corliss, J. B., 1976. Magma types of early Paleozoic altered volcanic rocks of the eastern Klamath Mountains, northern California: further results. EOS, 57: 1023 (abstr.).

Roberts, R. J., 1968. Tectonic framework of the Great Basin, in A coast to coast tectonic study of the United States. Univ. Mo., Rolla Jour., 1: 101-119.

Schmidt, R. G., 1957. Geology of Saipan, Mariana Islands--Part 2. Petrology of the volcanic rocks. U.S. Geol. Surv. Prof. Pap., 280-B: 127-175.

Staatz, M. H., Conklin, N. M. and Brownfield, I. K., 1977. Rare earths, thorium, and other minor elements in sphene from some plutonic rocks in west-central Alaska. U.S. Geol. Surv. J. Res., 5: 623-628.

Strand, R. G., 1962. Geologic map of California, Redding Sheet, scale 1:250,000. Calif. Div. Mines Geol.

Yajima, T., Higuchi, H. and Nagasawa, H., 1972. Variation of rare earth concentrations in pigeonitic and hypersthene rock series from Izu-Hakone Region, Japan. Contrib. Miner. Pet., 35: 235-244.

APPENDIX

Locations of samples:

1.   Roadcut, Highway 299W, 0.6 km northwest of Whiskeytown.
2.   See Kinkel et al. (1956).
3.   Roadcut, 0.34 km southwest of Shasta Dam.
4.   Roadcut, Highway 299W, opposite Crystal Creek Campground, 8.9 km airline distance northwest of Whiskeytown.
5.   Roadcut, opposite View Point on Highway 151, and 1.4 km southwest of east end of Shasta Dam.
6.   See Kinkel et al. (1956).
7.   East bank, Clear Creek, 6.1 km airline distance south-southeast of Whiskeytown.
8.   North side of pit, Iron Mountain Mine (for location see Kinkel et al., 1956), NW 1/4 French Gulch quadrangle.
9.   See Kinkel et al. (1956).
10. Summit, Mammoth Butte, SW 1/4 Lamoine quadrangle.
11. 200 m north of Sample No. 8.

Chapter 19

PETROLOGY, GEOCHEMISTRY AND ORIGIN OF THE SPARTA QUARTZ DIORITE-TRONDHJEMITE COMPLEX, NORTHEASTERN OREGON

D. Phelps

ABSTRACT

The Sparta complex in northeastern Oregon consists of a sequence of Triassic gabbro, quartz diorite and trondhjemite. The trondhjemite was previously thought to have formed by Na-metasomatism of the quartz diorite, but new textural and mineralogical evidence indicate a magmatic origin for the Sparta trondhjemite. Whole-rock major- and trace-element data are also compatible with a magmatic origin.

The quartz diorite and trondhjemite are genetically related, but the exact nature of the relationship is not clear. Major-element data and field observations are consistent with magmatic differentiation from either a low-K_2O basaltic or andesitic magma, but complications arise when the rare-earth element (REE) data are considered. Despite evidence of hornblende fractionation, the REE patterns of the trondhjemite do not show the expected increase in the Ce/Yb ratio relative to the quartz diorite. Alternatively, an origin involving two partial melts, one of trondhjemitic and one of quartz dioritic composition, is consistent with most of the geochemical and petrologic data.

INTRODUCTION

The origin of trondhjemites has received considerable attention in recent geologic literature; however, most of the recent studies have concentrated on Precambrian occurrences. Barker et al. (1976) have divided trondhjemites in general into two groups: a high-Al_2O_3 type containing 15% or more Al_2O_3, and a low Al_2O_3 type containing less than 15% Al_2O_3. The two types of trondhjemite have distinct trace element characteristics which have been interpreted to indicate different modes of origin (Barker et al., 1976; Barker and Arth, 1976). The low Al_2O_3 type of trondhjemite is known from Precambrian terrains (Barker et al., 1976; Barker and Arth, 1976), and is also found in Phanerozoic complexes associated with island arcs (Ishizaka and Yanagi, 1977; Barker, Millard, and Knight, this volume) and ophiolite complexes (Coleman and

Peterman, 1975; Coleman, 1977). The high-Al_2O_3 type of trondhjemite is known from both Precambrian and Phanerozoic terrains (Arth and Barker. 1976; Barker and Arth, 1976; Arth et al., 1978).

In this paper the results of a study on a low-Al_2O_3 type trondhjemite-quartz diorite complex from a postulated Triassic island arc in eastern Oregon are presented. The complex was first studied in detail by Gilluly (1933) and later by Prostka (1963). Both authors concluded that the trondhjemite (albite granite of Gilluly and Prostka) formed through Na-metasomatism of the associated quartz diorite. New petrographic, microprobe and whole-rock major- and trace-element chemical data presented in this report suggest that the quartz diorite-trondhjemite complex is a cogenetic suite formed either by magmatic differentiation or by partial melting of a basaltic source terrain. The new data indicate that Na-metasomatism played an insignificant role in the formation of the quartz diorite-trondhjemite complex.

GEOLOGIC SETTING

The Sparta quartz diorite-trondhjemite complex is located 32 km east of Baker, Oregon (Fig. 1). It is separated from the Jurassic-Cretaceous stocks and batholiths of the Wallowa Mountains to the north by a sequence of Mesozoic rocks. To the south the trondhjemite and quartz diorite are separated from the upper Paleozoic Burnt River Schist and Elkhorn Argillite by gabbros and ultramafic rocks. The Mesozoic rocks to the north consist of Upper Triassic volcanic and sedimentary rocks (Clover Creek Greenstone, Gold Creek Greenstone, Lower Sedimentary Series, Martin Bridge Limestone, and Hurwal Formation; Prostka, 1963). The Upper Triassic volcanic rocks are basalt, spilite, andesite, and keratophyre (Clover Creek Greenstone; Prostka, 1963). The relationship of the Clover Creek Greenstone to the trondhjemite and quartz diorite is problematic (Vallier et al., 1977; Phelps, 1978).

Upper Triassic volcanic rocks occur throughout eastern Oregon (Brooks, 1976; Vallier, 1977; Vallier et al., 1977) and are interpreted as an Upper Triassic volcanic arc sequence (Brooks, 1976; Vallier, 1977; Vallier et al., 1977). $^{40}Ar/^{39}Ar$ age determinations of 218 mybp on hornblende separates from a quartz diorite and trondhjemite (Ave Lallemant et al., in preparation) and a K-Ar age of 215 mybp on a biotite separate from a quartz diorite from the Sparta Complex (Vallier et al., 1977) coincide with the age of blue schists (220 mybp, Hotz, et al., 1977) cropping out near Mitchell, central Oregon (Swanson, 1969). The geologic relationships are consistent with the Sparta quartz diorite-trondhjemite complex being the plutonic member of an Upper Triassic island arc formed in response to eastward subduction in central Oregon (Phelps, 1978).

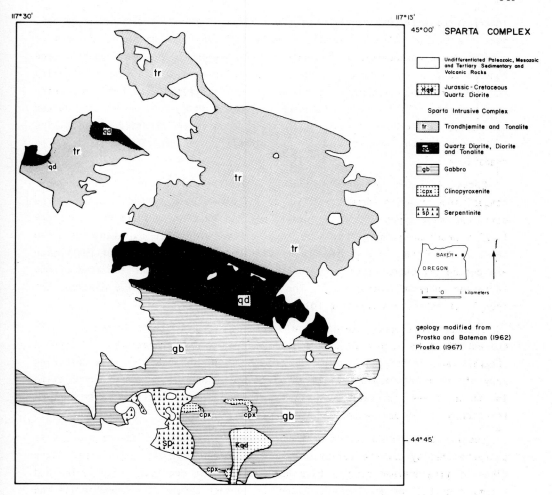

Figure 1.--Geologic map of the Sparta intrusive complex, eastern Oregon.

FIELD RELATIONSHIPS

Figure 1 is a simplified geologic map of the Sparta plutonic complex. Much of the Sparta complex is covered by Tertiary basalts and sediments, and for this reason the actual size and relative proportions of rock types of the Sparta complex are not known.

Ultramafic and mafic rocks crop out south of the trondhjemite and quartz diorite. The ultramafic rocks consist of clinopyroxenite, olivine clinopyroxenite and their serpentinized equivalents. The clinopyroxenite is interlayered with and overlain to the north by cumulus, two-pyroxene gabbro. Near the contact with the quartz diorite the two pyroxene-gabbro changes to ophitic two pyroxene-hornblende and two pyroxene-hornblende-quartz gabbro. The contact between the gabbro and quartz diorite is marked by a zone of shearing and intense alteration in both the gabbro and quartz diorite often obscuring the contact relationships. Although Prostka (1963) considered the quartz diorite to be intrusive into the gabbro, no unequivocal intrusive relationships were seen by the present author and in places the contact appears to be gradational.

Rocks included within the quartz diorite unit have variable modal compositions ranging from tonalite to meladiorite. Contacts between the different rock types within the quartz diorite unit are gradational, although locally pronounced changes in modal composition occur over a distance of a few meters. Xenoliths of diorite and meladiorite in various stages of resorption are common throughout the quartz diorite and probably account for much of the variation in modal composition. The quartz diorite is typically massive, but locally it exhibits a tectonic foliation.

The contact between the quartz diorite and trondhjemite is irregular and is characterized by a zone of complex and often ambiguous relationships. Intense shearing and faulting has occurred along much of the contact, thus obscuring many of the relationships. Alteration of the quartz diorite and trondhjemite in these areas is extreme. However, at a few locations the contact relationships can be reasonably evaluated.

Locally the contact is gradational. In these areas the quartz diorite is characterized by extreme variations in modal mineralogy and grain size. Rare dikes of fine-grained diorite have been observed to cut both trondhjemite and quartz diorite. At one locality along the contact between the trondhjemite and quartz diorite a small outcrop (<5 km^2) of a composite rock consisting of fine-grained diorite and aplite trondhjemitic in modal composition) is exposed (Fig. 2A). The two rock types are interfingered on a scale varying from a few millimeters to tens of centimeters. Contacts are either sharp and angular or diffuse and show evidence of mixing between the two rock types; no evidence of chilling of either rock type was observed.

Northward from the contact between the quartz diorite and trondhjemite, trondhjemite crops out for 10 to 12 km until it is overlain by keratophyres of the Clover Creek Greenstone. The trondhjemite is generally massive, but in places it shows evidence of shearing and exhibits a weak foliation. Near the contact with the quartz diorite the trondhjemite changes locally into quartz diorite or tonalite. Fine-grained irregular and pod-like leucocratic

Figure 2.--A. Mixed rock occurring in the contact zone between the quartz
diorite and trondhjemite. B. Xenoliths of diorite in hornblende-bearing
trondhjemite near the contact with the quartz diorite.

segregations a few centimeters to meters across are common throughout the
trondhjemite. Contacts of the leucocratic segregations may be either sharp or
gradational with no evidence of chilling against the coarser grained
trondhjemite. Similar appearing leucocratic rocks also occur as dikes showing
sharp contacts with or without chilled margins. Xenoliths of diorite and
meladiorite with sharp, angular contacts are common in the trondhjemite near
the quartz diorite contact (Fig. 2B).

The trondhjemite and quartz diorite were intruded by numerous mafic and felsic dikes. These dikes are one to two meters wide and may or may not show evidence of chilling against the wall rock. The mafic dikes are diabase or gabbro. The siliceous dikes are keratophyre and quartz keratophyre. Rare andesite dikes occur.

The contact between the the Clover Creek Greenstone and the trondhjemite is poorly exposed and the nature of the contact has been debated by several authors (Prostka, 1963; Vallier et al., 1977; Phelps, 1978). No unequivocal relationships were seen in the Sparta quadrangle to indicate whether the contact is intrusive or depositional.

PETROGRAPHY

Quartz diorite and related rock types consist of plagioclase, quartz, hornblende, biotite, minor Fe-Ti oxide minerals and trace amounts of sphene, zircon, and epidote. Textures are hypidiomorphic granular, porphyritic to mylonitic. Hornblende varies from 10% in tonalite to 50% in meladiorite; however, most of the rocks are quartz diorite and contain 15% to 30% modal hornblende. Plagioclase is characterized by partially resorbed cores with well developed oscillatory zoning and normally zoned rims. Near the contact with the trondhjemite patchy zoned subhedral phenocrysts of plagioclase 7 mm in length are set in a groundmass of plagioclase laths (1 mm to 2 mm long), hornblende and poikilitic quartz. Quartz is almost always interstitial to plagioclase, although rare phenocrysts of bluish quartz surrounded by hornblende occur near the trondhjemite contact. Green hornblende, typically poikilitically enclosing plagioclase laths, is the dominant mafic phase in the quartz diorite, although locally biotite may equal or exceed the modal hornblende content.

Alteration of the quartz diorite has been minor. Plagioclase cores in most samples are variably sericitized, but only rarely is the alteration severe. Biotite and hornblende may be altered to chlorite around the edges or along cleavage traces. Veinlets of epidote and quartz are present in some thin sections. Alteration tends to be more severe in the mylonitic quartz diorite.

A variety of rock types and textures are represented in the area mapped as trondhjemite. The most common rock type is a coarse-grained hypidiomorphic or xenomorphic trondhjemite. Other rock types found in the area mapped as trondhjemite include tonalite, quartz diorite, and porphyritic to fine-grained trondhjemite. The latter occurs as crosscutting dikes or local segregations within the coarser grained trondhjemite. The common coarse-grained (grain size up to 1 cm) trondhjemite consists of greater than 90% plagioclase and quartz and less than 10% mafic minerals. Plagioclase typically shows oscillatory and patchy zoned, slightly resorbed cores with normally zoned rims. Quartz occurs both as large, polycrystalline grains and in the interstices between plagioclase. In hand specimen the quartz has a bluish hue. Biotite is the most abundant primary mafic mineral except near the contact with the quartz diorite where hornblende is the dominant mafic phase and may comprise up to 40% of the rock.

Porphyritic texture is common, especially in the fine-grained leucocratic segregations and dikes found within the coarse-grained trondhjemite. Porphyritic trondhjemite contains phenocrysts of quartz and oscillatory zoned plagioclase set in a groundmass of phaneritic quartz and plagioclase. The groundmass consists of either subhedral laths of plagioclase and anhedral quartz or quartz and plagioclase in graphic and micrographic intergrowth. The graphic intergrowth may be concentrated around phenocrysts, but does not embay the phenocrysts. In some rocks phenocrysts may be absent and the entire thin section consists of fine-grained quartz and plagioclase with or without graphic intergrowth. Subhedral groundmass plagioclase laths not graphically intergrown with quartz are normally zoned and may contain an outer rim of antiperthite.

Some of the trondhjemite shows evidence of shearing. These rocks contain porphyroclasts of quartz and plagioclase in a groundmass of granulated quartz and plagioclase. A weak foliation has developed in some of the sheared trondhjemite. Veinlets of secondary quartz and albite are especially common in the sheared trondhjemite. Some rocks have been converted to a massive quartz-albite rock containing essentially no mafic minerals.

Alteration of the trondhjemite has been variable. In the sheared trondhjemite all mafic minerals have been converted to epidote and much of the plagioclase has been sericitized. In the undeformed trondhjemite plagioclase is in part converted to sericite. In many cases, cores of zoned grains are clouded whereas rims are clear. Some thin sections contain fresh biotite and hornblende with very little epidote and chlorite. Frequently biotite and hornblende have been completely or nearly completely converted to chlorite or epidote. Veinlets of prehnite, epidote, calcite, and quartz are present in many thin sections.

WHOLE-ROCK CHEMISTRY

Whole-rock major-element compositions for 15 samples from the quartz diorite unit, four coarse-grained trondhjemites, one sheared trondhjemite, two tonalites from the trondhjemite unit, seven fine-grained trondhjemites and related dike rocks, and five cross-cutting dikes are given in Table 1. Analyses of the trondhjemites and quartz diorites are displayed on a SiO_2 variation

TABLE 1. Whole-rock major-element compositions and C.I.P.W. norms of Sparta samples. All analyses are by X-ray fluorescence unless otherwise noted.

	Low-K_2O dikes		Keratophyric dikes				Mafic dike	High-K_2O dikes
	108B	205	184G	199	202A	202B	195A°	191
SiO_2	75.71	75.00	74.75	75.83	75.99	66.06	53.14	75.85
TiO_2	0.04	0.32	0.35	0.24	0.82	0.78	1.73	0.13
Al_2O_3	13.22	13.03	12.98	11.68	12.32	14.80	15.41	12.71
FeO*	0.74	1.64	1.71	1.23	1.84	5.52	10.41	0.92
MnO	0.05	0.03	0.02	0.04	0.07	0.18	0.23	N.D.
MgO	N.D.	0.08	0.71	N.D.	0.09	1.31	4.35	N.D.
CaO	4.95	2.33	0.76	1.91	1.56	4.46	8.08	1.02
Na_2O[1]	4.88	5.37	6.03	5.22	5.16	3.90	3.90	3.21
K_2O	0.06	0.26	0.12	0.22	0.20	1.08	0.70	4.42
P_2O_5	0.03	0.03	0.05	0.05	0.02	0.17	---	0.03
S	N.D.	N.D.	N.D.	0.02	N.D.	0.02	---	N.D.
H_2O′	0.75	0.71	1.16	0.77	0.76	1.77	---	0.88
Cr_2O_3[1]	N.D.	---	---	---	---	---	0.45	N.D.
TOTAL	100.43	98.90	98.64	97.21	98.24	100.05	98.40	99.17
Apatite	0.07	0.07	0.12	0.12	0.46	0.39	0.00	0.07
Ilmenite	0.08	0.61	0.67	0.46	0.61	1.48	3.29	0.25
Orthoclase	0.34	1.54	0.71	1.30	1.18	6.38	4.14	26.12
Nepheline	0.00	0.00	0.00	0.00	0.00	0.00	0.00	0.00
Albite	41.29	45.44	51.03	44.17	43.66	33.00	33.00	27.16
Anorthite	13.99	10.68	3.45	7.79	7.61	19.69	22.48	4.87
Corundum	0.00	0.00	1.67	0.00	0.84	0.00	0.00	0.86
Quartz	38.18	36.73	35.48	40.08	40.43	24.31	0.18	37.49
Forsterite	0.00	0.00	0.00	0.00	0.00	0.00	0.00	0.00
Fayalite	0.00	0.00	0.00	0.00	0.00	0.00	0.00	0.00
Diopside (Wo)	1.22	0.29	0.00	0.57	0.00	0.56	7.35	0.00
Diopside (En)	0.00	0.02	0.00	0.00	0.00	0.15	2.92	0.00
Diopside (Fs)	1.39	0.29	0.00	0.66	0.00	0.43	4.51	0.00
Enstatite	0.00	0.18	1.77	0.00	0.22	3.11	7.91	0.00
Ferrosillite	0.00	2.25	2.60	1.26	2.98	8.75	12.18	1.48

* Total Fe as FeO
1 Determined by INAA
╱ Total H_2O determined gravimetrically by the method described in Shapiro (1975)

High-K$_2$O dikes				Coarse-grained trondhjemite				Sheared trondhjemite	Tonalite
194B	194C	200A	201B	209B	196	193	201A	192	197A
74.62	75.98	77.07	77.86	73.35	72.88	72.82	72.93	80.58	67.91
0.42	0.17	0.24	0.20	0.35	0.45	0.43	0.39	0.25	0.41
11.92	11.87	11.89	11.92	12.66	12.50	13.22	13.40	10.90	15.05
3.34	1.08	1.61	1.37	2.68	3.37	2.90	3.06	0.58	4.44
N.D.	N.D.	0.04	0.06	0.07	0.12	0.09	0.13	0.02	0.14
0.24	N.D.	0.04	N.D.	0.51	0.64	0.54	0.56	N.D.	1.10
1.00	1.22	1.36	0.76	2.83	2.35	3.16	3.28	1.55	5.10
3.87	4.15	4.44	4.55	3.71	3.95	3.68	3.83	5.14	3.49
2.91	2.66	1.65	2.36	1.61	1.37	1.25	1.04	0.07	0.31
N.D.	N.D.	0.01	0.03	0.05	0.07	0.06	0.06	0.05	0.12
N.D.	N.D.	N.D.	N.D.	N.D.	0.01	N.D.	0.01	0.02	N.D.
0.93	0.80	0.96	0.93	0.91	1.27	1.22	1.33	0.86	1.25
N.D.	---	N.D.	N.D.	0.03	N.D.	N.D.	N.D.	---	---
99.25	97.93	99.27	100.04	98.76	98.98	99.28	100.03	100.02	99.38
0.00	0.00	0.02	0.07	0.12	0.16	0.14	0.14	0.12	0.28
0.80	0.32	0.46	0.38	0.07	0.86	0.82	0.74	0.48	0.89
17.20	15.72	9.75	13.95	9.52	8.10	7.39	6.15	0.41	1.83
0.00	0.00	0.00	0.00	0.00	0.00	0.00	0.00	0.00	0.00
32.75	35.12	37.57	38.50	31.39	33.42	31.14	32.41	43.49	29.53
4.96	5.91	6.68	3.58	13.14	11.21	15.29	15.88	6.46	24.87
0.59	0.00	0.35	0.57	0.00	0.41	0.21	0.15	0.00	0.06
35.99	38.30	40.78	39.77	37.01	36.28	37.04	36.60	47.11	30.72
0.00	0.00	0.00	0.00	0.00	0.00	0.00	0.00	0.00	0.00
0.00	0.00	0.00	0.00	0.00	0.00	0.00	0.00	0.00	0.00
0.00	0.60	0.00	0.00	0.24	0.00	0.00	0.00	0.38	0.02
0.00	0.00	0.00	0.00	0.06	0.00	0.00	0.00	0.00	0.01
0.00	0.07	0.00	0.00	0.20	0.00	0.00	0.00	0.43	0.13
0.60	0.00	0.10	0.00	1.21	1.59	1.35	1.40	0.00	2.74
5.44	1.63	2.64	2.30	4.27	5.67	4.78	5.22	0.26	7.63

° All elements except Na$_2$O, Cr$_2$O$_3$ and H$_2$O determined by electron microprobe
   analysis of fused glass beads; D. Gust, analyst.

▫ Diorite dike intruding quartz diorite and trondhjemite along the contact
   between the quartz diorite and trondhjemite.

TABLE 1, continued

	Tonalite	Quartz diorites and related rocks						
	210	208B	209	189	206	111B	111D	112B
SiO$_2$	65.65	54.23	48.91	56.48	51.76	58.31	55.45	66.94
TiO$_2$	0.62	0.71	0.26	0.99	0.96	1.16	0.88	0.60
Al$_2$O$_3$	14.46	15.84	16.01	19.28	17.77	15.06	16.51	14.34
FeO*	5.79	9.10	6.99	7.36	9.03	8.76	7.59	4.77
MnO	0.12	0.21	0.20	0.13	0.22	0.20	0.15	0.12
MgO	1.91	5.26	9.21	2.26	4.24	2.72	3.89	1.62
CaO	5.76	9.10	13.10	8.35	8.94	5.63	9.15	4.93
Na$_2$O'	2.98	2.55	3.69	3.33	3.20	3.75	3.08	3.65
K$_2$O	0.53	0.59	0.30	0.88	1.25	0.38	0.37	1.12
P$_2$O$_5$	0.10	0.05	0.01	0.15	0.14	0.28	0.18	0.12
S	0.00	N.D.	N.D.	0.02	N.D.	0.07	N.D.	0.03
H$_2$O'	1.21	2.24	1.66	1.53	1.57	2.84	2.50	1.24
Cr$_2$O$_3$[1]	0.05	0.84	0.03	0.07	0.58	---	---	---
TOTAL	99.18	100.72	100.37	100.83	99.66	99.16	99.75	99.48
Apatite	0.23	0.12	0.02	0.35	0.32	0.65	0.42	0.28
Ilmenite	1.18	1.35	0.49	1.88	1.82	2.20	1.67	1.14
Orthoclase	3.13	3.49	1.77	5.20	7.39	2.25	2.19	6.62
Nepheline	0.00	0.00	8.68	0.00	0.00	0.00	0.00	0.00
Albite	25.22	21.58	15.20	28.18	27.08	31.73	26.06	30.87
Anorthite	24.52	30.03	26.24	35.06	30.43	23.14	30.13	19.44
Corundum	0.00	0.00	0.00	0.00	0.00	0.00	0.00	0.00
Quartz	27.64	5.88	0.00	8.54	0.00	13.73	8.45	26.06
Forsterite	0.00	0.00	9.20	0.00	1.03	0.00	0.00	0.00
Fayalite	0.00	0.00	5.46	0.00	1.66	0.00	0.00	0.00
Diopside (Wo)	1.43	6.18	16.15	2.51	5.43	1.25	5.89	1.77
Diopside (En)	0.48	2.77	9.81	0.74	2.23	0.41	2.54	0.61
Diopside (Fs)	0.99	3.37	5.46	1.59	3.25	0.88	3.35	1.21
Enstatite	4.28	10.33	0.00	4.89	6.86	6.37	7.15	3.42
Ferrosillite	8.84	12.56	0.00	10.53	10.01	13.67	9.42	6.78

Quartz diorites and related rocks

113	115	117C	187	190B	208A	209C	111A
56.92	56.12	59.42	62.22	63.78	57.29	49.97	52.87
0.96	0.87	1.53	0.71	0.71	0.59	0.90	0.88
16.89	17.20	13.77	15.46	15.49	14.84	17.18	17.85
7.67	8.15	8.83	5.81	5.55	8.06	9.23	8.78
0.17	0.17	0.19	0.05	0.16	0.22	0.19	0.16
3.15	3.71	2.87	2.25	1.97	5.05	7.31	3.90
7.10	8.03	6.52	5.04	5.24	8.48	9.31	8.56
3.47	2.97	3.04	3.69	3.72	2.76	2.42	3.40
1.50	0.84	1.45	1.40	0.98	0.71	0.66	0.31
0.15	0.16	0.28	0.14	0.13	0.03	0.15	0.02
0.01	0.02	N.D.	0.01	N.D.	0.02	N.D.	N.D.
2.04	1.14	1.77	1.92	2.10	1.84	0.84	2.45
---	0.36	---	---	---	---	---	---
100.03	99.74	99.67	98.70	99.83	99.89	98.16	99.18
0.35	0.37	0.65	0.32	0.30	0.07	0.35	0.05
1.82	1.65	2.91	1.35	1.35	1.12	1.71	1.67
8.87	4.96	8.57	8.27	5.79	4.20	3.90	1.83
0.00	0.00	0.00	0.00	0.00	0.00	0.00	0.00
29.36	25.13	25.72	31.22	31.48	23.36	20.48	28.77
26.08	31.12	19.65	21.49	22.68	26.01	34.07	32.53
0.00	0.00	0.00	0.00	0.00	0.00	0.00	0.00
7.43	8.69	14.68	17.83	20.88	9.85	0.00	3.11
0.00	0.00	0.00	0.00	0.00	0.00	2.62	0.00
0.00	0.00	0.00	0.00	0.00	0.00	2.50	0.00
3.41	3.21	4.55	1.09	1.04	6.63	4.66	4.10
1.32	1.30	1.58	0.41	0.37	3.08	2.42	1.63
2.15	1.94	3.09	0.70	0.70	3.48	2.11	2.51
6.53	7.94	5.57	5.19	4.54	9.50	12.05	8.08
10.67	11.91	10.95	8.89	8.62	10.75	10.47	12.46

558

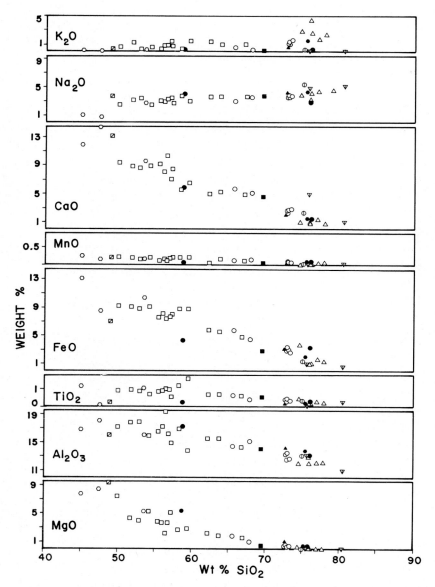

Figure 3.--Major-element SiO₂ variation diagram for rocks from the Sparta complex. □ = quartz diorite; ○ = tonalite and trondhjemite; ⬠ = gabbro; △=high-K₂O, fine-grained dike or segregation; ⏀ and ▽ = low-K₂O dike; ⊠ = diorite dike cutting trondhjemite and quartz diorite. Shown for comparison are a trondhjemite and quartz diorite from the Canyon Mountain ophiolite (●)Thayer and Himmelberg, 1968), trondhjemite from the Troodos complex (■) (Coleman and Peterman, 1975), Mule Mountain trondhjemite (▲) (Barker and others, 1978), and Rio Brazos trondhjemite (⬤) Barker and others, 1976).

diagram in Figure 3. The trondhjemites have been divided into coarse-grained and fine-grained types according to their field occurrences and petrography. The fine-grained trondhjemite has been further divided into a low-K_2O group and a high-K_2O group. The high-K_2O group was found to occur as pod-like segregations within the coarse-grained trondhjemite or as cross-cutting dikes, whereas the low-K_2O group occurs only as cross-cutting dikes.

Fifteen samples from the trondhjemite-quartz diorite suite were selected for trace-element analyses on the basis of field occurrence, petrography and major element chemistry. Results are presented in Table 2. Rare earth element (REE) concentrations normalized to chondrites (Haskin et al., 1968) are shown in Figures 4a-f.

The trondhjemite contains less than 15% Al_2O_3, Na_2O from 3.0% to 5.5%, high Na_2O/K_2O ratios and flat REE patterns with pronounced negative Eu anomalies (Eu/Eu* = 0.347 to 0.763; Eu* is the Eu content that a particular sample would have if it had no Eu anomaly. Eu* is derived by interpolating between Sm and Tb). Samples from the quartz diorite unit show a wide range of major-element chemistry. The SiO_2 content varies from 66% in quartz-rich samples to less than 50% in hornblende-rich samples. The Na_2O content increases while the content of all other major oxides decreases with increasing SiO_2. The scatter exhibited on the K_2O versus SiO_2 diagram suggests that K_2O has been affected by alteration. The high-SiO_2, low-MgO samples (tonalite) from the quartz diorite unit overlap in major- and trace-element composition with the hornblende-bearing trondhjemite and tonalite from the trondhjemite unit. REE patterns of the quartz diorite and tonalite are nearly flat (Ce/Yb = 0.92 to 1.24) with negative Eu anomalies (Eu/Eu* = 0.688 to 0.855).

Two of the quartz diorite samples (Sp206 and Sp115) have distinctly different REE patterns with light REE enrichment (Ce/Yb = 1.417 and 1.853) and small or nonexistent negative Eu anomalies. These samples were collected less than 500 m from one another in an area of poor outcrop; it is considered likely that they are intrusive into the main quartz diorite unit and are not directly related to it.

Two other samples (a high-K_2O dike, Sp191, and a mafic dike, Sp195) also have light REE-enriched profiles with very small Eu anomalies. Sample Sp191 is chemically and petrographically distinct from the other high-K_2O dikes and is not considered cogenetic with the trondhjemite-quartz diorite complex. The REE chemistry of the mafic dike suggests that it also is not related to the main quartz diorite-trondhjemite suite, but probably represents a separate magmatic event.

TABLE 2.--Trace element composition of selected samples from the Sparta complex. Analyses are by instrumental neutron activation analysis (all values in ppm).

	Quartz diorites					Tonalite	Mafic dike	Standard
	Sp115	Sp189	Sp206	Sp208B	Sp209	Sp210	Sp195A	BCR-1 (this study)
La	7.33	5.63	10.84	3.99	6.41	4.89	8.20	24.83
Ce	17.93	14.46	20.47	10.91	16.33	12.28	21.67	53.58
Sm	3.22	3.46	2.99	2.19	4.04	2.68	4.94	6.85
Eu	0.96	1.02	1.00	0.69	1.02	0.84	1.54	1.92
Tb	0.72	0.85	0.60	0.52	0.96	0.67	1.02	1.11
Yb	2.77	2.65	2.51	2.05	4.03	2.73	3.49	3.38
Lu	0.42	0.42	0.41	0.33	0.65	0.46	0.55	0.52
Ni	N.D.	N.D.	N.D.	N.D.	N.D.	N.D.	N.D.	N.D.
Co	29.30	26.30	26.10	47.53	48.14	25.51	36.62	35.77
S	25.93	24.92	31.10	37.48	15.39	20.60	36.75	31.86
Th	2.07	0.43	1.03	0.64	1.04	0.39	0.73	6.09

	Coarse-grained Trondhjemites				High-K$_2$O fine-grained Trondhjemites			High-K$_2$O dike
	Sp193	Sp196	Sp201A	Sp209B	Sp194B	Sp200A	Sp201B	Sp191
La	6.66	5.61	5.51	10.57	17.27	11.59	12.25	22.58
Ce	17.81	14.11	15.29	27.16	46.95	29.49	33.57	46.22
Sm	3.65	3.14	3.84	5.08	5.80	5.27	6.05	3.06
Eu	0.88	0.90	0.92	0.91	0.78	1.03	0.87	0.82
Tb	0.93	0.80	1.08	1.29	1.18	1.32	1.69	
Yb	4.05	3.53	4.82	5.55	5.88	7.10	8.11	2.00
Lu	0.64	0.60	0.75	0.95	1.00	1.16	1.38	0.43
Ni	N.D.	N.D.	N.D.	N.D.	N.D.	N.D.	N.D.	N.D.
Co	47.80	21.77	21.88	63.20	53.90	24.62	45.71	65.70
S	12.17	12.89	13.78	12.34	8.30	7.88	9.57	1.92
Th	1.24	1.47	1.15	2.52	2.92	2.62	3.23	12.32

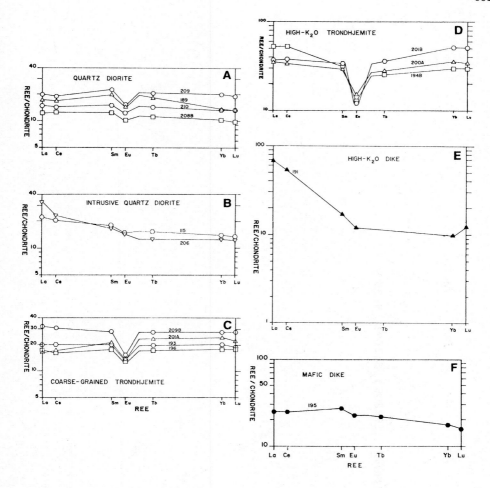

Figure 4.--REE concentrations normalized to chondrites (Haskin and others, 1968) for the Sparta complex. A. Quartz diorite (210 is a tonalite from within the area mapped as trondhjemite). B. Quartz diorite. C. Coarse-grained trondhjemite. D. High-K_2O, fine-grained trondhjemite. E. High-K2O dike. F. Mafic dike.

MINERAL CHEMISTRY

Plagioclase from a thin section of quartz diorite (Sp189), coarse-grained biotite-bearing trondhjemite (Sp209B), fine-grained graphic trondhjemite (Sp201B) and a quartz diorite from the trondhjemite-quartz diorite contact (Sp208-1) were analyzed. The results are presented in terms of the Ab-An-Or components in Figure 5 and representative analyses are given in Table 3.

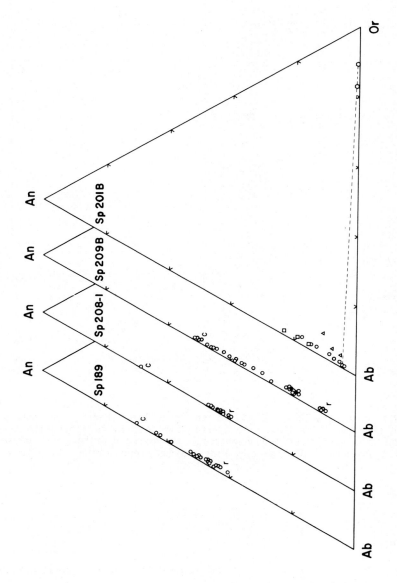

Figure 5.--Plagioclase analyses in terms of their An-Ab-Or components: c = core, r = rim; solid circles in Sp209B are analyses of patchy zoning. In Sp201B open squares are analyses from graphic plagioclase-quartz intergrowth, open hexagons are K-feldspar lamallae in albite (connected by dashed line); open triangles are analyses of clouded grains.

In the quartz diorite, cores of composition An_{60-70} are zoned to rims of composition An_{35-40}. Plagioclase in the coarse-grained trondhjemite is zoned from An_{45-50} to rims of An_{10}. Fine-scale oscillatory zoning is superimposed on the characteristic normal zoning in plagioclase from both the quartz diorite and trondhjemite. Patches of oligoclase with the same composition as rim plagioclase occur within calcic rich cores in the trondhjemite. Zoned plagioclase from fine-grained leucocratic trondhjemite has cores of composition An_{15-20} and rims of composition An_{10-15}. An outermost rim on some grains consists of albite (An_{4-5}) with lamellae of K-feldspar ($An_1Ab_{10}Or_{89}$). Plagioclase from graphic intergrowth of quartz and plagioclase is oligoclase (An_{15-25}). The Or component is uniformly low in all fresh plagioclase analyzed. The three analyses from sample Sp201B with Or >3% are from cloudy grains and may be the result of alteration.

Hornblende from a quartz diorite (Sp189) was analyzed. Results are presented in Table 4. All analyzed grains are Fe-rich (18% to 20% FeO) and contain significant quantities of Na_2O. No zoning was detected; variations between individual analyses probably result from submicroscopic exsolution.

DISCUSSION

Textural Evidence for a Magmatic Origin of the Sparta Trondhjemite

The trondhjemite of the Sparta area was studied by Gilluly (1933) who concluded it was formed through Na-metasomatism of the nearby quartz diorite. Later, Prostka (1963) mapped the Sparta quadrangle and supported Gilluly's contention that the Sparta trondhjemite represented metasomatized quartz diorite. Both Gilluly (1933) and Prostka (1963) based their conclusions on detailed field descriptions and petrography with little supporting geochemical data.

In order to evaluate Gilluly's hypothesis, it is necessary to consider the origin of the textural and petrographic features found in the Sparta trondhjemite that were cited by Gilluly (1933) as evidence for metasomatism. Gilluly considered the presence of graphic and irregular intergrowths of quartz and sodic plagioclase as strong evidence of a metasomatic origin for the Sparta trondhjemite. However, as shown by Barker (1970), Cerny (1971), and Smith (1974), the presence of graphic and irregular intergrowth of quartz and plagioclase is not a valid argument in support of a replacement origin for the rock in which it occurs. It may in fact argue in favor of a magmatic origin.

Plagioclase in the Sparta quartz diorite and coarse-grained trondhjemite is often characterized by an irregular shaped andesine or labradorite core with an oligoclase rim. Embayment of the rim plagioclase into the core is common.

TABLE 3.--Selected microprobe analyses of plagioclase and one K-feldspar lamallae. Samples 189 and 208-1 are quartz diorites, 209B is a coarse-grained trondhjemite, 201B is a high K_2O, fine-grained dike.

	core 189	rim 189	rim 208-1	core 209B	rim 209B	graphic 201B	rim 201B	lamallae 201B
SiO_2	50.38	57.08	59.52	56.00	64.85	63.44	68.24	63.60
Al_2O_3	30.54	25.72	26.23	28.02	21.72	23.10	20.23	18.04
Na_2O	3.32	6.72	6.69	5.36	9.98	7.56	9.61	1.20
K_2O	0.11	0.22	0.14	0.15	0.19	0.19	0.14	15.83
CaO	14.42	8.53	8.25	10.33	2.43	4.17	0.79	0.16
FeO	---	---	0.13	---	---	---	---	---
Total	98.78	98.26	100.97	99.86	99.17	98.46	99.01	98.82
Cations								
Si	9.293	10.414	10.527	10.075	11.498	11.300	11.964	11.963
Al	6.638	5.528	5.467	5.938	4.536	4.851	4.182	3.989
Na	1.188	2.375	2.294	1.868	3.431	2.612	3.268	0.436
K	0.025	0.050	0.031	0.035	0.042	0.043	0.032	3.789
Ca	2.850	1.668	1.564	1.991	0.462	0.796	0.149	0.032
Fe	---	---	0.020	---	---	---	---	---
Total/32oxy	19.994	20.035	19.902	19.908	19.970	19.602	19.595	20.182
Ab	29.05	58.03	59.00	47.96	81.17	75.69	94.75	10.24
Or	0.62	1.23	0.78	0.90	1.08	1.25	0.93	89.01
An	70.33	40.75	40.22	51.14	11.75	23.07	4.32	0.76

TABLE 4.--Microprobe analyses of hornblende from quartz diorite sample 189

SiO_2	47.20	46.36	44.55	44.74	46.28	45.93	46.30	45.99
Al_2O_3	6.75	5.16	8.31	8.76	7.21	8.18	7.40	7.41
TiO_2	1.31	1.23	1.38	1.10	1.18	1.17	1.19	1.37
FeO	18.95	19.11	20.04	19.28	18.84	18.92	18.17	19.28
MnO	0.44	0.46	0.52	0.40	0.37	0.37	0.38	0.40
CaO	10.60	10.67	10.59	11.35	11.36	11.64	11.29	10.44
MgO	10.63	10.17	9.57	9.76	10.20	10.00	10.51	10.13
Na_2O	1.11	1.25	1.44	1.14	0.99	0.83	0.96	1.19
K_2O	0.19	0.27	0.35	0.69	0.56	0.62	0.39	0.27
Total	97.18	96.70	96.74	97.23	97.00	97.65	96.59	96.48

Isolated patches of oligoclase of the same composition and in optical continuity with the rim oligoclase occur within the andesine or labradorite core. Gilluly (1933) suggests that such relationships are evidence for Na-metasomatism in the Sparta complex. However, Vance (1965) put forth an alternative hypothesis for the origin of this type of patchy zoning. According to Vance (1965) changes in the physiochemical conditions of a melt crystallizing plagioclase result in partial resorption of preexisting plagioclase. Renewed crystallization under the new conditions allows for the precipitation of more sodic plagioclase on the partially resorbed and irregular shaped crystal. The isolated patches of oligoclase found within the calcic core are embayments which presumably connect with rim oligoclase in the third dimension. The zoning relationships observed by the present author and described by Gilluly (1933) fit well with Vance's (1965) model. Furthermore, Vance (1965) has described 'veinlets' of sodic rim plagioclase cutting calcic cores along fractures (Vance, 1965, Fig. 10) in rocks of undoubted igneous origin. Similar features in plagioclase from the Sparta trondhjemite were attributed by Gilluly (1933) to Na-metasomatism.

Fine-scale oscillatory and normal zoning is common to most plagioclase of the Sparta trondhjemite and provides strong evidence for an igneous origin. Fine-scale oscillatory zoning in plagioclase from coarse-grained trondhjemite is similar to that described by Hills (1936) and Vance (1962) and attributed to a diffusion-controlled mechanism operative during magmatic crystallization. Fine-scale oscillatory zoning of this type is generally considered a characteristic of igneous rocks, and in the rare cases where it is found in metamorphic rocks it is thought to represent relic igneous plagioclase (Cannon, 1966).

Normal zoning in groundmass plagioclase of the porphyritic trondhjemite and the fine-grained dikes and segregations is continuous and may terminate in an outermost rim of antiperthite. Such zoning is consistent with crystallization of plagioclase from a melt in which potassium is concentratd in the liquid phase. The last plagioclase to crystallize is enriched in potassium and upon cooling exsolves K-feldspar in accordance with the subsolidus relationships in the system $NaAlSi_3O_8-KAlSi_3O_8$ (Smith, 1974). The slight increase in Or-component of plagioclase with increasing Ab-content supports such a crystallization history (Fig. 5).

Field Evidence for a Magmatic Origin of the Sparta Trondhjemite

In addition to the textural and mineralogical evidence discussed above, field observations also support an igneous origin for the trondhjemite. The presence of abundant dioritic xenoliths with sharp, angular contacts in the trondhjemite near the contact with the quartz diorite suggests that the trondhjemite is intrusive into the quartz diorite. The occurrence of the xenoliths is not consistent with a metasomatic origin for the trondhjemite. The composite rock exposed in the contact zone between the quartz diorite and trondhjemite is interpreted as an intrusive feature, although it is not possible to tell which rock type is intrusive and which is intruded. However, at other locations the contact is gradational and it is in these areas that rocks intermediate in composition and texture between quartz diorite and trondhjemite are often found. Several hypotheses might be evoked to explain the ambiguous contact relationships. The first hypothesis evoked by Gilluly (1933) proposes that the trondhjemite is metasomatized quartz diorite. This hypothesis explains the gradational nature of much of the contact zone, but does not account for xenoliths of diorite in the trondhjemite, the intrusive relationships (however rare) of the quartz diorite and trondhjemite, and the textural evidence discussed above. A second hypothesis, that of trondhjemite intruding quartz diorite and partially metasomatizing the quartz diorite near the contact, is not favored due to lack of textural evidence of metasomatism in the quartz diorite near the contact with the trondhjemite The preferred hypothesis is one of in situ magmatic differentiation and the resultant formation of the suite of rocks ranging in composition from diorite to trondhjemite. Local 'auto-intrusion' of trondhjemite into earlier formed quartz diorite could account for the intrusive relationships found sporadically along the contact. Similar relationships have been described from the Duluth Complex (Taylor, 1964) where late granophyre intrudes earlier differentiates of the same magma.

Chemical Evidence for Magmatic Differentiation

Whole-rock major-element data do not provide unequivocal support for either the magmatic or metasomatic hypotheses. On the SiO_2 variation diagram all the major oxides (except K_2O) fall approximately on straight lines; this could be the result of mixing of a Na-rich fluid and quartz diorite as suggested by Gilluly (1933). However, the major-element data are not only consistent with a metasomatic hypothesis, but they are also consistent with the quartz diorite and trondhjemite forming a differentiation suite.

On the SiO_2 variation diagram (Fig. 3) all the major oxides show a smooth transition from quartz diorite to coarse-grained trondhjemite compatible with a magmatic differentiation model for the origin of the quartz diorite-trondhjemite suite. The decrease in Al_2O_3, CaO, FeO, and MgO with increasing SiO_2, the abundant hornblende-rich meladiorite xenoliths in the quartz diorite, and the presence of hornblende as the dominant mafic phase in all the quartz diorites and even in some of the coarse-grained trondhjemites, suggests that differentiation was probably controlled by hornblende and plagioclase fractionation. The FeO versus MgO variation diagram (Fig. 6A) demonstrates that fractionation controlled by subtraction of hornblende can account for much of the variation in the FeO/MgO ratios of the quartz diorite-trondhjemite suite. Hornblende along with plagioclase fractionation in the approximate proportions of plagioclase-60:hornblende-40 is consistent with the CaO versus MgO and CaO versus Al_2O_3 variation diagrams (Figs. 6B and 6C).

The REE data are inconsistent with the metasomatic hypothesis. The immobility of the intermediate and heavy REE during metamorphism up through greenschist facies has been demonstrated by a number of studies (Menzies et al., 1977; Wood et al., 1976; Frey et al., 1974; Kay et al., 1970). Immobility of the REE during metamorphism and metasomatism related to the formation of spilite and keratophyre was shown by Herrmann et al. (1974) and Kay and Senechal (1976). As seen in Figure 4, both the coarse-grained trondhjemite and quartz diorite from Sparta have similar REE patterns and concentrations. However, with one exception, the trondhjemite has significantly larger negative Eu anomalies than does the quartz diorite. The fine-grained high-K_2O trondhjemite of the pod-like segregations and cross-cutting dikes has larger negative Eu anomalies and significantly different total REE concentrations than either the quartz diorite or the coarse-grained trondhjemite. Kay and Senechal (1976) have shown that there was no change in the REE content and no increase in the size of the negative Eu anomaly of basalt from the Troodos Complex which is thought to have undergone extensive metasomatism and which may contain up to 70% SiO_2 and 4.5% Na_2O. The significant increase in the magnitude of the negative Eu anomaly of the trondhjemite over the quartz diorite would not be expected if the trondhjemite was formed by Na-metasomatism of the quartz diorite.

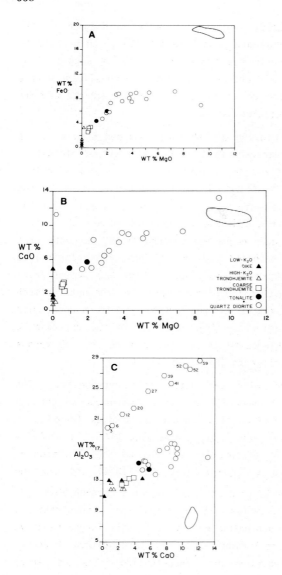

Figure 6.--Major-element variation diagrams for the Sparta quadrangle. The horizontally ruled field in each diagram is the range of hornblende analyses from quartz diorite sample Sp189. The open hexagon in 6B is the composition of plagioclase (An_{50}). The open hexagons in 6C are microprobe analyses of plagioclase; the normative An component is given beside each analysis.

However, the REE data are compatible with magmatic differentiation. One can calculate the partition coefficients and the proportions of the phases which must be fractionated in order to derive a liquid with a REE profile like the trondhjemites from a liquid with a REE profile similar to a tonalite. Results of calculations using a tonalite (Sp210) and trondhjemite (Sp193) are shown in Figure 7. If only hornblende and plagioclase are allowed to fractionate the calculated partition coefficients for plagioclase fall within the range of values reported in the literature (Arth and Barker, 1976; Schnetzler and Philpotts, 1970). The calculated partition coefficients for hornblende are similar to those reported for hornblende from dacite and rhyolite (Arth and Barker, 1976; Nagasawa and Schnetzler, 1971), except the calculated values for the Sparta rocks do not display a strong depletion in the light REE. The differences in the calculated hornblende partition coefficients from Sparta and those reported in the literature are probably the result of using simplistic modelling techniques for complex systems. The observed differences are not considered significant when the total number of possible variables affecting the calculations are considered.

Although the REE data are consistent with hornblende and plagioclase fractionation, the proportions of plagioclase to hornblende required by the REE data are different from those required by the major-element data. Whereas the major-element data require plagioclase to hornblende ratios ranging from 6:2 to 3:2, the REE data require plagioclase to hornblende ratios of approximately 17:2 to 10:2. The presence of cumulus hornblende and plagioclase in the analyzed samples will affect the calculations somewhat; however, it is not possible to evaluate the magnitude of this effect or whether it could account for the above discrepancy.

The high-K_2O group of fine-grained dikes and segregations are the most differentiated of any of the major rock types in the Sparta complex. The high-K_2O, fine-grained trondhjemite is enriched in K_2O, Na_2O, SiO_2, Th and REE, depleted in the other major oxides and Sc, and has a larger negative Eu anomaly relative to the coarse-grained trondhjemite. The field relationships and the major- and trace-element chemistry are consistent with the fine-grained, high-K_2O trondhjemite representing residual liquid remaining after crystallization of the quartz diorite and coarse-grained trondhjemite.

The possibility that the gabbro, quartz diorite and trondhjemite are a comagmatic suite resulting from differentiation of a low-K_2O, basaltic or andesitic melt cannot be overlooked. Relationships in the Sparta complex are similar to those described from the Smartville complex where quartz diorite (with trondhjemite segregations) grades into hornblende-pyroxene gabbro (Menzies and Blanchard, 1977). Quartz diorite and trondhjemite dikes occurring in ophiolite complexes have been interpreted as differentiates of basaltic liquid (e.g., Menzies et al., 1977; Kay and Senechal, 1976; Coleman and Peterman, 1975). Qualitatively, the flat REE patterns with pronounced negative Eu anomalies of the Sparta quartz diorite are consistent with fractionation of plagioclase, augite and hypersthene from a more mafic magma with a flat or slightly light-depleted REE pattern. Barker and Arth (1976) suggest fractionation of plagioclase, augite and hypersthene from a low-K_2O, andesitic magma as one possible mechanism for generating the low-Al_2O_3 type of trondhjemite. Such a model is consistent with the cumulus phases observed in the Sparta gabbro (plus a minor amount of olivine in the clinopyroxenite).

Normative Mineralogy and the Ab-An-Or-Q System

The normative composition of the high-K_2O, fine-grained trondhjemites, coarse-grained trondhjemites and two tonalites are shown plotted on the Ab-Or-Q and Ab-An-Q diagrams in Figure 8. The Ab-Or-Q and Ab-An-Q systems comprise two sides of the Quaternary Ab-An-Or-Q system, a schematic diagram of which is also shown in Figure 8. The phase relationships shown in Figure 8 were determined for water-saturated conditions (see James and Hamilton, 1969). Whitney (1975)

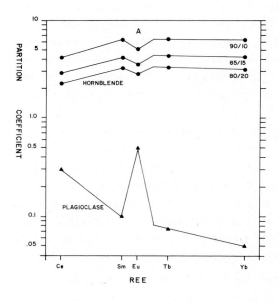

Figure 7.--Calculated REE partition coefficients of plagioclase and hornblende assuming fractionation is controlled entirely by plagioclase and hornblende. Three sets of partition coefficients have been calculated for hornblende assuming three different proportions of plagioclase to hornblende. The plagioclase to hornblende ratio is given to the right of each hornblende profile.

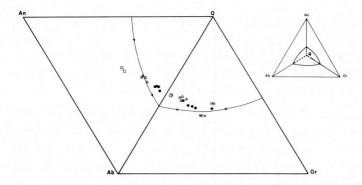

Figure 8.--Normative composition of two tonalites (□), four coarse-grained trondhjemites (△), four fine-grained, high-K_2O trondhjemites (●), and the high-K_2O, pegmatitic dike, Sp191, plotted on the Ab-Or-Q and Ab-An-Q diagrams. The Quaternary Ab-An-Or-Q system is shown in the inset. All phase boundaries are for water-saturated conditions (after James and Hamilton, 1969).

has shown that for a synthetic tonalite variations in the water content change the relative size of the plagioclase, quartz and alkali feldspar fields, but do not change the order of appearance of the phases (Whitney, 1975, Figs. 12 and 13). Therefore, the phase diagrams for water-saturated conditions can be used for a first order approximation of the phase relationships in the Sparta tonalites and trondhjemites. As can be seen in Figure 8, when projected into the Ab-An-Or-Q system the two tonalites fall in the volume of primary plagioclase crystallization, consistent with their petrography which shows quartz to be interstitial to plagioclase. The coarse-grained and fine-grained trondhjemites fall on or very near to the quartz-plagioclase cotectic surface (surface abc, Fig. 8), and the high-K_2O, fine-grained trondhjemites fall closest to the low temperature minimum. The fact that the fine-grained trondhjemites fall slightly below the quartz-plagioclase cotectic surface (in the volume of primary quartz crystallization) may be the result of the introduction of a small amount of secondary quartz into the fine-grained trondhjemites. The behavior of the Sparta tonalites and trondhjemites in the Ab-An-Or-Q system is consistent with differentiation controlled by plagioclase fractionation in the tonalites and by plagioclase and quartz fractionation in the trondhjemite. The residual liquids are represented by the high-K_2O group of fine-grained trondhjemite dikes and segregations.

Origin of the Quartz Diorite and Trondhjemite by Partial Melting

An alternative hypothesis for the origin of the quartz diorite-trondhjemite suite involves generation of a quartz dioritic _and_ trondhjemitic magma by different degrees of partial melting with subsequent differentiation of both magmas to create the observed range of rock types. Generation of a tonalitic or trondhjemitic melt by partial melting of a basaltic, amphibolitic or eclogitic source has been proposed by Arth and Hanson (1972, 1975), Arth and Barker (1976), Barker and Arth (1976), and Barker et al. (1976).

In order to test the partial melting hypothesis, calculation of REE behavior during partial melting was performed using the equations of Shaw (1970) with modifications by Hertogen and Gijbels (1976). The REE profiles of the quartz diorite and trondhjemite were used to place constraints on the mineralogy of the theoretical source material. The relatively flat REE profiles and the negative Eu anomalies of the quartz diorite and trondhjemite require that plagioclase and no garnet or hornblende remain as residual phases in the source rock. Sedimentary rocks were excluded since they generally contain higher REE contents than those observed in the trondhjemite (Haskin, 1968; Herrmann, 1970; Montigny, 1973). Geologically reasonable source rocks are then limited to plagioclase peridotite (representing an upper mantle composition) or basalt (representing lower continental crust or oceanic crust). Experimental studies have shown that trondhjemitic liquid can be generated by partial melting of hydrous tholeiitic basalt (Helz, 1976) or gabbro (Lambert and Wyllie, 1972), whereas the generation of a high-SiO_2 melt from a peridotite is unlikely. The material chosen as a theoretical source rock for the calculations was an average oceanic tholeiite depleted in the light REE. Normative composition and REE concentrations chosen for the starting material, distribution coefficients and melting proportions used in the calculations are given in Table 5.

TABLE 5.--Normative composition and REE concentrations of the starting material, and the partition coefficients used in the partial melting calculations

Norm	REE (x chondrite)		Partition coefficients			
			Pl[1]	Di[1]	Hy[1,2,3]	Ol[1]
Pl 56.2	CE 9.7	Ce	0.141	0.143	0.089	0.009
Di 23.3	Sm 11.5	Sm	0.085	0.471	0.160	0.011
Hy 9.5	Eu 12.8	Eu	0.399	0.454	0.114	0.010
Ol 11.0	Tb 13.1	Tb	0.080	0.633	0.274	0.013
	Yb 13.1	Yb	0.097	0.595	0.651	0.023

[1] Schnetzler and Philpotts (1970)

[2] Nagasawa and Schnetzler (1971)

[3] Arth and Hanson (1975)

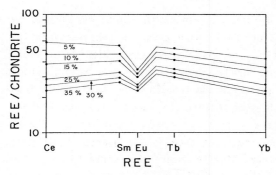

Figure 9.--Calculated REE profiles of liquids generated by partial melting of an oceanic tholeiite. Percent partial melt used in each calculation is given along the left side of the diagram.

Figure 9 shows the calculated REE concentrations for different degrees of partial melting of an oceanic tholeiite. The overall shape of the calculated REE profiles is similar to the observed profiles of the quartz diorite and trondhjemite, but the REE are enriched by a factor of almost 2 in the calculated liquid relative to the quartz diorite and trondhjemite. Negative Eu anomalies calculated for small amounts of partial melting (5%-15%) are similar in magnitude to those observed in the trondhjemite, while the negative Eu anomaly calculated for higher degrees of partial melting (20%-35%) have similar magnitudes to those observed in the quartz diorite. Although the calculated REE concentrations are too high by a factor of nearly 2, it is possible to reduce them considerably by changing one or more of several poorly controlled variables in the equations: First, the distribution coefficients used in the calculations may not be correct. Published REE distribution coefficients show considerable variation (compare Tanaka and Nishizawa, 1975; Grutzek, 1974; Schnetzler and Philpotts, 1970). A second possibility is that the REE content of the theoretical source rock may be too high. Reducing the REE content of the starting material by approximately one-half will result in REE contents in the calculated liquids equal to those of the quartz diorite and trondhjemite. However, there is no independent evidence to suggest that the source rock had such low REE concentrations. Finally, the normative composition of the starting material may not be correct. Changes in the proportion of the minerals present in the starting material will have a small but significant effect on the calculated REE composition of the partial melt.

On the basis of the above calculations one cannot eliminate the possibility that the trondhjemite and quartz diorite are descendents of two magmas generated by different degrees of partial melting. By choosing the appropriate values for the distribution coefficients and starting composition, REE profiles can be calculated which will match the profiles observed for the quartz diorite and trondhjemite. The two-magma hypothesis avoids the problems created by hornblende fractionation on the REE profiles which arise in the fractionation model. The two-magma hypothesis is also consistent with the field relationships. The presence of both gradational and intrusive relationships along the contact between the quartz diorite and trondhjemite could result from nearly simultaneous intrusion with some mixing to create the gradational features. Nearly simultaneous intrusion and the resultant mixing could also account for some of the more unusual features such as the quartz phenocrysts ringed by hornblende in the quartz diorite near the contact with the trondhjemite.

CONCLUSIONS

1. The Sparta trondhjemite is not the product of Na-metasomatism as suggested by Gilluly (1933). Most of the textural and mineralogical features cited by Gilluly (1933) as evidence of Na-metasomatism are now interpreted as the result of magmatic processes. Furthermore, the presence of well developed oscillatory and normal zoned plagioclase provides strong support for an igneous origin.

2. The quartz diorite and trondhjemite are genetically related, probably through the process of magmatic differentiation. Decreasing Al_2O_3 and CaO contents and increasing size of the negative Eu anomaly suggests that plagioclase was involved in the fractionation process. Hornblende fractionation is indicated by field observations and major-element chemistry; however, the lack of a significant increase in the Ce/Yb ratio of the more differentiated rock types is problematical. The most differentiated liquids are represented by fine-grained trondhjemite dikes and segregations occurring within the coarse-grained trondhjemite. The trondhjemite dikes and segregations are enriched in SiO_2, K_2O, Na_2O, REE, and have the largest negative Eu anomaly of any rocks in the complex. The cumulate gabbros cropping out to the south of the quartz diorite-trondhjemite complex may be the mafic cumulates of a low-K_2O, andesitic magma parental to the entire complex. At the present time the evidence on this point is not clear.

3. Liquids with REE concentrations similar to the trondhjemite and quartz diorite could be generated by partial melting of an oceanic tholeiite. This provides an alternative to the differentiation hypothesis. To generate negative Eu anomalies in the liquids plagioclase must remain as a residual phase in the source rock, thus limiting partial melting to depths no greater than 40 to 50 km (Lambert and Wyllie, 1972; Wyllie, 1971).

ACKNOWLEDGMENTS

The research was partially funded by a NSF Research Grant awarded to Dr. H. G. Ave Lallemant (EAR76-13372). Support for field work was provided by Penrose Bequest Grants (numbers 1988-75 and 2079-761) and a Sigma Xi Research Grant. Whole-rock chemical analyses were carried out in the NASA-JSC laboratories with the assistance of Dr. J. M. Rhodes and K. Rodgers (major-element XRF analyses) and Dr. D. Blanchard and J. Brannon (trace-elements by INAA). Without the assistance of these individuals the research would not have been possible. The first draft of this manuscript was greatly improved by discussions with Drs. R. J. Arculus and H. G. Ave Lallemant. The author kindly thanks Drs. M. Menzies and M. A. Dungan for reviews of the manuscript. Research for this project was carried out while the author was a graduate student at Rice University.

REFERENCES

Arth, J. G. and Hanson, G. N., 1972. Quartz diorites derived by partial melting of eclogite or amphibolite at mantle depths. Contrib. Miner. Pet., 37: 161-174.

Arth, J. G. and Hanson, G. N., 1975. Geochemistry and origin of the early Precambrian crust of northeastern Minnesota. Geochim. Cosmochim. Acta, 39: 325-362.

Arth, J. G. and Barker, F., 1976. Rare-earth partitioning between hornblende and dacitic liquid and implications for the genesis of trondhjemitic-tonalitic magmas. Geology, 4: 534-536.

Arth, J. G., Barker, F., Peterman, Z. E. and Friedman, I., 1978. geochemistry of the gabbro-diorite-tonalite-trondhjemite suite of Southwestern Finland and its implications for the origins of tonalitic and trondhjemitic magmas. J. Pet., in press.

Barker, D. S., 1970. Composition of granophyres, myrmekite, and graphic granite. Geol. Soc. Am. Bull., 81: 3339-3350.

Barker, F. and Arth, J. G., 1976. Generation of trondhjemitic-tonalitic liquids and Archean bimodal trondhjemite-basalt suites. Geology, 4: 596-600.

Barker, F., Arth, J. G., Peterman, Z. E. and Friedman, I., 1976. The 1.7- to 1.8-b.y.-old trondhjemites of southwestern Colorado and northern New Mexico: Geochemistry and depth of genesis. Geol. Soc. Am. Bull., 87: 189-198.

Batiza, R. and Vallier, T. L., 1976. Petrology and initial tectonic setting of Permian and Triassic volcanic rocks, northeastern Oregon and western Idaho (abs.). Geol. Soc. Am. Abs. with Programs, 8: 353.

Brooks, H. G., 1976. Pre-Cenozoic tectonic framework, eastern Oregon and western Idaho (abs.). Geol. Soc. Am. Abs. with Programs, 8: 357.

Cannon, R. T., 1966. Plagioclase zoning and twinning in relation to the metamorphic history of some amphibolites and granulites. Am. J. Sci., 264: 526-542.

Cerny, P., 1971. Graphic intergrowths of feldspar and quartz in some Czechoslovak pegmatites. Contrib. Miner. Pet. 30: 343-355.

Coleman, R. G., 1977. Ophiolites-Ancient Oceanic Lithosphere? Springer-Verlag, Berlin, Heidelberg, New York, 229 pp.

Coleman, R. G. and Peterman, Z. E., 1975. Oceanic plagiograrite. J. Geophys. Res., 80: 1099-1108.

Frey, F. A., Bryan, W. B. and Thompson, G., 1974. Atlantic ocean floor: Geochemistry and petrology of basalts from legs 2 and 3 of the Deep Sea Drilling Project. J. Geophys. Res., 79: 5507-5527.

Gilluly, J., 1933. Replacement origin of the albite granite near Sparta, Oregon. U.S. Geol. Surv. Prof. Pap., 1750: 65-81.

Grutzeck, M., Kridelbaugh, S. and Weill, D. F., 1974. The distribution of Sr and REE between diopside and silicate liquid: Geophys. Res. Lett., 1: 273-275.

Haskin, L. A., Haskin, M. A., Frey, F. A. and Wildeman, T. R., 1968. Relative and absolute abundances of the rare earths. In L. H. Ahrens (Ed), Origin and distribution of the elements: 889-912.

Helz, R. T., 1976. Phase relations of basalts in their melting ranges of P_{H_2O} = 5 kb. Part II. Melt compositions. J. Pet., 17: 139-193.

Herrmann, A. G., 1970. Yttrium and Lanthanides. In K. H. Wedepohl (Ed,), Handbook of Geochemistry, #2, 39: 57-71.

Hertogen, J. and Gijbels, R., 1976. Calculation of trace element fractionation during partial melting. Geochim. Cosmochim. Acta, 40: 312-322.

Hills, E. S., 1936. Reverse and oscillatory zoning in plagioclase feldspar. Geol. Mag., 73: 49-56.

Hotz, P. E., Lanphere, M. A. and Swanson, D. A., 1977. Triassic blue-schists from northern California and north-central Oregon. Geology 5: 659-663.

Ishizaka, K. and Yanagi, T., 1977. K, Rb and Sr abundances and Sr isotopic composition of the Tanzawa Granitic and associated gabbroic rocks, Japan: Low-potash island arc plutonic complex. Earth Planet Sci. Lett., 33: 345-352.

James, R. S. and Hamilton, D. L., 1969. Phase relations in the system $NaAlSi_3O_8-KAlSi_3O_8-CaAl_2Si_2O_8-SiO_2$ at 1 kb H_2O vapour pressure. Contrib. Miner. Pet., 21: 111-141.

Kay, R. and Senechal, R. G., 1976. The rare earth geochemistry of the Troodos ophiolite. J. Geophys. Res., 81: 964-970.

Ray, R., Hubbard, N. J. and Gast, P. W., 1970. Chemical characteristics and origin of ocean ridge volcanic rocks. J. Geophys. Res., 75: 1585-1613.

Korotev, R. L., 1976. Geochemical modeling of the distribution of rare-earth and other elements in a basalt and grain size fractions of soils from Apollo 17 valley floor and a well-tested procedure for accurate instrumental neutron activation analysis of geologic materials. Ph. D. Thesis, University of Wisconsin, Madison.

Lambert, I. B., and Wyllie, P. J., 1972. Melting of gabbro (quartz eclogite) with excess water to 35 kilobars, with geologic applications: J. Geol., 80: 693-708.

Menzies, M., Brannon, J. and Korotev, R., 1977. Rare earth and trace element geochemistry of a fragment of Jurassic seafloor, Point Sal, California. Geochim. Cosmochim. Acta., 41: 1419-1430.

Menzies, M. and Blanchard, D., 1977, The Smartville arc-ophiolite, Sierra Nevada, California: Geochemical Evidence. EOS, 58: 1245.

Montigny, R., Bougault, H., Bottinga, Y. and Allegre, C. J., 1973. Trace-element geochemistry and genesis of the Pindos ophiolite suite. Geochim. Cosmochim. Acta, 37: 2135-2147.

Nagasawa, H. and Schnetzler, C. C., 1971. Partitioning of rare earth, alkalic and alkaline earth elements between phenocrysts and acidic igneous magma. Geochim. Cosmochim. Acta, 35: 953-968.

Orville, P. M., 1960. Petrology of several pegmatites in the Keystone District, Black Hills, South Dakota. Geol. Soc. Am. Bull., 71: 1467-1490.

Phelps, D., 1978. Petrology, geochemistry, and structural geology of Mesozoic rocks in the Sparta quadrangle, and the Oxbow and Brownlee Reservoir areas, eastern Oregon and western Idaho. Ph. D. Thesis, Rice University.

Prostka, H. J. and Bateman, R. L., 1962. Geology of the Sparta quadrangle, Oregon. State of Oregon Department of Geology and Mineral Industries: GMS 1.

Prostka, H. J., 1963. Geology of the Sparta quadrangle, Oregon. Ph. D. Thesis, John Hopkins University.

Prostka, H. J., 1967. Preliminary geologic map of the Durkee quadrangle, Oregon. State of Oregon Department of Geology and Mineral Industries: GMS 3.

Schnetzler, C. C. and Philpotts, J. A., 1970. Partition coefficients of rare-earth elements between igneous matrix material and rock forming mineral phenocrysts--II. Geochim. Cosmochim. Acta, 34: 331-340.

Shapiro, L., 1975. Rapid analysis for silicate, carbonate and phosphate rocks--revised edition. U.S. Geol. Surv. Bull., 1401: 76 p.

Smith, J. V., 1974. Feldspar Minerals. II. Chemical and textural properties. Springer-Verlag, Heidelberg, 690 p.

Swanson, D. A., 1969. Lawsonite blue schist from north-central Oregon. U.S. Geol. Surv. Prof. Pap., 650-B: 8-11

Taylor, R. B., 1964. Geology of the Duluth Gabbro Complex near Duluth, Minnesota. Minn. Geol., Surv. Bull., 44: 63 p.

Tanaka, T. and Nishizawa, O., 1975. Partitioning of REE, Ba, and Sr between crystal and liquid phases for a natural silicate system at 20 kb pressure. Geochem. J., 9: 161-166.

Thayer, T. P. and Himmelberg, G. R., 1968. Rock succession in the alpine-type mafic complex at Canyon Mountains, Oregon. 23d Int. Geol. Conf., Prague: 175-186.

Vallier, T. L., 1976, Pre-Tertiary stratigraphy in the Snake River Canyon and adjacent Sevewn Devils and Wallowa Mountains, northeastern Oregon and western Idaho. Geol. Soc. Am. Abs. with Programs, 8: 417.

Vallier, T. L., 1977. The Permian and Triassic Seven Devils Group, western Idaho and eastern Oregon. U.S. Geol. Surv. Bull., B-1437.

Vallier, T. L., Brooks, H. C. and Thayer, T. P., 1977. Paleozoic rocks of eastern Oregon and western Idaho: In J. H. Stewart, C. H. Stevens and A. E. Fritsche (Eds.), Paleozoic Paleogeography of the Western United States: Pacific Coast Paleogeography Symposium, 1: 455-466.

Vance, J. A., 1962. Zoning in igneous plagioclase: Normal and oscillatory zoning. Am. J. Sci., 160: 746-760.

Vance, J. A., 1965. Zoning in igneous plagioclase: patchy zoning. J. Geol., 73: 636-651.

Whitney, J. A., 1975. The effects, of pressure, temperature, and X_{H_2O} on phase assemblage in four synthetic rock compositions. J. Geol. 83: 1-31.

Wood, D. A., Gibson, I. L. and Thompson, R. N., 1976. Elemental mobility during zeolite facies metamorphism of the Tertiary basalts of eastern Iceland. Contrib. Miner. Pet., 55: 241-254.

Wyllie, P. J., 1971. The Dynamic Earth: Textbook in Geosciences. Wiley, New York: 416 p.

Chapter 20

LOW-K$_2$O DACITE FROM THE TONGA-KERMADEC ISLAND ARC: PETROGRAPHY, CHEMISTRY, AND PETROGENESIS

W. B. Bryan

INTRODUCTION

The dacitic rocks of Tonga were first described in detail as drift pumice attributed to Falcon Island (Lacroix, 1939) and later as drift pumice recovered from the Great Barrier Reef and the Fiji Islands (Bryan, 1968). Melson et al. (1970) described the eruption, petrography, and major element chemistry of dacite pumice from Metis Shoal. Subsequently, comprehensive geologic studies of the major volcanic islands have provided a much more complete collection of these unusual rocks. Bryan (1971) provided details of petrography and mineralogy of drift pumice recovered from Eua Island, Tonga, and Ewart et al. (1973) have summarized the mineralogy and geochemistry of the volcanic rocks of Tonga, including the dacites. Ewart (1976) gives further information on the mineralogy of these rocks, with special emphasis on groundmass phases. Comprehensive chemical data and a petrographic summary of the Kermadec volcanic rocks is given by Ewart et al. (1977). Because these other papers have been concerned with broader geologic and geochemical problems, petrographic and genetic details of the dacites have been outlined only briefly. The purpose of this paper is to summarize the petrography and mineralogy of the dacites, their problems of nomenclature, and some further details of their petrogenesis. Many of the samples discussed in this paper are included in the collection of the U.S. National Museum, as indicated in Table 1. Maps showing locations of the principal volcanic islands of the Tonga-Kermadec system are given by Bryan et al. (1972) and by Ewart et al. (1977). In Tonga, dacites are present on the islands of Fonualei, Tofua, and Eua, and on the active submarine volcanoes at Metis Shoal and Falcon Bank. In the Kermadec Islands, dacites have been documented on Curtis, Raoul, and McCauley Islands.

PETROGRAPHY AND NOMENCLATURE

The dacitic rocks from Tonga are among the most calcic of their kind in the world. Indeed, classic rock nomenclature is severely strained to accommodate them; a typical dacite should contain plagioclase in the andesine-oligoclase range, and should not be an especially mafic rock. The Tonga "dacites" combine plagioclase in the labradorite-bytownite range with intermediate augite and hypersthene, and quartz and alkali feldspar are largely occult in the groundmass. Although there may be more than 20% quartz in the norm, free silica typically does not appear as phenocrysts. An exception is a dacite (keratophyre) from Eua Island, which contains rounded quartz phenocrysts. These

TABLE 1 : Sample numbers, location and source references for dacite samples collected in situ in the Tonga and Kermadec Islands. "USNM" refers to sample numbers in collection of the U.S. National Museum.

TONGA ISLANDS (Bauer, 1970; Ewart and Bryan, 1972; Ewart et al., 1973)

USNM	Field No.	Location
111108	MS	1967-68 dacite pumice eruption, Metis Shoal.
111549-8	E-8	Altered dacite, loose boulder in soil, Lakupo Beach, Eua Island.
111548-4	F-4	Dacite fragment in ash southeast edge of caldera rim, Fonualei Island.
111548-5	F-5	Young dacite lava flow on southeast coast, Fonualei Island.
111548-6	F-6	Yound dacite lava flow on southwest coast, Fonualei Island.
111548-8	F-8	Glassy lava block in explosion pit, west flank of central cone.
111548-20	F-20	Pre-caldera flow, northwest coast, Fonualei Island.
111548-32	F-32	Glassy spatter on older lava, northwestern slope of central cone.
111548-37	F-37	Basal pumice in caldera rim deposit, northwest coast, Fonualei Island.
111548-39	F-39	Young lava flow on coast, northwestern shore.
111548-40	F-40	Young flow on southwest flank of central cone, Fonualei Island.
111548-41	F-41	Pre-caldera flow on western coast, Fonualei Island.
	T-57	Dacite from Hamatua Formation, Tofua Island.

KERMADEC ISLANDS (Brothers and Searle, 1970; Brothers and Martin, 1970; Ewart et al., 1977)

USNM	Field No.	Location
-	7005	Obsidian block, Ngaio formation, Raoul Island.
-	10384	Pumice block, Sandy Bay Tuff, Macauley Island.
-	14864	
-	14849	Dacite from Curtis Island; no specific locations published.
-	14868	

are evidently very dry magmas; amphiboles and micas never appear as phenocrysts and are rarely detected in the groundmass. Titanomagnetite is sparsely present as a phenocryst phase. Forsteritic olivine, probably xenocrystal, appears in the dacite from Metis Shoal.

The term "dacite" has been applied to these rocks by all recent workers in Tonga, mainly in the sense that these are siliceous rocks in which plagioclase is the predominant feldspar, and mafic phases are subordinate in both the mode and the norm. Application of strict modal classification schemes to these rocks is limited by their fine-grained groundmass texture, which makes it difficult to determine overall mineral abundances and compositions. Where chemical data are available, rocks with wt.% SiO_2 in the range 63-69% generally satisfy the broader mineralogical requirements of the term dacite (see also discussion by Ewart, this volume.)

Highly calcic, siliceous rocks have been reported from other island arc systems, notably Japan, the Marianas, Bonin Islands, the South Sandwich Islands, and the West Indies. Although none of these rocks is as extreme in composition (in the sense of high calcium combined with high silica) as those of Tonga, some of these rocks have been thought sufficiently distinct from classic dacite to merit special nomenclature. In general these 'bandaites', 'boninites', and 'peleeites' are chemically and mineralogically closer to the siliceous andesites of Tonga than to the dacites. Kuroda and Shiraki (1975) present major element data for glass separated from the groundmass of a boninite. The anhydrous glass reembles the dacites of Tonga, except that Al_2O_3 is much higher (18.04 wt.%) and MgO is much lower (1.63 wt.%).

Most of the Tongan dacites are porphyritic rocks in which phenocrysts total less than 10% by volume. These are often clustered together as plagioclase-pyroxene-magnetite glomerocrysts (Fig. A, Plate 1). Plagioclase is always the most abundant phenocryst, while augite commonly exceeds hypersthene in abundance. Hypersthene phenocrysts may be surrounded by overgrowths or reaction rims of pigeonitic augite (Fig. B, Plate 1). Modal analyses are given in Table 2. The Metis Shoal dacite is exceptional in its high content of phenocrysts, and especially in the abundance of pyroxene. Forsteritic olivine with chrome spinel is also present in this rock (Melson et al., 1970; Ewart et al., 1973), although amounts are too small to be included in the mode. Bauer (1970) gives a mode for a largely crystalline dacite from Tofua as: feldspar, 42.4%; clinopyroxene, 30.0%; orthopyroxene, 0.8%; silica minerals, 6.1%; opaque minerals, 9.2%; glass, 9.8%; vesicles, 1.6%.

Phenocryst compositions are given in Tables 2-5. Plagioclase phenocrysts

584

A

B

Plate 1. Photomicrographs of dacite F-4, Fonualei Island, Tonga. A. Glomero-
cryst of augite and plagioclase in aphanitic groundmass. Width of field =
2.5 mm. B. Hypersthene phenocryst rimmed by overgrowth of clinopyroxene.
Width of field = 1.0 mm.

TABLE 2 : Electron microprobe analyses of plagioclase phenocrysts from Tongan dacite

	1	2	3	4	5
SiO_2	48.23	47.61	46.99	48.29	48.60
Al_2O_3	32.37	32.66	32.73	31.73	32.30
FeO	.87	.80	.71	.82	.77
MnO	.00	.01	-	-	.00
MgO	-	.06	.08	.08	.08
CaO	16.83	16.78	17.09	16.14	16.83
Na_2O	2.04	2.00	1.76	2.30	1.76
K_2O	.02	.04	.04	.06	.05
	100.36	99.96	99.41	99.42	100.38

Cations/32 Oxygens

Si	8.846	8.771	8.710	8.930	8.894
Al	7.000	7.094	7.154	6.916	6.970
Fe	.133	.124	.110	.126	.117
Mn	.000	.002	-	-	.000
Mg	.000	.018	.022	.022	.023
Ca	3.308	3.312	3.396	3.198	3.299
Na	.727	.716	.632	.826	.625
K	.005	.008	.008	.007	.011
	20.019	20.045	20.032	20.025	19.939

1. Dark pumice, Eua Island. Drift pumice on Lakupo beach.
2. Dacite F-4, Fonualei Island.
3. Dacite F-40, Fonualei Island.
4. Dacite F-41, Fonualei Island.
5. Dacite pumice, Metis Shoal.

are typically in the range An_{80}-An_{85} with minor oscillatory zoning (Table 2). Clinopyroxenes are Ti-poor, moderately aluminous augites, with Fe/(Fe + Mg) generally less than 0.5. Orthopyroxene is typically an intermediate to iron-rich hypersthene, with the notable exception of the xenocrystal bronzite in the Metis Shoal dacite (Table 4). Magnetite phenocrysts (Table 5) contain 30-40 mol.% ulvospinel.

Ewart (1976) has provided an extensive comparison of phenocryst and groundmass phases in all Tongan lavas. In the dacites, groundmass plagioclase

TABLE 3 : Electron microprobe analyses of clinopyroxene in Tongan dacite

	1	2	3	4	5
SiO_2	50.69	50.87	50.92	52.71	48.62
TiO_2	0.27	0.26	0.26	0.18	0.32
Al_2O_3	1.58	1.36	2.33	1.89	1.00
FeO	16.73	14.85	14.41	9.39	32.90
MnO	0.51	0.62	0.49	0.31	1.15
MgO	12.46	13.28	12.73	15.54	10.10
CaO	17.44	17.94	17.99	20.64	4.99
Na_2O	0.10	0.18	0.32	0.15	0.07
	99.79	99.35	99.57	100.82	99.15

Cations/6 Oxygens

	1	2	3	4	5
Si	1.945 ⎱ 2.000	1.948 ⎱ 2.000	1.939 ⎱ 2.000	1.945 ⎱ 2.000	1.965 ⎱ 2.000
Al	.055 ⎰	.052 ⎰	.061 ⎰	.055 ⎰	.035 ⎰
Al	.017	.009	.043	.027	.013
Ti	.008	.007	.011	.005	.010
Fe	.537 ⎱ 2.015	.475 ⎱ 2.018	.459 ⎱ 2.008	.290 ⎱ 2.015	1.112 ⎱ 2.003
Mn	.017	.020	.016	.010	.039
Mg	.712	.758	.722	.855	.608
Ca	.717	.736	.734	.817	.216
Na	.007	.013	.023	.011	.005

1. Phenocryst in dark drift pumice, Lakupo beach, Eua Island.
2. Phenocryst, dacite F-4, Fonualei Island.
3. Phenocryst, dacite F-40, Fonualei Island.
4. Phenocryst, Metis Shoal dacite pumice.
5. Groundmass pigeonite, dacite F-20, Fonualei Island (Ewart, 1976).

ranges between An_{45} and An_{65}. The author has detected K_2O-rich areas in the groundmass of several Fonualei dacites which appear to be potassic alkali feldspar, but no grains suitable for reliable analysis have been found. The few groundmass pyroxenes which have been analyzed are subcalcic ferroaugites or pigeonites; in contrast to common experience with basaltic rocks, they do not

TABLE 4 : Electron microprobe analyses of orthopyroxene phenocrysts in Tongan dacite, and an olivine xenocryst in Metis Shoal pumice.

	1	2	3	4	5	6
SiO_2	52.28	52.27	52.17	52.69	55.85	41.26
TiO_2	.15	.14	.19	.14	.06	-
Al_2O_3	.81	.71	.77	.92	1.03	-
FeO	25.64	25.45	26.53	21.26	11.41	7.10
MnO	.98	.92	.90	.53	.24	.13
MgO	19.51	19.28	18.40	22.66	28.94	50.64
CaO	1.82	1.91	1.97	1.63	1.85	.14
Na_2O	.02	.02	.02	.02	.00	-
	101.22	100.71	100.93	99.84	99.38	99.27
O	6.000	6.000	6.000	6.000	6.000	4.000
Si	1.966	1.974	1.975	1.964	1.989	1.003
Al	.034	.026	.025	.036	.011	-
Al	.002	.006	.009	.004	.032	-
Ti	.004	.004	.005	.004	.002	-
Fe	.807	.804	.840	.663	.340	.144
Mn	.031	.030	.029	.017	.007	.003
Mg	1.093	1.085	1.038	1.259	1.537	1.836
Ca	.073	.077	.080	.065	.070	.004
Na	.001	.001	.001	.001	.000	-

Si + Al braces = 2.000; lower groups: 2.001, 2.007, 2.002, 2.013, 1.988, 1.987

1. Hypersthene phenocryst, dacite F-4, Fonualei Island.
2. Hypersthene phenocryst, dacite F-40, Fonualei Island.
3. Hypersthene phenocryst, dacite F-41, Fonualei Island.
4. Hypersthene phenocryst, Metis Shoal dacite pumice.
5. Xenocrystal bronzite, Metis Shoal dacite pumice.
6. Forsterite xenocryst, Metis Shoal dacite pumice.

TABLE 5 : Electron microprobe analyses of magnetite and spinel in Tongan dacite and pumice. Molecular proportions are based on 32 oxygens.

	1	2	3	4	5	6	7	8
SiO_2	0.31	0.22	0.31	0.16	0.24	0.15	0.29	0.22
TiO_2	9.22	8.84	10.20	14.24	18.00	10.72	16.99	-
Al_2O_3	3.40	3.03	2.83	1.68	0.78	2.71	1.72	7.31
V_2O_3	0.87	0.75	0.72	0.80	0.26	0.91	0.44	.08
Fe_2O_3	45.88	47.30	44.64	39.39	32.34	44.01	32.61	7.36
FeO	38.83	37.63	39.66	44.60	47.44	40.53	46.65	11.00
MnO	0.39	0.41	0.42	0.41	0.47	0.30	0.36	.28
MgO	0.85	1.21	0.61	0.13	0.09	0.52	0.15	14.27
Cr_2O_3	-	-	-	-	-	-	-	59.79
	99.78	99.39	99.39	101.54	99.78	99.95	99.34	100.54
Si	.093	.066	.094	.047	.072	.045	.087	.058
Ti	2.075	1.987	2.301	3.174	4.088	2.413	3.855	-
Al	1.192	1.067	1.002	.587	.278	.956	.612	2.234
V	.208	.180	.173	.190	.062	.218	.106	.016
Fe^{3+}	10.284	10.645	10.079	8.784	7.350	9.912	7.404	1.436
Fe^{2+}	9.673	9.410	9.948	11.054	11.982	10.145	11.771	2.385
Mn	.098	.104	.106	.103	.120	.076	.092	.061
Mg	.378	.539	.272	.057	.041	.232	.067	5.514
Cr	-	-	-	-	-	-	-	12.255
	24.000	23.998	23.975	23.998	23.994	23.998	23.996	23.972

1. Phenocryst magnetite, dacite F-4, Fonualei Island total includes .03% CaO.
2. Phenocryst magnetite, dacite F-40, Fonealei Island.
3. Phenocryst magnetite, dactie F-41, Fonualei Island.
4. Phenocryst, dacite F-20, Fonealei Island; includes .05 Cr_2O_3 and .08 ZnO (Ewart, 1976).
5. Groundmass grain, dacite F-20, Fonualei Island includes .03 Cr_2O_3 and 0.13 ZnO (Ewart, 1976).
6. Phenocryst, dacite F-39, Fonualei Island (Ewart, 1976).
7. Groundmass grain, dacite F-39 (Ewart, 1976).
8. Spinel inclusion in olivine, Metis Shoal dacite pumice. Total includes ZnO = .06, CaO = .01.

show enrichment in TiO_2 and Al_2O_3 relative to the phenocryst pyroxenes (Table 4). Although the author has tentatively identified groundmass orthopyroxene optically in Fonualei dacite, and Bauer (1970) reported orthopyroxene in his mode of the Tofua dacite, no orthopyroxene was detected by detailed microprobe analyses of groundmass phases (Ewart, 1976). Groundmass magnetite resembles the phenocryst magnetite, except that there appears to be a systematic increase in ulvospinel in the groundmass magnetite (Table 5).

In order to account for the distinctive compositional features of the Tongan dacites without introducing new "place-name" nomenclature, Bryan et al. (1972) used mineralogical modifiers combined with the base name dacite. Under this scheme, the Tongan dacites are bytownite- or labradorite-dacites. The nature of the dominant phenocryst pyroxene can be indicated in the same way; thus, most Tongan dacites are bytownite-augite dacite, but a few, such as F-5 or F-40 (Table 6) are bytownite-hypersthene dacite.

Bryan et al. (1972) and Ewart et al. (1977) noted that the Tongan lavas conform petrographically to the "pigeonitic" series of Kuno (1959). Bauer (1970) showed, however, that rocks of Tofua (including the dacite) are systematically even more calcic and lower in total alkali than those of the Japanese "pigeonitic" series. Recently it has been the fashion to refer to calcic island arc series such as those of Tonga or the Japanese pigeonitic series as "tholeiitic" (Jakes and Gill, 1970). However, one of the major remaining petrogenetic problems in the Tonga-Kermadec arc, and perhaps in many other island arcs, concerns the relation, if any, between the genesis of the island arc lavas and the subducted sea-floor plate composed in part of tholeiitic sea-floor basalt. Bryan et al. (1972) noted that the iron

TABLE 6 : Modal analyses of phenocrysts and groundmass in dacites from Tonga (Ewart and Bryan, 1972; Ewart et al., 1973)

	F-5	F-8	F-20	F-32	F-39	F-40	F-41	MS	E-8*
Plagioclase	5.43	4.42	6.80	4.34	4.20	3.57	6.47	11.85	26.0
Augite	0.17	1.15	1.85	0.49	0.54	0.19	1.20	6.51	5.4
Hypersthene	0.31	0.53	0.51	0.39	0.36	0.26	0.76	7.43	
Magnetite	0.19	0.41	0.54	0.22	0.31	0.16	0.55	0.22	1.1
Groundmass	93.90	93.50	90.30	94.56	94.60	95.81	91.02	73.91	59.9

*Includes quartz, 7.6%; ferromagnesian pseudomorphs assumed to have been pyroxene.

enrichment typical of the pigeonitic series is not a uniquely tholeiitic characteristic; further, the highly calcic residual liquids represented by the Tongan and Kermadec dacites contrast with the alkalic or peralkaline residual liquids found in some continental tholeiitic basalts (Lindsley et al., 1971). Bryan et al. (1977) also showed that significant differences exist in critical geochemical parameters between continental tholeiitic basalt and sea-floor basalt in the western North Atlantic. These inconsistencies, of course, reflect the manner in which the term "tholeiite" has been expanded in recent years to include rocks which are well outside the composition range included in the original definition of tholeiite (Chayes, 1966). For island arc rocks, such as those of Tonga, it would be preferable to abandon the use of the term "tholeiitic" in favor of the established and purely descriptive term "pigeonitic." No misleading genetic implications are likely to arise if the dacites of the Tonga-Kermadec arc are recognized members of a pigeonitic suite.

CHEMICAL COMPOSITION

The major element chemistry and norms of dacites from the Tonga-Kermadec area are given in Tables 7, 8, and 9. The glass from Metis Shoal (Table 7) is well outside the SiO_2 range defined earlier, but is included because of the unusual nature of the Metis dacite and its possible relevance to petrogenesis of silicic rocks in Tonga. The Kermadec data (Table 8) also include two analyses which also are slightly outside the SiO_2 limits, but are useful in establishing some subtle chemical features of the Kermadec dacites. The dacite from Eua (Table 7) is distinguished from all other analyses in its unusually high Na_2O; as noted previously (Ewart and Bryan, 1972), it might more properly be called a keratophyre. This sample shows considerable secondary alteration and its chemistry could reflect these alteration processes to an unknown degree. The Metis Shoal pumice shows relatively high MgO, CaO, and low Na_2O, which can be attributed to the greater abundance of pyroxene and plagioclase phenocrysts (Table 6). The bulk analysis is in strong contrast to that of the glass; and it is evident that this "dacite" is a hybrid mixture of rhyolitic glass and a gabbroic phenocryst assemblage (Ewart et al., 1973).

Comparisons of data in the tables reveal subtle contrasts between the Kermadec dacites and those of Tonga. The Kermadec data are dominated by analyses from Curtis Island, while Fonualei accounts for most of the Tonga data; yet the few analyses from the other islands in each group tend to show the same characteristics. The Tonga dacites have distinctly higher total iron, higher CaO and K_2O, and lower Na_2O compared to the Kermadec dacites. Ewart et al. (1977) show that these features separate the dacites in an AFM diagram. These differences also are emphasized in the norms, with the Kermadec dacites

TABLE 7 : Chemical analyses and CIPW norms of dacite drift pumice and dacite from Eua, Tofua, and Metis Shoal.

	1	2	3	4	5	6	7	8	9
SiO_2	64.82	65.84	67.20	65.86	65.62	64.01	63.66	73.38	73.60
TiO_2	0.78	0.76	0.62	0.67	0.46	0.32	0.39	0.45	0.52
Al_2O_3	11.95	12.02	12.13	13.27	15.83	12.95	12.42	12.66	12.29
Fe_2O_3	1.53	1.05	0.52	1.83	3.44	1.51	1.35	1.11	1.31
FeO	8.16	8.25	8.47	6.12	1.08	5.43	5.22	2.84	2.71
MnO	0.15	0.13	0.13	0.16	0.09	0.13	0.12	0.06	0.06
MgO	1.19	1.29	1.30	1.84	2.24	5.47	5.10	0.84	1.07
CaO	6.54	6.22	5.60	6.01	3.22	7.51	6.97	3.79	3.61
Na_2O	2.64	2.66	2.62	3.13	5.36	1.83	2.58	3.09	3.17
K_2O	0.85	0.77	0.63	0.88	0.30	0.95	0.90	1.52	1.47
P_2O_5	Tr.	Tr.	0.16	0.23	0.06	0.06	0.07	0.00	0.07
H_2O^+	1.16	0.84	0.34	0.53	1.71	0.00	} 0.91	<0.13	} 0.13
H_2O^-	0.20	0.16	–	0.24	0.50	0.00		0.03	
	99.97	99.99	99.72	100.77	99.91	100.17	99.69	99.77	100.01
Q	27.70	28.78	31.07	27.11	23.44	24.52	22.32	39.11	39.49
Or	5.02	4.55	3.72	5.20	1.67	5.61	5.32	8.98	8.68
Ab	22.34	22.51	22.17	26.49	45.11	15.49	21.83	26.15	26.82
An	18.25	18.58	19.48	19.56	15.58	24.32	19.65	16.19	14.96
Di { Wo	5.93	5.12	3.07	3.72	–	5.26	6.06	1.09	1.06
Di { En	1.20	1.07	.61	1.30	–	3.09	3.53	.40	0.48
Di { Fs	5.15	4.42	2.69	2.52	–	1.91	2.24	.71	0.57
Hy { En	1.76	2.14	2.63	3.29	5.62	10.53	9.17	1.69	2.18
Hy { Fs	7.56	8.85	11.65	6.40	–	6.52	5.81	2.96	2.58
Mt	2.22	1.52	0.75	2.65	2.31	2.19	1.96	1.61	1.90
Il	1.48	1.44	1.18	1.27	0.91	0.61	0.74	0.85	0.99
Ap	0.00	0.00	.38	.54	<0.15	0.14	0.17	0.03	0.17
C	–	–	–	–	1.02	–	–	–	–
He	–	–	–	–	1.92	–	–	–	–

1,2: Pumice from 1928 eruption of Falcon Island (LaCroix, 1939).
3: Dark pumice attributed to Tonga, Herald Cays, Queensland (Bryan, 1968).
4: Dacite, Hamatua formation, Tofua Island (Bauer, 1970).
5: Dacite E-8 (Keratophyre), Lakupo Beach trail, Eua Island (Ewart and Bryan, 1972).
6: Dacite, Metis Shoal (Melson et al., 1970).
7: Dacite, Metis Shoal (Ewart et al., 1973).
8: Glass matrix, Metis Shoal dacite (Melson et al., 1970).

TABLE 8 : Chemical analyses and CIPW norms of dacite from the Kermadec
Islands (Ewart et al., 1977)

	Raoul Is.	Mccauley Is.	Curtis Is.		
	7005	10384	14864	14849	14868
SiO_2	66.78	68.0	64.5	65.35	70.5
TiO_2	0.61	0.65	0.57	0.75	0.55
Al_2O_3	13.65	11.57	16.73	15.77	13.51
Fe_2O_3	1.56	1.07	1.57	1.86	1.57
FeO	4.38	3.44	3.34	3.51	2.17
MnO	0.18	0.14	0.13	0.17	0.13
MgO	1.21	0.79	1.52	1.54	0.93
CaO	4.66	2.98	5.20	5.31	3.66
Na_2O	3.84	4.95	3.66	3.94	4.55
K_2O	0.60	1.40	0.62	0.38	0.64
P_2O_5	0.10	0.09	0.09	0.15	0.12
H_2O^+ H_2O^-	1.84	5.01	1.64	1.34	1.30
	99.41	100.09	99.57	100.07	99.63
Q	28.77	26.36	25.76	26.13	32.36
Or	3.54	8.27	3.66	2.24	3.78
Ab	32.49	41.89	30.97	33.34	38.50
An	18.24	5.22	25.23	24.22	14.55
Di { Wo	1.79	3.77	-	.52	1.21
En	.61	1.17	-	.25	.63
Fs	1.23	2.75	-	.26	.55
Hy { En	2.40	.80	3.79	3.59	1.69
Fs	4.85	1.87	4.14	3.73	1.47
Mt	2.26	1.55	2.27	2.70	2.28
Il	1.16	1.23	1.08	1.42	1.04
Ap	.24	.21	.21	.36	.28
C	-	-	.79	-	-

showing very low diopside or traces of corundum. In both sets of analyses,
however, the low normative diopside relative to hypersthene is unexpected in
view of the dominance of modal augite over hypersthene among the phenocryst
assemblages, and the tendency of hypersthene phenocrysts to react to form
augite overgrowths (Fig. B, Plate 1).

Other subtle differences appear among the dacite samples from Tonga, with
Falcon Island and other drift pumice samples showing lower K_2O and Na_2O and

TABLE 9 : Chemical analyses and CIPW norms of dacites from Fonualei Island, Tonga. F-4, F-20, and F-40 are classical gravimetric analyses by E. Jarosewich. F-39 is a classical gravimetric analyses by B.D. Kay. Remainder are x-ray fluorescence analyses by A. Ewart and S. Bagley. Data from Ewart et al., 1973. Eruption ages from Brodie (1970) and Bryan et al. (1972).

		Prehistoric			1846-47(?)	1939	
	F-20	F-41	F-4	F-37	F-39	F-5	F-40
SiO_2	64.79	64.89	65.09	64.34	65.34	66.26	65.17
TiO_2	0.55	0.56	0.56	0.58	0.60	0.59	0.51
Al_2O_3	14.48	14.16	14.39	13.77	14.12	14.18	13.92
Fe_2O_3	1.91	2.48	1.78	2.27	1.06	1.72	1.55
FeO	6.07	5.48	6.16	5.79	6.76	6.34	6.41
MnO	.16	.19	0.17	0.19	0.19	0.19	0.16
MgO	1.45	1.58	1.38	1.61	1.54	1.64	1.52
CaO	6.04	6.03	5.90	6.11	5.87	5.73	5.79
Na_2O	3.03	3.02	3.00	2.90	3.06	2.79	3.11
K_2O	1.11	1.06	1.13	1.08	1.13	1.03	1.15
P_2O_5	0.11	0.18	0.17	0.20	0.19	0.21	0.18
H_2O^+	<0.10	0.04	<0.10	0.76	0.15	n.d.	0.15
H_2O^-	0.10	0.14	0.14	0.16	0.16	n.d.	0.12
	99.80	99.81	99.81	99.76	100.17	100.68	99.74
Q	25.45	26.55	26.18	26.32	25.27	28.40	25.45
Or	6.56	6.26	6.68	6.38	6.68	6.09	6.79
Ab	25.64	25.56	25.39	24.54	25.89	23.61	26.32
An	22.63	21.95	22.46	21.37	21.46	23.13	20.63
Di { Wo	2.79	2.88	2.43	3.24	2.73	1.70	2.94
Di { En	.84	1.02	.67	1.10	.75	.53	.85
Di { Fs	2.07	1.93	1.88	2.24	2.12	1.24	2.23
Hy { En	2.78	2.91	2.62	2.91	3.09	3.56	2.94
Hy { Fs	6.89	5.51	7.36	5.91	8.78	8.36	7.72
Mt	2.77	3.60	2.58	3.29	1.54	2.49	2.25
Il	1.04	1.06	1.06	1.10	1.14	1.12	.97
Ap	.26	.43	.40	.47	.45	.50	.43

higher total iron than the samples from Fonualei. The one dacite analysis from Tofua is intermediate in these features. The data of Table 7 suggest that Raoul, Macauley, and Curtis Islands in the Kermadecs may also produce dacite with distinctive characteristics, but the relatively high degree of alteration in several of these samples prevents detailed comparisons.

The Fonualei dacites have been very consistent in composition in eruptions spanning a period of at least several hundred years (Brodie, 1970; Bryan et al., 1972). The four oldest samples (cols. 1-4, Table 8) show slightly higher CaO and lower SiO_2 than the samples attributed to the most recent eruptions in 1938. This suggests a large, compositionally homogeneous source area which is thermally stable and undergoing little, if any, variation by crystallization or partial melting processes.

All lavas from the Tonga-Kermadec arc, including the dacites, are characterized by unusually low concentrations of large-ion-lithophile trace elements. These geochemical peculiarities have been discussed in some detail by Ewart et al. (1973, 1977). Typical examples are given in Table 10. The dacites are more depleted in rare earth elements than most oceanic tholeiitic basalts, but do have somewhat higher Ba, Zr, and Y, which is consistent with their higher K_2O.

TABLE 10 : Selected trace element analyses of Kermadec and Togan dacites. Cols. 1-2 from Ewart et al., 1977; Cols. 3-7 from Ewart et al., 1973, 1977. Rare earth data for Metis Shoal from Melson et al., 1970. See Ewart et al. (1977) for additional limited rare earth data and U, Th data for dacites from Raoul, Curtis, and Fonualei Islands. n.d. = not determined.

	Raoul 7005	Curtis 14868	Fonualei F-6	Fonualei F-20	Eua E-8	Metis Shoal Rock	Metis Shoal Glass
Rb	10	6.8	17	14	1.7	14	21
Ba	210	345	305	270	60	360	610
Sr	160	175	300	305	135	140	130
Zr	75	84	47	48	100	46	68
Y	31	41	22	25	27	21	25
Zn	96	84	120	115	n.d.	58	46
Cu	9	21	28	28	7	88	120
Ni	5	5	n.d.	3	3.5	53	4
Co	11	7	13	14	8	25	10
V	39	19	95	100	88	175	130
Sc	n.d.	n.d.	26	25	14	29	12
Cr	3.2	n.d.	6	4	20	230	7
Ga	n.d.	n.d.	18	18	12	14	13
B	n.d.	n.d.	23	17	n.d.	53	105
La	4.2	4.8	4	3.7	-	2.7	-
Ce	13.1	14.0	9.5	10	-	7.31	-
Nd	10.0	10.5	7	8	-	-	-
Th	.54	2.10	.92	.81	-	-	-
U	.23	0.84	.42	.34	-	-	-

PETROGENESIS

The petrogenetic relations among the Tongan lavas have been discussed in some detail by Ewart et al., 1973. Least-squares calculations utilizing major element data for rocks and phenocrysts showed that, at least from a compositional point of view, the Tongan dacites can easily be interpreted as products of high-level fractional crystallization of the basaltic andesites. The sum of squares of residuals for the various solutions generally are below 0.10 and many are below 0.05, these being among the best fits ever demonstrated for assumed co-magmatic rock and mineral data (Table 11). The fractionation process is further supported by trace element data available for both rocks and minerals. In general, trace element concentrations are satisfied by the same mineral proportions required to explain the major element variations.

One unsettling feature of the Tongan suite is the apparent division into a bimodal rock assemblage dominated by basaltic andesite and dacite, with few examples of andesite of intermediate composition. This has been demonstrated in

TABLE 11 : Least squares approximation to basaltic andesite L-5 calculated as a linear combination of Metis Shoal glass and augite, hypersthene, plagioclase and magnetite phenocrysts (Ewart et al., 1973). Data recalculated to 100%, all Fe as FeO.

	A	B	C	D
SiO_2	54.11	54.11	Metis Glass	0.329
Al_2O_3	17.03	17.03	Plagioclase	0.375
FeO	9.65	9.64	Augite	0.192
MgO	4.87	4.87	Hypersthene	0.033
CaO	11.28	11.28	Magnetite	0.071
Na_2O	1.75	1.64		1.000
K_2O	0.49	0.52		
MnO	0.16	0.10		
TiO_2	0.58	0.72		
P_2O_5	0.07	0.02		

A. Basaltic andesite L-5, Late Island, Tonga.

B. Least-squares estimate of basaltic andesite L-5 (Bryan et al., 1968).

C. Components combined to form composition in column B

D. Weight fractions of components in Column C used to calculate column B. Sum of squares of residuals = 0.0408.

histograms of SiO_2 abundance (Ewart et al., 1977). An implication is that the dacite and basaltic andesite may be separate mantle-derived magma batches, although there is certainly no _a priori_ reason to suppose magmas are always erupted and sampled in proportion to their abundances within the crust.

Some further insight into the relationship of the dacites to andesite and basaltic andesite may be gained by looking at variation in composition as a function of the degree of crystallization required to generate each derivative liquid from the assumed basaltic andesite parent. The "percent crystallized" is readily obtained from the sum of the mineral weight fractions required to obtain the least squares fit to the parent composition.

Variation trends for a representative selection of compositions is shown in Figure 1. The assumed parent L-5 is a basaltic andesite from Late Island; HH-3, L-13, and F-31 are andesites, and F-20 is a typical dacite from Fonualei. The Metis Shoal glass(MG) is the "most fractionated" composition known from Tonga. This illustration indicates that the Fonualei dacite and Metis Shoal rhyolitic glass are logical extensions of the curvilinear variation trends extending from basaltic andesite through the andesites. It is interesting that, in terms of percent crystallized, the largest "data gap" lies within the andesites, not between andesite and dacite, as implied by SiO_2 frequency data.

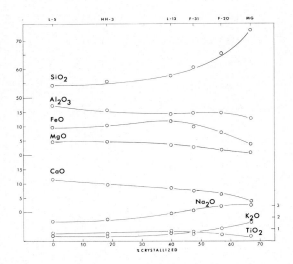

Figure 1. Variation of minor element oxides as a function of percent crystallization, assuming dacite and andesite are derived from a common basaltic andesite parent. See Table 11 for a typical least-squares solution, on which percent crystallized is based.

TONGAN DACITE AND PLATE TECTONICS

The geologic setting of Tonga arc is of special interest because it is apparently developed within a region of oceanic crust (Bryan et al., 1972). Thus, the development of siliceous magmatic liquids within this setting may be an example of an early stage in the genesis of primitive continental crust. It has already been noted that the basaltic andesite appears to be a reasonable parental magma from which dacite could be derived by crystallization in high-level magma chambers. The ultimate origin of the basaltic andesite, then, is a fundamental problem in the petrogenesis of Tongan lavas.

Geochemical data for Tongan lavas provide only limited support for the popular view that island arc magmas are directly derived by partial melting of subducted oceanic lithosphere. For example, rare earth elements in the dacites show chondritic patterns at 12-15 times chondritic concentrations. The basaltic andesites also have flat chondritic rare earth patterns at concentrations of 5-10 times chondritic. These patterns and concentrations are difficult to derive from the typical light-rare-earth depleted patterns at 15-25 times chondritic concentrations which are typical of oceanic basalts. Since rare earths would be strongly partitioned into any partial melt, island arc lavas derived from oceanic lithosphere should be significantly enriched in rare earths compared to sea-floor basalt; this is not observed in Tonga (Ewart and Bryan, 1973). Similar conclusions are required by the very low concentrations of Rb, Y, Zr, and K, which should also be significantly enriched by low degrees of partial melting.

Isotopic data bearing on this problem have recently been reviewed by Ewart et al. (1977). The average lead isotope ratios are similar to those observed in presumably mantle-derived ocean ridge basalts, although the Kermadec data show greater scatter than Tonga. These isotopic data, again considered along with the low concentrations of elements such as Ba, Rb, and Cs, suggest that sediment contribution to Tongan magmas could not be more than a few percent (Sinha and Hart, 1972). Strontium isotope ratios tend to be more radiogenic in the dacites than in the basaltic andesites of Tonga, and the latter are, in turn, slightly more radiogenic than typical ocean floor basalts. Ewart et al. (1973) showed that this could best be reconciled with other geochemical data by assuming small amounts of limestone assimilation in high-level magma chambers. Thus, geochemical contributions to the lavas by subducted sea-floor sediments appear to be minimal. This could mean that little sediment is transported down the Benioff Zone, or that subducted material is not the principal source of the lavas.

The absence of hydrous minerals in the lavas, and the high magmatic temperatures implied by the dominance of calcic plagioclase in the phenocryst assemblages, seem to preclude hydrous partial melting of peridotite as a source for the Tongan magmas, and at the same time do favor derivation of the magmas from depths approaching those of the Benioff Zone (Ewart, 1976). As shown by Ewart et al. (1977), the Tonga-Kermadec lavas become isotopically and compositionally more heterogeneous to the south, with the most fundamental differences appearing between the southern Kermadecs and the North Island of New Zealand. The New Zealand lavas are systematically more enriched in large-ion-lithophile elements, and are isotopically more radiogenic than the island arc lavas to the north. These differences can most reasonably be attributed to fundamental differences in the crust beneath New Zealand compared to the Tonga-Kermadec region, and the geochemical contrasts here resemble, in many respects, those noted by Bryan et al. (1977) between continental and oceanic basalts in the western Atlantic.

Taken together, the evidence to date suggests that lavas in the Tonga-Kermadec arc are generated at or near the Benioff Zone within a region of oceanic crust and mantle. The magmas may originate by essentially anhydrous melting of peridotite mantle overlying the Benioff Zone, or may include a significant contribution from partial melting of an amphibolitized lithospheric plate. Whatever the ultimate source, the rising magma diapirs must further interact with the surrounding upper mantle peridotite during their ascent. Thus, the isotopic ratios and other geochemical parameters in the Tonga-Kermadec lavas approach those typical of magmas derived by relatively high degrees of partial fusion of depleted mantle. Although the New Zealand magmas may have a similar source, interaction with pre-existing continental-type crust during ascent contributes significant radiogenic lead, strontium and large-ion-lithophile elements to the magma (Ewart et al., 1977).

This indicates then, that the dacites of Tonga are appropriately regarded as "first cycle" siliceous derivatives generated by interaction between subducted, mantle-derived oceanic lithosphere and overlying mantle peridotite. Significant contributions to dacite geochemistry by marine sediment or pre-existing continental crust is not indicated. There can be no assurance, of course, that the mantle beneath the Tonga-Kermadec arc has not undergone one or more previous episodes of partial melting in the past, either at an ocean ridge or subduction zone. Hence, this mantle, and consequently, the dacites which may reflect its composition, could be relatively more depleted geochemically than the primitive mantle and its siliceous derivatives involved in early stages of continental nucleation. Nevertheless, the Tonga arc may provide one of the best modern examples of the magmatic processes and products to be expected in the formation of new continental lithosphere.

The Tonga Island Arc also provides little support for the popular "geostill" concept, in which island arc magmatism is presumed to play a critical role in scavenging economically valuable metals from the subducted oceanic lithosphere (Rona, 1973). The low concentrations of elements such as Pb, Zn and Cu, and the low concentrations of water, as exemplified even in the most "evolved" magmatic products, indicate that these magmas would be a poor source of mineralizing solutions. This, in turn, suggests that oceanic lithosphere is not a major contributor to mineralization associated with subduction zones. It seems more likely that mineralization is developed where island arc magmatism mobilizes and redistributes volatiles and rare elements dispersed in pre-existing continental lithosphere.

REFERENCES

Bauer, G. R., 1970. The geology of Tofua Island, Tonga. Pacific Sci., 24: 333-350.

Brodie, J. W., 1970. Notes on volcanic activity at Fonualei, Tonga. New Zealand J. Geol. Geophys., 13: 30-38.

Brothers, R. N., and Martin, K. R., 1970. The geology of Macauley Island, Kermadec group, southwest Pacific. Bull. Volc., 34: 330-346.

Brothers, R. N., and Searle, E. J., 1970. The geology of Raoul Island, Kermadec group, southwest Pacific. Bull. Volc., 34: 7-37.

Bryan, W. B., 1968. Low-potash acite drift pumice from the Coral Sea. Geol. Mag., 105: 431-439.

Bryan, W. B., 1971. Coral Sea drift pumice stranded on Eua Island, Tonga, in 1969. Geol. Soc. Am. Bull., 82: 2799-2812.

Bryan, W. B., Finger, L. W. and Chayes, F., 1969. Estimating proportions in petrographic mixing equations by least-squares approximation. Science, 163: 926-927.

Bryan, W. B., Frey, F. A. and Thompson, G., 1977. Oldest Atlantic seafloor: Mesozoic basalts from western North Atlantic margin and eastern North America. Contrib. Miner. Pet., 64: 223-242.

Bryan, W. B., Stice, G. D., and Ewart, A., 1972. Geology, petrography, and geochemistry of the volcanic islands of Tonga. J. Geophys. Res., 77: 1566-1585.

Chayes, F., 1966. Alkaline and subalkaline basalts. Am. J. Sci., 264: 128-145.

600

Ewart, A., 1976. A petrological study of the younger Tongan andesites and dacites, and the olivine tholeiites of Niva Fo'ou Island, S.W. Pacific. Contrib. Miner. Pet., 58: 1-21.

Ewart, A., Brothers, R. N. and Mateen, A., 1977. An outline of the geology and geochemistry, and the possible petrogenetic evolution of the volcanic rocks of the Tonga-Kermadec-New Zealand Island Arc. J. Volc. Geotherm. Res., 2: 205-250.

Ewart, A. and Bryan, W. B., 1972. Petrography and geochemistry of the igneous rocks from Eua, Tongan Islands. Geol. Soc. Am. Bull., 83: 3281-3298.

Ewart, A. and Bryan, W. B., 1973. The petrology and geochemistry of the Tongan Islands. In: Coleman, P. J., (Ed.), The Western Pacific. Island Arcs, Marginal Seas, Geochemistry, 503-522. U. West. Aust. Press, Perth.

Ewart, A., Bryan, W. B. and Gill, J., 1973. Mineralogy and geochemistry of the younger volcanic islands of Tonga, S.W. Pacific. J. Pet., 14: 429-465.

Jakes, P. and Gill, J. B., 1970. .Rare earth elements and the island arc tholeiitic series. Earth Planet. Sci. Lett., 9: 17-28.

Kuno, H., 1968. Origin of andesite and its bearing on the island arc structure. Bull. Volc., 32: 141-176.

Kuroda, N. and Sheraki, K., 1975. Boninite and related rocks of Chichi-jima, Bonin Islands, Japan. Rept. Fac. Sci. Shizuoka Univ., 10: 145-155.

La Croix, A., 1939. Composition mineralogique et chimique des laves des volcans des iles de l'ocean Pacifique situees entre l'Equateur et le tropique du Capricorne. Mem. Acad. Sci. Paris, 63: 1-97.

Lindsley, D. A., Smith, D. and Haggerty, S. E., 1971. Petrography and mineral chemistry of a differentiated flow of Picture Gorge basalt near Spray, Oregon. Carn. Inst. Wash. Yrbk., 69: 264-285.

Melson, W. G., Jarosewich, E., and Lundquist, C. A., 1970. Volcanic eruption at Metis Shoal, Tonga, 1967-1968: Description and petrology. Smiths. Contrib. Earth Sci., 4: 1-18.

Rona, P., 1973. Plate tectonics and mineral resources. Sci. Am., 229: 86-95.

Sinha, A. K. and Hart, S. R., 1972. A geochemical test of the subduction hypothesis for generation of island arc magmas. Carn. Inst. Wash. Yrbk., 71: 309-312.

Chapter 21

DACITE OF THE LESSER ANTILLES

J. F. Tomblin

ABSTRACT

The dacites of the Lesser Antilles represent the acid end-members of a calc-alkaline, island arc volcanic suite. Rocks containing 65% or more silica by wet chemical analysis form an estimated 7% of the surface area of the volcanic Lesser Antilles, and are relatively more abundant in the central part of the island arc. Most of them are strongly porphyritic, with abundant plagioclase but widely varying percentages of quartz phenocrysts. Geochemically, they have low alkalis and low iron to magnesium ratios. Strontium isotope ratios for some of the dacites suggest that these were derived in part from ocean-floor sediments including ancient continental crust, whilst others represent the fractionation products of primary oceanic material. The systematic decrease in potassium and rubidium contents northward along the arc is attributed to the relative youth of the present subduction zone in this part of the arc, and the consequent failure of oceanic crust and overlying sediments to have reached the depth at which they partially melt.

BACKGROUND
The Lesser Antilles

The Lesser Antilles (Fig. 1) form an island arc of Tertiary to Recent age situated along the eastern margin of the Caribbean plate, immediately above the subduction zone boundary between the Caribbean and western Atlantic plates. The rocks are a typical orogenic assemblage consisting mainly of calc-alkaline volcanics of which less than 10% are sufficiently high in silica to be called dacites. Rare plutonic rocks of tonalitic composition are also present.

Definition of dacite

For the purpose of this chapter, dacites will be defined as all volcanic rocks of calc-alkaline type with silica content of 63% or greater by wet chemical analysis. The division between dacite and andesite (which has lower silica) is an arbitrary one, and often cannot be applied in the field. The dacites according to the above chemical definition include almost all of the rocks with conspicuous (more than 5%) quartz phenocrysts, but in addition to these quartz-rich rocks, which are identifiable in hand specimen and form about

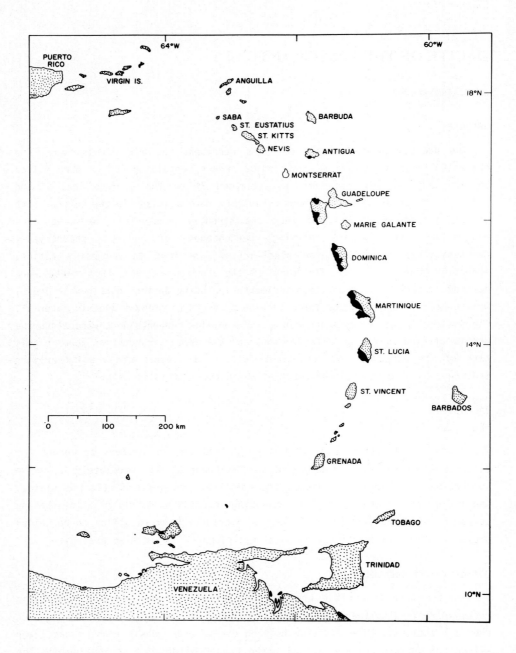

Figure LA.1.--Map of the Lesser Antilles. Solid shading indicates volcanic centres which contain dacite.

half of the total dacite population in the Lesser Antilles, there is a second and equally abundant type of dacite which is poor in quartz phenocrysts and which in hand specimen is indistinguishable from typical andesite. The use of a chemical classification is justifiable on the grounds that many hundreds of dacite and acid andesite analyses have now been made, thereby enabling the identification and quantitative assessment of dacite in this way. However, another problem has arisen in the form of a systematic difference between silica abundance as determined by X-ray fluorescence (XRF) and by wet chemical analysis, involving silica readings which by XRF in the dacite range, are on average about 3% higher (Fig. 2), of which only 1% is the result of the volatile-free recalculation to 100%. For the purposes of this chapter, therefore, the boundary between andesite and dacite is set at 6% silica for wet chemical analyses but at 66% silica where determined by XRF with total adjusted to 100%.

For field identification, there is little alternative but to recognize the conspicuously quartz-phyric rocks as dacites, and all others as andesites pending analysis. This classification was the one adopted by Lacroix (1904) who used the term dacite for strongly quartz-phyric rocks and dacitoide for those with similar chemical composition but without abundant modal quartz.

At the highest end of the silica scale, a few rocks (less than 1%) from the Lesser Antilles have more than 70% SiO_2 and have elsewhere been called rhyolites (Tomblin, 1968b) or rhyodacites (Brown et al., 1977). Some of these have a distinctive, almost aphyric texture and well-developed, "rhyolitic" flow banding.

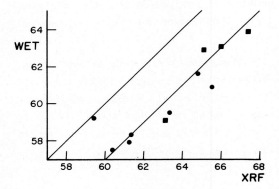

Figure LA.2.--Comparison of wet chemical and XRF determinations of silica abundance in dacites and acid andesites from Montserrat (circles) and St. Lucia (squares). Data are from Rea (1970), Holland and Tomblin (unpublished).

Brief history of research on the dacites of the Lesser Antilles

One of the first descriptions of dacites in the Lesser Antilles was that of Sapper (1903) who briefly outlined the geology of St. Lucia and identified dacite as abundant in the Soufriere region.

Lacroix (1904, p. 501) gave a more detailed account of the dacites of Martinique. He described the petrography of these rocks, noted the mineralogical and geochemical continuity between the andesites and dacites, and presented eight analyses of dacitic rocks. Lacroix (1926) gave additional petrographic data and three new analyses of dacites. MacGregor (1938) described the petrography and presented analyses of Montserrat rocks which included one dacite.

From the early 1960's, a sequence of detailed studies was made through the combined efforts of the Universities of Oxford and later Durham (England) and the West Indies (Trinidad) on the eruptive history, petrology, and geochemistry of younger Lesser Antillean volcanic centres. Doctoral theses on centres which contained dacites were produced by Tomblin (1964), Rea (1970), and Wills (1974). Comparable studies on the islands of Martinique and Guadeloupe have been carried out by Gunn, Roobol, and Smith (1974), Westercamp (1975), and Clocchiatti and Mervoyer (1976). A summary of the eruptive history and petrology of the recently active volcanoes has been given by Robson and Tomblin (1966).

A comprehensive geochemical study of major and minor elements by X-ray fluorescence analysis was made between 1967-1975, by the Universities of Durham and the West Indies. In all, 1,518 rocks from the Lesser Antilles have been analyzed (Brown et al., 1977), and this has made possible a reasonably definitive description of the geochemistry of the Lesser Antilles, including the establishment of the overall field distribution and range of chemical composition of the dacites.

Isotopic analyses of strontium, uranium, and lead, with discussions of their genetic significance, have been published by Pushkar (1968), Hedge and Lewis (1971), Donnelly et al. (1971), Pushkar et al. (1973), and Cheminée (1973). Isotopic age determinations on rocks from Martinique, including dacites, have been made by Andreieff et al. (1976), and on rocks from the arc as a whole by Nagle et al. (1976) and by Briden et al. (in press).

FIELD OCCURRENCE
Geographic distribution

Dacites are present in small quantities in most of the volcanic Lesser Antilles, having been identified in all islands except St. Vincent, Nevis, and

Saba. The number of dacite analyses and the estimated areas and ages of dacite outcrops in the Lesser Antilles are given in Table I. This table contains, on an island-by-island basis from the north (above) to the south (below), the numbers of XRF analyses with silica above 66%, expressed as percentages of all analyses and estimated area of outcrop. The equivalent data are also given for wet chemical analyses with silica above 63% (see the earlier section of this chapter on definition of dacite, and Fig. 2, for the significance of these silica pecentages). The XRF analyses provide a more reliable basis for estimating relative abundances of dacite, because they are more numerous and were made on samples selected to give the most uniform possible areal coverage of all volcanic materials. The wet chemical measurements in the three islands for which 40 or more analyses are available, give results which correspond well with the dacite proportions estimated from the XRF data.

From Table I and from the histogram in Figure 3, it can be seen that the great majority of the dacite occurs in the central part of the arc. From the analyses, St. Lucia has the highest percentage of dacite at the surface (16%), whilst Martinique, which is a bigger island, has the largest estimated surface area of dacite (106 km^2). The next two islands northward, Dominica and Guadeloupe, are the only others in the Lesser Antilles which contain substantial outcrops of dacite.

In St. Lucia, the dacites almost all come from one volcanic center which is the only center known to have been active within the Pleistocene. In the other islands near the middle of the arc, dacites are present in all the younger volcanic complexes, including three in Martinique (Mt. Pelée, Pitons du Carbet, and Diamant-Gros Ilet) and four in Dominica (Morne Patates, the Micotrin-Trois Pitons complex, Morne Diablotins, and Morne aux Diables).

Age

The age of the oldest rocks in each island, and the age of the oldest dacites, is given to the right of Table I. Comparison of these ages illustrates that the dacites are present in slightly higher abundance in these younger rocks of the arc than in the pre-Pleistocene formations. In St. Lucia, almost all of the dacites have been erupted from the youngest volcanic centre within the last 0.25 Ma (million years). In Martinique, all dacites except a minor outcrop of aphyric rock in the southeast have known ages extending back to 6.8 Ma, and exactly half of the 22 dated rocks from the three volcanic centres containing dacite are older than 2.5 Ma, so that it can be assumed that approximately half of the Martinique dacites are younger than 2.5 Ma. The writer has calculated, on the basis of all known isotopic dates and from geological maps showing the formations represented by the dated samples, that

TABLE 1. Estimated areas and ages of dacitic rocks in the Lesser Antilles.

	XRF ANALYSES					WET ANALYSES				AGES (MILLION YEARS)			
	Area of Volc. rocks km²	No. of Anals	No. of Dacites	% of Dacites	Area of Dacites km²	No. of Anals	No. of Dacites	% of Dacites	Area of Dacites km²	Oldest Rocks	Oldest Dacites	Area >2.5Ma km²	Area <2.5Ma km²
Saba	12	58	0	0	0	4	0	(0)	(0)	?	---	0	0
St. Eustatius	21	73	3	4	1	1	0	(0)	(0)	?	?	0	1
St. Kitts	174	178	3	2	3	25	0	(0)	(0)	7.5	?	0	3
Nevis	44	80	0	0	0	15	0	(0)	(0)	?	---	0	0
Montserrat	82	120	6	5	4	45	2	4	3	4	0.2	0	4
Antigua	100[a]	0	---	?	(10)	10	3	(33)	(33)	39	20	0	0
Guadeloupe	940	81	4	5	46	14	4	(35)	(330)	2.5	?	0	46
Desirade	5	14	11	(79)[b]	(4)	1	1	(100)	(100)	142	90	0	0
Dominica	781	301	22	8	61	16	0	(0)	(0)	(1.7)	?	0	57
Martinique	986	65	7	11	106	56	7	13	123	36	7	53	53
St. Lucia	596	88	14	16	95	25	9	(36)	(215)	18	0.25[c]	53	93
St. Vincent	384	90	0	0	0	67	0	0	0	2.7	---	0	0
Grenadines	100[a]	125	2	2	2	22	0	(0)	(0)	18	?	0	0
Grenada	340	263	1	0.4	1	33	1	(3)	(10)	21	2.5	0	1
TOTAL	4,565	1,518	63		333								258

NOTES: a Approximate area of volcanics
b Parentheses indicate estimate is based on too few analyses to be reliable
c Excepting a small outcrop of aphyric, high-silica dacite intrusive into Miocene volcanics

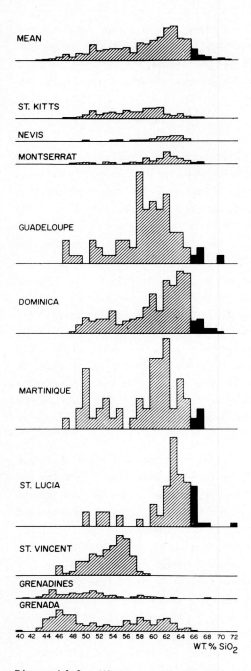

Figure LA.3.--Histogram showing frequency distribution of silica percentage by island in the Lesser Antilles. The area of each histogram is proportional to the area of volcanic rocks in the island. Data are from XRF analyses made by Holland and others (unpublished).

approximately 70% of all volcanics at the surface in the Lesser Antilles have ages of less than 2.5 Ma, and these outcrops include 75% of all the dacite. The main uncertainty in these estimates is the age of the volcanic rocks in Dominica, a large island for which only two age measurements exist and no pre-Pleistocene rocks have been identified.

Mode of Occurrence

The dacites in the Lesser Antilles occur mainly as pyroclasts, especially pumice from air fall and nuee ardente deposits. Massive dacites mostly occur as lava domes, which at the Qualibou caldera in St. Lucia have been estimated by Tomblin (1964) to form 1.5 km^3 out of a total of 8 km^3, i.e., about one-fifth of the dacite. These 8 km^3 of dacite are the only rock type erupted during the last quarter million years. A map of the Qualibou caldera showing the distribution of the various dacite units is presented in Figure 4, whilst Figure 5 provides a view of the interior of the caldera. This volcanic center appears to be unusual in the Lesser Antilles in that over the last 2.5 million years it has erupted material which has been virtually constant in composition during individual eruptive episodes (possibly up to thousands of years long), but which has gradually advanced in composition from acid andesite (58% SiO_2) to dacite (63% SiO_2) and during the last 0.25 Ma has continued to rise, in consecutive eruptions, from about 63% to 66% SiO_2. The larger eruptive episodes have involved mainly pyroclastic deposits of air fall and nuée ardente type (Figs. 6 and 7), apparently emanating from craters which in several cases have later been filled by domes.

The above type of activity closely resembles the two major historic eruptions of 1902-05 and 1929-32 at Montagne Pelée in Martinique, in which the magma composition was close to the boundary between andesite and dacite (Lacroix, 1904; Robson and Tomblin, 1966), and the similar prehistoric eruptions, one of which has been dated at 29,000 years b.p. (Tomblin, 1970; Sigurdsson, 1972) from Morne Micotrin in Dominica where, as in Martinique, the rock composition lies close to the arbitrary border between andesite and dacite. The proportion of clastic to massive dacites in Martinique is probably similar to that in St. Lucia. Of the seven Martinique samples determined as dacite from XRF analyses, two are from Montagne Pelée and consist of one pumice flow and one pumice fall deposit; at the Pitons du Carbet centre, three are pumice flow deposits and two are denser blocks believed to be from lava domes.

In Dominica, 19 out of a total of 281 analyses fall narrowly within the compositional range of dacite on the basis of XRF measurements by Wills (1974). Eighteen of these samples are pumice flows or falls, and only one is from a massive dome.

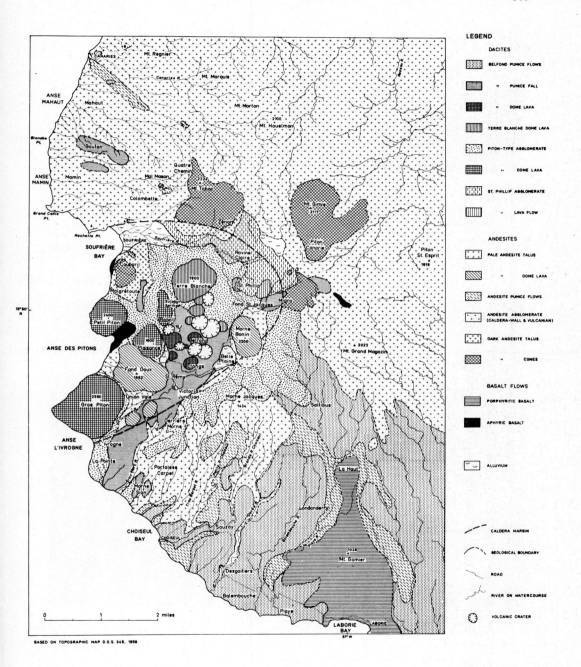

Figure LA.4.--Geological map of the Qualibou Caldera, St. Lucia, after Tomblin
(1964).

Figure LA.5.--Interior of the Qualibou caldera, St. Lucia, seen from the northern rim. The large, rounded hill in the centre is Terre Blanche (600 m a.s.l) which represents a young and morphologically intact dacite dome. The two pointed peaks of the Petit Piton (750 m a.s.l., on the right) and the Gros Piton (80 m a.s.l., behind) are the massive cores of dacite domes from which most of the original blocky flanks have been eroded. An active solfatara is marked by the white patch in the valley to the right of Terre Blanche.

Figure LA.6.--Dacite pumice fall deposit, St. Remy River, St. Lucia. Stratified lapilli and ash layers are each between 3 and 30 cm thick. Dips are variable but generally conform with the present land surface, i.e., the pumice layers mantled the pre-existing topography.

Figure LA.8.--Isopach map of Belfond dacite pumice flow, St. Lucia, modified from Tomblin (1964). Numbers mark observed thicknesses in metres. The deposit thickens with increasing distance from the Belfond craters which were the source. Contours offshore are hypothetical.

Figure LA.7.--Dacite pumice flow deposit, Londonderry, St. Lucia. Rounded to subangular pumice blocks, up to 30 cm across, i.e., in an unstratified matrix containing a high proportion of flour-like dust. The dark shadows are pick-marks.

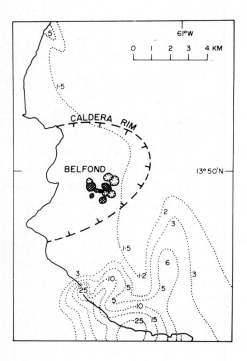

The very large size of individual pyroclastic emissions is illustrated by the youngest large pumice flow in St. Lucia (Fig. 8) which, according to Tomblin (1964), deposited an estimated 0.1 km^3 of material on land (and probably a similar or larger volume at sea), leaving deposits locally 25 m thick in pre-existing valleys at distances of up to 8 km from the source. Associated dacite pumice fall deposits in St. Lucia were estimated to have been of the order of six times the volume of the pumice flows.

Minor intrusives of dacitic composition include one of porphyritic, quartz-rich dacite into Eocene-Oligocene volcanics at Crab Point in the south-west of Antigua (Martin-Kaye, 1959), plugs of aphyric, high-silica dacite intrusive into rocks of Miocene age in the north of St. Lucia (Tomblin, 1970), and a pre-Tertiary, coarse-grained intrusive of tonalite composition in Désirade (Barrabé, 1954; Fink, 1970; Briden et al., in press.)

PETROGRAPHY

Hand specimen petrography

Among the material from the Lesser Antilles identified geochemically as dacite, three types are distinguishable in hand specimen: (i) Porphyritic, with numerous (5-25%) large quartz phenocrysts; (ii) Porphyritic with rare (<5%) quartz phenocrysts; (iii) Nearly aphyric.

Quartz-rich dacites of type (i) occur only in St. Lucia (1 volcanic centre), Martinique (2 volcanic centres), and in Antigua. They are easily identifiable in the field because they contain quartz phenocrysts 5-10 mm in diameter, generally accompanied by biotite phenocrysts which in the Pitons du Carbet centre (Martinique) reach the unusually large size of 2 cm across.

Quartz-poor dacites of type (ii), which occur at all of the other centres except northern St. Lucia, mostly contain less than 2% of quartz as small (<2 mm) phenocrysts which are difficult to distinguish in hand specimen from fresh plagioclase. These rocks closely resemble many of the acid andesites in texture and mineralogy, and are separated from these andesites on the arbitrary basis of their higher percentage of silica in the chemical analysis. These dacites are the only type present in the Montague Pelée centre of Martinique, in Dominica, Montserrat, St. Kitts, St. Eustatius, and Grenada.

The nearly aphyric dacites of type (iii) occur in minor quantities in two areas of Miocene rocks in the north of St. Lucia and in the nearby south-east of Martinique. Texturally, they are dense rocks and exhibit strongly developed, "rhyolitic" flow banding.

Almost all of the porphyritic dacites, including the dome rocks, are at least mildly vesicular, with irregular-shaped cavities and a slightly friable texture. In the clastic blocks, strongly vesicular, pumice texture is common and these rocks are nearly white in color whilst the massive rocks are mostly pale gray or pinkish.

Microscopic petrography

Under the microscope, the phenocrysts in typical order of abundance are plagioclase (25-40%), quartz (up to 25%), amphibole (up to 10%), orthopyroxene (up to 10%), biotite (up to 5%), opaque oxide (up to 2%), and rarely clinopyroxene (up to 2%), olivine and garnet. The groundmass of the massive rocks is typically microcrystalline and equigranular (felsitic), whilst that of the pyroclasts is mostly cryptocrystalline or glassy. Some examples of modal and mineral compositions are given in Table II.

Plagioclase

Plagioclase is the commonest phenocryst and groundmass mineral component. It generally forms euhedral, elongate prisms often up to 5 mm and rarely 10 mm long, with cores of bytownite or anorthite which may be deeply corroded and outer parts consisting of many thin, oscillatory zones (Fig. 11) showing a

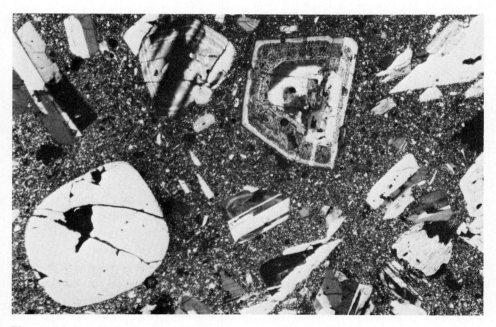

Figure LA.9.--Photomicrograph of dacite dome lava from Petit Piton, St. Lucia (sample L13). Plagioclase phenocrysts show a great variety of zonal patterns. A rounded quartz crystal occupies the lower left of the photograph. Magnification X 23.

TABLE II. Phenocryst mineral abundances in dacites of the Lesser Antilles.

	MONTS	DOMIN	MARTQ	ST. LUCIA			
	F4347	SD4	MW15B	L329	L13	L267	L205
Plagioclase	31.8	27.9	32.5	35.4	38.2	30.5	1
Quartz	1.1	--	16.7	7.8	9.6	13.0	1
Amphibole	2.9	2.5	tr	0.6	0.1	5.9	--
Biotite	--	--	4.6	2.8	0.1	1.3	--
Orthopyroxene	6.0	8.9	--	1.2	4.3	0.3	--
Ore	2.2	1.6	1.0	--	0.5	0.5	--
Clinopyroxene	--	2.7	2.2	2.1	--	--	1
Olivine	--	--	--	0.2	--	--	--
Garnet	--	--	tr	--	--	--	--
Zeolites	--	--	--	--	--	--	4
Groundmass	56.0	56.4	43.6	49.9	47.2	48.5	93.0

MONTS = Montserrat   DOMIN = Dominica   MARTQ = Martinique

F4347   Orthopyroxene-hornblende dacite, quartz-poor, minor intrusion, south-west of Landing Bay, Montserrat, 16°41.4'N, 62°11.5'W. (MacGregor, 1938).

SD4   Orthopyroxene-hornblende-clinopyroxene dacite, quartz-poor, block in pyroclast flow, Ravine Blanche, Morne Patates, Dominica, 15°13.4'N, 61°07.7'W. (Wills, 1974).

MW15B   Biotite-clinopyroxene-garnet dacite, dome lava, Gros Ilet, Martinique. 14°33.8'N, 61°01.3'W. (Westercamp, 1975).

L329   Clinopyroxene-biotite-orthopyroxene-hornblende-olivine dacite, quartz-rich, dome lava, east flank of Gros Piton, St. Lucia, 13°48.4'N, 61°03.7'W. (Tomblin, 1964).

L13   Orthopyroxene-hornblende-biotite dacite, quartz-rich, dome lava, Northwest flank of Petit Piton, St. Lucia, 13°50.2'N, 61°03.9'W. (Tomblin, 1964).

L267   Cummingtonite-biotite-orthopyroxene dacite, quartz-rich, dome lava, Belfond Hill, St. Lucia, 13°49.5'N, 61°02.4'W. (Tomblin, 1964).

L205   Aphyric high-silica dacite, dome lava, Bisé Quarry, St. Lucia, 14°01.3'N, 60°58.4'W. (Tomblin, 1968b).

descent from about An_{70} at the innermost zone to about An_{40} at the outer margin. Phenocrysts of plagioclase may be poikilitic to pyroxene, amphibole or opaque oxides, and some contain glassy or inclusion-filled zones (Fig. 9). Groundmass plagioclase ranges in composition from about An_{60} through An_{40}. The strong oscillatory zoning of the plagioclase phenocrysts is generally regarded as evidence that the crystals have grown in a high viscosity magma with fluctuating water vapour pressure.

Quartz

Quartz phenocrysts vary in abundance over a wide range and more-or-less independently of whole-rock silica percentage, although the abundance of quartz is relatively constant at individual volcanic centres. The rocks rich in quartz phenocrysts are usually also richer in hornblende and biotite.

Quartz phenocrysts range in texture from euhedral bipyramids to mildly resorbed or almost globular and deeply embayed relics. This variation can often be seen in a single thin section (Fig. 10). In general, quartz phenocrysts tend to be more resorbed in massive dome rocks where they have cooled more slowly in a large volume of liquid at shallow depth (i.e., low water vapour pressure). This corresponds to the experimental evidence (Tuttle and Bowen, 1958) that the field of stability of quartz, in appropriate silicate systems, becomes smaller with decreasing water vapour pressure.

That the quartz in the Lesser Antillean dacites is of magmatic origin has been shown by studies of the chemical composition of minute glassy inclusions in the phenocrysts (Clocchiatti and Mervoyer, 1976). These inclusions have a composition corresponding closely to the late magmatic liquids, i.e., the groundmass, of the rocks in which they occur (see Table III, sample CW12G).

Figure LA.10. Photomicrograph of dacite dome lava from agglomerate, St. Phillip, St. Lucia (sample L81), showing the contrasting euhedral and embayed texture of adjacent quartz phenocrysts. Magnification X14.

TABLE III. Major Element Abundances in Dacitic Rocks from the Lesser Antilles.

	ANTIQUA		MONTS	GUADELOUPE		DESIR	MARTINIQUE				ST. LUCIA				VINCT
	A0015	A0003	F4347	MB106	CW12G	LB423	L531J	MW5Z	MW15B	MW4D	L13	L267	L267G	L205	37104G
	Q	Q	P	P	G	C	P	Q	Q	A	Q	Q	G	A	G
SiO_2	67.8	76.2	64.2	64.5	72.9	71.2	63.7	64.4	64.6	69.8	63.9	64.9	69.6	70.7	65.5
Al_2O_3	14.8	12.6	16.8	15.7	12.0	14.0	18.2	15.6	15.5	16.0	16.8	17.1	15.2	13.4	15.9
Fe_2O_3	1.8	2.5	3.7	3.2		2.2	2.6	1.9	3.1	2.1	1.0	0.4	0.3	1.2	2.4
FeO	2.4	0.8	1.8	4.1	1.7	1.7	2.3	2.9	2.0	1.7	3.0	3.1	1.1	2.5	2.9
MgO	2.0	0.0	2.2	1.4	?	1.1	2.3	1.9	1.4	0.3	1.5	1.5	0.7	0.0	1.4
CaO	2.1	2.9	6.0	4.6	2.0	2.0	5.1	4.8	4.9	2.9	6.2	6.0	3.5	2.8	5.0
Na_2O	4.6	4.0	3.4	4.4	3.5	6.2	3.5	3.9	2.7	5.6	3.4	3.0	2.8	4.9	4.4
K_2O	1.7	1.1	1.1	1.1	2.6	0.3	1.1	1.5	2.1	1.5	1.6	1.6	3.7	2.0	1.1
H_2O	2.6	0.4	0.4	0.4	?	1.0	0.3	1.2	2.2	1.3	1.2	2.4	2.1	2.3	0.2
TiO_2	0.5	0.3	0.3	0.6	?	0.4	0.3	0.3	0.1	0.2	0.4	0.4	0.1	0.3	0.7
P_2O_5	0.1	tr	0.1	0.1	?	0.1	0.1	0.3	0.1	0.0	0.1	0.1	0.1	tr	0.2
MnO	0.1	0.1	0.1	0.1	?	0.1	?	tr	tr	tr	0.1	0.1	0.1	0.3	0.1
TOTAL	100.5	100.9	100.1	100.2	(94.7)	100.3	99.5	98.7	98.7	101.4	99.2	100.6	99.3	100.4	99.8

N.B. All analyses are by wet chemical methods, except CW12G which is by electron microprobe.

MONTS	= Montserrat		P	= Quartz-poor
DESIR	= Desirade		G	= Groundmass
VINCT	= St. Vincent		C	= Coarse-grained
Q	= Quartz-rich		A	= Aphyric

LEGEND FOR TABLE III

A0015   Chlorite-clacite dacite, dome lava, Crab Point, Antigua, 17° 02.3'N, 61° 53.3'W. Chlorite and iron oxide appear to pseudomorph amphibole. (Tomblin, 1968b).

A0003   High-silica dacite, block in agglomerate, north of Sweets, Antigua, 17° 03.6'N, 61° 48.1'W. Quartz phenocrysts form more than 20% of the slide. Mafic phenocrysts are altered to chlorite and iron oxide. (Tomblin, 1968b).

F4347   Orthopyroxene-hornblende dacite, quartz-poor, minor intrusion, southwest of Landing Bay, Montserrat, 16° 41.4'N, 62° 11.5'W. (MacGregor, 1938).

MB106   Dacite, quartz-poor, Riviere du Plessis, Guadeloupe, 16° 03'N, 61° 44'W.

CM12G   High-silica dacite glass, inclusion in quartz phenocryst, from pumice flow, Pointe de la Grande Anse. 15° 57.9'N, 61° 39.3'W. (Clocchiatti and Mervoyer, 1976).

LB423   Hornblende-tonalite, intrusion, Desirade. 16° 20'N, 61°W (approximately). (Barrabe, 1942).

L531J   Dacite, quartz-poor, pyroclast flow 25 January 1903, Riviere Blanche, Martinique. 14° 46'N, 61° 12'W. (Lacroix, 1904).

MW5Z   Biotite dacite, quartz-rich, spine of Rocher du Diamant, Martinique. 14° 26.5'N, 61° 02.6'W (Westercamp, 1975).

MW15B   Biotite-clinopyroxene-garnet dacite, dome lava, Gros Ilet, Martinique. 14° 33.8'N, 61° 51.7'W (Westercamp, 1975).

L13   Orthopyroxene-hornblende-biotite dacite, quartz-rich, dome lava, Northwest flank of Petit Piton, St. Lucia, 13° 50.2'N, 60° 03.9'W. (Tomblin, 1964).

L267   Cummingtonite-biotite-orthopyroxene dacite, quartz-rich, dome lava, Belfond Hill, St. Lucia, 13° 49.5'N, 61° 02.4'W. (Tomblin, 1964).

L267G   Glassy groundmass from L267 (Tomblin, 1964).

L205   Aphyric high-silica dacite, dome lava, Bise quarry, St. Lucia, 14° 01.3'N, 60° 58.4'W. (Tomblin, 1968b).

37104G   Groundmass from clinopyroxene-orthopyroxene lava flow, Belleisle Gutter, St. Vincent, 13° 21.5'N, 61° 08.6'W. (Tomblin, 1968b).

Figure LA.11.--Photomicrograph of dacite dome lava from Belfond Hill St. Lucia (sample L267), showing strong oscillatory zoning in plagioclase, subhedral quartz, and cummingtonite (below bubble). Magnification X 23.

Amphibole

Amphibole is the most abundant mafic phenocryst mineral in many of the Lesser Antillean dacites, reaching 6% in the Belfond (youngest) dacite of St. Lucia (Tomblin, 1968a) and with a mean modal abundance of 8.4% in six samples from the Diamant centre in southwestern Martinique (Gunn, Roobol and Smith, 1974). Some phenocrysts are very large (up to 10 mm long), forming the most conspicuous crystals in the rock. The amphibole ranges widely in composition from common hornblende through oxyhornblende, and rarely cummingtonite. The latter mineral has been identified only in the youngest dacites of St. Lucia, where it occurs as large phenocrysts, some of which have cores of green hornblende (Fig. 12).

Orthopyroxene

In some of the dacites, especially the quartz-poor variety, orthopyroxene with an abundance of up to 9% (see Table II, sample SD4) is the dominant mafic mineral. The ratio of iron to magnesium content is relatively constant, varying from about En_{50} in the Dominica and older St. Lucia dacites to En_{40} in the younger St. Lucia dacites. Orthopyroxene occurs as prisms up to 2 mm long which are often euhedral and sometimes poikilitic to small grains of opaque

Figure LA.12. --Photomicrograph of dacite dome lava from Belfond Hill, St. Lucia (sample 1267), showing a large large phenocryst of cummingtonite grown around a core of common hornblende. Magnification X25.

oxide and plagioclase. It also occurs as an alteration product after hornblende, forming aggregates of minute granules intergrown with opaque oxide.

Biotite

Biotite phenocrysts occur only in the quartz-rich dacites, forming subhedral plates, which are commonly up to 22 mm across. They are poikilitic to small plagioclases and opaque oxide. Pleochroism is usually from dark to pale brown. In some rocks the biotites are rimmed by finely granular opaque oxide and orthopyroxene. In the Pitons du Carbet center in Martinique, very large, euhedral prisms of biotite reach 20 mm in diameter and occupy nearly 5% of the rock.

Olivine

Olivine occurs rarely in dacites from Martinique (Lacroix, 1904) and St. Lucia (Tomblin, 1964). In the latter island, it occurs as anhedral crystals up to 3 mm across, rimmed by coronas of finely granular hornblende, orthopyroxene and opaque oxide. The high magnesium content, the reaction rims and the silica-rich groundmass indicate that the olivine was not in equilibrium with the host magma.

Garnet

Almandine garnet has been reported from dacites in Martinique (Lacroix, 1904; Westercamp, 1976), where it occurs as xenocrysts with reaction rims of plagioclase and biotite. A chemically analyzed sample from Gros Ilet (Westercamp, 1976) corresponded to a molecular composition of 62% almandine, 18% pyrope, 17% grossularite, and 3% spessartine. These xenocrysts are interpreted on the basis of their plagioclase and glass inclusions as having had a magmatic origin under hydrous conditions with an upper pressure limit of 10 kilobars.

GEOCHEMISTRY
Major Elements

Many analyses have been made of Lesser Antillean dacites. A list of 344 wet chemical analyses, including 33 of dacitic composition, has been compiled by Tomblin (1968b). A further 45 wet chemical analyses from Montserrat including two dacites were presented by Rea (1970), and 26 from Martinique including five dacites by Westercamp (1975). A much larger number of analyses has been made by XRF methods in recent years, including 1,518 at the University of Durham (Brown et al., 1977), of which 59 are dacites according to the criterion adopted in this chapter (66% or more SiO_2 for volatile-free XRF measurements). Additional XRF data have been presented by Wills (1974) on 281 Dominica rocks including 19 dacites. Analyses of six major oxides by microprobe on 39 samples of inclusions in quartz phenocrysts from Guadeloupe and Martinique, all of high-silica dacite composition, have been published by Clocchiatti and Mervoyer (1976). A selection of existing wet chemical analyses of the dacites is given in Table III.

The main geochemical features of the dacites are their relatively high abundance of alumina and lime, corresponding to the abundant calcic plagioclase phenocrysts, and their low potash, titania, and low iron-to-magnesium ratios. These features are characteristic of the acid members of the calc-alkaline assemblage which is typical of island arcs and other subduction zones.

It can be seen from Table III that there is no geochemical distinction between the two types of porphyritic dacite identified earlier in this chapter on the basis of the abundance or rarity of quartz phenocrysts. However, there are differences between the porphyritic and aphyric rocks, involving higher Na_2O which reflects the more sodic plagioclase. The sample of ancient metatonalite from Désirade is distinguished by its very high soda and extremely low potash, whilst the two analyses of interstitial glass from dacite lava (L267G) and from quartz phenocrysts (CW12G) have relatively high potash.

The rapid impoverishment in iron relative to magnesium in the more acid rocks is a distinctive feature of the calc-alkaline rock assemblage. Figure 13 shows that this characteristic is well exemplified both in the whole rocks and in the whole rock to groundmass relationships in Lesser Antillean dacites. The early removal of iron in greater amounts than magnesium is attributed by Brown and Schairer (1968) to the early separation of amphibole and iron oxide under conditions of high water vapour pressure and oxygen fugacity. The high proportion of amphibole in the accumulative xenoliths which are common in several islands (Lewis, 1973; Baker, 1968) confirms the early separation of this mineral, whilst the high water vapour content of Lesser Antillean magmas is illustrated by the highly explosive, gas-rich nature of many of the historic eruptions, and of the prehistoric eruptions involving dacites.

The potash to silica ratio in different islands of the Lesser Antilles is illustrated in Figure 14 from which it can be seen that the content of potash ranges widely from a minimum of about 0.8% at 63% SiO_2 in St. Kitts, to about 1.8% for the same silica percentage in Grenada. Rocks from the central part of the Lesser Antilles (Martinique, St. Lucia and Dominica), where the dacites are most abundant, fall between the extremes of St. Kitts and Grenada, and contain between 1.2 and 1.5% potash at 63% silica. The metatonalites of Désirade, by contrast, contain extremely low potash (maximum of 0.3% for between 66 and 75% silica), and in this respect belong to a completely different geochemical assemblage.

Trace elements

Trace element data on Lesser Antillean dacites include emission spectrograph measurements by Nockolds and Allen (1953), Tomblin (1964) and Rea (1970). More recently, a large number of XRF analyses for certain trace elements has been made at the University of Durham on the same 1,518 samples as were measured for major oxides (Brown et al., 1977). Table IV gives the mean trace element compositions by island in the dacites, for a total of 43 samples. The variation in trace element composition from north (Saba) to south (St. Lucia) involves a factor of two increase in barium and, most notably, a factor of ten increase in rubidium, the abundance of which rises southward in a striking and systematic way.

Studies on thorium and uranium for Lesser Antillean rocks have been carried out by Donnelly et al. (1971) and by Cheminée (1973). The reported abundances of these elements in the dacites range from 1.7 through 8.7 ppm for thorium, and from 0.9 through 3.3 ppm for uranium. The Th/U ratios in the dacites (maximum 3.4) as well as the abundances, are very low compared with continental igneous rocks. Donnelly et al. (1971) conclude that these differences alone rule out the involvement of continental crust in the generation of the majority of Lesser Antillean magmas.

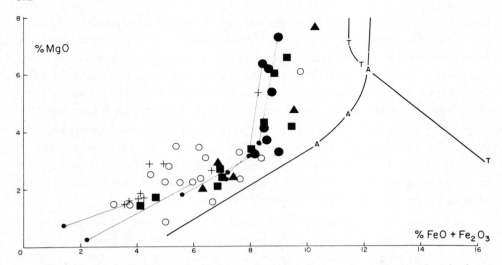

Figure LA.13.--Variation of magnesia against total iron in dcites and andesites of the Lesser Antilles (selected from Tomblin, 1968b). Triangles = Grenada; large solid circles = St. Vincent; crosses = St. Lucia; squares = St. Kitts; open circles = other islands; small solid circles = ground masses. Curves through A represent Hawaiian alkali and through T represent Hawaiian tholeite series from Tilley, Yoder and Schaver (1968).

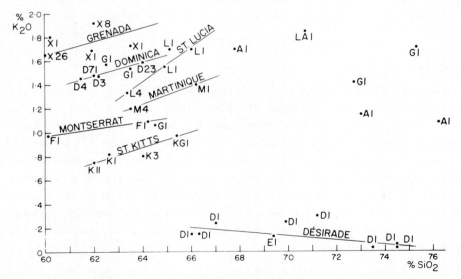

Figure LA.14.--Potash-silica variation in dacitic and acid andesitic rocks of the Lesser Antilles. X = Grenada; D = Dominica; L = St. Lucia; LA = St. Lucia aphyric; M = Martinique; F = Montserrat; G = Guadeloupe; K = St. Kitts; KG = St. Kitts groundmass; A = Antigua; D (less than 0.4% K_2O) = Désirade; E = St. Eustatius. The number following the code letter(s) gives the number of analyses represented by the dot. About half of the dots represent XRF analyses: 3% was subtracted from the silica measurement for these before they were plotted.

TABLE IV. Trace Element Abundances in Dacites of the Lesser Antilles.

	EUS	SKI	GUA	DOM	MTQ	SLU	MEAN	ALL
	2	3	4	23	7	4	43	1518
Ba	136	194	166	248	303	243	240	247
Nb	7	2	4	4	6	(5)	4	5
Zr	136	129	155	103	122	88	113	107
Y	29	27	52	21	25	(18)	26	24
Sr	269	278	223	284	312	277	282	387
Rb	12	13	32	57	67	112	56	27
Zn	27	53	64	47	70	?	52	72
Cu	11	24	36	42	30	5	33	57
Ni	35	4	32	33	38	5	29	75
Cr	?	11	?	119	?	27	(96)	?
V	?	35	?	?	?	?	(35)	?
U	?	?	1.4	?	1.9	(2.5)	(1.8)	?
Th	?	?	2.4	?	5.3	(7.0)	(4.6)	?

EUS = St. Eustatius   DOM = Dominica

SKI = St. Kitts   MTQ = Martinique

GUA = Guadeloupe   SLU = St. Lucia

MEAN = Arithmetic mean of all Lesser Antilles dacite analyses

ALL   = Arithmetic mean of all XRF analyses for basalts, andesites, and dacites from the Lesser Antilles.

N.B.   The second line of each column shows the number of analyses from which the mean abundance was calculated. Parentheses indicate that fewer analyses were available than the number given in the second line.

Isotopic ratios

Studies on the relative abundances of certain isotopes serve to determine not only the age, but also the parent materials of igneous rocks. For the latter purpose, the ratio of Sr^{87}/Sr^{86} which increases primarily as a function of the amount of continental material or calcareous sediment involved in the genesis of the new magma, is an important guide. Studies on this ratio in the Lesser Antilles have been carried out by Pushkar (1968), Hedge and Lewis (1971) and Pushkar et al. (1973). Of the 41 strontium isotope ratios reported in these papers, thirty-five including two dacites fall between 0.7035 and 0.7054 and are compatible with a fairly recent, primary mantle origin. The remaining six

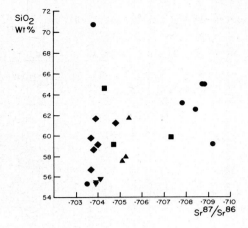

Figure LA.15.--Distribution of strontium isotopic ratios as a function of silica percentage in dacites and acid andesites of the Lesser Antilles. Circles = St. Lucia; squares = Dominica; diamonds = Martinique; triangles = Grenadines; inverted triangles = St. Vincent.

analyses, including three dacites from St. Lucia, have considerably higher Sr^{87}/Sr^{86} ratios of between 0.7073 and 0.7092, which cannot be explained as the result of simple differentiation of any of the analyzed basalts or basaltic andesites. Plots of strontium isotopic ratios as a function of silica percentage in the andesites and dacites of the Lesser Antilles are shown in Figure 15.

PETROGENESIS

Distinctive features of Lesser Antillean dacites

The main features of the dacites in the Lesser Antilles which impose constraints on the source material and physical conditions of magma genesis are:

1. The chemical and mineralogical continuity between andesite and dacite, sometimes seen within the products of a single eruption, and more generally within a series of eruptions from one volcano.

2. The presence of a much higher proportion of dacitic rocks in the central sector of the island arc.

3. The tendency for dacites to occur more abundantly among the younger products of a given volcanic centre, i.e., as the result of a mature stage of evolution at that centre.

4. The tendency for dacites to be erupted in large volume with little change of chemical composition, e.g., in prehistoric eruptions in St. Lucia and historic activity in Martinique. This contrasts with the strong variation of magma composition in the basalt to andesite range during the 1902 eruption of

St. Vincent (Tomblin, 1975), during the prehistoric eruptions of the Mansion pyroclastics of St. Kitts (Baker, 1968) and the White River pyroclasts of Montserrat (Rea, 1970).

5. The dichotomy of strontium isotopic ratios, with some of the dacites showing high Sr^{87}/Sr^{86} values diverging widely from those for the basalts for most of the andesites and a few of the dacites from the Lesser Antilles.

6. The high rubidium content of certain of the dacites, especially those from St. Lucia which also have high Sr^{87}/Sr^{86} ratios.

7. The wide range (factor of ten) in rubidium content of the dacites and remarkably uniform increase in abundance of this element from north to south along the arc.

8. The systematic although less dramatic change in potassium content of the dacites, involving a factor of two increase from north to the south along the arc.

9. The absence of significant differences along the active volcanic arc in the depth to the seismically active zone.

10. The presence of notably more intermediate depth earthquakes (between 70-200 km), at least in the last two decades during which higher quality hypocenter determinations have been made, beneath the central part of the arc.

11. The presence of minor amounts of olivine and garnet as xenocrysts in a few of the dacites.

12. The occurrence of aphyric, high-silica dacites in small volume among the older (Miocene) volcanics of two islands.

13. The existence of pre-Tertiary intrusive rocks (metatonalites) and keratophyres in one island.

14. The identification, in andesites and basaltic andesites, of groundmass or glass inclusions with compositions closely similar to dacitic whole rocks.

15. The presence of coarse-grained xenoliths, or blocks in clastic deposits, containing accumulative textures and rich in amphibole.

Possible genetic processes

It is evident that in the Lesser Antilles, two types of source material are available for partial melting. The first is the oceanic mantle forming the base of the overriding Caribbean plate, which is likely to be of primitive composition, i.e., low in potash, rubidium and Sr^{87}/Sr^{86} ratio. The second type of material is the Atlantic oceanic crust plus ocean-floor calcareous and siliceous sediments, including continental material carried northward from South America, all of which are substantially higher in potash and radioactive elements.

In the Lesser Antilles or in any island arc, a progressive magmatic evolution can be expected to take place with time. In the earlier magmas, there will be no contribution from the oceanic crust for the first several millions of years until this has been subducted to the depths required for fusion. When the latter does finally occur, the contribution of oceanic crust is likely to be a gradually increasing one, which is subject to fluctuations according, for example, to the amount and composition of crustal material subducted, and the efficiency of migration of water to the overlying plate.

The greater abundance of dacite in the central Lesser Antilles may be a result of the steeper angle and deeper penetration of the subducted Atlantic floor in this sector of the arc, and the consequently higher proportion of crust and oceanic sediments available for melting. It is likely also that in the case of a more steeply inclined subducting crustal slab with a faster vertical component of motion, more water will remain in this slab and less will permeate upward into the overlying slab of Caribbean mantle.

The notably lower potassium and rubidium contents in the northern Lesser Antilles can be explained not only because the subduction zone is at a lower angle and subduction is oblique, not perpendicular, to the axis of the arc, but also, and more importantly, because subduction is known to have operated beneath these northern islands only since the Pliocene when the active volcanic arc was displaced southwestward from Antigua-Anguilla to its present position beneath Montserrat-St. Kitts. Allowing for subduction along the newly established plate boundary for 10 million years at 1 cm/year, which are near the maximum probable values, the Atlantic crust will only have travelled 100 km down the subduction zone and will hardly yet have reached the depth necessary for partial fusion.

REFERENCES

Andreieff, P., Bellon, H. and Westercamp, D., 1976. Chronometrie et stratigraphie comparée des édifices volcaniques et formations sedimentaires de la Martinique (Antilles francaises). Trans. 7th Caribbean Geol. Conf., Guadeloupe: pp. 345-356.

Baker, P. E., 1968. Petrology of Mt. Misery volcano, St. Kitts. Lithos, 1: 124-150.

Barrabé, L., 1942. La signification structurale de l'arc des Petites Antilles. Geol. Soc. France Bull., 5: 143-157.

Barrabé, L., 1954. Observations sur la constitution géologique de la Désirade (Guadeloupe). Geol. Soc. France Bull., 3: 613-626.

Briden, J. C., Rex, D. C., Faller, A. M. and Tomblin, J. F., in press. K-Ar geochronology and palaeomagnetism of volcanic rocks in the Lesser Antilles. Phil. Trans. Roy. Soc. Lond.

Brown, G. M., Holland, J. G., Sigurdsson, H., Tomblin, J. F. and Arculus, R. J., 1977. Geochemistry of the Lesser Antilles volcanic island arc. Geochim. Cosmochim. Acta, 41: 785-801.

Brown, G. M. and Schairer, J. F., 1968. Chemical and melting relations of some calc-alkaline volcanic rocks. Carnegie Inst. Yearbook, 66: 460-463.

Cheminèe, J. L., 1973. Contribution a l'etude des comportements du potassium, de l'uranium et du thorium dans l'evolution des magmas. Thèse de doctorat, Univ. de Paris, 396 + 50 pp.

Clocchiatti, R. and Mervoyer, B., 1976. Contribution a l'etude de cristaux de quartz de la Guadeloupe. Trans. 7th Caribbean Geol. Conf., Guadeloupe: pp. 357-370.

Donnelly, T. W., Rogers, J. J. W., Pushkar, P. and Armstrong, R. L., 1971. Chemical evolution of the igneous rocks of the eastern West Indies: an investigation of thorium, uranium, and potassium distributions, and lead and strontium isotopic ratios. Geol. Soc. Am. Mem., 130: 181-224.

Fink, L. K., 1970. Evidence for the antiquity of the Lesser Antilles island arc. Trans. Am. Geophys. Union, 51: 326.

Gunn, B. M., Roobol, M. J. and Smith, A. L., 1974. Petrochemistry of the Pelean-type volcanoes of Martinique. Geol. Soc. Am. Bull., 85: 1023-1030.

Hedge, C. E. and Lewis, J. F., 1971. Isotopic composition of strontium in three basalt-andesite centers along the Lesser Antilles arc: Contrib. Miner. Pet., 32: 39-47.

Lacroix, A., 1974. La Montagne Pelée et ses éruptions. Masson et Cie, Paris, 662 pp.

Lecroix, A., 1926. Les caracteristiques lithologiques des Petites Antilles. Soc. Geol. Belg., Livre Jubilaire, pp. 387-405.

Lewis, J. F., 1973. Petrology of ejected plutoic blocks of the Soufriere volcano. St. Vincent, West Indies J. Pet., 14: 81-112.

MacGregor, A. G., 1938. The volcanic history and petrology of Montserrat. Phil. Trans. Roy. Soc. London, Ser. B, 229: 1-90.

Martin-Kaye, P. H. A., 1959. The geology of the Leeward and British Virgin Islands. Voice Pub. Co., St. Lucia, 117 pp.

Nagle, F., Stipp, J. J. and Fisher, D. E., 1976. K-Ar geochronology of the Limestone Caribbees and Martinique, Lesser Antilles, West Indies. Earth Planet. Sci. Lett., 29: 401-412.

Nockolds, S. R. and Allen, R., 1953. The geochemistry of some igneous rock series. Geochim. Cosmochim. Acta, 4: 105-142.

Pushkar, P., 1968. Strontium isotope ratios in volcanic rocks of three island arc areas. J. Geophys. Res., 73: 2701-2714.

Pushkar, P., Steuber, A. M., Tomblin, J. R. and Julian, G. M., 1973. Strontium isotopic ratios in volcanic rocks from St. Vincent and St.Lucia, Lesser Antilles. J. Geophys. Res., 78: 1279-1287.

Rea, W. J., 1970. The geology of Montserrat, British West Indies. Ph. D. Thesis, Univ. of Oxford, England, unpublished, 196 pp.

Robson, G. R. and Tomblin, J. F., 1966. Catalogue of active volcanoes of the world including solfatara fields, Part XX, West Indies. Internat. Assoc. Volcanology, Rome, 56 pp.

Sapper, K., 1903. Zur Kenntnis der Insel S. Lucia in Westindien. Zbl. Miner. Geol. Palaont., pp. 273-278.

Sigurdsson, H., 1972. Partly welded pyroclast flow deposits in Dominica, Lesser Antilles. Bull. Volc., 36: 148-163.

Tomblin, J. F., 1964. The volcanic history and petrology of the Soufriere region, St. Lucia. Phil. Thesis, Univ. of Oxford, England.

Tomblin, J. F., 1968a. The geology of the Soufriere volcanic centre, St. Lucia, Trans. 4th Caribbean Geol. Conf., Trinidad, 1965. Caribbean Printers, Trinidad, pp. 367-376.

Tomblin, J. F., 1968b. Chemical analyses of volcanic rocks from the Lesser Antilles. Univ. West Indies Seismic Res. Unit Spec. Publ. 15, 23 pp.

Tomblin, J. R., 1970. Field guides to Dominica, Martinique, St. Lucia, etc., in International Field Institute guidebook to theCaribbean island-arc system. Am. Geol. Inst., Washington, D.C.

Tomblin, J. F., 1975. The Lesser Antilles and Aves Ridge. In, the Ocean Basins and Margins (ed., A.E.M. Nairn and F. G. Stehli), Vol. 3, Chapt. 11, Plenum, New York.

Tuttle, O. F. and Bowen, N. L., 1958. Origin of granite in the light of experimental studies in the system $NaAlSi_3O_8$-$KAlSi_3O_8$-SiO_2-H_2O. Geol. Soc. Am. Mem., 74, 13 pp.

Westercamp, D., 1975. Petrology of the volcanic rocks of Martinique, West Indies. Bull. Volc., 39: 1-26.

Westercamp, D., 1976. Petrologie de la dacite a grenat de Gros Ilet, Martinique, Petites Antilles Francaises. Trans. 7th Caribbean Geol. Conf., Guadeloupe, pp. 413-424.

Wills, K.J.A., 1974. The geological history of southern Dominica and plutonic nodules from the Lesser Antilles. Ph. D. thesis, Univ. of Durham, England, 414 + 202 pp.

Chapter 22

MIOCENE LOW-K DACITES AND TRONDHJEMITES OF FIJI

J. B. Gill and A. L. Stork

ABSTRACT

High-Si dacites comprise one mode in each of two bimodal volcanic rock suites in Fiji. Both suites are low-K throughout but differ in level of iron-enrichment and light REE-enrichment. Sparsely-phyric dacite lava and tephra cover 10^2-10^3 km^2 in each suite, apparently having erupted in shallow marine environments. Tephra predominates. Typical phenocrysts are plagioclase >>quartz >>Fe-Ti oxides and augite; hypersthene and hornblende are rare and biotite is absent. Most samples have >72% SiO_2, <15% Al_2O_3, and <0.8% K_2O. Normatively, most have 6% Or and An x 100/(Ab + An) ratios of 20 over a wide range in Ab/Qz ratios; thus they cross the feldspar-quartz cotectic at a high angle. Their compositions are similar to those of 20 to 40% partial melts of basalt at P_{H_2O} = 5 kb. Tonalite-trondhjemite and gabbro plutons also form a bimodal suite. Trondhjemite and dacite mineralogy and compositions are analogous although trondhjemites contain primary hornblende. REE patterns vary considerably in the three otherwise similar suites, ranging from light REE-depletion with $La_{e.f.}$ = 8, to middle REE-enrichment with $Nd_{e.f.}$ = 360, to middle-REE depletion with $Dy_{e.f.}$ = 7 (Fig. 5). The latter characterizes all trondhjemites analyzed and is compatible with fusion of lower Fijian crust.

INTRODUCTION

Voluminous high-Si, low-K dacites and trondhjemite plutons of Tertiary age are uncommon. However, three exceptions of Miocene age occur in Fiji: high-Si dacites which constitute 30 to 40% of the basement Wainimala Group of Viti Levu island; high-Si dacites of the Undu Group which cover 750 km^2 of northeastern Vanua Levu island as domes, breccias, and tuffs; and about ten trondhjemite plutons, each about 100 km^2 which intrude the Wainimala Group basement of Viti Levu and are the principal plutonic rock type of Fiji (Fig. 1).

Throughout the time of emplacement of these exceptional rocks, Fiji probably was an ordinary island arc on the eastern boundary of the Indian plate which was being underthrust from the east by the Pacific plate (Gill and Gorton, 1973). This tectonic configuration is thought to have continued until about 5 m.y.B.P., after which Fiji became separated from the plate boundary by opening of an intervening interarc basin (Gill, 1976b). Thus, high-Si, low-K magmatism in Fiji occurred during the surge of mid-miocene igneous activity which affected many other convergent boundaries within the Pacific plate (Kennett et al., 1977), including the Green Tuff region of Japan where rocks of similar composition were emplaced (Tatsumi and Clark, 1972).

The thickness and velocity structure of crust in Fiji is poorly known. Thicknesses of 30 km beneath Viti Levu and Vanua Levu are suggested by gravity models (Robertson, 1967; Worthington, pers. comm., 1971), whereas only 15 km of crust were found in the only available refraction profile which was obtained just to the southwest of the area shown in Figure 1 (Shor et al., 1971). However, no salic crustal layer having P wave velocities of 6 km/sec was found, nor have pre-Eocene or K-feldspar-rich sediments been reported. Thus, Fiji can be considered an ensimatic island arc built on ocean crust during the last 50 m.y.

We will summarize preliminary data concerning the geology, mineralogy, and composition of the high-Si dacites and trondhjemites of Fiji. However, because

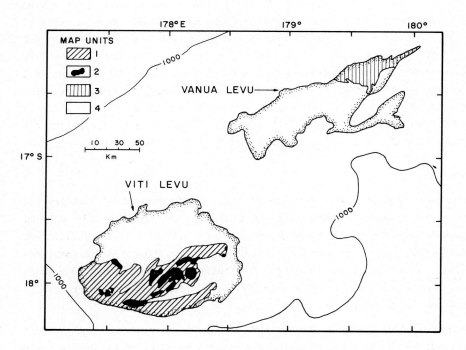

Figure 1.--Generalized geological map of Fiji showing 1000 fathom isobath and distribution of rock units discussed in text. Map units: 1, Wainimala Group (area of dacites not differentiated); 2, Tholo plutons (gabbro plus trondhjemite); 3, Undu Volcanic Group; 4, other.

we recently began a more detailed study of these suites, this paper is only an introduction.

HIGH-Si DACITES OF THE UNDU VOLCANIC GROUP

The Undu Volcanic Group covers 750 km^2 of northeastern Vanua Levu and is the youngest, largest, and freshest occurrence of high-Si dacite in Fiji. This group interfingers with the upper portions of the more basic Natewa Volcanic Group to the west; together these units constitute the Mathuandrove Supergroup. The Undu Group is largely unfossiliferous but the age of silicic volcanism is bracketed by Upper Miocene faunas (Foram Zone N.17 to N.18) in the Natewa Group and by an Upper Pliocene fauna (Foram Zone N.20) from the Malau Formation of the Undu Volcanic Group (Blow, 1969; Ibbotson, 1969). This Group probably was deposited in a complicated near shore and shallow submarine environment. Ash turbidites and interbedded marine sediments indicate that it was partly subaqueous while infrequent welded ash flows indicate it was partly subaerial.

Rickard (1970) divided the Undu Volcanic Group into three formations which interfinger to some extent, record lateral facies from near-vent to more distal regions, and also may record temporal changes in the style of volcanism. They are presented here in order of decreasing age. The Nasavu Flow and Tuffs, approximately 53% of the outcrop area, consist of massive dacite lavas with occasional breccia, glass, and tuff (e.g., sample B535) horizons. The Vunivia Breccia, 17% of the outcrop area, are massive, poorly-bedded, often monomict breccias. The breccia usually contains subrounded to angular vitric dacite clasts 5 to 15 cm in diameter, but clasts up to two meters occur. Domes and lassive lavas are poorly developed but the breccias often are cut by dacite dikes. This formation is overlain by the Malau Formation, 30% of the outcrop area, which is dominantly massive pumice breccia interlayered with epiclastic sediments and minor lenses of dacite and dacite breccia. In addition to pumice, clasts in the pumice breccias are dominantly aphyric to porphyritic dacite (e.g., sample H26) with some vesicular obsidian.

Phenocrysts usually occupy <10 volume percent, although dacites in some horizons contain 40 to 60 percent phenocrysts. Plagioclase (An$_{50}$ to An$_{38}$) is the most abundant and often the only phenocryst phase. Crystals commonly are 0.5 to 5 mm in length, clear, euhedral, and occasionally twinned, with Carlsbad twinning more abundant than albite. Normal and oscillatory zoning are common. Quartz is not a common phenocryst but accompanies plagioclase in highly porphyritic rocks. Crystals are 3 to 10 mm, subhedral, and embayed.

Fe-Ti oxides occur as microphenocrysts in all porphyritic samples and often are the only mafic phase present. Augite occurs erratically; hypersthene is

632

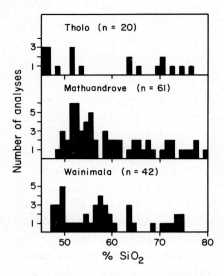

Figure 2.--Histogram of SiO_2 content of Fijian igneous rocks. Analyses from Rodda (1969), Hindle (1970), Gill (1970, 1972), and Colley and Rice (1975). Class width is 1 wt % SiO_2.

rare. Hornblende is found in only a few samples and biotite is absent. Apatite is a common inclusion in plagioclase.

The groundmass usually is glassy with microphenocrysts, in order of decreasing abundance, of plagioclase (An_{44} to An_{28}), Fe-Ti oxides, pyroxene, quartz, and apatite. Groundmass textures are felty to trachytic.

The Mathuandrove Supergroup contains a continuum of rock types from basalt to high-Si dacite (Fig. 2), although the volume distribution probably is bimodal with basaltic andesite and high-Si dacite predominating. The overall suite is low-K according to Taylor et al. (1969), calc-alkaline according to Miyashiro (1974), and a dilemma for Jakes and Gill (1970). Mean analyses are given in Table 1 and representative REE patterns in Figure 5.

HIGH-Si DACITES OF THE WAINIMALA GROUP

The basement of Viti Levu island is a mildly-deformed and unfossiliferous assemblage of tuffs, breccias, wackes, marls, and subordinate lavas collectively called the Wainimala Group (First Period group of Gill, 1970). Over 20 km of section (including lateral equivalents) has been mapped in this Group, resulting in subdivision into eight formations (Rodda and Band, 1967). All are considered submarine on the basis of pillow lavas and interbedded marine sediments, but poor exposure and lack of marker horizons has precluded detailed stratigraphy or inferences of paleo-environments.

Three formations within the Group (the Lokalevu Keratophyre, Metawailevu Dacite, and Wainimbuka Trachyte) consist of high-Si dacite and related rocks. Each contains, in order of decreasing volume, tuffs, volcaniclastic sediments, and flows or domes with columnar jointing. Each formation has an estimated thickness of 3 to 5 km, such that the three may constitute up to 30 volume percent of the Group. The formations occur as lenses up to 125 km^2 in outcrop area within more mafic units, and are thought to reflect the distribution of centers of silicic volcanism even though only one lens immediately surrounds an exposed trondhjemitic pluton. The lithology, distribution, and relative volume of rock types are similar to, though less well known than, those included in the Undu Volcanic Group. Limestones apparently interbedded with some of the Wainimala dacites contain early middle Miocene fauna (Hirst, 1965; Band, 1968; J. Stoen, pers. comm., 1974); no dacites have been dated radiometrically.

The dacites are sparsely-phyric, fine-grained, light-gray to light-green, and sometimes amygdaloidal. Phenocrysts are euhedral, often unzoned plagioclase (An_{30} to An_4), and subhedral, sometimes embayed quartz, which together constitute 20 volume percent and often <5 percent of samples. Augite and Fe-Ti oxides occur infrequently as phenocrysts; primary hornblende is rare and neither hypersthene nor primary biotite is known. Chlorite, epidote, sericite, and calcite are common constituents, reflecting regional greenschist facies metamorphism; actinolite is absent.

The Wainimala Group contains a bimodal distribution with few rocks having between 64 and 68% SiO_2 (Fig. 2). Composition of the overall suite is discussed by Gill (1970). It is low-K according to Taylor et al. (1969), tholeiitic according to Miyashiro (1974, Fig. 1), and an island arc tholeiitic series according to Jakes and Gill (1970). Mean analyses for the suite are given in Table 1 and REE patterns for an andesite and dacite are given in Figure 5.

THOLO GROUP TRONDHJEMITES

The discovery of "granitic" plutons in interior Viti Levu led nineteenth century geologists to consider Fiji continental. Subsequent mapping defined about ten plutons, some lying in cores of broad anticlines, where they intrude early to middle Miocene or older rocks of the Wainimala Group but are overlain by late Miocene sediments. The intrusion and deformation are known as the Tholo Orogeny. The plutons range from 75 to 150 km^2 in outcrop area, but several contain roof pendants and are flanked by satellite plugs, indicating larger areal extent at depth, incomplete unroofing, and epizonal conditions.

Contacts often are sharply discordant and steeply dipping, and surrounding rocks usually are metamorphosed to hornblende-hornfels facies assemblages.

TABLE 1. Mean analyses of suites containing high-Si dacite or trondhjemite. Analyses from Gill (1972) except for > 68% SiO_2 category which include, in addition, analyses from Rodda (1969) and Colley and Rice (1975). All are recalculated to an anhydrous basis with original LOI (loss on ignition) values given as ancillary information only.

	SiO_2 < 53	SiO_2 53-64	SiO_2 > 68	SiO_2 < 53
	A. Mathuandrove Supergroup			B. Wainimala Group
n	8	9	7	12
$SiO_2(\%)$	51.3	56.9	75.8	49.5
TiO_2	.87	.88	.36	1.1
Al_2O_3	16.1	17.0	13.0	18.4
Fe_2O_3*	10.1	8.8	2.0	11.3
MnO	.18	.15	.04	.20
MgO	7.3	4.1	.34	5.4
CaO	10.9	8.1	2.4	10.0
Na_2O	2.3	2.5	4.5	3.3
K_2O	.64	.79	.86	.85
P_2O_5	.19	.18	.11	.21
(LOI)	2.1	2.3	1.8	3.4
Rb(ppm)	13	13	9	10
Sr	420	354	100	379
Ba	257	280	117	128
Th	0.6	0.5	0.4	0.6[3]
U	0.2	0.25	0.4	0.3[3]
Pb	2	2	2.5	2
Y	23	28	43[1]	26
Zr	57	78	146	65
Ni	73	15	< 5	25
Co	35	24	< 5	37
Cr	198	26	3	73
Sc	35	26	8	35
V	253	225	4	267
Cu	106	120	6	80
K/Rb	424	636	1062	865
$^{87}Sr/^{86}Sr$	.7038(3)[2]	.7041(3)	.7040(3)	.7035(3)

* All Fe as Fe_2O_3
[1] H26 excluded

SiO$_2$ 53-64	SiO$_2$ > 68	SiO$_2$ < 53	SiO$_2$ 64-68	SiO$_2$ > 68
B. Wainimala Group		C. Tholo Plutonics		
18	8	9	3	6
58.2	72.3	48.7	64.4	72.4
.95	.50	.72	.51	.43
16.9	14.3	20.1	16.9	14.1
8.4	3.0	7.7	5.7	3.4
.19	.10	.16	.14	.07
3.2	.66	6.5	2.2	.89
6.9	2.3	13.1	6.2	3.2
3.9	5.5	1.8	3.2	4.6
.64	1.1	.17	.67	1.0
.26	.14	.09	.14	.07
3.0	1.5	1.8	1.1	0.8
7.5	9	2	8	9
236	155	190	349	160
138	228	41	171	210
0.7[3/]	1.5	< 0.2	0.6	2.0
0.3[3/]	0.6	< 0.2	0.2	0.7
2	2	< 1	1	2
37	52	15	22	35
88	150	45	82	125
< 5	< 5	40	< 5	< 5
20	< 5	35	12	5
5	2	164	7	4
30	12	29	12	9
172	14	253	66	32
60	4	67	28	4
769	888	930	594	1252
.7036(8)	.7044(3)	.7037(3)	----	.7039(2)

[2/] Parentheses include n for isotope ratios
[3/] Mean excludes samples (about n/3) with undetectable Th (<0.3 ppm) and U (<0.1 ppm).

Although some field descriptions suggest pluton zonation to more quartz-rich cores (Band, 1968), the trend has not been striking in our reconnaissance study. Mafic inclusions up to 30 m in diameter, apparently of country rock, occur along many pluton margins but amphibolite clots are not distributed ubiquitously throughout the plutons.

In eastern Viti Levu, plutons intrude formations containing fauna as young as Foram Zone N.12 (J. Stoen, pers. comm., 1974), whereas plutonic detritus occurs in conglomerates which grade upward into sediments containing fauna as old as Foram Zone N.17 (Rodda, in press); this implies intrusion between 13 and 7 m.y.B.P. Eight K-Ar age determinations have been made and at least two episodes of intrusion are suggested. Hornblende from one trondhjemite in western Viti Levu is 33 ± 1 m.y. old (McDougall, 1963), whereas hornblende and biotite from seven plutons of central and eastern Viti Levu yield concordant 7.5 to 11 m.y. ages (Rodda et al., 1967; and unpub. results). The closeness in age between plutons and sediments derived therefrom confirms epizonal emplacement and implies rapid erosion.

Note that there is no evidence for contemporaneity between the high-Si dacites of the Wainimala Group and either episode of trondhjemite intrusion, despite their broadly similar spatial distribution (Fig. 1) and composition (Tables 1 and 2).

The plutons are a bimodal assemblage of gabbros, which constitute 10 to 20% of the outcrop area, and tonalites to trondhjemites (Fig. 2); intermediate diorites occur but are less common. The gabbros contain olivine, augite and orthopyroxene sometimes rimmed by hornblende or biotite or both; some have cumulate textures. Where relative ages are known, gabbros are older.

Mineralogically, the salic plutons contain 40 to 70% plagioclase (An_{65} to An_{15}), 15 to 50% quartz, 0 to 20% hornblende, and 0 to 10% biotite. K-feldspar is minor or absent. Thus, the rocks are tonalites or trondhjemites depending on color index (Streckeisen, 1973) or normative plagioclase composition (O'Connor, 1965). Both modal and normative plagioclase usually are andesine.

Maximum dimensions of plagioclase and quartz crystals typically are 5 and 10 mm, respectively. Plagioclases usually are subhedral, normally zoned with albite rims, and turbid. Quartz typically is anhedral and strained. Myremekite intergrowths of the two are common in some plutons. Largely interstitial green hornblende <4 mm in length is the most ubiquitous mafic mineral and usually is accompanied by biotite; both together usually constitute 10-15 volume percent of rocks containing 20-40 percent of quartz. It is unclear texturally whether either mineral was a liquidus phase or, instead, a product of subsolidus reaction. Magnetite, apatite, and sphene are common accessories. Epidote, chlorite, sericite, calcite, or sulfides occur in most samples, usually replacing hornblende or in interstices and occupying 1 to 10 volume percent.

The mean compositions of gabbro, tonalite, and trondhjemite are given in Table 1.

CHEMICAL COMPOSITION

Mean analyses of the two dacite and one trondhjemite-containing suites are given in Table 1. New analyses and re-analyses of dacites and trondhjemites are given in Tables 2 and 3; twelve additional analyses are available in Rodda (1969), Gill (1970), and Colley and Rice (1975). Locations and petrographic descriptions of newly analyzed samples are provided in Appendix 1.

All of the analyses reported here were made between 1970 and 1972 at the Australian National University. Analytical techniques, precision, and accuracy are as discussed by Gill (1976a). Of the analyses given in Table 3, samples H26 and M96 were analyzed during 1971 using Mix E; the rest were analyzed in late 1972 using Mix F and the data reduction techniques of Taylor and Gorton (1976). Analyses 48, 51, and 59 in Table 3 are re-analyses of samples from Gill (1970) using these improved techniques; resulting REE patterns are more even.

The seven analyzed Undu dacites are unmetamorphosed; several are only slightly devitrified obsidian clasts from breccia. Thus, most analyses are likely to be of liquid compositions. All samples have >72% SiO_2, <15% Al_2O_3, and 4.0 to 4.7% Na_2O. Five have <0.8% K_2O. Available data suggest that (B535 and M96) are more siliceous, potassic, and radiogenic than lavas (H26 and others) as is often true in continental calderas (e.g.. Bailey et al., 1976), but the contribution of seawater to these differences is not yet known

Normative compositions seem unrelated to phase boundaries in the salic tetrahedron (Figs. 3 and 4), having a uniform An x 100/(Ab + An) ratio of 20±5 over a range in Ab/Qz ratios of 1.2 to 0.7, and lying prallel to the Ab-An-Qz face of the tetrahedron with 6±2 percent Or. Five of the seven dacites are peraluminous with small percentages of normative corundum.

Many LIL element (K, Rb, Ba, Th, U, Pb, Nb, and LREE) concentrations are very low for such high-Si igneous rocks, as are Th/U and Ba/Sr ratios. K/Rb ratios are anomalously high. Zr, Hf, and ferromagnesian trace element concentrations are more typical. $^{87}Sr/^{86}Sr$ ratios are slightly above those of more mafic members of the Mathuandrove Supergroup (Table 1), but the samples with higher ratios are tephra and may contain seawater Sr.

TABLE 2. New analyses of Fijian high-Si dacites, tonalites, trondhjemites.**

	Undu			Wainimala				Tholo					
	H26++	B535	M96	901	856	387	854	909	910	908	858	867	848
SiO_2	75.1	77.8	79.4	68.6	70.7	72.1	74.3	64.0	63.7	69.7	70.2	72.5	74.6
TiO_2	0.50	0.30	0.20	1.04	0.38	0.43	0.36	0.50	0.47	0.61	0.37	0.31	0.38
Al_2O_3	13.5	11.4	10.4	15.5	15.4	14.6	13.9	16.7	17.3	14.8	14.9	14.4	12.8
$Fe_2O_3^*$	2.64	1.72	2.49	3.59	3.87	2.91	2.33	5.89	5.59	4.57	3.57	2.94	3.42
MnO	0.01	0.03	0.05	0.09	0.09	0.11	0.11	0.16	0.13	0.11	0.07	0.09	0.09
MgO	0.34	0.81	0.28	0.28	0.80	1.19	0.48	2.13	2.16	0.78	1.16	0.82	0.68
CaO	2.45	2.50	1.76	3.90	2.41	1.21	0.58	6.44	6.62	3.41	3.94	2.90	3.16
Na_2O	4.71	4.01	4.08	5.30	5.33	7.08	6.49	3.48	3.40	5.06	4.04	4.73	4.48
K_2O	0.64	1.45	1.17	1.21	0.87	0.27	1.40	0.57	0.49	0.87	1.76	1.20	0.32
P_2O_5	0.14	0.07	0.18	0.43	0.11	0.09	0.07	0.19	0.13	0.13	0.08	0.07	0.06
(LOI)	1.85	1.66	2.32	0.42	3.25	0.63	1.17	1.54	0.72	0.74	0.65	1.34	0.66
Rb	8	12	6	16	6	3	15	8	7	9	21	13	1
Sr	108	94	97	277	203	91	120	360	338	150	207	193	111
Ba	90	138	123	305	214	55	299	180	162	274	315	340	91
Th	0.5	0.4	0.4	1.3	0.8	--	2.5	0.6	0.6	1.0	1.7	2.3	--
U	0.4	0.4	0.4	1.3	0.5	--	1.0	0.2	0.2	0.4	0.8	0.6	--
Pb	1	4	3	2	2	2	2	--	2	2	2	2	--
Zr	177	142	119	177	162	189	224	87	76	190	104	118	77
Hf	3.0	2.1	2.9	--	--	--	--	--	1.0	--	--	2.3	--
Nb	1.2	1.2	1.3	--	--	--	--	--	1.3	--	--	--	--

	560	34	52	63	47	44	68	23	20	56	22	22	55
Y	560	34	52	63	47	44	68	23	20	56	22	22	55
Ni	--	<5	<5	<5	<5	<5	<5	<5	<5	<5	<5	<5	<5
Co	--	<5	<5	<5	<5	<5	<5	12	13	5	6	7	<5
Cr	--	3	3	4	2	3	3	6	8	5	4	8	3
Sc	--	7	9	18	6	6	7	10	13	15	9	5	14
V	--	7	<5	43	5	8	7	48	83	15	64	31	22
Cu	--	7	6	9	3	9	4	4	51	8	8	3	3
$^{87}Sr/^{86}Sr$	.7036	.7043[+]	.7042[+]	--	--	.7045	--	--	--	.7035	--	--	--
K/Rb	654	982	1550	617	1140	700	764	628	561	830	684	747	2950
Ba/Sr	0.8	1.5	1.3	1.1	1.0	0.6	2.5	0.5	0.5	1.8	1.5	1.8	0.8
Th/U	1.2	1.0	1.0	1.0	1.6	--	2.5	3.0	3.0	2.5	2.1	3.8	--
Zr/Hf	59	68	41	--	--	--	--	--	76	--	--	51	--

** Data recalculated on an anhydrous basis; original LOI values for reference only.
* All Fe as Fe_2O_3
+ From Gill and Compston (1973)
++ Major elements from Hindle (1970)

TABLE 3. Rare earth element analyses of Fijian high-Si and related rocks.
Major element analyses in Table 2 or Gill (1972).

	Undu			Wainimala		Tholo		
	H26	B535	M96	48	51	910	867	59
SiO_2	75.1	77.8	79.4	57.5	73.4	63.7	72.5	76.7
K_2O	0.6	1.4	1.2	0.8	1.1	0.5	1.2	0.2
$^{87}Sr/^{86}Sr$	.7036	.7043*	.7042*	.7039[+]	.7043[+]	----	----	.7044[+]
La	76	4.3	7.8	1.7	2.4	5.0	7.9	11.4
Ce	----	12.7	23	5.1	7.1	12.3	18.3	23
Pr	41	1.3	3.5	.85	1.2	1.7	2.4	2.5
Nd	210	5.8	17.0	4.2	6.2	7.5	9.0	8.4
Sm	71	1.6	6.8	1.6	2.6	2.0	2.2	1.8
Eu	8.4	.45	2.0	.60	.84	.72	.70	.58
Gd	81	2.3	5.8	2.6	4.0	2.3	3.0	1.9
Tb	12	.37	.89	.44	.76	.31	.42	.32
Dy	70	2.4	6.0	3.0	4.9	1.9	2.7	2.1
Ho	15.6	.62	1.3	.82	1.3	.46	.61	.55
Er	37	1.8	3.6	2.4	3.9	1.4	2.0	1.6
Yb	27	1.9	3.0	2.4	4.0	1.6	2.2	1.7
La/Yb	2.8	2.3	2.6	0.7	0.6	3.1	3.6	6.7
Eu/Eu*	0.38	0.80	?	1.0	0.85	1.14	1.0	1.07

*From Gill and Compston (1973)

[+]From Gill (1970)

The three REE patterns shown in Figure 5 are perplexing in their diversity, despite all having La/Yb ratios of 2.3 to 2.8. For example, those of M96 and H26 are somewhat parallel except for Eu, but differ ten times in concentration. These differences correlate with no other compositional variable except Y contents. The pattern of H26 looks suspiciously like an apatite distribution coefficient and, indeed, is approximately what an apatite in equilibrium with B535 should be Fig. 5). However, the high Y (and, by analogy, high REE) content of H26 characterizes a 2-gram sample mass whose low P_2O_5 and Sr contents restrict apatite to <0.4 wt percent; consequently the REE pattern is thought to represent a liquid composition rather than an unlucky concentrate of apatite.

The compositions of dacites of the Wainimala Group differ from those of the fresher Undu dacites in several respects. Wainimala dacites have higher average Na/Ca, Ab/An, and Ab/Qz ratios (Figs. 3 and 4), higher Fe_2O_3*, MgO, Sr, Ba, and Th contents, and LREE-depletion. Presumably the difference in Na/Ca ratios reflects metasomatism, as may the more variable LIL-element concentrations. However, differences in Ba and Th contents and Th/U ratios are consistent and thought primary. No similar differences separate the mafic members of the two bimodal suites. The only REE analysis of a Wainimala Group dacite is of sample 51 (Table 3; Fig. 5), which supersedes that of sample 50, from the same locality, in Gill (1970). It resembles the REE patterns of ophiolite keratophyres and plagiogranites (Coleman, 1977, p. 78). Silica metasomatism of basalt, advocated by Kay and Senechal (1976) to explain some such rocks, is inapplicable to sample 51 which contains phenocrysts of quartz but of no mafic minerals.

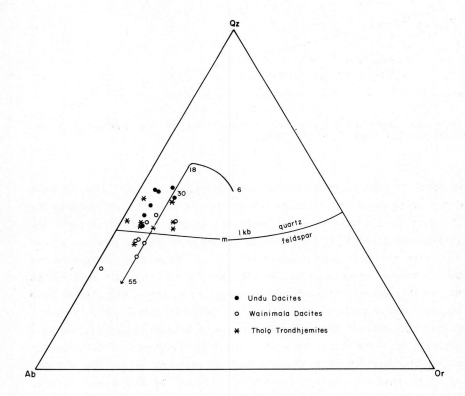

Figure 3.--CIPW norms of Fijian rock compositions plotted in the system Ab-Or-Qz-H_2O. Phase boundary and minimum (m) at 1 kb from Luth et al. (1964). Line with arrow connects compositions of partial melts of a 1921 Kilauea olivine tholeiite at P_{H_2O} = 5 kb from Helz (1976); numbers indicate percent of melt formed.

642

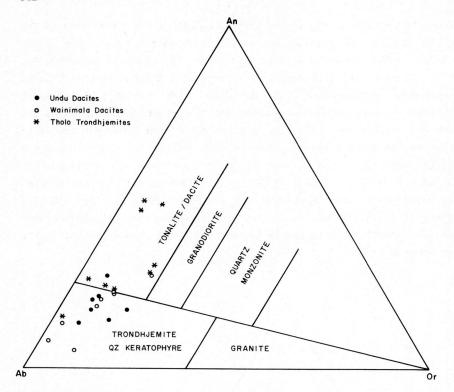

Figure 4.--CIPW norms of Fijian rock compositions in the system Ab-Or-An. Field boundaries from O'Connor (1965).

Tholo tonalites and trondhjemites of both intrusive episodes also resemble Undu dacites in composition, although the greater range of K_2O contents in the plutonics leads to a distribution of normative components which straddle the plagioclase-quartz cotectic in the Ab-Or-Qz system more than is true for either of the extrusive suites discussed above (Fig. 3). The plutons share with the contiguous Wainimala Group dacites Sr, Ba, and Th contents and Th/U ratios which consistently exceed those of Undu dacites. In contrast, the plutons have higher Co, Cr, and V contents than do either volcanic suite. All three REE patterns are LREE-enriched (Fig. 5) and have minima between Tb and Ho; two have slight positive Eu anomalies. There is a two-fold enrichment of LREE between tonalite and trondhjemite with a cross-over of patterns between Nd and Sm. Thus, the three resemble the REE pattern of Undu dacite B535 except for Eu, even though Y contents are lower in the plutonics.

In summary, high-Si dacites and trondhjemites from three separate spatio-temporal environments in Fiji have similar compositions except for some trace

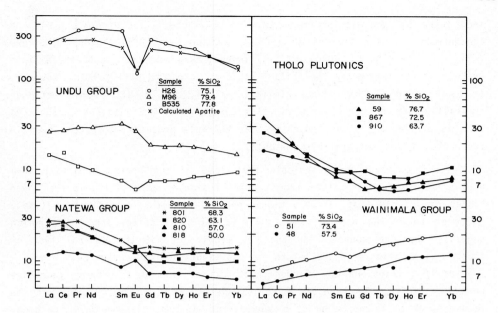

Figure 5.--REE of Fijian samples from Table 3 and Gill (1972) normalized to values given in Gill (1976a, Table 3). "Calculated apatite" is REE of apatite equilibrated with B535 using the lowest distribution coefficients of Nagasawa (1970).

elements. The Fijian rocks apparently ignore cotectic surfaces in the salic tetrahedron. All have nearly constant Ab/An ratios and Or contents rather than the nearly constant Qz/(Ab + Or) ratios which characterize many granites and rhyolites. All have low LIL-element contents and high K/Rb but low Th/U and Ba/Sr ratios for high-Si igneous rocks. The Wainimala dacites and Tholo trondhjemites contain chlorite, epidote, sericite, and calcite, and have somewhat higher and more variable Na/Ca ratios and LIL-element concentrations than the unmetamorphosed Undu dacites. However, the higher Ba and Th contents and Th/U ratios in both Viti Levu suites seem to be primary features. Plutonic samples have higher Co, Cr, and V contents than either volcanic suite. Most plutonic samples have slight (<15%) positive Eu anomalies; most volcanic samples have more pronounced (>15%) negative anomalies. REE patterns and Y contents vary considerably without recognized correlation with other aspects of composition or mineralogy (Fig. 5). However, all plutonic rocks and one Undu dacite have a concave-up pattern with $Dy_{e.f.}$ of 6 to 9 as a minimum.

DISCUSSION

A close genetic link between all three Fijian high-Si rock units and their more mafic associates is indicated by the similarity of the two populations of each suite in such distinctive geochemical characteristics as low LIL-element concentrations, high K/Rb ratios (>600), and low La/Yb (<4), Ba/Sr (<2), Th/U (<3), and $^{87}Sr/^{87}Sr$ (<0.7045) ratios. Indeed, the rocks seem to be the silicic members of the island arc tholeiitic series of Jakeš and Gill (1970). However, it is unknown whether these similarities in Fiji result from fractional crystallization or partial fusion. The diversity of REE patterns encountered in this preliminary study indicates that multiple processes operated, even in restricted spatio-temporal circumstances.

Several observations indicate that some of the rocks, especially the plutonics, may have resulted from partial fusion of amphibolite in the lower Fijian crust, i.e., of suitably metamorphosed Wainimala Group basement (Table 1) or of underlying oceanic crust. First, all three suites are bimodal which suggests separate sources for the two modes. Second, the general lack of clustering or alignment parallel to the quartz-plagioclase cotectic in Figure 3 implies that fractionation of phenocryst minerals was of secondary importance at most. Third, the high Ab/Or ratios clearly rule out equilibrium with K-feldspar, which is not surprising considering its modal absence from the high-Si suites and from Fijian rocks generally. However, the high Ab/Or ratios, coupled with peraluminous character, suggest equilibrium with hornblende (Brown and Fyfe, 1970; Helz, 1976). Because hornblende was not a consistent liquidus mineral in either volcanic suite, its role is more conveniently ascribed to an inaccessable residuum. Fourth, the general REE patterns of the plutonics, including the slight positive Eu anomaly, could characterize melts resulting from 15 to 25% fusion of a source initially having ten times chondritic concentrations and leaving an amphibole >>plagioclase >clinopyroxene >magnetite residuum, if maximum amphibole/liquid distribution coefficients are <2 and change from <1 to >1 between Nd and Sm. Either the Wainimala Group or underlying oceanic crust could be such a source, although both may be characterized by LREE-depletion on a regional scale. However, neither differences between the three plutonic samples nor the extent of LREE-enrichment can be modelled successfully in detail in this way.

Clear problems for this interpretation include the high K/Rb ratios of the trondhjemites which require the source's average to be >1500. Also, the near constancy of Ab/Or ratios implies the absence of refractory plagioclase (Helz, 1976), whereas this is unlikely near the solidus of basalt compositions if P_{H_2O} <P_{TOTAL} (which is implied if amphibole is not a liquidus phase in derivative magmas and which is suggested by epizonal emplacement), and some refractory plagioclase is necessary to minimize positive Eu anomalies in the derivative melt.

Derivation from a LREE-depleted precursor is necessary to explain the

La$_{e.f.}$ <Sm$_{e.f.}$ features observed in dacites H26, M96, and 51, but no likely crystal-liquid equilibria explain any one of these patterns, much less all. By analogy with oceanic plagiogranites, the REE pattern and K/Rb ratio of sample 51 should be derivable from a LREE-depleted parent magma. However, only <50% crystallization with X$_{pl}$ >0.8 could relate the REE patterns of samples 48 and 51, and this is inconsistent with the large changes in major element composition and the small Eu anomaly observed. Thus, we prefer to learn more about each suite before proposing genetic models.

However, if any of these magmas result from crustal anatexis, three implications merit brief comment. First, if water-undersaturated amphibolite crust fused, then thermal gradients between 30 and 70°C/km (depending on crustal thickness) characterized parts of Fiji between 15 and 5 m.y.B.P. This bears on the petroleum potential of Fiji. Second, if fusion of primitive island arc crust yields LIL-element depleted sialic magmas, then crustal fusion alone cannot be invoked to explain the derivation of post-Archean upper continental crust or Andean-type volcanics from an island arc basement, as it has by Jakes and White (1971) or Taylor (1977.) Finally, although low-K, high-Si magmas accompanied subduction in Fiji, the association is unnecessary, which implies that Archean analogues could arise without contemporaneous plate tectonics.

ACKNOWLEDGMENTS

M. Rickard, W. Hindle, and P. Rodda of the Mineral Resources Division of Fiji donated samples, and many Division personnel provided logistical support and geological advice. Residents of Wainiika and Tawake villages on Undu Peninsula housed and humored us. Drs. S. R. Taylor and W. Compston provided access to laboratories at the A.N.U. P. Muir and W. Nance analyzed some of the samples in Table 3. Financial support came from NSF Grant EAR 76/84065.

REFERENCES

Bailey, R. A., Dalyrymple, G. B., and Lanphere, M. A., Volcanism, structure, and geochronology of Long Valley Caldera, Mono County, California. J. Geophys. Res., 81: 725-744.

Band, R. B.. 1968. The geology of southern Viti Levu and Mbengga. Geol. Surv. Fiji Bull., 15.

Blow, W. H., 1969. Late Middle Eocene to Recent planktonic foraminiferal biostratigraphy. First Int. Conf. Planktonic Microfossils, Geneva, 1967. E. J. Brill Pub. Co., 199-422 pp.

Brown, G. C. and Fyfe, W. S., 1970. The production of granitic melts during ultrametamorphism. Contrib. Miner. Pet., 28: 310-318.

Coleman, R. C., 1977. Ophiolites. Berlin, Springer- Verlag, pp. 229.

Colley, H., and Rice, C. M., 1975. A Kuroka-type ore deposit in Fiji. Econ. Geol., 70: 1373-1386.

Gill, J. B., 1970. Geochemistry of Viti Levu, Fiji, and its evolution as an island arc. Contrib. Mineral. Pet. 27: 179-203.

Gill, J. B., 1972. The geochemical evolution of Fiji. Unpub. Ph.D. thesis, A.N.U.

Gill, J. B., 1976a, Composition and age of Lau Basin and Ridge volcanic rocks: implications for evolution of an interarc basin and remnant arc. Geol. Soc. Am. Bull., 87: 1384-1395.

Gill, J. B., 1976b. From island arc to oceanic islands: Fiji, southwestern Pacific. Geology, 4: 123-126.

Gill, J. B., and Compston, W., 1973. Stontium isotopes in island arc volcanic rocks. In: The Western Pacific-island arcs, marginal seas, geochemistry, P. Coleman (Ed.). W. Austral. Univ. Press. pp. 483-496.

Gill, J. B., and Gorton, M., 1973. A proposed geological and geochemical history of Eastern Melanesia. In: The Western Pacific-island arcs, marginal seas, geochemistry, P. Coleman (Ed.), W. Austral. Univ. Press, pp 543-566.

Helz, R. T. 1976. Phase relations of basalts in their melting ranges at $P_{H_2O} =$ 5 kb. Part II. Melt composition. J. Pet., 17: 139-193.

Hindle, W. H., 1970. Geochemistry of samples from Vanua Levu and other islands in the Fiji Group. Unpub. M.Sc. thesis, Leeds Univ.

Hirst, J. A., 1965. Geology of East and Northeast Viti Levu. Geol. Surv. Fiji Bull., 12.

Ibbotson, P., 1969. The geology of east-central Vanua Levu. Geol. Surv. Fiji Bull., 16.

Jakes, P. and Gill, J., 1970. Rare earth elements and the island arc tholeiitic series. Earth Planet. Sci. Lett., 9: 17-28.

Jakes, P. and White, A. J. R., 1971. Composition of island arcs and continental growth. Earth Planet. Sci. Lett., 12: 224-230.

Kay, R. W. and Sernechal, R. G., 1976. The rare earth geochemistry of the Troodos ophiolite complex. J. Geophys. Res., 81: 964-970.

Kennett, J. P., McBirney, A. R. and Thunell, R. C., 1977. Episodes of Cenozoic volcanism in the circum-Pacific region. J. Volc. Geotherm. Res., 2: 145-163.

Luth, W. C., Jahns, R. H., and Tuttle, O. F., 1964. The granite system at 4 to 10 kilobars. J. Geophys. Res., 64: 759-773.

McDougall, I., 1963. K-Ar ages of some rocks from Viti Levu, Fiji. Nature, 198: 677.

Miyashiro, A., 1974. Volcanic rock series in island arcs and active continental margins. Am. J. Sci., 274: 321-355.

Nagasawa, H., 1970. Rare earth concentration in zircon and apatite and their host dacites and granites. Earth Planet. Sci. Lett., 5: 47-51.

O'Connor, J. T., 1965. A classification of quartz-rich igneous rocks based on feldspar ratios. U.S. Geol. Surv. Prof. Pap., 525B: 79-84.

Richard, M. J., 1970. The geology of northeastern Vanua Levu. Geol. Surv. Fiji Bull., 14: 12 pp.

Robertson, E. I., 1967. Bouguer anomaly map of Viti Levu, Fiji. N. Z. Jl. Geol. Geophys., 10: 1309-1312.

Rodda, P., 1967. Outline of the geology of Viti Levu. N. Z. Jl. Geol. Geophys., 10: 1260-1273.

Rodda, P., 1969. Analyses of rocks from Fiji. Geol. Surv. Dept., Fiji.

Rodda, P. and Band, R. B., 1966. Geology of Viti Levu. Fiji. Geol. Surv. Ann. Report for 1966, pp. 8-16.

Rodda, P., Snelling, N. J. and Rex, D. C., 1967. Radiometric age data on rocks from Viti Levu, Fiji. N. Z. Jl. Geol. Geophys., 10: 1248-1259.

Shor, G. G., Jr., Kirk, H. K. and Menard, H. W., 1971. Crustal structure of the Melanesian area. J. Geophys. Res., 76: 2562-2586.

Streckeisen, A. L., 1973. Plutonic rocks classification and nomenclature recommended by the IUGS Subcommission on the Systematics of Igneous Rocks. Geotimes, 23: 26-30.

Tatsumi, T. and Clarke, L. A., 1972. Chemical composition of acid volcanic rocks genetically related to formation of the Kuroko deposits. J. Geol. Soc. Japan, 78: 191-201.

Taylor, S. R., 1977. Island arc models and the composition of the continental crust. In: Island Arcs, Deep Sea Trenches and Back-Arc Basins, M. Talwani and W. C. Pitman III (Eds.): Washington, AGU, pp. 325-336.

Taylor, S. R., Capp, A. C., Graham, A. L. and Blake, D. H., 1969.Trace element abundancies in andesites II. Saipan, Bougainville, and Fiji. Contrib. Miner. Pet., 23: 1-26.

Taylor, S. R. and Gorton, M. P., 1977. Geochemical application of spark source mass spectrography -- III. Element sensitivity, precision and accuracy. Geochim. Cosmochim. Acta, 41: 1375-1380.

APPENDIX 1: Locality and petrography of samples from Table 2.

Undu

H26   Porphyritic obsidian clast in bedded pumice breccia.
       Undu mine: E179°91', S16°10'. Source: W. Hindle.

B535   Bedded lapilli tuff with 2% plagioclase >quartz>> pyroxene
       crystal fragments. Ndronga Bay: E179°55', S16°13'. Source:
       M. Rickard.

M96   Crystal tuff(?) with 3% zoned oligoclase and <1% augite
       phenocrysts in a mosaic of devitrified glass and unspecified
       zeolites. Location unknown. Source: M. Rickard.

Wainimala

901   Porphyritic lava with 10% andesine, <1% augite (some
       altered), <1% opaque phenocrysts in trachytic groundmass of
       plagioclase, devitrified glass, and unspecified zeolites.
       Waisa Creek stream cobble: E167°24.0, S17°42.1'.

856   Porphyritic lava with 10% zoned andesine-oligoclase, 2%
       pseudomorphed pyroxene or hornblende, <1% opaque
       phenocrysts in altered groundmass of feldspar, quartz,
       pyroxene, opaques, and devitrified glass. Navuwai Peak:
       E177°34.2', S18°3.9'.

387   Porphyritic lava with 6% plagioclase phenocrysts in altered
       groundmass of feldspar, quartz, opaques, chlorite, apatite,
       and white mica. Mataweilevu Keratophyre. Location unknown.
       Source: P. Rodda sample C1277.

754   Porphyritic lava with 10% sericitized oligoclase, 15% quartz,
       and 2% opaque phenocrysts in groundmass of the same minerals.
       Lokalevu Keratophyre. Near Kubunataba Peak: E177°40.5',
       S18°3.7'.

Tholo Plutonics

909   Medium-grained trondhjemite with 57% turbid and sericitized
       plagioclase, 30% quartz, 4% opaques, 6% chlorite, and 3%
       epidote and calcite. Stream cobble in Wailotu River:
       E178°29.9', S17°43.9'.

910   Medium-grained trondhjemite with 55% labradorite to andesine, 35% quartz, 7% hornblende altered to chlorite, and 3% opaques. Location as for 909.

908   porphyry with 25% plagioclase, 30% hornblende (some alteration), and 3% opaques in fine-grained matrix of feldspar, quartz, opaques, and devitrified glass. Waimaro River: E178^{o}28.0', S17^{o}46.9'.

858   Coarse-grained trondhjemite with 45% andesine (frequently sericitized), 35% quartz, 10% K-feldspar, 2% hornblende, 2% opaques, and 6% chlorite and unspecified zeolites. Lato Creek: E177^{o}50.9', S17^{o}56.1'.

867   Coarse-grained trondhjemite with 50% andesine-oligoclase about half dusted with sericite or calcite, 40% quartz, 8% hornblende with occasional pyroxene inclusions and mostly altered to chlorite, epidote, and opaques; 2% opaques, and a trace of biotite. Namosi Creek near Yavuna village: E177^{o}32.5', S17^{o}49.8'.

SUBJECT INDEX